ONE WEEK

Commercial Enforcement

Commercial Enforcement

Sarah Payne
Allen & Overy LLP

assisted by

Michael Godden
Allen & Overy LLP

ALLEN & OVERY®

Tottel Publishing, Maxwelton House, 41–43 Boltro Road, Haywards Heath, West Sussex, RH16 1BJ

A CIP Catalogue record for this book is available from the British Library.

ISBN 1-84592-037-6

9 781845 920371

Typeset by Doyle & Co, Colchester
Printed and bound in Great Britain by The Bath Press, Bath, Avon

Preface

Effective enforcement is integral to the effectiveness of any civil court system. Without the means of recovering sums owed under a judgment, a claimant may find that his day in court amounts to a pyrrhic victory. Recognition of this fact underlies the historical antecedents of modern methods of civil enforcement, many of which have their roots in antiquity. However, the law of enforcement of money judgments has not been surveyed in detail for a long time. Recognition of its importance formed the basis for the Government's Civil Enforcement Review, which began in March 1998 and concluded with the March 2003 'Effective Enforcement' White Paper. Similarly, a text book attempting to piece together the forms of enforcement available in respect of money judgments and subject them to detailed analysis has long been called for. That endeavour is the aim of this book, which seeks to provide a detailed, systematic and practical account of the law of enforcement of high value money judgments in the High Court of England and Wales.

One of the difficulties with the law on enforcement is that the court rules explaining the procedural manner of seeking enforcement often mask a developed corpus of underlying substantive law, which can be difficult to locate. Commentary on such law often proves even more elusive. While this book is written by practitioners for practitioners, it is an unashamedly legal book, as the sheer number of authorities referred to illustrates. There are an enormous number of cases on enforcement and a degree of selection has necessarily been made to keep this book to a manageable size. In making that selection, we have focused on those issues which, in our view, are most likely to be relevant in the context of commercial enforcement. Inevitably, given the scope and novelty of the task undertaken, there will be areas which have been overlooked and where mistakes have been made. We would therefore welcome any comments, criticisms and suggestions on how this text can be improved.

The law as known to the authors is stated as at 4 January 2005.

SP/MDG
March 2005

Acknowledgments

Any undertaking of this size inevitably involves the help and support of many others, which we gratefully acknowledge.

We are particularly grateful for the assistance of the following past and present colleagues from the litigation department at Allen & Overy LLP, who assisted in the preparation of a number of the chapters: Paul Adams, Oliver Browne, Amy Buchanan, Jemma Clamp, Owain Morgan, Piers Reynolds, Holly Vandeleur-Kauenhoven, Camilla Macpherson, Andrew Pullen, Angeline Welsh, Russell Williams, Guy Wilkes and Jon Witts.

In addition, numerous trainee solicitors at Allen & Overy LLP assisted us by researching discrete points and checking the text, for which we are grateful. We are particularly grateful to Jennifer Bowers, Sophie Levy, Clare Ludlam and Katie Spooner who no doubt learned more about the law of enforcement than they could ever wish to know.

The ever resourceful Library Enquiries team at Allen & Overy LLP were a source of unwavering support and assistance. Similarly, the enormous professionalism and efficiency of Allen & Overy LLP's Document Checking team greatly assisted in preparing the manuscript.

Last but not least, the Allen & Overy LLP professional support lawyers (in particular Joanna Hughes, Karen Birch and Richard Bethell-Jones) and Michael Green of Fountain Court Chambers, were kind enough to review drafts of a number of the chapters and provided useful comments. Any errors that remain are of course our own.

Contents

Chapter 3 Third party debt orders

Table of statutes

Paragraph references printed in **bold** type indicate where the Act is set out in part or in full.

Table of statutory instruments

Those paragraph numbers in **bold** type indicate where a Statutory Instrument is set out in part or in full.

Table of European legislation

Table of conventions

Paragraph references printed in **bold** type indicate where the Convention is set out in part or in full.

Table of cases

C

PARA

E

F

CHAPTER 1

General rules about enforcement of judgments

'As many a claimant has learned to his cost, it is one thing to recover a favourable judgment; it may prove quite another to enforce it against an unscrupulous defendant. But an unenforceable judgment is at best valueless, at worst a source of additional loss.'

Lord Bingham in *Société Eram Shipping Co Ltd v Cie Internationale de Navigation* [2003] UKHL 30; [2004] 1 AC 260.

INTRODUCTION

1.1 As the quotation from Lord Bingham above illustrates, a court judgment affords a judgment creditor no guarantee that payment will actually be made by the judgment debtor. All too often, the process of obtaining judgment is only the first step in successfully recovering the amounts owed to a claimant. Litigation can be a time-consuming and expensive business, not just in terms of legal costs but also in lost management time and lost revenue from profitable activities. Where the defendant is a wealthy individual or organisation, the availability of assets to satisfy the judgment may be less of a concern. However, a claimant faced with an impecunious or unscrupulous defendant may find that his day in court amounts to a pyrrhic victory if there are no assets against which to enforce. To compound matters, he will also have incurred the costs of pursuing litigation which, without an effective means of recovery, is nothing more than a further source of loss.

1.2 The prospects of successful enforcement should therefore always be considered at the outset, before proceedings are even issued, rather than as an afterthought once judgment has been obtained. This will involve careful consideration of the judgment debtor's assets, the location of those assets, his solvency, the existence of other creditors and any impediments to enforcement peculiar to the judgment debtor or his assets.

1.3 It is an integral feature of the English civil justice system that the court does not automatically enforce its judgments. The courts provide various procedures for the enforcement of judgment debts and it is up to the judgment creditor to choose the most effective and appropriate means to do so when a judgment debtor fails to pay. Making an informed choice between the various procedures available in light of the judgment debtor's means lies at the heart of effective enforcement.

1.4 It will also be important to distinguish between judgment debtors who 'can't pay' and those who 'won't pay'. Judgment creditors will not wish to waste further time and money pursuing enforcement against debtors who genuinely lack the means to pay. However, distinguishing between judgment debtors who are in genuine financial difficulty and those who are deliberately evading payment is often problematic, particularly at the start of enforcement proceedings. Accurate information as to a judgment debtor's true means is fundamental to effective enforcement.

1.5 There are also strong public policy reasons for ensuring that effective methods are available to facilitate the enforcement of civil judgments. Without effective methods of enforcing the court's judgments, the court system would become discredited and ultimately unworkable. Recognition of this fact was central to the government's Civil Enforcement Review, which began in March 1998. The March 2003 'Effective Enforcement' White Paper represents the government's conclusions from that Review and states at the outset:

> 'People ordered to pay a court judgment ... have little or no incentive to do so if they know there is no effective means of enforcing it. Unless there is prompt and effective enforcement the authority of the courts, the effectiveness of penalties, and the public confidence in the justice system are all undermined.'[1]

The steps that have so far been taken to reform the law on enforcement as part of the Civil Enforcement Review are considered towards the end of this chapter.[2]

[1]   Effective Enforcement: Improved methods of recovery for civil court debt and commercial rent and a single regulatory regime for warrant enforcement agents (March 2003) Cm 5774, para 2.
[2]   See paras 1.231–1.237.

1.6 The enforcement of civil judgments has also been recognised as integral to the right to a fair trial under art 6 of the European Convention for the Protection of Human Rights and Fundamental Freedoms, which now forms part of English law following the entry into force of the Human Rights Act 1998. The human rights considerations that arise in the context of court enforcement procedures are considered towards the end of this chapter.[1]

[1]   See paras 1.151–1.156.

1.7 This book is concerned with the subject of commercial enforcement in the English courts, that is, the enforcement of high value, English, money judgments in the High Court. The means by which a judgment creditor can elicit information as to a judgment debtor's assets, and thus ascertain what methods of enforcement are likely to prove the most fruitful, are described in Chapter 2 of this book. Chapters 3 to 5 cover the most common methods of enforcement available in the

High Court for the enforcement of judgment debts, namely third party debt orders (Chapter 3), charging orders (Chapter 4) and writs of fieri facias (Chapter 5). Chapter 6 considers the law relating to the appointment of a receiver by way of equitable execution, which may assist a judgment creditor collecting in a judgment debtor's assets to satisfy a judgment debt where no other method of enforcement is available. Since the circumstances in which a judgment creditor has to resort to enforcement proceedings will, by definition, mean that there is delay in payment of the judgment debt, Chapter 7 considers the law relating to interest on judgment debts.

1.8 The remainder of this chapter considers the general rules relating to the enforcement of money judgments and provides an overview of the methods of enforcement covered in this book, together with other considerations that may be relevant to a judgment creditor in seeking to choose which method of High Court enforcement to employ.

Insolvency as a means of enforcement?

1.9 It is worth noting at the outset that the use of insolvency proceedings as a means of exerting pressure on a judgment debtor to pay a judgment debt should also be given due consideration at the start of any enforcement process. Insolvency is a collective realisation of the assets available for the benefit of all creditors, rather than a method of enforcement solely for the benefit of a single judgment creditor. Detailed consideration of the law on insolvency is therefore outside the scope of this book. However, an outline of key considerations from an enforcement perspective is provided.

1.10 Bankruptcy proceedings can be initiated in the case of an individual judgment debtor where the judgment debt exceeds £750.[1] Alternatively, where execution or other process issued on a judgment debt is returned unsatisfied in whole or in part this can be used for grounds to issue a bankruptcy petition.[2] The prospect of bankruptcy can be a useful tactic where the judgment debtor's profession makes it difficult for him to be adjudged bankrupt, as is the case with many professionals and company directors. Similarly, a company registered in England and Wales is deemed unable to pay its debts if a judgment creditor with the benefit of a judgment debt exceeding £750 has served on the company a written demand for payment (in the prescribed form) and the company has failed to meet that payment.[3] Alternatively, the company will be deemed unable to satisfy its debts if execution or other process issued on a judgment debt is returned unsatisfied in whole or in part.[4] The High Court has jurisdiction to wind up any company registered in England and Wales and may do so under the Insolvency Act 1986 (IA 1986), s 122 where the company is unable to pay its debts.

---

[1]   IA 1986, s 267(2).
[2]   IA 1986, ss 267(2)(c) and 268(1)(b). See also Insolvency Rules 1986, SI 1986/1925, r 6.8(3).
[3]   IA 1986, s 123(1)(a).
[4]   IA 1986, s 123(1)(b).

If insolvency is a possibility, should enforcement be attempted?

1.11 More generally, where the judgment creditor has doubts as to the solvency of the judgment debtor he should consider seriously whether there is likely to be any merit in bringing enforcement proceedings at all. Bankruptcy and winding up effectively operate as an automatic stay on enforcement proceedings and a judgment creditor who has not completed the enforcement before the commencement of the bankruptcy or winding up will not be entitled to retain the benefit of it. As will be seen, less formal forms of insolvency can also have serious effects on a judgment creditor's ability to enforce his judgment. The interrelation between the insolvency regime and the law on enforcement in this regard is considered at paras 1.157–1.215. The impact of the commencement of bankruptcy or winding up on each of the methods of enforcement considered in this book is discussed in more detail in each of the relevant chapters. Chapter 2 (paras 2.10–2.23 and 2.38) describes the methods by which a judgment creditor can seek to ascertain whether a judgment debtor is insolvent.

Time for payment of a money judgment

1.12 Before considering the steps which a judgment creditor can take to enforce a judgment, it is worth noting at the outset that enforcement procedures are generally not available before the judgment debt is actually due.[1] A judgment or order for the payment of an amount of money may specify the date by which payment must be made.[2] Where no such time limit is imposed,[3] a party must comply with the judgment or order (including a costs order) within 14 days of the date of the judgment or order.[4]

[1] However, a charging order can be obtained in respect of a judgment debt which is not immediately payable: Charging Orders Act 1979, s 1(1). See further Chapter 4.

[2] CPR 2.9 provides that the court should, wherever practicable, specify the calendar date (and time of day) by which an act must be completed when it gives a time limit for doing any act. In practice, judgments or orders for the payment of money often do not specify such a time limit.

[3] Where no other part of the CPR specifies a date for compliance and the court has not stayed the proceedings (see CPR 40.11).

[4] CPR 40.11.

Judgments in a foreign currency

1.13 The English court can award judgment for a sum of money expressed in a foreign currency.[1] This power may be exercised irrespective of whether the applicable law of the contract is English law[2] or foreign law.[3] It is not restricted to claims for payment of debts[4] and extends to claims for damages for breach of contract whether the claim is for liquidated[5] or unliquidated damages.[6] Enforcement of an English judgment which is expressed in a foreign currency should not be confused with the enforcement of foreign judgments (see further paras 1.242–1.260). However, English judgments awarded in a foreign currency raise particular administrative issues.

[1] *Miliangos v George Frank (Textiles) Ltd* [1976] AC 443, HL.

[2] *Federal Commerce and Navigation Co Ltd v Tradax Export SA, The Maratha Envoy* [1977] 1 QB 324, CA (reversed subsequently but on grounds not bearing on this point: [1978] AC 1).

3   *Miliangos v George Frank (Textiles) Ltd* [1976] AC 443, HL.
4   *Miliangos v George Frank (Textiles) Ltd* [1976] AC 443, HL.
5   *Federal Commerce and Navigation Co Ltd v Tradax Export SA, The Maratha Envoy* [1977] 1 QB 324, CA.
6   *Services Europe Atlantique Sud (SEAS) v Stockholms Rederiaktiebolag at Stockholm SVEA, The Folias* [1979] AC 685, HL.

1.14   The judgment will be for payment of the amount of the foreign currency or the sterling equivalent at the time of payment. The order should be in the following terms:[1]

'It is ordered that the defendant pay the claimant [state the sum in the foreign currency] or the sterling equivalent at the time of payment.'

The 'time of payment' means that:[2]

'... if the defendant fails to deliver the foreign currency, the date for its conversion into sterling should be the date when the plaintiff is given leave to levy execution for a sum expressed in sterling.'

1   PD 40B, para 10.
2   *Miliangos v George Frank (Textiles) Ltd* [1976] AC 443 at 497–498, per Lord Cross of Chelsea, HL.

1.15   This reflects the fact that:[1]

'... if the judgment is one expressed in foreign currency, it *must* be converted into sterling so that those responsible for enforcing the judgment (whether by levying execution or otherwise) may know what steps are open to them and how far they can go.'

1   *Miliangos v George Frank (Textiles) Ltd* [1976] AC 443 at 498, per Lord Edmund-Davies, HL.

1.16   In other words, it is not possible to *enforce* a judgment expressed in a foreign currency, it must first be converted into sterling to allow those enforcing the judgment to know whether they have satisfied the judgment or not. The conversion date for the purposes of enforcement will be the 'time of payment', that is, the date when the court authorises enforcement of the judgment in sterling since '[t]his date gets nearest to securing the creditor exactly what he bargained for'.[1]

1   *Miliangos v George Frank (Textiles) Ltd* [1976] AC 443 at 469, per Lord Wilberforce, HL.

GENERAL RULES ON ENFORCEMENT

1.17   The Civil Procedure Rules 1998[1] (CPR), Pt 70 contains general rules about the enforcement of judgments and orders.[2] By virtue of the rules contained in CPR Pt 40 and Pt 70 an order may be enforced in the same manner as a judgment.[3] The general rules, relating to the enforcement of judgments and orders were formerly contained in the Rules of the Supreme Court 1965[4] (RSC), Ord 45. However, Pt 70 did not fully replace RSC Ord 45, which is partially preserved in CPR Sch 1 and which must be read in conjunction with Pt 70.

1   SI 1998/3132.
2   CPR Pt 70 came into force on 25 March 2002: SI 2001/2792, para 1(c).

³   See further Civil Procedure 2004, vol 1, paras 40.1.1 and 40.2.3.
⁴   SI 1965/828.

Use of any method of enforcement available

1.18   A judgment creditor is free to use any method of enforcement which is available, save where an enactment, rule or practice direction provides otherwise.[1]

¹   CPR 70.2(2).

Multiple enforcement proceedings

1.19   Similarly, except where an enactment, rule or practice direction provides otherwise, a judgment creditor may use more than one method of enforcement either at the same time or one after the other.[1] As will be seen, the method of enforcement chosen by the judgment creditor will be determined by the assets of the judgment debtor that are available for enforcement. However, the judgment debtor may have a number of different assets which are amenable to different methods of enforcement. In the context of commercial enforcement, the costs incurred in connection with enforcement proceedings are likely to be small in comparison to the size of the judgment debt, which may in any event exceed the value of any one of the judgment debtor's assets. The use of concurrent enforcement proceedings should therefore be considered.

¹   CPR 70.2(2).

Enforcement against a non-party

1.20   Where a judgment or order is made in favour of a person who is not a party to the proceedings, it may be enforced by that person in exactly the same way as if he had been a party.[1] Permission to enforce the judgment or order is not required. Similarly, a judgment or order made against a non-party may be enforced against that person by the same methods as if he had been a party.[2]

¹   CPR 70.4.
²   CPR 70.4.

Interest on judgments

1.21   As has been noted in the introduction to this chapter, interest on judgment debts is considered in detail in Chapter 7. On enforcement, the interest which has accrued since judgment is recoverable together with the principal judgment debt.

THE JUDGMENT DEBTOR'S ASSETS

1.22   Information is the key to effective enforcement. It will both enable a judgment creditor to avoid wasting time and resources on fruitless enforcement proceedings when faced with a judgment debtor without the means to pay, and to select the method or methods of enforcement most likely to result in satisfaction of his judgment where the judgment debtor does have assets amenable to enforcement.

1.23   Information relating to the judgment debtor's means may have come into the judgment creditor's possession during the course of the litigation. However, given the importance of proper information about the judgment debtor's assets in the context of enforcement, Chapter 2 is devoted to the various methods by which a judgment creditor can obtain further information through public sources, the use of inquiry agents, and orders to obtain information from the judgment debtor. It also describes the methods by which a judgment creditor can check whether a judgment debtor is insolvent, since the judgment debtor's insolvency may mean that effort spent on taking enforcement steps is wasted[2]. Where a judgment creditor decides to conduct a court examination of a judgment debtor to obtain information on his assets by making a Pt 71 application, the questions put to the judgment debtor should be tailored by reference to information already known to the judgment creditor.

METHODS OF ENFORCEMENT COVERED BY THIS BOOK

1.24   Once a judgment creditor has information as to the judgment debtor's assets and means, he can consider which method or methods of enforcement will be most likely to result in the satisfaction of his judgment debt.

Third party debt order

1.25   A third party debt order directs a third party who itself owes a debt to the judgment debtor to discharge that debt by paying it directly to the judgment creditor. The fact that virtually every judgment debtor will maintain a bank account is likely to make this method of enforcement always worth considering.[3] Whether it is worth applying for such an order is likely to depend on the health of the judgment debtor's bank balance. Use of the third party debt order procedure is not confined to bank accounts and it can be used to attach any debt owed to the judgment debtor by a third party.[1] However, the procedure cannot be used to attach future wages and salaries, for which an attachment of earnings order is needed (an outline of which is provided at paras 1.49–1.63).

[1]   Apart from the Crown. The debt must also be properly recoverable within the jurisdiction. See further Chapter 3.
[2]   See paras 1.157–1.215.
[3]   A bank account which is in credit is a debt due by the bank to its customer. See further Chapter 3.

Charging order

1.26   A charging order is a means of securing a judgment debt by imposing a charge over a judgment debtor's property. They are commonly used to impose a charge over a judgment debtor's house or commercial premises, but are also available in relation to securities and funds in court. The charging order places the judgment debtor in the position of a secured creditor. With such security in place, the judgment creditor may be content to wait until the judgment debtor sells the property, when the sale proceeds will be used to discharge the charge and satisfy the judgment debt. However, if the judgment debtor is not prepared to wait for such a sale, he can himself apply to the court for a sale of the charged property. A charging order is likely to be a particularly useful method of enforcement where the judgment debtor owns land or property which is not mortgaged or where the value of the property to be charged significantly exceeds charges already held over the property.

Writ of fieri facias

1.27   A writ of fieri facias (or writ of fi fa, as it more commonly known) is a method of seizing the judgment debtor's goods to satisfy a money judgment. In the context of commercial enforcement, writs of fi fa are likely to be worth considering where the judgment debtor owns high value goods that would raise good prices at a public auction or if sold by private tender. In the case of corporate judgment debtors, the use of writs of fi fa to seize company property such as stock, machinery, office equipment or vehicles may also be considered.

Appointing a receiver by way of equitable execution

1.28   Appointing a receiver by way of equitable execution is an often-overlooked procedure that can provide access to a judgment debtor's assets that cannot be reached through other methods of enforcement. It can be used to collect assets such as rental income, future debts or to enforce contractual rights which the judgment debtor is refusing to enforce. Effectively, equitable execution operates as a residual form of enforcement because it is only available where other methods of enforcement are not available.

1.29   Each of the procedures outlined above are considered in more detail in Chapters 2 to 6.

COMPARISON OF ASSETS REACHED BY EACH FORM OF ENFORCEMENT

1.30   The following table illustrates the main assets against which third party debt orders, charging orders, writs of fieri facias and receivers by way of equitable execution can be used. It is intended as a broad overview – the individual chapters should be consulted for further details of the operation of the method of enforcement and for any restrictions and difficulties that might apply.

Asset	Third party debt order	Charging order	Writ of fi fa	Equitable execution[1]
Aircraft	✗	✗	✓	✗
Bank accounts	✓	✗	✗	-
Bank notes	✗	✗	✓	✗
Claim under an indemnity	✗	✗	✗	✓
Crown assets[2]	✗	✗	✗	✗
Crown debt owed to judgment debtor[3]	✗	✗	✗	✗
Damages (pre-assessment)	✗	✗	✗	✓
Damages (post-assessment)	✓	✗	✗	-
Debts (present)	✓	✗	✗	-
Debts (future)	✗	✗	✗	✓
Dividends	✗[4]	✓[5]	✗	✓[6]
Funds in court	✗[7]	✓	✗	-
Goods	✗	✗	✓	✗
Government stock	✗	✓	✗	✗
Interest under a trust	✗	✓	✗	-
Interest under a will	✗	✗	✗	✓
Land (freehold interest)	✗	✓	✗	✗
Land (leasehold interest)	✗	✓	✗	✗
Land (rents)	✗[8]	✗	✗	✓[9]
Machinery	✗	✗	✓[10]	✗
Pensions[11]	✗	✗	✗	✗
Shares	✗	✓	✗	✗
Ships	✗	✗	✓	✗
Units in a unit trust	✗	✓	✗	✗
Vehicles	✗	✗	✓	✗
Wages / salary[12]	✗	✗	✗	✗

[1] As explained further in Chapter 6, the appointment of a receiver by way of equitable execution is a residual method of enforcement. In general, equitable execution is only available where: (a) the asset cannot be reached using another method of enforcement; or (b) the asset can theoretically be reached using another method of enforcement but this would be practically very difficult if not impossible. For this reason, where the dash (-) symbol appears, this indicates that equitable execution may theoretically be possible but would not normally be granted because another enforcement method is available.

[2]   As explained in paras 1.130–1.131, the Crown is immune from all normal methods of enforcement available to a subject. Instead a statutory procedure for obtaining payment of judgment debts owed by the Crown exists, which is explained at paras 1.132–1.134.

[3]   As explained in paras 3.83–3.85, a special procedure exists under the Crown Proceedings Act 1947, s 27 to attach debts owed by the Crown to a judgment debtor.

[4]   Unless the dividend is due at the time the interim third party debt order is served. A third party debt order cannot be used in respect of future dividends.

[5]   Dividend income can only be charged under a charging order over certain government stock, stock of various English and foreign bodies and units in a unit trust.

[6]   Future dividends in respect of securities which cannot be subject to a charging order could in principle be subject to equitable execution.

[7]   However, CPR 72.10 provides a procedure whereby a judgment creditor can apply for an order that money in court be paid to him in satisfaction of a judgment debt. See further paras 3.61–3.62.

[8]   Unless the rent is due at the time the interim third party debt order is served. A third party debt order cannot be used in respect of future rent.

[9]   Future rent cannot be attached under a third party debt order and can only be attached by appointing a receiver by way of equitable execution.

[10]   However, the machinery must not be or have become a fixture to the land. See further para 5.25.

[11]   The correct method of attaching pensions is an attachment of earnings order. See paras 1.49–1.63.

[12]   The correct method of attaching wages and salary is an attachment of earnings order. See paras 1.49–1.63.

JUDICIAL STATISTICS ON ENFORCEMENT

1.31   It is instructive to consider data on the methods of enforcement most commonly favoured by judgment creditors. Each year judicial statistics about the courts are published by the Department for Constitutional Affairs. The following table sets out a comparison of enforcement proceedings issued in the Queen's Bench Division of the High Court[1] with those of the county court.

High Court - Queen's Bench Division

	1999	2000	2001	2002	2003
All claims	72,161	26,876	21,613	18,624	14,191
Money judgments over £50,000	580	928	550	620	490
Oral examinations	360	44	46	7	18
Writs of fieri facias	44,592	49,465	53,248	50,687	41,652
Charging orders	1,005	446	581	361	330
Third party debt orders	458	412	169	104	136

[1]   The Queen's Bench Division is used because the vast majority of commercial claims will be issued in this division, which encompasses the Commercial Court. An exact comparison cannot be made because the judicial statistics are presented in different ways for the High Court and county court.

County court

	1999	*2000*	*2001*	*2002*	*2003*
Money claims	1,760,308	1,631,966	1,502,879	1,395,754	1,354,446
Money claims over £50,000	Not available	Not available	Not available	Not available	14,899
Oral examinations	Not available	Not available	Not available	Not available	Not available
Warrants of execution	538,337	470,270	394,611	372,505	355,476
Charging orders	3,357	16,357	22,098	30,389	34,756
Third party debt orders	13,600	3,174	4,139	5,499	6,019
Attachment of earnings	34,399	35,545	42,011	39,855	40,384

1.32   The decline in the number of enforcement proceedings issued over the past five years is in line with the decline in the number of claims issued over that period. It is clear that the overwhelming majority of claims and enforcement proceedings are issued in the county court, although the majority of these are for relatively small sums.[1]

[1]   So much so that the judicial statistics for county court claims over £50,000 were only made available for the first time in 2003.

1.33   It is also clear that in both the High Court and the county court, the use of writs of fi fa or the county court equivalent, warrants of execution, are overwhelmingly the most commonly used methods of enforcement. In the High Court the number of writs of fi fa issued significantly exceeds the number of claims made. The likely explanation for this apparent anomaly is that many of these writs of fi fa represent judgments that were originally made in the county court that have been 'transferred up' see (paras 1.75–1.80).

1.34   Leaving aside attachment of earnings orders, which are generally only available in the county court,[1] charging orders and third party debt orders are the next most widely used method of enforcement, and in the county court there is a trend towards increasing use of these methods of enforcement. Appointment of a receiver by way of equitable execution seems to be so rare that there is not even a category for it.

[1]   See para 1.50.

1.35   The prevalence of writs of fi fa and warrants of execution is likely to have a number of explanations. A public visit by an enforcement officer to the judgment debtor's home or business followed by seizure and the threat of the sale of the judgment debtor's goods may be seen as more likely to induce payment of the debt than other enforcement procedures. In addition, the issue of a writ of fi fa is an administrative procedure that does not generally involve further court hearings. This may be a perceived benefit to a judgment creditor with litigation fatigue. However, in the context of commercial enforcement and high value debts, charging orders or third party debt orders may prove a more efficient means of satisfying the judgment debt unless particularly high value goods can be identified.

COMMITTAL AND WRITS OF SEQUESTRATION

1.36 Historically, orders for payment of money were ultimately enforced through imprisonment. However, Dickensian images of debtors languishing in Newgate prison became a thing of the past with the introduction of the Debtors Act 1869. The general object of the Debtors Act 1869 was to abolish imprisonment for non-payment of debts, with certain limited exceptions.[1] Section 5 of the Act preserved the court's powers to commit a judgment debtor in default of payment of a judgment debt or instalment order to prison for a term not exceeding six weeks. However, those powers were severely curtailed by the Administration of Justice Act 1970.[2] The High Court's jurisdiction to commit to prison for defaults in payment of a judgment debt or instalment order is now confined to defaults in respect of High Court maintenance orders.[3] As Wilson J observed in *B v B (injunction: restraint on leaving jurisdiction)*:[4]

'... Parliament has clearly determined that such invasion of personal liberty should be strictly limited even in the cause of enforcing judgment debts.'

[1] See *Middleton v Chichester* (1871) 6 Ch App 152. Debtors Act 1869, s 4 provides: 'With the exceptions herein-after mentioned, no person shall ... be arrested or imprisoned for making default in payment of a sum of money. There shall be excepted from the operation of the above enactment: 1. Default in payment of a penalty, or sum in the nature of a penalty, other than a penalty in respect of any contract. 2. Default in payment of any sum recoverable summarily before a justice or justices of the peace. 3. Default by a trustee or person acting in a fiduciary capacity and ordered to pay by a court of equity any sum in his possession or under his control. 4. Default by any attorney or solicitor in payment of costs when ordered to pay costs for misconduct as such, or in payment of a sum of money when ordered to pay the same in his character of an officer of the court making the order. 5. Default in payment for the benefit of creditors of any portion of a salary or other income in respect of the payment of which any court having jurisdiction in bankruptcy is authorised to make an order. 6. Default in payment of sums in respect of the payment of which orders are in this Act authorised to be made. Provided, first, that no person shall be imprisoned in any case excepted from the operation of this section for a longer period than one year; and, secondly, that nothing in this section shall alter the effect of any judgment or order of any court for payment of money except as regards the arrest and imprisonment of the person making default in paying such money.'

[2] Administration of Justice Act 1970, s 11(a).

[3] Similarly, Administration of Justice Act 1970, s 11 confines the county court's jurisdiction under Debtors Act 1869, s 5 to defaults in respect of High Court or county court maintenance orders or judgments in respect of taxes, social insurance contributions and other liabilities specified in Administration of Justice Act 1970, Sch 4. A person entitled to enforce a judgment or order under the Debtors Act 1869, s 5 will issue a judgment summons although the court has discretion to make an attachment of earnings order instead of an order of committal on such application (Attachment of Earnings Act 1971, s 3(6)).

[4] [1998] 1 WLR 329 at 331.

1.37 Non-payment of a judgment debt will constitute civil contempt of court and may be punishable by writ of sequestration. RSC Ord 45, r 5 provides the procedural machinery for the court to enforce its judgments or orders in circumstances that constitute contempt of court. A writ of sequestration[1] may be available with the permission of the court where a person who is required by a judgment or order to do an act within a time specified in that judgment or order (as extended or abridged by the court or agreed in writing by the parties) fails or neglects to do it within that time.[2] In any event, neither committal nor sequestration are direct means of enforcing a judgment debt and contempt of court does not itself give rise to any claim in damages.

Rather, sequestration may potentially form a means of exerting pressure on a judgment debtor to meet his judgment debt to avoid sequestration of his assets.

[1]   RSC Ord 45, r 5 also makes provision for an order of committal to be available but states that this remedy is subject to the provisions of the Debtors Act 1869 and 1878 which, as has been noted, abolished imprisonment for non-payment of debts.

[2]   RSC Ord 45, r 5.

1.38   Modern practice is for the last date for compliance with an order to be specified in the order.[1] Where a judgment or an order for the payment of money does not specify the time by which payment should be made, it will not be enforceable by writ of sequestration unless or until such a time limit is specified. RSC Ord 45, r 6 makes provision for the court to make an order setting a time limit for an act to be done where the original order does not specify such a time limit. If such an order is sought with a view to seeking an order for sequestration in the event of non-compliance, the judgment creditor should also ensure that the order prominently displays on the front cover a warning to the judgment debtor that disobedience is punishable by sequestration. RSC Ord 45, r 5 should be read in conjunction with RSC Ord 45, r 7, and a writ of sequestration will not be issued unless the order has been served personally on the judgment debtor[2] (or) before the expiration of the time limit for payment and is endorsed with a prominent penal notice warning the judgment debtor of the consequences of non-compliance.[3]

[1]   CPR 2.9.

[2]   Or on the officer of a company where sequestration of his assets in that capacity is sought.

[3]   RSC Ord 45, r 7. Where a further order of the court has been sought under RSC Ord 45, r 6 specifying the time limit by which payment must be made, a copy of that order must also be served on the judgment debtor.

1.39   A writ of sequestration can be obtained against the judgment debtor's property or, in the case of a corporate judgment debtor, the property of any director or other officer of the body.[1] However, sequestration is a severe remedy and, as with civil contempt generally, will only be granted in serious cases. Leave of the court is required to issue a writ of sequestration and the application must be made in accordance with Pt 23 and be heard by a judge.[2] The procedural rules relating to the application and issue of a writ of sequestration are set out in RSC Ord 46, rr 5 and 6.

[1]   RSC Ord 45, r 5.

[2]   RSC Ord 46, r 5.

1.40   The effect of a writ of sequestration is to place the contemnor's property into the hands of sequestrators, who will manage the property and receive rents or profits until the court orders how the property should be dealt with. However, the property remains in the contemnor's ownership and no title to or interest in the property is conferred upon the judgment creditor. The remedy may prove most useful where the defaulting judgment debtor is a company since it may act as a means of putting pressure on the officers of that body to take the necessary steps to ensure that the company complies with the judgment.

1.41   The court also has specific powers of committal in relation to Pt 71 proceedings (orders to obtain information from judgment debtors) (see Chapter 2) and attachment of earnings orders (see paras 1.49–1.63).

HIGH COURT MONEY JUDGMENTS

1.42   As has been noted in the introduction to this chapter, the focus of this book is commercial enforcement. It is concerned with methods of enforcement that are available in the High Court for the enforcement of judgments for the payment of a sum of money. Some enforcement procedures therefore fall outside the scope of this book, namely certain forms of writs of execution, distress, judgment summonses, attachment of earnings orders and self-help remedies. However, an outline of each of these procedures is provided in paras 1.44–1.63 below together with an indication of when they are likely to be relevant in a commercial enforcement scenario.

Payments into court

1.43   The rules relating to the enforcement of judgments or orders for the payment of money include judgments or orders for the payment of costs.[1] However, they do not apply to judgments or orders for the payment of money into court.[2] Accordingly, a party cannot apply to enforce an order for a payment into court through a third party debt order, a charging order or a writ of fieri facias. An order for the payment of money into court may be enforced by the appointment of a receiver,[3] by a writ of sequestration or by an order of committal.[4] However, the most appropriate form of sanction is likely to be an application to strike out the defaulting party's claim or defence, as appropriate.

1   CPR 70.1(2)(d).
2   CPR 70.1(2)(d).
3   In accordance with the court's jurisdiction under Supreme Court Act 1981, s 37.
4   RSC Ord 45, r 5.

Writs of execution

1.44   Writs of execution encompass writs of fieri facias, writs of possession, writs of delivery, writs of sequestration and any further writ in aid of one of these writs.[1] The enforcement of money judgments by writs of fieri facias is covered in Chapter 5 of this book. An outline of the circumstances in which writs of sequestration may be available in aid of the enforcement of a judgment debt has been provided in paras 1.36–1.40.

1   RSC Ord 46, r 1.

Writs of possession

1.45   A writ of possession is a method of enforcing a judgment or order for the giving of possession of land.[1] It is therefore outside the scope of this book, which is concerned with the enforcement of money judgments.

1   RSC Ord 45, r 3. Judgments for the giving of possession of land may also be enforced by an order of committal and writs of sequestration in certain circumstances: see RSC Ord 45, rr 3, 5 and 7.

Writs of delivery

1.46 Where a judgment is given or order is made for the delivery of any goods which does *not* give the person against whom judgment is made the alternative of paying the assessed value of the goods, it may be enforced by 'writ of specific delivery'. A judgment or order that requires delivery of any goods *or* payment of their assessed value may be enforced by 'writ of delivery'.[1] Writs of delivery for the recovery of goods (or their assessed value) are outside the scope of this book, which is concerned with the enforcement of money judgments.

1   RSC Ord 45, r 4. In certain circumstances such judgments or orders may also be enforced through orders of committal and writs of sequestration: see RSC Ord 45, rr 3, 5 and 7.

Judgment summons

1.47 A judgment summons orders a judgment debtor in default of an order to pay a sum of money to attend court to be examined as to his means of complying with the order and to give reasons why he should not be committed to prison for the default. However, in the High Court these are only available in relation to defaults in respect of High Court maintenance orders[1] and are not therefore relevant in the context of commercial enforcement.

1   See further para 1.36.

Distress

1.48 In certain circumstances an injured party is entitled to seek redress for the wrong done to him himself rather than take recourse through the courts. One example is the right of distress damage feasant, whereby a man who finds another's chattel on his land unlawfully may impound it to compel the owner of the chattel to make good any damage done.[1] Similarly, distress for rent[2] is an ancient remedy which entitles a landlord who is owed unpaid rent to enter the demised premises and seize and sell goods found there to satisfy the unpaid rent.[3] Such self-help remedies are outside the scope of this book.

1   See further *Clerk and Lindsell on Torts* (18th edn, 2000) pp 1683–1686.
2   *The Law Commission Report on Landlord and Tenant Distress for Rent* 4 February 1991 (Law Com No 194) recommended the abolition of distress for rent as a remedy once improvements had been made to the court system to provide landlords with effective alternatives to distress. Professor Beatson QC's *Independent Review of Bailiff Law Report*, June 2000, which was commissioned as part of the Civil Enforcement Review, recommends fundamental reform to the law on distress for rent.
3   See further *Woodfall on Landlord and Tenant*.

Attachment of earnings orders

1.49 Although this book is concerned with methods of enforcement that are available in the High Court, a judgment creditor may wish to give some consideration to attachment of earnings orders in the context of commercial enforcement. In terms of popularity, attachment of earnings orders are second only to warrants of execution as a method of enforcement used in the county court.[1] Where the judgment debtor is a highly paid employee or likely to be in receipt of a high pension, an attachment of earnings order may prove attractive.

[1]   See the table at para 1.31.

1.50 The statutory provisions relating to the attachment of earnings orders as a means of enforcing the discharge of monetary obligations were consolidated in the Attachment of Earnings Act 1971 (AEA 1971). The High Court only has jurisdiction to make an attachment of earnings order to secure payments under a High Court maintenance order.[1] It has no such jurisdiction in relation to judgment debts. However, a county court may make an attachment of earnings order to secure the payment of a judgment debt[2] of £50 or more.[3] It is possible for High Court judgments to be transferred to the county court for the purposes of enforcement (see paras 1.65–1.70).

[1]   AEA 1971, s 1(1).
[2]   High Court or county court.
[3]   AEA 1971, s 1(2) and CPR Sch 2, CCR Ord 27, r 7(9). County courts may also make attachment of earnings orders in respect of maintenance orders and county court administration orders.

Interrelation with other methods of enforcement

1.51 Where an attachment of earnings order has been made to secure payment of a judgment debt,[1] no order or warrant of commitment shall be issued in consequence of any enforcement proceedings relating to the judgment debt that were begun before the attachment of earnings order was made.[2] Further, AEA 1971, s 8(2)(b) provides that 'so long as the [attachment of earnings] order is in force, no execution for recovery of the [judgment] debt shall issue against any property of the [judgment] debtor without the leave of the county court'.[3] There are no cases interpreting this provision and it is unclear whether 'execution' is used in its narrow sense to mean seizure of goods (ie a writ of execution or writ of fi fa) or its wider sense to mean all forms of enforcement.[4] Where a judgment creditor is therefore contemplating using a number of enforcement methods to secure payment of a judgment debt, he should be aware that using an attachment of earnings order may preclude the use of other forms of enforcement. From a practical perspective, an attachment of earnings order should therefore only be sought after other methods of enforcement have been given due consideration.[5] It may also be worth nothing that where an application is made for an attachment of earnings orders to secure payment of a judgment debt and it appears to the court that the judgment debtor has other creditors, the court must consider whether the case is one in which all the debtor's liabilities should be dealt with together under a county court administration order[6]. However, given that such orders can only be made where the judgment debtor's total indebtedness does not exceed £5,000, this is unlikely to be relevant in a commercial enforcement scenario (see para 1.214).

[1]   References in AEA 1971 to sums payable under a judgment debt include a reference to the payment of costs (AEA 1971, s 25(2)).
[2]   AEA 1971, s 8(2)(a).
[3]   AEA 1971, s 8(2)(b).

4   The Interpretation Act 1978 does not assist as it does not define 'execution'.
5   A further drawback of using the attachment of earnings procedure is that interest ceases to
     accrue on the judgment debt once the order is in place. County Courts (Interest on Judgment
     Debts) Order 1991, SI 1991/1184, art 4(3).
6   AEA 1971, s 4.

Earnings

1.52 'Earnings' are defined in AEA 1971, s 24 as any sums payable to a person by
way of wages or salary (including bonuses and overtime), pension (including
annuities) and statutory sick pay, after deduction of tax and National Insurance
contributions.[1] Certain types of payments are specifically excluded and are not
attachable under the provisions of the AEA 1971, including pay to members of Her
Majesty's forces, social security benefits and disability payments.[2] Attachment of
earnings orders are available in respect of persons in the employment of the Crown.[3]

1   AEA 1971, Sch 3.
2   AEA 1971, s 24(2).
3   AEA 1971, s 22 contains provisions as to the operation of attachment of earnings orders in
     respect of Crown employees.

1.53 Before considering whether to apply for an attachment of earnings order, it will
bc important for the judgment creditor to ascertain not only the amount but also the
exact nature of the income received by the judgment debtor to determine whether it
constitutes 'earnings' for the purposes of AEA 1971. The attachment of earnings
procedure cannot be used where, for example, the judgment debtor is self-employed
or where he is a partner who withdraws his share of the profits through drawings on
account. The court has a power to determine whether payments are earnings for the
purpose of an attachment of earnings order and an application for such a determination
can be made by the judgment debtor, the judgment creditor or the judgment debtor's
employer.[1]

1   AEA 1971, s 16.

1.54 Information as to the judgment debtor's earnings may have been obtained
through the prior use of Pt 71 proceedings (see Chapter 2). Alternatively, the judgment
debtor may provide the relevant information following service of the application for
an attachment of earnings order (see para 1.58). In addition, each county court
maintains an index of all attachment of earnings orders for that district. The index may
be searched free of charge and will reveal whether other attachment of earnings
orders have been against that judgment debtor.

Consolidated attachment of earnings order

1.55 If there are existing attachment of earnings orders, the judgment creditor may
apply for his judgment to be consolidated with those other judgments under a
consolidated attachment of earnings order. The sums paid under a consolidated
attachment of earnings order will be distributed in proportion to the amounts payable
under the respective judgments.[1] However, the existence of other attachment of

earnings orders is likely to indicate that this method of enforcement will entail some delay before the whole of the judgment debt is repaid.

[1]   CCR Ord 27, r 22.

Procedure

1.56   The procedural rules relating to attachment of earnings orders are contained in the County Court Rules 1984 (CCR) Ord 27.[1] The application should be made to the county court for the district in which the judgment debtor resides.[2] If necessary, the judgment should first be transferred to that county court (see paras 1.65-1.70). Form N337 should be filed, which certifies the amount of money remaining due under the judgment, together with a certified copy of the judgment and a witness statement or affidavit verifying the amount due under the judgment.[3]

[1]   Preserved in CPR, Sch 2.
[2]   CCR Ord 27, r 3(1). If the judgment debtor does not reside in England and Wales or the judgment creditor does not know where he lives, the application should be made to the county court which made the order or, where the order is an order of the High Court, the county court for that district: CCR Ord 27, r 3(2).
[3]   CCR Ord 27, r 4.

1.57   The fee for lodging an application for an administration of earnings order is £60.[1] From 1 April 2005, all cheques should be made payable to 'HMCS' or 'Her Majesty's Courts Service' instead of 'Her Majesty's Paymaster General' or 'HMPG' as was previously the case.

[1]   Civil Proceedings Fees Order 2004, SI 2004/3121, Sch 1, para 7.7.

1.58   The court will issue the application and serve a copy on the judgment debtor informing him that he should either pay the judgment debt or furnish the information requested as to his earnings (in Form N56, known as a 'statement of means') within eight days.[1] If the judgment debtor fails to pay the judgment debt or to provide a statement of means within that eight-day period, the court may make an order requiring him to do so.[2] The court has power to enforce the requirements for provision of information, which ultimately may lead to imprisonment of the judgment debtor for up to 14 days.[3] In addition, the court has power to order the judgment debtor's employer to provide specified particulars of the judgment debtor's earnings and anticipated earnings.[4]

[1]   AEA 1971, s 14 and CCR Ord 27, r 5. This usually takes the court between five and ten working days after filing.
[2]   AEA 1971, s 14.
[3]   AEA 1971, s 23 and CCR Ord 27, r 7B.
[4]   AEA 1971, s 14 and CCR Ord 27, r 6.

1.59   The court has a discretion to make an attachment of earnings order but to do so it must appear to the court that the judgment debtor has failed to make one or more payments required by the judgment.[1] The standard attachment of earnings order is Form N366 and will be directed to the judgment debtor's employer. It will direct the employer to make periodic deductions from the judgment debtor's earnings and pay the amounts specified to the collecting officer of the court.[2] The order will specify both the normal deductions rate (that is, the rate at which the court thinks it is reasonable for the judgment debtor's earnings to be applied to meet the judgment debt) and the protected earnings rate (that is, the rate below which the court thinks the judgment debtor's earnings should not be reduced having regard to the judgment debtor's earnings and needs).[3] The court collecting officer will pay the sums received under the attachment of earnings order to the judgment creditor[4] and payments made to the court collecting officer under the attachment of earnings order will be deemed to be payments made by the judgment debtor so as to discharge the judgment debt.[5] Both the judgment debtor and his employer are obliged to inform the court in the event of any change in his employment and earnings while an attachment of earnings order is in force.[6]

[1]   AEA 1971, s 3(3).
[2]   AEA 1971, s 6. The order will be sent by the Centralised Attachment of Earnings Payment System in Northampton.
[3]   AEA 1971, s 6 and Sch 3. The employer will also be allowed to deduct £1 from the judgment debtor's earnings towards his clerical and administrative costs on making each deduction (AEA 1971, s 7(4) and SI 1991/356). The judgment creditor may also be allowed his costs of making the application: see CCR Ord 27, r 9.
[4]   After deducting court fees, if any.
[5]   AEA 1971, s 13.
[6]   AEA 1971, s 15.

1.60   The judgment debtor may apply on notice for the attachment of earnings order to be reconsidered.[1] In practice, the judgment debtor often makes such application to suspend the attachment of earnings order to permit him to make payments direct to the judgment creditor without having to involve his employer. Where a judgment debtor does not wish his employer to know about the judgment debt, an application for an attachment of earnings order may therefore be a means of exerting pressure on the judgment debtor to pay the judgment debt and a suspended order may result in the debt being paid off more quickly.

[1]   CCR Ord 27, r 7(2).

Offences

1.61   It is an offence for a judgment debtor who has been given notice of a hearing of an application for an attachment of earnings order or variation of such an order to fail to attend the hearing.[1] A judgment debtor also commits an offence if he fails to provide the information required by the court or to notify the court of changes in his employment details.[2] An employer who fails to comply with an attachment of earnings order or to fail to notify the court of a change in a judgment debtor's employment and earnings, or to provide false particulars of these matters to the court will also be guilty of an offence.[3]

[1]   AEA 1971, s 23(1).
[2]   AEA 1971, s 23.
[3]   AEA 1971, s 23. AEA 1971, s 23(5) sets out certain defences to these offences.

Reform of the attachment of earnings procedure

1.62   The Effective Enforcement White Paper published in March 2003 reviewed the current operation of attachment of earnings orders and sought to identify aspects in which it could be improved. The paper noted that the current procedure has certain failings from the judgment creditor's perspective in that it is initially dependent on the judgment debtor to both provide a statement of means and to do so accurately. It also identified significant regional variation in the court's assessment of what is considered reasonable for protected earnings.

1.63   The White Paper proposes a fixed table process setting out a sliding scale of deductions dependent on the net amount earned per month by the judgment debtor, with the option for both the judgment creditor and the judgment debtor to apply for a review if they can show that the table deduction rates fall well below or above what the judgment debtor can afford. The White Paper also proposes tracking the judgment debtor's employment through Inland Revenue records to provide the courts with a reliable source of employment details. It is envisaged that amendments will be needed to AEA 1971 through primary legislation to effect these changes.[1]

[1]   Paragraph 324.

TRANSFER OF PROCEEDINGS BETWEEN THE HIGH COURT AND THE COUNTY COURT

1.64   The question as to which court the judgment creditor should issue his enforcement proceedings in is dealt with in each of the relevant chapters. Although this book is concerned with High Court methods of enforcement, transfer of proceedings between the High Court and the county court may be relevant in the context of commercial enforcement where the judgment creditor seeks to utilise the attachment of earnings order (which will necessitate transfer of a High Court judgment to a county court) or where the judgment creditor seeks to enforce a judgment for more than £5,000 by writ of fieri facias (when the judgment can be 'transferred up' to the High Court for the purposes of utilising this method of enforcement). An outline of the general rules on transfer is therefore set out below.

High Court to county court

1.65   As has been noted, the most common reason to transfer a High Court judgment to the county court for enforcement is to enable the judgment creditor to apply for an attachment of earnings order.

1.66   County Courts Act 1984 (CCA 1984), s 40 gives the High Court the power to transfer any proceedings before it, including enforcement proceedings, to the county court where statute provides that such proceedings are required to be brought before a county court. Subject to any such statutory provisions, the High Court may also order the transfer of any proceedings before it to a county court at its discretion. The transfer shall be to such county court that the High Court considers appropriate having taken into account the convenience of the parties and that of any person likely to be affected.[1]

[1]   CCA 1984, s 40(4). CCA 1984, s 40(6)(b) and (7) provides that, once transferred, the judgment will be treated for 'all purposes' as a judgment of the county court although any rights to set aside or appeal remain unaffected.

1.67 A judgment creditor wishing to enforce a High Court judgment or order in a county court must apply to the High Court for an order transferring the proceedings to that county court.[1] The High Court order for transfer will be in Form PF 168.

1   CPR 70.3.

1.68 Once the High Court order for transfer has been made, the judgment creditor must file the following documents in the county court with his request for enforcement:[1]

(1) a copy of the judgment;
(2) a certificate verifying the amount due under the judgment or order;
(3) if a writ of execution has previously been issued in the High Court to enforce the judgment or order, a copy of the relevant enforcement officer's return to the writ; and
(4) a copy of the High Court order transferring the proceedings to the county court.

1   PD 70, para 3.1.

1.69 Form N322H should be used to make the request to the county court to register the High Court judgment for enforcement, which contains a helpful checklist.

1.70 Upon transfer, the High Court judgment can be enforced as a judgment of the county court.[1]

1   CCA 1984, s 40(6).

County court to High Court

1.71 The procedure for transfer from the county court to the High Court varies according to whether the transfer is to enable execution by writ of fieri facias against the judgment debtor's goods[1] or whether the purpose of the transfer is to seek other forms of enforcement.

1   The same rules also apply to a transfer for a writ of possession, although as these are outside the scope of this book they are not considered further here.

Transfer to High Court for all forms of enforcement except execution against goods

1.72 An application for transfer of a county court judgment to the High Court to seek a method of enforcement other than a writ of fieri facias should be made under CPR Pt 23 relying on CCA 1984, s 42(2). Having issued the application, the judgment creditor should make a request in writing to the county court for a certificate of judgment[1] stating:

(a) that the certificate is required for the purpose of enforcing the judgment in the High Court;[2] and
(b) confirming that an application has been made under CCA 1984, s 42 and attaching a copy of the application to the request.[3]

1   CCR Ord 22, r 8(1).
2   CCR Ord 22, r 8(1)(a)(ii).
3   CCR Ord 22, r 8(1A)(b).

1.73   No fee is payable for the issue of the certificate of judgment by the county court or the registration of the judgment in the High Court (although a fee is payable for the issue of the Pt 23 application).

1.74   Once the county judgment has been transferred to the High Court, it will be treated as a judgment of the High Court judgment and all the methods of enforcement available in the High Court can be used.[1]

[1]   CCA 1984, s 42(5)(a). However, the judgment will remain a judgment of the county court for the purposes of appeals (CCA 1984, s 42(6)).

Enforcement against the judgment debtor's goods by writ of fieri facias - 'transfer up'

1.75   The most common reason to transfer a county court judgment to the High Court for enforcement is so that the judgment creditor can issue a writ of fieri facias for execution against goods. Judgments over £5,000 *must* be transferred to the High Court for execution against goods to take place.[1] For this reason, a streamlined procedure exists to allow the issue a writ of fieri facias in respect of a county court judgment which circumvents the procedure for transfer set out in CCA 1984, s 42(2).

[1]   High Court and County Courts Jurisdiction Order 1991, SI 1991/724, art 8(1)(a).

1.76   The judgment creditor should make a request in writing for a certificate of judgment[1] stating:

(a)   that the certificate is required for the purpose of enforcing the judgment in the High Court;[2] and
(b)   confirming that it is intended to enforce the judgment by execution against goods.[3]

[1]   CCR Ord 22, r 8(1).
[2]   CCR Ord 22, r 8(1)(a)(ii).
[3]   CCR Ord 22, r 8(1A)(a)(i).

1.77   The transfer to the High Court takes effect, from the grant of the certificate of judgment, as an order to transfer the proceedings to the High Court. However, the judgment is only sent to the High Court for the limited purpose of enforcement by writ of fieri facias.[1] Once transfer has taken place, the court will notify the judgment debtor of the transfer[2] using Form N328.[3]

[1]   CCR Ord 25, r 13(1).
[2]   CCR Ord 25, r 13(2).
[3]   'Notice of transfer of proceedings to the High Court.'

1.78   Form N293A is a combined certificate of judgment and request for writ of fieri facias. The first page of the Form is the certificate of judgment and must be signed by an officer of the county court from which judgment is being transferred. The second page is effectively a simplified version of Form PF 53 (writ of fieri facias) and will be issued by the High Court once the first page of the Form has been signed by the county court. The Form contains detailed guidance notes[1] as to how to issue the writ of fieri facias in the High Court once the certificate of judgment has been completed by the county court.

[1]   These are based on Practice Direction (County Court Order: Enforcement) (No 2) [1998] 1 WLR 1557.

1.79 No fee is payable for the issue of the certificate of judgment by the county court or the registration of the judgment in the High Court, although a fee is payable for the issue of the writ of fieri facias (see further Chapter 5).

Limitations on transfer up

1.80 There are a number of situations in which a certificate of judgment will not be granted and in which transfer up to the High Court for the purposes of execution by a writ of fieri facias is not available. These are set out in CCR Ord 25, r 13(3) and include a situation where there is an application either to set aside the judgment or for a stay of execution under CCA 1984, s 88. In such circumstances the request for the certificate will not be dealt with until those proceedings are determined.[1]

1   CCR Ord 25, r 13(3).

County court to another county court

1.81 For completeness, an outline of the procedure for transfer between county courts is given. If a judgment creditor is required by a rule or practice direction to enforce a judgment or order of one county court in a different county court, he must make a request in writing to the court in which the case is proceeding to transfer the proceedings to that other court.[1] CCR Ord 25, r 2 sets out the procedure for transfer of proceedings between county courts for enforcement where such transfer is required by the provisions of the CPR. A court officer will transfer the proceedings to the other court unless a judge orders otherwise and the court will give notice of the transfer to all the parties.[2] When the proceedings have been transferred, the parties must take any further steps in the proceedings in the county court to which they have been transferred, unless a rule or practice direction provides otherwise.[3]

1   PD 70, para 2.1.
2   PD 70, paras 2.2–2.3.
3   PD 70, para 2.4.

PROCEDURES IN AID OF ENFORCEMENT

1.82 As well as steps to enforce the judgment debt, a judgment creditor may also need to consider whether any ancillary measures in support of enforcement should be utilised.

1.83 As has been noted at the start of this chapter, one of the main perils facing a claimant is the prospect that following judgment he may be unable to obtain satisfaction of that judgment, either in full or at all. From the 1970s onwards, a body of case law has developed to prevent a defendant artificially creating such a situation by dissipating his assets so as to make himself 'judgment proof' through the use of injunctions and other interim remedies. Where the judgment creditor suspects that the judgment debtor may dissipate his assets to frustrate enforcement, steps to preserve those assets in the interim should be considered. In addition, where a judgment creditor believes he may be in competition with others who claim a beneficial interest in securities or funds in court against which he seeks enforcement, the use of a stop order or stop notice should be considered to prevent dealings in those assets.

Freezing injunctions

1.84   The court has jurisdiction to grant an interim injunction restraining the disposal of assets over which the claimant has a proprietary claim (a 'proprietary injunction'). However, even where the claimant asserts no proprietary claim over the defendant's assets but after judgment those assets may be used to satisfy a money judgment, an interim remedy may be available. The court may grant the claimant an interim injunction restraining a party from removing assets located in England and Wales from the jurisdiction, or restraining a party from dealing with any assets whether located in the jurisdiction or not. Such injunctions are known as 'freezing injunctions' (formerly known as 'Mareva injunctions') and the court's jurisdiction to grant freezing injunctions is now recognised in Supreme Court Act 1981, s 37(3).[1] The procedural regime relating to freezing injunctions is contained in CPR Pt 25.

[1]   Supreme Court Act 1981, s 37(3) provides: 'The power of the High Court under subsection (1) to grant an interlocutory injunction restraining a party to any proceedings from removing from the jurisdiction of the High Court, or otherwise dealing with, assets located within that jurisdiction shall be exercisable in cases where that party is, as well as in cases where he is not, domiciled, resident or present within that jurisdiction.'

1.85   Freezing injunctions are potentially available at all stages in the litigation but are most frequently sought at a very early stage, usually before the claim form has been issued. However, the court's power to grant an injunction may also be granted after judgment to assist the process of enforcement.[1] Although in some cases seeking a freezing injunction after judgment may amount to locking the stable door after the horse has bolted, it may be that a judgment debtor will only take steps to dissipate his assets once judgment has been given against him.

[1]   See eg *Orwell Steel (Erection and Fabrication) Ltd v Asphalt and Tarmac (UK) Ltd* [1985] 3 All ER 747 and *Mercantile Group (Europe) AG v Aiyela* [1994] 1 All ER 110.

1.86   In *Orwell Steel (Erection and Fabrication) Ltd v Asphalt and Tarmac (UK) Ltd*,[1] the judgment debtor attempted to sell various asphalt machines and vans to another company after judgment had been awarded to frustrate the execution of a writ of fieri facias. The court granted a freezing injunction restraining the judgment debtor from dealing with assets up to the value of the judgment.

[1]   [1985] 3 All ER 747.

1.87   The granting of a freezing injunction in aid of enforcement of a judgment is discretionary and such orders are not granted lightly.[1] The court may take into account not just the effect on the judgment creditor and judgment debtor of granting the injunction, but also the consequences for third parties.[2]

[1]   See further *Gee on Commercial Injunctions* (5th edn, 2004).
[2]   See eg *Camdex International Ltd v Bank of Zambia (No 2)* [1997] 1 WLR 632, CA, where the court found that the considerable hardship that would have been caused in Zambia by an injunction relating to (worthless) Zambian bank notes held in England meant that the injunction should be varied to enable the bank to deal with the notes.

Further injunctions in support of freezing injunctions

1.88 Debtors Act 1869, s 6 provides that where a claimant can show that a defendant is about to leave England unless apprehended and the defendant's absence will 'materially prejudice' the claimant's prosecution of his action, the court may make an order for the defendant's arrest. However, this section does not apply post-judgment and will not assist a judgment creditor in enforcing a judgment.[1] A writ ne exeat regno is also available to prevent a person leaving the jurisdiction where it can be shown that his absence from the jurisdiction will materially prejudice the claimant in prosecution of his claim.[2] However, again, such a writ is only available to facilitate the obtaining of a judgment. It is not available in aid of enforcement proceedings.[3]

[1]   Debtors Act 1869, s 6 provides that the power is available 'at any time before final judgment'. See also *Yorkshire Engine Co v Wright* (1872) 21 WR 15.
[2]   The availability of a writ ne exeat regno is limited by analogy with Debtors Act 1869, s 6. See *Drover v Beyer* (1879) 13 Ch D 242.
[3]   *Hume v Druyff* (1873) LR 8 Exch 214. In the words of Megarry J in *Felton v Callis* [1968] 3 All ER 673 at 680: 'The writ [ne exeat regno] is very far from being a form of execution.'

1.89 However, Supreme Court Act 1981, s 37(1) provides:

'The High Court may by order (whether interlocutory or final) grant an injunction ... in all cases in which it appears to the court to be just and convenient to do so.'

1.90 The jurisdiction granted to the court under this statutory provision has been developed to provide ancillary remedies to prevent a defendant leaving the jurisdiction. The circumstances in which such an order would be made in support of enforcement proceedings were considered in *B v B* (*injunction: restraint on leaving jurisdiction*).[1] In that case, a husband, who was resident abroad, had been ordered to pay his wife's costs after a failed application under the Married Women's Property Act 1882. He failed to comply with the order and while he was visiting London on one occasion, his wife obtained an order for an oral examination as to his means and also to restrain him from leaving the jurisdiction until the hearing and to surrender his passport. The husband contended that the court had no jurisdiction to grant the injunction.

[1]   [1998] 1 WLR 329.

1.91 Having observed that the court's jurisdiction to restrain a party from leaving the jurisdiction and to make a consequential order for the surrender of his or her passport should exist in principle in aid of all the court's procedures leading to the disposal of proceedings, Wilson J continued:[1]

'I consider that the jurisdiction is also available in some circumstances after judgment. To be specific, it can be invoked to aid the court's established procedures for enforcement of the judgment.'

[1]   [1998] 1 WLR 329 at 334.

1.92 He therefore considered that the court had the power to make an order obliging the husband to remain within the jurisdiction pending the oral examination:[1]

'A judgment summons and an oral examination are both established procedures for enforcement and they should not be permitted to be frustrated by the debtor's departure from the jurisdiction.'

He further concluded the court had been right to make such an order in the circumstances.

1   [1998] 1 WLR 329 at 334.

1.93   However, while the court's powers under the Supreme Court Act 1981, s 37(1) could restrain a debtor from leaving the jurisdiction in aid of enforcement proceedings, it did not amount to a freestanding enforcement procedure in its own right. Accordingly, it could not be used to restrain a judgment debtor within the jurisdiction indefinitely until the judgment debt was paid. Such an injunction is not therefore available as a means of putting pressure on a judgment debtor to pay his judgment debts. The injunction sought in such terms by the judgment creditors in *B v B* was therefore refused even though Wilson J 'would have been pleased' to make it and was of the view that it would have induced the judgment debtor to pay the debt immediately. Wilson J observed that provision of such an order would entail a change in the law, which was properly a matter for Parliament, and that in light of the growing trend in the reciprocal enforcement of the orders of other jurisdictions, the power to restrain a judgment debtor within the jurisdiction until the judgment debt was paid seemed less necessary than in former times.

Interim receivers to preserve assets

1.94   Interim receivers to preserve assets fulfil a similar function to that of a freezing injunction and their appointment is granted on similar grounds. The purpose of the order is to preserve assets so that they are available to meet a judgment.

1.95   The appointment will prohibit the respondent from dealing with the receivership assets. As with a freezing injunction, were a respondent to deal with assets in breach of the order then the respondent may be found in contempt of court. However, a receiver offers a greater degree of protection than a freezing injunction, at least in respect of assets within the jurisdiction of the court, because the receiver will take control[1] of the respondent's assets, thereby making it harder for assets to be dissipated. Appointing a receiver will involve the added expense of the receiver's costs and for this reason it would have to be shown that an injunction would not suffice to preserve assets and that the added protection of a receiver is needed.[2]

1   *Derby & Co Ltd v Weldon (Nos 3 and 4)* [1990] Ch 65, CA. The Court of Appeal upheld the appointment of an interim receiver which ordered two individual defendants to do all within their power to vest assets in the receiver.
2   Commercial Litigation: Pre-emptive remedies, para A2–369.

Interim receivers to preserve assets in aid of enforcement

1.96   An interim receiver to preserve assets in aid of enforcement should not be confused with a receiver by way of equitable execution, who is appointed to aid the enforcement of judgments. Once a receiver by way of equitable execution is appointed, one effect of the order is to prohibit the judgment debtor dealing with the assets covered by the receivership order. In *Manchester and Liverpool District Banking Co v Parkinson*[1] the Court of Appeal held that evidence of dissipation of assets was a potential factor in the court exercising its discretion to appoint a receiver by way of equitable execution. The court applied this in *Goldschmidt v Oberrheinische Metallwerke*[2] where there was reason to believe that the German judgment debtor was endeavouring to collect all debts due to it in England in order to avoid enforcement. If dissipation is feared in the period between judgment and the hearing of the application to appoint a receiver by way of equitable execution, the application can be made without notice for an injunction prohibiting dissipation pending the hearing of the application. The appointment of a receiver by way of equitable execution is considered in Chapter 6.

[1]   (1888) 22 QBD 173 at 177, per Fry LJ, CA.
[2]   [1906] 1 KB 373 at 375, CA.

Stop orders and stop notices

1.97 A stop order is an order which has the effect of prohibiting dealings in securities and may also prohibit the payment of any dividend or interest relating to such securities. Stop orders may also be obtained in relation to funds in court to prohibit dealing with the funds or any income on them. The purpose of a stop order is to afford the applicant an opportunity to take whatever further steps he considers appropriate to secure his claim to the relevant assets. In many cases, the next step is likely to be an application for a charging order over the securities or funds in court.

1.98 A stop notice has the effect of preventing any dealings in the securities without first giving 14 days' notice to the person who obtained the order. The requirement to provide notice to the party who obtained a stop notice before dealing in securities affords the applicant the opportunity to assert his claim to the securities.

1.99 Stop orders and stop notices may be obtained on the application of a person claiming to have an interest in securities, which would include a judgment creditor whose judgment has not been satisfied. They are therefore a means whereby a judgment creditor can takes steps to preserve a judgment debtor's assets so that they are available for enforcement. The rules relating to stop orders and stop notices are considered further in Chapter 5.

PAYMENT OF JUDGMENT DEBT AFTER ENFORCEMENT COMMENCED

1.100 One important question which may arise in practice is what happens if the judgment debtor pays the judgment debt after enforcement proceedings have been issued. Double recovery will not be permitted and in the event that the judgment debt or part of it is paid after the judgment creditor has issued an application for enforcement proceedings but before the date for the hearing of the application, the judgment creditor must immediately notify the court in writing.[1] In the case of a writ of fieri facias, if full or partial payment of the judgment debt is made after an application to the High Court for a writ but before the writ has been executed, the judgment creditor must instead notify the relevant enforcement officer.[2]

1   PD 70, para 7.
2   Since there is generally no hearing required in the process of applying for a writ of fieri facias. See further Chapter 5.

APPROPRIATION OF PAYMENTS

1.101   A further question arises where a judgment debtor is indebted to a judgment creditor under two or more judgments and makes a partial payment towards the total indebtedness. Which judgment is deemed satisfied? The law of appropriation of payments was considered by the House of Lords in *Cory Brothers & Co Ltd v Owners of the Turkish Steamship 'Mecca'*.[1] Although their Lordships' comments in that case were in a different context they are of general application:[2]

> 'Now, my Lords, there can be no doubt what the law of England is on this subject. When a debtor is making a payment to his creditor he may appropriate the money as he pleases, and the creditor must apply it accordingly. If the debtor does not make any appropriation at the time when he makes the payment the right of application devolves on the creditor. In 1816, when Clayton's Case[3] was decided, there seems to have been authority for saying that the creditor was bound to make his election at once according to the rule of the civil law, or at any rate, within a reasonable time, whatever that expression in such a connection may be taken to mean. But it has long been held and it is now quite settled that the creditor has the right of election "up to the very last moment," and he is not bound to declare his election in express terms. He may declare it by bringing an action or in any other way that makes his meaning and intention plain. Where the election is with the creditor, it is always his intention expressed or implied or presumed, and not any rigid rule of law that governs the application of the money. The presumed intention of the creditor may no doubt be gathered from a statement of account, or anything else which indicates an intention one way or the other and is communicated to the debtor, provided there are no circumstances pointing in an opposite direction. But so long as the election rests with the creditor, and he has not determined his choice, there is no room, as it seems to me, for the application of rules of law such as the rule of the civil law, reasonable as it is, that if the debts are equal the payment received is to be attributed to the debt first contracted.'

1   [1897] AC 286, HL.
2   [1897] AC 286 at 293–294, per Lord MacNaughten, HL.

1.102   In other words, the general rule is that (apart from where the rules of insolvency apply) a person may pay his debts in any order he pleases.[1] If the judgment debtor owes multiple judgment debts to a judgment creditor, he can appropriate a payment towards a particular judgment debt. The intention to do so can be express or by implication. If the debtor fails to make an election, then the election passes to the judgment creditor who may elect which judgment debt the payment satisfies. Again, the intention can be express or it can arise by implication.[2] To avoid any ambiguity, the judgment debtor should specify which judgment debt he is paying when he makes the payment and should choose which payment will most be to his advantage. For example, if the judgments carry different rates of interest, he should pay the debt bearing the highest rate first. The position in the county court is dealt with slightly differently by statutory instrument.[3]

1   Although this case did not concern a judgment debt and there is no direct authority on this point on judgment debts, the same principles should apply by analogy.
2   See further *Chitty on Contracts* (29th edn, 2004) paras 21-059–21-061.
3   In the county court, this is dealt with in the County Courts (Interest on Judgment Debts) Order 1991, SI 1991/1184, art 6(1) of which provides that: '[w]here the debtor is indebted to the same judgment creditor under two or more judgments or orders, money paid by him shall be applied to satisfy such of the judgments as the debtor may stipulate or, where no such stipulation is made, according to their priority in time.'

Appropriation of payments – interest

1.103   The question remains of whether a partial payment satisfies the principal or interest component of the debt. In the absence of a contrary intention, the payment will discharge interest first and then the earliest items of principal.[1] The position in the county court is dealt with slightly differently by statutory instrument.[2]

1   *Chitty on Contracts* (29th edn, 2004), para 21-067.
2   County Courts (Interest on Judgment Debts) Order 1991, SI 1991/1184, art 6(2) provides that: '[m]oney paid by the debtor in respect of any judgment debt shall be appropriated first to discharge or reduce the principal debt and then towards the interest.'

JUDGMENTS THAT ARE SET ASIDE AND STAYS OF EXECUTION

1.104   The impact on enforcement proceedings of a judgment being set aside is considered next, together with the circumstances in which the court will halt the enforcement process by granting a stay of execution.

Judgments that are set aside

1.105   If a judgment or order is set aside, any enforcement of the judgment or order ceases to have effect unless the court orders otherwise.[1] Accordingly, if a judgment is set aside enforcement steps should cease immediately.

1   CPR 70.6.

Stays of execution

1.106   Once a judgment has been obtained and has become enforceable[1] the successful party can take enforcement steps at any time. There are a number of rules which deal with the circumstances in which the judgment debtor may ask the court to make an order granting a stay of execution.

1   See para 1.12.

1.107   Although the court has a general case management power to grant a stay under CPR 3.1(2)(f), this section is concerned with the specific rules which govern stays of execution. In the context of enforcement, the court can order a stay of execution in three situations:

(a)   where an appeal of the judgment is pending;
(b)   with respect to a writ of fieri facias, where there are either special circumstances rendering it inexpedient to enforce the judgment or where the applicant is unable to pay the money; or
(c)   where matters have occurred since the date of the judgment.

These are considered in turn.

Appeals

1.108   Stays of execution are sometimes encountered when the original decision is subject to appeal. CPR 52.7 states that an appeal does not operate as a stay of any order or decision of the lower court. The general rule is not to grant a stay of execution pending the hearing of the appeal.[1] This reflects the principle that the successful party is entitled to the fruits of the judgment.[2] However, the court has an unfettered discretion as to whether to grant a stay pending the hearing of an appeal.[3]

[1]   *Leicester Circuits Ltd v Coates Brothers plc* [2002] EWCA Civ 474 at [12], CA.
[2]   *Contract Facilities Ltd v Estate of Rees (deceased)* [2003] EWCA Civ 1105 at [12].
[3]   *Leicester Circuits Ltd v Coates Brothers plc* [2002] EWCA Civ 474 at [12], CA.

1.109   A useful summary of the approach of the court was given by Clarke LJ in *Hammond Suddard Solicitors v Agrichem International Holdings Ltd*:[1]

'By CPR r 52.7, unless the appeal court or the lower court orders otherwise, an appeal does not operate as a stay of execution of the orders of the lower court. It follows that the court has a discretion whether or not to grant a stay. Whether the court should exercise its discretion to grant a stay will depend upon all the circumstances of the case, but the essential question is whether there is a risk of injustice to one or other or both parties if it grants or refuses a stay. In particular, if a stay is refused what are the risks of the appeal being stifled? If a stay is granted and the appeal fails, what are the risks that the respondent will be unable to enforce the judgment? On the other hand, if a stay is refused and the appeal succeeds, and the judgment is enforced in the meantime, what are the risks of the appellant being able to recover any monies paid from the respondent?'

[1]   [2001] EWCA Civ 2065 at [21].

1.110   Where a party claims that they will be financially unable to pursue the appeal if made to pay the judgment or order, the court will expect full, frank and clear evidence of its financial means to substantiate that claim.[1] In making an assessment of the financial position of a party, the court can take into account not just the means of the party itself but whether the funding can be raised by its directors, shareholders, other backers and interested persons.[2]

1   *Hammond Suddard Solicitors v Agrichem International Holdings Ltd* [2001] EWCA Civ 2065 at [12].
2   *Contract Facilities Ltd v Estate of Rees (deceased)* [2003] EWCA Civ 1105 at [10].

1.111   It may be that a stay would be more readily granted where the application relates to a non-money judgment, say to hand over an irreplaceable item. Where the application for a stay relates to a money judgment, the applicant is likely to face an uphill struggle.

House of Lords

1.112   CPR 52.7 does not apply to civil appeals to the House of Lords. However, there is a similar rule in House of Lords Practice Directions and Standing Orders applicable to Civil Appeals which provides that the presentation of a petition of appeal, or a petition for leave to appeal, does not in itself place a stay of execution on any appealed order.[1] A party seeking such a stay should apply to the court appealed from, not to the House of Lords.[2]

1   House of Lords Practice Directions and Standing Orders applicable to Civil Appeals, para 43.1.
2   House of Lords Practice Directions and Standing Orders applicable to Civil Appeals, para 43.1.

Stay of execution with respect to writs of fieri facias

1.113   Stays of execution for writs of fieri facias are governed by RSC Ord 47, r 1, which states:

> 'Where a judgment is given or an order made for the payment by any person of money, and the court is satisfied, on an application made at the time of the judgment or order, or at any time thereafter, by the judgment debtor or other party liable to execution–
> (a)   that there are special circumstances which render it inexpedient to enforce the judgment or order; or
> (b)   that the applicant is unable from any cause to pay the money,
> then … the court may by order stay the execution of the judgment or order by writ of fieri facias either absolutely or for such period as the court thinks fit.'

1.114   A judgment debtor can apply for such a stay of execution notwithstanding that he did not acknowledge service of the claim form or serve a defence or take any previous part in the proceedings.[1]

1   RSC Ord 47, r 1(2).

1.115   It may be that orders staying execution on the 'special circumstances' or 'inability to pay' grounds set out in RSC Ord 47, r 1 should be granted less frequently now that the debtor can apply to pay the judgment debt by instalments.[1] Indeed, this may prove more straightforward for the judgment debtor than applying for a stay.

1   The power to order payment of a judgment debt by instalments is set out in CPR 40.11.

1.116   The courts have recognised that RSC Ord 47, r 1 gives them a wide discretion as to whether to grant or deny a stay.[1] It is clear from the wording of the rule that the onus is on the party applying for the stay to demonstrate that the tests set out in (a) or (b) are satisfied.

1   *Canada Enterprises Corpn Ltd v MacNab Distilleries Ltd* [1987] 1 WLR 813 at 818, CA, per Browne LJ.

1.117   If a judgment creditor is out of the jurisdiction and has failed to authorise anyone in England to accept payment of the money, the judgment debtor would be entitled to a stay of execution on a writ of fieri facias on paying the money into court.[1] A judgment debtor is not automatically entitled to a stay of execution simply by virtue of the fact that it is a statutory body because execution may be levied against statutory bodies.[2]

1   *Re a Debtor (No 1838 of 1911)* [1912] 1 KB 53, CA.
2   *Marine and General Mutual Life Assurance Society v Feltwell Fen Second District Drainage Board* [1945] KB 394 (a statutory drainage board).

Cross-claims by the judgment debtor

1.118   If a third party is associated with the judgment debtor[1] and has made a separate claim against the judgment creditor, the court has jurisdiction to stay execution under a writ of fi fa under RSC Ord 47, r 1.[2] The court also has jurisdiction to pierce the corporate veil, which it will do in these instances to find out which party is in fact controlling those companies.[3] Although the courts have in the past granted stays of execution by reason of these triangular 'cross-claims', they are nonetheless very reluctant to do so. Courts will insist that the requirement of 'special circumstances' be strictly shown. In *Burnet v Francis Industries plc*[4] Lord Justice Bingham set out a non-exhaustive list of factors which should be considered in deciding whether special circumstances can be found to exist in such cases.[5]

1   For example, the third party is the parent or subsidiary of the corporate debtor.
2   *Canada Enterprises Corpn Ltd v MacNab Distilleries Ltd* [1987] 1 WLR 813, CA. In that case, another relevant consideration in granting the stay was that the judgment debtor had already paid the money into court.
3   *Canada Enterprises Corpn Ltd v MacNab Distilleries Ltd* [1987] 1 WLR 813, CA.
4   *Burnet v Francis Industries plc* [1987] 1 WLR 802, CA.
5   *Burnet v Francis Industries plc* [1987] 1 WLR 802 at 811, CA.

Matters which have occurred since the date of the judgment

1.119   Even where no appeal is pending, and without prejudice to the power to stay in respect of writs of fieri facias, RSC Ord 45, r 11 provides that the court has a general discretion to grant a stay of execution in respect of matters that have occurred since judgment:

> 'Without prejudice to Order 47, r 1, a party against whom a judgment has been given or an order made may apply to the court for a stay of execution of the judgment or order or other relief on the ground of matters which have occurred

since the date of the judgment or order, and the court may by order grant such relief, and on such terms, as it thinks just.'

1.120   However, it seems the rule is more limited in scope than it might first appear. The meaning of RSC Ord 45, r 11 was considered by Plowman J in *London Permanent Benefit Building Society v de Baer*:[1]

'The power conferred by that rule to grant relief is a power to do so, and I quote, "on the ground of matters which have occurred since the date of the judgment or order."
   It is implicit in the rule that the matters referred to are matters which would or might have prevented the order being made, or would or might have led to a stay of execution if they had already occurred at the date of the order.'

[1]   [1969] 1 Ch 321 at 334.

Stay of execution by operation of law

1.121   Certain events operate as a stay of execution as a matter of law. The most obvious examples which are relevant to commercial enforcement are certain insolvency steps (see paras 1.157-1.215). However, another example is the issue of interpleader proceedings in connection with writs of execution, which have the effect of a stay of execution over the affected goods until the proceedings are resolved.[1]

[1]   *Re Ford, ex p Ford* (1886) 18 QBD 369 at 371. See further Chapter 5.

GENERAL RESTRICTIONS ON ENFORCEMENT

1.122   There are a number of statutes which provide restrictions on the availability of enforcement. These include the Limitation Act 1980, the Crown Proceedings Act 1947, the State Immunity Act 1978, the Diplomatic Privileges Act 1964, the Consular Relations Act 1968 and the International Organisations Act 1968. These are each considered in turn in paras 1.124–1.149.

1.123   The provisions of human rights and insolvency law raise more pervasive questions on possible limitations of the law on enforcement. The enactment of the Human Rights Act 1998 raises the possibility of human rights challenges to enforcement proceedings, which are considered in paras 1.151–1.156. As has been noted, a judgment debtor's bankruptcy or winding up effectively stays enforcement proceedings. The provisions of IA 1986 which are relevant to enforcement are considered in paras 1.157–1.215.

Limitation issues

1.124   Limitation Act 1980 (LA 1980), s 24 (1) provides:

'An action shall not be brought upon any judgment after the expiration of six years from the date on which the judgment became enforceable.'

1.125 LA 1980, s 24 was considered by the House of Lords in *Lowsley v Forbes*.[1] In that case the plaintiffs had obtained judgment by consent for £70,000 on 2 February 1981. For reasons not relevant to the decision, the defendant then left the country. Some 11 years later, the plaintiffs sought to enforce the judgment and obtained leave to issue a writ of execution. They also obtained a charging order on the defendant's share of the matrimonial home and a garnishee order over the defendant's bank account. One of the questions before their Lordships was whether LA 1980, s 24(1) bars execution of a judgment after six years, or whether it only bars the bringing of a fresh action on the judgment.[2]

1   [1999] 1 AC 329, HL.
2   An action on a judgment is a fresh proceeding commenced using the original judgment as a cause of action.

1.126 After extensive consideration of the confusing and sometimes contradictory earlier case law on this point, and having reviewed the relevant sections of the report of the Law Reform Committee on Limitation of Actions (1977) which foreshadowed LA 1980,[1] Lord Lloyd of Berwick, who gave the lead judgment, concluded the matter succinctly:

> '"[a]ction" in s 24(1) means a fresh action, and does not include proceedings by way of execution.'

1   Law Com No 6923. In particular, paras 4.13 and 4.14.

1.127 However, where six years or more have elapsed since the date of the judgment or order the court rules provide that permission is needed to issue a writ of execution.[1] While there is no equivalent provision in relation to other methods of execution such as third party debt orders or charging orders, the amount of time which has elapsed since the date of the judgment may be a factor the court takes into account in exercising its discretion to grant the order. Where a judgment or order which has not yet been enforced is approaching its sixth anniversary, a judgment creditor who wishes to preserve his full rights of enforcement may be well advised to being a fresh action on the judgment to preserve their options on enforcement.

1   RSC Ord 46, r 2(1)(a). See further paras 5.73–5.78.

Crown privilege

1.128 The Crown can use any method of enforcement available to a subject.[1] However, the Crown also maintains a number of privileges and immunities in relation to enforcement. In a nutshell, the Crown is immune from all methods of enforcement and, in certain cases, the Crown's attempts to enforce judgments take priority over those of a subject.

1   CPA 1947, s 26(1).

Meaning of the 'Crown'

1.129 Claims by and against the Crown are governed by the Crown Proceedings Act 1947 (CPA 1947). For the purposes of CPA 1947, the 'Crown' refers to *claims* brought by or against an 'authorised Government department'.[1] The Minister for the Civil Service must publish a list of authorised government departments which is admissible in evidence to establish which departments are authorised government departments.[2] Included in the list are the Commissioners of the Inland Revenue and the Commissioners for Customs. The 'Crown' does not include enforcement by or against Her Majesty in her private capacity.[3]

1   CPA 1947, s 17(2).
2   CPA 1947, s 17(1). This list is available for download from the Treasury Solicitor's Department website: www.treasury-solicitor.gov.uk/Publications/CPA_Jan_2004.pdf.
3   CPA 1947, s 40(1). For the meaning of Her Majesty in her private capacity see CPA 1947, s 38(3).

Crown immunity from enforcement

1.130   The basic immunity of the Crown from enforcement is set out in CPA 1947, s 25(4). This provides:

> '… no execution or attachment or process in the nature thereof shall be issued out of any Court for enforcing payment by the Crown of any such money or costs as aforesaid, and no person shall be individually liable under any order for the payment by the Crown, or any Government department, or any officer of the Crown as such of any money or costs.'

1.131.   This statutory provision is amplified by the court rules, which provide that equitable execution, oral examination, third party debt orders, charging orders, writs of execution[1] and committal cannot be exercised against the Crown.[2]

1   This includes writs of fieri facias and sequestration.
2   RSC Ord 77, r 15(1). Note that where the Crown owes a debt to a judgment debtor, while the third party debt order procedure is not available, there is a limited procedure for attachment of Crown debts under a process analogous to third party debt order proceedings. This is considered at paras 3.81–3.85.

Certificate containing particulars of the judgment

1.132   However, the provisions of CPA 1947, s 25(4) do not mean that judgments or orders made against the Crown are worthless. Although court methods of enforcement are unavailable, a procedure exists in their place whereby a certificate stating the amount of the Crown's indebtedness under the judgment or order is issued, which is then presented to the Crown for payment.

1.133   The court may issue such a certificate to a judgment creditor on his application of the Crown at any time after 21 days from the date of the judgment.[1] The standard form certificate is either Form No 95 or 96 (as appropriate).[2] If the judgment or order provides for the payment of any money by way of damages or otherwise, or of any costs, the certificate shall state the amount so payable.[3] However, a certificate for a costs order made against the Crown will only be issued after the costs have been assessed.[4] The court also has power to direct that a separate certificate shall be issued for any costs order.[5]

¹   CPA 1947, s 25(1).
²   RSC Ord 77, r 15(3). Form No 95 is a Certificate of order against the Crown and Form No 96 is a Certificate of order for costs against the Crown.
³   CPA 1947, s 25(3).
⁴   CPA 1947, s 25(1).
⁵   CPA 1947, s 25(1).

1.134   A copy of the certificate should be served by the judgment creditor upon the person for the time being named in the record as the solicitor, or as the person acting as solicitor, for the Crown.¹ Upon receipt of the certificate, the appropriate government department will pay to the person entitled or his solicitor the amount appearing by the certificate to be due to him together with any interest.² If an appeal is pending, the court may direct that payment of the whole or part of the amount payable shall be suspended and may insert directions to that effect in the certificate if it has not yet been issued.³

¹   CPA 1947, s 25(2).
²   CPA 1947, s 25(3).
³   CPA 1947, s 25(3).

State immunity

1.135   The State Immunity Act 1978 (SIA 1978) provides that a state is immune from the jurisdiction of the courts of the United Kingdom except as is provided in the Act.¹ Detailed consideration of the concept of state immunity is outside the scope of this book. However, from an enforcement perspective it is important to note that one aspect of the jurisdictional immunity enjoyed by states is that, subject to a number of important exceptions considered below, the property of a state is immune from any process for the enforcement of a judgment.²

¹   SIA 1978, s 1(1).
²   SIA 1978, s 13(2)(b).

1.136   A 'state' for the purposes of SIA 1978 means any foreign or Commonwealth state other than the UK.¹ It includes the sovereign or other head of that state in his public capacity, the government of that state and any department of that government.² A state does not include any entity which is distinct from the executive organs of the government of the state and capable of suing or being sued.³ However, such an entity can still be immune from enforcement if, and only if, the proceedings relate to anything done by it in the exercise of sovereign authority and the circumstances are such that a state would have been so immune.⁴ The state's central bank or other monetary authority, even where it is distinct from the executive organs of the government of the state and capable of suing or being sued, is immune from execution because it is treated as a state for the purposes of immunity from execution.⁵

¹   SIA 1978, s 14(1). The UK government can claim Crown immunity, see paras 1.128–1.134.
²   SIA 1978, s 14(1).
³   SIA 1978, s 14(1). See also SIA 1978, s 14(2).
⁴   SIA 1978, s 14(2).
⁵   SIA 1978, s 14(4). Note that it can waive immunity by express agreement although the 'commercial purposes' exception in SIA 1978, s 13(4) does not apply (considered further below).

1.137 There are two important exceptions to state immunity from execution.

Agreement to enforcement by the state

1.138 The first exception is that enforcement is permitted with the written consent of the state concerned (which may be contained in a prior agreement).[1] The head of a state's diplomatic mission in the UK is deemed to have authority to give such consent on behalf of the state.[2] These types of agreements are commonly included as part of the choice of jurisdiction clause in commercial contracts.[3] However, a provision merely submitting to the jurisdiction of the courts of a country is not to be regarded as consent for the purposes of enforcement of the judgments of that court. Rather, an express submission to the enforcement of the judgments of that court against the state should be included.[4]

[1]   SIA 1978, s 13(3). The state can also make an agreement by treaty – see SIA 1978, s 17(2).
[2]   SIA 1978, s 13(5).
[3]   A typical clause might read: 'The State irrevocably waives all immunity to which it may be or become entitled in relation to this Agreement, including immunity from jurisdiction, enforcement, prejudgment proceedings, injunctions and all other legal proceedings and relief, both in respect of itself and its assets, and consents to such proceedings and relief.'
[4]   SIA 1978, s 13(3). See previous footnote for specimen wording.

Property used for commercial purposes by the state

1.139 The second exception is that the state's 'property which is for the time being in use or intended for use for commercial purposes' is not immune from execution.[1] The expression 'in use for or intended for use for commercial purposes' does not include property of a state's central bank or other monetary authority.[2] 'Commercial purposes' is defined to include the following transactions or activities:

(a) any contract for the supply of goods or services;
(b) any loan or other transaction for the provision of finance and any guarantee or indemnity in respect of any such transaction or of any other financial obligation; and
(c) any other transaction or activity (whether of a commercial, industrial, financial, professional or other similar character) into which a state enters or in which it engages otherwise than in the exercise of sovereign authority.[3]

[1]   SIA 1978, s 13(4).
[2]   SIA 1978, s 14(4).
[3]   SIA 1978, s 3(3).

1.140 In principle, the commercial property exception was held by the House of Lords in *Alcom Ltd v Republic of Columbia*[1] to permit a garnishee order (now a third party debt order) in respect of a bank account held by a state with a commercial bank which is earmarked solely[2] for the discharge of liabilities incurred in commercial transactions.[3] The onus of establishing this lies with the judgment creditor.[4] The head of a state's diplomatic mission in the UK can issue a certificate confirming that certain property is not in use or intended for use by or on behalf of the state for commercial purposes.[5] Such a certificate must be accepted as sufficient evidence of that fact unless the contrary is proved.[6] In *Alcom Ltd v Columbia* the attempt to obtain a garnishee order against the state failed because, among other reasons, the head of the mission certified that the bank issued a certificate certifying that the account in question was not in use nor intended for use for commercial purposes but only to meet the expenditure necessarily incurred in the day-to-day running of the diplomatic mission.

1   [1984] AC 580, HL.
2   Subject to de minimus exceptions.
3   [1984] AC 580 at 604, HL. Lord Diplock gave the example of account used to issue
    documentary credits in payment of the price of goods sold to the state.
4   *Alcom Ltd v Columbia* [1984] AC 580 at 604, HL.
5   SIA 1978, s 13(5).
6   SIA 1978, s 13(5).

Diplomatic immunity

1.141   The Diplomatic Privileges Act 1964 (DPA 1964) governs issues of diplomatic immunity. It gives those articles of the Vienna Convention on Diplomatic Relations signed in 1961, which are set out in DPA 1964, Sch 1, the force of law in the UK (the Diplomatic Convention).[1]

1   DPA 1964, s 2(1).

1.142   Detailed consideration of the law on diplomatic immunity is outside the scope of this book.[1] However, from an enforcement perspective, the Diplomatic Convention provides that premises of a diplomatic mission are inviolable. The agents of the receiving state[2] may not enter them except with the consent of the head of the mission.[3] The Convention further provides that the premises of the mission, their furnishings and other property thereon and the means of transport of the mission shall be immune from attachment or execution.[4] This has the effect of prohibiting all forms of enforcement with respect to the property of the mission.

1   See further *Dicey & Morris on The Conflict of Laws* (13th edn, 2000) pp 235–252 and
    Cheshire & North's Private International Law (13th edn, 1999) pp 388–395.
2   Defined at DPA 1964, s 2(2).
3   Diplomatic Convention, art 22(1).
4   Diplomatic Convention, art 22(3).

1.143   The Diplomatic Convention also grants qualified immunity from execution to diplomatic staff falling into three categories. The category attracting greatest protection are 'diplomatic agents', which means the head of the mission or a member of the diplomatic staff of the mission.[1] The private residence of a diplomatic agent enjoys the same inviolability and protection as the premises of the mission.[2] In other words, the private residence of a diplomatic agent is wholly immune from enforcement.

1   Diplomatic Convention, art 1. Members of administrative and technical staff of the mission
    and their families, the service staff of the mission and private servants of members of the
    mission attract a lesser degree of immunity as set out in Diplomatic Convention, art 37.
2   Diplomatic Convention, art 30(1).

1.144   Enforcement proceedings may be brought against a diplomatic agent[1] where it relates to an action relating to any professional or commercial activity exercised by the diplomatic agent in the receiving state outside his official functions.[2] However, even in these circumstances, enforcement is only permitted provided that the measures concerned can be taken without infringing the inviolability of the diplomatic agent's person or residence.[3] The same immunity extends to members of the family of a diplomatic agent forming part of his household provided they are not nationals of the receiving state.[4]

[1] Diplomatic Convention, art 31(3).
[2] Diplomatic Convention, art 31(1)(c).
[3] Diplomatic Convention, art 31(3).
[4] Diplomatic Convention, art 37(1).

1.145 The immunity of a diplomatic agent and his family from enforcement can be expressly waived by the sending state.[1] However, waiver of immunity from jurisdiction in respect of civil proceedings does not impliedly waive immunity in respect of enforcement of the judgment, for which a separate waiver is necessary.[2]

[1] Diplomatic Convention, art 32(1)–(2).
[2] Diplomatic Convention, art 32(4).

1.146 Diplomats can be identified using the London Diplomatic List. This is an alphabetical listing compiled by the Foreign and Commonwealth Office of all the representatives of foreign states and Commonwealth countries in London, with the names and designations of their diplomatic staff.[1] If in any proceedings any question arises whether or not any diplomat is entitled to any privilege or immunity, a certificate issued by or under the authority of the Secretary of State shall be conclusive evidence of that fact.[2]

[1] The London Diplomatic List is printed by The Stationery Office (ISBN 0 11 59177 99) and is available for £8.99 from: TSO, PO Box 29, Norwich NR3 1GN, Tel: 0870 600 5522, Fax: 0870 600 5533. The following lists are also available from the Foreign and Commonwealth website: Heads of Mission and their Spouses and Representatives in London of Foreign States & Commonwealth Countries in order of Precedence. The Foreign and Commonwealth Offices website also allows a search by country for details of the name of the Ambassador or High Commissioner, the address, telephone and fax numbers of the Embassy or High Commission in London, and, where available, the website and email address. The Foreign and Commonwealth website can be found at: www.fco.gov.uk where there is a link to Foreign Embassies in the UK.
[2] DPA 1964, s 4.

Consular immunity

1.147 Foreign consuls are not within the scope of DPA 1964. Instead, the Consular Relations Act 1968 (CRA 1968) governs issues of immunity enjoyed by foreign consuls. It gives those articles of the Vienna Convention on Consular Relations signed in 1963 and set out in Sch 1 to the Act the force of law in the UK (the Consular Convention).[1] Detailed consideration of the concept of consular immunity is outside the scope of this book.[2] However, from an enforcement perspective, foreign consuls enjoy similar, although somewhat reduced, immunities to those enjoyed by diplomats.[3]

[1] CRA 1968, s 1(1).
[2] *Dicey & Morris on The Conflict of Laws* (13th edn, 2000) pp 256–258 and *Cheshire & North's Private International Law* (13th edn, 1999) pp 401–402.
[3] For further detail reference should be made to the CRA 1968.

1.148 If in any proceedings any question arises whether or not any consul is entitled to any privilege or immunity, a certificate issued by or under the authority of the Secretary of State shall be conclusive evidence of that fact.[1]

1   CRA 1968, s 11.

International organisations immunity

1.149 A further dimension to sovereign immunity is that a number of international organisations of which the UK and a foreign sovereign or government are members are granted various privileges under the International Organisations Act 1968. The scheme of the Act is to specify by an Order in Council the privileges and immunities that are to apply to a particular international organisation.[1] A large number of such Orders in Council have been made. One of the immunities granted is immunity from suit and legal process,[2] which would make the international organisation immune from enforcement proceedings. When dealing with such an organisation, the relevant Order in Council should be consulted to check the extent of any immunities from enforcement.[3]

1   International Organisations Act 1968, s 1(2). The various Orders in Council are conveniently collected together in the notes to the International Organisations Act 1968 in *Halsbury's Statutes*.
2   International Organisations Act 1968, s 1(2)(b) and Sch 1, Part I, para 1.
3   See further *Dicey & Morris on The Conflict of Laws* (13th edn, 2000) pp 258–262 and *Cheshire & North's Private International Law* (13th edn, 1999) pp 399–401.

CRIMINAL OFFENCES - HARASSMENT OF DEBTORS

1.150 Under the Administration of Justice Act 1970, s 40(1) it is an offence to harass a person who owes a debt under a contract with demands for payment with the object of coercing the debtor to pay the money claimed. However, sub-s 40(3) provides that the offence does not apply to anything done by a person which is reasonable (and otherwise permissible in law) for the purpose of the enforcement of any liability by legal process. Accordingly, enforcement proceedings do not fall foul of this provision.

HUMAN RIGHTS

1.151 With the entry into force of the Human Rights Act 1998 (HRA 1998) the operation of the law relating to enforcement must be viewed in the light of the provisions of the European Convention for the Protection of Human Rights and Fundamental Freedoms (ECHR). HRA 1998, s 6(1) provides:

'It is unlawful for a public authority to act in a way which is incompatible with a convention right.'

1.152 A court is included in the definition of a public authority by virtue of HRA 1998, s 6(3). Accordingly, there is an obligation on the courts of England and Wales to apply the law and otherwise act in accordance with the ECHR.

1.153 The particular human rights implications potentially raised by each of the methods of enforcement considered in this book are dealt with in each of the relevant chapters. A judgment debtor may seek to argue that certain types of enforcement proceedings infringe his rights under ECHR, art 8 (the right to respect for private family life and the home) and the First Protocol, art 1 of (the right to peaceful enjoyment of possessions). However, it is important to note at the outset that powerful human rights arguments also operate in favour of the judgment creditor. ECHR, art 6(1) provides:

'In the determination of his civil rights and obligations … everyone is entitled to a fair and public hearing within a reasonable time by an independent and impartial tribunal established by law.'

1.154 In a number of judgments, the European Court of Human Rights has recognised that the enforcement of judgments is an integral part of the right to a fair trial under ECHR, art 6(1).[1] Similarly, excessive delays in enforcement will be a breach of a judgment creditor's rights under art 6(1), although the reasonableness of the length of enforcement proceedings must be assessed in the light of the particular circumstances of the case, and in particular the complexity of the case, the conduct of the judgment creditor and the conduct of the relevant authorities.[2]

[1] See eg *Silva Pontes v Portugal* (1994) 18 EHRR 156, paras 35–42.
[2] See eg *Silva Pontes v Portugal* (1994) 18 EHRR 156 and *Zappia v Italy* [1996] ECHR 43 in which the court found that a period of more than 23 years for enforcement proceedings that were still pending and were of no particular complexity could not be regarded as reasonable.

1.155 In *Hornsby v Greece*[1] the European Court of Human Rights set out the rationale for this principle:[2]

'The Court reiterates that, according to its established case-law, Article 6(1) secures to everyone the right to have any claim relating to his civil rights and obligations brought before a court or tribunal; in this way it embodies the "right to a court", of which the right of access, that is the right to institute proceedings before courts in civil matters, constitutes one aspect (see the *Philis v Greece (No 1)* (1991) 13 EHRR 741, para 59). However, that right would be illusory if a Contracting State's domestic legal system allowed a final, binding judicial decision to remain inoperative to the detriment of one party. It would be inconceivable that Article 6(1) should describe in detail procedural guarantees afforded to litigants – proceedings that are fair, public and expeditious – without protecting the implementation of judicial decisions; to construe Article 6 as being concerned exclusively with access to a court and the conduct of proceedings would be likely to lead to situations incompatible with the principle of the rule of law which the Contracting States undertook to respect when they ratified the Convention (see, mutatis mutandis, the *Golder v United Kingdom* (1980) 1 EHRR 524, paras 34-36). Execution of a judgment given by any court must therefore be regarded as an integral part of the "trial" for the purposes of Article 6; moreover, the Court has already accepted this principle in cases concerning the length of proceedings (see, most recently, the *Di Pede v Italy* and *Zappia v Italy* judgments of 26th September, 1996, Reports of Judgments and Decisions 1996-IV, pp 1383–1384, paras. 20-24 and pp. 1410–1411, paras 16–20 respectively).'

¹   (1997) 24 EHRR 250.

²   (1997) 24 EHRR 250, para 40.

1.156 While HRA 1998 does not make decisions of the European Court of Human Rights binding on the English courts, both its decisions and the opinions of the European Commission on Human Rights must, where relevant, be taken into account where the court is determining a question that has arisen in connection with an ECHR right.¹

¹   HRA 1998, s 2(1).

INSOLVENCY AND ITS AFFECT ON ENFORCEMENT

1.157 As has been noted in paras 1.9–1.11 an issue of fundamental importance for all the methods of enforcement is the question of the effect of the judgment debtor's insolvency. The insolvency regimes for companies and individuals are considered separately. In addition to insolvency, a number of anti-avoidance rules exist to prevent assets being transferred to defeat execution.¹

¹   Perhaps most important are those contained in the Insolvency Act 1986, s 423-424 which would allow a judgment creditor prejudiced by a transaction entered into at an undervalue by a judgment debtor to apply to set it aside. In spite of being contained in the Insolvency Act 1986, these provisions apply irrespective of whether the individual or company is insolvent: IA 1986, s 424(1)(c). Another anti-avoidance provision is contained in the Married Women's Property Act 1882, s 10, which provides that a gift by a husband to his wife will not be exempt from seizure if it remains in his 'order, disposition or reputed ownership'. However, personal chattels will not be deemed to fall foul of this provision simply because they continue kept in the house in which they both live after the gift: *French v Gething* [1922] 1 KB 236, CA.

CORPORATE JUDGMENT DEBTORS

1.158 The insolvency legislation provides for four types of proceedings that relate to companies in financial difficulty: winding up, administration, company voluntary arrangements and administrative receivership. These are considered in turn.

WINDING UP

1.159 Winding up can either be voluntary or compulsory. Although both methods have the same basic objective of collecting and distributing the assets of the company for creditors, certain provisions that affect enforcement only apply to a compulsory winding up.

Application for a stay on presentation of a winding up petition

1.160 At any time after the presentation of a petition for a compulsory winding up, and before a winding up order has been made, the company, or any creditor or contributory, may ask the court to stay any execution on such terms as it thinks fit.¹

In the absence of special circumstances, the court will ordinarily exercise its discretion to stay execution with a view to securing equal distribution of the assets among creditors of the same class.[2]

[1]   IA 1986, s 126.
[2]   *Bowkett v Fuller's United Electric Works Ltd* [1923] 1 KB 160, CA (decided under Companies (Consolidation) Act 1908, s 140, which contained a similarly worded provision).

1.161   If no stay is obtained, the execution may be continued until a winding up order is made, at which time the leave of the court will be needed to continue it (see paras 1.171–1.172). However, given the rules on execution steps that are uncompleted by the commencement of the winding up (which are considered next), there may be no benefit in continuing the execution as the proceeds may be required to be handed to the liquidator.

Execution not completed before the commencement of the winding up

1.162   The Insolvency Act 1986 (IA 1986), s 183(1) provides:

'Where a creditor has issued execution against the goods or land of a company or has attached any debt due to it, and the company is subsequently wound up, he is not entitled to retain the benefit of the execution or attachment against the liquidator unless he has completed the execution or attachment before the commencement of the winding up.'

1.163   Accordingly, the commencement of the winding up prevents the judgment creditor from retaining the benefit of any execution or attachment unless completed before that time.

Meaning of 'retain the benefit of the execution or attachment'

1.164   The reference to 'retain the benefit of the execution or attachment' has been held to refer to the benefit of the charge which the creditor obtains by the issue of his execution or attachment and does not include money already received by the creditor.[1] This issue is considered more fully at paras 1.204–1.207 with respect to the equivalent wording that applies to bankruptcy.

[1]   *Re Caribbean Products (Yam Importers) Ltd* [1966] 1 Ch 331, CA.

Meaning of 'commencement of the winding up'

1.165   IA 1986, s 183(1) applies to all forms of winding up, although the meaning of 'commencement of the winding up' varies according to how the winding up is brought about:

(a)   A voluntary winding up is deemed to commence at the time of the passing of the resolution for voluntary winding up.[1] However, where a creditor has had notice of a meeting having been called at which a resolution for voluntary winding up is to be proposed, the date on which he had notice is substituted for the date of commencement of the winding up.[2]

(b) If, before the presentation of a petition for the winding up of a company by the court, a resolution has been passed by the company for voluntary winding up, the winding up of the company is deemed to have commenced at the time of the passing of the resolution; and unless the court, on proof of fraud or mistake, directs otherwise, all proceedings taken in the voluntary winding up are deemed to have been validly taken.[3]

(c) Where the court makes a winding up order by virtue of para 13(1)(e) Sch B1 IA 1986, which allows the court on an application for an administration order to make a winding up order instead, the winding up is deemed to commence on the making of such winding up order.[4]

(d) In any other case, the winding up of a company by the court is deemed to commence at the time of the presentation of the petition for winding up.[5]

[1] IA 1986, s 86.
[2] IA 1986, s 183(2)(a).
[3] IA 1986, s 129(1).
[4] IA 1986, s 129(1A).
[5] IA 1986, s 129(2).

1.166 It should be noted that, in contrast with the equivalent bankruptcy provision, the date for commencement of a winding up is usually earlier than the date of the court order.

Meaning of 'completed the execution or attachment'

1.167 The key question is the point at which a judgment creditor has 'completed' the execution or attachment. The time of completion is defined in IA 1986, s 183(3) and depends upon the type of property that is subject to enforcement. IA 1986, s 183(3) provides:

'(a) an execution against goods is completed by seizure and sale, or by the making of a charging order under s 1 of the Charging Orders Act 1979;

(b) an attachment of a debt is completed by receipt of the debt; and

(c) an execution against land is completed by seizure, by the appointment of a receiver, or by the making of a charging order under s 1 of the Act above-mentioned.'

1.168 The application of these rules to third party debt orders, charging orders and writs of fieri facias is considered further in each of the relevant chapters.

1.169 Under IA 1986, s 183(2)(c) the court has a discretion to set aside the rights of the liquidator under IA 1986, s 183(1)[1] in favour of an execution creditor to such extent and subject to such terms as it sees fit. It seems that the words 'to such extent' permit the court to allow an execution creditor a proportion of the amounts due.[2] However, in practice it would be rare for the court to make such an order because it would run contrary to the pari passu principle.[3]

[1] See para 1.162.

2　*Re Grosvenor Metal Co Ltd* [1950] Ch 63 at 64.
3　See further Bailey, Groves and Smith *Corporate Insolvency: Law and Practice* (2nd edn, 2001) pp 532–534 which gives some examples under previous insolvency legislation of where the court might exercise its discretion in favour of an execution creditor.

History of the statutory provisions relating to the completion of enforcement

1.170　IA 1986, s 183 has long history.[1] However, as the provisions which are now contained in IA 1986, s 183 have been re-enacted over time they have not been fully updated to reflect changes in enforcement law that have taken place. This creates the potential for confusion and misinterpretation. For example, the reference to 'execution against land is completed by *seizure*' in IA 1986, s 183(3)(a) refers to a sheriff's seizure of land by writ of elegit, which was abolished in 1956.[2] A further oddity is that 'goods' are defined in an unusually wide sense to include '*all* chattels personal',[3] thereby including choses in action such as debts as well as choses in possession such as money.

1　It derives from similar provisions in Companies Act 1928, ss 69–70; Companies Act 1929, ss 268–269; Companies Act 1948, ss 325-326; and Companies Act 1985, ss 621-622.
2　Administration of Justice Act 1956, s 34.
3　IA 1986, s 183(4).

Enforcement after the commencement of compulsory winding up is void

1.171　IA 1986, s 128(1) provides that in the case of a compulsory winding up, any attachment, sequestration, distress or execution put in force against the estate or effects of the company after the commencement of the winding up is void. 'Commencement of the winding up' in this context means the time of the presentation of the petition for winding up.[1] This provision does not apply to a voluntary winding up by the court and there is no equivalent provision for a voluntary winding up.

1　IA 1986, s 129(2).

Enforcement after the making of the winding up order

1.172　IA 1986, s 130(2) provides that once a winding up order has been made, or a provisional liquidator has been appointed, no action or proceeding shall be proceeded with or commenced against the company or its property, except with the leave of the court and subject to such terms as the court may impose. Enforcement proceedings fall within the expression 'action or proceeding'. Again, it is unlikely that leave would be granted because it would upset the pari passu principle.

ADMINISTRATION

1.173　As originally enacted, IA 1986 introduced administration as an alternative to winding up with the primary objective of trying to salvage the company as a going concern. Under the original regime, an administrator could only be appointed by an order of the court after a somewhat involved court application.

1.174   The Enterprise Act 2002 introduced a new and more flexible regime for the administration of companies, which is found in IA 1986, Sch B1. This procedure applies to most administrations after 15 September 2003[1] although the old administration regime continues to apply to insolvent partnerships, limited liability partnerships, certain bodies that are insurers under the Financial Services and Markets Act 2000[2] and various types of public utility company and building societies.[3]

[1]   Enterprise Act 2002, s 248 inserted a new IA 1986, Pt II (administration) with effect from 15 September 2003.
[2]   Enterprise Act 2002 (Commencement No 4 and Transitional Provisions and Savings) Order 2003, SI 2003/2093, art 3(2) and Sealy and Milman *Annotated Guide to the Insolvency Legislation* (2nd revd 7th edn, 2004) p 706.
[3]   Enterprise Act 2002, s 249(1).

1.175   The new regime allows an administrator to be appointed in a wider variety of circumstances and without the need to petition the court in every case. As will be seen, the lynchpin of both the original and new form of administration is an all-embracing moratorium preventing any judgment creditor from taking enforcement steps to allow the administrator the opportunity to try and salvage the company as a going concern. The original and new forms of administration are considered in turn.

Original company administration regime

1.176   During the period beginning with the presentation of a petition for an administration order, and ending with the making of an administration order or the dismissal of the petition, no execution or other legal process can be commenced or continued against the company or its property except with the leave of the court and on such terms as the court may impose.[1] This operates as an interim moratorium against all forms of enforcement. It is unlikely the court would grant such permission to commence or continue enforcement proceedings given that the court has yet to consider the merits of the application. After filing the petition for an administration order, the petitioner must give notice to place the company into administration of its presentation to an enforcement officer known to be charged with an execution against the company or its property.[2]

[1]   IA 1986, s 10(1)(c).
[2]   Insolvency Rules 1986, r 2.6A(a).

1.177   Once an administration order had been made and continues in force, no execution or other legal process can be commenced or continued against the company or its property except with the leave of the administrator or the court, and, where the court gives leave, on such terms as the court may impose.[1] This operates a moratorium against all forms of enforcement. It is unlikely that leave would be granted to commence or continue enforcement proceedings once an administration order has been made because it would defeat the objective of administration. An administrator must advertise the making of an administration order once in the Gazette and once in such newspaper as he thinks most appropriate for ensuring that the order comes to the notice of the company's creditors.[2] In contrast to the new administration regime, the administrator does not have a separate duty to give notice of the making of the order to an enforcement officer known to be charged with execution against the company or its property.

1   IA 1986, s 11(3)(c).
2   Insolvency Rules 1986, r 2.10(2).

Company administration regime introduced by Enterprise Act 2002

1.178 Where the new procedure is applicable, in addition to being appointed by order of the court, an administrator can be appointed without the need to petition the court by the holder of a qualifying floating charge[1] or the company or its directors.[2] However, an administrator is an officer of the court whether or not appointed by an order of the court.[3] While a court application for an administration order is pending, or for the brief period of time before an out of court appointment takes effect, no legal process (which includes legal proceedings, execution, and distress) may be instituted or continued against the company or property of the company except with the permission of the court.[4] This operates as an interim moratorium against all forms of enforcement. Where an application is made to the court for an administration order, or where the company or its directors seek to appoint an administrator, an enforcement officer known to be charged with execution against the company or its property must be given notice of the application for an order to appoint an administrator or the intention to seek to appoint an administrator, as the case may be.[5] No notice needs to be given in the case of an administrator appointed by the holder of a floating charge.

1   As defined in IA 1986, Sch B1, para 14.
2   IA 1986, Sch B1, para 2.
3   IA 1986, Sch B1, para 5.
4   IA 1986, Sch B1, para 44(5).
5   Insolvency Rules 1986, rr 2.7(application for an administration order) and 2.20 (administration by the company or its directors).

1.179 While a company is in administration, no legal process (which includes legal proceedings, execution and distress) may be instituted or continued against the company or property of the company except with the consent of the administrator or with the permission of the court.[1] This provision operates as a moratorium against all forms of enforcement. It is unlikely that the administrator would consent, or the court would grant leave, to commence or continue enforcement of a judgment once a company is in administration because it would defeat the objective of administration. The administrator must advertise his appointment once in the Gazette, and once in such newspaper as he thinks most appropriate for ensuring that the appointment comes to the notice of the company's creditors.[2] Upon appointment, the administrator also has a separate duty to give notice of his appointment to an enforcement officer known to be charged with execution against the company or its property.[3]

1   IA 1986, Sch B1, para 43(6).
2   Insolvency Rules 1986, r 2.27(1).
3   Insolvency Rules 1986, r 2.27(2)(c).

Administrator's powers to deal with security

1.180 The moratorium which takes effect during an administration does not necessarily mean that all is lost for a judgment creditor who has taken enforcement steps. Both forms of administration allow an administrator to sell assets which are subject to security provided the proceeds of sale are applied towards discharging the sums due on the security.[1] The meaning of security for these purposes is 'any mortgage, charge, lien or other security'.[2] This definition has the effect that certain forms of enforcement constitute 'security' for the purposes of an administration and therefore imposes an obligation on an administrator to apply the proceeds towards the discharge of the security held by the judgment creditor.

1   IA 1986, s 15 (original administration) and IA 1986, Sch B1, para 71 (new administration).
2   IA 1986, s 248(b).

Charging order

1.181   A charging order takes effect as an equitable charge.[1] A final charging order clearly constitutes security for the purposes of administration and would be valid even if the judgment debtor was subsequently wound up.[2]

1   Charging Orders Act 1979, s 3(4) states that 'a charge imposed by a charging order shall have the like effect and shall be enforceable in the same courts and in the same manner as an equitable charge created by the debtor by writing under his hand'. See further Chapter 4.
2   *Clarke v Coutts & Co* [2002] EWCA Civ 943 at [39].

1.182   However, it is less clear whether an interim charging order will put the judgment creditor in the position of a secured creditor for the purposes of administration. An interim charging order certainly imposes an immediate charge on the judgment debtor's interest in the asset to which the application relates.[1] While this is not sufficient to constitute making the execution 'completed' for the purposes of bankruptcy or winding up,[2] it has to be remembered that those provisions[3] have the effect of depriving the judgment creditor of security rights which he would otherwise have.[4] However, while an interim charging order undoubtedly constitutes a charge, the charge is of a defeasible nature and a court may refuse to exercise its discretion not to make the final charging order in the event of the judgment debtor's intervening administration. The effect of a judgment debtor's insolvency on the granting of a charging order is considered in Chapter 4.

1   *Roberts Petroleum Ltd v Bernard Kenny Ltd* [1983] 2 AC 192 at 209, HL; *Clarke v Coutts & Co* [2002] EWCA Civ 943 at [39] and CPR 73.4(2).
2   *Clarke v Coutts & Co* [2002] EWCA Civ 943 at [39].
3   Ie IA 1986, ss 183(1) and 346(1).
4   *Peck v Craighead* [1995] 1 BCLC 337 at 342.

Third party debt order

1.183   Although CPR Pt 72 has removed the references to the proprietary consequences of a third party debt order from the procedural rules, the making of an interim third party debt order still constitutes an equitable charge on the judgment debtor's property.[1]

1   *Société Eram Shipping Co Ltd v Cie Internationale de Navigation* [2004] 1 AC 260 at 292, per Lord Millett, HL. Lord Millett added (at 299) that 'RSC Ord 49 has now been replaced by Part 72 of the Civil Procedure Rules, which is cast in more modern language. It is

common ground that, as the editorial introduction states, the basic purpose of the rule remains unchanged. Unfortunately all reference to attachment has been dropped, and there is no longer any indication that the order has proprietary consequences. The words which formerly created an equitable charge at the interim stage have been replaced by a power to grant an injunction, which is normally a personal remedy. The straightforward language of Part 72 is deceptive. Its true nature cannot easily be understood without a knowledge of its history and antecedents. I do not, with respect, regard this as an altogether satisfactory state of affairs.' See further Chapter 3.

1.184 As Lord Millett explained in *Société Eram Shipping Co Ltd v Cie Internationale de Navigation*[1] a charging order operates in two stages:

'The first stage takes the form of an order nisi (or interim order) which creates a charge on the asset to be executed against and gives the judgment creditor priority over other claimants to the asset; and the second stage takes the form of an order absolute (or final order) which brings about the realisation of the asset and the payment of the proceeds to the judgment creditor.'

[1]   [2004] 1 AC 260 at 292.

1.185 It would therefore seem that the interim order constitutes 'security' for the purposes of administration. It is, however, important to note that although an interim third party debt order operates as a charge, the charge is defeasible in nature and a court may refuse to exercise its discretion to make the final third party debt order in the event of the judgment debtor's intervening administration. The effect of a judgment debtor's insolvency on the granting of a third party debt order is considered further in Chapter 3.

Writ of fieri facias

1.186 In *Peck v Craighead*[1] the court had to construe the similarly worded definition of security for the purposes of an individual voluntary arrangement (or IVA). Under IA 1986, s 383(2), which refers to 'a mortgage, charge, or other security', the court held that where goods were seized under a writ of fieri facias (in that case under a walking possession agreement) the judgment creditor was as regards those goods in the position of a secured creditor before the goods were sold. M E Mann QC, sitting as a deputy judge of the High Court, held that:[2]

'I infer that the security right which an execution creditor has under a fieri facias, which has been acted upon by seizure, is not unlike a lien, which is a security right expressly contemplated by s 383(2). The fact that such a security right has not been enforced is nothing to the point. It is enough that the debtor's property in the goods is bound. It is clearly irrelevant that the property has not yet passed out of the debtor's hands as on completion of the execution by sale.'

[1]   [1995] 1 BCLC 337.
[2]   [1995] 1 BCLC 337 at 341.

1.187 This decision is consistent with a number of other authorities pointing to the same conclusion.[1] It follows that, after the judgment debtor's goods have been seized by an enforcement officer, a judgment creditor will be a secured creditor in an administration of the company.

1   See further Chapter 5 (Writs of fieri facias).

1.188   None of these considerations are relevant in winding up proceedings because statute provides that nothing short of *sale* will do.

Equitable execution

1.189   It is clear in the case of equitable execution that the order appointing a receiver does not constitute a 'mortgage, charge, lien or other security'.[1] Accordingly, where a receiver has been appointed by way of equitable execution, the judgment creditor will not be in the position of a secured creditor on administration.

1   See eg *Re Pearce* [1919] 1 KB 354, CA (construing the similarly worded Bankruptcy Act 1914, s 167).

COMPANY VOLUNTARY ARRANGEMENTS

1.190   Company voluntary arrangements (CVAs) are available to allow proposals to be put to creditors of the company either to avoid insolvency or to compliment other forms of insolvency.

1.191   The original CVA regime made no provision for a moratorium. For this reason, it was common for an administration order to be obtained first (which imposed a moratorium) and then for the administrator to seek the creditors' agreement to a CVA.

Company voluntary arrangements for small companies

1.192   The Insolvency Act 2000 introduced a new moratorium regime if the debtor is a small company.[1] The procedure allows eligible companies to obtain a moratorium against enforcement to allow them time to put their proposal to creditors.

1   Subject to a number of exceptions, IA 1986, Sch A1, para 3(2) provides that to qualify as a small company, it must meet two or more of the qualifying criteria: (a) a turnover of not more than £5.6m; (b) a balance sheet total of not more than £2.8m; (c) not more than 50 employees.

1.193   The moratorium begins once the company files its proposals for a CVA with the court.[1] During the period that the moratorium is in force, no execution or other legal process may be commenced or continued against the company or its property except with the leave of the court and subject to such terms as the court may impose.[2]

1   IA 1986, Sch A1, para 8(1).
2   IA 1986, Sch A1, para 12(1)(h).

1.194   Once the moratorium is in force it must be advertised forthwith,[1] once in the Gazette and once in such newspaper as is most appropriate for ensuring that its coming into force comes to the notice of the company's creditors.[2] There is also a requirement to notify any enforcement officer known to be charged with an execution against the company or its property of the coming into force of the moratorium.[3]

1   IA 1986, Sch A1, para 10(1)(a).
2   Insolvency Rules 1986, r 1.40(2).
3   Insolvency Rules 1986, r 1.40(4). The notification should specify the date on which the moratorium came into force.

1.195   The moratorium lasts for 28 days unless a meeting of the company and its creditors is arranged for a time after that period, in which case it ends at the end of the day arranged for such meeting.[1]   The end of the moratorium must be advertised forthwith and the court, registrar of companies and any creditor of the company must be notified.[2]

1   IA 1986, Sch A1, para 8(3).
2   IA 1986, Sch A1, para 11.

Administrative receivers

1.196   An administrative receiver is defined in IA 1986, s 29(2) as:

'(a) a receiver or manager of the whole (or substantially the whole) of a company's property appointed by or on behalf of the holders of any debentures of the company secured by a charge which, as created, was a floating charge, or by such a charge and one or more other securities; or
(b) a person who would be such a receiver or manager but for the appointment of some other person as the receiver of part of the company's property.'

1.197   Floating charges are the security of choice of banks when lending to corporates.   The Enterprise Act 2002 has severely curtailed the circumstances in which a qualifying floating charge holder can appoint an administrative receiver (with the intention of promoting the new administration procedure set out in paras 1.78–1.79 above).   In future, an administrative receiver can only be appointed by a floating charge created prior to 15 September 2003 or in respect of specified transactions.

Priority of floating charge holders and execution creditors

1.198   There is limited authority on the question of the effect of a floating charge on a judgment creditor's ability to enforce his judgment.   Such authority that there is lacks coherence.   It does, however, seem clear that if a judgment creditor completes the enforcement before the charge crystallises, he gets priority over the floating charge holder.[1]   However, where a charge specifies that steps to enforce a judgment will automatically crystallise the charge this may be effective to defeat an attempt by a judgment creditor to enforce his judgment.[2]   This is a clause that is usually included in the debenture.   The priority between floating charge holders and execution creditors is considered in more detail in specialist works.[3]

1   *Robson v Smith* [1895] 2 Ch 118 (garnishee order obtained and paid before charge crystallised) and *Evans v Rival Granite Quarries Ltd* [1910] 2 KB 979, CA (garnishee order absolute made before charge was crystallised).

²   *Davey & Co v Willamson & Sons* [1898] 2 QB 194 (sheriff's attempt to levy execution
     defeated because the charge had already automatically crystallised). In *Evans v Rival Granite
     Quarries Ltd* [1910] 2 KB 979, CA, the decision was doubted by Fletcher Moulton LJ (at
     997) although not by Buckely LJ (at 1000) who said 'I have no fault to find with the
     decision'.

³   Gough *Company Charges* (2nd edn, 1996), pp 319–328 and Goode *Legal Problems of
     Credit and Security* (3rd edn, 2003), pp 179–180.

INDIVIDUAL JUDGMENT DEBTORS

1.199 Legislation essentially provides three forms of insolvency procedures for
individuals in financial difficulties that are of practical significance: bankruptcy,
individual voluntary arrangements and county court administration orders.[1] These
are considered in turn.

¹   Deeds of Arrangement under the Deeds of Arrangement Act 1914 have in practice been
     supplanted by Individual Voluntary Arrangements and are outside the scope of this book.

BANKRUPTCY

1.200 Where a bankruptcy petition has been presented, or an individual has been
adjudged bankrupt, the court that has bankruptcy jurisdiction over the individual has
a discretion to stay any 'execution or other legal process' against the property of the
debtor or the bankrupt as the case may be.[1] Similarly, any other court in which any
enforcement proceedings are pending against an individual also has a power to stay
them, or allow them to continue on such terms as it thinks fit, once it has been proven
that a bankruptcy petition has been presented against that individual or that he is an
undischarged bankrupt.[2]

¹   IA 1986, s 285(1).
²   IA 1986, s 285(2).

1.201 Once a bankruptcy order has been made, IA 1986, s 285(3) provides that no
judgment creditor shall have a remedy against the property of the bankrupt except
with the leave of court and on such terms as the court may impose.

Execution not completed before bankruptcy

1.202 IA 1986, s 346 provides that:

'… where the creditor of any person who is adjudged bankrupt has, before the
commencement of the bankruptcy—
(a) issued execution against the goods or land of that person, or
(b) attached a debt due to that person from another person,
that creditor is not entitled, as against the official receiver or trustee of the
bankrupt's estate, to retain the benefit of the execution or attachment, or any
sums paid to avoid it, unless the execution or attachment was completed, or the
sums were paid, before the commencement of the bankruptcy.'

1.203 The 'commencement of a bankruptcy' is the day on which the bankruptcy order was made.[1] Accordingly, this section deprives a judgment creditor of the benefit of any enforcement which was not completed before the bankruptcy order was made. This section (like IA 1986, s 183 which applies to a winding up) has long history.[2]

[1]   IA 1986, s 278(a).
[2]   Bankruptcy Act 1861, s 73; Bankruptcy Act 1869, s 87; Bankruptcy Act 1883, s 45; Bankruptcy Act 1914, s 40; and Insolvency Act 1985, s 179.

Meaning of 'retain the benefit of the execution or attachment'

1.204 The meaning of 'retain the benefit of the execution or attachment' was considered in *Re Andrew*[1] where the court was construing the similarly worded Bankruptcy Act 1914, s 40(1). In that case, a sheriff had seized goods under a writ of fieri facias and an arrangement was made whereby the sheriff withdrew from possession in return for a number of part payments by the judgment debtor. A number of payments were made before the judgment debtor became bankrupt. The trustee contended that the 'benefit of the execution' meant all the part payments.

[1]   [1937] Ch 122, CA.

1.205 The trustee's argument failed and the court held that 'benefit of execution' referred not to moneys actually received by the creditor in whole or partial satisfaction of his debt, whether under or in consequence of an execution or not, but rather to the charge which the judgment creditor obtained by the issue of the execution. The benefit of the execution could only refer to the charge *still remaining* after taking into account any payments which would reduce the amount of the charge.[1]

[1]   [1937] Ch 122 at 130, CA. Approved in *Marley Tile Co Ltd v Burrows* [1978] QB 241, CA.

1.206 It seems the same principle applies to any other form of enforcement which allows part payments without the execution being completed,[1] such as charging orders, where a number of payments may be received but not enough to pay the whole amount of the judgment debt. However, it is unclear to what extent this principle is still good law in the light of the wider changes made to the insolvency legislation.

[1]   *Re Caribbean Products (Yam Importers) Ltd* [1966] 1 Ch 331 at 351, per Russell LJ, CA.

1.207 Sums paid to avoid execution are now specifically dealt with by IA 1986, s 346, which provides that they may be retained provided they were paid before the bankruptcy order was made. Any sums paid after the making of the bankruptcy order must be handed to the official receiver or trustee. (By contrast, the equivalent provision applicable to a winding up[1] does not expressly mention payments made to avoid execution.)

[1]   IA 1986, s 183.

Completion of execution

1.208 The meaning of 'completion' of execution and attachment is defined in IA 1986, s 346(5):

'(a) an execution against goods is completed by seizure and sale or by the making of a charging order under s 1 of the Charging Orders Act 1979;

(b) an execution against land is completed by seizure, by the appointment of a receiver or by the making of a charging order under that section;

(c) an attachment of a debt is completed by the receipt of the debt.'

1.209   The application of these rules to third party debt orders, charging orders, writs of fieri facias and appointing a receiver by way of equitable execution is considered further in the relevant chapters. It should be noted that 'goods' are not given the artificially wide definition they are given under the equivalent provision applicable to a winding up (see paras 1.170).[1] This does, however, render the reference in IA 1986, s 346(5)(a) to execution against goods being completed by the making of a charging order meaningless because a charging order cannot be made over goods.[2]

[1]   IA 1986, s 183(4).
[2]   In Goode *Legal Problems of Credit and Security* (3rd edn, 2003) p 179 it is suggested that the provision is a drafting error.

1.210   Under IA 1986, s 346(6) the court may set aside the rights of the official receiver or trustee under IA 1986, s 346(1) in favour of an execution creditor on such terms as it sees fit. However, it would be rare for the court to make such an order in favour of a judgment creditor because it would run contrary to the pari passu principle.[1]

[1]   See further Berry, Bailey and Miller *Personal Insolvency: Law and Practice* (3rd edn, 2001) pp 499–500 which gives some examples under previous insolvency legislation of where the court might exercise its discretion in favour of an execution creditor.

1.211   The joint effect of IA 1986, ss 285(3) and 346(1) is that the making of a bankruptcy order prevents any further enforcement steps except with the leave of court and deprives the judgment creditor of any benefit of any enforcement unless it was completed by that time.

INDIVIDUAL VOLUNTARY ARRANGEMENTS

1.212   Individual voluntary arrangements are an alternative procedure to bankruptcy for individual debtors. It allows a debtor to avoid some of the restrictions imposed on a bankrupt, such as acting as a director of a company.

1.213   If a debtor applies for an interim order to make a proposal for a voluntary arrangement, the court that has jurisdiction over the interim order may at any time stay any 'execution or other legal process' against the property of the debtor.[1] The court in which any enforcement proceedings are pending against an individual also has a power to stay them, or to allow them to continue on such terms as it thinks fit, once it has been proven that an application for an interim order has been made.[2]

[1]   IA 1986, s 254(1)(b).
[2]   IA 1986, s 254(2).

COUNTY COURT ADMINISTRATION ORDERS

1.214 Although not contained in IA 1986, s 112, CCA 1984 provides that where an *individual* judgment debtor is unable to pay a judgment obtained against him and the judgment debtor's total indebtedness (including the judgment debt) is not more than £5,000, the county court has power to make an order for the administration of his estate.[1] If a county court administration order is in place, although execution of debts over £50 is still possible,[2] from a practical perspective this is likely to prove pointless given the debtor's perilous financial position and may end up being a further source of expense to the judgment creditor.

1   CCA 1984, s 112(1).
2   CCA 1984, ss 114–115.

CONCLUSION: THE INTERACTION OF THE INSOLVENCY AND ENFORCEMENT REGIMES

1.215 The insolvency provisions as they apply to methods of enforcement have developed on a piecemeal basis and lack consistency. While bankruptcy and winding up effectively nullify any uncompleted enforcement steps, in an administration a judgment creditor implementing certain forms of enforcement is treated as secured creditor. It is somewhat disappointing that the relationship between insolvency and enforcement has not been properly addressed and the fact this interface did not form part of the Civil Enforcement Review was perhaps a missed opportunity for a long overdue need to rationalise the law in this area.[1]

1   For a more detailed critique, see Walton 'Execution Creditors—(almost) the Last Rights in Insolvency' (2003) 32 CLWR 179.

ASSIGNMENT OF A JUDGMENT DEBT

1.216 A judgment debt is a chose in action and may be assigned by way of legal assignment or equitable assignment. Where a judgment creditor is able to assign the judgment debt to a third party for valuable consideration, he may consider doing so, even where the consideration received represents a considerable discount to the monetary value of the judgment debt, in order to avoid the delay, expense and uncertainty that may be associated with enforcing the judgment himself. An outline of the principles of legal and equitable assignment is provided below. Detailed reference should be made to specialist works.[1]

1   See *Chitty on Contracts* (29th edn, 2004).

Legal assignment

1.217 In order for there to be a valid legal assignment, the assignment must take place in accordance with the Law of Property Act 1925 (LPA 1925), s 136. The following conditions must therefore be met:[1]

(1)   the assignment must be in writing under the hand of the assignor;
(2)   the assignment must be absolute and not purporting to be by way of charge only; and
(3)   express notice of the assignment in writing must to be given to the judgment debtor.

[1]   LPA 1925, s 136.

1.218   If these conditions are complied with, the judgment debt transfers to the assignee from the date of notice to the judgment debtor the legal right to the judgment debt, all legal and other remedies for the same, and the power to give good discharge for the debt without the concurrence of the assignor.[1] Consideration is not necessary for legal assignment under LPA 1925. The assignee may enforce the judgment debt by all the methods of enforcement that would have been available to the assignor (the judgment creditor) and may do so in his own name and he does not have to bring proceedings in the judgment creditor's name.[2]

[1]   LPA 1925, s 136. Stamp duty of £5 was chargeable on an assignment of a debt executed before 1 December 2003 as a 'conveyance of property other than on sale' (Finance Act 1999, s 16(1), Sch 13). Stamp duty is not chargeable on an assignment of a debt executed on or after 1 December 2003 (Finance Act 2003, s 125).

[2]   *Goodman v Robinson* (1886) 18 QBD 332. That case was only concerned with whether garnishee proceedings (now third party debt orders) were available to the legal assignee of a debt which had been assigned under the Supreme Court of Judicature Act 1873, s 25(6) (now replaced by LPA 1925, s 136). However, the court saw no reason why writs of fi fa and oral examinations should not equally be available to the legal assignee of a debt, though such comments are strictly obiter. The same principles should apply to charging orders although these were not considered in the judgment.

Equitable assignment

1.219   An equitable assignment will transfer the equitable (though not legal) right to the judgment debt. Consideration may be given for the assignment. However, provided that the assignor has done everything required of him to make the assignment complete in equity,[1] consideration is not required for the assignment. No particular form of words is necessary provided there is shown a clear intention to assign the benefit of the judgment debt to the assignee. Notice of the equitable assignment to the judgment debtor is not necessary for an equitable assignment but is preferable. The assignor should be joined to any proceedings brought by the assignee to enforce payment of the judgment debt.

[1]   Eg where a holder of a judgment debt declares that he holds it on trust for another.

1.220   *Glegg v Bromley*[1] is illustrative of an equitable assignment of a judgment debt. A wife had assigned to her husband as security for a debt[2] she owed to him any interest, money or premises to which she may become entitled as a consequence of an action she was bringing against a third party. The action was successful and she was awarded damages. Separately, a judgment creditor of the wife sought to garnish the judgment debt owed to her as a result of the action. The Court of Appeal held that there had been a valid assignment of the judgment debt in equity since the husband had given good consideration for the judgment debt in forbearing to take action on the debt on the strength of the security given by his wife. Accordingly, the judgment creditor could not garnish the judgment debt.

1   [1912] 3 KB 474, CA.
2   The assignment could not therefore operate as a legal assignment, see para 1.217.

Assignment of judgment debts – maintenance and champerty

1.221   The courts have considered the question of whether the assignment of judgment debt is void for illegality because it involves maintenance or champerty. Maintenance is the giving of assistance to a party to litigation by a person who has no interest in the litigation or other motive recognised by the law as justifying his interference. Champerty is an aggravated form of maintenance in which the assistance is given in return for the promise of a share in the proceeds of the action. A contract involving maintenance or champerty is contrary to public policy and void for illegality.

1.222   However, the rule against maintenance or champerty does not prevent the assignment of a judgment debt, even prior to judgment, provided the assignee has no right to control or influence the conduct of the proceedings. In *Glegg v Bromley*[1] the facts of which have been described above, the court held:

> 'I think that all that was assigned was the fruits of an action. I know no rule of law which prevents the assignment of the fruits of an action. Such an assignment does not give the assignee any right to interfere in the proceedings in the action. The assignee has no right to insist on the action being carried on; in fact, the result of a compromise is actually included as a subject of the assignment. There is in my opinion nothing resembling maintenance or champerty in the deed of assignment.'

1   [1912] 3 KB 474.

ENFORCEMENT OF MONETARY AWARDS MADE BY BODIES OTHER THAN THE HIGH COURT AND COUNTY COURTS

1.223   This chapter has so far considered the enforcement of judgments and orders of the court. However, a number of statutes provide that decisions by tribunals (or other bodies) constituted under their ambit may be enforced by the court as if they were orders of the court if the court so orders.[1] Where such a tribunal has made an award for a sum of money, an application to enforce the award should be made in accordance with CPR 70.5.[2] This rule does not apply to awards made by arbitration tribunals (see para 1.229) or to foreign judgments (which are registrable for enforcement in England and Wales under the provisions of Pt 74: see paras 1.240–1.260).[3]

1   See eg Value Added Tax Act 1994, s 87 in relation to decisions of VAT and Duties Tribunals and Employment Tribunals Act 1996, s 15 in relation to Employment Tribunals.
2   Such an application can also be made to enforce decisions of tribunals etc other than monetary awards.
3   CPR 70.5(2). Neither does the rule apply to orders made in connection with criminal investigations and proceedings, which can be registered in the High Court pursuant to RSC Ord 115.

1.224   The application should be made by filing an application using Form N322A[1] in the court for the district where the person against whom the award was made resides or carries on business (unless the court orders otherwise).[2] It may be made without notice[3] and should state the name and address of the person against whom enforcement is sought together with a statement of how much of the award remains unpaid.[4] The costs of making the application for an order to enforce an award may also be recovered and should be stated in the application notice.

1   PD 70, para 4.1.
2   CPR 70.5(4)(b).
3   CPR 70.5(4)(a).
4   PD 70, para 4.2.

1.225   A copy of the award should be filed with the application notice.[1] The fee for issuing the application is £30[2] and the application may be dealt with by a court officer without a hearing.[3]

1   CPR 70.5(6).
2   Civil Proceedings Fees Order 2004, SI 2004/3121, Sch 1, para 7.9.
3   CPR 70.5(7).

Judgments of the House of Lords

1.226   The Civil Procedure Rules 1998 do not apply to civil appeals to the House of Lords.[1] Where a judgment creditor seeks to enforce a judgment of the House of Lords he should apply under Pt 23 for an order that the House of Lords judgment be made an order of the High Court. The application should be made to the procedural judge in the Division, District Registry or court in which the proceedings are taking place.[2]

1   CPR 2.1. Civil appeals to the House of Lords are governed by the House of Lords Practice
     Directions and Standing Orders Applicable to Civil Appeals November 2003 (the Blue Book).
2   PD 40B, para 13.1.

1.227   The application must be supported by:[1]

(a)   details of the order which was the subject of the appeal to the House of Lords;
(b)   details of the order of the House of Lords (with a copy annexed); and
(c)   a copy annexed of the certificate of the Clerk of Parliaments of the assessment of
       the costs of the appeal to the House of Lords.

1   PD 40B, para 13.2.

1.228   The order that the House of Lords judgment be made an order of the High Court should take the form of PF 68.

Arbitration awards

1.229   Detailed consideration of the statutory provisions and procedural rules relating to enforcement of arbitration awards is outside the scope of a book on the enforcement of English judgments in the High Court. However, for present purposes it is worth nothing that under the provisions of the Arbitration Act 1996, an award made by an arbitration tribunal pursuant to an arbitration agreement may, by leave of the court, be enforced in the same manner as a judgment or order of the court to the same effect.[1] Where leave is so given, judgment may be entered in terms of the award.[2] The procedural rules relating to arbitration claims[3] are set out in Pt 62. An application for permission to enforce an arbitration award as an order of the court should be made in accordance with CPR 62.18. It may be made without notice and a Pt 8 claim form should be issued.

1   Arbitration Act 1996, s 66(1).
2   Arbitration Act 1996, s 66(2).
3   Ie applications to the court under the Arbitration Act 1996 or other claims connected to
     arbitration proceedings: see CPR 62.2.

LAW REFORM

1.230   Many of the methods of enforcement covered in this book have historical antecedents dating back to the Middle Ages and in some cases beyond. The editorial introduction to Pt 70 in the White Book states:[1]

'The law on enforcement of judgments is out of date, unsatisfactory and in need of reform. Rather more than rule changes will be required (legislation has been promised). Nothing was done on enforcement in the original CPR 1998 and even now the rule changes are disappointing.'

1   Civil Procedure 2004, vol 1, para 70.0.2.

The Civil Enforcement Review

1.231   In March 1998 the government launched the Civil Enforcement Review as part of its 'access to justice' initiative. The Review's terms of reference included an examination of the present methods of enforcement available in the county court and High Court to assess their effectiveness and identify means through which this could be improved. The first phase of the Enforcement Review concluded in July 2000, with the publication of a number of proposals for primary and secondary legislation.[1]

1   Report of the First Phase of the Enforcement Review, July 2000.

1.232   A number of changes to the procedural rules relating to enforcement have so far been effected through secondary legislation. The Civil Procedure (Amendment No 4) Rules 2001[1] inserted Pts 70 to 73 into the CPR. These Parts came into force on 25 March 2002,[2] and apply to enforcement proceedings commenced after that date. Part 70 contains general rules about the enforcement of judgments and orders. However, as has been noted, it did not replace the whole of RSC Ord 45, which formerly contained the general rules relating to the enforcement of judgments, and with which Pt 70 must therefore be read in conjunction.

1   SI 2001/2792.
2   SI 2001/2792, r 1(c). Some amendments were effected by SI 2001/4015.

1.233   CPR Pts 71 to 73 contain the procedural rules relating to orders to obtain information from judgment debtors, third party debt orders and charging orders. They replaced RSC Ords 48 to 50 respectively. Similarly, Pt 69 updated the rules relating to the court's powers to appoint a receiver and was introduced by the Civil Procedure (Amendment) Rules 2002.[1]

[1]   SI 2002/2058. Part 69 replaced RSC Ord 30 and RSC Ord 51.

1.234   RSC Ord 46 and RSC Ord 47 remain in force.[1] The procedural rules relating to writs of execution and writs of fieri facias have not yet been updated. However, the second phase of the Enforcement Review focused on proposals for primary legislation. This has now effectively concluded with the publication of the March 2003 White Paper on Effective Enforcement.[2] A number of the White Paper's proposals relating to a new class of enforcement agents to replace High Court sheriffs have now been enacted in the Courts Act 2003. The White Paper also included proposals for a single piece of legislation to codify the law relating to enforcement agents and provide a unified regulatory regime and fee structure. An Enforcement Officer Bill has been suggested for some time in 2005[3] and reform of the procedural rules should follow.

[1]   Preserved in Sch 1 to the CPR.
[2]   Cm 5744.
[3]   Wilson 'Who shot the sheriff' LSG 2004, 101(16), 31.

1.235   The particular implications of the White Paper's proposals for reform in relation to each of the methods of enforcement covered in this book are considered in each of the relevant Chapters. The White Paper also proposed a unified register of county court and High Court judgments, which was also enacted under the Courts Act 2003.[1] However, as yet no draft regulations have been published as to the format or workings of the register.

[1]   Courts Act 2003, s 98(1). See further paras 2.28–2.30.

1.236   The White Paper's proposals for Data Disclosure Orders (DDOs) arguably represent the most far reaching change to enforcement law that the Review envisages. The proposals for DDOs outline a new court procedure to obtain access to information from third parties to assist with the enforcement of judgments. The role envisaged for court service officers in assessing the information retrieved and informing the judgment creditor of the methods of enforcement available in light of it perhaps marks a first, if small, departure from the principle that the judgment debtor is left to ascertain the most appropriate means by which to enforce his judgment without the court's involvement.

1.237   However, leaving aside DDOs, one criticism which could be made of the Civil Enforcement Review is that it did not seek to challenge some of the bedrock foundations of English enforcement law, such as considering whether the court could play a more proactive role in the enforcement of its judgments. Similarly, the interaction between the law on enforcement and the insolvency regime, particularly outside the realm of the onset of formal insolvency proceedings, appears to lack rationale and coherence in a number of respects. Some aspects of the law in this regard are ripe for reform.

PRE-CPR AUTHORITIES

1.238   One final point should be made in the context of reform of the law on enforcement in that the introduction of Pts 70 to 73 raises questions as to the relevance of pre-CPR authorities. The CPR introduced a new procedural code with the overriding objective of enabling the court to deal with cases justly.[1] In a number of judgments given by the Court of Appeal shortly after the CPR entered into force, the Court held that authorities under the former rules are generally no longer relevant; rather it is necessary to concentrate on the intrinsic justice of the case by reference to the overriding objective.[2]

1   CPR 1.1(1).
2   See *Biguzzi v Rank Leisure plc* [1999] 1 WLR 1926, CA; *Purdy v Cambran* [1999] All ER (D) 1518, CA and *Walsh v Misseldine* [2000] All ER (D) 261, CA.

1.239   However, these Court of Appeal judgments all concerned the approach the court should take in applying the test to strike out proceedings: that is, they were concerned with entirely procedural matters. On questions of substantive law the validity of pre-CPR authorities remains. The point is of importance since in the law relating to enforcement, perhaps more than any other area, the distinction between procedural and substantive law is often fine at best. Thus, where a pre-CPR authority is confined to procedural matters alone, it should rightly be treated with due scepticism, if not ignored, in the context of considering the operation of the modern rules. However, the extensive consideration and discussion given to a wealth of pre-CPR authorities in the 2003 judgment of the House of Lords in *Société Eram Shipping Co Ltd v Cie Internationale de Navigation*[1] is illustrative of the fact that consideration of earlier cases on the substantive law may often be necessary or helpful in arriving at the correct interpretation of the operation of the modern rules. As Lord Millet observed in *Société Eram*:[2]

> 'I wish to add one thing more. RSC, Order 49[3] has now been replaced by Part 72[4] of the Civil Procedure Rules, which is cast in more modern language. It is common ground that, as the editorial introduction states, the basic purpose of the rule remains unchanged. Unfortunately all reference to attachment has been dropped, and there is no longer any indication that the order has proprietary consequences. The words which formerly created an equitable charge at the interim stage have been replaced by a power to grant an injunction, which is normally a personal remedy. The straightforward language of Part 72 is deceptive. Its true nature cannot easily be understood without a knowledge of its history and antecedents. I do not, with respect, regard this as an altogether satisfactory state of affairs.'

1   [2004] 1 AC 260, HL.
2   [2004] 1 AC 260 at 298, HL.
3   The rule formerly governing garnishee orders.
4   The rules now governing third party debt orders, which have replaced garnishee orders.

LOCATION OF THE JUDGMENT DEBTOR'S ASSETS

1.240   This chapter has attempted to survey the general rules which apply to the enforcement of English judgments in the High Court. However, before it concludes, it is worth saying a few words about the enforcement of foreign judgments. As has been noted in the introduction to this chapter, the location of a judgment debtor's assets should be considered even before proceedings are issued since it is here that a claimant will wish to bring proceedings in order for the judgment to be effective. The location of assets may also affect the choice of jurisdiction in which to commence proceedings.

1.241   The principle of reciprocal enforcement of judgments is intended to provide claimants with a streamlined mechanism for the enforcement of a judgment obtained in one country in the courts of another country. Detailed consideration of the law relating to the reciprocal enforcement of judgments is the subject of specialist works[1] and is outside the scope of this book. However, an outline of the various regimes and key considerations relating to both the enforcement of English judgments overseas and the enforcement of foreign judgments in England and Wales is provided below.[2] The following commentary is intended by way of summary only and detailed reference should be made to the relevant Regulations, Conventions, statutes and procedural rules.

[1]   See *Dicey and Morris on the Conflict of Laws* (13th edn, 2000) or *European Civil Practice* (2nd edn, 2004).
[2]   There is an entirely separate regime for the international enforcement of arbitration awards from that applicable to court judgments. International Conventions (such as the New York Convention) mean that in many instances an arbitral award is more widely enforceable than an English court judgment.

ENFORCEMENT OF AN ENGLISH JUDGMENT OVERSEAS

1.242   Where enforcement of an English judgment in another jurisdiction is contemplated local law advice on the enforceability of an English judgment in that jurisdiction should be sought at the outset. Failure to do so may result in a judgment creditor pointlessly incurring time and expense in obtaining judgment to no end because the judgment is unenforceable in the jurisdiction where the defendant's assets are located.

1.243   There are three broad regimes which govern whether an English judgment will be recognised and enforced in another jurisdiction:

(a)   where the Brussels Regulation,[1] the Brussels Convention[2] or the Lugano Convention[3] apply (the Convention Regime);
(b)   where the Convention Regime does not apply, but there is a bilateral treaty or arrangement between the UK and the state in which enforcement is sought; or
(c)   where the law of the state in which enforcement is sought otherwise permits enforcement.

[1]   That is, the Regulation on Jurisdiction and the Enforcement of Judgments in Civil and Commercial Matters (Regulation 44/2001 of 22 December 2000).
[2]   That is, the Convention on Jurisdiction and the Enforcement of Judgments in Civil and Commercial Matters 1968.
[3]   That is, the Lugano Convention on Jurisdiction and the Enforcement of Judgments in Civil and Commercial Matters 1988.

The Convention Regime

1.244   The enforcement regime under the Brussels Regulation is a simplified and streamlined version of the enforcement regime under the Brussels and Lugano

Conventions, which are similar. The Brussels Regulation governs issues of enforceability as between all EU states, except for Denmark.[1] The Brussels Convention now only applies between Denmark and other EU states. The Lugano Convention applies as between EU states and EFTA countries.[2]

[1]   That is, between Austria, Belgium, Republic of Cyprus (not including Turkish Cyprus), Czech Republic, Estonia, Finland, France, Germany, Greece, Hungary, Ireland, Italy, Latvia, Lithuania, Luxembourg, Malta, Netherlands, Portugal, Poland, Slovakia, Slovenia, Spain, Sweden, and the United Kingdom.
[2]   That is, between Iceland, Switzerland and Norway and all EU states (including Denmark).

1.245   The aim of the Convention Regime is to provide a system whereby a claimant who has obtained a judgment from the courts of a member state may enforce that judgment in all other member states without issuing separate proceedings there. The courts of the enforcing state must first declare the judgment to be enforceable. The judgment must relate to a 'civil or commercial matter' and there are further restrictions as to the types of claim that can be enforced within the Convention Regime.[1]

[1]   The Convention Regime does not apply to bankruptcy or insolvency proceedings, claims relating to the status or legal capacity of natural persons, rights in property arising out of a matrimonial relationship, wills and succession, or arbitration. Further reference should be made to the detail of the Brussels Regulation and the Brussels and Lugano Conventions in this regard.

1.246   The procedure for enforcing an English judgment in a member state will be governed by local law and local law advice should be sought in this regard. The Brussels Regulation and the Brussels and Lugano Conventions also set out certain requirements on an application for recognition or declaration of enforcement of a judgment in a foreign jurisdiction.[1]

[1]   See arts 53–54 of the Regulation and arts 46–48 of the Conventions.

1.247   Theoretically, the process of recognition is straightforward. However, in practice it may take some time and interim measures in the foreign court to prevent the dissipation of assets may need to be considered. A refusal by the courts of the state in which enforcement is sought to recognise or enforce the English judgment can be appealed under the Convention Regime.[1] The judgment debtor cannot make an appeal on the merits to the court in which enforcement is sought against the decision of the English court. Similarly, the courts of the enforcing state may not review the jurisdiction of the English court in reaching the judgment.[2]

[1]   See arts 33 and 34 of the Brussels Regulation or arts 27 and 28 of the Brussels and Lugano Conventions.
[2]   Other than satisfying themselves that the matter was within the scope of the Conventions.

1.248   If the recognition procedure is successful, separate enforcement proceedings will then need to be brought in the member state in question, which may entail further delay and expense.

European Enforcement Order

1.249   From 21 October 2005 a streamlined procedure will exist for enforcement of uncontested judgments by virtue of Regulation (EC) No 805/2004 (the European

Enforcement Order Regulation).[1] The European Enforcement Order Regulation allows uncontested claims[2] to be enforced automatically in another member state without the need for a declaration of enforceability and without any possibility of opposing its recognition once the order has been certified as a European Enforcement Order by the court of origin.[3] The European Enforcement Order should greatly simplify the enforcement of uncontested judgments throughout the EC.

[1]   European Enforcement Order Regulation, art 33.
[2]   Defined in European Enforcement Order Regulation, art 3 as claims on admission or a consent order approved by the court, claims which the debtor never objected to, and claims where the debtor did not appear after initially objecting.
[3]   European Enforcement Order Regulation, art 5. European Enforcement Order Regulation, art 6 sets out the requirements for certification.

Bilateral treaty on enforcement of judgments

1.250   If the UK and the state in which enforcement is sought are signatories to a bilateral treaty on enforcement of judgments, the terms of that treaty should be referred to determine the enforceability of the English judgment in that country. Local law advice should be sought on both enforceability and procedure. If under the terms of a bilateral treaty the judgment of the courts of a foreign country are enforceable in England, it is more likely that enforcing an English judgment in that country will be straightforward under the principle of reciprocity.

Law of the state in which enforcement is sought

1.251   Where the state in which enforcement of a foreign judgment is sought is not party to either the Convention Regime or a bilateral treaty on the enforcement of judgments, enforcement will be a matter of local law in the foreign state. Local law advice on the enforceability of English judgments and the procedure for enforcement should be sought.

ENFORCEMENT OF FOREIGN JUDGMENTS IN ENGLAND

1.252   The common law rule is that fresh proceedings must be issued in England to enforce a foreign judgment. However, there are a number of important exceptions to this rule that in practice will apply to the majority of countries in which enforcement of a foreign judgment is sought. Where an exception does apply, the foreign judgment simply needs to be registered in England, following which it is possible to proceed to enforce the judgment as if it were an English judgment. Notably, the common law procedure still governs the enforceability of US judgments in England and thus fresh proceedings must be issued to enforce a US judgment.

The Convention Regime

1.253   The first major exception to the common law rule applies to judgments from the courts of countries falling under the Convention Regime.

1.254 The question of whether a foreign judgment issued by the courts of an EU member state (other than Denmark) will be enforceable in England is governed by the Brussels Regulation and Civil Jurisdiction and Judgments Act 1982 (CJJA 1982), s 4. In the case of Danish judgments, this will be governed by the rules of the Brussels Convention and CJJA 1982, s 4. The enforceability of judgments of the courts of Lugano Convention countries will be governed by the Lugano Convention and CJJA 1982, s 4.

1.255 Application for recognition and enforcement of a judgment of an EU state should be made to the High Court. The application should be made under the Brussels Regulation or CJJA 1982, s 4, as applicable, and the procedure is governed by Pt 74.

The 1920 and 1933 Acts

1.256 In the case of Commonwealth (and some other) countries, the enforceability of judgments given by the courts of the foreign state in England will be governed by either the Administration of Justice Act 1920 (AJA 1920) or the Foreign Judgments (Reciprocal Enforcement) Act 1933 (FJ(RE)A 1933).

1.257 Application for recognition and enforcement of a judgment of a country to which the AJA 1920 or FJ(RE)A 1933 apply should be made to the High Court. The applications should be made under AJA 1920, s 9 or FJ(RE)A 1933, s 2 respectively and the procedure is governed by Pt 74. The grounds for non-registration are set out in AJA 1920, s 9(2) and FJ(RE)A 1933, s 4.

Common law

1.258 In the case of judgments which do not fall under the Convention Regime, AJA 1920 or FJ(RE)A 1933, enforcement is governed by the English common law rules. A foreign judgment which is enforceable at common law creates an obligation that is actionable in England. However, it cannot be enforced here except by the institution of fresh legal proceedings.

1.259 The foreign judgment should be sued upon as a debt. Permission to serve out may be required. Once proceedings have been commenced, the judgment creditor should make an application for summary judgment on the basis that there is no defence to the claim. A number of defences are available at common law (for example, on the grounds that enforcement is contrary to public policy, that the judgment was obtained by fraud or that the proceedings were not sufficiently served and reference should be made to the relevant authorities in this regard).

The UK internal convention

1.260 Finally, it is worth noting that the enforcement of UK judgments in other parts of the UK is governed by CJJA 1982, s 18 and Schs 6 and 7. Again, the procedural rules are contained in Pt 74.

CHAPTER 2

Obtaining information about a judgment debtor's assets

INTRODUCTION

2.1 As has been noted in Chapter 1, it is for the judgment creditor, not the court, to enforce his judgment. The civil justice system provides various procedures to assist the judgment creditor in this process, which form the subject of this book. However, enforcement can be an expensive and time-consuming process and ineffective or abortive enforcement amounts to nothing more than an additional source of loss for the judgment creditor.

2.2 Where a judgment creditor is faced with a judgment debtor who will not pay it will often be prudent to take steps to obtain information about the judgment debtor's assets before commencing proceedings for enforcement. The ability to select an effective method of enforcement depends fundamentally on the information the judgment creditor possesses on the assets held by the judgment debtor. Taking steps to obtain such information will allow the judgment creditor to make an informed decision as to whether to pursue enforcement, and if so, which method or methods of enforcement are likely to prove most fruitful.

2.3 For the reasons discussed in Chapter 1, the claimant should consider the availability of assets for enforcement at the outset of any litigation. Steps to preserve assets[1] may have been necessary before or during proceedings in the event that the claimant suspects the defendant may attempt to dissipate his assets in order to render himself 'judgment-proof'. Disclosure during the course of litigation by the defendant or third parties may also have provided the judgment creditor with valuable information relating to the judgment debtor's assets.

[1] Such as freezing injunctions or other without notice injunctions.

2.4 As well as direct investigations into the judgment debtor's means, it may also be worth considering whether there are any assets belonging to the judgment debtor that are being held in another person's name, particularly where the judgment creditor knows or suspects that the judgment debtor has concealed assets in an attempt to evade payment. For example, it may be possible to establish that money held in a bank account in the name of the judgment debtor's spouse is actually beneficially owned by the judgment debtor, and thus held on trust for the judgment debtor by the spouse. Alternatively, it may be the case that a company is so closely associated with the judgment debtor that there is a complete merger of interests or unfettered control of the company by the judgment debtor so as to enable the court to treat the company as the judgment debtor's alter ego. If so, the company's assets may be liable to execution.[1]

[1] The test for whether the court will 'lift the corporate veil' is a high one and will be a question of fact in every case. See further *Lonrho Ltd v Shell Petroleum Co Ltd* [1980] QB 358 and *Trustor AB v Smallbone (No 2)* [2001] 1 WLR 1177.

2.5 This chapter describes various methods a claimant can use to obtain information about a defendant's assets once judgment has been obtained. While the judicial machinery of Pt 71 of the Civil Procedure Rules 1998 (CPR) (which provides for orders for a court examination of a judgment debtor to obtain information about his assets) is only available after judgment, there are a variety of public sources of information that may reveal important information about a judgment debtor's means even prior to judgment. In certain circumstances, it may also be worth considering instructing an inquiry agent to carry out more detailed investigations. Each of these three routes of inquiry is dealt with in this chapter.

2.6 It is worth noting that the procedure for a court examination of judgment debtors has been the subject of considerable discussion in the context of reform. The March 2003 White Paper on Effective Enforcement states: 'Access to better information is the key to effective enforcement.'[1] The premise that effective enforcement is unlikely without accurate information underlies many of the proposals for reform of the law on enforcement currently being considered by the Department of Constitutional Affairs.

While the procedure set out in Pt 71 can form the cornerstone to a successful enforcement process, it has itself been the subject of some criticism, particularly from a human rights perspective.[2] Some of the criticisms which have been made of the oral examination process and some of the proposals for its reform are considered at the end of this chapter.

[1] Chapter 3, executive summary.
[2] See 'The Legality of Debt Enforcement', a discussion paper published by Joseph Jacob of the London School of Economics.

2.7 It is also notable that the commentary to Pt 71 in the White Book states that:[1] 'The new procedure is clearly intended to be ECHR compliant and it is submitted that it is.' Whether further reform of the process will be required as a consequence of human rights challenges remains to be seen.

[1] Civil Procedure 2004, vol 1, para 71.8.1.

PUBLIC SOURCES OF INFORMATION

2.8 Before incurring the expense of instructing inquiry agents or commencing Pt 71 proceedings, it is worth noting that considerable information relating to a judgment debtor's assets is potentially available through public sources. Much of the information available through public sources is either free or relatively inexpensive to obtain. The use of such sources is likely to be a relatively painless and prudent first step that should avoid wasting costs in fruitless enforcement proceedings. It should also be noted that an increased amount of information held by public authorities has been made available under the Freedom of Information Act 2000 (FIA 2000) from 1 January 2005. Under the terms of the FIA 2000, any person making a request for information to a public authority[1] is entitled (subject to be exemptions set out in the FIA 2000) to be informed in writing by the authority whether it holds information of the description specified in the request and, if that is the case, to be provided with that information.[2] This may create further opportunities for judgment creditors to access information about a judgment debtor that is held by a public authority.

1   Defined in FIA 2000, s 3(1) and Sch 1.
2   FIA 2000, s 1(1).

2.9   Recourse to public sources of information may also have been made prior to the commencement of litigation, particularly where there are doubts about a potential defendant's solvency or worth. It may be the case that the information available from some of the sources outlined in this chapter can be employed much more usefully at an earlier stage in the litigation. However, for completeness, those sources which are most likely to be useful in the context of commercial enforcement are included here.

Insolvency

2.10   Before taking any enforcement steps it is worth considering whether the judgment debtor is solvent. If not, enforcement proceedings are unlikely to be worth pursuing.[1]

1   In such circumstances, it may be worth considering whether to initiate bankruptcy or winding up proceedings, or to file a proof of debt where such proceedings are already under way. See further Chapter 1.

2.11   The interplay between the insolvency regime and enforcement proceedings is considered generally in Chapter 1 and in each of Chapters 3 to 6 which deal with the various methods of enforcement. However, for present purposes, it is worth noting that a judgment creditor who has issued execution against the property of a judgment debtor or attached any debt due to the judgment debtor who is subsequently wound up (in the case of a company) or made bankrupt (in the case of an individual) is not entitled to retain the benefit of the execution or attachment against the liquidator or trustee in bankruptcy unless he has completed the execution or attachment before the commencement of the winding up or bankruptcy.[1]

1   IA 1986, ss 183(1) and 346(1).

2.12   As a consequence, if there are any doubts as to the judgment debtor's solvency, the judgment creditor should check whether a petition for bankruptcy or winding up has been presented before enforcement proceedings are commenced. Where the judgment debtor is an individual, a bankruptcy search should be carried out. In the case of a company, a winding up search should be made. A range of insolvency notices are required to be published in the London Gazette. A great deal of historical information is also freely available from the London Gazette website, although the most recent information requires a subscription.[1]

1   Full details are available from the London Gazette website: www.gazettes-online.co.uk.

Bankruptcy searches

2.13 Bankruptcy searches can be undertaken using the Land Charges Register or the Individual Insolvency Register.

Land Charges Register

2.14 All bankruptcy petitions[1] and bankruptcy orders[2] filed in England and Wales are automatically notified to the Chief Land Registrar to be registered in the register of pending actions[3] and the register of writs and orders affecting land[4] respectively. Both of these registers are held at the Land Charges Department.

1 Insolvency Rules 1986, SI 1986/1925, r 6.13 (Creditor's Petition) and r 6.43 (Debtor's Petition)
2 Insolvency Rules 1986, r 6.34(2)(a) (Creditor's Petition) and r 6.46(2)(a) (Debtor's Petition).
3 Land Charges Act 1972, s 5(1)(b).
4 Land Charges Act 1972, s 6(1). The register is something of a misnomer given that the Land Charges Act 1972, s 6(1)(c) provides that a bankruptcy order may be registered 'whether or not the bankrupt's estate is known to include land'.

2.15 The search can be made over the telephone.[1] However, in order to use the telephone service a key number is needed which can only be obtained by opening a credit account. The full name of the individual(s) the judgment creditor wishes to search against should be given. The cost is £2 per name searched against. A verbal answer will be given immediately and a certificate will follow by document exchange or post.

1 Land Registry Practice Guide 61 (July 2004): Telephone services (credit account holders only), para 3.

2.16 Alternatively, the search can be made by post or fax using form K16. The cost is £1 per name by post or £2 per name by fax. Contact details for the Land Charges Department are given in Appendix 1.

Individual Insolvency Register

2.17 Searches for both bankruptcy orders and individual voluntary arrangements in England and Wales can be made by searching the Individual Insolvency Register.[1] Unlike the Land Charges Register, this search will not reveal bankruptcy petitions[2] and thus gives no warning of an impending bankruptcy. However, it does reveal individual voluntary arrangements[3] and therefore indicates when a judgment debtor is in financial difficulties. The register is updated daily.

1 Insolvency Rules 1986, rr 6A.1–6A.8.
2 Insolvency Rules 1986, r 6A.4(2).
3 Insolvency Rules 1986, r 6A.2(1).

2.18 The search can be made free of charge online,[1] by post or fax to the Insolvency Service's headquarters in Birmingham, or in person at the office of the local Official Receiver.[2] An online search can be performed against just a surname (or part of a surname) for either the whole of England and Wales or, if desired, an area covered by an individual Official Receiver's Office.

1   www.insolvency.gov.uk/eiir.
2   Details of the nearest Official Receiver's Office can be obtained by calling the Insolvency
     Service's Central Enquiry Line or online at: www.insolvency-service.co.uk/officemap.htm.
     Contact details for the Insolvency Service appear in Appendix 1.

2.19   In the case of a postal or fax search, the appropriate form can be downloaded from the Insolvency Service website.[1] The details provided about the individual to be searched against should be as full as possible. The minimum required is the full name of the individual. However, where other details are known (such as aliases, gender, date of birth, address, occupation or trading name) these should also be provided since they will help narrow the search.

1   www.insolvency.gov.uk/pdfs/insolvencyregister.pdf.

2.20   The results form will be despatched by post and will either indicate that there is no trace of a bankruptcy order or individual voluntary arrangement, or that there is a match or close possible match and provide details. In the latter case, further enquiries should be made by telephoning the relevant court.[1] Contact details for the Insolvency Service are given in Appendix 1.

1   Inspection of court records for insolvency proceedings is dealt with by Insolvency Rules
     1986, rr 7.28–7.32.

Insolvency searches

2.21   Where the judgment debtor is a company, an insolvency search can be carried out at the Central Registry of Administration and Winding Up Petitions at the Companies Court in London. The search will reveal any petition or orders for the winding up of the company made in England and Wales. However, in the case of companies in administration, only administrations in the High Court in London will be revealed.

2.22   The Central Registry can be searched by either personal attendance at Companies Court Central Office or by telephone. Telephone searches are free of charge for up to three company names. Contact details for the Companies Court Central Registry are provided in Appendix 1.

2.23   The Central Registry only maintains records of compulsory winding up petitions or orders. To find out whether a company has commenced a voluntary winding up, a search should be made at Companies House (see para 2.35).

Register of county court judgments

2.24   Where there are doubts about a judgment debtor's solvency, it may also be worth making a search of the Register of County Court Judgments. This contains details of all county court judgments[1] in England and Wales. It will therefore provide information about other creditors of the judgment debtor and may serve as an early warning signal that further pursuit of a judgment debtor is unlikely to be worthwhile. The Register of County Court Judgments is maintained by Registry Trust Ltd.[2] The information held in the register is public.[3]

1   Also included are administration orders made under the County Courts Act 1984, s 112 and an order restricting enforcement under County Courts Act 1984, s 112A.

2   County Courts Act 1984, ss 73 and 73A and the Register of County Court Judgments Regulations 1985, SI 1985/1807. Certain information is also available from Scotland, Ireland, Northern Ireland, the Isle of Man and Jersey-see further the Registry Trust Ltd's website under the FAQs section: www.registry-trust.org.uk.

3   Register of County Court Judgments Regulations 1985, SI 1985/1807, reg 11. Credit reference agencies buy the information in bulk by virtue of this regulation.

2.25 The information held on the register comprises the judgment debtor's name and address, the amount of the judgment (including costs), the county court which entered the judgment, and the case number.[1] Entries are kept on the register for a period of six years from the date of the judgment before they are cancelled.[2] Claims satisfied within one calendar month of the judgment being entered can be removed from the register. If the judgment debtor satisfies the judgment after one calendar month, the entry will remain on the register for six years (although the judgment debtor can apply for a note to be made on the register denoting the satisfaction of the judgment).[3]

1   Register of County Court Judgments Regulations 1985, reg 6.

2   Register of County Court Judgments Regulations 1985, reg 9.

3   Register of County Court Judgments Regulations 1985, reg 8.

2.26 Certain judgments or orders are exempt from registration.[1] Where a judgment or order was made after a contested hearing, the judgment or order will not be entered on the register until the judgment creditor takes steps to enforce the judgment.[2] Other judgments and orders exempt from registration include those where there is an application for a new trial,[3] where there is an appeal pending and a stay has been granted or a deposit or security has been given,[4] and interim orders for costs following summary assessment.[5] As the nature of the exemptions illustrates, the purpose behind the register is to identify persons who are uncreditworthy, not to identify parties who legitimately dispute liability.

1   County Courts Act 1984, s 73(2) and Register of County Court Judgments Regulations 1985, SI 1985/1807.

2   Register of County Court Judgments Regulations 1985, reg 5(2). Note under reg 5(2), a request for the oral examination of the judgment debtor or an application for the payment of a money judgment or order by instalments also triggers registration.

3   Register of County Court Judgments Regulations 1985, reg 5(3)(a).

4   Register of County Court Judgments Regulations 1985, reg 5(3)(b).

5   Register of County Court Judgments Regulations 1985, reg 5(3A).

2.27 The register may be inspected by personal attendance at Registry Trust Ltd and paying a fee of £4 per name and address. Requests can also be made by post for a search against a named person, company or firm at a stated address.[1] In this case the fee is £4.50 per name and address and a certified copy of any entry on the register will be provided.[2] Contact details for the Registry Trust Ltd are provided in Appendix 1.

Attachment of earnings orders are not included in the Register of County Court Judgments. However, the court for the district in which the judgment debtor resides must maintain a register of all attachment of earnings orders in force against the judgment debtor which either that court made against him or, where the order was made by another court, of which the court has been notified.[3] This can be searched by any person having a judgment or order against a person believed to be residing within the district of the court and the court will issue a certificate of the result of the search.[4]

1　　Register of County Court Judgments Regulations 1985, reg 11(1)(a). The form is available at: www.registry-trust.org.uk/search.aspx.
2　　Register of County Court Judgments Regulations 1985, reg 11(2).
3　　Note that CCR Ord 27, r 2(2) imposes an obligation on any court in which the judgment debtor does not reside to inform the county court in which the judgment debtor resides of the making of an attachment of earnings order.
4　　CCR Ord 27, r 2.

Register of High Court judgments

2.28　In contrast to the county court, there is no equivalent register for High Court judgments. Therefore, while a judgment for £10,000 obtained against a judgment debtor in the county court could easily be located, a judgment for £10m obtained in the High Court would not appear on any equivalent register.

2.29　This anomaly will be rectified once the Courts Act 2003 (CA 2003), s 98 enters into force. This gives effect to one of the recommendations of the First Phase of the Enforcement Review.[1] Following consultation,[2] the Court Service recommended an expansion of the county court register to include High Court judgments.[3] CA 2003, s 98 will introduce a unified register of county court and High Court judgments by re-enacting the provisions concerning registration of county court judgments and including High Court judgments.[4]

1　　See *Enforcement Review – Report of the First Phase of the Enforcement Review* (July 2000) p 16.
2　　Registration of County Court Judgments – a consultation paper (July 2000) p 16.
3　　Register of County Court Judgments – a consultation paper (June 2003).
4　　CA 2003, s 98(1).

2.30　Under CA 2003, s 98, the Lord Chancellor has the power to issue regulations implementing the unified register of judgments. At the time of writing, no draft regulations had yet been published and so it is not clear how the register will work. The indications given in the consultation paper *Register of County Court Judgments and Responses to consultation on service and methods of service delivery*[1] are that the register will be made more widely available via the internet, email and telephone.

1　　November 2003, pp 28–33.

Companies

2.31　Where the judgment debtor is a company, considerable information as to its assets may be available through public sources of information.

Companies House

2.32　The Companies Act 1985 (CA 1985) requires that all companies formed and registered under CA 1985 deliver certain documentation to the Registrar of

Companies.[1] In addition, oversea companies which have an established place of business in Britain are required to deliver certain documents.[2] Some of this information may provide an indication of the financial health or assets of a company. An outline of that which is likely to prove most useful to a judgment creditor is given in paras 2.34-2.40.

[1]   A more comprehensive summary of the documents required to be sent to the Registrar of Companies can be found in Appendix 6 to *Tolley's Company Law Service*.
[2]   CA 1985, Pt XXIII.

2.33   Companies House Information Centres are located in Cardiff, Edinburgh and London and maintain records of every registered company's documents. The public has a right to inspect and obtain copies of documents held by the Registrar.[1] Information can be requested and accessed by personal visit to one of the Information Centres, by telephone to the call centre in Cardiff, or online. The Companies House website[2] provides free access to certain basic company information and also provides a full list of fees for providing copies of other documents filed with the Registrar of Companies. Contact details for Companies House are provided in Appendix 1 to this chapter.

[1]   CA 1985, s 709.
[2]   www.companieshouse.co.uk.

Company accounts

2.34   A summary of the information available from Companies House is set out in Appendix 2 to this chapter. The information of most interest to a judgment creditor is likely to be contained in the company accounts, which every company is required to deliver to the Registrar of Companies under CA 1985, s 242. The accounts comprise the company's audited balance sheet and profit and loss account, together with the directors' and auditors' reports and, in the case of quoted companies, the directors' remuneration report. Where appropriate, the accounts will include group accounts.[1]

[1]   It should be noted that the accounts held at Companies House may not be fully up to date. Under CA 1985, s 244, public limited companies are required to file their accounts within seven months after the end of the accounting reference period and private limited companies within ten months. The late filing of accounts may sometimes suggest that a company is in financial difficulties and the company's accounting reference date (which can be found on the Companies House website) should be checked to ascertain how current the accounts are. There are certain exceptions in terms of filing requirements for small to medium-sized companies, unlimited companies and dormant companies.

Company insolvency information available from Companies House

2.35   Companies House also holds certain information which may be useful where the solvency of a company is of concern. All companies are required to file notice of appointment of a receiver or manager[1] and the appointment of an administrative receiver.[2] Details of any voluntary resolutions[3] or orders[4] for the winding up of the company and notice of the appointment of a liquidator[5] must also be filed.

1   CA 1985, s 405(1).
2   IA 1986, s 43(5).
3   CA 1985, s 380(1) and IA 1986, s 84(3).
4   IA 1986, s 130(1) and Insolvency Rules 1986, r 4.21(3).
5   IA 1986, s 109(1).

Company charges

2.36   Some information can be obtained from Companies House as to the registered charges of a company. This will be relevant where there is a risk that the company may become insolvent since a judgment creditor will generally rank behind secured creditors in any claim to the company's assets.

2.37   Although the instrument creating a company charge is required to be sent to the Registrar of Companies as part of the process of registration, the instrument itself is returned to the company and only Form 395, setting out particulars of the charge, is retained. Form 395 and the register of charges can be obtained from Companies House but often will not contain vital information, in particular the amount of the charge.

2.38   A company must retain a copy of the instrument creating a charge at its registered office which is available for inspection by any creditor or shareholder of the company.[1] Whether the charge instrument itself will reveal the actual amount secured will depend on the type of security. If it secures 'all monies', the judgment creditor will be none the wiser. It may, however, secure a loan of a fixed amount which will prove more useful if that amount is set out in the charge (although the charge may simply refer to amounts owed under a separate loan agreement).

1   CA 1985, s 408(1).

Statutory records

2.39   In addition to filing various documents with the Registrar of Companies, CA 1985 also requires a company to keep certain information in the form of registers. These are usually required to be kept at the registered office of the company. Some of this information is open to inspection by the public.[1]

1   Other information is only available to a company's members, creditors or debenture holders. For a summary of the statutory records required to be kept by a company and rights of inspection, see Chapter 3 of *Tolley's Company Secretary's Handbook 2003–2004* (13th edn, 2003) and Appendix 6 of *Tolley's Company Law Service*.

2.40   It may also be worth noting that CA 1985 makes provision for additional rights to inspect company documents in the case of a company's members, creditors and debenture holders, and that directors have a common law right to inspect a company's books (subject to the court's discretion). Where the judgment creditor falls into one of these categories, these additional rights to inspect documents may be useful when it comes to enforcement (to the extent that they have not already been utilised during the course of litigation).

Common law rights of inspection of company books and records

2.41 At common law the shareholders of a company have a right to inspect the documents of the company, including legal advice paid for using company funds.[1] This principle applies to all companies irrespective of size or importance[2] although it is subject to any contrary provision in the company's articles of association.[3]

[1] Unless that legal advice was prepared to advise the company on hostile litigation between the company and the shareholder), *Woodhouse and Co Ltd v Woodhouse* (1914) 30 TLR 559, CA. See also Hollander *Documentary Evidence* (8th edn, 2003) para 6-06.

[2] *CAS (Nominees) Ltd v Nottingham Forest plc* [2001] 1 All ER 954 at 958–959.

[3] *Gourand v Edison Gower Bell Telephone Co of Europe Ltd* (1888) 59 LT 813. If a company has 1985 Table A articles of association, the articles will contain the following: 'No member shall (as such) have any right of inspecting any accounting records or other book or document of the company except as conferred by statute or authorised by the directors or by ordinary resolution of the company.' This provision is similar to a provision considered in *Gourand* and which the court held was insufficient to resist disclosure of legal advice on the basis it was not framed with litigation in mind.

2.42 At common law the directors of a company have the right to inspect the company's books of account and other records so as to enable them to carry out their duties as a director. This right ceases upon the director's removal from office. The court retains a residual discretion whether or not to order inspection to be allowed. However, where there is no reason to suppose that a director is likely to be removed from office, the court will assume that a director is exercising his right in the interests of the company unless the court is satisfied that the director's intention is to abuse the confidence reposed in him as a director and to injure the company.[1]

[1] *Conway v Petronius Clothing Co Ltd* [1978] 1 WLR 72 at 89–90.

Other public sources

2.43 Finally, it is worth remembering that Bloomberg, Reuters and the London Stock Exchange may also be a source of information relating to transactions a company has entered into or its likely financial health. The internet may also provide general information about a company, particularly where the company or its group has its own website.

Limited Liability Partnerships

2.44 Limited Liability Partnerships (LLPs) were introduced by the Limited Liability Partnerships Act 2000 (LLPA 2000) and the Limited Liability Partnerships Regulations 2001,[1] which both came into force on 6 April 2001. LLPs are an alternative corporate business vehicle that can be seen as a hybrid between a company and a partnership. LLPs and companies have broadly similar accounting and filing requirements. However, LLPs are organised internally like partnerships and have no shareholders.

[1] SI 2001/1090.

2.45 The Limited Liability Partnerships Regulations 2001 provide that amended versions of certain designated provisions of, among other things, CA 1985 and

IA 1986 apply to LLPs. Under this modified legislation, LLPs are required to file certain documents at Companies House which are available to the public in the same way as are certain company documents. The key filing requirements under LLPA 2000 are similar to those applicable to companies and are set out in Appendix 3.[1]

---

[1]   Note that all statutory references in Appendix 3 are to the legislation as modified by the Limited Liability Partnerships Regulations 2001, SI 2001/1090.

2.46   As with companies, certain basic information relating to LLPs can be freely accessed from the Companies House website. Other documents can be ordered in the same way as documents for companies. The relevant fees for copies of documents filed with the Registrar of Companies are available on the Companies House website. Contact details for Companies House and details of the LLP inquiry line are provided in Appendix 1.

Dun & Bradstreet

2.47   Dun & Bradstreet is a commercial source of company information designed to be used for credit, marketing, purchasing and management decision purposes. Companies are given a number of ratings including payment performance and likelihood of success or failure. The ratings are used as predictive indicators for assessing company risk and business failure. The Dun & Bradstreet report may therefore provide some useful information to a judgment creditor who is considering whether the pursuit of enforcement proceedings against a judgment debtor company is likely to be worthwhile. There are various forms of report which often conveniently collect together public information and which may be purchased from their website.[1] Contact details for Dun & Bradstreet are set out in Appendix 1.

---

[1]   http://dbuk.dnb.com/english/default.htm.

Land

2.48   The land and buildings owned by a judgment debtor may be one of its most substantial assets and the availability of charging orders over land (see further Chapter 4) means that such assets are potentially available for enforcement by a judgment creditor. The judgment creditor will need to check that the land is in fact owned by the judgment debtor and it will also be prudent to check the extent of any prior charges over the land. This will enable the judgment creditor to ascertain the extent of the remaining equity in the property so as to form a view whether execution against land is worthwhile since a charging order will take effect subject to any prior charges over the property.

2.49   The means by which ownership is ascertained will depend on whether the land is registered or unregistered. To determine whether land is registered, any person may apply for a search of the index map.[1] The Land Registry form for a search of the index map is form SIM.[2] Credit Account holders can apply for a search of the index map by telephone or online at Land Registry Direct.[3] The certificate of result will reveal whether or not title to the land is registered and, if it is so registered, the title number(s).[4] If the land is known to be registered but the title number is unknown, a different procedure applies.[5]

1   The index map is a computerised map based on the Ordnance Survey Map providing an index
     of the land comprised in every registered title and pending application for first
     registration: Land Registration Rules 2003, SI 2003/1417, r 145. See further *Land Registry
     Practice Guide 10* (April 2004): Official searches of the index map.
2   Land Registration Rules 2003, r 145(2). The form can be downloaded from the Land Registry
     website: www.landreg.gov.uk/publications/?pubtype=1.
3   Land Registry Practice Guide 10 (April 2004): Official searches of the index map, para 4.
4   Land Registry Practice Guide 10 (April 2004): Official searches of the index map, paras 1.2
     and 8.
5   An application for official copies can be made as normal using Land Registry Form OC1 with
     the words 'please supply the title number' written boldly at the head of the form: *Land
     Registry Practice Guide 10* (April 2004): Official searches of the index map, para 4.

Registered land: HM Land Registry

2.50   Where land is registered copies of the register of title for an individual property
may be obtained from HM Land Registry. This may be helpful where the judgment
creditor knows or suspects a property to be owned by the judgment debtor. Any
person may inspect and take copies of any register of title of an individual property
and any document referred to in the register of title.[1] It is not possible for a judgment
creditor to search for *all* land registered in the name of a particular person.[2]

1   Land Registration Act 2002, s 66.
2   Although there is an index of proprietors' names maintained by the Land Registrar which
     would potentially allow a search of all land registered in the name of a particular judgment
     debtor, this is not a public index. Land Registration Rules 2003, r 11(3) provides that a
     person may apply using Form PN1 for a search to be made of the index of proprietors'
     names against 'the name of some other person in whose property he can satisfy the registrar
     that he is interested generally (for instance as trustee in bankruptcy or personal
     representative)'. The practice of HM Land Registry is not to recognise a judgment creditor
     as a person 'interested generally' in the property of a judgment debtor and to refuse to allow
     a search of the index without a court order specifically authorising a search of the index of
     proprietors' names and detailing the names to be searched.

2.51   Searches to obtain the register of title can be performed in person, by post, fax,
telephone[1] and online.[2] The register will identify the registered proprietor(s), any
leasehold interests registered against that property and any registered charges over
the property. The fee varies from £2 to £4 per individual register of title depending on
how the request is made.[3]

1   However, in order to use the telephone service a key number is needed which can only be
     obtained by opening a credit account.
2   Members of the public may use the Land Register Online (www.landregisteronline.gov.uk)
     and there is a subscription service aimed at professionals known as Land Registry Direct
     (www.landreg.gov.uk/direct).
3   Land Registration Fee Order 2004, SI 2004/595, Sch 3, part 2.

2.52   Where the charges register refers to a charge on the property the judgment
creditor may wish to inspect the charge document to ascertain whether there is
sufficient equity in the property to satisfy the judgment debt, either in whole or in
part, after that charge has been paid off. A charge document received by HM Land
Registry after 13 October 2003 may be inspected as of right.[1] An application to view a
charge document is made using Form OC2[2] and the fee per document is £4.[3]

1   Land Registration Rules 2003, r 135(1).
2   Land Registration Rules 2003, r 135(4). For a transitional period, ending on 13 October 2005, charge documents received by HM Land Registry before 13 October 2003 may only be inspected at the discretion of the Land Registrar (Land Registration Rules 2003, r 135(3)). If applying for documents to be disclosed at the discretion of the Land Registrar, the manner in which the application should be made is explained in Land Registry Practice Guide 11 (December 2004): Inspection and applications for official copies, para 4. The fee for each document made available at the discretion of the Land Registrar is £8: Land Registration Fee Order 2004, SI 2004/595, Sch 3, Pt 4.
3   Land Registration Fee Order 2004, SI 2004/595, Sch 3, Pt 2.

2.53 Any person filing documents with the Land Registrar who claims that a document contains 'prejudicial information' can ask that it is designated as an 'exempt information document' and thus not made publicly available.[1] It may be the case that the party who registered the charge document applied for it to be an exempt information document. In such case the judgment creditor should apply to the Land Registrar to obtain a full copy of the document using Form EX2.[2] The Land Registrar will consider the application and will serve a notice on the person who initially applied to designate the document as an Exempt Information Document allowing them to make representations.[3] The fee for each official copy provided of an Exempt Information Document is £40.[4]

1   Land Registration Rules 2003, r 136.
2   Land Registration Rules 2003, r 137(2). The application should explain why the edited version of the document is 'insufficient for their purposes' and why 'none of the information omitted is prejudicial commercial or personal information, or why the public interest in allowing a full copy to be issued outweighs the public interest in not doing so' (Land Registry Fact Sheet 9: Information to aid retrieval, p 2).
3   Land Registration Rules 2003, r 137(3).
4   Land Registration Fee Order 2004, SI 2004/595, Sch 3, pt 2.

Unregistered land

2.54 Where the index map search reveals that the land is unregistered, the only means whereby a judgment creditor may be able to confirm that the judgment debtor owns the land is through requiring him to attend court with the relevant title documents using the Pt 71 procedure described in paras 2.130–2.265.

High value goods

2.55 High value goods, such as ships, yachts, motor boats, aeroplanes, paintings or motor vehicles, may go some way to payment of a judgment debt and can be subject to execution through writs of fieri facias. It may therefore be worth investigating whether the judgment debtor owns any such items. While an inquiry agent or an oral examination may be needed to elicit this information, there are also a number of public and commercial registers available for inspection.

2.56 One preliminary point that should be noted as regards execution against goods is that an injunction can be obtained to restrain an enforcement agent from remaining in possession of, and from selling, goods which do not belong to the judgment debtor.[1] During the tenure of a hire purchase agreement, the legal title to the goods remains with the owner, with title only being transferred to the hirer at the end of the hire purchase period. Thus where it is intended to levy execution against a class of goods which are commonly subject to a hire purchase agreement, it is advisable first to check that the asset is not subject to a hire purchase agreement. This may be done through inquiries of the judgment debtor[2] or, in the case of motor vehicles, through checking with HPI Limited (see para 2.66).

[1]   See further Chapter 5.
[2]   If necessary, through Pt 71 proceedings. See paras 2.130–2.265.

Ships – Register of British Ships

2.57   The Registrar General of Shipping and Seamen maintains a Register of British Ships, which is a central register of UK merchant ships, fishing vessels and pleasure vessels. The Register is divided into four parts:

Part 1 for merchant ships and pleasure vessels;
Part 2 for fishing vessels;
Part 3 for small ships; and
Part 4 for bareboat charter ships.[1]

[1]   Merchant Shipping (Registration of Ships) Regulations 1993, SI 1993/3138, reg 2.

2.58   The register is a public record[1] and any person is entitled on application to the Registrar General of Shipping and Seamen to obtain a certified transcript of the entries in the Register or to inspect entries in the Register during the official opening hours of the General Registry of Shipping and Seamen.[2] The certified transcript of the entries in the Register sets out details of the ship and the owner. Ships may also be subject to mortgages and details of any registered mortgages will also be provided in the certified transcript of entries in the Register. However, the details of the mortgage are fairly brief and reveal little more than the identity of the mortgagor and mortgagee, the date of its execution and the number of shares in the ship that are mortgaged.

[1]   Merchant Shipping Act 1995, s 8(7).
[2]   Merchant Shipping (Registration of Ships) Regulations 1993, SI 1993/3138.

2.59   There is no online search facility for the Register of British Ships. However, enquiries can be made by telephone to determine whether any ships are owned by an individual or company. No fee is charged for this search. If any matches are revealed, then the name of the ship and its official number will be provided. A request for a certified transcript of the entries in the Register can then be made. There is no official form for the search and the request should be made by letter which can either be posted or faxed to the Registry of Shipping and Seamen. The fee is currently £13. Contact details for the Registry of Shipping and Seamen are set out in Appendix 1.

Ships and Lloyd's Register

2.60   Lloyd's maintains both a Register of Ships and a List of Ship Owners, the hard copies of which are published annually. The List of Ship Owners provides details of ship owners worldwide and acts as a companion volume to the Register of Ships. The Register of Ships is a commercial register and, although there is no statutory requirement for registration of a vessel in the Register of Ships, this may be required by a bank or insurance company. Trading vessels will usually be registered with Lloyd's as a consequence and the Register of Ships contains details of some 98% of the world's vessels of 100 gross tons or greater. Unlike the Register of British Ships, it is not confined to British registered ships and covers ships wherever registered in the world.

2.61 A search of the List of Ship Owners can be made through Lloyd's Information Services under the name of the individual or company to determine any ships owned. Searches can be ordered over the telephone, by post or by fax. Inquiries made by telephone, fax or post currently cost £125 plus VAT per ship. A search can also be made free of charge by personal attendance. A daily updated version of the registers are available online[1] although this service is only available to subscribers. Contact details for Lloyd's Information Services are provided in Appendix 1.

[1]   www.lrfairplay.com.

Tracking a ship

2.62 If a ship is identified either from the Register of British Ships or the Lloyd's Register, Lloyd's Maritime Intelligence Unit offers a vessel tracking service. The service currently costs £100 per vessel per week. The service includes:

(a)   last reported location (arrived/sailed);
(b)   if the vessel is in port, the expected sailing date;
(c)   the next port of call; and
(d)   the estimated time of arrival.

Contact details for the Lloyd's Marine Intelligence Unit are set out in Appendix 1.

Aircraft

2.63 The Aircraft Registration Section of the Civil Aviation Authority (CAA) maintains a register of UK registered aircraft.[1] Searches can be carried out against a person's name to identify any aircraft owned by an individual or company and can be made free of charge using the CAA's website, by post, fax, telephone or inspection of the register.

[1]   UK registration of aircraft is governed by the Air Navigation Order 2000, SI 2000/1562. See generally *Halsbury's Laws of England* vol 2(3), paras 633–640.

2.64 For the same reasons as set out in para 2.56 above, it is also likely to be worth enquiring whether there is a mortgage over the aircraft. The CAA also maintains a register of mortgages over aircraft registered in the UK,[1] known as the UK Register of Aircraft Mortgages. A search of the UK Register of Aircraft Mortgages can be requested by phone, fax, letter or email. The form to be used is CA350 and the current fee for the service is £20 per aircraft. Contact details for the CAA are provided in Appendix 1.

[1]   Mortgaging of Aircraft Order 1972, SI 1972/1268.

Vehicles

2.65 The Driver and Vehicle Licensing Agency (DVLA) maintains registers of drivers and vehicles. It does not provide a search facility against the names of registered keepers but does have a facility to allow vehicle registration numbers to be searched by any person who can show 'reasonable cause' for wanting the particulars.[1] Any request should be made by writing a letter to the DVLA and enclosing a cheque of £5 per registration number to be searched. The DVLA will then make a decision as to whether the information is to be released. Telephone inquiries indicate that the DVLA generally considers a judgment creditor to have 'reasonable cause' although it requires a copy of the judgment before releasing any information. Contact details for the DVLA are provided in Appendix 1.

[1]   Road Vehicles (Registration and Licensing) Regulations 2002, SI 2002/2742, reg 27(1)(e). See also the Information Commissioner's Compliance Advice: Implications of the use and disclosure of vehicle keepers information.

Vehicles subject to finance

2.66 As noted in para 2.56, it is important to ascertain whether a vehicle is subject to hire purchase or a leasing agreement. HPI Limited provides a service to check whether a vehicle is subject to a credit or leasing agreement.[1] Details for HPI Limited are provided in Appendix 1.

[1]   The vehicle registration and chassis numbers are required for maximum accuracy, although a search can be carried out against just the vehicle registration.

Other judgment debtors

Mutual societies

2.67 Unincorporated mutual societies commonly include building societies, friendly societies,[1] industrial and provident societies and housing associations, but also include credit unions, benevolent societies and working men's clubs.

[1]   Friendly societies and building societies also exist in incorporated form.

2.68 Friendly societies and certain other mutual societies are required to file certain documents at the Mutual Societies Registry.[1] Since 1 December 2001, the Financial Services Authority (FSA) has taken over the functions of the Central Office of the Registry of Friendly Societies.[2]

[1]   Formerly the Friendly Societies Registry.
[2]   Financial Services and Markets Act 2000, s 335.

2.69 The fee to search a file at the Mutual Societies Registry is currently £26.50.[1] In addition, copies of documents held on a Society's public record file can also be obtained.[2] The records which can be obtained include the latest annual return, latest accounts, mortgages and charges, society rules and any winding up documents. Contact details for the Mutual Societies Registry are included in Appendix 1.

[1]   Scale of Fees as of 1 September 2002.
[2]   The relevant fee is set out in the Scale of Fees as of 1 September 2002.

Partnerships

2.70   Subject to an express or implied agreement to the contrary, partnership books are to be kept at the partnership's place of business and every partner may have access to and inspect and copy them.[1] However, partnerships (other than limited liability partnerships – see paras 2.44–2.46)[2] are not required to make their accounts or partnership documents public.[3] As a consequence it may be difficult to ascertain the assets of a partnership. However, individual partners remain jointly liable for the contractual debts and obligations of the partnership where the partnership has insufficient assets.[4] A judgment creditor can therefore seek to obtain payment from the private estates of individual partners where the partnership has insufficient assets to satisfy a judgment debt. RSC Ord 81[5] provides special machinery for claims brought by or against partners in their firm's name.

1   Partnership Act 1890, s 24.
2   See paras 2.44–2.45 and Appendix 3.
3   The only publicity requirements relate to the publication of the name of each partner with an address for service in Great Britain on business letters, invoices etc and at their place of business. See Business Names Act 1985, ss 1–4.
4   Partnership Act 1890, s 9.
5   Preserved in CPR, Sch 1.

INQUIRY AGENTS

2.71   Where investigation of the public sources of information outlined above has not revealed significant assets for the purposes of enforcement, a judgment creditor may wish to consider using an inquiry agent to elicit further information about a judgment debtor's assets.

2.72   In practice, inquiry agents are frequently instructed in commercial litigation to attempt to identify the ownership of assets as part of the process of both obtaining judgment and its subsequent enforcement. If used properly, inquiry agents can be an invaluable resource for the location of assets both in the UK and abroad, particularly in the case of assets which the judgment debtor has attempted to conceal.

2.73   In the popular imagination inquiry agents often conjure up seedy images of men in macs investigating allegations of marital infidelity. The modern reality is very different. There are now a number of large international firms of inquiry agents who specialise almost exclusively in conducting inquiries of a commercial nature. They are made up of people from a wide range of backgrounds, from accountants to policemen, military and intelligence personnel. Instructing inquiry agents raises a number of legal and professional conduct issues, both for the judgment creditor and his legal representatives.

Means used by inquiry agents

2.74   There are a large number of reported cases which refer to the use of inquiry agents in both a civil[1] and criminal[2] context. The disreputable and unlawful means adopted by some inquiry agents have been the subject of trenchant judicial criticism. In

Dubai Aluminium Co Ltd v Al Alawi,[3] a case in which the court considered at length the role of inquiry agents in the conduct of litigation and the impact their actions can have on proceedings, the defendant alleged that detailed information had been obtained from his bank, credit card and telephone accounts by the use of 'pretext calls' to the companies concerned. The court proceeded on the basis that there was strong prima facie evidence of criminal or fraudulent conduct in obtaining the information. In another case, an inquiry agent, accompanied by the plaintiff's wife, forced entry to the plaintiff's flat for the purpose of obtaining evidence of the plaintiff's alleged adultery and was found liable for both trespass and assault.[4]

1   See eg *Tomlinson v Tomlinson* [1980] 1 WLR 322 at 325.
2   See eg *R v Nugent* [1977] 1 WLR 789 at 791.
3   [1999] 1 WLR 1964. This case is considered in detail in paras 2.122–2.128.
4   *Jolliffe v Willmett & Co* [1971] 1 All ER 478. See further paras 2.83–2.87.

2.75   Many inquiry agents, however, rely on entirely legitimate means of acquiring information, using both public sources of information and traditional methods such as interviewing potential witnesses. Although such methods could also be used by a solicitor, it will often be much cheaper and more cost effective for the work to be performed by an inquiry agent in the first instance. This is particularly the case where information or witnesses are located overseas, since many of the larger firms of inquiry agents have offices or contacts abroad.

2.76   Judicial attitudes to inquiry agents are not invariably hostile and they are often referred to in reported cases without comment, or occasionally even suggested by the judge as a means of ascertaining information.[1] In *Rank Film Distributors Ltd v Video Information Centre (a firm)* [2] Lord Denning MR referred, apparently without comment, to entrapment methods being used by inquiry agents to catch persons making pirate videos.[3]

1   See eg *Re St Michael and All Angels, Tettenhall Regis* [1995] Fam 179 at 197, an ecclesiastical case where Judge John Shand Ch suggested instructing an inquiry agent to trace relatives of those buried in the last 50 years in a churchyard that was due to be redeveloped.
2   [1980] 3 WLR 487, CA.
3   [1980] 3 WLR 487 at 503, CA.

2.77   However, it is far from the case that a judge will assume, without more, that the ends justify the means when it comes to the use of inquiry agents. In one case concerning an appeal relating to judicial bias, an inquiry agent posed as a judge's accountant to obtain information from the judge's solicitors as to whether he had paid for an amendment to his will. Lord Woolf CJ summed up the Court of Appeal's attitude to this method of obtaining information as 'disgraceful'.[1]

1   *Taylor v Lawrence* [2002] 3 WLR 640 at 644. The court decided 'to overlook the discreditable manner in which that information was … obtained' and hear the appeal on its merits.

2.78   The trend of recent case law has highlighted the importance of ensuring that inquiry agents only employ legitimate means to obtain information. In the *Dubai Aluminium* case, Rix J made the following telling comment:[1]

'It seems to me that if investigative agents employed by solicitors for the purpose of litigation were permitted to breach the provisions of such statutes [the Data

Protection Act 1984] or to indulge in fraud or impersonation without any consequence at all for the conduct of the litigation, then the courts would be going far to sanction such conduct.'

¹   [1999] 1 WLR 1964 at 1969.

2.79   The last few years have seen the enactment of legislation such as the Data Protection Act 1998, the Human Rights Act 1998 and the Regulation of Investigatory Powers Act 2000, all of which have a potential impact on the means used by inquiry agents. The changing legal landscape has therefore increased the importance of the proper use of inquiry agents.

Legal risk

2.80   It is often the case that the solicitor acting for the judgment creditor will instruct the inquiry agent on behalf of his client. Some of the more dubious means used by inquiry agents therefore potentially expose the solicitor and client alike to both legal and regulatory risk. The solicitor will therefore need to ensure that improper means are not used by the inquiry agent. If the client chooses to instruct the inquiry agent direct, the solicitor should advise him of the potential consequences of illegal means being used by inquiry agents. An overview of some of the legal risks and pitfalls is set out below.

Civil liability

2.81   Where a solicitor or his client instructs an inquiry agent they may become exposed to civil liability for the acts and omissions of the inquiry agent through the law of agency.¹

¹   Detailed consideration of the law of agency is outside the scope of this book - see generally *Bowstead and Reynolds on Agency* (17th edn, 2001).

Trespass

2.82   Inquiry agents will commonly put the judgment debtor and his home and business under surveillance. If they enter onto the land of the judgment debtor to carry out such surveillance or to search through the judgment debtor's rubbish, this may amount to the tort of trespass and form the basis of an action for damages. Surveillance conducted on the judgment debtor's land, even from a highway crossing the land, may also amount to trespass.¹

¹   See eg *Hickman v Maisey* [1900] 1 QB 752, CA, where a racing tout was found liable for trespass for standing on a highway running across the plaintiff's land to observe horse-training taking place on the land.

2.83   In *Jolliffe v Willmett & Co*¹ a husband and wife who lived apart were seeking a divorce. The wife believed that the husband was committing adultery with a Miss Henderson, the husband's part-time secretary. The wife's solicitors instructed an inquiry agent, an ex-policeman, to gather evidence of the alleged adultery. The matrimonial proceedings had been going on for a number of years and the husband had previously complained to the wife's solicitors of trespass by other inquiry agents. The letter of instruction from the wife's solicitors to the inquiry agent stated:

'We must stress that the [husband] has instructed solicitors, and therefore no direct approach must be made. In any event a direct approach would be useless as only stealth and cunning are likely to serve in this case.'

1   [1971] 1 All ER 478.

2.84   The husband was living in a flat which the wife had not lived in for many years and to which she had never possessed a key. In the course of his inquiries, the inquiry agent knocked on the door of the flat which was answered by Miss Henderson. (It was disputed whether the inquiry agent had posed as a policeman for this purpose.) Following this incident, the inquiry agent reported back to the wife's solicitor and it was agreed that the wife would accompany the inquiry agent on the next visit. The solicitor at no point instructed or gave permission for the inquiry agent to enter the husband's flat. A few days later, the inquiry agent and the wife returned to the husband's flat and, after posing as the postman, the inquiry agent forced entry when Miss Henderson answered the door. The wife and inquiry agent then proceeded to inspect the flat in spite of Miss Henderson's protests that they were trespassing. The husband, who was in bed upstairs, awoke to find the inquiry agent in his bedroom. Having indicated that the inquiry agent was trespassing and asking him to leave several times, a scuffle then broke out during which the inquiry agent struck the husband on the head.

2.85   The husband sued both the inquiry agent and the wife's solicitors seeking damages for trespass and assault. Geoffrey Lane J found the inquiry agent liable for trespass and assault, having held that the wife had no authority to grant the inquiry agent a licence to enter the flat.

2.86   As to the claim against the solicitor, Geoffery Lane J held:

'Now I turn to the question of the [solicitors'] responsibility for these matters. The [inquiry agent] was, vis-à-vis the [solicitors], an independent contractor and not a servant. Consequently, looked at strictly, there is no question of any vicarious liability on the part of the [solicitors]. Were they then equally responsible with the [inquiry agent] for the trespass that took place? There are, in my judgment, only two ways in which the [solicitors] can be made liable to the plaintiff. The first way is if they were negligent in their selection of the [inquiry agent] as an independent contractor, and if that negligence was the cause of the trespass. The second way in which they could be made liable would be if they expressly ordered or authorised or ratified the unlawful trespass of the [inquiry agent]. So far as negligence is concerned ... there is no evidence that [the solicitor], or anyone else in the [solicitors'] firm, was negligent in selecting the [inquiry agent]. They had recommendations from [a reputable firm of inquiry agents they had previously used], and indeed if they had gone further and listened to the catalogue of the [inquiry agent's] excellencies which he gave me in evidence, they would have had no hesitation in engaging him. There is no question of negligence. Secondly, did they authorise, order or ratify his conduct? I have said sufficient about the facts and sufficient about the way in which I treat the subsidiary dispute between the [inquiry agent] and [the solicitor] to show that, in my judgment, [the solicitor] did not know that the second defendant was going to the flat in the first place and, even if he did know that he was going there, he never authorised nor ordered the [inquiry agent] to enter the flat and would not, in any circumstances, have done so. Accordingly, so far as this action against the [solicitors] is concerned, that fails.'[1]

[1]   [1971] 1 All ER 478 at 484.

2.87   This case illustrates the importance of both taking care in the selection of an inquiry agent and providing the inquiry agent with instructions in writing, making clear that only legal means must be employed by the inquiry agent in the pursuit of his enquiries. Where oral instructions are given, it would seem sensible for the solicitor to confirm these in writing or make an attendance note of the call in order to be able to demonstrate subsequently, where necessary, that nothing was done or said by the solicitor to suggest or encourage the use of illegal means.

Private nuisance

2.88   It is possible that certain sorts of surveillance might amount to private nuisance. In *Baron Bernstein of Leigh v Skyviews*,[1] flying over the plaintiff's property at a reasonable height for the purpose of commercial photography was held to be neither trespass nor private nuisance. However, the obligation of the court under the Human Rights Act 1998 to apply art 8 of the European Convention for the Protection of Human Rights and Fundamental Freedoms (ECHR) (right to respect for private and family life) could possibly lead to a different result where the purpose of the flight was covert surveillance of a judgment debtor.

[1]   [1978] QB 479.

Copyright

2.89   If an inquiry agent copies documents to which another person owns the copyright, he may be liable for breach of copyright to the copyright holder. This could lead to damages being awarded and/or an injunction for delivery up and destruction of the material subject to copyright.

Breach of confidence

2.90   A duty of confidence can arise in a variety of different circumstances. The leading case in this regard is *Coco v AN Clark (Engineers) Ltd*.[1] Megarry J held that there are three elements essential to a cause of action for breach of an implied duty of confidence, namely:

(a)   that the information was of a confidential nature;

(b) that it was communicated in circumstances importing an obligation of confidence; and

(c) that there was an unauthorised use of the information.

1   [1969] RPC 41.

2.91   Where a third party receives information knowing it to have been obtained in breach of confidence to another he will owe a duty of confidence to the confider.[1] Unauthorised use of such information may render the third party liable for breach of confidence, which carries the risk of an order for compensation or an account of profits. The court might also grant an injunction restraining the use of the confidential information and/or an order for delivery up and destruction of the material containing the confidential information.

1   *A-G v Guardian Newspapers Ltd (No 2)* [1990] 1 AC 109 at 261, per Lord Keith of Kinkel and at 281, CA, per Lord Goff.

Breach of confidence to protect privacy?

2.92   The House of Lords decision in *Campbell v Mirror Group Newspapers Ltd*[1] poses a risk for private investigators that an action may be brought based on disclosure of information about a person's private life. In *Campbell* the court awarded damages for the disclosure of certain information about Naomi Campbell's private life on the basis of breach of confidence. The exact ambit of this case is uncertain and will require clarification by subsequent case law.

1   [2004] 2 WLR 1232, HL.

Criminal liability

2.93   In addition to civil liability, an inquiry agent's activities could potentially expose the solicitor or his client to criminal liability. While the criminal offences within the Proceeds of Crime Act 2002 (PCA 2002) seek to criminalise the activities of money launderers, PCA 2002 is very widely drafted. Under PCA 2002, s 329 it is an offence to acquire, use or possess criminal property. Criminal property is defined in PCA 2002, s 340(3) and could include documents or information obtained through illegal means if the information or documents represented a person's benefit from criminal conduct. Thus, aside from any reputational or professional considerations, where a judgment creditor seeks to use information that has been obtained as a consequence of criminal conduct, the judgment creditor (or his solicitor) could, in theory, be criminally liable under PCA 2002.[1]

1   How great the practical risk of prosecution may be is a different matter.

Data Protection Act 1998

2.94   The Data Protection Act 1998 (DPA 1998) provides certain safeguards to individuals relating to the use which can be made by others of personal data[1] relating to that individual. The provisions of DPA 1998 only apply to individuals and do not apply to companies. A breach of certain sections of DPA 1998 is an offence and, in light of the wide-ranging provisions regarding the processing[2] of personal data under DPA 1998, it is advisable to include a clear statement that the inquiry agent should pay due regard to the provisions of DPA 1998 in his written instructions.

1   'Data' and 'personal data' have specific definitions set out in DPA 1998, s 1. There is a further sub-category of 'sensitive personal data' defined in DPA 1998, s 2, in relation to which further safeguards apply.

2   'Processing' is defined in DPA 1998, s 1 and includes: obtaining, recording, holding, organising, adapting, altering, retrieval, consultation, use and disclosure of information or data.

2.95   Detailed consideration of the provisions of DPA 1998 is outside the scope of this book. However, it is worth noting that an inquiry agent will invariably obtain personal data as a consequence of his investigations into an individual judgment debtor's assets. DPA 1998 requires that personal data should be obtained fairly and lawfully.[1] An inquiry agent should therefore give details of his identity, the uses to which the personal data may be put and any proposed disclosures of personal data to the provider of the information when required to do so. It should also be noted that DPA 1998, s 55 makes it an offence knowingly or recklessly to obtain disclosure, or procure the disclosure of, personal data without the consent of the data controller.[2]

1   DPA 1998, s 4(4) requires a data controller to comply with the data protection principles set out in DPA 1998, Sch 1, Pt I. The first data protection principle provides that personal data 'shall be processed fairly and lawfully'.

2   The Information Commissioner's Annual Report 2004 at p 35 refers to the conviction of an inquiry agent under DPA 1998, s 55 for obtaining information from the DVLA by providing misleading information.

Protection from Harassment Act 1997

2.96   Surveillance of a judgment debtor could, if badly managed, not only result in a civil liability (see paras 2.82-2.88) but fall foul of the harassment legislation. The Protection from Harassment Act 1997[1] (PHA 1997) makes it both an offence[2] and a civil wrong[3] for a person to pursue a course of conduct which amounts to the harassment of another and which he knows or ought to know would amount to such harassment.[4] Harassing a person includes alarming the person or causing the person distress.[5] A course of conduct must involve conduct on at least two occasions[6] and conduct includes speech.[7]

1   For more detail see *Archbold Criminal Pleading Evidence and Practice 2005*, para 19-277.

2   PHA 1997, s 2. A conviction for an offence under PHA 1998, s 2 carries a maximum penalty of six months' imprisonment.

3   PHA 1997, s 3. Section 3(2) gives the court a power to award damages for '(among other things) any anxiety caused by the harassment and any financial loss resulting from the harassment'. By virtue of s 3(3) the court has a power to grant an injunction to restrain any conduct which amounts to harassment. Any breach of the injunction is an offence under PHA 1997, s 3(5) and the court can grant a warrant for the arrest of the defendant for a breach of the injunction.

4   PHA 1997, s 1(2) provides that 'the person whose course of conduct is in question ought to know that it amounts to harassment of another if a reasonable person in possession of the same information would think the course of conduct amounted to harassment of the other'.

5   PHA 1997, s 7(2).
6   PHA 1997, s 7(3).
7   PHA 1997, s 7(4).

Computer Misuse Act 1990

2.97   Seeking to obtain unauthorised access to computer material is an offence under the Computer Misuse Act 1990 (CMA 1990).[1] It is an offence intentionally to cause a computer to perform any function to secure unauthorised access[2] to any program or data held in any computer.[3] The intent does not need to be directed at securing access to any particular program or data, a program or data of any particular kind, or a program or data held in any particular computer.[4]

1   For more detail see *Archbold Criminal Pleading, Evidence and Practice 2005* paras 23-87–23-101.
2   'Secure access' is given a wide meaning under CMA 1990, s 17(2).
3   CMA 1990, s 1(1).
4   CMA 1990, s 1(2).

Regulation of Investigatory Powers Act 2000

2.98   Under the Regulation of Investigatory Powers Act 2000 (RIPA 2000), s 1, it is an offence intentionally and without lawful authority to intercept in the course of its transmission post, telephone calls and emails (although this is subject to a number of exceptions provided for by the statute and regulations made under it).[1]

1   For more detail see *Archbold Criminal Pleading, Evidence and Practice 2005* paras 25-367–25-380.

Theft

2.99   The fact that individuals often throw away items such as bank statements may tempt an inquiry agent to inspect a judgment debtor's rubbish in the search for information about his assets or finances. The taking of rubbish can amount to theft. In *Williams v Phillips*[1] a number of dustmen were convicted of theft for taking items from rubbish bins. The Divisional Court held that the rubbish had not been abandoned as it had been left for the purpose of allowing the local authority to collect it, not for anybody to take it away. The rubbish therefore remained the householders' property until collected, at which point ownership passed to the local authority. The dustmen were therefore convicted of theft.[2]

1   (1957) 41 Cr App Rep 5 at 8–9.
2   The judgment in *Williams* may explain why the inquiry agents in *Dubai Aluminium* took documents obtained from the plaintiff's dustbins, copied them, and then returned them. However, such conduct is not without its own potential pitfalls: see paras 2.105-2.129.

Proceeds of Crime Act 2002

2.100   See para 2.93.

Professional conduct

2.101   The potential civil and criminal liability which may arise as a consequence of using an inquiry agent means that careful consideration must be given to both their instruction and management. A further consideration for the solicitor is that the improper use of inquiry agents is likely to be a breach of professional conduct.

2.102   There is no specific guidance in the Guide to the Professional Conduct of Solicitors as to how to approach the instruction of inquiry agents. However, in certain circumstances, the Law Society has a statutory power to prevent a solicitor from employing or remunerating a person guilty of a crime or misconduct. Under the Solicitors Act 1974, s 43, where the Law Society considers that a person has been convicted of a criminal offence which discloses such dishonesty that, in the opinion of the Society, it would be undesirable for him to be employed or remunerated by a solicitor in connection with his practice, it can impose a ban on that person being employed or remunerated by a solicitor in future. This power would extend to the use of inquiry agents.

2.103   Once such a banning order has been made by the Law Society or the Solicitors' Tribunal, it is an offence for a person subject to the order to seek or accept employment by a solicitor without first informing the solicitor.[1] A solicitor who knowingly employs a person in contravention of an order may be disciplined.[2]

[1]   Solicitors Act 1974, s 44(1).
[2]   Solicitors Act 1974, s 44(2). A solicitor may employ such a person with the prior consent of the Law Society.

Bar Council guidance

2.104   While the Guide to the Professional Conduct of Solicitors lacks specific guidance on these matters, in September 2003 the Bar Council produced guidance on the use of illegally obtained evidence in civil and family proceedings which is available from the Bar Council website.[1]

[1]   Bar Council Guidance on Illegally Obtained Evidence in Civil and Family Proceedings, available at www.barcouncil.org.uk.

Admissibility of illegally obtained evidence

2.105   Aside from legal and professional conduct risks, the further question arises as to whether the fact that information has been obtained illegally will prevent it from being used in evidence in civil proceedings. Evidence will inevitably be required in support of any court based method of enforcement. As will be seen, there seems to be an increasing judicial recognition that the chances of civil or criminal sanction where inquiry agents have obtained evidence illegally are remote, and that the court therefore needs to exercise greater vigilance in the use which may be made of illegally obtained evidence to deter such conduct. This trend further highlights the need to ensure that inquiry agents use only legitimate means of investigation.

Admissibility – pre-CPR

2.106 Prior to the introduction of the CPR, it had long been the rule that illegally obtained evidence was admissible provided it was relevant. *Kuruma, Son of Kaniu v R*[1] contains one of the more robust judicial statements of this rule:[2]

'In their Lordships' opinion the test to be applied in considering whether evidence is admissible is whether it is relevant to the matters in issue. If it is, it is admissible and the court is not concerned with how the evidence was obtained.'

1   [1955] AC 197, PC.
2   [1955] AC 197 at 203, per Lord Goddard.

2.107 In one of the cases cited by their Lordships in *Kuruma* one judge even went so far as to say:[1]

'It matters not how you get it; if you steal it even, it would be admissible.'

1   *R v Leatham* (1861) 8 Cox CC 498, per Crompton J.

Admissibility – under the CPR

2.108 Under CPR Pt 32 the court now has an express power granting it a wide discretion to exclude evidence. CPR 32.1 provides:

'(1) The court may control the evidence by giving directions as to
(a) the issues on which it requires evidence;
(b) the nature of the evidence which it requires to decide those issues; and
(c) the way in which the evidence is to be placed before the court.
(2) The court may use its power under this rule to exclude evidence that would otherwise be admissible.'

Jones v University of Warwick

2.109 The leading case on how the court will use this discretion to exclude evidence that has been illegally obtained by inquiry agents is the Court of Appeal decision in *Jones v University of Warwick*.[1] The facts of the case were that the claimant had injured her hand in an accident at work. The defendant admitted liability but it was disputed whether the injury had the continuing debilitating effects alleged by the claimant. On two occasions inquiry agents acting for the defendant's insurers gained access to the claimant's home by posing as market researchers and used a hidden camera covertly to film the defendant in her own home. Having been shown the covertly recorded footage, the defendant's medical expert formed the view that the claimant's hand functioned entirely satisfactorily.

1   [2003] 1 WLR 954, CA.

2.110 When the defendant attempted to rely on the evidence, the claimant applied to exclude it on the basis that the inquiry agent had obtained entry to her home by trespass and her right to privacy had been infringed under ECHR, art 8, which provides for the right to respect for private and family life. The right provided in art 8 is a qualified right such that it can only be interfered with by a public authority where such interference is in accordance with the law and necessary in a democratic society for certain specified purposes. Counsel for the claimant argued that since the court was a public authority[1] it must exercise its discretion to exclude the evidence obtained by the insurer's inquiry agents in order to comply with ECHR, art 8.

[1]   Human Rights Act 1998, s 6(3)(a).

2.111   The unanimous judgment of the Court of Appeal was given by Lord Woolf CJ, who summed up the balancing exercise the court had to perform:[1]

'… the issue on the appeal requires this court to consider two competing public interests: the interests of the public that in litigation the truth should be revealed and the interests of the public that the courts should not acquiesce in, let alone encourage, a party to use unlawful means to obtain evidence.'

[1]   [2003] 1 WLR 954 at 956.

2.112   On this occasion the Court of Appeal decided not to exclude the evidence. Lord Woolf CJ observed:[1]

'The significance of the evidence will differ as will the gravity of the breach of art 8, according to the facts of the particular case. The decision will depend on all the circumstances. Here, the court cannot ignore the reality of the situation. This is not a case where the conduct of the defendant's insurers is so outrageous that the defence should be struck out. The case, therefore, has to be tried. It would be artificial and undesirable for the actual evidence, which is relevant and admissible, not to be placed before the judge who has the task of trying the case. We accept [counsel for the defendant's] submission that to exclude the use of the evidence would create a wholly undesirable situation. Fresh medical experts would have to be instructed on both sides. Evidence which is relevant would have to be concealed from them, perhaps resulting in a misdiagnosis; and it would not be possible to cross-examine the claimant appropriately. For these reasons we do not consider it would be right to interfere with the judge's decision not to exclude the evidence.'

[1]   [2003] 1 WLR 954 at 962.

2.113   However, the Court of Appeal did not leave the matter there. In what must be read as a warning to future litigants seeking to rely upon evidence which has been illegally obtained by inquiry agents Lord Woolf CJ went on to say:

'While not excluding the evidence it is appropriate to make clear that the conduct of the insurers was improper and not justified. … The fact that the insurers may have been motivated by a desire to achieve what they considered would be a just result does not justify either the commission of trespass or the contravention of the claimant's privacy which took place. We come to this conclusion irrespective of whether [counsel for the claimant] is right in contending that in this particular case the evidence could be obtained by other means.'[1]

[1]   [2003] 1 WLR 954 at 962–963.

2.114 Lord Woolf CJ then observed that excluding the evidence is not the only weapon in the court's armoury. In particular, the court can reflect its disapproval of such conduct in the orders for costs which it makes in order to discourage future litigants from contemplating such steps. The Court of Appeal held that because the conduct of the insurers had given rise to litigation over the admissibility of the evidence, they should have to pay the costs of the proceedings to resolve that issue at first instance and on appeal, even though the appeal was otherwise dismissed. The Court also indicated to the trial judge that when he came to dealing with the question of costs he should take into account the defendant's conduct, and may consider that the costs of the inquiry agent should not be recovered. Further, if the trial judge found in favour of the claimant, he may wish to award her costs on an indemnity basis.

2.115 Lord Woolf CJ concluded:[1]

'In giving effect to the overriding objective, and taking into account the wider interests of the administration of justice, the court must, while doing justice between the parties, also deter improper conduct of a party while conducting litigation. We do not pretend that this is a perfect reconciliation of the conflicting public interests. It is not; but at least the solution does not ignore the insurers' conduct.'

[1]   [2003] 1 WLR 954 at 963.

2.116 A litigant who obtains evidence illegally therefore runs the risk not only of the evidence being held inadmissible but, even when the court will hear the evidence, facing severe cost sanctions.

Improper and unjustified conduct

2.117 Whether the conduct is so 'improper and unjustified' that a costs sanction should be imposed will be a question of fact in each case. In the Scottish case of *Martin v McGuiness*[1] (where the relevant evidence had been held admissible by the lower court), the Scottish Outer House found that even if an inquiry agent had committed trespass by entering the claimant's house, it did not warrant the description of 'improper and unjustified conduct'. Similarly, engaging the claimant's wife in conversation did not amount to breach of the peace, not least since she did not ask the inquiry agent to leave. In the circumstances, there was no reason therefore to depart from the usual rule that costs follow the case. While the case could therefore be distinguished from *Jones*, Lord Bonomy stated:

'My decision following debate and my decision on this motion, are based entirely on the circumstances of the present case. Neither should be regarded, as was feared by the counsel for [the claimant], as an indication that "anything goes" in carrying out inquiries in the course of adversarial litigation.'

[1]   2003 SLT 1136.

Loss of privilege

2.118 In addition to questions of admissibility, the fact that evidence has been obtained illegally may cause a loss of legal professional privilege over reports and other documents relating to the investigations carried out by inquiry agents.

2.119 The well-established exception to legal professional privilege where there is fraud was summed up by Lord Sumner in *O'Rourke v Darbishire*:[1]

'No one doubts that the claim for [legal] professional privilege does not apply to documents which have been brought into existence in the course of or in furtherance of a fraud to which both solicitor and client are parties. To consult a solicitor about an intended course of action, in order to be advised whether it is legitimate or not, or to lay before a solicitor the facts relating to a charge of fraud, actually made or anticipated, and make a clean breast of it with the object of being advised about the best way in which to meet it, is a very different thing from consulting him in order to learn how to plan, execute, or stifle an actual fraud.'

[1]   [1920] AC 581 at 613, HL.

2.120 In *Ventouris v Mountain, The Italia Express*[1] Bingham LJ referred to legal professional privilege existing 'in the absence of iniquity'.[2] The iniquity which may lead to a loss of legal professional privilege has been held to cover 'crime or fraud',[3] the 'criminal or unlawful',[4] and 'all forms of fraud and dishonesty such as fraudulent breach of trust, fraudulent conspiracy, trickery and sham contrivances'[5] and the effecting of transactions at an undervalue for the purpose of prejudicing the interests of a creditor.[6]

[1]   [1991] 1 WLR 607, CA.
[2]   [1991] 1 WLR 607 at 611.
[3]   *R v Cox and Railton* (1884) 14 QBD 153 at 165.
[4]   *Bullivant v A-G for Victoria* [1901] AC 196 at 201, HL.
[5]   *Crescent Farm (Sidcup) Sports Ltd v Sterling Offices Ltd* [1972] Ch 553 at 565.
[6]   *Barclays Bank plc v Eustice* [1995] 1 WLR 1238, CA.

2.121 Whether the iniquity involved will cause the privilege to be lost will be determined on a case by case basis. As Goff LJ explained in *Gamlen Chemical Co (UK) Ltd v Rochem Ltd*:[1]

'[T]he court must in every case, of course, be satisfied that what is prima facie proved really is dishonest, and not merely disreputable or a failure to maintain good ethical standards and must bear in mind that legal professional privilege is a very necessary thing and is not lightly to be overthrown, but on the other hand, the interests of victims of fraud must not be overlooked. Each case depends on its own facts.'

[1]   (Unreported, 7 December 1979), CA.

Dubai Aluminium Co Ltd v Al Alawi

2.122 The leading case on whether the iniquity exception will lead to a loss of legal professional privilege where evidence has been illegally obtained by inquiry agents is the decision of Rix J in *Dubai Aluminium Co Ltd v Al Alawi*.[1] The plaintiffs had brought a fraud claim against Mr Al Alawi and others and had obtained a freezing injunction against Mr Al Alawi. Mr Al Alawi applied to discharge the freezing injunction.

1   [1999] 1 WLR 1964.

2.123   One of the grounds relied upon by Mr Al Alawi to discharge the freezing injunction was that:

'... in investigating his finances and assets, [the plaintiff] has employed agents who have acted in contravention of the Data Protection Act 1984[1] or Swiss banking laws, or have trespassed on Mr Al Alawi's property and converted documents fetched out of his dustbins.'[2]

1   Now the Data Protection Act 1998.
2   [1999] 1 WLR 1964 at 1966.

2.124   In support of this ground for discharging the freezing injunction, Mr Al Alawi sought disclosure of the reports and other documents relating to the investigations of his financial affairs by the plaintiff's inquiry agents. It was accepted by the plaintiff that these documents were relevant and discloseable but it was contended that legal professional privilege attached to them. Mr Al Alawi accepted that on the face of it legal professional privilege would attach to the documents but contended that it did not apply in these circumstances because they were part of or relevant to criminal or fraudulent or otherwise iniquitous acts or purposes. The acts complained of were first, that detailed information had been obtained about the defendant's bank, credit card and telephone accounts by the use of 'pretext calls' to the companies concerned and, secondly, that documents had been removed from Mr Al Alawi's dustbins and copied before being replaced. Mr Al Alawi alleged that the evidence had been obtained in contravention of the Data Protection Act 1984 or Swiss banking laws, or through trespass and conversion. The plaintiff put no evidence in opposition and indeed previous evidence from the plaintiff had admitted the use of 'pretext calls'.

2.125   The plaintiff submitted that no authority had extended the exception to privilege this far and that all the cases involving the exception concerned instances where solicitors had become involved, innocently or otherwise, with the planning or carrying out of iniquitous acts which were the subject matter of litigation.

2.126   The plaintiff's submission was rejected and the court ordered disclosure of the documents. Rix J first recognised that deciding this question involved balancing a number of competing public interests – the public interest in legal professional privilege, in combating crime and fraud, and in trying cases on all the relevant evidence. His observations that an approach where statutes were breached without any consequence for the conduct of the litigation could not be sanctioned have been noted in para 2.78. He continued:[1]

'Of course, there is always the sanction of prosecutions or civil suits, and those must always remain the primary sanction for any breach of the criminal or civil law. But it seems to me that criminal or fraudulent conduct for the purposes of acquiring evidence in or for litigation cannot properly escape the consequence that any documents generated by or reporting on such conduct and which are relevant to the issues in the case are discoverable and fall outside the legitimate area of legal professional privilege. It is not as though there are not legitimate avenues which can be sought with the aid of the court to investigate (for instance) banking documents. That apparently is true in Switzerland as well. In any event, the material being investigated is usually material which falls within the other party's possession or control, and which in all probability he will in due course be obliged to disclose himself. In such circumstances, it does not seem to me to be too great an intrusion on legal professional privilege to require that documentation such as is in question in this case should be disclosed. Otherwise the position would be that the party employing the criminal or fraudulent agent would have it entirely within his own power to decide which of the criminally or fraudulently acquired information he was willing to rely on and disclose and which he was not. Where such a party will be asking the court to make inferences from such material, it is only fair that such material should be seen as a whole.'

1   [1999] 1 WLR 1964 at 1969.

2.127   However, as regards the information obtained from a search of Mr Al Alawi's dustbins, the court found that although it had been obtained through activities which constituted the torts of conversion and trespass, such civil wrongs do not fall within the crime, fraud or iniquity exception and thus the documents remained privileged.

2.128   The clear message from this case is that that reports or documents relating to the investigations carried out by inquiry agents which have been obtained through crime, fraud or iniquity are unlikely to be protected by legal professional privilege.

Inquiries abroad

2.129   *Dubai Aluminium* illustrates that practitioners should also be alert to the possibility of unlawful means being used by inquiry agents in making investigations abroad. The law of the country where the inquiries are being made may impose severe criminal penalties for breach of data protection, banking secrecy or other laws. In *Dubai Aluminium* there were allegations that information had been obtained in breach of Swiss laws of banking secrecy. This was central in the court's finding that legal professional privilege would not apply to documents generated as a result.

PART 71 ORAL EXAMINATION

2.130   In addition to publicly available information or the use of inquiry agents, the judgment creditor may wish to consider making an application for a court examination of the judgment debtor under the procedure set out in CPR Pt 71.

Introduction

2.131   The purpose of Pt 71 is to provide a procedure 'for a judgment debtor to be required to attend court to provide information, for the purpose of enabling a judgment creditor to enforce a judgment or order against him'.[1]

1   CPR 71.1.

2.132 Part 71 therefore is not in itself a method of enforcement. Rather, it is a tool available to the judgment creditor to enable him to obtain information about the judgment debtor's assets so that he can best decide which enforcement procedure(s) to use. However, the threat of an oral examination may in some cases prove sufficient for the judgment debtor to pay the sums owed.

The procedure is only available post-judgment and, in contrast with the methods described earlier in this chapter, the information gathered under Pt 71 is obtained directly from the judgment debtor. The rules provide for questioning of the judgment debtor in the forum of a courtroom but the procedure nevertheless demands a relatively high degree of co-operation from the judgment debtor. However, a judgment debtor who refuses to co-operate may find himself liable for contempt of court.

2.133 Part 71 was enacted with the 26th set of amendments to the CPR under the Civil Procedure (Amendment No 4) Rules 2001,[1] which came into force on 25 March 2002. These provisions repealed and replaced RSC Ord 48.

1   SI 2001/2792.

2.134 RSC Ord 48 originated from Common Law Procedure Act 1854, s 60, which was later re-enacted in amended form as Rules of Court of 1875, Ord XLV, r 1. However, while the modern form of the procedure has simplified the rules, the basic purpose of the procedure is unchanged. This is evident from the terms of s 60 of the 1854 Act, which provided:

'It shall be lawful for any Creditor who has obtained a Judgment in any of the Superior Courts to apply to the Court or a Judge for a Rule or Order that the Judgment Debtor should be orally examined as to any and what Debts are owing to him … and the Court or Judge may make such Rule or Order for the Examination of such Judgment Debtor, and for the Production of any Books or Documents …'

Part 71 substantially reproduces this section.

PROCEDURE

2.135 As has been noted, it is necessary that a judgment or order has been made against the judgment debtor for the Pt 71 procedure to be available.[1] The procedure is not available before judgment has been given.

1   CPR 71.1 states that the procedure is available 'for the purpose of enabling a judgment creditor to enforce a judgment or order'.

2.136 However, following judgment, the judgment creditor can utilise the procedure at any time. There is nothing in the rules which require that, for example, where an order has been made for payments by instalments the judgment debtor should be behind with payments, or have refused to pay, or otherwise be behaving in an obstructive manner for the procedure to be available.[1]

1   However, see para 2.254 for a discussion of human rights considerations in this regard.

Application by the judgment creditor

Which court?

2.137   The application must be issued in the court which made the judgment or order which the judgment creditor seeks to enforce (unless the proceedings have since been transferred to a different court, in which case the application must be made in that court).[1] The order will ordinarily require the judgment debtor to attend the county court for the district in which he resides or carries on business,[2] although there is no requirement to transfer the proceedings to the judgment debtor's home court before the application is issued.

1   CPR 71.2(2)(b).
2   Unless the court orders otherwise: PD 71, para 2.1.

Application notice

2.138   An application for an order under Pt 71 may be made without notice.[1] The application must be made using Form N316 if the judgment debtor is an individual, or Form N316A if the judgment debtor is an officer of a company or other corporation.[2]

1   CPR 71.2(2).
2   CPR 71.2(3) and PD 71, para 1.1.

2.139   CPR 71.2(3) and Practice Direction to Pt 71, para 1.2 stipulate certain information which the application notice must contain. This consists of:

(a)   the judgment debtor's name and address;
(b)   the judgment or order of which enforcement is sought;
(c)   in the case of money judgments,[1] the amount presently owed by the judgment debtor (including any costs and interest);
(d)   where the judgment debtor is a company or corporation, providing details of the company officer who the judgment creditor wishes to attend court including his position in the company (see further para 2.149);
(e)   where the judgment creditor wishes the questioning to be conducted before a judge, providing reasons why this is necessary (see further paras 2.142–2.143); and
(f)   the identification of any specific documents the judgment creditor wishes the judgment debtor to produce at court.[2]

1   In the case of non-money judgments the application should stipulate what the order required the judgment debtor to do.
2   In the case of non-money judgments the application should also identify the matters about which the judgment creditor wishes the judgment debtor to be questioned.

Additional questions from the judgment creditor

2.140   The standard form records of examination, Form EX140 (in the case of an individual judgment debtor) and Form EX141 (in the case of an officer of a company or corporation), list the standard questions which will be asked where an officer of the court conducts the examination. In the case of an individual, these relate to matters such as employment details, income, property, investments and other debts. Where the judgment debtor is a corporation, the officer will be asked about the company's operational and financial status and questioned about the company's assets and relationships with other group companies. The judgment debtor or company officer will also be required to produce certain documents at the hearing and the application Forms N316 and N316A list the types of document the order to attend court will include.

2.141 The standard questions asked and documents required at the hearing are discussed further in paras 2.169-2.172. However, in high value or complex litigation where the nature and holding of the judgment debtor's assets may well be more complex, the judgment creditor may not consider the standard form questions and document requests sufficient to extract useful information from the judgment debtor. He may therefore wish to file additional questions or requests for documents to be asked or made by the court officer when making his application, or alternatively attend the actual hearing to ask questions himself.[1] Such questions should relate to the judgment debtor's ability to pay the judgment debt and questions which do not relate to this may be disallowed by the court. The scope of the questions which may be asked of the judgment debtor is considered further in paras 2.176–2.219.

[1]   CPR 71.6(3)(a) provides that a judgment creditor may ask questions when the questioning takes place before a court officer.

Seeking a hearing before a judge

2.142 A further consideration for the judgment creditor is the issue of who should carry out the questioning. The judgment debtor will be questioned by a court officer unless the court has ordered that the questioning shall be before a judge.[1] The order will provide for the questioning to take place before a judge only if there are 'compelling reasons' to do so.[2] Where the judgment creditor wishes to conduct the questioning himself (or through his counsel) before a judge, he must set out his reasons for this request in the application notice.[3]

[1]   CPR 71.6(2).
[2]   PD 71, para 2.2.
[3]   See para 2.139.

2.143 No guidance is provided on what constitutes 'compelling reasons'. However, in high value or complex litigation where the nature and holding of the judgment debtor's assets may be complex, the judgment creditor is likely to want to obtain an order that the questioning is conducted before a judge. This will allow the judgment creditor to retain control of the questioning process and utilise his full knowledge of the facts of the case to tailor specific questions to the judgment debtor's circumstances. A court officer, who will not have this detailed knowledge and who is working from a list of standard questions will not be able to conduct the examination with the same vigour. The reasons why the order is sought should therefore be carefully explained. However, it is important to note that while the examination may be carried out by counsel for the judgment creditor, the judge ultimately determines what questions can be put to the judgment debtor. As Hughes J observed in *Mubarak v Mubarak:*[1]

'Although in the present case the examination was carried out by counsel for the judgment creditor, and the district judge no doubt exercised a proper judicial restraint himself, the oral examination is conducted by the district judge. It is for him to say what questions need answering and for him to say when it is over.'

[1]   [2002] EWHC 2171 (Fam), a case which related to RSC Ord 48.

Fee

2.144   The fee for issuing an application under Pt 71 is £50.[1] From 1 April 2005, all cheques should be made payable to 'HMCS' or 'Her Majesty's Courts Service' instead of 'Her Majesty's Paymaster General' or 'HMPG' as was previously the case.

[1]   The Civil Proceedings Fees Order 2004, SI 2004/3121, Sch 1, para 6.2. In the county court the fee is £40.

Order to attend court

2.145   The application for an oral examination may be dealt with by a court officer without a hearing.[1] However, the court officer considering the application notice may refer it to a judge for consideration and will do so where the judgment creditor requests the judgment debtor to be questioned before a judge.[2]

[1]   CPR 71.2(4).
[2]   PD 71, para 1.3.

2.146   Provided that the application notice satisfies the requirements set out in PD 71, an order requiring the judgment debtor to attend court to provide information will be issued.[1]

[1]   The wording of CPR 71.2(5) gives the judgment creditor a *right* to an order provided the application complies with the formal requirements. This marks a change from the former rule under RSC Ord 48 which provided the court with a discretion to make the order.

2.147   The order requiring the judgment debtor to attend court for questioning will be in Form N39. The examination will take place in the county court for the district in which the judgment debtor resides or carries on business, unless the judge decides otherwise.[1] The order will provide that a person served with the order must:

(a)   attend court at the time and place specified in the order;
(b)   produce the documents in his control which are described in the order; and
(c)   answer on oath such questions as the court may require.[2]

[1]   CPR PD 71, para 2.1.
[2]   CPR 71.2(6).

2.148   An order made under Pt 71 will also contain a notice in the following terms:[1] 'You must obey this order. If you do not, you may be sent to prison for contempt of court.' This wording is usually termed the 'penal notice' and its inclusion is critical if the order subsequently needs to be enforced by committal for contempt of court (see further paras 2.224–2.236). The standard order to attend court for questioning, Form N39, includes this wording in bold towards the bottom of the front page.

[1]   CPR 71.2(7).

Who can be examined?

2.149 Where the judgment debtor is an individual, the question of who can be examined under Pt 71 is straightforward. In the case of a company or corporation, the rule provides that '*an officer*' may be required to attend court for questioning.[1] Before making the application, the judgment creditor should consider which officer of the company is most likely to be able to answer questions on the company's operational and financial status and assets. The company secretary or finance director may prove a more useful source of information than a non-executive director. A search at Companies House will provide a full list of the company directors and the secretary.

[1]   CPR 71.2(1)(b).

Former officers of a company

2.150 In *Société Générale du Commerce et de l'Industrie en France v Johann Maria Farina & Co*[1] it was held that the words 'an officer' of a body corporate included former officers of the company. In that case, judgment had been obtained against a company and an order had been made under one of the predecessor rules to Pt 71[2] directing the examination of a named director of the company as to what debts were owing to it and whether the company had the means to satisfy the judgment debt. Upon examination, the director named in the order admitted that he was a director of the company at the time the judgment was made but refused to answer any further questions as to the debts due to and property of the company on the ground that he had ceased to be a director after the date of the judgment. The matter came before a judge who made an order that the director should attend to be examined. The director appealed against that order on the grounds that since the words of the rule were in the present tense, there was no power to order the examination of anyone who at that time was not an officer of the judgment debtor company.

[1]   [1904] 1 KB 794, CA.
[2]   Rules of the Supreme Court 1887, Order XLII, r 32 (the immediate predecessor to RSC Ord 48).

2.151 The Court of Appeal dismissed the director's appeal. Lord Collins MR held:[1]

'I am of [the] opinion that this construction which is sought to be put upon the rule is too narrow. There is nothing in the rule which restricts it to an existing officer of the corporation, and there is nothing in the wording of the rule incompatible with its application to a person who has been an officer of the corporation. The construction of the rule that is contended for might work serious injustice if an officer of a corporation merely by resigning his position could get rid of the responsibility of giving the information that is sought by a plaintiff.'

[1]   [1904] 1 KB 794 at 797.

2.152 Matthew LJ agreed:[1]

'The object of Order XLII., R 32 [a predecessor rule to Pt 71], is to permit the examination of officers connected with a corporation as to its property and assets.

I cannot see any reason why a company should escape liability to disclosure by accepting the resignation of a director, who might be the sole manager and the only person acquainted with details. I find nothing in the language of the rule which compels us to place on the rule an interpretation which would have that effect, and I see no reason why this order should not be enforced.'

¹   [1904] 1 KB 794 at 797-798.

2.153   Equally, there is nothing in the modern day language of Pt 71 which should preclude the examination of former officers of a company in such circumstances.

Unincorporated associations

2.154   In *Maclaine Watson & Co Ltd v International Tin Council (No 2)*¹ the Court of Appeal had to consider whether the RSC Ord 48 procedure applied to unincorporated associations. Order 48, r 1 provided for the examination of '*the judgment debtor or, if the judgment debtor is a body corporate, an officer thereo*'. At first instance² Millett J had (regretfully) upheld the master's decision that the International Tin Council (ITC) could not be examined under RSC Ord 48 since the wording of the Order did not give the court the power to order this.³ This was notwithstanding the fact that the ITC had been granted the legal capacities of a body corporate by statutory instrument because the statutory instrument fell short of deeming that the ITC was, or should be treated as, a body corporate. However, he ordered that the court had an inherent jurisdiction under Supreme Court Act 1981 (SCA 1981), s 37(1) to order the ITC to make full disclosure of its assets to the judgment creditors and that it was in accordance with the policy of the law to assist judgment creditors to do so.

¹   [1989] Ch 286, CA.
²   [1987] 1 WLR 1711.
³   At [1987] 1 WLR 1711 at 1714, Millett J also rejected an argument by the judgment creditor that the proper construction of the word 'person' in accordance with the Interpretation Act 1978 should mean that 'judgment debtor' in RSC Ord 48 should include an unincorporated association as a forced and unnatural construction of the Order rendering one of its express provisions meaningless.

2.155   On appeal, the correctness of Millett J's construction of RSC Ord 48 (as not applicable to unincorporated associations) was not challenged and the Court of Appeal upheld his decision to order the disclosure of ITC's assets under the inherent jurisdiction of the court. Both Millett J and the Court of Appeal appeared to be heavily influenced by the behaviour of the ITC, which Millett J noted:¹

'... has behaved more like a disreputable private debtor concerned only to hinder and delay his creditors than the responsible international organisation it claims to be.'

¹   [1987] 1 WLR 1711 at 1713.

2.156   The wording of Pt 71 refers to 'a judgment debtor or if a judgment debtor is a company or other corporation, an officer of that body'.¹ It therefore seems that this 'lacuna' in the rules has been preserved and, although Pt 71 is no more concerned with the judgment debtor's legal status than was its predecessor RSC Ord 48, the correct means by which to seek to elicit information as to the assets of an unincorporated association is to ask the court to make an order requiring disclosure of its assets under SCA 1981, s 37(1).

1   CPR 71.2(1).

Partnerships

2.157   While there is no case law on the availability of the oral examination procedure where the judgment debtor is a partnership, in light of the wording of Pt 71 and the judgment in *Maclaine Watson*, a judgment creditor who seeks to examine a partner as to the partnership assets would be well advised to make an application under Pt 71 and SCA 1981, s 37(1) in the alternative.

The Crown

2.158   The procedure in Pt 71 cannot be used in respect of any order against the Crown.[1] As already noted in Chapter 1, under CPA 1947, s 25(4) 'no execution or attachment or process in the nature thereof shall be issued out of any court for enforcing payment by the Crown of any such money or costs'. This is also reflected in RSC Ord 77, r 15(1)(a),[2] which expressly disapplies Pt 71 as against the Crown.

1   *Franklin v R (No 2)* [1974] QB 205, CA.
2   Preserved in CPR, Sch 1.

Service of the order

2.159   It is vital that proper service of the order is effected.[1] This is because, if proper service cannot be shown, the court will not impose the sanction of committal on a judgment debtor who fails to attend court.[2]

1   Equally important is the payment of the judgment debtor's travelling expenses when requested: see paras 2.163–2.164.
2   CPR 71.8(3). See also *Beeston Shipping Ltd v Babanaft International SA (The Eastern Venture)* [1985] 1 All ER 923, CA.

2.160   Once the order to attend court has been issued, it must be served personally on the judgment debtor not less than 14 days before the hearing, unless the court orders otherwise.[1] Service of the order must be carried out by the judgment creditor or someone acting on his behalf.[2] A judgment creditor may wish to instruct a process server to effect service of the order, though it should be noted that only limited costs will be recoverable in this regard (see further paras 2.256–2.258).

1   CPR 71.3(1).
2   PD 71, para 3. The only exception is where the judgment creditor is an individual litigant in person in county court proceedings, when the county court bailiff will serve the order on the judgment debtor.

2.161   If the judgment creditor has been unable to serve the judgment debtor personally with the order, the judgment creditor must inform the court of this no less than seven days before the date of the hearing.[1] The words 'unless the court orders otherwise' in CPR 71.3(1) make provision for service by an alternative method under CPR 6.8 where personal service is not possible. CPR 6.8 provides that where it appears to the court that there is a good reason to authorise service by a method not permitted by the CPR, the court may make an order permitting service by an alternative method. An application for an order under CPR 6.8 must be supported by evidence (usually in the form of a witness statement or affidavit) clearly stating the problems that have been encountered in trying to effect personal service. This evidence will then be put on the court file to provide a record of the facts upon which the court relied in making the order for substituted service. The order which permits service by an alternative method must specify the method of service and the date when the document will be deemed to be served.[2]

[1]   CPR 71.3(2).
[2]   CPR 6.8(3)(a)–(b).

2.162   However, although CPR 71.3(1) and CPR 6.8 provide a possible solution for a judgment creditor who is unable to effect personal service of the order on the judgment debtor, depending on the reasons why personal service has not been possible, the judgment creditor may wish to consider carefully at this point whether to proceed with the oral examination. Although the order for substituted service will allow the process to continue, if the judgment debtor is deliberately evading service, this may indicate that the procedure under Pt 71 will not be successful since it requires a significant degree of co-operation from the judgment debtor. While continued non-co-operation may result in a committal order against the judgment debtor, this may prove cold comfort to the judgment creditor seeking financial redress. The cost of continuing what may turn out to be a fruitless procedure may ultimately be a further source of financial loss.

Requirement to pay reasonable travelling costs

2.163   Once the judgment debtor has been served with the order, he may, within seven days, ask the judgment creditor to pay a sum reasonably sufficient to cover his travelling expenses to and from court. The judgment creditor must pay such a sum if requested.[1]

[1]   CPR 71.4. Absent such request, there is no requirement to pay conduct money.

2.164   The provision to provide the judgment debtor with reasonable travelling expenses when requested should be taken seriously. This is because an order for committal will not be made where they have not been tendered.[1]

[1]   CPR 71.8(3). See also *Beeston Shipping Ltd v Babanaft International SA (The Eastern Venture)* [1985] 1 All ER 923, CA, in which the Court of Appeal considered (in the context of RSC Ord 48) but ultimately did not need to decide this issue.

Judgment creditor's affidavit(s)

2.165   At least two days before the hearing, the judgment creditor must file at court an affidavit or affidavits dealing with service of the order, the provision of travelling expenses to the judgment debtor and how much of the judgment debt remains unpaid.[1] Alternatively, the affidavit or affidavits may be produced at the hearing.[2]

[1]   CPR 71.5(1).
[2]   CPR 71.5(2).

Affidavit evidence dealing with service

2.166 The affidavit evidence of service must be sworn by the person who served the order – either the judgment creditor himself or his process server.[1] The affidavit must provide details of how and when the order was served and should attach a copy of the order served.

[1]   CPR 71.5(1)(a), unless the order was served by the court in the case of a county court litigant in person: see para 2.160, n 2.

Affidavit evidence dealing with travelling expenses

2.167 Where service was effected through a process server, the judgment creditor must also file affidavit evidence stating either that the judgment debtor has not requested payment of his travelling expenses, or alternatively that the judgment creditor has paid a sum in accordance with such a request.[1] Given that CPR 71.4(1) provides that the judgment debtor has seven days from service of the order in which to request a sum in payment of his travelling expenses, this affidavit evidence cannot be sworn before that time. The affidavit evidence should also confirm either that all the money owing to the judgment creditor when the application was issued remains unpaid or, alternatively, provide details of the balance owing if any payments have been received in the meantime.[2] This evidence can either be in a separate affidavit to the affidavit on service or included in the process server's affidavit on the basis of information and belief. The affidavit for use in the country court (EX550) is a single affidavit in this form and could be used as a precedent for these purposes.

[1]   CPR 71.5(1)(b).
[2]   CPR 71.5(1)(c).

The hearing

2.168 At the start of the hearing the judgment debtor will be asked to swear on oath or to affirm before the questioning begins.[1] A court officer will explain the purpose of the oath and the questions.

[1]   CPR 71.6(1).

Questions asked by a court officer

2.169 Where the questioning is conducted by a *court officer* he will ask a standard set of questions set out in Forms EX140 or EX141.[1]

[1]   PD 71, para 4.1.

2.170   Where the judgment debtor is an individual (Form EX140) the questions cover matters such as his employment details, salary, benefits, other income, property, investments, other debts and any offer of payment the judgment debtor is prepared to make. In addition, the order to attend court for questioning will require the judgment debtor to produce certain documents at the hearing, including: pay slips, bank statements, building society books, share certificates and rent books, together with documents evidencing the judgment debtor's out-goings (such as his mortgage statement and utilities bills). He will also be required to bring documents relating to his business where he is operating as a sole trader (for example, bills owed to the business and its accounts).

2.171   Where the judgment debtor is a company or corporation (Form EX141) the company officer will be asked about the company's current operational status, its current financial status, its assets, its property, the company's liabilities and other matters such as details of other group companies and loans to employees. The officer will also be asked what, if any, offer of payment the company is prepared to make. The order to attend court will require the company officer to produce certain of the company's documents at the hearing, including bank statements, accounts, bills owed to the company, outstanding bills and other documents evidencing other liabilities owed by the company.

2.172   The judgment creditor or his representative may attend the hearing (although there is no requirement to do so) and may ask additional questions if he wishes to do so.[1] Alternatively, he may ask the court officer to ask additional questions by attaching a list of proposed additional questions when filing the application.[2]

[1]   CPR 71.6(3)(a).
[2]   PD 71, para 4.2(2).

2.173   The court officer will make a written record of the answers given on Form EX140/EX141 (unless the hearing is tape recorded). At the end of the questioning the court officer will read the record of the evidence given and ask the judgment debtor to sign it. If the judgment debtor refuses, the court officer will note the refusal on the record of evidence.[1]

[1]   PD 71, para 4.3.

Questions where the hearing is before a judge

2.174   Where the hearing is before a *judge* the judgment creditor (or his representative) must attend and conduct the questioning.[1] The standard questions in forms EX140 and EX141 will not be used.[2] The proceedings will be tape recorded and the court will not make a written record of the evidence.[3]

[1]   CPR 71.6(3)(b). In this context 'judge' includes masters and district judges: CPR 2.3(1).
[2]   PD 71, para 5.1.
[3]   PD 71, para 5.2.

2.175   Where the questioning is conducted by the judgment creditor's representative there is greater scope for the questioning to take the form of a vigorous cross-examination with questions tailored to the specific facts or circumstances of the judgment debtor. In high value or complex litigation, particularly where fraud is involved, this more testing form of examination may be necessary if the judgment creditor is to elicit useful information.

What questions may be put to the judgment debtor?

2.176   The scope of the questions which can be put to the judgment debtor has been the subject of some debate. It is for the court to determine the scope of the questions the judgment debtor must answer.[1]

[1]   See para 2.143.

2.177   In the 1880 case of *Republic of Costa Rica v Strousberg*,[1] the Court of Appeal had to consider whether the questions which could be asked of a judgment debtor under one of the predecessor rules to Pt 71[2] should be confined to asking the judgment debtor 'whether any and what debts are due to him'. The judgment debtor had attended before the court examiner but had refused to answer, among others, questions as to whether he had any other bank account than the one named, whether he was carrying on business, whether he had any contracts pending, whether any money was due to him for rent, or in fact any question other than what debts were due to him. The judgment creditor brought an application before the Vice-Chancellor for an order that the judgment debtor should be further examined and should answer those questions he had previously refused to answer.

[1]   (1880) 16 Ch D 8, CA.
[2]   Rules of Court of 1875, Ord XLV, r 1.

2.178   The Vice-Chancellor observed:[1]

'The object of this examination evidently is for the purpose of ascertaining from the judgment debtor what debts are owing to him, in order that the judgment creditor may attach those debts. It is in the nature of a discovery; and it appears to me very much like the discovery of documents where a defendant is asked what documents he has, and he sets out what documents he has: but you cannot cross-examine him upon that.'

[1]   (1880) 16 Ch D 8 at 10.

2.179   He went on:[1]

'However, my construction of the Act is that [the judgment creditors] were not at liberty to make a general examination … Therefore I think the examination went beyond its just bounds.'

[1]   (1880) 16 Ch D 8 at 11.

2.180   The judgment creditor appealed the Vice-Chancellor's decision on the basis that if the judgment debtor were entitled to restrict the examination to the simple question of whether any debts are due to him, the order would be a nullity. The Court of Appeal agreed. Lord Jessel MR observed:[1]

'Any question, therefore, fairly pertinent to the subject-matter of the inquiry, which means put with a view to ascertain so far as possible, by discovery from a reluctant defendant, what debts are owing to him, ought to be answered by the defendant.'

1   (1880) 16 Ch D 8 at 12.

2.181   He continued:[1]

'He must answer all questions fairly directed to ascertain from him what amount of debts is due, from whom due, and to give all necessary particulars to enable the Plaintiffs to recover under a garnishee order.'

1   (1880) 16 Ch D 8 at 12.

2.182   James LJ and Cotton LJ agreed, the former adding:[1]

'The examination is not only intended to be an examination, but to be a cross-examination, and that of the severest kind.'

1   (1880) 16 Ch D 8 at 12.

2.183   *Strousberg* was cited with approval in *Mubarak v Mubarak*,[1] where Hughes J observed that under RSC Ord 48: 'The process is intended to be a severe and testing one.'

1   [2002] EWHC 2171 (Fam).

2.184   CPR 71.2(1) provides that the order will require a judgment debtor to attend court to provide information about 'the judgment debtor's means or any other matter about which information is needed to enforce a judgment or order.' The wider form of the modern wording would therefore in any event appear to preclude a judgment debtor from arguing that he is not obliged to answer a question on a technical interpretation of the rules.

2.185   A judgment creditor who intends to carry out an oral examination of a judgment debtor should tailor the questions asked with a view to eliciting information as to the assets of the defendant which may be available for enforcement. Reference to the types of assets amenable to third party debt orders, charging orders, writs of fieri facias and equitable execution as described in Chapters 3 to 6 of this book should inform the examination.[1]

1   The assets amenable to the various methods of enforcement covered in this book are summarised in tabular form at para 1.30.

What documents must the judgment debtor produce?

2.186   *Mubarak* also considered the power of the court to order a judgment debtor to produce documents under RSC Ord 48, which are now contained in CPR 71.2(6)(b). It is worth quoting from the judgment at length since Hughes J neatly summarises both the purpose of the oral examination procedure and the ancillary nature of the power to require the judgment debtor to produce documents as part of that process.

2.187   In considering the court's power to order the production of documents, Hughes J first observed the integral nature of the power to require the production of documents to the oral examination process:

'I accept the submission of ... [counsel for the judgment debtor], that Order 48 does not authorise a freestanding process of specific discovery. The oral examination is, however, a process of considerable potential utility to a judgment creditor in a case where the judgment debtor is deliberately evading his obligation to pay. Whilst the obligation on the judgment debtor to produce books or documents is necessarily ancillary to the process of examination and not independent of it, that does not mean that it is anything other than an important and often vital part of the process. It is a significant tool in the enforcement of the court's order in relation to which, ex hypothesi, the judgment debtor is in default.'

2.188 He then went on to observe the flexible nature of the process:

'I do not accept [the judgment debtor's] further submission that the only time when the court can order production of documents is on first ordering attendance for oral examination, nor that order can only be a generalised one in the terms of Ord 48, that is to say, to produce anything relevant to any debts owing or other assets. It is no doubt the case that the great majority of Ord 48 oral examinations are quite brief and the documents relating to them comparatively few.

... That, however, is not to say that the process is not available in and adaptable to the very complex case, such as the present, where the debt and the assets are counted in millions and the potential relevant documents require a trolley rather than an envelope to bring them to court. Indeed, it may be all the more important a process in a case of that kind.'

2.189 He further observed that orders for the production of documents can be adjourned and can be both general and specific:

'I am quite satisfied that the rules permit the examination to be adjourned from time to time, if that is necessary, and that orders for the production of relevant documents may also be made from time to time. Such orders may be specific as well as general, providing of course that what is specified for production is relevant to the two questions to which the examination is directed, that is to say, debts owing to the judgment debtor and his property or other means of paying what he owes. If it were not so, a judgment debtor in a complex case such as the husband here, and even if benefiting from skilled advice, which is often not the case, would be faced with real doubt about what documents to bring.'

2.190 The court went on to examine the ambit of the expression relating to documents 'in the possession' of the judgment debtor in RSC Ord 48. CPR 71.2(6)(b) refers to documents in the judgment debtor's 'control'. Hughes J observed that since the present case concerned family proceedings it was not yet governed by Pt 71, but noted the different wording between the two rules and observed that the new rule in Pt 71 was consistent with the requirement for the judgment debtor to produce documents in his possession or power. His judgment stated:

'It is of course true that the range of documents which are relevant to oral examination under Order 48 will often be narrower than the range of documents relevant to pre-trial discovery, for the former must be relevant to enforcement and to the ability to pay.'

And concluded:

'What is, however, clear is that to be in the possession or power of a judgment debtor the document must be one which he has the necessary enforceable right to call for, and in his personal capacity not merely qua director or agent. This is further consistent with the actual decision in *B v B*,[1] where Dunn J held that, absent the case of a one-man company, which is the alter ego of the party, a party who has the physical holding of documents or a right to inspect them simply as a director, will, although obliged to disclose their existence at the discovery stage, not be ordered to produce them for inspection.'

[1]   [1978] 3 WLR 624.

2.191   In the present case, although the judgment debtor had great influence over the companies concerned and an apparent ability to manipulate their affairs in many ways, there was not such a complete merger of interests or unfettered control to enable the court to treat the companies as his alter ego and require production of the company accounts. This was the case notwithstanding the fact that he found the judgment debtor to have been on occasion evasive and untruthful since:

'the [the judgment debtor's] behaviour, however disgraceful, is not a reason to justify going beyond what can legitimately be achieved in the particular process before the court.'

2.192   Finally, Hughes J observed two limitations to the procedure:

(a)   there was no power under RSC Ord 48 (and thus presumably under Pt 71) to direct that a new document be brought into existence (in that case a list of the judgment debtor's expenditure). The court can only order the judgment debtor to produce an existing document which is in his possession; and

(b)   there is no power to order the judgment debtor to use all necessary endeavours to obtain documents which are not in his possession.

Questions about a judgment debtor's foreign assets

2.193   The question of the court's power under RSC Ord 48 to examine a judgment debtor as to his foreign assets was considered by the Court of Appeal in *Interpool Ltd v Galani*.[1]

[1]   [1988] QB 738, CA.

2.194   Interpool Ltd was a US company which had obtained a French judgment in the sum of US$8,196,000 against a Greek judgment debtor, Galani, in respect of guarantees he had given. Following the judgment, Mr Galani moved from Paris to London and the judgment was registered as a judgment of the High Court under the Foreign Judgments (Reciprocal Enforcement) Act 1933.[1]

[1]   The French judgment of which enforcement was sought was given in 1985, prior to the Brussels Convention entering into force between France and the United Kingdom under the

Civil Jurisdiction and Judgments Act 1982. The Foreign Judgments (Reciprocal Enforcement) Act 1933 was therefore the legislation applicable to the enforcement of a French judgment in England. This is now governed by Council Regulation (EC) 44/2001 of 22 December 2000 on jurisdiction and the recognition and enforcement of judgments in civil and commercial matters (the Brussels Regulation).

2.195   An order was made for Mr Galani's oral examination in relation to debts owed to him and as to his other property under RSC Ord 48. Mr Galani objected to answering any questions except those relating to any assets he may have within the jurisdiction of the English courts. This was on the grounds that the English court does not exercise extra-territorial jurisdiction and will not enforce its judgments by way of execution save as to assets which are within the jurisdiction. Since RSC Ord 48 was merely part of the machinery for the enforcement of judgments, any examination under RSC Ord 48 should be limited to assets within the jurisdiction.

2.196   While commending the attractive simplicity of the judgment debtor's arguments, the Court of Appeal rejected them. First, because it found that certain English enforcement procedures were not confined to English assets and, secondly, because there were policy reasons for rejecting the narrow construction of the rule for which the judgment debtor contended.

2.197   As regards the use of English enforcement proceedings to execute against foreign assets, Balcombe LJ first observed that RSC Ord 48[1] contained no express reference to the locality of debts. He then made various observations on the jurisdictional scope of English enforcement procedures. He noted that there was no limitation in the provisions of RSC Ord 49, which at the time governed garnishee proceedings,[2] that the garnished debt must be properly recoverable within the jurisdiction. Rather the court had a jurisdiction to garnish a foreign debt, albeit that it may choose not to exercise its discretion to do so. However, these observations must now be seen as wrong in light of their Lordships' decision in *Société Eram Shipping Co Ltd v Compagnie Internationale de Navigation*.[3] (See further paras 3.67–3.79.)

Balcombe LJ then considered the court's jurisdiction to make a charging order. He commented that he could see no reason why the jurisdiction to make a charging order should be construed more narrowly than the garnishee jurisdiction and should therefore encompass foreign assets. Again, these observations must now be seen as wrong given the recent developments in the law relating to third party debt orders noted in the previous paragraph. However, Balcombe LJ considered that there were other reasons why there should be jurisdiction to examine a judgment debtor as to his interests under a foreign trust. First, such examination may be necessary to discover the nature and extent of the judgment debtor's interest in that trust, in part to see whether it is in fact a 'foreign' trust. Secondly, Charging Orders Act 1979, s 1(5) requires the court to consider all the circumstances of the case and, in particular, any evidence as to the personal circumstances of the debtor. The existence or otherwise of a judgment debtor's interest in foreign trusts or properties may be relevant to the court's determination of whether a charging order should be made.

---

1   The same is true of Pt 71.
2   The predecessor to Pt 72, which is considered in detail in Chapter 3.
3   [2004] 1 AC 260.

2.198 Having concluded that the judgment debtor was therefore wrong in his submission that English enforcement procedure is confined to English assets, the Court of Appeal considered that there were also policy reasons for giving RSC Ord 48 the wider meaning for which the judgment creditor contended. Balcombe LJ noted that the provisions for the reciprocal enforcement of judgments between states were continuously expanding, as evidenced by the Civil Jurisdiction and Judgments Act 1982 (CJJA 1982), which had largely come into force the previous year. The court accepted counsel for the judgment creditor's submission that:[1]

'[I]t is entirely consistent with this pattern of legislation that the judgment creditor should have available to him a procedure, under Order 48, which he can utilise to find out whether, in default of any English assets, there are foreign assets available to satisfy his judgment. The use of Order 48 for this purpose is not regulating the conduct of the judgment debtor abroad so as to be contrary to the principle considered by Hoffmann J in *Mackinnon v Donaldson, Lufkin and Jenrette Securities Corpn* [1986] Ch 482.'

1   [1988] QB 738 at 742.

2.199 While not applicable in *Interpool*,[1] the court also considered the provisions of art 16(5) of the Brussels Convention, which had since come into force by virtue of CJJA 1982, s 2(c). Article 16(5) provides that:[2]

'The following courts shall have exclusive jurisdiction, regardless of domicile:....
5. in proceedings concerned with the enforcement of judgments, the courts of the Contracting State in which the judgment has been or is to be enforced.'

1   See para 2.194, n 1.
2   Lugano Convention, art 16(5) and Brussels Regulation, reg 22(5) contain identical provisions.

2.200   Balcombe LJ observed that:[1]

'Article 16(5) provides that, in proceedings concerned with the enforcement of judgments, the courts of the contracting state in which the judgment has been or is to be enforced shall have exclusive jurisdiction, regardless of domicile. But this provision must be read in the light of the fact that it is possible, as [counsel for the judgment debtor] conceded, for the same debt to be simultaneously enforced by judgments obtained, or registered, in more than one country. So this provision can only relate to the enforcement proceedings in a particular state. The use of Order 48, in English enforcement proceedings, in order to discover the existence of foreign assets, does not confer, or purport to confer, jurisdiction on the English court in relation to enforcement proceedings in any other country in which those assets may be situate.'

1   [1988] QB 738 at 742–743.

2.201   Accordingly, the provisions of RSC Ord 48 were not limited to debts owed and assets located within the jurisdiction and the court had power to order a judgment debtor to answer questions intended to discover his assets outside as well as within the jurisdiction.

2.202   The decision in *Interpool* was considered by the Court of Appeal in *Babanaft International Co SA v Bassatne*,[1] a case concerning the court's jurisdiction under

SCA 1981, s 37(1) to issue an injunction restraining a defendant from dealing with its overseas assets. Accordingly, the court's comments on the *Interpool* decision in the *Babanaft* case are strictly obiter. Lord Justice Kerr specifically noted that the orders for the disclosure of assets abroad pursuant to RSC Ord 48 were not in issue in that appeal and added an 'emphatic note of caution'[2] in relation to those parts of his judgment which had not been canvassed in the arguments of counsel. However, he observed:[3]

'In *Interpool Ltd v Galani* [1988] Q.B. 738 this court ordered the defendant to make a full disclosure after judgment of his assets abroad, clearly in order to enable the plaintiff to use the disclosure for the purpose of enforcement proceedings in the jurisdictions where the disclosed assets were situated. The court also held, at p 1046D-G, that an order for disclosure by the defendant of his assets worldwide pursuant to Order 48 did not infringe article 16(5) of the European Judgments Convention. In my view, the correctness of that decision is not open to doubt.'

1   [1990] Ch 13, CA.
2   [1990] Ch 13 at 36.
3   [1990] Ch 13 at 34.

2.203 Lord Justices Neill and Nicholls agreed that *Interpool* had established that there is no objection in principle to the judgment debtor being required to disclose overseas assets under RSC Ord 48. However, the latter added an addendum to his judgment in the following terms:[1]

'I say nothing concerning the circumstances in which it will be proper for the court to make an order for the disclosure of information regarding assets situated abroad, either before judgment or after judgment. That is not a matter which arose, or was argued, on this appeal. But in all cases where such an order is sought or made the court will need to be alive to the importance of exercising control over the use of information disclosed compulsorily about assets situated overseas. It is obvious that such information can be used by a plaintiff in a manner that, in some circumstances, would be unjust to the defendant who has been compelled to disclose it.'

1   [1990] Ch 13 at 46.

2.204 He concluded that in light of the unforeseen consequences that an order for the disclosure of information could potentially have, the court may need to take steps to control the use made of such information overseas.[1]

1   Neill LJ did not elaborate on the type of 'unjust' circumstances he envisaged. While there may be circumstances where, for example, a judgment debtor cannot reveal the existence of foreign debts he is owed without being in breach of foreign law obligations to another party (such that the court may decline to order the judgment debtor to answer questions in that regard), this is likely to be the exception rather than the norm. Alternatively, in such circumstances the position could be addressed by requiring appropriate undertakings from the judgment creditor as to the disclosure and use made of any information relating to the judgment debtor's foreign assets.

2.205 *Interpool* was also cited with approval by the Court of Appeal in *Maclaine Watson*.[1] As discussed at paras 2.154–2.156, that case considered the court's jurisdiction to order a judgment debtor to disclose his assets under SCA 1981, s 37(1). Kerr LJ observed:[2]

> 'Finally, as regards, the extension by Millett J of his first order so as to include the disclosure of the [judgment debtor's] assets outside the jurisdiction, there can be no doubt that he had the necessary jurisdiction for this purpose: see in particular the decision of this court in *Interpool v Galani*.'

1   [1989] Ch 286, CA.
2   [1989] Ch 286 at 306.

2.206   The Court of Appeal's decision in *Interpool* was considered by the House of Lords in *Société Eram Shipping Company v Compagnie Internationale de Navigation*.[1] Their Lordships noted that the *Interpool* decision had considered RSC Ord 48 procedure rather than the garnishee jurisdiction, which was the subject of the *Société Eram* appeal.[2] In their Lordships' view the comments made in *Interpool* as to the nature of the garnishee jurisdiction (see para 2.197) were erroneous.[3] However, as has been noted, the Court of Appeal did not base its decision in *Interpool* solely on the availability of English execution steps against foreign assets. The Court also took into consideration wider policy arguments. One of the principal reasons for their Lordships' finding in *Société Eram* that the English courts have no jurisdiction to garnish a foreign debt was that the garnishee process operates not as an in personam order against a third party but rather has proprietary consequences and takes effect as an order in rem against the debt owed by the third party.[4] Their Lordships' criticisms of the *Interpool* Court of Appeal's analysis of the garnishee jurisdiction would not seem to extend to that Court's finding that oral examination proceedings may be used in relation to overseas assets, since, in contrast to garnishee proceedings, neither RSC Ord 48 nor Pt 71 proceedings seek to assert any in rem jurisdiction over assets (whether located in the UK or overseas). Accordingly, the Pt 71 procedure should be available to elicit information as to a judgment debtor's foreign assets.

1   [2004] 1 AC 260, HL.
2   [2004] 1 AC 260 at 272, per Lord Bingham.
3   [2004] 1 AC 260 at 283, per Lord Hoffmann, and at 289, per Lord Hobhouse.
4   [2004] 1 AC 260 at 292, per Lord Millett. See further Chapter 3.

Use of Part 71 in connection with foreign enforcement proceedings

2.207   In an article written shortly after the Court of Appeal's decision in *Interpool*,[1] Peter Kaye reviewed the *Interpool* judgment and the comments passed on it in *Babanaft*. Kaye concludes that while the English Court has the power to order disclosure of foreign assets under the RSC Ord 48 procedure, it lacks jurisdiction to do so where the application is being brought for the purpose of foreign enforcement proceedings.

1   'Examination of judgment debtors as to their assets abroad: courts' powers and jurisdiction' [1989] LMCLQ 465.

2.208   Kaye draws a distinction between those cases outside and cases governed by the Brussels Convention (and by implication the Lugano Convention and the Brussels Regulation, which contain equivalent provisions).[1] However, in both cases Kaye concludes that the English courts lack jurisdiction to order the examination of a judgment debtor to the extent that those proceedings contemplate enforcement proceedings overseas.

¹ See Lugano Convention, art 16(5) and Brussels Regulation, art 22(5).

2.209 As regards jurisdictions outside the Brussels regime, from the passage from *Interpool* cited in para 2.200, Kaye concludes that:

'… it may be deduced from *Interpool v Galani* that orders for examination of judgment debtors as to their foreign assets, under RSC Ord. 48 fall within the national jurisdiction of the English courts whenever these are made for the purposes of orders in English enforcement proceedings'

and continues:¹

'However, where the RSC Ord. 48 order is sought in aid of judgment-enforcement proceedings taking place not in England but in a foreign state (not party to the Brussels Convention), the English court would appear to lack jurisdiction to make such order.'

¹ [1989] LMCLQ 465 at 470.

2.210 In Kaye's view, the 'clear implication' of the passage in *Interpool* cited in para 2.200,¹ is that the English court would *lack* jurisdiction to make an order under RSC Ord 48 for the purpose of foreign enforcement proceedings. However, it is questionable whether Kaye's interpretation is in fact the 'clear implication' of that passage. The court may simply have meant that by asking a question of a judgment debtor over whom it has personal jurisdiction about the existence of foreign assets, the English court is *not* asserting jurisdiction over any overseas assets which that person may hold.

¹ Namely that the use of RSC Ord 48 in English enforcement proceedings to discover the existence of foreign assets does not confer, or purport to confer, jurisdiction on the English courts in relation to enforcement proceedings in another country where those assets are situate.

2.211 As regards the position under the Brussels Convention, Kaye concludes:

'The answer, it is believed, is that *to the extent* that proceedings brought before the English courts for enforcement of an English or foreign judgment may be said to *contemplate enforcement* thereof in a *foreign* Contracting State, rather than in the United Kingdom, both the enforcement measures sought and, more particularly in present context, RSC Order 48, R 1 powers in relation to discovery of foreign (or even, in the circumstances, United Kingdom) assets of the judgment debtor lie beyond the jurisdiction of the English courts in accordance with art 19 of the Brussels Convention and, correspondingly, by virtue of art 16(5), within the exclusive jurisdiction of the courts of the foreign Contracting State or states in which the judgment is to be enforced and in which the foreign assets may be situated.'¹ (Emphasis added.)

¹ [1989] LMCLQ 465 at 471.

2.212 Thus he concludes that rather than the oral examination procedure being available in support of foreign proceedings:¹

'On the contrary, it is felt, the plain meaning and intent of the words used in art 16(5) should be taken to be that measures of enforcement and orders relating thereto are to be limited exclusively to the enforcement in the United Kingdom – as the Contracting State of the forum – of the English or foreign judgment, and that to the extent that applications relate to foreign Contracting State enforcement, the English courts must decline jurisdiction to grant the relief requested, of their own motion, under art 19 of the Brussels Convention.'

[1]   [1989] LMCLQ 465 at 471.

2.213   Accordingly, Kaye concludes that oral examination orders are prohibited where they are sought for the purposes of enforcement proceedings taking place outside the jurisdiction of England and Wales.

2.214   Kaye notes that this situation appears unsatisfactory, partly because it is at odds with the position under the Conventions in relation to disclosure ancillary to interim injunctions,[1] and further because this interpretation raises both the cost and complexity of discovering the location of a judgment debtor's assets. It would mean that the judgment creditor[2] may have to go to each of the EU states to obtain an order for examination as to the judgment debtor's assets so as to discover what, if any, assets are located in that particular EU state before issuing execution proceedings. Further, Kaye's conclusion that oral examination proceedings are precluded to the extent that they 'contemplate' foreign enforcement[3] begs the very question: until a judgment creditor has information as to the location of a judgment debtor's assets, he will not be able to 'contemplate' enforcement proceedings, whether in the UK or anywhere else.

[1]   Where disclosure *can* be obtained where it is ancillary to an interim protective measure in support of proceedings in another Contracting State under the Brussels Convention, art 24. Lugano Convention, art 24 and Brussels Regulation, reg 31.

[2]   Or at least one who has not been able to obtain post-judgment disclosure in support of a freezing injunction.

[3]   See para 2.211.

2.215   While Kaye may be correct that amendment of the Brussels and Lugano Conventions and the Brussels Regulation is necessary to avoid this spectre,[1] his interpretation of the RSC Ord 48 procedure is manifestly at odds with the purposes and intent behind the Convention regimes.[2] Section 5 of the Jenard Report,[3] which by virtue of CJJA 1982, s 3 is admissible in the English courts as an aid to the construction of the Brussels Convention, discusses what meaning is to be given to the expression 'proceedings concerned with the enforcement of judgments':

'It means those proceedings which can arise from 'recourse to force, constraint or distraint on moveable or immovable property in order to ensure the effective implementation of judgments and authentic instruments.'

Problems arising out of such proceedings come within the exclusive jurisdiction of the courts of the place for enforcement.

'Provisions of this kind appear in the internal law of many Member States.'

The footnote to the last paragraph adds:

'... French courts have exclusive jurisdiction over measures for enforcement which is to take place in France (preventative measures, distress levied on a tenant's chattels, writs of attachment and applications for enforcement of a foreign judgment); over distraint levied on immovable or moveable property, and over proceedings concerned with the validity of measures for enforcement.'

1   Or a direct ruling from the European Court of Justice.
2   Under what is now the Treaty Establishing the European Community, art 293, the member states agreed to enter into negotiations with a view to securing the *simplification* of formalities governing the reciprocal recognition and enforcement of judgments.
3   Report by Mr P Jenard on the Convention of 27 September 1968 on Jurisdiction and the Enforcement of Judgments in Civil and Commercial Matters (OJ 1979 C 59, p 1).

2.216   The oral examination procedure would not obviously seem to fall within the types of proceedings listed in s 5 of the Jenard Report or the footnote to that section.

2.217   Further, as Kaye himself observes, the European Court of Justice's favoured approach of adopting a strict construction of art 16 is based upon proximity of subject-matter of the types of dispute prescribed in that article to the territories of competent courts. In *Reichert v Dresdner Bank AG*,[1] a case decided after Kaye's article was published, the European Court of Justice was asked to consider whether the '*action paulienne*' under French law (which allows a creditor to obtain the revocation of a transaction whereby the debtor has effected a disposition in fraud of the creditor's rights) qualified as 'proceedings concerned with the enforcement of judgments'. The European Court of Justice held, in a passage that sheds considerable light on the scope of art 16(5), that:

'22 The Dresdner Bank claims that the action paulienne, *in so far as it is preparatory to the enforcement of a decision*, does come within the exceptions set out in Article 16(5) of the Convention. ...

24 It should be pointed out, in the first place, that ... Article 16 of the Convention makes a number of exceptions to the general rule set out in Article 2 of the Convention by granting exclusive jurisdiction to the courts of a Contracting State other than that specified under Article 2 in proceedings which have a particular connection with that other State, on the basis of the location of immovable property, the seat of a company, an entry in a public register or, in the case of paragraph (5), the place where a judgment is to be enforced.

25 In the second place it should be pointed out that Article 16 must not be given a wider interpretation than is required by its objective, since it results in depriving the parties of the choice of forum which would otherwise be theirs and, in certain cases, in their being brought before a court which is not that of the domicile of any of them ....

26 From that point of view it is necessary to take account of the fact that the essential purpose of the exclusive jurisdiction of the courts of the place in which the judgment has been or is to be enforced is that it is only for the courts of the Member State on whose territory enforcement is sought to apply the rules concerning the action on that territory of the authorities responsible for enforcement.' (Emphasis added.)

1   [1992] ECR I-2149, ECJ.

2.218   The court then referred to s 5 of the Jenard Report quoted in para 2.215 and concluded that although the '*action paulienne*' under consideration:[1]

> 'thus preserves the interests of the creditor with a view in particular to a subsequent enforcement of the obligation, it is not intended to obtain a decision in proceedings relating to "recourse to force, constraint or distraint on movable or immovable property in order to ensure the effective implementation of judgments and authentic instruments" and does not therefore come within the scope of Article 16(5) of the Convention.'

[1]   In the opinion of Mr Advocate General Gulamm, the position is stated rather more categorically: 'The Dresdner Bank claims that that provision must not be restrictively interpreted and that it may cover a revocatory action such as the action paulienne because the purpose of the action to set the transaction aside is to *prepare for enforcement* of the creditor's claim to the property in question ... Clearly it should be accepted that courts in the State in which the judgment has been or is to be enforced have exclusive jurisdiction under Article 16(5) of the Convention *only in cases directly connected with the enforcement of judicial decisions already taken* or with other enforceable instruments.' (Emphasis added)

2.219   The procedure which was set out in RSC Ord 48, and which is now contained in Pt 71, is not strictly a method of enforcement at all, since it is not in itself designed to extract payment from the judgment debtor. While Pt 71 proceedings may be a precursor or 'preparatory' to the enforcement steps contemplated by art 16(5) of the Brussels Convention[1] (as was the action paulienne, in *Dresdner*), they are not enforcement proceedings in their own right. While it seems obvious that proceedings to *seize* an asset owned by a UK domiciliary which is located in Germany should be brought in Germany, the provisions of art 16(5) should not override the bedrock provisions of art 2 of the Convention regime[2] to require that proceedings to *examine* that UK domiciliary as to what assets he has in Germany should be held in Germany simply by virtue of the fact that he holds *some* assets which are located in Germany.[3]

In conclusion, the better view would appear to be that the English courts should have jurisdiction over UK domiciliaries to order disclosure of foreign assets under Pt 71 for the purpose of foreign enforcement proceedings.

[1]   Or the Lugano Convention, art 16(5) or the Brussels Regulation, art 22(5).
[2]   That persons should be sued in the Contracting State in which they are domiciled. Identical provisions appear as the Lugano Convention, art 2 and the Brussels Regulation, art 2.
[3]   The House of Lords decision in *Kuwait Oil Tanker Company SAK v Qabazard* [2004] 1 AC 300 considered the provisions of art 16(5) in the context of garnishee proceedings and concluded that the effect of this provision was that the English court did not have jurisdiction to make a garnishee order in respect of a foreign debt. However, the question of whether the oral examination procedure provided under CPR Pt 71 should be considered 'proceedings concerned with the enforcement of judgments' under art 16(5) was not considered.

Subsequent hearings

2.220   Part 71 contains no limitation that an order for oral examination may be made only once. In *Sturges v Countess of Warwick*[1] it was held that where an oral examination had been held under one of the predecessors to Pt 71,[2] a further examination may be ordered in special circumstances. The commentary to the White Book notes that the new rule places no restriction on repeat examinations and suggests that the court's case management and costs powers should be used to prevent abuse.[3]

1   (1914) 30 TLR 112, CA.
2   Rules of the Supreme Court 1883, Ord XLII, r 32.
3   Civil Procedure 2004, vol 1, para 71.2.7.

Adjournment of the hearing

2.221   Adjournment of the oral examination hearing is also possible, where, for example the judgment creditor requires the judgment debtor to produce relevant documents before the examination can proceed. CPR 71.7 makes specific provision for adjournment and states that the court will give directions as to how notice of the new hearing is to be served on the judgment debtor in the case of adjournment. As has been noted, in *Mubarak* Hughes J said:

'I am quite satisfied that the rules [Order 48] permit the examination to be adjourned from time to time, if that is necessary, and that orders for the production of relevant documents may also be made from time to time.'

2.222   A judgment creditor may be well advised to apply for an adjournment where this is necessary to ensure that complete or truthful answers are being provided by the judgment debtor.

2.223   Where a hearing has been adjourned, it is vital that the judgment debtor is served with the amended order indorsed with the new date of examination. If this is not done, the judgment debtor's failure to attend on the new date will not constitute contempt of court. This was the Court of Appeal's decision in *Beeston Shipping Ltd v Babanaft International SA, The Eastern Venture*,[1] notwithstanding the fact that the judgment debtor's legal representatives were aware of the adjourned date, were in communication with their client, and had confirmed to the judgment creditor's solicitors that it was not necessary to re-serve the judgment debtor with the order adjourning the hearing. Dunn LJ observed:[2]

'... committal for contempt of court is an extreme remedy and, whatever the relationship between the solicitors may be and whatever knowledge in fact the person to be proceeded against for contempt of court has, none the less the committal proceedings will be bad unless the rules are strictly complied with.'

1   [1985] 1 All ER 923, CA.
2   [1985] 1 All ER 923 at 927.

Failure to comply with the order

2.224   It is the sanction of committal in the event of non-compliance with an order to attend court that gives the oral examination procedure teeth. The penal notice contained in the order[1] warns the judgment debtor that if he does not obey the order, he may be sent to prison for contempt of court.

1   See para 2.148.

2.225   CPR 71.8 sets out what will happen in the event of failure to comply with the order. If the judgment debtor:

(a)   fails to attend court;
(b)   refuses at the hearing to take the oath or to answer any question; or
(c)   otherwise fails to comply with the order;

the court will refer the matter to a High Court judge or circuit judge.[1] The judge or court officer making the referral must certify in writing in which respect the judgment debtor failed to comply with the order.[2] The commentary to the White Book[3] states that the most common type of non-compliance is the debtor's failure to attend court to be examined.

[1]   CPR 71.8(1).
[2]   CPR PD 71, para 6.
[3]   Civil Procedure 2004, vol 1, para 71.8.1.

Suspended committal order

2.226   CPR 71.8(2) gives the judge to whom the matter is referred discretion to make a committal order against the judgment debtor, subject to the provisions of CPR 71.8(3) and 71.8(4):

(a)   CPR 71.8(3) provides that a committal order may not be made unless the judgment creditor has complied with the rules for payment of the judgment debtor's travelling expenses[1] and filed affidavits as to service of the order and payment of travelling expenses.[2]
(b)   CPR 71.8(4) states that if a committal order is made, it will be suspended provided that the judgment debtor attends court for examination at a subsequent time and place, which will be specified in the order, and complies with the terms of that order and the original order. This hearing will be before a judge if either the original order was to attend before a judge or the judge making the suspended committal order directs that this should be the case.[3]

[1]   Set out in CPR 71.4.
[2]   Set out in CPR 71.5.
[3]   PD 71, para 7.1.

2.227   Once the suspended committal order has been made it must be personally served on the judgment debtor in accordance with the rule in CPR 71.3, and an affidavit of service must be filed in accordance with CPR 71.5(1) and (2).[1] However, there is no requirement to offer the judgment debtor travel expenses to attend the subsequent hearing.

[1]   PD 71, para 7.2.

2.228   If the judgment debtor attends court in accordance with the terms of the suspended committal order, the examination will then take place and the suspended committal order will be discharged.

2.229   If, however, the judgment debtor fails to attend court at the time and date specified in the suspended committal order and it appears to the judge or the court officer that the judgment debtor has been duly served with the order, the failure to attend will be certified in writing.[1] Alternatively, if the judgment debtor fails to comply with any other term on which the committal order was suspended, this will also be certified in writing and the judge or court officer will set out details of the non-compliance.[2]

1   PD 71, para 8.1.
2   PD 71, para 8.2.

Committal hearing

2.230 If the judgment debtor fails to comply with any term on which the committal order is suspended, he shall be brought before a judge to consider whether the committal order should be discharged.[1] A warrant for the judgment debtor to be brought before the court (rather than being taken to prison) may be issued by the court on the basis of a court certificate that the judgment debtor failed to comply with the terms of a suspended committal order (see previous paragraph).[2] The judge[3] will then consider whether or not the committal order should be discharged.

1   CPR 71.8(4)(b).
2   PD 71, para 8.3.
3   PD 71, para 8.4 provides that the hearing may take place before a master or district judge.

2.231 The judge will discharge the committal order unless he is satisfied beyond reasonable doubt that the judgment debtor has failed to comply both with the terms of the original order to attend court and the terms on which the committal order was suspended and that both orders have been duly served on the judgment debtor.[1] A criminal standard of proof is therefore imposed and the judge may discharge the committal order for procedural irregularity if, for example, he is not satisfied that the orders have been properly served. Committal is an extreme remedy and will not be used unless the rules are strictly complied with.[2] The notes to the White Book observe that, in practice, the committal order is invariably discharged at this hearing because the judgment debtor agrees to be examined there and then, thus completing the purpose of Pt 71.[3]

1   PD 71, para 8.5.
2   *Beeston Shipping Ltd v Babanaft International SA, The Eastern Venture* [1985] 1 All ER 923, CA, a case in which a judgment debtor was held not to be in contempt by failing to attend court on the adjourned hearing date since he had not been served with the amended order.
3   Civil Procedure 2004, vol 1, para 71.8.1.

Warrant for committal

2.232 If the judge decides that the committal order should not be discharged, a warrant for committal will be issued immediately[1] and the judgment debtor will be taken to prison to serve the sentence. The sentence for committal is a maximum of two years.[2]

1   PD 71, para 8.6.
2   Contempt of Court Act 1981, s 14(1).

Truthfulness of the judgment debtor's answers

2.233 Much of the effectiveness of Pt 71 will depend on the nature of the questions asked and, of equal importance, truthful answers being given. This raises the question of whether a judgment debtor who can be shown to have given untruthful answers during an oral examination can be liable for committal. Although the provisions of CPR 71.8(1)(c) that the matter may be referred to a judge where a judgment debtor '*otherwise fails to comply with the order*' might be read as suggesting that the power of committal extends to untruthful answers being given, it would seem that committal is not available in these circumstances.

2.234 The Report on the First Phase of the Enforcement Review published in July 2000 specifically considered the question of whether the sanction of committal should be available in the event of a judgment debtor providing untruthful answers during the oral examination procedure. It noted that reaction to the proposal to extend the committal power to a judgment debtor who had given untruthful answers had been mixed. The majority of panel members were concerned that a civil procedure with equivalent effect to trying a judgment debtor for perjury may not maintain the strict criminal standard of proof and that civil judges may be over-eager to impose a custodial sentence.[1]

[1]   Paragraph 101.

2.235 However, the Report also noted the merit in the argument that the court should take responsibility for ensuring its own integrity and punishing those who seek to abuse that integrity,[1] pointing out that lying in a civil court should be punished as a civil offence (particularly if the criminal justice system was unwilling or unable to take responsibility for doing so). It was also argued that lying during the course of an oral examination should be viewed as a contempt of court in the same way as failing to attend or refusing to answer questions.

[1]   This argument was made by (amongst others) the Civil Justice Council. See para 102.

2.236 The Report concluded with a specific recommendation that the committal power be extended to situations in which the debtor fails to answer questions truthfully,[1] but suggested that this would need to be taken forward by enacting primary legislation as part of a more general streamlining of the contempt procedures.[2] In the absence of such legislation, it seems that committal is not available, and the somewhat unsatisfactory distinction remains between a judgment debtor who refuses to answer questions and one who avoids the sanctions for contempt by attending the hearing and providing untruthful answers.

[1]   Paragraph 99.
[2]   Paragraph 105.

Perjury

2.237 In the absence of committal, the only sanction against a judgment debtor who gives untruthful answers during an oral examination may be a criminal prosecution for perjury. However, as the *Report on the First Phase of the Enforcement Review* notes:[1]

'At present there is an existing criminal penalty of perjury, but anecdotal evidence suggests that it is hardly ever used … it is far too cumbersome a weapon to be of any use in combating the casual untruths which are probably much more of a feature of the oral examination process.'

[1]   Paragraph 100.

2.238   A conviction for the offence of perjury must satisfy the criteria under Perjury Act 1911, s 1(1), that the witness: (a) was lawfully sworn in a judicial proceeding; (b) made a false statement wilfully (rather than by mistake); (c) knew it was false or did not believe it to be true; and (d) that the statement was material to the proceedings.

2.239   The case would have to satisfy strict evidential requirements[1] and the Crown Prosecution Service (CPS) will not prosecute if they do not think it is in the public interest. As the Report states:[2]

'The CPS and the police would need to be convinced that a serious transgression had occurred if they were to devote the resources necessary to bring a criminal prosecution.'

[1]   The Crown Prosecution Service Code for Crown Prosecutors states that there must be sufficient evidence to provide 'a realistic prospect of conviction'.
[2]   Paragraph 100.

2.240   However, there have been cases where a conviction for perjury has been made where a defendant has lied about assets. In *R v Shamj*[1] an appellant was examined before a master and told various lies about his assets. In convicting him to 15 months' imprisonment for perjury, the court commented:[2]

'Sometimes in civil proceedings, as these were, the effect of perjury is to cause financial loss to others … but there is … in cases of this kind one victim of perjury. That victim is the course of justice and its proper administration. It is because of that inevitable feature of the offence that a conviction for perjury must always be visited …, save in the most exceptional circumstances … with an immediate custodial sentence.'

[1]   (1989) 11 Cr App Rep (S) 587.
[2]   (1989) 11 Cr App Rep (S) 587 at 589–590.

2.241   While the prospect of a conviction for perjury may encourage a judgment debtor to tell the truth under oral examination, this may seem a remote risk and is likely to occur only in the most serious cases or when the court is faced with a judgment debtor who has a history of dishonest conduct. A prosecution for perjury cannot force a judgment debtor to tell the truth and a conviction for perjury may do little to enhance the chances of a judgment creditor successfully enforcing his judgment.

Possible limitations on Part 71 procedure

2.242   The common law privilege against self-incrimination and the provisions of the ECHR may both impact upon the operation of the Pt 71 procedure.

Privilege against self-incrimination

2.243   Under the privilege against self-incrimination, no person can be compelled to answer questions or produce documents, in civil or criminal proceedings, which may expose him to criminal proceedings.[1] The privilege is set out in the Civil Evidence Act 1968, s 14[2] which provides the privilege excuses the production of documents or the answering of questions which, but for the privilege, would have to be produced/answered. However, it does not excuse the disclosure of the *existence* of such documents, only their *production*.

1   *Blunt v Park Lane Hotel Ltd* [1942] 2 KB 253, CA and, more recently, *Den Norske Bank ASA v Antonatos* [1998] 3 WLR 711, CA.
2   'The right of a person in any legal proceedings ... to refuse to answer any question or produce any document or thing if to do so would tend to expose that person to proceedings for an offence or for the recovery of a penalty: (a) shall apply only as regards criminal offences under the law of any part of the United Kingdom and penalties provided for by such law; and (b) shall include a like right to refuse to answer any question or produce any document or thing if to do so would tend to expose the husband or wife of that person to proceedings for any such criminal offence or for the recovery of any such penalty.'

2.244   There have been a number of statutory modifications to the privilege whereby defendants who make disclosures are given specific statutory protection in relation to the prosecution of particular offences.[1]

1   See eg Criminal Damage Act 1971, s 9; Supreme Court Act 1981, s 72 and Theft Act 1968, s 31.

2.245   Although the privilege against self-incrimination can be invoked by a person for his own protection or that of his spouse it cannot be invoked for the protection of a third party.[1] Although there seems to be no reason why the privilege should not apply where disclosure of information by a director, servant or agent of a company would tend to incriminate the company, this has so far been left undecided.[2]

1   *British Steel Co v Granada Television Ltd* [1981] AC 1096, HL.
2   The question was left open in *Re Westinghouse Uranium Contract* [1978] AC 547, HL and *Sociedade Nacional de Combustiveis de Angola UEE v Lundqvist* [1991] 2 WLR 280, CA.

2.246   A person relying on the privilege must satisfy the court that disclosure of the information would tend to expose him to proceedings for a criminal offence or the recovery of a penalty. There must be a reasonable risk that self-incrimination would be the result of providing the information;[1] the privilege may not be claimed on the basis of a mere possibility that the facts might lead to exposure to criminal proceedings.[2]

1   *Sociedade Nacional de Combustiveis de Angola UEE v Lundqvist* [1991] 2 WLR 280 at 290.
2   *Tarasov v Nassif* (11 February 1994, unreported), CA.

2.247   In *Den Norske Bank ASA v Antonatos*[1] the Court of Appeal thought that in cases where possible self-incrimination issues existed, it would also be inappropriate to make disclosure orders under asset-freezing injunctions and orders for cross-examination on disclosure affidavits.[2] By analogy, a judgment debtor ordered to attend court pursuant to Pt 71 proceedings could therefore potentially invoke the privilege against self-incrimination to refuse to answer questions.

One way round this possible obstacle to obtaining information may be to seek an assurance from the CPS that they would not use information disclosed in the examination for the purposes of prosecuting the person who made the disclosure. In *United Norwest Co-operatives Ltd v Johnstone*[3] the Court of Appeal considered the right of defendants to civil fraud proceedings to invoke the privilege against self-incrimination in the context of an order for a disclosure ancillary to Anton Piller and Mareva injunctions. The Court held that where the CPS had given an assurance that it would not use the information disclosed for the purposes of prosecuting the defendant, and in reliance on that assurance or a court order made as a result of it the defendant disclosed self-incriminatory information, the court would not assist the CPS to obtain the information by the exercise of its statutory powers. However, where no assurance had been given by the CPS and the CPS had not consented to the order for disclosure in these terms, the court would not withhold its assistance.

1   [1998] 3 All ER 74 at 90, CA.
2   See also *Cobra Golf Inc v Rata* [1998] Ch 109 at 126–128 in relation to search orders.
3   (1994) Times, 24 February, CA.

2.248   The privilege against self-incrimination may potentially therefore frustrate a judgment creditor's attempts to enforce his judgment using the Pt 71 procedure (see also para 2.250). A further consideration is that a judgment creditor who obtains information from a judgment debtor as to his assets which is self-incriminatory would need to be mindful of the provisions of PCA 2002 (see para 2.93) which criminalises, among other things, the acquisition, use and possession of criminal property.[1]

1   PCA 2002, s 329. Criminal property is defined in PCA 2002, s 340 and includes documents and information.

Human rights

2.249   As has been noted in Chapter 1 The European Convention for the Protection of Human Rights and Fundamental Freedoms (ECHR) may also potentially impact upon the operation of Pt 71. The ECHR now forms part of English law following the entry into force of the Human Rights Act 1998 (see further Chapter 1). Those arts of the ECHR which might potentially be infringed by the provisions of Pt 71 are art 6 (the right to a fair trial) and art 8 (the right to respect for private and family life).

ECHR, art 6

2.250   As regards art 6, the possibility that the Pt 71 procedure could lead to a defendant incriminating himself would seem to be the most likely potential infringement of art 6. In *Saunders v UK*[1] the European Court of Human Rights held that evidence obtained under compulsion cannot be used in subsequent criminal proceedings. As has been noted in para 2.243, a number of statutes have been amended to provide that, whilst the privilege against self-incrimination is abrogated in respect of disclosure in civil proceedings, the evidence will not be admissible in subsequent criminal proceedings. Case law in relation to search orders and freezing injunctions suggests that a court would be unlikely to order a judgment debtor to answer a question put to him in an oral examination under Pt 71 where self-incrimination issues may arise.[2] The likelihood of an art 6 infringement during the course of Pt 71 proceedings therefore seems remote.

1   (1997) 23 EHRR 313.
2   See para 2.247.

ECHR, art 8

2.251   Under art 8 ECHR, everyone has the right to respect for his private and family life, his home and his correspondence. A procedure for compulsory examination and production of documents could therefore potentially infringe this right.

2.252   However, the right to respect for private and family life under art 8 is qualified. The second part of art 8 states:

'There shall be no interference by a public authority with the exercise of this right, except such as is in accordance with the law and is necessary in a democratic society in the interests of national security, public safety or the economic well-being of the country, for the prevention of ... crime ... or for the protection of the rights and freedom of others.'

2.253   A number of these qualifications may be relevant in the context of Pt 71 proceedings. A system whereby judgment creditors can recover sums rightfully due to them by recalcitrant judgment debtors is likely to be necessary 'in the economic well-being of the country'. Similarly, an infringement of the judgment debtor's right to privacy in relation to his assets is likely to be necessary to protect the rights and freedom of the judgment creditor to obtain the sums rightfully due to him. The Strasbourg jurisprudence recognises as a necessary incident of the right to a fair trial the right of a judgment creditor to obtain effective enforcement of his judgment (see further Chapter 1).

2.254   One possible situation where art 8 infringements may apply is where an oral examination is sought in relation to a judgment debtor who has been ordered to pay a judgment debt by instalments and is up to date with the schedule of payments. While the Pt 71 procedure is available in such circumstances, it is less clear that the infringement to the judgment debtor's right to privacy would be justified in such circumstances, not least since the court would be likely to have taken the judgment debtor's circumstances into account in ordering payment by instalments. In any event, instalment orders are unlikely to apply in high value commercial litigation.

2.255   As has been noted at the start of this chapter, the notes to the White Book[1] submit that the Pt 71 procedure is compliant with Strasbourg jurisprudence. To date there have been no challenges to the Pt 71 procedure from a human rights perspective, though some commentators[2] have suggested the procedure is not compliant. Whether such challenges will follow remains to be seen.

1   Civil Procedure 2004, vol 1, para 71.8.1.
2   See eg 'The Legality of Debt Enforcement', a discussion paper published by Joseph Jacob of the London School of Economics.

Costs

2.256 Where the court makes an order under Pt 71 to obtain information from a judgment debtor, the judgment creditor will only be entitled to fixed costs for the application unless the court orders otherwise.[1] The amount of fixed costs are the court fee of £50[2] together with the judgment creditor's fixed costs shown in the table to CPR 45.6. These fixed costs will be £15 for each half hour (or part) where the questioning takes place before a court officer. Where the questioning takes place before a judge, the judge may summarily assess the costs. In addition, CPR 45.5 prescribes a fee of £15 for effecting personal service of the order to attend court on the judgment debtor. As the notes to the White Book observe,[3] where process servers are instructed to effect service, this figure is likely to be substantially less than the fee charged for doing so.

[1]   CPR 45.1(2)(c).
[2]   CPR 45.1(3) allows court fees to be recovered in addition to any fixed costs set out in CPR Pt 45. Court fees have already been considered in para 2.144.
[3]   Civil Procedure 2004, vol 1, para 71.3.3.

2.257 Where the application is entirely straightforward and the amounts in issue are relatively modest, the court's award of costs is likely to be confined to fixed costs. However, in a complex case, where the examination takes place before a High Court Judge, the successful judgment creditor should seek an order at the hearing in relation to the recovery of those additional costs which are outside the fixed costs regime.

2.258 The general rule is that the court should make a summary assessment of the costs at the conclusion of a hearing lasting not more than one day unless there is good reason not to.[1] Each party who intends to claim costs should prepare a written statement of costs which should follow as closely as possible Form N260. The statement must be signed by the party or his legal representative and must be filed at court with copies served on any party from whom recovery of costs is sought. Filing and service must be done as soon as possible and in any event at least 24 hours before the date fixed for the hearing.[2]

[1]   See Pt 44.
[2]   General rules about costs are set out in Pt 44 and the accompanying Practice Direction, which should be referred to for the specific provisions.

Reform

2.259 The effectiveness of the oral examination procedure has been criticised for a number of reasons. These centre on three key aspects of the procedure:

(a) the degree of co-operation required from the judgment debtor to attend court at the outset;
(b) the fact that the judgment debtor may outwardly seem to comply with the order by providing answers, but the answers may be incomplete, unhelpful, untruthful or may otherwise defeat the judgment creditor's purpose; and
(c) the inability of either the court or the judgment creditor to verify the information given by the judgment debtor at the oral examination.

2.260   A number of proposals for reform of the oral examination procedure were considered as part of the Lord Chancellor's Department's[1] review of the civil enforcement system, which began in March 1998 and concluded with the government's White Paper in March 2003 'Effective Enforcement', setting out the government proposals for reform of civil enforcement law (see further Chapter 1).

[1]   Now known as the Department of Constitutional Affairs.

First Phase of the Enforcement Review

2.261   The First Phase of the Enforcement Review[1] made various recommendations for reform of the oral examination procedure. A number of these (such as the introduction of a standard oral examination questionnaire and the replacement of postal service of the order to attend court with the requirement for personal service) have been implemented with the introduction of Pt 71 under the Civil Procedure (Amendment No 4) Rules 2001.[2] However, some proposals remain recommendations. The most important of these is the proposal for the introduction of Data Disclosure Orders (DDOs), whereby the court would have the power to require *third parties* to provide information about a judgment debtor's assets to aid the enforcement process.[3]

[1]   Report on the First Phase of the Enforcement Review, July 2000.
[2]   SI 2001/2792.
[3]   See Chapter 3 of the March 2003 White Paper on Effective Enforcement. At present, while a court may order a defendant to sign a letter of instruction authorising certain individuals to obtain information relating to his assets from third parties such as banks, the third party will not be compelled to comply. Such letters are primarily sought during the course of litigation in conjunction with freezing injunctions to prevent a defendant from dissipating his assets, rather than at the enforcement stage.

2.262   The DDO proposal specifically responds to two of the key criticisms of the oral examination procedure, namely that it requires a high degree of co-operation from the judgment debtor and that there is no way for the judgment creditor to check the information obtained from the judgment debtor.

2.263   The March 2003 White Paper on Effective Enforcement envisages a number of post-judgment situations in which a DDO might be available, although the possibility of obtaining a DDO before judgment was rejected,[1] largely on the grounds that to allow a judgment creditor to ask for such information before a judgment would raise concerns in the areas of data protection and human rights. Notably, the White Paper envisages that a DDO should be available where either the judgment creditor or the judge believes that the judgment debtor has lied on oath at the oral examination hearing. Potentially, this not only provides a viable alternative to prosecuting the judgment debtor for perjury but may also mean that the judgment debtor will be less inclined to perjure himself in the first place (since he will know that a DDO could result in the truth being obtained).

[1]   See further Consultation Paper No 4, Chapter 4 ('The Oral Examination'), para 4.17.

2.264   In order to limit any abuses and ensure the process is compliant with data protection and human rights concerns it is not proposed that information received pursuant to a DDO will be released directly to the judgment creditor. Rather the court will consider the information and the results of the DDO will be sent to the judgment creditor in a form which will also indicate the enforcement methods which the court considers are available. It is not intended that the DDO should result in any automatic enforcement rights; the judgment creditor will need to take enforcement steps on the basis of the information supplied pursuant to the DDO.

2.265 Primary legislation would be needed to implement the DDO proposals contained in the White Paper. At the time of writing, inquiries at the Department of Constitutional Affairs revealed that there are plans to put legislation before Parliament but it is not clear when this will happen.

APPENDIX I

Useful contact details

2.266

Central Registry of Administration and Winding Up Petitions
(Companies Court)
Companies Court General Office
Room TM 2.09
The Royal Courts of Justice
Thomas More Building
The Strand
London WC2A 2LL
Telephone: 020 7947 7328

Civil Aviation Authority
Aircraft Registration Section
CAA House
45-59 Kingsway
London WC2B 6TE
Telephone: 020 7453 6666
Fax: 020 7453 6670
www.caa.co.uk

Companies House
www.companieshouse.co.uk

Cardiff Information Centre
Crown Way
Cardiff CF14 3UZ
DX 33050 Cardiff
Telephone: 0870 333 3636
Fax: 029 2038 0900
Opening hours: Monday to Friday 9.00 am - 5.00 pm

London Information Centre
PO Box 29019
21 Bloomsbury Street
London WC1B 3XD
Telephone: 0870 333 3636
Fax: 029 2038 0900
Opening hours: Monday to Friday 8.30 am - 5.00 pm

Edinburgh Information Centre
37 Castle Terrace
Edinburgh EH1 2EB
Telephone: 0870 333 3636
Fax: 029 2038 0900
Opening hours: Monday to Friday 9.00 am - 5.00 pm

Limited Liability Partnerships Inquiry Line
Telephone: 029 2038 0744

Dun & Bradstreet
Customer Service Department
Westminster House
Portland Street
Manchester M1 3HU
Telephone: 0870 243 2344
http://dbuk.dnb.com/english/default.htm

DVLA
Vehicle Record Enquiries
Vehicle Customer Services
DVLA
Swansea SA99 1AJ
www.dvla.gov.uk

HPI Limited
Dolphin House
New Street
Salisbury
Wiltshire SP1 2PH
Telephone: 01722 422 422
www.hpicheck.com

Insolvency Service
Bankruptcy Public Search Room
The Insolvency Service
4th Floor, East Wing
45-46 Stephenson Street
Birmingham B2 4UZ
Telephone: 0121 698 4000 (general enquiries)
Fax: 0121 698 4407
www.insolvency.gov.uk

Land Charges Department
The Superintendent
Land Charges Department
Search Section
Plumer House
Tailyour Road
Crownhill
Plymouth PL6 5HY
DX 8249 Plymouth (3)
Telephone: 0870 908 8063
Fax: 01752 636699

Lloyd's Register
Information Services
Lloyd's Register
71 Fenchurch Street
London EC3M 4BS
Telephone: 020 7423 2475
Fax: 020 7423 2039
Email: ageinfo@lr.org
www.lr.org

Lloyd's Marine Intelligence Unit
Sheepen Place
Colchester
Essex CO3 3LP
Telephone: 01206 772410
Fax: 01206 772580
Email: enquiries@lloydsmiu.com
www.lloydsmiu.com/tracker

Mutual Societies Registry
Mutual Societies Search and Copy
9th Floor
Financial Services Authority
25 The North Colonnade
Canary Wharf
London E14 5HS
Helpline: 020 7066 4916
Fax: 020 7066 4909
Email: mutual.societies@fsa.gov.uk
www.fsa.gov.uk/industry/psc_ms.html

Registry of Shipping and Seaman
MCA Cardiff
Ground Floor
Anchor Court
Keen Road
Cardiff CF24 5JW
Telephone: 029 2044 8800
Fax: 029 2044 8820
www.mcga.gov.uk

Registry Trust Ltd
Registry of County Court Judgments
173-175 Cleveland Street
London W1T 6QR
Telephone: 020 7380 0133
www.registry-trust.org.uk

APPENDIX 2

Company information available from Companies House

Information	Details
Basic company details available from Companies House website, www.companieshouse.co.uk	Includes: • Company number • Company type • Date of incorporation • Registered address • Previous registered names • Accounting reference date • Date last annual return is made up to and next return date • Date last accounts made up to and next accounts date • Branch details and oversea company information
Company appointments (CA 1985, s 288)	Details of the company's director(s) and secretary[1]
Personal appointments (CA 1985, ss 288-289)	Details of any other directorships held or previously held by the director(s)
Charges register (CA 1985, s 401)	Brief details of all registrable charges and whether the charges have been fully or partially satisfied
Insolvency details (See para 2.35 for statutory references)	Details of: • Appointment of a receiver or manager • Appointment of an administrative receiver • Voluntary resolutions to wind up the company • Orders for the winding up of the company • Appointment of a liquidator
Company Accounts (CA 1985, s 242)	Includes: • Company's annual accounts • Directors' report • Directors' remuneration report (for quoted companies only)
Company Annual Return (CA 1985, ss 363-365)	Includes: • Registered office • Name and address of every director of the company and other prescribed details about the director(s) • Details of share capital and list of shareholders • Changes since last annual return

[1]   It should be noted that under CA 1985, s 723B, a serving or prospective director may apply to the Secretary of State for a confidentiality order where making his residential address available to members of the public is likely to expose him, or a person who lives with him, to a serious risk of violence or intimidation. Where a confidentiality order is in place, the residential address of a director will not be available from Companies House.

APPENDIX 3

LLP information available from Companies House

2.268   [Note that all statutory references in this table are to the legislation as modified by the Limited Liability Partnerships Regulations 2001.]

Information	Details
Basic LLP details available from Companies House website, www.copmanieshouse.co.uk	Includes: • LLP number • LLP type • Date of incorporation • Registered address • Previous registered names • Accounting reference date • Date last annual return is made up to and next return date • Date last accounts made up to and next accounts date
LLP appointments (CA 1985, s 288)	Details of the LLP's members and designated members
Charges register (CA 1985, s 401)	Brief details of all registrable charges and whether the charges have been fully or partially satisfied
Insolvency details (See para 2.35 for statutory references unless the item is footnoted to the contrary)	Details of: • Appointment of a receiver or manager • Appointment of administrative receiver • Voluntary winding up of the LLP[1] • Orders for the winding up of the LLP • Appointment of a liquidator
LLP Accounts (CA 1985, s 242)	Includes: • LLP's annual accounts • Auditors' report
LLP Annual Return (CA 1985, ss 363-364)	Includes: • Registered office • Name and address of every member of the LLP and who are designated members • Changes since last annual return

[1]   This is provided for by the modified IA 1986, s 84(3). CA 1985, s 380 has not been applied to LLPs.

Third party debt orders

INTRODUCTION

3.1 The fact that virtually every person, body corporate or human being, maintains a bank account makes the third party debt order process one of the most useful methods of execution available to a judgment creditor. A bank account in credit is a debt due by the bank to its customer. Disclosure during the course of litigation or the use of orders to obtain information from judgment debtors (see Chapter 2) may provide the judgment creditor with information on the judgment debtor's bank details. The third party debt order procedure allows a judgment creditor to apply to the court for an order that a third party (such as a bank) should discharge a debt it owes to the judgment debtor by direct payment to the judgment creditor.

3.2 There are two essential features of the process. First, a third party debt order is a proprietary remedy which operates by way of attachment against the property of the judgment debtor (namely the debt owed by the third party, which is a chose in action). The first stage of the process, the interim third party debt order, freezes the debt in the hands of the third party. Subject to any monetary limit specified in the order, the third party cannot pay the debt away without risk of having to pay it over again to the judgment creditor. The second essential feature of the process is that it extinguishes the debt owed. The final third party debt order obliges the third party, subject to any monetary limit specified in the order, to make payment to the judgment creditor and not to the judgment debtor. In making that payment, the third party is discharged from his debt to the judgment debtor.

3.3 The procedure for obtaining third party debt orders is set out in Pt 72 of the Civil Procedure Rules 1998 (CPR), which came into force as part of the 26th set of amendments to the CPR on 25 March 2002. The new procedural regime repealed and replaced the long-standing method of enforcement known as 'garnishee proceedings' detailed in Rules of the Supreme Court 1965 (RSC), Ord 49.[1] However, the historical antecedents of the third party debt order process go back much further in English legal history and have been traced to Roman occupation and beyond.[2] The provisions of RSC Ord 49 were derived from the Common Law Procedure Act 1854, ss 61-70,[3] which were themselves modelled on a procedure called 'foreign attachment' which existed in the Mayor's court in London and some other cities. The new regime is set out in straightforward, modern language but contains little, if any, material difference in the underlying rules. As the editorial introduction to Pt 72 observes, the basic purpose of third party debt orders remains unchanged.[4] As their Lordships have noted:[5]

> 'The straightforward language of Part 72 is deceptive. Its true nature cannot easily be understood without a knowledge of its history and antecedents.'

[1]　And in the County Court Rules 1981, Ord 30, which were also repealed and replaced.
[2]　See *London Corpn v Cox* (1867) LR 2 HL 239 at 256.
[3]　The procedure was subsequently contained in RSC Ord 45 scheduled to the Supreme Court of Judicature Act (1873) Amendment Act 1875.
[4]　Civil Procedure 2004, vol 1, para 72.0.2.
[5]　*Société Eram Shipping Company Ltd v Cie Internationale de Navigation* [2004] 1 AC 260 at 298, per Lord Millett.

3.4　Two decisions of the House of Lords in June 2003 have clarified how this venerable procedure should operate in the light of modern, multi-jurisdictional banking operations and practices. It had always been clear that a third party who owed a debt to the judgment debtor must be within jurisdiction of the court for a third party debt order to be made against it.[1] However, following what must now be seen as erroneous obiter dicta by the Court of Appeal in two cases in the late 1980s, *SCF Finance Co Ltd v Masri (No 3)*[2] and *Interpool Ltd v Galani*,[3] the received wisdom was that there was no limitation that the third party debt must also be properly recoverable within the jurisdiction.[4] As will be seen,[5] following their Lordships' decisions in *Société Eram Shipping Company Ltd v Cie Internationale de Navigation*[6] and *Kuwait Oil Tanker Company SAK v UBS AG*,[7] it now seems clear that judgment creditors *cannot* use the third party debt order process to enforce against foreign debts.

[1]　See CPR 72.1(1), which mirrors the requirement set out in the Common Law Procedure Act 1854, s 61 that 'any other Person is indebted to the Judgment Debtor, and is *within the Jurisdiction*'. (Emphasis added.)
[2]　[1987] QB 1028.
[3]　[1988] QB 738.
[4]　See eg the former notes to RSC Ord 49: Supreme Court Practice 1999, vol 1, para 49.1.12.
[5]　See paras 3.67–3.78.
[6]　[2004] 1 AC 260.
[7]　[2003] UKHL 31.

Part 72: a two-stage process

3.5　Part 72 sets out a two-stage process for applying for a third party debt order.

Interim third party debt order

First, the judgment creditor must make an application to the court for an interim third party debt order (formerly a garnishee order nisi). The application notice should be in the prescribed form and contain the prescribed information. The application may be made without notice and will initially be dealt with by the judge without a hearing. If the judge makes an interim third party debt order, the judgment creditor must then serve the order on the third party and the judgment debtor.

Final third party debt order

Following service of the interim order a hearing takes place to consider whether a final third party debt order (formerly a garnishee order absolute) should be made. Both the third party and the judgment debtor may attend the hearing if they wish to object to the court making the final order. If the court makes a final third party debt order, the third party must pay over the amount specified in the order to the judgment creditor. The effect of that payment is to extinguish the debt owed by the third party to the judgment debtor to the extent of the amount paid over to the judgment creditor.

3.6 The steps which must be taken at each stage of the procedure, the obligations which arise and the effect of those steps are considered in detail in this chapter.

DEBT OWED BY A THIRD PARTY

3.7 Before making the application, the judgment creditor should consider whether the debt he seeks to attach falls into a category which is attachable under Pt 72. While bank and building society accounts are likely to provide the most fertile ground for use of the procedure, with certain exceptions, a judgment creditor can apply for a third party debt order in relation to 'any debt due or accruing due'[1] to the judgment debtor from a third party.

¹   CPR 72.2(1)(a).

Debt 'due or accruing due'

3.8 The relationship of creditor and debtor must exist between the judgment debtor and the third party in order for the procedure to be used. A third party debt order can only be used to attach money due to the judgment debtor. It cannot be used to enforce against any of the judgment debtor's other property.

3.9 The debt must be in existence at the date the interim third party debt order is made. Provided the debt is in existence, the fact that it is payable in the future[1] will not be a bar to its being attached under the third party debt order procedure. However, as an analysis of the case law shows:[2]

'It is very often difficult to distinguish between a case where a debt has not accrued and there is no actual debt, and the case where there is a debt debitum in praesenti solvendum in futuro.'

¹   Sometimes referred to in the case law as a debt 'debitum in praesenti solvendum in futuro'.
²   *Dunlop & Ranken Ltd v Hendall Steel Structures Ltd (Pitchers Ltd Garnishees)* [1957] 3 All ER 344 at 345.

Deferred payment

3.10 In *Tapp v Jones*[1] a judgment creditor sought to garnish sums payable to the judgment debtor under an agreement whereby the garnishee had agreed to pay to the judgment debtor a sum of money by monthly instalments of £10 each. The court considered what was the true construction of the Common Law Procedure Act 1854, s 61, forebear of Pt 72,[2] which permitted the attachment of 'all Debts owing or accruing'. Blackburn J stated:[3]

'It is evident that the legislature had in view both present debt and future debt, debita in praesenti, solvenda in futuro, for it speaks in the earlier part of the section of "debts owing and accruing".'

He continued:

'I have come to the conclusion that the true construction is that there is power to make an order against the garnishee for payment of his debts as and when they become payable, instead of making a fresh order as each falls due.'

[1]   (1874-75) LR 10 QB 591.
[2]   See para 3.3.
[3]   (1874-75) LR 10 QB 591 at 592–593.

3.11   Field J concurred. Accordingly, an order could be made for payment of the accruing debt as and when it became payable by the garnishee. It was not necessary to wait until the debt had actually become payable before making the order, or to make a fresh order as each instalment fell due.

Interest in a trust

3.12   By contrast, in *Webb v Stenton*[1] the Court of Appeal had to consider whether a judgment debtor's life interest in the income arising from a fund vested in trustees was attachable. The income was payable half-yearly in February and August. At the time the judgment creditor applied for a garnishee order to attach the judgment debtor's share of the income in the hands of the trustees (in November), the last half-yearly payment had been made and the trustees held no income from the trust property.

[1]   (1882-83) LR 11 QBD 518.

3.13   On this occasion, the court had to construe the words of Ord 45, r 2 of the Judicature Act of 1873 (which had replaced the Common Law Procedure Act 1854, s 61, but was in the same terms as its predecessor, providing for the attachment of 'all debts owing or accruing' to the judgment debtor). Brett MR considered the meaning of 'accruing debt':[1]

'Now can it mean any debt which may at any future time arise between the judgment debtor and the person sought to be made a garnishee, there being no contract at that time between the judgment debtor and such person, or anything which can make any relation of any kind, legal or equitable, between them? To state the proposition is to shew its absurdity. Then can it be this, that it may be a debt which there is some probability may in future arise? Who can say where there is nothing out of which a debt can be said in law to arise, that it is probable that a debt may arise, as for instance a probability that the parties will make a contract. If it is not a debt it will not do. It must be something which the law recognises as a debt.'

[1]   (1882-83) LR 11 QBD 518 at 523.

3.14 As regards the relationship between the trustees and the judgment debtor (as cestui que trust), until money came into the hands of the trustees then no debt existed between the trustees and the judgment debtor. Brett MR stated:[1]

'Therefore there are contingencies upon which no debt may ever arise, and all that can be said of it is, that it is probable that at the end of half-a-year money will come into the hands of the trustees, but until it does come into their hands, there is no debt existing between them and their cestui que trust.'

[1]   (1882-83) LR 11 QBD 518 at 525–526.

3.15 Fry LJ and Lindley LJ concurred, the latter stating:[1]

'I should say, apart from any authority, that a debt legal or equitable can be attached whether it be a debt owing or accruing; but it must be a debt, and a debt is a sum of money which is now payable or will become payable in the future by reason of a present obligation, debitum in presenti, solvendum in futuro. An accruing debt, therefore, is a debt not yet actually payable, but a debt which is represented by an existing obligation.'

[1]   (1882-83) LR 11 QBD 518 at 527.

3.16 *Webb v Stenton* was also followed in *Re Greenwood*,[1] where it was held that since a garnishee order absolute could only garnish a debt due, it could not operate as a forfeiture of a life interest in a trust. In *Re Sampson, Sampson v Sampson*[2] the court considered whether funds in the hands of trustees could be attached where the terms of the trust were that the judgment debtor's interest in the income from the trust arose only as it came into the hands of the trustees, following which it should be dealt with in one of two ways: if the judgment debtor had not done or suffered an act which would prevent his personal enjoyment of the income, that portion of the income should be paid to him; if he had, then it should be applied at the discretion of the trustees for the benefit of the judgment debtor's wife and children.

[1]   [1901] 1 Ch 887.
[2]   [1896] 1 Ch 630.

3.17 The court held that since at the time the trustees were served with the garnishee order nisi the judgment debtor had not done anything to deprive himself of the income from the trust, the wife had not become entitled to the benefit of the discretionary trust in her favour and the funds could be attached.

3.18 Where a judgment creditor therefore seeks to attach funds payable to the judgment debtor under the terms of a trust, only funds currently in the hands of the trustees will be attachable, not future income, and the terms of the trust will need to be examined to ascertain whether the judgment debtor is presently entitled to those funds.

Executors

3.19 Where judgment has been obtained against an executor of a deceased person's estate in their capacity as executor, the third party debt order procedure can be used to execute against debts owed to the estate.[1] A third party debt order can also be made against personal representatives where the deceased was indebted to the judgment debtor. However, care should be taken to address the order to the executors in their capacity as executors (and not personally).[2]

1   *Burton v Roberts* (1890) 29 LJ Exch 483.
2   *Stevens v Phelips* (1875) LR 10 Ch App 417.

Bills of exchange

3.20   In *Hyam v Freeman*[1] the court made a garnishee order in respect of money which became payable on maturity of two bills of exchange. The order suspended execution until maturity and an injunction was also granted to restrain the judgment debtor negotiating the bills in the interim. The only reported instance of this case is a short summary in the Solicitors' Journal of December 1890, so Pollock J's reasoning behind the judgment is not detailed. However, it is notable that under Bills of Exchange Act 1882, s 3, a bill of exchange is an unconditional order in writing to pay a certain sum, in this instance at maturity. Like the agreement for payment by instalments in *Webb v Stenton*, a bill of exchange therefore represents an existing obligation and payment is not contingent on any supervening event.

1   (1890) 35 Sol Jo 87.

Rent

3.21   Rent is attachable.[1] Where the judgment debtor is a landlord, particularly in the case of commercial premises, it may be worth considering whether there is attachable rent. However, although rent accrues from day to day and is apportionable accordingly under the Apportionment Act 1870, s 2 , it cannot be attached unless it is actually payable by the tenant on the date the interim order was served.[2] Future rent *cannot* be attached using the third party debt order procedure.[3] It is likely to be more appropriate to appoint a receiver by way of equitable execution to receive rent payable to a judgment debtor (see Chapter 6).

1   *Mitchell v Lee* (1867) LR 2 QB 259.
2   *Barnett v Eastman* (1898) 67 LJQB 517.
3   In contrast to a debt payable by instalments as in *Tapp v Jones*, future rent may be probable but is not certain. See *Barnett v Eastman* (1898) 67 LJQB 517.

Unascertained debts

3.22   In *O'Driscoll v Manchester Insurance Committee*,[1] the Court of Appeal had to consider whether the fact that the amount of a debt was not ascertained should prevent a garnishee order nisi being made. The judgment debtor was one of a panel of doctors who had done work under an agreement with the insurance committee. The committee had received funds with which to pay the panel doctors under their contracts with them and were indebted to the judgment debtor in respect of his work. However, the committee's liability to pay the panel doctors was limited to the amount it received from the National Insurance Commissioners and the exact amount owed to the judgment debtor would have to be calculated in terms of his proportionate share of the panel fund.

1   [1915] 3 KB 499. See also *Lucy v Wood* [1884] WN 58, in which the court held that given the fact that the judgment creditor is reliant on the judgment debtor for information about the judgment debt 'it would be an absolute denial of justice if he could not get this order without swearing to the amount of the debt'.

3.23   The court found that funds received by the committee to pay the judgment debtor were attachable, even though the precise sum payable to him had not yet been ascertained. Swinfen Eady LJ held that although the amount owing to the judgment debtor had not yet been ascertained:[1]

'There was, however, no contingency which could happen to deprive him of his right to payment on the figures being finally adjusted ... there was a debt owing or accruing from the Insurance Committee to the panel doctors. It was not presently payable, the amount not being ascertained, but it was a debt to which the doctors were absolutely and not contingently entitled. The only question was as to the amount of the debt, the debt not being payable until the amount had been ascertained.'

1   [1915] 3 KB 499 at 511–512.

3.24   Phillimore LJ and Bankes LJ concurred and, in an often-cited passage, the latter stated:[1]

'It is well established that "debts owing or accruing" include debts debita in praesenti solvenda in futuro. The matter is well put in the Annual Practice, 1915[2], p.808: "But the distinction must be borne in mind between the case where there is an existing debt, payment whereof is deferred and the case where both the debt and its payment rest in the future. In the former case there is an attachable debt, in the latter case there is not." If, for instance, a sum of money is payable on the happening of a contingency, there is no debt owing or accruing. But the mere fact that the amount is not ascertained does not show that there is no debt.'

1   [1915] 3 KB 499 at 516–517.
2   The forerunner of the White Book.

Judgment debts

3.25   A judgment debt owed by a third party to the judgment debtor can be attached under the third party debt order procedure.[1] However, the damages must be liquidated damages at the time the interim order is made, whereas unliquidated damages cannot be attached.[2]

1   *Dawson v Preston (Law Society, Garnishees)* [1955] 3 All ER 314, in which there was held to be an attachable debt payable by the Law Society to a legally aided plaintiff in respect of damages he had won which had been paid to the Law Society, notwithstanding the fact that that debt could not yet be paid because the amount of the charge on the damages in favour of the Law Society in respect of costs had not yet been determined.

²   *Jones v Thompson* (1858) EB & E 63, in which the court refused to attach an amount for which the judgment debtor had obtained unliquidated damages since although a verdict had been given in the judgment debtor's favour, the judgment had not yet been signed and thus there was not yet a debt due. Crompton J held: 'I have always acted on the principle that it is not enough to shew that it is very probable that there soon will be a debt, but that it must be shewn that there is a debt, though it need not be yet due.' Note that this case may now be of limited relevance given the modern practice on when a judgment is effective (see para 7.11). See also *Holt v Hodgson* (1889) 24 QBD 103.

Contingent events

3.26 It was key to the court's ruling in *O'Driscoll*¹ that it found that the third party (the insurance committee) was in fact indebted to the judgment debtor at the date the garnishee order nisi was served. Where the obligation to pay is contingent on another event taking place, there is only an attachable debt once that condition has been met. In *Dunlop & Ranken Ltd v Hendall Steel Structures Ltd (Pitchers Ltd, Garnishees)*,² judgment creditors of sub-contractors nominated under a standard form RIBA³ building contract sought to garnish monies in the hands of the principal contractors. The judgment creditors claimed that sums were owed to the sub-contractors by the principal contractors in respect of work done under the building contract.

¹   See paras 3.22–3.25.
²   [1957] 3 All ER 343.
³   Royal Institute of British Architects.

3.27 The court noted that it was often difficult to distinguish between cases where there was a debt accruing and where no debt existed¹ and cited the passage from *O'Driscoll* quoted to at para 3.24. The court found that under the terms of the RIBA building contract the sub-contractor had no right to receive any sum of money at all from the principal contractor until a certificate had been issued by the architect and referred to a statement in the notes to Ord 45, r 1 in the Annual Practice 1957,² which stated:

> 'In the case, for example, of a building contract in the RIBA form, where the builder is paid on the certificate of the architect, it is plain that money in the hands of the building owner cannot be attached until a certificate is issued, and then only for the amount mentioned in that certificate.'

¹   See the quote from Lord Goddard CJ referred to at para 3.9.
²   The forerunner of the White Book.

3.28 Accordingly, the court held that until a certificate was issued, the sub-contractors had no right to be paid and there was no debt.

3.29 The decision in *Dunlop* appears to rest on the court's construction of the contract. It held that the fact that payment under the contract was to be made 'in accordance with the certificates' issued by the architect meant that payment should be made 'if and when a certificate is given'.¹ The architect's certificate was thus a condition precedent to the debt becoming due.

¹   [1957] 3 All ER 344 at 348. In fact no written contract was entered into between the sub-contractors and the principal contractors but that the RIBA form of contract clearly

contemplated this should have been entered into and that the principal terms of the RIBA contract would be incorporated.

3.30 The decision in *Dunlop* was distinguished in the Canadian case of *Sandy v Yukon Construction Co Ltd and Rush and Tompkins Construction Ltd*,[1] which also concerned a judgment creditor seeking to garnish amounts due to a sub-contractor from the principal contractor in respect of work done under a building contract. The Canadian garnishee rules were equivalent to the English rules in permitting the attachment of 'debts, if any, due or accruing due' and the court considered both the *O'Driscoll* and *Dunlop* cases. As in *Dunlop*, no architect's certificate in relation to the work done by the sub-contractor had been issued in accordance with the terms of the tender and it was argued that, as a result, no debt had come into existence.

[1]   (1961) 26 DLR (2d) 253.

3.31 The Alberta Supreme Court rejected that argument and found that the giving of the certificate was not a condition precedent to the debt coming into existence. It first held that an examination of the terms of the contract did not support the interpretation that the contract was an entire contract in which no debt could arise until the whole work was done since the contract provided for interim payments with only the final payment being retained until the work was complete and accepted. Johnson JA went on:[1]

'There is nothing to suggest in the granting or refusing of a certificate that there is 'the happening of any contingency' (mentioned by Bankes LJ in the *O'Driscoll* case, supra) preventing the establishment of a debt as the work is done, although, of course, the absence of the certificate in most cases will prevent the contractor from being able to sue. I say in most cases, for there are cases where the Courts have permitted recovery even where no certificate has been given.'

[1]   (1961) 26 DLR (2d) 254 at 258.

3.32 The cases Johnson JA referred to were a decision of the Canadian Supreme Court in *Oshawa v Brennan Paving Co*[1] and a decision of the House of Lords in *Panamena Europea Navigacion Compania v Frederick Leyland & Co*.[2] Johnson JA observed:[3]

'It is inherent, I think, in both of these judgments that a prior debt existed before the certificate came into existence and that the certificate requirement merely postponed the payment until the certificate had been given. If the indebtedness was conditional upon the certificate, it would have been impossible for the Courts to have given the judgments they did in these cases.'

Accordingly, he concluded a debt was owed to the sub-contractor in *Sandy* which could be attached by garnishee proceedings and the judgment creditor could apply to the court for a determination of the amount of that debt. However, it is worth noting that the *Panamena* case concerned a contract for the repair of a ship and there were differences between the court's construction of the role of the surveyor in that case and the role of the architect in *Dunlop*.

[1]   [1955] 1 DLR 321.

²   [1947] AC 428.
³   (1961) 26 DLR (2d) 254 at 259.

3.33   It therefore seems that in all cases where a judgment creditor seeks to attach a debt due to a judgment debtor under this type of building contract, the contract concerned will need to be carefully interpreted to ascertain whether delivery of the architect's certificate (or equivalent document) is a condition precedent on which the existence of the debt depends. The building industry has many standard form building contracts which contain complex series of interrelated provisions setting out the rights and obligations of the parties by reference to decisions of an architect, engineer or other third party. Each case will turn on its own facts.

3.34   Where the judgment debtor could sue the third party to recover the debt, it is clear there is an attachable debt. However, this is not an infallible test. Where the money is not payable until maturity of a bond, or the requisite date for the payment of the next instalment of a debt has not yet fallen, such analysis sheds little light on the question of whether there is an attachable debt.

Debts created after service of the interim order

3.35   In *Heppenstall v Jackson and Barclays Bank Ltd (Garnishees)*¹ Barclays were served with a garnishee order nisi attaching all debts owed by the bank to the judgment debtor on the date of service. In between the date of service of the order nisi and the date of the hearing of the application, the judgment debtor paid further sums into his account. The Court of Appeal held that there was clear authority *'that a garnishee order attaches no debts which do not exist at the moment when the order is made and served.'*² If the judgment creditor wished to attach subsequent debts, he should have issued a further application.

¹   [1939] 1 KB 585.
²   [1939] 1 KB 585 at 592.

Bank and building society accounts

General

3.36   The fact that Pt 72 contains specific rules which apply only to third party banks and building societies served with an interim third party debt order¹ recognises that it is the ubiquitous nature of bank accounts that renders this method of enforcement so useful to the judgment creditor.

¹   See further paras 3.123–3.133.

3.37   Before a credit balance on a bank account becomes payable (ie a debt due) to a customer, the customer must first have made a demand for payment. However, in *N Joachimson v Swiss Bank Corporation*¹ the court held that service of a garnishee order nisi (now an interim third party debt order) constitutes such demand.²

¹   [1921] 3 KB 110.
²   In *Rekstin v Severo Sibirsko Gosudarstvennoe Akcionernoe Obschuestvo Komseverput; and Bank for Russian Trade Ltd* [1933] 1 KB 47, the court held that service of the garnishee

order nisi operates to revoke an account holder's instructions to transfer funds which had not been fully carried out. See further paras 3.110–3.111.

3.38 *Joachimson* is also authority for rendering current accounts liable to attachment. The Supreme Court Act 1981 (SCA 1981), s 40 and the County Courts Act 1984 (CCA 1984), s 108 extend the types of accounts which can be attached to deposit accounts[1] and withdrawable share accounts.

[1] However, note the anomalous position of National Savings Bank deposit accounts, which cannot be attached using the third party debt order procedure. See further para 3.80–3.81.

3.39 Under CPR 72.2(3) and SCA 1981, ss 40(2) and 40(3) (and equivalent provisions in CCA 1984, s 108), various prescribed conditions which must otherwise be met before money can be withdrawn from an account may be disregarded in third party debt order proceedings. These include any prior condition that:

(a) a receipt for money deposited in the account be produced;
(b) notice be given;
(c) a personal application be made; or
(d) a deposit or share account book be produced.

3.40 As will be seen[1], the judgment creditor must, where possible, give details in the application notice of the name and address of the branch at which the judgment debtor's account is believed to be held and the account number.[2]

[1] See paras 3.90–3.94.
[2] Case law previously stated that a garnishee order nisi would not attach the balance of a bank account unless it correctly stated the name of the account as it appears in the books of the bank. Where the judgment debtor has and operates an account in a name other than his own, that name must appear in the order. See *Koch v Mineral Ore Syndicate* (1910) 54 Sol Jo 600 and para 3.93.

Foreign currency accounts

3.41 A debt held in a foreign currency account within the jurisdiction is also attachable. *Choice Investments Ltd v Jeromnimon*[1] sets out the machinery by which a debt payable in England and Wales in a foreign currency should be attached to satisfy an English sterling judgment:

(a) As soon as reasonably practicable after service of the interim order, the bank should ascertain (at its then normal buying rate of exchange against sterling) the amount of foreign currency that would, if converted at that rate, equal the amount of judgment debt and costs. That amount of foreign currency in the account should then be attached by a 'stop order' on the requisite amount of currency.
(b) As soon as the final order has been served, the bank should purchase (at its normal buying rate of exchange against sterling) the sterling equivalent of the attached amount of foreign currency (or, if the exchange rate has changed, so much as by that date would be equal to the sterling judgment debt and costs), and should pay that amount of sterling into court or to the judgment creditor.
(c) The bank should also inform the court of the amount of foreign currency attached and the rate of exchange used so that the terms of the final order can be adapted to reflect this procedure, namely by ordering the bank to pay the sterling equivalent

of the attached amount of foreign currency or the judgment debt and costs, whichever is less.[2]

1   [1981] QB 149.

2   The reasoning behind this adaptation of the wording of the final order is that if between the date of the attachment and the date of the final order exchange rate fluctuations are such that the attached amount of foreign currency is now more than enough to meet the sterling judgment debt and costs, the bank must release the balance of the foreign currency to the judgment debtor. Alternatively, if exchange rate fluctuations mean that the attached amount of currency is now less than the sterling judgment debt and costs, the bank is not prejudiced since it will be ordered to pay whichever is the lesser of the two.

Monies held as agent for others

3.42   In *Hancock v Smith*[1] a judgment creditor sought to attach a bank balance held in the name of the judgment debtor, a stockbroker. All the money paid into the account represented funds received by the stockbroker on behalf of clients. The court held that execution can only take effect on property which the debtor has a right to dispose of for his own purposes,[2] and thus the account could not be attached.

1   [1889] LR 41 Ch D 456.

2   See also *Roberts v Death* (1881-82) LR 8QBD 319, discussed further in para 3.156.

Joint debts

3.43   Where a debt is due to the judgment debtor jointly with another person it cannot be attached under the third party debt order procedure.[1]

1   Unless that other person is a joint judgment debtor. See para 3.49, n 1.

3.44   In *MacDonald v The Tacquah Gold Mines Company*,[1] the third party, The Tacquah Gold Mines Company, had covenanted by mortgage deed to pay a sum to two individuals (Horton and Fitzgerald) jointly and not to either of them alone. The plaintiff, who was a judgment creditor of Fitzgerald, sought to garnish Fitzgerald's share of the sum owing under the mortgage deed. The Court of Appeal unanimously held that the debt could not be garnished. Bowen LJ stated:[2]

'Where money is due on a covenant made with two persons jointly by which it is to be paid to such two jointly, no one of those two has any right to that money without the other of them.' Accordingly, the debt was 'therefore not a sum capable of being attached.'

1   (1884) 13 QBD 535.

2   (1884) 13 QBD 535 at 539.

3.45   Brett MR and Fry LJ concurred, the latter stating in his judgment:[1]

'I adhere to what was said by this Court in *Webb v Stenton* as to the word "indebted" in that rule.[2] Then can it be said that the defendant company was indebted to the judgment debtor when they were indebted to him and another person jointly only? It seems clearly it cannot, and that the words of the rule are not applicable to such a case. If they were, the result would be to enable a judgment creditor to attach a debt due to two persons in order to answer for the debt due to him from the judgment debtor alone, which would be altogether contrary to justice.'

1   (1884) 13 QBD 535 at 539.
2   Namely Ord 65 of the Rules of 1875, which then contained the rules relating to garnishee orders and mirrored the provisions of the earlier Common Law Procedure Act 1854.

3.46   *MacDonald* was followed in *Beasley v Roney*[1] and then in *Hirschorn v Evans*,[2] which considered the position in relation to joint bank accounts. A husband and wife opened a joint bank account with Barclays Bank upon terms that the signature of either would be a sufficient discharge for the repayment of money deposited with the bank. The judgment creditor sought to garnish the account as a debt owed to the husband, the judgment debtor. The Court of Appeal held (Greer LJ dissenting) that:[3]

'one has to look at the account as a whole, and, looking at the account as a whole, I think it is in the nature of a joint account on which the bank are jointly liable to both parties and, consequently, the garnishee summons is misconceived in stating that the bank are indebted to the said judgment debtor in the sum there stated, whereas, in reality, they are jointly indebted both to the judgment debtor and to his wife.'

1   [1891] 1 QB 509, in which Pollock B stated at 512 that the *MacDonald* case 'is a distinct authority to shew that the debt owing by a garnishee to a judgment debtor which can be attached to answer the judgment debt must be a debt due to the judgment debtor alone, and that where it is only due to him jointly with another it cannot be attached'.
2   [1938] 2 KB 801.
3   [1938] 2 KB 801 at 812–813.

3.47   Mackinnon LJ concurred and also held that:[1]

'As the account was in the joint names and not in the name of the judgment debtor, the bank took the view that the summons did not attach any part of their debt on the joint account, and they could not dishonour cheques drawn on the joint account. I think they were right in that view. Indeed, if they had dishonoured cheques, I think they could have been sued by the joint creditors for so doing.'

1   [1938] 2 KB 801 at 814.

3.48   Arguably, the wording of the Practice Direction to Pt 72 creates some ambiguity as to whether the third party debt order procedure can apply to joint accounts, since at para 3.1 it states:

'A bank or building society served with an interim third party debt order is only required by rule 72.6, *unless the order states otherwise,*

(1) to retain money in accounts held solely by the judgment debtor (or, if there are joint judgment debtors, accounts held jointly by them or solely by either or any of them);' (Emphasis added.)

3.49   It could be argued that the inclusion of the words 'unless the order states otherwise' means that the CPR envisages that it is possible to make third party debt orders in respect of joint accounts in certain circumstances. However, the fact that, immediately following these words, para 3.1(1) of the Practice Direction states in parentheses '(or, if there are joint judgment debtors, accounts held jointly by them or solely by either or any of them)' suggests that the better view is that the Practice Direction only envisages the attachment of a joint account where both the account holders are joint judgment debtors.[1] This view is further supported by the direction in the following paragraph (3.2) that a bank or building society served with an interim third party debt order is *not* required to retain money in accounts in the joint names of the judgment debtor and another person.

[1]   In *Miller v Mynn* (1859) 28 LJQB 324 the court held that where a judgment creditor has a joint judgment against several judgment debtors, a debt due to any one or more of them may be attached.

3.50   *MacDonald* and *Hirschorn* were decided long before modern jurisprudence on freezing injunctions had developed. The standard form freezing injunction extends to assets held jointly by a respondent and another person.[1] However, it appears that for the time being at least the position will remain that a joint account cannot be attached under a third party debt order. In March 2003 the Government published a White Paper on 'Effective Enforcement' as part of the Civil Enforcement Review arising from the Government's 'access to justice' initiatives (see Chapter 1). Chapter 4 of the White Paper sets out the Government's reasons for not proceeding with one of the proposals from the first phase of the Enforcement Review, namely that joint accounts should be subject to third party debt orders, and observes that any changes to this position would require primary legislation.

[1]   See para 6 of the specimen freezing injunction in the Practice Direction to Pt 25. In *Z Ltd v A-Z and AA-LL* [1982] QB 558 CA, it was argued by counsel for the applicant banks that joint accounts present difficulties for banks and should not be caught by *Mareva* injunctions unless the judge in the exercise of his discretion so directs. It was expressly submitted that a different position should not arise under a *Mareva* injunction than under a garnishee order which, under *Hirschorn v Evans*, could not be garnished. The judgments of Lord Denning MR, Eveleigh LJ and Kerr LJ concur that joint accounts should be subject to *Mareva* injunctions where this is justifiable for the protection of the plaintiff but none expressly considered the submission as to the inconsistency which thus arises between the position in relation to garnishee orders and *Mareva* injunctions.

3.51   The principal reasons stated in the White Paper for rejecting the proposal are the difficulties in coming up with a statutory definition of 'joint account', the operational difficulties for financial institutions in identifying joint accounts, difficulties in allocating ownership of funds in joint accounts, and addressing the rights of 'innocent' third parties to the account (who would need to be notified of the order so that they could challenge the deemed proportion of ownership and be made aware that the account had been frozen). It is notable that Fry LJ's statement in *MacDonald* that garnishing joint accounts would be 'altogether contrary to justice' was made notwithstanding the fact that the plaintiff sought only to garnish that portion of the debt to which the judgment debtor was entitled, which was agreed between Horton and Fitzgerald to be two thirds of the total sum. One of the reasons given in *Hirschorn* for the Court of Appeal's refusal to garnish a joint bank account was the 'unjustified and intolerable burden' this would impose upon banks.[1] The White Paper concludes that any change in the law to make joint accounts attachable would lead to an increased administrative burden on the courts and financial institutions, contrary to the aims of the Civil Enforcement Review.

[1]   MacKinnon LJ at 815.

3.52 Many if not all of the objections to attaching joint debts can be made in relation to freezing injunctions, which do extend to joint accounts. 'Innocent' third parties with an interest in a frozen account may apply to the court for an appropriate variation of the order and the standard from freezing injunction expressly provides this.[1] Given that the purpose of a freezing injunction is to preserve assets for the purposes of satisfying a judgment when it appears likely that a claimant will succeed in his claim, this inconsistency in the court's approach to joint accounts may seem illogical. However, there are a number of notable differences between a freezing injunction and an interim third party debt order. An applicant for a freezing injunction is required to provide an undertaking in damages in respect of any costs or loss caused to a third party as a result of the order. Freezing injunctions are not granted lightly and the applicant for a freezing injunction is under a 'high duty' to make full and frank disclosure of all material information.[2] Were the law in relation to the attachment of joint debts under the third party debt order process to change, this would invariably entail the court having to direct a trial of an issue at the hearing to consider whether a final order should be made whenever the debt involved is a joint debt (see paras 3.155–3.156) to enquire what share of that debt rightly belongs to the judgment debtor. Such proceedings would entail further time and costs for both the judgment creditor and 'innocent' third parties such as the joint debtor or financial institutions. The effect would inevitably be to complicate and protract the enforcement process.

---

[1]   CPR 40.9 provides: 'A person who is not a party but who is directly affected by a judgment or order may apply to have the judgment or order set aside or varied.' Paragraph 13 of the specimen freezing injunction in the Practice Direction to Pt 25 provides: 'Anyone served with or notified of this order may apply to the court at any time to vary or discharge this order (or so much of it as affects that person), but they must first inform the Applicant's solicitors.'

[2]   *Ninemia Maritime Corpn v Trave GmbH ('The Niedersachsen')* [1983] 1 WLR 1412.

Wages

3.53 Wages or salaries which are not presently payable cannot be attached under the third party debt order procedure since future unearned salary is not a debt 'due or accruing due'.[1] In *Hall v Pritchett*[2] the court held that the future salary of a medical officer could not be attached. In *Mapleson v Sears*[3] the court held that a proportion of the salary of a music hall artiste who had been engaged for a week could not be attached since under the terms of his contract there was no debt due to the artiste that was liable to attachment until the expiration of his week's engagement.

---

[1]   The proper method for the attachment of wages is an attachment of earnings order – see para 3.60.

[2]   (1877-78) LR 3 QBD 215.

[3]   (1911) 56 Sol Jo 54.

3.54 The position in relation to future unearned salary should be contrasted with that where fees have been earned but are unpaid. In *Edmunds v Edmunds*[1] a public vaccinator earned fees under a contract which specified that he should perform certain ministerial acts before becoming entitled to payment of the fees. Gorell Barnes J held that whether or not the fees were attachable depended upon the terms of the contract and, after a careful examination of its terms, he held:[2]

'The effect of my decision on this point is that the amount of 381. 18s. 6d was effectually earned for fees under this contract up to March 24, and that nothing which might happen afterwards could prevent that money becoming payable; and that although it was not to be payable, according to the terms of the contract, until one calendar month after Lady Day, it was, within the meaning of the garnishee order and the rules by analogy to which we act, a debt due or accruing due.'

1   [1904] P 362.
2   [1904] P 362 at 373.

3.55   Subsequent smaller amounts which were also earned but not payable until later in the year only involved a question of suspension of the order.[1] The Court of Appeal held the same view in relation to fees payable to a panel doctor by the Manchester Insurance Committee in *O'Driscoll* (see paras 3.22–3.24).

1   [1904] P 362 at 373.

Wages of Crown servants

3.56   The anomalous position of servants of the Crown should also be noted. In *Lucas v Lucas*[1] the court held that 'sterling overseas pay' payable to an Indian civil servant from the High Commissioner for India was not attachable since public servants have no right to their remuneration but rather are employed at the pleasure of the Crown. Pilcher J held:[2]

'I am satisfied that the rule of public policy to which Lord Blackburn refers would prevent Mr Lucas from successfully prosecuting any action against any officer of the Crown in respect of unpaid salary. There can, therefore, never be any "debt owing or accruing" from such an officer to Mr Lucas which can be attached by his wife under the machinery provided by [a predecessor to Pt 72].'

1   [1943] P 68.
2   [1943] P 68 at 78.

3.57   In summary, salaries of public servants are not due from the Crown or the ministers of the Crown as a debt and cannot be sued for, providing a further reason why they cannot be attached under the third party debt order procedure.[1]

1   They can, however, be obtained in satisfaction of a judgment debt using the procedure set out in the Attachment of Earnings Act 1971. See Chapter 1.

3.58   It should also be noted that certain salaries are protected from attachment by statute.[1]

1   See further Chapter 1.

Pensions

3.59   Pensions, like earnings, are not attachable in so far as they represent sums which may become due in the future.[1] However, where a pension has accrued due, it is attachable. In *Booth v Trail, Corporation of Sunderland (Garnishees)*[2] the court considered whether a sum already accrued due to a retired police constable in respect of his superannuation allowance was attachable. Lord Coleridge CJ held:[3]

> 'I am of the opinion that the judgment creditor is entitled to an order attaching so much of the pension as had already accrued due at the date of the summons. We are, however, bound by the decision of the Court of Appeal in *Webb v Stenton*, and independently of that decision it seems to me clear that sums which may or may not become due in the future are not debts owing or accruing within the meaning of the rules relating to the attachment of debts. Therefore, so much of the application as seeks to attach the pension prospectively as it falls due from time to time must be refused.'

[1]   However, pensions are amenable to the procedure set out under the Attachment of Earnings Act 1971. See Chapter 1.
[2]   (1883-84) 12 QBD 8.
[3]   (1883-84) 12 QBD at 10.

Attachment of Earnings Act 1971

3.60   As regards future earnings, the Attachment of Earnings Act 1971 (AEA 1971) makes provision for the attachment of the wages or salary[1] of an employed person as a means of enforcing the discharge of monetary obligations. This procedure is covered in Chapter 1.

[1]   Under AEA 1971, s 24(1), 'earnings' includes any sums payable to a person by way of wages or salary (including fees, bonus, commission, overtime or other emoluments), pension and statutory sick pay. However, under s 24(2), certain payments are not to be treated as earnings for the purposes of the AEA 1971, including sums payable by a Government department, sums payable to members of HM forces, social security pensions or benefits, disability pension or benefits, seaman's wages and the guaranteed minimum pension. See further Chapter 1.

Money in court

3.61   The third party debt order cannot be used to attach money standing to the credit of the judgment debtor in court procedure[1] (on the basis that it is not appropriate for the court itself to be the subject of court proceedings). However, there is a simple, alternative procedure available to a judgment creditor to obtain funds in court in satisfaction of his judgment, which is set out in CPR 72.10.

[1]   CPR 72.10(1)(a). *Re Greer* [1895] 2 Ch 217 also states that a sum of money which has been ordered to be paid into court cannot be attached.

3.62   Under CPR 72.10(1)(b) a judgment creditor may apply for an order that money in court, or so much of it as is needed to satisfy the judgment and the costs of the application, be paid to him. The application should be made in accordance with CPR Pt 23 and the application notice must be served on both the judgment debtor and the Accountant General at the Court Funds Office. The judgment creditor is then protected from any attempt by the judgment debtor to seek payment out of funds held in court.[1] Once the application notice has been issued, the money in court must not be paid out until the application has been disposed of.[2]

1   CPR 72.10(3).
2   CPR 72.10(3).

'Within the jurisdiction'

3.63   As noted in para 3.4, it is stipulated in CPR 72.1(1) that the third party who owes the debt which the judgment creditor seeks to attach must be 'within the jurisdiction'.

3.64   In *SCF Finance Co Ltd v Masri (No 3)*[1] the garnishee was within the jurisdiction on the day that the application for a garnishee order nisi was made and had instructed her solicitors to accept service of that order. However, by the time the garnishee order nisi was made later that day, the garnishee had boarded an aircraft flying to Jordan. The garnishee then sought to appeal the order on the grounds, among others, that the judge was wrong in law in holding that she was a person 'within the jurisdiction' for the purposes of RSC Ord 49.

1   [1987] 1 QB 1028.

3.65   The Court of Appeal held that, subject to the court's discretion, the mere 'temporary physical presence of the garnishee within the territorial limits of England and Wales' at the time the interim order is made is sufficient to found jurisdiction for the purposes of garnishee proceedings. Ralph Gibson LJ stated:[1]

'We have no doubt that physical presence of the garnishee in this country at the time of the making of the order nisi is sufficient to found jurisdiction which would not be lost by subsequent departure of the garnishee.'

1   [1987] 1 QB 1028 at 1041.

3.66   In addition, where the third party has agreed to submit to the jurisdiction of the English court for the purposes of third party debt proceedings before the interim third party debt order is made, he will be within the jurisdiction for the purposes of Pt 72.[1] It is worth noting that the Court in *SCF Finance* rejected counsel's submission that for physical presence to found jurisdiction for a garnishee order it must exist at the time of service of the interim order or the making of the final order. Because in that case the garnishee had instructed her solicitors to accept service of the order, the question of how service of an interim order on a third party who is within the jurisdiction at the time the interim order is made but who has left before service of that order is effected did not arise. However, in such circumstances, permission to serve out would presumably be needed and complicated questions of how the final order should be enforced against the overseas third party would be likely to arise.

1   *SCF Finance Co Ltd v Masri (No 3)* at 1041–1042.

Foreign debts

3.67   While it was clear that the third party must be within the jurisdiction for garnishee proceedings to be used, prior to two 2003 judgments of the House of Lords it seemed that there was no limitation that the third party debt must also be properly recoverable[1] within the jurisdiction.[2]

1   See further para 3.79, n 1 for a discussion of their Lordships' analysis of what is meant by a debt being 'properly recoverable'.
2   See also the former notes to RSC Ord 49 at 49.1.12.

3.68   The 1927 case of *Richardson v Richardson*[1] concerned the attachment of a foreign debt, namely credit balances held with the foreign branches of the National Bank of India Ltd. In his judgment, Hill J, following the earlier case of *Martin v Nadel*[2] (which concerned a German debt), held that the foreign balances could not be attached. He stated:[3]

'The bank is no doubt indebted to the judgment debtor and the bank is within the jurisdiction. The Order deals with the case where "any other person is indebted to the judgment debtor and is within the jurisdiction." But both in principle and upon authority, that means "is indebted within the jurisdiction and is within the jurisdiction." The debt must be properly recoverable within the jurisdiction. In principle, attachment of debts is a form of execution, and the general power of execution extends only to property within the jurisdiction of the court which orders it. A debt is not property within the jurisdiction if it cannot be recovered here.'

1   [1927] P 228.
2   [1906] 2 KB 26. See in particular the judgment of Vaughan Williams LJ at [1906] 2 KB 26 at 29.
3   [1927] P 228 at 235.

3.69   However, two judgments of the Court of Appeal in the late 1980s cast doubt on this judgment. In *SCF Finance v Masri*[1] the court held that it was not bound by the decision in *Richardson* and that RSC Ord 49:[2]

'contains no express requirement that the garnishee be indebted within the jurisdiction and we see no reason to read in words to that effect. We accept that in a case where the garnishee is not "indebted within the jurisdiction" this may be relevant to the exercise of the court's discretion.[3]'

1   [1987] QB 1028.
2   [1987] QB 1028 at 1044.
3   That is, the court's discretion to make the garnishee order absolute.

3.70   *SCF Finance* was followed in *Interpool Ltd v Galani*,[1] where the Court of Appeal held that:[2]

'Garnishee proceedings are governed by Ord 49, and we have already referred to the provisions of Ord 49, r.1(1) that the garnishee must be within the jurisdiction. There is no similar limitation that the garnished debt must be properly recoverable within the jurisdiction. The decision at first instance of *Richardson v Richardson*, that there is no jurisdiction to garnish a debt which is not recoverable within the jurisdiction is no longer good law.'

1   [1988] QB 738.
2   [1988] QB 738 at 741.

3.71   However, in *SCF Finance* the debt concerned *was* treated as properly recoverable in England[1] and *Interpool* was not concerned with garnishee proceedings but rather the oral examination of the judgment debtor under RSC Ord 48.[2] Thus, strictly, the observations of the Court of Appeal that the court had a discretion to garnish foreign debts (though it would not do so where this would be inequitable)[3] were obiter in both of those cases.

1   [1987] QB 1028 at 1044. Similarly, in *Deutsche Schachtbau-und-Tiefbohrgesellschaft mbH v Ras Al Khaimah National Oil Co and Shell International Petroleum Co Ltd* [1988] 2 Lloyd's Rep 293, which was appealed to the House of Lords, it was agreed that the debt concerned was an English debt.
2   Now contained in Pt 71. See Chapter 2.
3   Eg because it may expose the garnishee to the risk of having to pay the debt twice.

3.72   In any event, the position taken by the Court of Appeal in *SCF Finance* and *Interpool* regarding the attachment of foreign debts must now be seen as incorrect following their Lordships' decisions in *Société Eram Shipping Co Ltd v Cie Internationale de Navigation*[1] and *Kuwait Oil Tanker Co SAK v UBS AG*.[2]

1   [2004] 1 AC 260, HL, [2003] UKHL 30.
2   [2004] 1 AC 300, HL, [2003] UKHL 31.

3.73   In *Société Eram* the debt concerned was held with the Hong Kong branch of HSBC. Their Lordships unanimously found that no garnishee order should have been made in respect of that debt, although the reasoning given differed subtly in some respects. Discharge of the debt by virtue of the garnishee order was fundamental to the process. Lord Bingham stated that:[1]

'It is not in my opinion open to the Court to make an order in a case, such as the present, where it is clear or appears that the making of the order will not discharge the debt of the third party or garnishee to the judgment debtor according to the law which governs that debt.'

1   [2004] 1 AC 260 at [26]. Lord Hoffmann agreed that the discharge of the debt was an essential part of the process (at [63]), as did Lord Millett (at [97]).

3.74   He continued that while, in practical terms, it does not much matter whether the court rules it has no jurisdiction to attach a foreign debt or that it should never exercise its discretion to do so, the former was the preferable analysis and he found himself in close agreement with the judgment of Hill J in *Richardson*.[1] Similarly, Lord Hobhouse agreed that the criticism of Hill J expressed in *SCF Finance* and *Interpool* was mistaken.[2]

1   [2003] UKHL 30 at [26]
2   [2003] UKHL 30 at [75].

3.75   Other of their Lordships' judgments also emphasised the need for the English courts to refrain from exerting exorbitant extraterritorial jurisdiction. Lord Hoffmann observed that:[1]

'The execution of a judgment is an exercise of sovereign authority. It is a seizure by the state of an asset of the judgment debtor to satisfy the creditor's claim. And it is a general principle of international law that one sovereign state should not trespass upon the authority of another, by attempting to seize assets situated within the jurisdiction of the foreign state or compelling its citizens to do acts within its boundaries.'

1   [2003] UKHL 30 at [54].

3.76 He went on to say that there are strong reasons of principle for not making a garnishee order in respect of a foreign debt and that, while the application of such principles is not the same as exercising a discretion, it also is not the same as a statutory rule restricting the discretion.[1] He thus concurred with Lord Millett, who observed:[2]

'If the debt is situated and payable overseas, however, it is beyond the territorial reach of our Courts'

and later in his judgment said:[3]

'Our Courts ought not to exercise an exorbitant jurisdiction contrary to generally accepted norms of international law and expect a foreign Court to sort out the consequences.'

1   [2003] UKHL 30 at [59].
2   [2003] UKHL 30 at [98].
3   [2003] UKHL 30 at [109].

3.77 The decision in *Kuwait Oil* concerned a Swiss debt. The UK and Switzerland are both signatories to the Lugano Convention,[1] so the question of jurisdiction before their Lordships was not simply a matter of English or private international law but was also governed by the Convention regime. Article 16(5) of the Lugano Convention[2] provides:

'The following courts shall have exclusive jurisdiction, regardless of domicile:

...

5.   in proceedings concerned with the enforcement of judgments, the courts of the Contracting State in which the judgment has been or is to be enforced.'

1   That is, the Lugano Convention on Jurisdiction and the Enforcement of Judgments in Civil and Commercial Matters 1988.
2   Equivalent provisions are contained in the Brussels Convention, art 16(5) and the Brussels Regulation, reg 22.

3.78 Since the judgment creditor was seeking to enforce against a debt situated in Switzerland, their Lordships held that the Swiss courts had exclusive jurisdiction over the enforcement proceedings and the English courts were bound to decline jurisdiction in favour of the Swiss courts in accordance with art 19 of the Convention.[1] Their Lordships also held that, had the case not been governed by the Lugano Convention regime, they would have refused to make a garnishee order absolute for the reasons given in the *Société Eram* judgment.

1   Equivalent provisions are contained the Brussels Convention, art 19 and Brussels Regulation, reg 25. By analogy, the same principles should therefore apply in the case of a debt situated in a Brussels regime state.

The courts' approach to extraterritorial orders

3.79 It now seems clear that judgment creditors cannot use the third party debt order process to attach foreign debts by way of third party debt order.[1] It also appears that the courts' approach to third party debt orders is now in line with that adopted in relation to the extra-territorial effect of freezing injunctions and orders requiring banks to produce documents relating to foreign branches. The standard form wording of world-wide freezing injunctions was modified following Kerr LJ's observations in *Babanaft International Co SA v Bassatne*[2] that unqualified world-wide freezing injunctions 'can never be justified, either before or after judgment, because they would involve an exorbitant assertion of jurisdiction of an in rem nature over third parties outside the jurisdiction of our courts'.[3] Similarly, in *R v Grossman*[4] and *MacKinnon v Donaldson, Lufkin & Jenrette Securities Corp*[5] orders for the production of documents in relation to foreign accounts were refused on the basis that jurisdictional conflict may otherwise follow and that a state should not demand obedience from foreigners in respect of their conduct outside the jurisdiction. Passages from these judgments were cited by their Lordships in *Société Eram*, and chime with the observations of Lord Hoffmann in that judgment:[6]

> 'If the Courts of one country in which a bank operates exercise no restraint about using their sovereign powers of compulsion in relation to accounts maintained with that bank at branches in other countries, conflict and chaos is likely to follow.'

[1]   The only judgment in the *Société Eram* judgment which expressly discussed the proper analysis of the 'situs' of a debt was Lord Hobhouse's, which approved the Dicey and Morris formulation for the situs of a debt at Rule 112, which states that 'choses in action generally are situate in the country where they are properly recoverable or can be enforced' at [72]–[73]. Lord Bingham observed (at [2004] UKHL 30 at [26]) that an order attaching a foreign debt may be made if it appears by the law applicable in that situs that the English third party debt order would be recognised as discharging the third party liability to the judgment debtor, though this distinction was likely to be *'of little or no practical importance'*. Lord Hoffmann recognised that different considerations may apply in cases where the 'foreign' debt either is not payable in a foreign country or is not governed by foreign law (at [32]), but said that he found it hard to think of a principle which might override the strong reasons of principle for not making a third party debt order in respect of a foreign debt (at [59]). Their Lordships' comments suggest that while the possibility of attaching a foreign debt through third party debt order proceedings may remain as a theoretical possibility, in practical terms, it is unlikely to prove an option. For further discussion of what is the proper analysis of the situs of a debt and the considerations which could apply in third party debt order proceedings, see P J Rogerson 'The situs of debts in the Conflict of Laws' (1990) 49(3) CLJ 441 and Dickinson 'Now you seize it … Now you Don't, LQR 2004, 120 (JAN), 16–19.

[2]   [1990] Ch 13.

[3]   [2003] UKHL 30 at [35]. See also the decision of the Court of Appeal in *Bank of China v NBM LLC* [2001] EWCA Civ 1993; [2002] 1 WLR 844. It is now clear that the court's freezing injunction jurisdiction is an in personam jurisdiction founded on the principle that a person who is subject to the jurisdiction of the court can be ordered to deal with his property in a certain way.

[4]   (1981) 73 Cr App R 302.

[5]   [1986] 1 Ch 42.

[6]   At [55].

Crown debts

3.80   Under the Crown Proceedings Act 1947 (CPA 1947), s 25(4) and RSC Ord 77,[1] the third party debt order procedure cannot be used to attach a debt payable by the Crown to a judgment debtor. This includes balances held with the National Savings

Bank which, although an institution that accepts deposits[2] and that would otherwise be subject to third party debt orders, is under the control of the Crown.[3] Accordingly, credit balances in deposit accounts with the National Savings Bank cannot be attached using the third party debt order procedure.

1   Rules 15(1)(a) and 16(1)(a).
2   'Accepting deposits' is a specified kind of activity which is now defined under the Financial Services and Markets Act 2000 (Regulated Activities) Order 2001, SI 2001/544, art 5. Under art 4 of the Financial Services and Markets Act 2000 (Exemption) Order 2001, SI 2001/1201, the exemption in respect of accepting deposits for the National Savings Bank, which was in place by virtue of it being listed in the Banking Act 1987, Sch II is preserved.
3   National Savings is a government department and an executive agency of the Chancellor of the Exchequer.

3.81   However, CPA 1947, s 27 provides a method of attaching monies payable by the Crown to a judgment debtor where the judgment creditor would be entitled to a third party debt order were the third party not the Crown.[1] The High Court may make an order restraining the judgment debtor from receiving the debt due from the Crown and directing payment of that debt to the judgment creditor.[2]

1   CPA 1947, s 27(1)(c), which formerly precluded the attachment of National Savings Bank deposits, was repealed by Supreme Court Act 1981, s 139(1). Under the Supreme Court Act 1981, s 139(2), the Lord Chancellor may, by statutory instrument, re-impose that restriction. No such order is currently in force and thus under CPA, s 27(3) the provisions of CPA, s 27 shall apply to National Savings Bank deposits.
2   The procedure cannot be used in respect of wages payable to officers of the Crown or money subject to statutory restrictions on assignment, charging or taking in execution (CPA 1947, s 27).

3.82   It can only be used where the judgment sought to be enforced is for more than £50.[1] The procedure for attaching Crown debts is set out in RSC Ord 77, r 16.[2]

1   RSC Ord 16, r 1A.
2   Preserved in CPR, Sch 1.

Procedure for attaching a Crown debt

3.83   The application must be made by claim form and must be served (unless the court otherwise directs):

(a) on the Crown, at least 15 days before the return day; and
(b) on the judgment debtor (or his solicitor), at least seven days after the claim form has been served on the Crown and at least seven days before the return day.[1]

1   RSC Ord 77, r 16(2).

3.84   The application must be supported by a witness statement or affidavit containing the following information:[1]

(a) the facts giving rise to the application;
(b) the name and last known address of the judgment debtor;
(c) the order to be enforced together with the amount of such order and the amount remaining unpaid at the date of the application;
(d) details of the particular debt from the Crown in respect of which the application is made; and

(e) where the debt is a deposit with the National Savings Bank, the name and address of the branch at which the account is believed to be held and the number of that account, or, where relevant, that all or part of this information is not known to the applicant.

1   RSC Ord 77, r 16(2A) and (2B).

3.85   The provisions of CPR 72.8, which contain rules about a judgment debtor or third party objecting to a third party debt order (see paras 3.140-3.141) apply to applications under RSC Ord 77, except that the court shall not have power to order enforcement to issue against the Crown.[1]

1   RSC Ord 77, r 16(3).

Judgment creditor takes subject to prior equities

3.86   It should also be noted that the judgment creditor can have no greater right in relation to the debt than the judgment debtor had.[1] In *Tapp v Jones*[2] an order was made for payment of the garnishee's debts 'as and when they became payable'. Blackburn J stated:[3] 'I agree that no greater right is given to the creditor than the debtor had.' In *Re General Horticultural Company, ex p Whitehouse*[4] a judgment debtor had earlier charged a debt owed to him by a third party. The judgment creditor obtained a garnishee order nisi without notice of two of the three charges on the debt. The court held that the charges had priority over the garnishee order nisi, even where the judgment creditor did not have notice of the charges, since the judgment creditor 'can only obtain what the judgment debtor could honestly give him.'[5]

1   *Tapp v Jones* (1874-75) LR 10 QB 591; In *O'Driscoll* Swinfen Eady LJ stated at 513: 'The judgment creditor who has obtained a garnishee order is in no better position in these respects than the judgment debtor.'
2   (1874-75) LR 10 QB 591.
3   (1874-75) LR 10 QB 591 at 593.
4   (1886) LR 32 Ch D 512.
5   (1886) LR 32 Ch D 512 at 516. See also *Badeley v Consolidated Bank* (1888) LR 34 Ch D 536, CA and *Davis v Freethy* (1890) 24 QBD 519, CA, which followed *ex p Whitehouse*. Similarly, in *Sinnott v Bowden* (1912) 2 Ch 414, the court held that a mortgagee's rights are not displaced by a garnishee order nisi.

PROCEDURE

3.87   The procedural rules relating to third party debt orders are set out in Pt 72.

Application by the judgment creditor

3.88   The first step is an application by the judgment creditor for an interim third party debt order. The rules relating to the application are set out in CPR 72.3 (as supplemented by the Practice Direction to Pt 72).

Which court?

3.89 The judgment creditor's application should be issued in the court which made the judgment or, where the proceedings have since been transferred to another court, the transferee court.[1] There is no provision for the automatic transfer of enforcement proceedings to the defendant's local court as applies in the case of a claim for a specified amount of money against an individual.[2] However, the court has a discretion to transfer the proceedings to the court where the judgment debtor resides or carries on business (or another court) on the application by a judgment debtor who wishes to oppose the judgment creditor's application for a third party debt order[3] (see paras 3.140–3.143)[4].

1   CPR 72.3(b).
2   CPR 26.2.
3   PD 72, para 4.
4   See further Chapter 1 for general commentary on the transfer of proceedings.

Without notice

3.90 The judgment creditor's application for a third party debt order may be made without notice to the judgment debtor.[1] The notes to Pt 72[2] state that applications for third party debt orders are treated by the court as urgent business and will be placed before the master[3] as soon as possible on the day they are received by the court. Current practice in the High Court is for the interim third party debt order to be issued between two to three days after the application is filed at court.

1   CPR 72.3(1)(a).
2   Civil Procedure 2004, vol 1, para 73.2.2.
3   Or district judge in the county courts.

Prescribed form

3.91 The application should be made on form N349[1] and must be verified by a statement of truth signed by the judgment creditor or the judgment creditor's solicitor. Form N349 contains or makes provision for the insertion of all the information required by CPR 72.3 and para 1.2 of the Practice Direction, namely:

(a) details of the judgment or order sought to be enforced;
(b) the name and address of the judgment debtor;
(c) the amount of money remaining due under the judgment or order (the form requires the applicant to state both the amount of money the judgment required the judgment debtor to pay (including any costs and interest) and the amount remaining due, which may include further interest accrued since the date of the judgment);[2]
(d) whether the judgment provided for payment by instalments and, if so, the amount of the instalments that have fallen due and remain unpaid;
(e) confirmation[3] that the third party is within England and Wales and owes money to, or holds money to the credit of, the judgment debtor;
(f) where the third party is a bank or building society:

(i) its name and the address of its head office in England and Wales;

(ii) the branch at which the account is held and its address, or alternatively that this information is not known; and

(iii) the account number and sort code, or alternatively that this information is not known;

(g) where the third party is not a bank or building society, the name and address of the third party;

(h) the names and addresses of any persons (other than the judgment debtor) who have a claim to the money owed by the third party and the information known to the judgment creditor about each such claim;

(i) the source and grounds of the judgment creditor's knowledge or belief that the third party is indebted to the judgment debtor and, where relevant, that another person has a claim to the money owed by the third party; and

(j) details of any other applications for third party debt orders the judgment creditor has made in respect of the same judgment debt.

1   Available at www.courtservice.gov.uk.
2   In *White, Son & Pill v Stennings* [1911] 2 KB 418 the Court of Appeal held that garnishee proceedings could not be commenced before the time given in a judgment for payment of the money had expired. This case concerned Ord XXVI, r 1 of the County Court Rules 1903, which required the applicant to swear an affidavit in support of the application stating that the judgment 'is still unsatisfied'. However, the same principles should apply under Pt 72. See para 1.12 for a discussion of when a judgment becomes payable.
3   The Practice Direction to Pt 72 requires that such confirmation is provided to the best of the judgment creditor's knowledge or belief. Section 5 of Form N349 requires the judgment creditor to state the source and grounds for his knowledge or belief that the third party is indebted to the judgment debtor.

3.92   The Practice Direction to Pt 72 states that the court will not grant speculative applications for third party debt orders and will only make third party debt orders against a bank or building society if the judgment creditor's application notice contains evidence to substantiate his belief that the judgment debtor holds an account with that institution.[1]

1   PD 72, para 1.3.

3.93   No such warning was provided under the old RSC Ord 49. However, the wording of the current Practice Direction is a reflection of the earlier position under case law. In *Koch v Mineral Ore Syndicate, London and South Western Bank Ltd, Garnishees*,[1] the judgment creditor obtained a garnishee order nisi attaching all monies owed by London and South Western Bank to 'Ernest Frederick Julius Berckhardt, trading as the Mineral Ore Syndicate'. The order was served on the bank, which informed the judgment creditor's solicitors that it held no account in either of those names. The judgment creditor's solicitors then told the bank that Mr Berckhardt had since informed them that the account was in fact in the name of the General Import Co. and was operated upon cheques drawn by 'Julius Berckhardt, managing director'. They asked the bank to attach the balance on that account under the order nisi.

1   (1910) 54 Sol Jo 600.

3.94   The bank refused to do so on the grounds that the order nisi did not attach the balance of an account unless the order correctly set forth the names of the account as it stood in the books of the bank, and also because it wanted to be satisfied that no other person had an interest in that account. Before the judgment creditor had the order amended (to correct the judgment debtor's name to Julius Berckhardt and insert the General Import Co's name), two cheques were drawn on the account which were honoured by the bank. The bank argued that unless the approach they had adopted was correct, banks would be placed in an exceedingly difficult and wholly untenable position since the onus would be on them to decide in all doubtful cases where there was a discrepancy in the names whether or not they should freeze the account pending the hearing of the application. The Court of Appeal agreed. Had the bank frozen the account it would have been exposed to an action from their customer for breach of mandate and they were right not to do so.

3.95 The court sanctioned the bank's approach notwithstanding the fact that it had a customer whose name was very similar to that mentioned in the order nisi and who the bank knew described his business as the Mineral Ore Syndicate. This case and the wording of the Practice Direction to Pt 72 suggest that the court will be unlikely to tolerate a 'scatter gun' approach in relation to third party debt orders, where a judgment creditor attempts to serve all the major clearing banks with an interim third party debt order in the hope that an account will be identified and attached. They also illustrate the importance of the applicant for a third party debt order substantiating his belief as to the identity of the judgment debtor's bank accounts in the application. This may entail the use of a court examination of the judgment debtor under the Pt 71 procedure to obtain information as to the judgment debtor's assets before making an application for a third party debt order where necessary.[1]

1   See Chapter 2.

Fee

3.96 The fee for issuing an application for a third party debt order is £100.[1] From 1 April 2005, all cheques should be made payable to 'HMCS' or 'Her Majesty's Courts Service' instead of 'Her Majesty's Paymaster General' or 'HMPG' as was previously the case.

1   See Civil Procedure Fees Order 2004, SI 2004/3121, Sch 1 para 6.3(a).

Interim third party debt order

3.97 The application will be dealt with by a master initially without a hearing.[1] The master will consider the information contained in the application notice and has discretion[2] to make an interim third party debt order. However, in practice, the court's discretion is likely to be exercised at the hearing for further consideration of the application.

1   CPR 72.4(1).
2   CPR 72.4(2) states that 'The judge *may* make an interim third party debt order.' (Emphasis added.)

Form of the order

3.98 The standard form interim third party debt order (Form N84) contains the information prescribed by CPR 72.4, together with certain other information. The order will:

(a) fix a date for a hearing on which the court will consider whether a final third party debt order should be made. The date of that hearing will be at least 28 days after the interim third party debt order is made; and

(b) direct that, until that hearing, the third party must not (unless the court orders otherwise) pay to the judgment debtor (or any other person) any sum of money owed to the judgment debtor which would reduce the amount owed by the third party to the judgment debtor to less than the amount specified in the order. The interim third party debt order will specify the amount of money which the third party must retain, which will be the total of:

    (i)   the amount now owing under the judgment (including costs and interest); and

    (ii) the amount of the judgment creditor's fixed costs which the court may eventually allow in respect of the application (see paras 3.183–3.189).

(c) The interim third party debt order contained in Form N84 also:

    (i)   notifies the third party that the interim third party debt order does not authorise the third party to pay any money to the judgment creditor at this stage (see paras 3.105–3.107);

    (ii) contains information as to hardship orders (see paras 3.116–3.121);

    (iii) notifies the third party of what it must now do (see paras 3.122–3.152); and

    (iv) states what will happen if a final third party debt order is made (see paras 3.173–3.178).

Service of the interim order

3.99   Under CPR 72.5, copies of the interim third party debt order, the application notice and any documents filed in support of the application must be served:

(a) on the third party, at least 21 days before the date fixed for the hearing; and

(b) on the judgment debtor, at least seven days after service on the third party and at least seven days before the date fixed for the hearing.

3.100   The interim third party debt order becomes binding on the third party when it is served on him.[1]

---

[1]   CPR 72.4(4).

3.101   If the third party in good faith pays the debt to the judgment debtor before service of the interim third party debt order, the order is inoperative.[1] Similarly, a bona fide assignment of the debt owed by the third party before service of the interim order will defeat attachment.[2] The third party should therefore be served as soon as possible after the interim order is obtained and before serving on the judgment debtor, since otherwise the judgment debtor may defeat the proceedings by instructing the third party to pay the funds away. The wording of CPR 72.5(1)(b)(i) would appear to impose a mandatory requirement that a copy of the order 'must' be served on the judgment debtor not less than seven days after a copy has been served on the third party. In any event, it may be self-defeating for the judgment creditor not to serve the third party first.

---

[1]   *Cooper v Brayne* (1858) 27 LJ Ex 446. Note that this report appears incorrectly to refer to the garnishee having paid the debt away to the 'official assignee of the *judgment creditor*'

(emphasis added). Presumably this should in fact have been a reference to the judgment debtor. See also paras 3.108 and 3.109.

2   *Hirsch v Coates* (1856) 25 LJCP 315; *Wise v Birkenshaw* (1860) 29 LJ Ex 240; *Holt v Heatherfield* [1942] 2 KB 1.

3.102   Service is governed by Pt 6. Particular care should be taken both as to the place and method of service chosen, depending on the nature of the person to be served and the date on which service will be deemed to have been effected, to ensure that the requisite time periods are allowed in accordance with CPR 72.5.

3.103   Banks and building societies are invariably incorporated. CPR 6.2(2) together with the Companies Act 1985, ss 725, 695 and 694A provide the methods for service on a company. The notes to Pt 72[1] recommend that banks and building societies should be formally served at their registered office[2] with a copy of the order and other documents also being sent to any branch where it is known or suspected that the judgment debtor has an account.

1   Civil Procedure 2004, vol 1, para 72.5.2.
2   An oversea company will not have a registered office in Great Britain but is required to deliver to the registrar of companies the name and address of person(s) resident in Great Britain and authorised to accept service on the company's behalf. Such address should be used for service on an oversea company, in addition to a copy of the order being sent to the relevant branch.

Certificate of service

3.104   CPR 6.3 makes provision for the court to serve the interim order. However, the judgment creditor may serve the order himself provided he notifies the court that he wishes to do so. The judgment creditor is likely to wish to take advantage of this provision so that he can retain control over the time and method in which service is effected. Where he does so, he must either file a certificate of service at court at least two days before the hearing or produce a certificate of service at the hearing.[1]

1   CPR 72.5(2).

Effect of service of the interim third party debt order

3.105   The effect of service of the interim third party debt order on the third party is to attach the debt owed by the third party to the judgment debtor to answer the judgment creditor's demand.[1] The order does not create any security for the debt[2] nor operate as a transfer of the debt, but creates an equitable charge on it.[3] It binds the property of the judgment debtor (namely the debt owed by the third party) in the hands of the third party. The property of the third party is in no way involved.[4] However, the third party cannot pay the debt away without risk of having to pay it over again to the judgment creditor.[5] In the case of bank and building society accounts, service of the interim third party debt order operates to freeze the account.[6] A bank served with an interim order may dishonour cheques drawn upon it by the judgment debtor.[7]

1   *Rogers v Whiteley* [1892] AC 118 at 123.
2   *Chatterton v Watney* (1881) 17 Ch D 259.

3   *Re Combined Weighing and Advertising Machine Company* (1889) 43 Ch D 99; *Galbraith v Grimshaw and Baxter* [1910] 1 KB 339, affirmed [1910] AC 508. However, note that such charge will rank subsequent to prior equitable charges on the debt – see *ex p Whitehouse* and para 3.86.
4   *Société Eram Shipping Co Ltd v Cie Internationale de Navigation* [2003] UKHL 30 at [28].
5   *Galbraith v Grimshaw* [1910] AC 508.
6   *Choice Investments Ltd v Jeromnimon* [1981] QB 149.
7   *Rogers v Whiteley* [1892] AC 118.

3.106   In *Société Eram*,[1] the House of Lords examined the nature of garnishee or third party debt proceedings in detail and both Lord Bingham and Lord Hoffmann recited key passages from the authorities on the effect of a garnishee order nisi (now interim third party debt orders) in their judgments.   Lord Bingham then neatly summarised the position:[2]

'A garnishee or third party debt order is a proprietary remedy which operates by way of attachment against the property of the judgment debtor. The property of the judgment debtor so attached is the chose in action represented by the debt of the third party or garnishee to the judgment debtor. On the making of the interim or nisi order that chose in action is (as it has been variously put) bound, frozen attached or charged in the hands of the third party or garnishee. Subject to any monetary limit which may be specified in the order, the third party is not entitled to deal with that chose in action by making payment to the judgment debtor or any other party at his request.'[3]

1   [2003] UKHL 30.
2   [2003] UKHL 30 at [24].
3   For a discussion of how the operation of third party debt orders may differ had the jurisdiction been developed as an 'in personam' rather than an 'in rem' jurisdiction, see Briggs *Owing, owning and the garnishing of foreign debts* [2003] LMCLQ 418. Briggs hypothesises that the development of an in personam jurisdiction whereby the judgment debtor is ordered to direct his civil debtor to make payment to the judgment creditor might have been preferable to the in rem operation of third party debt orders. However, such a perspective overlooks the fact that enforcement procedures are necessary precisely because a judgment debtor has failed to comply with an order of court namely that directing him to pay the judgment debt. A judgment creditor may well prefer the option of an order directed to a compliant third party than a further order against the judgment debtor, even where backed up by the coercive sanctions of the court.

3.107   Lord Bingham's summary was expressly stated to apply to both garnishee and third party debt orders. However, it is notable that Pt 72, unlike its predecessor, RSC Ord 49, contains no reference to attachment or the proprietary effect of the interim order, but simply directs that the third party must not reduce its liability to the judgment debtor to less than the amount specified in the order. Lord Millett sought to address this in his judgment:[1]

'I wish to add one thing more. RSC, Order 49 has now been replaced by Part 72 of the Civil Procedure Rules, which is cast in more modern language. It is common ground that, as the editorial introduction states, the basic purpose of the rule remains unchanged. Unfortunately all reference to attachment has been dropped, and there is no longer any indication that the order has proprietary consequences. The words which formerly created an equitable charge at the interim stage have been replaced by a power to grant an injunction, which is normally a personal remedy. The straightforward language of Part 72 is deceptive. Its true nature cannot easily be understood without a knowledge of its history and antecedents. I do not, with respect, regard this as an altogether satisfactory state of affairs.'

1   [2003] UKHL 30 at [112].

Debt paid by cheque before service of the interim order

3.108 As has been noted in para 3.101, where a third party has paid the debt to the judgment debtor in good faith before service of the interim order, there is no attachable debt. However, where the third party has paid the judgment debtor by cheque and is served with the interim order before the cheque is presented, the situation becomes a little more complicated. If the third party stops payment of the cheque, there will be an attachable debt on which the order can operate. This is what happened in *Cohen v Hale,*[1] where the court found that on the third party stopping the cheque it was 'as if it had never been given'[2] so that the debt could be attached under a garnishee order.

1   (1877-78) LR 3 QBD 371.
2   (1877-78) LR 3 QBD at 373.

3.109 However, the third party may have good reason for not wishing to stop the cheque given to the judgment debtor. Where the cheque has subsequently passed into the hands of a bona fide holder for value, stopping the cheque may render the third party liable to an action by the holder. The courts have held that there is no obligation on the drawer of a cheque to stop the cheque for the benefit of another person.[1] The giving of the cheque has the effect of payment of the debt so that the recipient no longer has the right to sue for the debt. This right is only revived in the event that the cheque is dishonoured. Therefore, if the third party chooses not to stop the cheque, there will be no attachable debt.[2]

1   *Re Palmer, ex p Richdale* (1881-82) LR 19 Ch D 409, which considered this question in the context of bankruptcy proceedings.
2   *Elwell v Jackson* (1885) 1 TLR 454.

Revocation of the account holder's instructions

3.110 As has been noted, *Joachimson* is authority for the proposition that service of the interim third party debt order operates as a demand for repayment of a customer's account (see para 3.37). In *Rekstin v Severo Sibirsko Gosudarstvennoe Akcionernoe Obschestvo Komseverputj and the Bank for Russian Trade Ltd*[1] the judgment debtors instructed their bank to close their account and transfer the funds to another entity, to whom they owed nothing. The bank made the relevant entries in its books for the purposes of closing the account on the same day as it received the instruction. Shortly afterwards that same day, and before notice had been given to the proposed transferees and the transfer accepted by them, the bank was served with a garnishee order nisi.

1   [1933] 1 KB 47.

3.111   The Court of Appeal held that the mere making of book entries to give effect to the account transfer without payment to the transferee meant that the judgment debtor's instruction to close the account was still revocable at the time the garnishee order nisi was served and that the order operated as a revocation of that instruction. In his judgment, Lord Hanworth MR considered the observations of the House of Lords in *Rogers v Whiteley*[1] and said:[2]

'That is a direct authority that the garnishee order nisi attaches the funds in the hand of the banker and acts as a revocation of any direction given by the judgment debtor in regard to the disposition of the funds.'

He concluded:[3]

'It appears to me that the House of Lords have definitely held that a garnishee order nisi revokes any order to transfer which has not been fully carried out.'

[1]   (1889) 23 QBD 236.
[2]   [1933] 1 KB 47 at 67.
[3]   [1933] 1 KB 47 at 67.

No obligation to pay under the interim order

3.112   As Lord Denning MR noted in *Choice Investments Ltd v Jeromnimon*,[1] the:

'"attachment" is not an order to pay. It only freezes the sum in the hands of the bank until the order is made absolute or is discharged. It is only when the order is made absolute that the bank is liable to pay.'

Thus the third party must *not* pay the judgment creditor on service of the interim order. Form N84 specifically draws this to the attention of the third party. The obligation to pay to the judgment creditor only arises once the *final* third party debt order has been made (see paras 3.174–3.178).

[1]   [1981] QB 149 at 155.

3.113   The need for the third party to refrain from making payment to the judgment creditor prior to the final order is illustrated by *Crantrave Ltd v Lloyds Bank plc*.[1] In that case the garnishee bank paid funds held by the judgment debtor with the bank to the judgment creditor following service of the garnishee order nisi. The garnishee order was not made absolute and the proceedings founded on it were stayed. The judgment debtor was subsequently wound up and the liquidator claimed repayment of the sum the bank had paid over to the judgment creditor. The Court of Appeal resoundingly rejected[2] the bank's argument that it genuinely believed that it was entitled to act as it did and that this should be a defence to the claim. The court found that the bank had no authority or purported authority from its customer to make the payment and 'there was no obligation imposed on them by due process of law to make the payment, since the garnishee order had not been made absolute.' Accordingly, the bank had no defence to the liquidator's claim for repayment of the money.[3]

[1]   [2000] QB 917.
[2]   [2000] QB 917 at 924, which states: 'It is a startling proposition that bankers can pay sums to a third party out of a customer's account because they believe the customer to be indebted

to that third party. I see no difference in principle between a judgment debt and other perceived debts. As against a customer, a contrary principle would place the bank in a position to act as debt collector for creditors of the customer.'

3   [2000] QB 917 at 925.

3.114   Similarly, in the earlier cases of *Turner v Jones*[1] and *Re Webster, ex p Official Receiver*,[2] garnishees of judgment debtors who paid sums over to the judgment creditors before the garnishee order was made absolute were found to have no answer to a claim for repayment of the debt when the judgment debtors subsequently became bankrupt. In the former case, Bramwell B stated:

'I own the inclination of my own opinion is, that the garnishee is not protected unless he gets a Judge's order directing payment as there mentioned.'

1   (1857) 1 H & N 878.
2   [1907] 1 KB 623.

3.115   The clear message is that a third party who pays sums over to the judgment creditor (or anyone else) prior to the court making a final third party debt order does so at his peril.

Debtors in hardship

3.116   The provisions for individual judgment debtors in hardship were a new introduction under Pt 72. As had been noted, service of an interim third party debt order on a bank or building society will freeze the judgment debtor's account and there must be at least 28 days after the interim order is made before the hearing at which the court will consider whether to make the order final.[1] Freezing the judgment debtor's bank account may leave him unable to pay his mortgage or meet ordinary living expenses for himself or his family. CPR 72.7 allows a judgment debtor who is an individual and is suffering hardship in meeting ordinary living expenses as a result of his bank or building society account being frozen to apply to the court for an order permitting the bank or building society to make one or more specified payments out of the account. An order for such a payment is called a hardship payment order and will be made based on Form N37.

1   CPR 72.4(5).

3.117   The judgment debtor's application for a hardship payment order should be made by application notice under Pt 23. The rules as to which court should hear the hardship order application are set out in CPR 72.7 and PD 72, paras 5.1–5.3. The judgment debtor does not have to make the application to the court in which the third party debt order proceedings are taking place, and where the application is made to a different court the application will not be transferred to that court. In High Court proceedings the application may be made at the Royal Courts of Justice or at any district registry,[1] but the judgment debtor may only apply to one court for the order.

1   CPR 72.7(2). In county court proceedings the application may be made to any county court.

3.118   Where the application for a hardship payment order is made in a different court to the court dealing with the third party debt order proceedings, the court dealing with the third party debt order will send copies of the original application notice (Form N349) and the interim third party debt order to the court dealing with the application for a hardship payment order. However, where both the application for a third party debt order and the application for a hardship payment order are proceeding in the same court, the notes to Pt 72[1] state that it is generally preferable to advance the hearing of the application to make the final third party debt order so that it is heard at the same time as the judgment debtor's application for a hardship payment order. This will save time and costs and will enable all the issues to be resolved at one hearing. The judgment creditor should ask the court to do this if the court has not already done so of its own initiative.

[1]   Civil Procedure 2004, vol 1, para 72.7.5.

3.119   The judgment debtor should file detailed evidence in support of the application for a hardship payment order explaining why he needs the payment and the application notice must be verified by a statement of truth. Paragraph 5.6 of the Practice Direction to Pt 72 states that the evidence filed in support of the application should include documentary evidence such as bank statements, wage slips and mortgage statements to enable the judgment debtor to prove his financial position and the need for the payment.

3.120   The application notice does not need to be served on the third party but must be served on the judgment creditor at least two days before the hearing unless the court orders otherwise.[1] In cases of exceptional urgency, the court may deal with the application without notice to the judgment creditor.[2] If the court decides to deal with the application without it being served on the judgment creditor, where possible it will normally direct that the judgment creditor be informed of the application and give him the opportunity to make representations by telephone, fax or other appropriate means.

[1]   CPR 72.7(5).
[2]   PD 71 Para 7.

3.121   The court has a discretion to make the order and may permit the third party to make one or more payments out of the account. The court may also specify to whom the payments are to be made, and, for example, may therefore specify that the bank make payment direct to the judgment debtor's mortgagee.

Obligations of a third party served with an interim third party debt order

3.122   The obligations of the third party served with an interim third party debt order are set out in CPR 72.6 and in Form N84, the standard form interim third party debt order. The exact nature of those obligations will depend on the nature of the third party. In summary, they consist of:

(a)   the obligation not to reduce the amount owed to the judgment debtor to less than the amount specified in the order;

(b)   in the case of banks and building societies, the obligation to search for accounts; and

(c)   the obligation to disclose certain information to the court and the judgment creditor.

Banks and building societies

3.123 The obligations on a third party bank or building society are set out in CPR 72.6(1)–(3).

Search for accounts

3.124 A bank or building society served with an interim third party debt order 'must carry out a search to identify all accounts held with it by the judgment debtor.' The wording of Form N84 and para 3.1(2) of the Practice Direction make it clear that the bank is only required to search for (or disclose information relating to – see paras 3.127-3.133) accounts held solely by the judgment debtor. The bank is not required to search for accounts held in the joint names of a judgment debtor and another person.[2]

1   CPR 72.6(1).
2   Unless that other person is a joint judgment debtor – see para 3.1(1) of the Practice Direction. See also paras 3.43–3.52.

Disclosure of accounts held with affiliated entities?

3.125 Given that the rules require the bank or building society to search for accounts held with '*it*', it seems that the search should be confined to accounts held by the judgment debtor with the legal entity named as the third party in the interim order and on whom the order has been served.[1] Were the bank to disclose information relating to accounts held with affiliated entities, for example, the affiliated entity with whom the account is held may face a claim from the account holder for breach of the contractual duty of confidentiality owed by a bank to its customer.[2]

1   Where there is any ambiguity in this regard, eg because the bank has been incorrectly named in the order, this should be addressed in the subsequent disclosure of information made by the bank – see para 3.132.
2   Such entity would not have a defence of falling within one of the exceptions to the duty of confidentiality owed by a bank to its customers set out in *Tournier v National Provincial and Union Bank of England* [1924] 1 KB 461, such as disclosure under compulsion of the law, since the order does not concern this entity.

Disclosure of accounts held with foreign branches or subsidiaries?

3.126 Similarly, while there is no express limitation in CPR 72.6 or Form N84 that the bank's search for accounts should be confined to accounts held with that entity that are within the jurisdiction, the dicta of the House of Lords in *Société Eram* and the court's ruling that the third party debt order procedure cannot be used to attach foreign debts[1] would suggest this is the better view. Given that following its search for accounts the bank must disclose each account identified to the court and the judgment creditor, there would appear to be further support for this interpretation of the rule in the Court of Appeal's ruling in *R v Grossman*.[2] In that case the Court held that an application under the Bankers' Book Evidence Act 1879 addressed to the

English branch of a bank for the inspection of documents held with the Isle of Man branch should not be allowed. The Court found that the fact that the Manx branch was subject to the laws and regulations of the Isle of Man meant that for these purposes the Manx branch should be treated as a separate legal entity from the head office in London.[3] Similarly, if a bank were to disclose information relating to foreign accounts held with it by the judgment debtor pursuant to an English interim third party debt order, this may place the bank in breach of the local law governing the account. The fact that the CPR provides a specific procedure for a judgment creditor to obtain information from the judgment debtor as to his assets (including overseas assets)[4] in Pt 71 arguably provides an additional reason for interpreting the requirement in this way.

1   See paras 3.67-3.78.
2   (1981) 73 Cr App Rep 302.
3   (1981) 73 Cr App Rep 302 at 308.
4   See paras 2.193–2.219.

Information to be disclosed

3.127   Within seven days of being served with the interim order in respect of each account identified, the bank or building society must disclose to the court and the judgment creditor:[1]
(a) the account number; and
(b) whether the account is in credit and, if so:
    (i)   whether the account balance is sufficient to cover the amount in the interim order;
    (ii) if it is not, the amount of the balance at the date the bank was served with the order; and
    (iii) whether the bank asserts any right to the money in the account, whether pursuant to a right of set off or otherwise, and the grounds for that assertion.

1   CPR 72.6(2).

3.128   Alternatively, if the judgment debtor does not hold an account with the bank or building society, or the bank or building society is unable to comply with the order for any other reason, it must inform the court and the judgment creditor of that fact within seven days of being served with the interim order.[1]

1   CPR 72.6(3).

3.129   As regards the obligations of third party banks and building societies, the wording of the standard form interim third party debt order, Form N84, states:

'If the third party *is a bank or building society*, it must search for all accounts held solely by the judgment debtor and, within 7 days of receiving this order, give details of them to the court and the judgment creditor, stating whether it holds sufficient to cover the total shown and, if not, the amounts in them.'

3.130   This wording does not make clear the obligation under CPR 72.6(3) for the third party bank or building society to inform the court and the judgment creditor where it does *not* hold an account for the judgment debtor or cannot comply with the order for some other reason. Third party banks and building societies should be made aware that they are *also* required to provide this information to the court and the judgment creditor where relevant.

3.131 The example given in CPR 72.6(3) of where a bank or building society is unable to comply with the order for 'any other reason' is where the bank has more than one account holder whose details match the information provided in the interim order and it cannot identify which one the order applies to. Alternatively, it may be that the order has been served on the wrong legal entity in a group of affiliated banking entities. The judgment creditor may apply to the court to vary the order or make a fresh application for a third party debt order once the correct information has been obtained.

3.132 It may be most convenient for the bank or building society to provide the information required by CPR 72.6 to the court and judgment creditor in writing (either by letter or fax), though there is no requirement to do so.[1] If a letter is sent, it would be advisable for the third party bank or building society on whom the order has been served to state clearly the name of the legal entity on whom the interim order was served and on whose behalf the letter is written. This will avoid any ambiguity where the order has been served on the wrong legal entity by the judgment creditor.

[1] By contrast, a third party other than a bank or building society *is* required to provide written notification if he claims not to owe the debt or to owe less than the amount specified in the interim order (CPR 72.6(4)).

3.133 The bank or building society is allowed to deduct a sum from the balance in the account for its administrative expenses in complying with the order (see para 3.188).

Other third parties

3.134 Where the third party is not a bank or building society he must notify the judgment creditor and the court in writing within seven days of the order if he claims:

(a) not to owe any money to the judgment debtor; or
(b) to owe less than the amount specified in the order.[1]

[1] CPR 72.6(4).

Where the judgment creditor disputes the third party's notice

3.135 Where the third party has given notice under CPR 72.6 that he does not owe any money to the judgment debtor, or that the amount owed is less than the amount specified in the interim order, and the judgment creditor wishes to dispute this, the judgment creditor must file and serve written evidence setting out the grounds on which he disputes the third party's case.[1] Such evidence is likely to take the form of a witness statement from the judgment creditor exhibiting documentary evidence in support. This evidence must be filed and served on each party as soon as possible and in any event at least three days before the hearing.[2]

¹   CPR 72.8(3).
²   CPR 72.8(4).

If the third party does not comply with the interim order

3.136   The notes to CPR 72.6[1] observe that: 'It is to be hoped that the third party will comply with his obligations under this new Rule ... but the inevitable question arises what if he does not?'

¹   Civil Procedure 2004, vol 1, para 72.6.1.

3.137   A third party other than a bank or building society is only required to notify the court and the judgment creditor where he claims *not* to owe any money to the judgment debtor or to owe less than the amount specified in the order. Thus where no such notification is received, the court will assume that the debt is not disputed and make a final third party debt order. It will then be for the third party to seek to set aside or appeal the order if no debt is owed. If he does not have a good explanation for why he did not make timely notification of this fact, he may face a costs sanction.

3.138   A bank or building society is required to inform the court of the position in relation to accounts held with it by the judgment debtor even where none exist. The discussion in the notes to the White Book[1] focuses largely on the question of whether the court will proceed to make a final third party debt order in the absence of such information, and this will depend on the particular facts of the case and evidence before the court. The notes observe that, if a bank does not comply or alternatively arrange to be represented to make submissions at the hearing, the court could telephone the bank to ascertain the position in accordance with the court's duty to actively manage cases under CPR 1.4. However, the obligation on the third party bank or building society to search for and disclose the position in relation to the judgment debtor's accounts arises pursuant to an order of the court and it follows that an institution that fails to provide the requisite notification or, alternatively, fails to attend the hearing to make a final third party debt order to make representations may face liability for contempt of court.[2]

¹   Civil Procedure 2004, vol 1, para 72.6.1.
²   In light of this, the fact that the interim third party debt order in Form N84 does not make clear the obligation on banks and building societies to inform the court and judgment creditor even where they hold no account for the judgment debtor or cannot comply with the order for some other reason is unsatisfactory.

Additional steps by the third party

3.139   Where the third party objects to the court making a final third party debt order or knows or believes that someone other than the judgment debtor has an interest in the money specified in the interim order, he must take certain further steps.

Objections to a final third party debt order

3.140   As will be seen,[1] the final third party debt order will direct the third party to pay the debt owed to the judgment creditor rather than to the judgment debtor and the third party will be discharged from his obligations to the judgment debtor to the same extent. As a result, the third party is not prejudiced by the order and in most cases the third party will have no objection to the order being made.

¹   See paras 3.173-3.178.

3.141   However, if the judgment debtor or third party objects to the court making a final third party debt order, the burden is on the judgment debtor or third party to show cause why the interim order should not be made final.¹ He must file and serve written evidence stating the grounds for his objections in accordance with CPR 72.8.² Such evidence must be filed and served on each party as soon as possible and in any event at least three days before the hearing.³ In such circumstances the judgment debtor or third party will inevitably also wish to attend the hearing to make representations as to why the final third party debt order should not be made. In *Newman v Rook*⁴ it was held that a garnishee must set up a prima facie case before the court would order trial of an issue (see paras 3.155–3.156).

¹   *Roberts Petroleum Ltd v Bernard Kenny Ltd* [1982] 1 WLR 301, a case concerning charging orders where the same principles apply. This principle was stated in the Court of Appeal judgment and was not affected by the reversal of this decision by the House of Lords.
²   CPR 72.8(1).
³   CPR 72.8(4).
⁴   (1858) 4 CBNS 434.

3.142   In *Vinall v de Pass*¹ the third party filed an affidavit denying that he owed the debt specified by the judgment creditor to the judgment debtor but declined, repeatedly, to deny that he owed *any* debt to the judgment debtor. The House of Lords held that garnishee order attaches all debts owed by the third party to the judgment debtor² and that given the third party's refusal to give any answer other than a denial that he owed that particular debt, the garnishee order absolute was properly made against him.

¹   [1892] AC 90
²   This would be subject to any limit specified in the order.

3.143   The circumstances in which the court may decline to make a final third party debt order are considered in paras 3.157–3.170.

Persons other than the judgment debtor with a claim to the debt

3.144   If the judgment debtor or third party knows or believes that a person other than the judgment debtor has a claim to the money specified in the interim order, he must file and serve written evidence stating his knowledge of that matter.¹ Such evidence must be filed and served on each party as soon as possible and in any event at least three days before the hearing.²

¹   CPR 72.8(2).
²   CPR 72.8(4).

3.145   If the court is notified that some person other than the judgment debtor may have a claim to the money specified in the interim order, it will serve notice of the application and hearing on that person.[1] That person may then wish to attend the hearing to provide evidence of his claim to the money.

1   CPR 72.8(5).

3.146   If the third party knows that some person other than the judgment debtor has a claim to the money and does *not* disclose that fact to the court, he may be liable to that person. In *Wood v Dunn*[1] the garnishee had been served with a garnishee order nisi and at that time had no reason to object to the order being made absolute nor knew of any other interest in the debt. The garnishee order absolute was made and served on the garnishee, following which he made payment to the judgment creditor in compliance with the order. However, during the interval between the interim and the final order, unbeknown to the garnishee, the judgment debtor was adjudged bankrupt. The court held that the garnishee was protected from any claim for the debt by the trustees in bankruptcy by the fact that he had paid in compliance with the garnishee order absolute. The court noted that it would be a hardship for the garnishee to have to apply to have the order set aside in these circumstances and that the relevant legislative provisions,[2] stated that payment in accordance with a garnishee order absolute shall be a valid discharge of the debt to the judgment debtor, even if the order is subsequently set aside or the judgment reversed. However, the court noted (obiter) that:[3]

> 'if the present defendants [the garnishee] had had notice of the trust deed [the bankruptcy] at the time, or after the ex parte order of attachment was served upon them, and before the time for shewing cause, they would have had good cause to shew, and the order for payment would not have been made; and we think that there can be no doubt that, in that case, the proper course to take would be to shew cause, and if the garnishee were to pay instead of shewing cause, that the assignees could recover against him.'

1   (1866-67) LR 2 QB 73 at 82.
2   The modern counterparts of which are contained in CPR 72.9(3). See further para 3.164.
3   (1866-67) LR 2 QB 73 at 82.

3.147   This is exactly what happened in *The Leader*.[1] In that case, the garnishee failed to inform the court of a lien which the judgment debtor's solicitors had over a sum owed by the garnishee (of which the garnishee had knowledge) before the garnishee order absolute was made and the sums were paid over to the judgment creditors.[2] The court held that the garnishee ought to have apprised the judge of the existence of the lien before the final orders were made and he was therefore liable to the judgment debtor's solicitors for that sum.

1   (1868) LR 2 A&E 314.
2   The facts in this case are complicated since the debt owed by the garnishee was itself a judgment debt owed in consequence of proceedings which had been brought against the garnishee (the defendant) by the plaintiff. After the plaintiff recovered judgment against the defendant, judgment creditors of the plaintiff sought to attach the judgment debt owed by the garnishee. These were the garnishee proceedings to which this case relates.

Right of set-off or counterclaim by the third party

3.148   If the third party is a bank or building society, it should have informed the court where it asserts any right to the money in the account, whether pursuant to a

right of set off or otherwise, and the grounds for that assertion.[1] The third party
should be allowed to avail himself of any right of set-off against the judgment debtor
which existed when the interim order was made. In *Tapp v Jones*[2] the court held:[3]

> 'I agree that no greater right is given to the [judgment] creditor than the
> [judgment] debtor had. It is obviously just that if a cross debt were due to the
> garnishee at the date of the attachment there should be a right of set-off in his
> favour, and I should strive hard to give effect to that if I could, though there
> would be difficulties in the way.'

[1]   See para 3.127.
[2]   (1875) LR 10 QB 591. See para 3.10.
[3]   (1875) LR 10 QB 591 at 593.

3.149   Where the third party has a counterclaim which could be set off against a
claim by the judgment debtor for repayment of the debt, the third party should be able
to avail itself of this counterclaim so that the amount the third party is ordered by the
court to pay over to the judgment creditor is reduced accordingly. The third party
should set out the nature and extent of its counterclaim in a witness statement filed
and served in accordance with CPR 72.8 (see para 3.141).

3.150   In *Hale v Victoria Plumbing Co Ltd*[1] the judgment creditor sought to attach
sums owed by the garnishee, a building contractor, to the judgment debtor, a plumbing
contractor. The garnishee filed an affidavit stating that it was not indebted to the
judgment debtor and had claims against the judgment debtor for breach of contract in
excess of the sum claimed by the judgment creditor. The Court of Appeal held that
since RSC Ord 18, r 17 provided that claims arising out of the same transaction between
two parties can be set off against each other, then, notwithstanding the fact that the
garnishee had not brought proceedings against the judgment debtor, the garnishee
order should be set aside. The same principles should apply under the CPR.[2]

[1]   [1966] 2 QB 746.
[2]   The modern counterpart of RSC Ord 18, r 17 is contained in CPR 16.6, which provides that
       where a defendant contends he is entitled to money from the claimant and relies on this as
       a defence to the claim, that contention may be included in the defence and set off against the
       claim, whether or not it is added as a counterclaim.

3.151   *Hale* distinguished the earlier Court of Appeal authority of *Stumore v
Campbell & Co*,[1] where the court held that a solicitor could not set off a claim for
costs against monies it held for a client for a special purpose which had failed, since
when the purpose failed a trust arose for repayment of that money to the client.
Danckwerts LJ stated in his judgment in *Hale* that the decision in Stumore 'may be
perfectly correct, and I say nothing against the decision whatever, but it seems to me
to be utterly different from the present case'.[2]

[1]   [1892] 1 QB 314.
[2]   [1966] 2 QB 746 at 751.

3.152   While the court may take into account claims which the third party has against
the *judgment debtor* in considering whether to make a final third party debt order, it
will not decide issues between the third party and the *judgment creditor* in third party
debt order proceedings. In *Sampson v The Seaton and Beer Railway Company*[1] a

garnishee refused to pay over to the judgment creditor the full amount of a debt owed to the judgment debtor on the grounds that it claimed the right to retain an amount owed to it by the judgment creditor. Lush J held:[2]

> 'The machinery provided [under garnishee proceedings] for determining questions of disputed liability has reference solely to cases where the garnishee disputes his liability to the judgment debtor. And although we have no doubt that the state of accounts between the garnishee and the judgment debtor may and ought to be gone into, so that the garnishee may not be in a worse position than if he had been sued for his debt by the judgment debtor, the case is different as between him and the judgment creditor. There is no place for the discussion of cross claims between the garnishee and the judgment creditor. If it had been intended to let in such claims, some mode of adjusting them in case of dispute would have been also provided. But there is none.'

However, it is questionable whether this remains good law in light of the provisions of CPR 72.8(6)(c), which allow the court to decide any issues between 'any of the parties and any other person who has a claim to the money specified in the interim order' at the hearing for further consideration of the application.[3] The overriding objective and the efficient administration of justice would suggest that such consideration could be best dealt with at such hearing.

[1]   (1874-5) LR 10 QB 28.
[2]   (1874-5) LR 10 QB 28 at 30.
[3]   See para 3.154.

Hearing for further consideration of the application

3.153   At least 28 days after the interim third party debt order is made there will be hearing at which the court will consider whether to make a final third party debt order.

3.154   CPR 72.8(6) provides:

> 'At the hearing the court may
> (a)   make a final third party debt order;
> (b)   discharge the interim third party debt order and dismiss the application;
> (c)   decide any issues in dispute between the parties, or between any of the parties and any other person who has a claim to the money specified in the interim order; or
> (d)   direct a trial of any such issues, and if necessary give directions.'

There is therefore a range of options open to the court at the hearing.

When will the court order a trial of the issues?

3.155   CPR 72.8(6)(c) makes it clear that the master[1] can decide the issues raised by the parties at the hearing for further consideration of the application. The notes to CPR 72.8[2] observe that only exceptionally will it be necessary for the master to give directions and order a trial of any issue between the parties pursuant to CPR

72.8(6)(d). In *Newman v Rook*[3] Willes J sitting in the Court of Common Pleas held that:

> 'I should say that the mere assertion by the garnishee that he disputes the debt amounts to nothing: there is no substantial dispute until some real answer or defence is set up.'

[1] Or district judge in the county court.
[2] Civil Procedure 2004, vol 1, para 72.8.1.
[3] (1858) 4 CB 434.

3.156 In *Wise v Birkenshaw*[1] the court held that where a garnishee had satisfied the master by affidavit that there was no attachable debt, there should be no trial of that issue. However, if there were any reasonable doubt as to whether a debt existed, the matter should be tried. Reasonable grounds for directing a trial to decide whether or not a debt exists will have to amount to more than an assertion of the judgment creditor's beliefs. In *Roberts v Death*[2] the court held that where there are reasonable grounds for suggesting that the judgment debtor is not entitled to money owed by a third party for his own use, the court ought not to make the final order until it has enquired whether or not the judgment debtor is so entitled. In that case, the money was owed to the judgment debtor as trustee for another and the Court of Appeal held that the garnishee order absolute ought not therefore to have been made. If there are serious doubts as to the solvency of the judgment debtor, the court should not make the order until there has been an enquiry into this matter.[3]

[1] (1860) 29 LJ Exch 240.
[2] (1881-82) LR 8 QBD 319.
[3] See para 3.171.

The court's discretion to make a final third party debt order

3.157 The use of the word 'may' in CPR 72.8(6) indicates that the court has a discretion to make the final third party debt order.

3.158 In *Roberts Petroleum Ltd v Bernard Kenny*[1] the Court of Appeal set out various general principles governing the court's discretion to make a charging order under the Charging Orders Act 1979. As Lord Brandon of Oakbrook observed, the same general principles should apply to third party debt orders:

> '(1) The question whether a charging order nisi should be made absolute is one for the discretion of the court.
>
> (2) The burden of showing cause why a charging order nisi should not be made absolute is on the judgment debtor.
>
> (3) For the purpose of the exercise of the court's discretion there is, in general at any rate, no material difference between the making absolute of a charging order nisi on the one hand and a garnishee order nisi on the other.[2]
>
> (4) In exercising its discretion the court has both the right and the duty to take into account all the circumstances of any particular case, whether such circumstances arose before or after the making of the order nisi.

(5) The court should so exercise its discretion as to do equity, so far as possible, to all the various parties involved, that is to say the judgment creditor, the judgment debtor, and all other unsecured creditors.'[3]

1   [1982] 1 All ER 685.
2   Similar sentiments were expressed in the earlier Court of Appeal decision in *Rainbow Properties v Moorgate* [1972] 2 All ER 821 where Buckley LJ at 824 expressed the view: 'I for myself can see no difference between those considerations which are relevant to the question whether the discretion should or should not be exercised to make absolute a garnishee order and those considerations which are relevant to the question whether the court should or should not make absolute a charging order.'
3   [1982] 1 All ER 685 at 689.

3.159   The Court of Appeal's decision in *Roberts v Kenny* was subsequently reversed in the House of Lords but the principles set out above were not effected by that reversal and remain good law.[1]

1   Two further principles were set out by Lord Brandon of Oakbrook at [1982] 1 All ER 685 at 689 but the House of Lords subsequently overturned these - see the judgment of Lord Brightman at [1983] 2 AC 192 at 213.

Third party debt order would be inequitable

3.160   An order will not be made where it would be inequitable. In *Kennett v Westminster Improvement Commissioners*[1] a number of bondholders had agreed to advance money to the commissioners on terms that all of the bondholders were to rank equally. One of the bondholders then sued the commissioners on one of the bonds and obtained judgment. He then sought to attach a debt owed to the commissioners through garnishee proceedings. The court held that it would be inequitable to make the garnishee order absolute since the effect of so doing would be to give that bondholder a priority over the other bondholders. This would be in violation of his agreement with the other bondholders.

1   1856 25 LJ ExCh 97.

Double jeopardy

3.161   Where there is a 'real or substantial risk' of the third party being required to pay the debt a second time it will be inequitable to make a final third party debt order. In *Deutsche Schachtbau und Tiefbohrgesellschaft mbH v Shell International Petroleum Co Ltd*[1] the House of Lords held (Lord Templeman dissenting) that a garnishee order absolute should not be made in respect of an English debt owed by Shell to the judgment debtor, since there was a 'real and substantial risk'[2] that Shell would be required by a foreign court to pay the debt over again to the judgment debtor.[3] Lord Goff also observed that:[4]

'as a general rule, commercial pressure cannot of itself be enough to render it inequitable to make an order absolute.'

1   [1990] 1 AC 295. Arguably, this case should still be seen as the leading authority on this point notwithstanding the obiter dicta the judgment contains on whether the court has

jurisdiction to garnish foreign debts. As Lord Hobhouse observed in *Société Eram* at [75]: 'It is unfortunate also that what Lord Goff said in *Deutsche Schachtbau und Tiefbohrgesellschaft mbH v Shell International Petroleum Co Ltd* [1990] 1 AC 295 should have been cited without having proper regard to what that case was about. The debt was a commercial debt with an admitted situs in England. It was properly recoverable in England and the order made by the English court would discharge the debt. The question which arose was the exceptional one, whether there was a real and substantial risk that the garnishee, Shell, would nevertheless in a foreign country, be compelled to pay the debt again. This did not raise a question of jurisdiction of lack of subject matter but more simply the, in that case, difficult question whether it was equitable in the discretion of the court to make the garnishee order.'

2   [1990] 1 AC 295 at 344.

3   The House of Lords held this view notwithstanding the fact that the foreign proceedings had been illegitimately started by the judgment debtor in breach of an arbitration agreement between the parties and that according to generally accepted rules of international law the foreign court did not have jurisdiction to make such an order.

4   [1990] 1 AC 295 at 352.

3.162 In *Soinco SACI and Eural Kft v Novokuznetsk Aluminium Plant (No 2)*[1] the Court of Appeal had to consider a similar scenario to that before their Lordships in *Deutsche Schactbau*. In this case the judgment creditors had brought proceedings to enforce a Zurich arbitration award against the judgment debtors, a Russian enterprise, relating to an aluminium smelting contract in Russia. The judgment creditors had obtained a garnishee order attaching all debts owed by the third party, a Guernsey company, to the judgment debtors. In the meantime, civil proceedings had been instituted by the Russian authorities before a Russian arbitral court seeking a declaration that the contract between the judgment creditor and judgment debtor was invalid. The third party's debt was admitted and had been paid into a London bank account but the third party sought to appeal the garnishee order absolute on the grounds that, notwithstanding the attachment of the debt by the English court, they might be compelled to pay that debt to the judgment debtors by some order to be made by the Russian courts.

1   [1998] 2 Lloyd's Rep 346.

3.163 Lord Justice Chadwick summarised the position:[1]

'It is common ground that the power of the Court to make a garnishee order, in circumstances in which it has jurisdiction to do so, remains discretionary. It is also common ground that the principles upon which that discretion should be exercised – at least for the purposes of the present proceedings – were considered exhaustively by the House of Lords in [Deutsche Schachtbau] ... In short, the Court, in the exercise of its discretion, should not make a garnishee order in circumstances in which it would be inequitable to expose the garnishee to the risk of being compelled to pay the attached debt twice over – the risk of "double jeopardy".'

1   [1998] 2 Lloyd's Rep 346 at 347–348.

3.164 Lord Justice Chadwick went on to point out that Lord Goff had been careful to stress in *Deutsche Schachtbau* that the third party does not have to establish certainty or even a very high risk of being compelled to pay the debt twice, but only a 'real risk' of being required to do so.[1]

1   [1998] 2 Lloyd's Rep 346 at 354.

3.165   In *Soinco*, in contrast to the *Deutsche Schachtbau* case, the court found that there was insufficient evidence to displace the assumption that the Russian courts would respect the accepted norms of international private law and refuse to recognise the arbitration award and the English garnishee order, thus the garnishee order absolute stood.   It was also of significance that the third party and the judgment debtor were closely linked and the history of their trading relationship suggested there was little risk of the judgment debtor taking steps in Russia or elsewhere to force the third party to make a second payment.

Insolvency of the judgment debtor

3.166   Where the insolvency of a judgment debtor is established, the court is unlikely to exercise its discretion to make the final third party debt order since to do so would effectively give the judgment creditor preference over other creditors of the judgment debtor's estate.   In *Pritchard v Westminster Bank Ltd*,[1] Lord Denning MR, sitting in the Court of Appeal, observed:[2]

'The general principle, when there is no insolvency, is that the person who gets in first gets the fruits of his diligence … But it is different when the estate is insolvent … The court will not allow one creditor, however diligent he may be, to get an advantage over the others by getting in first with a garnishee order.'[3]

[1]   [1969] 1 WLR 547.
[2]   [1969] 1 WLR 547 at 999–1000.
[3]   These dicta are now effectively reflected in the Insolvency Act 1986, s 183(2)(a), under which if a creditor has notice of a meeting having been called at which a resolution for winding up is to be proposed, he will not be entitled to retain the benefit of the attachment against a liquidator unless he has completed the attachment before he had notice of that meeting.

3.167   Similarly, in *Wilson (D) (Birmingham) Ltd v Metropolitan Property Development Ltd*[1] the Court of Appeal held:[2]

'The position is, I think, that a court in considering whether or not to exercise its discretion to make absolute a garnishee order in circumstances such as this, must bear in mind not only the position of the judgment creditor, the judgment debtor and the garnishee, but the position of the other creditors of the judgment debtor and must have regard to the fact that proceedings are on foot, and were on foot at the time the garnishee proceedings were launched, for ensuring the distribution of the available assets of the judgment debtor company among the creditors pari passu.'

[1]   [1975] 2 All ER 814.
[2]   [1975] 2 All ER 814 at 819, per Buckley LJ.

3.168   The same principles applied when the House of Lords decided that the liquidation of the defendants was sufficient cause for the court to exercise its discretion *not* to make a charging order absolute in *Roberts Petroleum Ltd v Bernard Kenny Ltd*.[1]   Both third party debt order and charging order proceedings are methods of enforcement that depend on the exercise of the court's discretion.   The same considerations apply in the exercise of that discretion in both types of proceedings.[2]

1   [1983] 2 AC 192.
2   See eg the judgment of Buckley LJ in *Rainbow v Moorgate Properties* [1975] 2 All ER 821 at 824.

3.169 In *Roberts,* in contrast to the earlier cases of *Pritchard* and *Wilson,* a resolution to wind up the judgment debtor company on grounds of insolvency intervened between the charging order nisi and the hearing for further consideration. Their Lordships held that while each case would be a matter for individual judgment in the particular circumstances,[1] the imposition of a statutory scheme for the distribution of assets among creditors *was* sufficient cause for the court to exercise its discretion not to make the charging order absolute. Lord Brightman, who gave the lead judgment, with which their Lordships unanimously agreed, stated that the purpose of the hearing for further consideration of the application was to enable the court to review the position inter partes.[2] Before reviewing the authorities Lord Brightman observed:[3]

'If the statutory scheme for dealing with the assets of the company has been irrevocably imposed on the company, by resolution or winding up order, before the court has irrevocably determined to give the creditor the benefit of a charging order, I would have thought that the statutory scheme should prevail.'

He went on:

'I do not see why a creditor should gain an advantage merely because he has a revocable order for security at the time when the statutory scheme comes into existence.'

1   [1983] 2 AC 192 at 212.
2   [1983] 2 AC 192 at 208.
3   [1983] 2 AC 192 at 209.

3.170 By analogy, the same principle should apply if an individual is adjudged bankrupt after the interim order but before the final order.[1]

1   *Roberts* disapproved the earlier Court of Appeal decision in *Burston Finance v Godfrey* [1976] 2 All ER 976, where the Court of Appeal upheld an order for a charging order absolute notwithstanding the fact that the judgment debtors had been adjudged bankrupt prior to the further hearing.

3.171 In *George Lee & Sons (Builders) v Olink*[1] the Court of Appeal held that where there was serious doubt as to whether an estate was solvent, a garnishee order absolute should not be made until there had been an enquiry into whether the estate was solvent or insolvent.

1   [1972] 1 WLR 214.

3.172 Finally, it is also worth noting in the content of insolvency that in *Lancaster Motor Company (London), Ltd v Bremith, Ltd. Barclays Bank, Ltd (Garnishees)*[1] the Court of Appeal held that where a liquidator of a company had been appointed, a judgment creditor of that company could not garnish a bank account held by the liquidator. In his judgment, with which Clauson and Goddard LJJ agreed, Sir Wilfrid Greene MR considered the position under the then current regime, RSC Ord 45, and stated:[2]

'Here the money held by the bank was not owing to the judgment debtors. The judgment debtors were the company and the account was in the name of the liquidator. The liquidator alone could sue the bank. His cheque alone would be honoured. There was no relationship of banker and customer or debtor and creditor between the bank and the company.'

He continued:[3]

'The crucial matter to be observed is what is the relationship of the alleged debtor to the judgment debtor. That relationship must be one of debtor and creditor and unless it falls within that description the rule does not apply.'

1   [1941] 1 KB 675.
2   [1941] 1 KB 675 at 677.
3   [1941] 1 KB 675 at 679.

Final third party debt order

Form of the order

3.173   Form N85 contains the standard form final third party debt order. This will order the third party to pay a specified sum of money to the judgment creditor by a certain date. It also provides that the judgment creditor's costs of the application are to be retained out of the money received by the judgment creditor in priority to the judgment debt (see para 3.183). Form N85 also states the effect of the order, namely:

(a)   to reduce the amount owed to the judgment debtor by the third party by the amount paid under the order plus any costs and expenses to which the third party is entitled; (see further paras 3.188 and 3.189); and

(b)   to reduce the amount owed by the judgment debtor to the judgment creditor by the amount paid by the third party less the judgment creditor's costs of the application (see further para 3.183).

Effect of a final third party debt order

3.174   As has been noted in para 3.112, the third party must not pay the debt to the judgment creditor *until* the final third party debt order has been made.

3.175   CPR 72.9(2) provides:

'If—
(a)   the third party pays money to the judgment creditor in compliance with a third party debt order; or
(b)   the order is enforced against him,
the third party shall, to the extent of the amount paid by him or realised by enforcement against him, be discharged from his debt to the judgment debtor.'

3.176   The effect of a final third party debt order was succinctly summarised by Lord Bingham in his judgment in *Société Eram*:[1]

'When a final or absolute order is made the third party or garnishee is obliged (subject to any specified monetary limit) to make payment to the judgment creditor and not to the judgment debtor, but the debt of the third party to the judgment debtor is discharged pro tanto.'

1   [2003] UKHL 30 at [24].

3.177   The discharge of the debt owed by the third party to the judgment debtor is an essential feature of the procedure. Its importance was highlighted by their Lordships in *Société Eram* and the fact that an English garnishee order would not operate to discharge a foreign debt was key to their Lordships' reasoning in that case. As has been noted,[1] Lord Bingham stated:[2]

'It is not in my opinion open to the Court to make an order in a case, such as the present, where it is clear or appears that the making of the order will not discharge the debt of the third party or garnishee to the judgment debtor according to the law which governs that debt.'

Lord Hoffmann concurred:[3]

'The discharge of the third party's indebtedness effected by rule 72.9(2) (formerly RSC, Ord 49, r 8) is therefore an essential part of the execution.'

As did Lord Millett:[4]

'The discharge of the debt owed by the third party to the judgment debtor is not, therefore, merely a fortunate consequence of the order but a necessary and integral part of it. It is what justifies the making of the order and makes it a process of execution against the assets of the judgment debtor.'

1   See para 3.73.
2   [2003] UKHL 30 at [26].
3   [2003] UKHL 30 at [63].
4   [2003] UKHL 30 at [97].

3.178   CPR 72.9(1) provides that a final third party debt order shall be enforceable as an order to pay money. It can therefore be enforced in the same way as any other order of the court and if the third party does not pay over the sums in accordance with the order, the judgment creditor can, for example, bring enforcement proceedings against the third party to enforce payment.

Setting aside the order

3.179   A third party who pays in compliance with a final third party debt order will be discharged from the debt owed to the judgment debtor even if the third party debt order (or original judgment) is subsequently set aside.

3.180   A third party who objects to a final third party debt order being made should file evidence stating his grounds for such objection in advance of the hearing and make representations at the hearing as necessary.[1] However, the court has jurisdiction to set aside a final third party debt order[2] and if the third party (or another party with an interest in the debt) was not present at the hearing or new information has come to light since the hearing, he should promptly apply for the order to be set aside.

1   See para 3.141.
2   See eg: *Moore v Peachey* (1892) 66 LT 198; *Burrell & Sons v Read* (1895) 11 TLR 36;
        Marshall v James [1905] 1 Ch 432; *O'Brien v Killeen* [1914] 2 Ir R 63.

Appealing the order

3.181   In addition, if the third party considers that the master should not have made
the order, he may appeal to a High Court judge in accordance with the procedure set
out in CPR 52.[1] However, a higher court will be reluctant to interfere with the master's
exercise of discretion[2] and the final order will not be interfered with by a higher court
unless wrong in principle.[3]

1   Appeal of the decision of a master is to be made to a High Court judge. A decision of a district
        judge of a county court is appealable to a circuit judge. See further PD Pt 52, para 2A.
2   See *Wise v Birkenshaw* (1860) 29 LJ Exch 240.
3   *Wicks v Shanks* (1893) 67 LT 109, a case concerning charging orders, where the same
        considerations apply.

Building society balances

3.182   A final third party debt order will not require a payment which would reduce
the amount in a judgment debtor's account with a building society or credit union to
less than £1.[1]

1   PD 72, para 6.

Costs

3.183   Where a judgment creditor is awarded costs on an application for a third
party debt order[1] he retains those costs out of the money recovered under the order.[2]
Such costs shall be deemed paid first out of the money recovered, in priority to the
judgment debt.[3] The effect of this provision is to reduce the amount of the judgment
debt by the amount received after the costs of making the application have been
deducted. Thus where the debt owed by the third party to the judgment debtor is less
than the total of the amount awarded by the court in respect of costs plus the judgment
debt, a portion of the judgment debt will remain outstanding.

1   Or an order for payment out of funds held at court in accordance with the procedure set out
        in CPR 72.10 – see paras 3.61–3.62.
2   CPR 72.11. Unless the court orders otherwise: see CPR 72.11(a).
3   CPR 72.11(b). These matters are also stated in the standard form final third party debt order
        contained in Form N85.

3.184   Where the court makes a final third party debt order under CPR 72.8(6)(a) it
will award the judgment creditor fixed costs of the application. The interim third party
debt order will have specified the amount secured by it and the amount ordered in this
regard will appear in the final third party debt order. The fixed costs are the court fee
(currently £100) together with the judgment creditor's fixed costs payable under CPR
45.6. These are:

(a) if the amount recovered is less than £150, one half of the amount recovered;

(b) if the amount recovered is more than £150, £98.50.

3.185   Where the application is unopposed and a final third party debt order is made at the hearing without further consideration of any issues, the court's award of costs is likely to be confined to these amounts. However, where the third party or judgment debtor (or some other person) objects to the final third party debt order being made, the judgment creditor may have incurred further costs in relation to the issues between the parties (for example, as a consequence of having to prepare and file written evidence disputing the third party's case). In such circumstances the successful judgment creditor should seek an order in relation to the recovery of those additional costs, which are outside the fixed costs regime, at the hearing.

3.186   Where a judgment creditor's application has been unsuccessful he may be ordered to pay the costs of the other parties, particularly in the case of a third party who has been put to the expense of filing evidence objecting to a final third party debt order being made. In such circumstances those parties should also be prepared to apply to the court for costs at the hearing. In addition, where the judgment debtor or third party disputes the liability and the judgment creditor declines to contest the issue and abandons the application, he may be liable for the costs incurred by the other parties.[1]

1   *Wintle v Williams* (1858) 3 H&N 288.

3.187   The general rule is that the court should make a summary assessment of the costs at the conclusion of a hearing lasting not more than one day unless there is good reason not to.[1] Each party who intends to claim costs should prepare a written statement of costs which should follow as closely as possible Form N260. The statement must be signed by the party or his legal representative and must be filed at court with copies served on any party from whom recovery of costs is sought. Filing and service must be done as soon as possible and in any event at least 24 hours before the date fixed for the hearing.[2]

1   See CPR Pt 44.
2   General rules about costs are set out in Pt 44 and the accompanying Practice Direction, which should be referred to for the specific provisions.

3.188   The interim third party debt order[1] also provides:

'A bank or building society may deduct an amount from any money held for the judgment debtor, for its expenses in complying with this order.'

1   Form N84.

3.189   While the wording of the order is not entirely clear, this would seem to be a reference to the fact that, independently of any award of costs, a deposit-taking institution[1] is entitled to deduct a 'prescribed sum' from the debt owed to the judgment debtor (ie the account balance) for administrative and clerical expenses in complying with a final third party debt order.[2] Such sum has been varied from time to time by statutory instrument and is currently set at £55.[3] The final third party debt order contained in form N85 also states that the amount owed by the third party to the judgment debtor will be reduced by the amount the third party pays under that order and any costs and expenses to which the third party is entitled.

1   Defined in SCA 1981, s 40(6). This includes banks and building societies.
2   SCA 1981, s 40A(1) and CCA 1984, s 109(1).
3   Attachment of Debts (Expenses) Order 1996, SI 1996/3098. Note that under SCA 1981, s 40A(1B) the institution may deduct this sum even where the debt owed is insufficient to cover both the deduction for expenses and the amount attached by the interim third party debt order in respect of the judgment debtor and costs.

Interplay with the insolvency regime

3.190   Chapter 1 considers generally the interaction between the law of enforcement and the insolvency regimes relating to corporate and individual judgment debtors. This section considers the application of the rules set out in the Insolvency Act 1986 (IA 1986), ss 183 and 346, to third party debt orders for the purposes of bankruptcy and winding up.

3.191   IA 1986, ss 183 and 346 provide that unless a judgment creditor has completed the attachment of a debt under third party debt order proceedings by receipt of the debt before the commencement of the winding up or bankruptcy of a judgment debtor, he will be deprived of the benefit of that attachment as against a liquidator or trustee in bankruptcy. For the purposes of these sections 'completed' means receipt of debt.[1]

1   IA 1986, ss 183(3) and 346(5).

CHAPTER 4

Charging orders

INTRODUCTION

4.1 A judgment debtor who is seeking to avoid paying a judgment debt is likely to find it harder to conceal the ownership of land than many other assets. In addition, subject to existing charges on the land, a judgment debtor's equity in his home or commercial premises is likely to be a significant asset available to the judgment creditor for the purposes of enforcement. Such considerations make charging orders an attractive form of enforcement to many judgment creditors who may have exhausted all other forms of enforcement and are faced with a judgment debtor who refuses to pay.

4.2 A charging order is a means of securing a judgment debt by imposing a charge over a judgment debtor's land, securities or certain other types of property. The charging order creates an equitable charge and therefore, subject to any prior charges affecting the property, places the judgment creditor in the position of a secured creditor. Such security may be sufficient for many judgment creditors, particularly large financial institutions who, with the assurance that if the property is sold the funds released will be used in discharge of the judgment debt, may be content to use the charging order as a form of long-term security. However, should the judgment creditor seek to satisfy the judgment debt, the charging order also provides a means whereby the judgment creditor can apply to the court for an order for sale of the charged property.

4.3 The modern form of a charging order over land has a historical antecedent in the (now abolished) writ of elegit, described in *Blackstone's Commentaries on the Laws of England* of 1768.[1] The nineteenth century saw the introduction of the Judgments Act 1838 (JA 1838), whereby every judgment, whether in law or in equity, operated to impose an equitable charge on all the landed interests (legal and equitable) of the judgment debtor.[2] However, the judgment creditor could not bring proceedings to enforce the charge until one year after the judgment and during that period had no priority over other creditors if the judgment debtor went into bankruptcy. Leaving to one side reform of the procedure for registration of charges, more than a century was to pass before Parliament reformed the law relating to charging orders by enacting the

Administration of Justice Act 1956 (AJA 1956). Under AJA 1956, s 35, a judgment creditor could only obtain a charging order over specified parcels of a judgment debtor's land, rather than the blanket charge over all the judgment debtor's landed interests obtainable under JA 1838.

¹   Vol 3, pp 418–420. The writ of elegit was abolished by the Administration of Justice Act 1956, s 34(1). See further para 6.68, n 1 for further background on writs of elegit.
²   JA 1838, s 13.

4.4   The modern form of charging order over securities similarly has historical antecedents. Charging orders over securities were available under JA 1838, s 14 (the effect of which was extended by the Judgments Act 1840, s 1). These statutory provisions were subsequently repealed but the power to make charging orders over securities were replaced by rules of court.

4.5   By the early 1970s a number of concerns had been raised about the operation of the law relating to charging orders in the wake of two Court of Appeal decisions. In *Re Overseas Aviation (GB) Ltd*¹ the Court of Appeal (by a majority) held that a charging order on land does not, of itself, operate to give the judgment creditor any preference in the event of the insolvency of the judgment debtor. In order to acquire a preference over other creditors it was necessary for the judgment creditor to take at least one further, often purely formal, step in appointing a receiver.

¹   [1963] Ch 24.

4.6   Separately, in *Irani Finance Ltd v Singh*¹ the Court of Appeal found that a beneficial interest in land held on trust for sale was not an 'interest in land' for the purposes of AJA 1956, s 35, the statutory regime then governing charging orders.² Accordingly, a charging order could not be obtained over a judgment debtor's interest in co-owned land.

¹   [1971] Ch 59.
²   The main ground for this decision was that, since the interest of a beneficiary under a trust for sale was technically an interest in the proceeds of sale of land, not the land itself, it was not land or an interest land for the purposes of the Administration of Justice Act 1956, s 35.

4.7   These 'defects'¹ in the law were referred to the Law Commission, together with a concern relating to the statutory provisions for the discharge of charging orders.² The Law Commission published its report into the operation of the law relating to charging orders in March 1976.³ The Report's key recommendations included that:

(a)   the effect of *Overseas Aviation* should be reversed, so that the making of a charging order should amount to completion of the execution for the purposes of insolvency legislation;

(b)   the court should have a 'full' discretion whether or not to make a charging order and, in exercising this discretion, the court should take into account any evidence before it on both the personal circumstances of the judgment debtor and any other creditors of the judgment debtor who might be unduly prejudiced by the making of a charging order;

(c)   the court should have power in all circumstances to make a charging order in respect of a beneficial interest of a judgment debtor arising under a trust of land;

(d)   the court's powers to charge a trustee's interest in securities should correspond with its power to charge a trustee's interest in land; and

(e) the court should have express power to make an order discharging the property subject to a charging order.

1   Law Commission Report, 1976, para 1.
2   Under the pre-1979 regime it was unclear whether a judgment debtor could obtain a court order formally discharging the charging order after satisfying the judgment debt.
3   Law Commission No 74, Cmnd 6412.

4.8   The 1976 Law Commission Report also proposed a draft charging orders bill, the text of which was largely enacted in the Charging Orders Act 1979 (COA 1979), the statutory regime now governing charging orders. However, while COA 1979 introduced a new statutory framework, much of the case law predating that Act considers equivalent or very similar former statutory provisions and therefore remains binding authority. Under COA 1979 a charging order takes effect as an equitable charge,[1] albeit a species which is imposed by statute and by a court, which is available only in relation to restricted categories of assets, and which has generated its own body of case law in addition to the general principles applying to equitable charges.

1   COA 1979, s 3(4).

4.9   The Civil Enforcement Review instituted by the Lord Chancellor's Department in March 1998 as part of the civil justice reforms[1] reviewed the existing charging orders regime. Its conclusions were published in the 'Effective Enforcement' White Paper in March 2003. The White Paper made a number of procedural recommendations but stated:[2]

'… the Review has identified no significant means by which the charging order procedure should be changed … It is our conclusion that the existing procedure works well in the main.'

1   See further Chapter 1.
2   At para 388.

4.10   The procedural rules for obtaining a charging order are contained in Pt 73 of the Civil Procedure Rules 1998 (CPR). Part 73 came into force on 25 March 2002[1] and replaced the former procedure under the Rules of the Supreme Court 1965 (RSC), Ord 50 and the County Court Rules 1981, Ord 31.[2]

1   Civil Procedure (Amendment No 4) Rules 2001, SI 2001/2792.
2   Formally preserved in CPR, Schs 1 and 2.

A two/three stage process

4.11   The process of enforcement, namely obtaining the charging order over the judgment debtor's assets, is a two-stage process. First, an application is made for an interim charging order, which is then followed by an application for a final charging order. Once the charging order has been obtained, it takes effect as an equitable charge over the judgment debtor's property and places the judgment creditor in the position of a secured creditor. Some judgment creditors, particularly banks or other financial institutions, are content to leave the matter there and use the charging order as a form of long term security for the debt.[1]

¹   See March 2003 White Paper, *Effective Enforcement* ch 4, section 2, para 374, which notes that from a sample of 800 charging order cases of one major creditor in only one instance was an application for an order for sale made. Rather, lenders with the security of a charging order will accept long term repayment agreements to clear the judgment debt.

4.12   However, unlike other processes of enforcement (such as third party debt orders or writs of fieri facias), completion of the process of enforcement with the final charging order will not realise funds to satisfy the judgment debt. In order to achieve this, this judgment creditor will need to take a further step, namely proceedings to enforce his rights as a secured creditor under that equitable charge by applying for an order for sale.

4.13   An outline of the process is set out in paras 4.14–4.17.

Interim charging order

4.14   The judgment creditor first makes an application for an interim charging order (formerly a 'charging order nisi'). The application notice must be in the prescribed form and contain the prescribed information. The application may be made without notice and will initially be dealt with by a judge without a hearing. If the judge makes an interim charging order, the judgment creditor must then serve the order on the judgment debtor and certain other parties.

Final charging order

4.15   Following service of the interim charging order a hearing takes place to consider whether a final charging order (formerly a 'charging order absolute') should be made. The judgment creditor, the judgment debtor and any person who objects to the court making a final charging order may attend the hearing. At the hearing the court may make a final charging order, discharge the interim charging order, decide any issues in dispute, or direct a trial of any such issues.

Order for sale

4.16   A judgment creditor who is not content with the position of secured creditor and seeks cash in satisfaction of the judgment debt must seek to realise his security and enforce the charging order by applying for an order for sale of the charged property. This involves bringing fresh proceedings under CPR Pt 8.

4.17   As will be seen, the court has a discretion as to whether to make the relevant order at each stage of this process. The steps which must be taken at each stage of the procedure, the obligations which arise and the effect of those steps are considered in detail later in this chapter.

JURISDICTION

4.18   The court's power to make a charging order over a judgment debtor's assets derives from COA 1979, s 1(1), which provides:

'Where, under a judgment or order of the High Court or a county court, a person (the "debtor") is required to pay a sum of money to another person (the "creditor") then, for the purpose of enforcing that judgment or order, the appropriate court may make an order in accordance with the provisions of this Act imposing on any such property of the debtor as may be specified in the order a charge for securing the payment of any money due or to become under the judgment or order.'

4.19 Accordingly, charging orders are available to secure a sum payable under a judgment or an order of the court, including assessed costs. The charging order must be made in accordance with the provisions of COA 1979 and may only be made in relation to those types of property of the judgment debtor specified in COA 1979 (see further paras 4.33–4.58).

4.20 It is key to note at the outset that COA 1979, s 1(1) provides that the court 'may' make a charging order.[1] As will be seen, statute therefore confers a discretion as to whether or not to make the order and the court must consider 'all the circumstances of the case' in so doing.[2]

[1]   COA 1979, s 1(3) provides that an order under COA 1979, s 1(1) is referred to as a 'charging order'.
[2]   COA 1979, s 1(5) and see further paras 4.148–4.193.

4.21 Pursuant to COA 1979, s 3(1) the charging order may be made either absolutely or subject to conditions, such as notifying the debtor when the charge is to become enforceable or as to other matters. As will be seen, in light of the potentially draconian nature of a charging order, a range of statutory and procedural safeguards are built in to the process in order to seek to ensure that the process is fair and that vulnerable judgment debtors are adequately protected.

Ascertained sum

4.22 It is a well-established principle that a charging order cannot be given except for an ascertained sum. In *Widgery v Tepper*[1] the court had declared that the plaintiffs were entitled to a share in the proceeds of sale of certain property that had been received by the defendants. The court directed an account of what was due to the plaintiffs and ordered that that the defendants should pay over what was found to be due, together with the costs of the suit. The plaintiff then obtained a charging order nisi. The defendants appealed against the charging order absolute being made on the grounds that the sum due to the plaintiffs had not yet been ascertained and costs had not been taxed.[2] The Court of Appeal upheld the defendants' appeal. James LJ held:

'The authorities are sufficient to shew that a charging order cannot be given except for an ascertained sum, and not for costs, charges and expense, until they have been taxed.'

[1]   (1877) LR 6 Ch D 364. It is interesting to note that the court stated that it could not consider the question of what steps the plaintiff ought to have taken to protect their entitlement to the funds in question but speculated that the plaintiffs may be entitled to an injunction in some other proceeding. See the judgments of James LJ and Cotton LJ at 369 and 370 respectively.
[2]   Such costs would now be assessed under the provisions of CPR Pt 44.

4.23   Similarly, in *A&M Records v Darakdjian*[1] the court held that a charging order could not be obtained in relation to an award of costs which had not yet been taxed since the court had no power to make a charging order for an unascertained sum. While *Widgery* and *A&M Records* are cases under the statutory regimes preceding COA 1979, the relevant statutory provisions are in the same form. *Widgery* was cited in the 1996 Court of Appeal decision in *Ezekiel v Orakpo*,[2] where Millett, LJ held:

'[The defendant's] submission was founded on the well-established principle that a Charging Order cannot be given except for an ascertained sum: see *Widgery v Tepper* (1877) LR 6 Ch D 364, a decision of this court. It is clear law, for example, that a charging order cannot be made for untaxed costs.'

1   [1975] 1 WLR 1610.
2   [1997] 1 WLR 340.

Interest on a judgment

4.24   COA 1979, s 1(1) provides that a court may make a charging order securing the payment of *'any money due or to become due under the judgment or order'*. Interest accrues on a Sterling High Court judgment under JA 1838, s 17.

4.25   In *Ezekiel v Orakpo*[1] the Court of Appeal considered whether a charging order secured the payment of interest on a judgment debt even though the charging order was silent as to interest. Millett LJ concluded that the charging order *did* secure the payment of interest on the judgment even though it contained no mention of interest for two different reasons. First, he cited the provisions of JA 1838, s 17[2] and held:

'It follows that there is no need to mention interest in the judgment itself, or in the Order carrying the judgment into effect, or in a Charging Order, since the reference to the judgment alone is enough. It is, of course, much the better practice to include an express reference to interest so that the effect of the Order is clear to the judgment debtor, but it is not strictly necessary.'

1   [1997] 1 WLR 340. This case is also discussed further at paras 7.103–7.112 in relation to the provisions of the Limitation Act 1980.
2   Which now states: 'Every judgment debt shall carry interest at the rate of 8% per annum from such time as shall be prescribed by the rules of court ... until the same shall be satisfied, and such interest may be levied under a writ of execution on such judgment.'

4.26   Secondly, he found that since COA 1979, s 3(4) provides that a charging order takes effect as an equitable charge created by the judgment debtor by writing under his hand:

'It must therefore be given the same effect, unless the Act itself provides otherwise, as would an equitable charge on the land in question to secure a stated principal sum but with no mention of interest. Such a charge would carry interest even though there were no words allowing interest in the charge itself.'[1]

1   It is also worth noting that the court rejected the judgment debtor's argument that a charging order cannot be made to secure future interest accruing under JA 1838 since the amount of such interest cannot be ascertained in advance (and thus does not constitute an

ascertained sum). Millet LJ held: 'However, the Charging Order Act itself entitles the court to make a Charging Order for monies due or to become due, and it appears to me that future interest at an ascertained rate (albeit a variable rate) from the date of judgment to the date of payment is an ascertained, or at least ascertainable, sum for the purpose of the rule in question.' This line of reasoning was cited in *Holder v Supperstone* [2000] 1 All ER 473, where the court rejected the argument that since a charging order could only be made in respect of ascertained indebtedness, a sum due in respect of untaxed costs specifically could not be added to the security conferred by a charging order. Rather, the court held that the costs of enforcing a charging order could be added to the sum secured by the charge made under such an order and the submissions to the contrary involved 'a confusion between the rules which govern the nature of the debts in respect of which there is a power to make charging orders under s 1(1) of the 1979 Act and the rules which apply to the holder of a charging order which govern what right he has to add to the security conferred by the charging order further sums for interest and costs, which are not found in s 1(1) but rather in the common law applicable to equitable chargees generally applied to charging orders by s 3(4) of the 1979 Act. It seems to me, with respect, that this is a contrast of which Millett LJ was fully aware when he gave judgment in Ezekiel's case. Although he treated the interest accruing on the judgment debt as being a debt in respect of which a charging order could be made because such interest was ascertainable at time of the making of the charging order, it seems clear that it also could have been added to the judgment debt by the holder of the charging order when its amount was subsequently ascertained.' (Evans-Lombe J at 478.)

4.27 As Millett LJ noted, however, as a matter of best practice the charging order should be drafted to state expressly that it covers interest on the judgment debt and the standard form final charging order (Form N87) expressly states this.[1]

[1] See further para 4.194.

Costs of enforcing the charge

4.28 The Court of Appeal in *Ezekiel* also considered whether a charging order secured the costs of enforcing the charge and concluded that, since by statute the charge took effect as if it were an equitable charge given by the judgment debtor, such costs were secured.[1] Millett, LJ stated:

'So far as the costs of enforcing the security are concerned, it is of course perfectly true that at the date of the Charging Order, or indeed subsequently, it was quite impossible to ascertain them. The judge came to the conclusion that the Charging Order must, by the provisions of the statute, be given the same effect as if it were an equitable charge under hand only. If it were, the chargee would have the right in equity to add the costs of enforcing the security to the security. He considered that that should be implied into the Charging Order by virtue of s 3(4). I agree with him and do not think it necessary to add anything further on the matter.'

[1] See also the commentary on *Holder v Supperstone* in para 4.26, n 1.

4.29 Again, as a matter of best practice the charging order should be drafted to expressly state that it covers the costs of the application and the standard form final charging order Form N87 expressly states this.[1]

[1] See further para 4.194.

Judgment debt payable by instalments

4.30 The fact that statute provides that a court may make a charging order for securing the payment of any money *'due or to become due under the judgment or order'*[1] means that the High Court[2] has the power to make an order to secure the whole of the judgment debt even where the judgment debt is payable by instalments which have not yet fallen into arrears.[2] However, whether the court will choose to exercise its discretion to make a charging order where the judgment debtor is not in default with his payments is a separate question (which is considered in para 4.189).

1.   COA 1979, s 1(1). See para 4.18.
2.   The position is different in the county court by virtue of County Courts Act 1984, s 86(1). This provides: '(1) Where the court has made an order for payment of any sum of money by instalments, execution on the order shall not be issued until after default in payment of some instalment according to the order.' Accordingly, a charging order cannot be obtained until after default on one or more instalments payable under the judgment. However, the position is different where the interim charging order is obtained prior to the instalment order – see *Ropaigealach v Allied Irish Bank plc* [2001] EWCA Civ 1790 and para 4.190. The 2003 White Paper recommended that enforcement by way of charging order should be made available in cases where the judgment debtor is not in arrears with the instalment order (paras 370–375). At the time of writing there were no proposals for the enactment of this recommendation.
3.   The application notice for a charging order (Form N379 or N380) requires the judgment creditor to state, if the judgment debt is payable by instalments, the amount of any instalments which have fallen due and remain unpaid. See further para 4.76.

Judgment debt not yet immediately payable

4.31 Similarly, the wording of the statute empowers the court to make a charging order in respect of a debt which is not yet immediately payable.[1] (Again, how the court will exercise its discretion in this regard is considered at paras 4.186–4.188.)

1.   *Robinson v Bailey* [1942] Ch 268, see further para 4.186.

Other types of charging order

4.32 Charging orders may also be obtained in certain circumstances under the Solicitors Act 1974,[1] the Partnership Act 1890, the Insolvency Act 1986 (IA 1986),[2] and the Council Tax (Administration and Enforcement) Regulations 1992.[3] These schemes for obtaining charging orders are outside the scope of this book and, except for charging partnership interests,[4] are not considered further.

1.   Solicitors Act 1974, s 73 provides that a solicitor may apply for a charging order on his client's property in order to enforce payment of his costs.
2.   IA 1986, s 313 makes provision for a trustee in bankruptcy to apply for a charging order over a bankrupt's interest in a dwelling house.
3.   SI 1992/613. Under the provisions of reg 50 a local authority may apply to the county court for a charging order over a dwelling in respect of which council tax arrears are outstanding in excess of £1,000. There are also provisions relating to the availability of charging orders in certain circumstances under the Agricultural Holdings Act 1986, s 85, Drug Trafficking Act 1994, s 27 and Child Support Act 1991, s 33.
4.   See further paras 4.59–4.61.

ASSETS THAT MAY BE CHARGED

4.33 The assets over which a charging order can be obtained[1] are set out in COA 1979, s 2. Section 2 states:

'(1) Subject to subsection (3) below, a charge may be imposed by a charging order only on:

(a) any interest held by the debtor beneficially –
   (i) in any asset of a kind mentioned in subsection (2) below, or
   (ii) under any trust; or

(b) any interest held by a person as trustee of a trust ("the trust"), if the interest is in such an asset or is an interest under another trust and-
   (i) the judgment or order in respect of which a charge is to be imposed was made against that person as trustee of the trust, or
   (ii) the whole beneficial interest under the trust is held by the debtor unencumbered and for his own benefit, or
   (iii) in a case where there are two or more debtors all of whom are liable to the creditor for the same debt, they together hold the whole beneficial interest under the trust unencumbered and for their own benefit.

(2) The assets referred to in subsection (1) above are –

(a) land,

(b) securities of any of the following kinds –
   (i) government stock,
   (ii) stock of any body (other than a building society) incorporated within England and Wales,
   (iii) stock of any body incorporated outside England and Wales or of any state or territory outside the United Kingdom, being stock registered in a register kept at any place within England and Wales,
   (iv) units of any unit trust in respect of which a register of the unit holders is kept at any place within England and Wales, or

(c) funds in court.

(3) In any case where a charge is imposed by a charging order on any interest in an asset of a kind mentioned in paragraph (b) or (c) of subsection (2) above, the court making the order may provide for the charge to extend to any interest or dividend payable in respect of the asset.'

[1] The importance of researching a judgment debtor's assets and means before issuing proceedings or instituting enforcement steps is considered in Chapter 2.

4.34 A charging order may therefore be imposed on any beneficial interest the judgment debtor holds in any asset of the kind mentioned in COA 1979, s 2(2), namely land, securities and funds in court. Alternatively, a charging order may be imposed on a judgment debtor's beneficial interest under a trust. A charging order may also be imposed on a judgment debtor's legal interest under a trust in certain circumstances. Each of these provisions is considered in turn below.

Charge can only be imposed on the judgment debtor's interest

4.35 As the wording of the statute makes clear, save in the restricted circumstances where a charging order can be obtained over a judgment debtor's legal interest in a trust, a charging order can only be obtained over the judgment debtor's own beneficial interest in a relevant asset. The charge imposed cannot extend further than that interest. This point was illustrated in *Gill v The Continental Union Gas Company Ltd*,[1] where a judgment creditor sought to obtain a charging order over shares which a judgment debtor held as bare trustee, having previously disposed of the shares for valuable consideration to a third party prior to the charging order nisi having been obtained.[2] The charging order was not allowed since the court found that a judgment creditor cannot by his charging order get any more than the debtor could honestly give him.

1   (1871-72) LR 7 Exch 332.
2   *Gill* concerned the provisions of JA 1838, which provided that in order for a charging order to be obtained the judgment debtor must have stock 'standing in his name in his own right, or in the name of any person in trust for him'. However, the fact that this was understood by the court to mean the judgment debtor's 'beneficial interest' (the wording used in the modern counterpart of COA 1979) is reflected by the headnote to Gill which states: 'In an action, under [JA 1838] against a company for permitting the transfer of shares after notice of a charging order nisi, and before the making of it absolute, it is a good answer to shew that the judgment debtor in whose name the shares stood had no *beneficial interest* in them.' (Emphasis added.)

4.36   The point was succinctly stated in *Hawks v McArthur*,[1] where Vaisey J held:

'The charging order affects only such interest, and so much of the property affected, as the person whose property is purported to be affected could himself validly charge.'

1   [1951] 1 All ER 22.

Land

4.37   Before considering the provisions of COA 1979 relating to charging a judgment debtor's interest in land, it is worth briefly outlining how an interest in land may be held.

4.38   The simplest case is where the judgment debtor is the sole owner of the property, ie the judgment debtor is both the legal and beneficial owner.

4.39   Commonly a judgment debtor will co-own land with another person, for example a spouse. In practice co-owned land is now held under either a joint tenancy or a tenancy in common.[1] Statute provides that *at law* co-owners must hold as joint tenants.[2] In equity, however, the co-owners may hold their interests either as joint tenants or tenants in common. The main difference between these forms of co-ownership is that joint tenants are considered to be a single owner and when one of them dies the property automatically vests in the other joint tenant (or joint tenants if there is more than one survivor). By contrast, tenants in common own undivided shares and are free to transfer their interest in the property individually either during their lifetime or in their wills.[3] An equitable joint tenancy of land can be converted into an equitable tenancy in common by a process known as severance and the imposition of a charging order against the interest of one equitable joint tenant is considered an act of severance.[4] In other words, once a charging order has been imposed upon the equitable interest of one joint tenant in the land, the co-owners will hold their equitable interests as tenants in common.

1   Megarry and Wade *The Law of Real Property* (6th edn, 2000) pp 475–482.
2   Law of Property Act 1925, ss 1(6), 34(1), 36(2) and the Settled Land Act 1925, s 36(4).
3   Megarry and Wade *The Law of Real Property* (6th edn, 2000) pp 475–480.
4   Megarry and Wade *The Law of Real Property* (6th edn, 2000) p 498; Gray and Gray *Elements of Land Law* (4th edn, 2005), p 1064.

4.40   Any co-owned land will almost invariably be held under a trust of land. The Trusts of Land and Appointment of Trustees Act 1996 (TLATA 1996), s 1 defines a trust of land widely as 'any trust of property which consists of or includes land' except settled land or land to which the Universities and College Estates Act 1925 applies. The trust can be of any description, whether express, implied, resulting or constructive, and includes a trust for sale and a bare trust and trusts which were created or arose before the commencement of TLATA 1996. The manner of holding follows the trust for sale (which TLATA 1996 replaced): the legal estate in land and all powers of disposition and management are vested in the trustees. Where the land is registered it will be registered in the name of the trustees.

4.41   Pursuant to COA 1979, s 2(1)(a)(i) and (2)(a), a charging order may be imposed on a judgment debtor's beneficial interest in land.[1] Further, pursuant to COA 1979, s 2(1)(a)(ii), a charging order may be imposed upon an judgment debtor's beneficial interest under any trust, which would include a beneficial interest under a trust of land where a judgment debtor co-owns land with another person. In certain circumstances, a charging order may also be imposed upon a judgment debtor's legal interest in land – for example, where there are co-owners of a property who together own the whole of the beneficial interest in the land and who are joint judgment debtors in respect of the same judgment debt.[2] 'Land' is not defined further in COA 1979[3] but includes freehold and leasehold land.[4]

1   While it may not often be relevant in the context of high value commercial enforcement, it should be noted that where a judgment creditor is seeking to enforce a costs order against a party who is an individual who receives funded services from the Legal Services Commission, the Community Legal Service (Cost Protection) Regulations 2000, SI 2000/824, reg 4 provides that where, for the purpose of enforcing a costs order against such a person (alone or together with any other judgment creditor), a charging order under COA 1979, s 1 is made in respect of the client's interest in the main or only dwelling in which he resides, that charging order shall operate to secure the amount payable under the costs order (including, without limitation, any interest) only to the extent of the amount (if any) by which the proceeds of sale of the client's interest in the dwelling (having deducted any mortgage debts) exceed £100,000. The regulations also provide that an order for sale of the dwelling shall not be made on the basis of the charging order.
2   Pursuant to COA 1979, s 2(1)(b)(iii). See also *National Westminster Bank Ltd v Allen* [1971] 2 QB 718.
3   See COA 1979, s 6 (Interpretation).
4   Interpretation Act 1978, s 5 provides: 'In any Act, unless the contrary intention appears, words and expressions listed in Schedule 1 to this Act are to be construed according to that Schedule.' Schedule 1 provides: '"Land" includes buildings and other structures, land covered with water, and any estate, interest, easement, servitude or right in or over land.'

4.42   The post-COA 1979 charging order regime differs significantly from its predecessor regime as regards beneficial interests in land. As has been noted in para

4.6, in *Irani Finance*, the Court of Appeal held that the beneficial interest under a trust for sale of land[1] could not be made the subject of a charging order under AJA 1956, s 35 . Following that decision, COA 1979 entered into force on 3 June 1980.[2] COA 1979, s 7 repealed AJA 1956, s 35 and, not least given the background to the new legislation as set out in the 1976 Law Commission Report, the provisions of s 2 of the new Act may have seemed clear. However, only two months after COA 1979 entered into force this very question came before the court. *National Westminster Bank Ltd v Stockman*[3] was an appeal against the refusal of a master to make a charging order nisi in respect of a beneficial interest in land where the master was not satisfied that the provisions of COA 1979, s 2 enabled the order to be made.

[1]   Trusts for sale have now been replaced by trusts of land under TLATA 1996. However, the
       trust of land follows the trust for sale in that the legal estate (and the powers of disposition
       and management) is vested in the trustees of land on trust for the beneficiaries.
[2]   Charging Orders Act 1979 (Commencement) Order 1980, SI 1980/627, para 2.
[3]   [1981] 1 WLR 67.

4.43   Russell J upheld the appeal in no uncertain terms:

'The ratio of the judgment of the court in the Irani case was that the words "interest in land" to be found in s 35 Administration of Justice Act 1956 did not include interests under trusts for sale of land. Such interests were not interests in land but interests in the proceeds of the sale of land. Those equitable interests, therefore, were not caught by the provisions of s 35 and no charging order could be made.

Section 35 of the 1956 Act has now been repealed by s 7 of the Charging Orders Act 1979. The short point for my consideration is whether s 2 of the 1979 Act has removed the limitations of s 35 of the 1956 Act, as interpreted by the Court of Appeal in the Irani case, so as to permit charges on the interests of those, such as the defendant in the instant case, who hold real property under the terms of a trust for sale.

In my judgment it was plainly the intention of Parliament that the availability of charging orders should be extended to cover cases in which the interest sought to be charged is a beneficial interest in the proceeds of sale of land held under a trust for sale. I think that that object has been achieved by the plain wording of s 2, despite the interesting arguments to the contrary advanced by counsel for the defendant.'

4.44   Accordingly, it is clear that a charging order may be imposed over a judgment debtor's beneficial interest in land.

Securities

4.45   Pursuant to COA 1979, s 2(2)(b) the kinds of securities over which a charging order may be imposed comprises: government stock, stock of corporates incorporated within England and Wales (other than building societies[1]), stock of overseas corporates (provided the stock register is kept within England and Wales), and units of any unit trust (provided the register of unit holders is kept within England and Wales).

[1]   Under COA 1979, s 6(1) 'building society' is defined to have the same meaning as in the
       Building Societies Act 1986.

4.46 'Government stock' is defined[1] as 'any stock issued by Her Majesty's government in the United Kingdom or any funds of, or annuity granted by, that government'.

[1] COA 1979, s 6(1).

4.47 The definition of corporate 'stock' under COA 1979 is remarkably wide. COA 1979, s 6(1) states:

> '"stock" includes shares, debentures and any securities of the body concerned, whether or not constituting a charge on the assets of that body.'

4.48 As has been noted in para 4.38, the 1976 Law Commission Report also recognised that any list of assets amenable to a charging order may well become out-dated over time with the development of completely new kinds of securities. The widely drafted ambit of 'securities' under COA 1979, s 6(1) is further recognition of this fact. A tighter definition of securities would arguably be overly prescriptive and would be unlikely to be able to keep pace with developments in modern financial instruments. Further, as will be seen, in the event that the corporate body which has issued the security felt that, for some reason, the imposition of a charging order in relation to a particular kind of financial instrument was inappropriate, the company would be afforded the opportunity to make representations to this effect at the hearing when the court considers whether to make a final charging order.[1]

[1] See further paras 4.136–4.140.

Dividends and interest

4.49 Where securities of the type listed in COA 1979, s 2(2)(b)[1] are charged by a charging order, the court has the power to order that the charge should extend 'to any interest or dividend payable in respect of the asset'.[2] Where appropriate the order should state that it also applies to such interest or dividend.

[1] Or funds in court – see para 4.51.
[2] COA 1979, s 2(3).

4.50 As will be seen at the end of this chapter, further protection against securities being transferred out of the hands of a judgment debtor is available in the form of stop orders and stop notices. Where dissipation of the securities is a real risk, the judgment creditor may also have sought a freezing injunction in relation to those assets (see further Chapter 1).

Funds in court

4.51 In addition to interests in land and securities, a judgment creditor can also obtain a charging order over any interest held by the judgment debtor beneficially in 'funds in court' pursuant to COA 1979, s 2(2)(c) .

4.52 Where funds in court are charged by a charging order, the court has the power to order that the charge should extend to interest payable on those funds.[1] Again, it is advisable for the order expressly to state that this is the case. (Alternatively, if money is standing to the credit of the judgment debtor in court, the judgment creditor may apply for an order that the funds be paid to him under the procedure set out in CPR 72.10 – see further Chapter 3 in this regard).

1   COA 1979, s 2(3).

Interest in a trust

Beneficial interest in a trust

4.53   A charging order may be imposed on any interest held by the judgment debtor beneficially under any trust.[1]

1   COA 1979, s 2(1)(a)(ii).

Interest under a foreign trust

4.54   In *Interpool Ltd v Galani*[1] the Court of Appeal speculated that an English court may have jurisdiction to charge a judgment debtor's beneficial interest under a 'foreign trust', but as a matter of discretion would not exercise that jurisdiction where it could expose the trustees to a risk of double jeopardy'.[2] However, the court in *Interpool* was concerned with the oral examination of the judgment debtor under RSC Ord 48[3] and thus the court's observations on charging order jurisdiction are strictly obiter.

1   [1988] QB 738.
2   [1988] QB 738 at 741–742, per Balcombe LJ.
3   The predecessor to Pt 71 proceedings.

4.55   While it is correct that COA 1979 contains no jurisdictional limitation as to the location of the assets subject to a charging order, the court's observations in *Interpool* as to the jurisdiction to charge to an interest under a foreign trust were predicated (in part at least) on the view that the court had jurisdiction to garnish[1] a foreign debt, and there was no reason that a more restrictive limitation should therefore apply to charging an interest under a foreign trust.[2] However, this obiter speculation must now be seen as wrong in light of the House of Lords' decisions in *Societe Eram Shipping Co. Ltd v Cie Internationale de Navigation*[3] and *Kuwait Oil Tanker Company SAK v Qabazard,*[4] which for all practical purposes concluded that the English court does *not* have jurisdiction to garnish a foreign debt.[5] Further, even if, which seems unlikely for the reasons given in those cases, the court does have jurisdiction to impose a charging order over a judgment debtor's beneficial interest in a 'foreign trust', there may be difficulties in establishing that English law trust concepts apply in relation to foreign assets and that the judgment debtor has the sort of beneficial interest that would be amenable to a charging order.

1   The predecessor to the third party debt order procedure under Pt 72.
2   Balcombe LJ at 741.
3   [2004] 1 AC 260.
4   [2003] UKHL 31.
5   These cases are discussed at paras 3.67–3.79. Alternatively, if the court has jurisdiction, it should not exercise it to garnish a foreign debt. Because the same principles apply as regards

the exercise of the court's jurisdiction in relation to third party debt order proceedings as those applicable to charging orders, the court should not exercise its jurisdiction to impose a charging order over and an interest in a foreign trust.

Constructive or resulting trusts

4.56 COA 1979 provides that a charging order may be imposed over an interest in 'any' trust and this would cover implied trusts such as a resulting or constructive trust.

4.57 Full consideration of the circumstances in which implied trusts may arise is outside the scope of this book and standard works on the law of trusts should be consulted. However, it may be worth the judgment creditor considering whether the judgment debtor holds any such interests which may be amendable to a charging order, particularly where he suspects that the judgment debtor may have been concealing assets. In such circumstances, the judgment creditor should provide detailed evidence to the court of the circumstances in which the trust and the judgment debtor's interest under that trust arose in the form of a witness statement in support of the application for a charging order.

Legal interest in a trust

4.58 In certain circumstances, a charging order may be imposed on a judgment debtor's legal interest in a trust. The interest in the trust of which the judgment debtor is trustee must be either an interest in an asset of the kind set out in COA 1979, s 2(2)[1] or an interest under another trust. If so, the judgment debtor's legal interest in the trust can be charged in three sets of circumstances, which are set out in COA 1979, s 2(1)(b)(i)–(iii):

(a) where 'the judgment or order in respect of which a charge is to be imposed was made against that person as trustee of the trust'.[2] Where a court has ordered that a trustee of a trust, in his capacity as trustee, must pay a sum of money to the judgment creditor, the judgment creditor may apply for a charging order over the trustee's legal interest in the trust.

(b) where 'the whole beneficial interest under the trust is held by the debtor unencumbered[3] and for his own benefit'.[4] In such circumstances there is no other beneficiary who may be disadvantaged by the charge and thus the court may charge the legal interest. Where a judgment debtor can show that he holds the legal interest on trust for a third party (and provide conclusive evidence), he may be able to resist the making of a final charging order.[5]

(c) where 'there are two or more debtors all of whom are liable to the creditor for the same debt, they together hold the whole beneficial interest under the trust unencumbered and for their own benefit'.[6] An obvious example of where this provision would apply is where there are joint judgment debtors who are co-owners of the land. In order for a charging order to be obtained over the legal estate there must be 'unity of the debt', ie the judgment debtors must be liable to the creditor for the same debt. If two judgment debtors who jointly hold the whole of the beneficial interest under a trust are both liable to the same judgment creditor but in respect of *separate* debts, the legal estate cannot be charged under this provision.

1   Since COA 1979, s 2(1)(b) refers to an interest in 'such an asset'.
2   COA 1979, s 2(1)(b)(i).
3   Ie the interest is not subject to some prior right such as a charge or mortgage.
4   COA 1979, s 2(1)(b)(ii).
5   *Barclays Bank v Forrester* [1987] CLY 2537. See further para 4.140. The burden of proving that the interim charging order should not be made final will rest on the judgment debtor in such circumstances: *Aero Properties Ltd v Citycrest Properties Ltd* [2003] All ER (D) 218.
6   COA 1979, s 2(1)(b)(iii).

Interest in a partnership

4.59   While COA 1979 contains no provision for a judgment debtor to apply to the court for an order charging a partner's interest in the partnership property, the Partnership Act 1890 (PA 1890) provides such a mechanism.[1] PA 1890, s 23(2) (as amended) states:

'The High Court or a judge thereof or a county court, may, on the application of any judgment creditor of a partner, make an order charging that partner's interest in the partnership property and profits with payment of the amount of the judgment debt and interest thereon, and may by the same or subsequent order appoint a receiver of that partner's shares of profits (whether already declared or accruing), and of any other money which may be coming to him in respect of the partnership, and direct all accounts and inquiries, and give all other orders and directions which might have been directed or given if the charge has been made in favour of the judgment creditor by the partner, or which the circumstances of the case may require.'

1   Under the previous law, a judgment obtained against a partner could be executed against the property of the partnership. PA 1890, s 23 now prohibits this but instead provides a mechanism whereby execution can be obtained against a partner's share in the partnership.

4.60   PA 1890, s 23(3) provides the other partner or partners with a statutory right to redeem the interest charged or, in case of a sale being directed, to purchase that interest. PA 1890, s 33 also provides that a partnership may, at the option of the other partners, be dissolved if any partner suffers his share of the partnership property to be charged under the Act for his separate debt. Accordingly, if a judgment creditor discovers that the judgment debtor acts in partnership with others, expressing an intention to charge the judgment debtor's interest in the partnership property may be a good way of bringing pressure to bear on the judgment debtor to settle his liability.

4.61   The procedure for obtaining a charging order under PA 1890, s 23(2) is set out in RSC Ord 80, r 10.[1] The application must be made in accordance with CPR Pt 23[2] and every application notice issued and order made on such application must be served on the judgment debtor and on such of his partners as are within the jurisdiction.[3]

1   Preserved in CPR, Sch 1.
2   RSC Ord 81, r 10(1).

³ RSC Ord 81, r 10(3). This provision affords the other partners the opportunity to exercise their statutory right to redeem the interest charged or purchase the partnership interest in the event of a sale.

Changes to the categories of prescribed assets

4.62 COA 1979, s 2(7) provides that:

'The Lord Chancellor may by order made by statutory instrument amend section 2(2) of the Act by adding to, or removing from, the kinds of asset for the time being referred to there, any asset of a kind which in his opinion ought to be so added or removed'.

4.63 As yet, no order has been made under this subsection. However, this statutory provision affords the Lord Chancellor the power to increase, or decrease, the scope of assets which may be subject to a charging order in the future should he consider that the circumstances warrant such a change.

4.64 The widening of the category of stock amenable to charging orders and the inclusion of unit trusts were both enacted in COA 1979, s 2(2) as a result of consultation in the production of the 1976 Law Commission Report, which concluded that the previous list was unnecessarily restrictive. The 1976 Law Commission Report also recognised that no such list was likely to remain appropriate for ever and that totally new kinds of 'securities' may develop. It therefore included a recommendation for a power to extend the list further from time to time, which eventually took the form of COA 1979, s 2(7).[1]

¹ See the 1976 Law Commission Report, para 86.

Application to the Crown

4.65 Charging orders are not available against the Crown by virtue of the Crown Proceedings Act 1947, s 47.[1] However, a procedure exists for the payment of judgment debts owed by the Crown (see paras 1.132–1.134).

¹ See also RSC Ord 77, r 15(1), preserved in CPR, Sch 1.

PROCEDURE FOR OBTAINING A CHARGING ORDER

4.66 The procedural rules which give effect to the provisions of COA 1979 are contained in CPR Pt 73 (as supplemented by the Practice Direction).

Application for interim charging order

4.67 The first step is an application by the judgment creditor for an interim charging order.

Which court?

4.68 COA 1979, s 1(1) provides that the 'appropriate court' may make a charging order in accordance with the provisions of COA 1979. COA 1979, s 1(2) sets out the definition of appropriate court as follows:

'The appropriate court is—

(a) in a case where the property to be charged is a fund in court, the court in which that fund is lodged;

(b) in a case where paragraph (a) above does not apply and the order to be enforced is a maintenance order[1] of the High Court, the High Court or a county court;

(c) in a case where neither paragraph (a) nor paragraph (b) above applies and the judgment or order to be enforced is a judgment or order of the High Court for a sum exceeding the county court limit,[2] the High Court or a county court; and

(d) in any other case, a county court.'

---

[1] 'Maintenance order' is defined in COA 1979, s 1(2) to have the same meaning as in the Attachment of Earnings Act 1971, s 2(a).

[2] COA 1979, s 1(2) continues: 'In this section "county court limit" means the county court limit for the time being specified in an Order in Council under section 145 of the County Courts Act 1984, as the county court limit for the purposes of this section.' At present, no order has been made under the relevant provisions of the County Court Act 1984 setting the county court limit for these purposes. However, under the Interpretation Act 1978, s 17(2)(b), the County Courts Jurisdiction Order 1981, SI 1981/1123 applies, of which s 2 sets a limit of £5,000 for these purposes.

4.69 Accordingly, under the provisions of COA 1979, the county court has concurrent jurisdiction to make a charging order in relation to High Court judgments save in the case where the property to be charged is a fund held in the High Court (in which case, the application must be made in the High Court). Where the judgment is a county court judgment, the application must be made in the county court.[1]

---

[1] COA 1979, s 1(2)(d).

4.70 However, CPR 73.3(2) provides:

'An application for a charging order must be issued in the court which made the judgment or order which it is sought to enforce, unless –

(a) the proceedings have since been transferred to a different court, in which case the application must be issued in that court;

(b) the application is made under the 1992 Regulations,[1] in which case it must be issued in the county court for the district in which the relevant dwelling (as defined in regulation 50(3)(b) of those Regulations) is situated;

(c) the application is for a charging order over an interest in a fund in court, in which case it must be issued in the court in which the claim relating to that fund is or was proceeding; or

(d) the application is to enforce a judgment or order of the High Court and it is required by section 1(2) of the 1979 Act to be made to a county court.[2]

---

[1] The Council Tax (Administration and Enforcement) Regulations 1992, SI 1992/613. See CPR 73.1(2)(b).

2   The rule in CPR 73.3(2)(d) would appear to be directed towards the situation where there is
     a judgment or order of the High Court for a sum which does not exceed the county court limit
     (£5,000 – see para 4.68, n 2), in which case the application for a charging order should be
     brought in the county court pursuant to COA 1979, s 1(2)(d).

4.71 Accordingly, the general rule is that the application for a charging order must
be issued in the court which made the judgment or order of which enforcement is
sought. However, where the judgment is for less than £5,000, the application must be
made in a county court. The two key exceptions from a commercial enforcement
perspective are when enforcement is sought against funds in court (in which case the
application for a charging order must be brought in the court in which the funds are
lodged) and where the proceedings have since been transferred to a different
court.[1] The court has a discretion to transfer an application for a charging order to the
court for the district where the judgment debtor resides or carries on business (or to
another court) on the application of a judgment debtor who wishes to oppose the
charging order.[2]

1   See further Chapter 1 on transfer of proceedings.
2   PD 73, para 3.

More than one judgment or order against the same judgment debtor

4.72 CPR 73.3(3) provides that (subject to the provisions of CPR 73.3(2) as to which
court the application for a charging order must be issued in), a judgment creditor may
apply for a single charging order in respect of more than one judgment or order
against the same debtor. Thus where, for example, a judgment creditor has obtained
two judgments against a judgment debtor issued by the same court, he need only
issue one application for a charging order in that court to enforce both judgments.

Application for charging orders in relation to more than one asset

4.73 Similarly, a judgment creditor may apply in a single application notice for charging
orders over more than one asset.[1] However, if the court makes interim charging orders
over more than one asset, it will draw up a separate order relating to each asset.
1   PD 73, para 1.3.

Without notice

4.74 The judgment creditor's application for an interim charging order may be made
without notice to the judgment debtor.[1]
1   CPR 73.3(1).

Prescribed form

4.75 The application notice must be in the form and contain the information required
by the Practice Direction to Pt 73[1] and must also be verified by a statement of truth.[2] The

prescribed form is Form N379 if the application relates to land, or Form N380 if the application relates to securities.

¹   CPR 73.3(4).
²   An affidavit in support of the application is no longer required – see Civil Procedure 2004, vol 1, para 73.3.2.

4.76   The information which Form N379/N380 must contain is as follows:

(a) the name and address of the judgment debtor;
(b) details of the judgment or order sought to be enforced;
(c) the amount of money remaining due under the judgment or order;
(d) if the judgment debt is payable by instalments, the amount of any instalments which have fallen due and remain unpaid;
(e) if the judgment creditor knows of the existence of any other creditors of the judgment debtor, their names and (if known) their addresses;
(f) identification of the asset or assets which it is intended to charge;
(g) details of the judgment debtor's interest in the asset; and
(h) the names and addresses of the persons on whom an interim charging order must be served under CPR 73.5(1) (see further paras 4.88–4.91).¹

¹   Forms N379 and N380 require the applicant to provide details of other persons who may have an interest in the property under the heading 'Other persons to be served'. In the case of securities, Form N380 suggests that this includes any co-owners and trustees. In the case of land, Form N379 suggests that this includes 'any co-owners, trustees and persons with rights of occupation'.

4.77   Forms N379 and N380 also make provision for any further information the judgment creditor wishes the court to take into account. The notes to the White Book¹ suggest that this section could be used by the judgment creditor to provide evidence that a judgment debtor has the means to satisfy a judgment but is refusing to do so, and/or to provide information about other methods of execution which have been tried and failed. The provision of such information is advisable in light of the court's duty to take into account all the circumstances of the case in considering whether to make a charging order (see further para 4.149).

¹   Civil Procedure 2004, vol 1, para 73.4.2.

4.78   Where the judgment creditor is a corporation, the person signing the application notice on behalf of the corporation must also state the sources of the information he has used to complete the form.

4.79   In the case of land, it is advisable for the judgment creditor to attach Office Copy Land Register entries to evidence the judgment debtor's interest in the property and Form N379 makes provision for this. Where the judgment creditor believes that the judgment debtor has a beneficial interest in the land which is not evidenced by the Land Register entries,¹ he will need to explain the reason for his belief. Relevant information may have been provided by the judgment debtor during the course of earlier Pt 71 proceedings (see Chapter 2).

¹   For example, where property is purchased in another party's name but the judgment debtor contributes to the purchase price so that he acquires an interest under a resulting trust proportionate to his contribution to the purchase price.

4.80 Similarly, in the case of securities, the judgment creditor will also need to state his reasons for believing the judgment debtor has the interest in the securities specified in Form N380. It is advisable for copies of the judgment debtor's share certificate or other documentary evidence of the holding in securities to be provided.

Fee

4.81 The fee for issuing an application for a charging order is £100.[1] From 1 April 2005, all cheques should be made payable to 'HMCS' or 'Her Majesty's Courts Service' instead of 'Her Majesty's Paymaster General' or 'HMPG' as was previously the case.

1   The Civil Proceedings Fees Order 2004. SI 2004/3121, Sch 1, para 6.3(b).

Interim charging order

4.82 The application for a charging order will initially be dealt with by a master[1] without a hearing.[2]

1   CPR 2.3(1) provides that 'judge' means, unless the context otherwise requires, '*a judge, Master or district judge or a person authorised to act as such*'. CPR 2.4(a) provides that where the CPR provide for the court to perform any act then, except where an enactment, rule or practice direction provides otherwise, that act may be performed in relation to proceedings in the High Court, by any judge, master or district judge of that court. In the High Court the practice is for such applications to be dealt with by a master.
2   CPR 73.4(1).

Discretion to make an interim charging order

4.83 COA 1979, s 1(1)[1] and CPR 73.4(2) provide that the judge 'may' make an interim charging order. The court therefore has a discretion to make the order. As will be seen, the court also has a discretion to make the final charging order. For the purpose of the exercise of the court's discretion there is, in general, no material difference between the making of an interim charging order and a final charging order.[2] However, in practice the court is likely to grant the interim charging order and consider fully the exercise of its discretion at the hearing for further consideration of the application. The principles governing the exercise of the court's discretion are considered in paras 4.148-4.193.

1   COA 1979, s 1(1) simply refers to 'an' order.
2   As per Lord Brandon of Oakbrook at 689 in the Court of Appeal decision in *Roberts Petroleum v Bernard Kenny* [1982] 1 All ER 685. See further paras 4.157-4.166.

4.84 If the court makes an interim charging order, the order will:[1]

(a) impose a charge over the judgment debtor's interest in the asset to which the application relates; and
(b) fix a hearing to consider whether to make a final charging order as provided by CPR 73.8(2)(a) (see paras 4.141–4.147). Such hearing will be at least 21 days after the date of the interim charging order.[2]

1   CPR 73.4(2).

²   And probably more, since CPR 73.5 provides that at least 21 days' notice of the hearing
      must be given to the person served with the interim charging order.

Form of the order

4.85   Form N86 contains the standard form interim charging order. The judgment
debtor's beneficial interest in the asset which is subject to the charge is described in
a schedule contained in the order.

Effect of the interim charging order

4.86   COA 1979, s3(4) provides that a charge imposed by a charging order takes
effect as an equitable charge created by the judgment debtor by writing under his
hand. The effect of the interim charging order is therefore to impose a charge over the
judgment debtor's property and convert the judgment creditor into a secured creditor
of the judgment debtor. The position was summarised by Buckley LJ in the Court of
Appeal decision in *Rainbow v Moorgate Properties Ltd*:¹

> 'The effect of the charging orders was not, I think, such as can be accurately
> described as conferring "additional security"; in fact it converted the plaintiffs,
> as unsecured creditors, into secured creditors for the amount of the charge, and
> to the extent that a secured creditor is better off than an unsecured creditor if
> the debtor is insolvent or likely to be insolvent, the effects of the orders must be
> to confer an advantage on the creditor to whom such an order is granted, and in
> that sense it does give a priority in favour of other unsecured creditors.'

¹   [1975] 2 All ER 821 at 823–824. This case considered the earlier statutory regime under
      AJA 1956, s 35 but the relevant statutory provisions are the same under COA 1979.

4.87   It is important to note that the charge is imposed from the date of the interim
charging order, not the subsequent final charging order (see further para
4.196). However, while the interim charging order creates an immediate charge over
the judgment debtor's property, that charge is defeasible since the interim charging
order is revocable at the hearing for further consideration of the application.¹ As is
discussed further in paras 4.157–4.166, in *Roberts Petroleum Ltd v Bernard Kenny
Ltd (in liquidation)*² the House of Lords had to consider whether a charging order
nisi should be made absolute when a creditor's voluntary liquidation had since
intervened. Lord Brightman found that the judgment creditor:

> 'had no more than a defeasible charge at the date of the commencement of the
> liquidation, so that the right of the receiver [ie the receiver appointed by the
> judgment creditor under the charging order]³ to retain the asset as against the
> liquidator was only a defeasible right. Neither the precarious existence of the
> charge nor the precarious possession of the receiver seems to me to afford a
> convincing reason for consolidating the position of the judgment creditor vis-
> à-vis the general body of unsecured creditors…'⁴

¹   *Roberts v Kenny* [1983] 2 AC 192 at 205, 208, 209, per Lord Brightman.
²   [1983] 2 AC 192.

3   See para 4.5.

4   [1983] 2 AC 192 at 209. As Judge Paul Baker QC (sitting as a judge of the High Court) observed in *Calor Gas Ltd v Piercy* [1994] 2 BCLC 321: 'The way the law has been relaxed is that prior to this, before a charging order nisi could be regarded as completed it had to be accompanied by the appointment of a receiver, and there was such a receiver in *Roberts Petroleum Ltd v Bernard Kenny Ltd*. All that the 1979 Act does is that it ensures that an order without a receiver is completion of the execution but, and this is where the case comes in, the initial order nisi is still defeasible in the sense as it was used by Lord Brightman in the *Roberts Petroleum Ltd's* case.'

Service of the interim charging order

Parties to be served

4.88   Under CPR 73.5(1), copies of the interim charging order, the application notice and any documents filed in support of the application must be served on the following persons:

(a) the judgment debtor;

(b) such other creditors as the court directs;

(c) if the order relates to an interest under a trust, on such of the trustees as the court directs;

(d) if the interest charged is in securities other than securities held in court, then -

  (i)   in the case of stock for which the Bank of England keeps the register, the Bank of England;

  (ii) in the case of government stock to which (i) does not apply, the keeper of the register;

  (iii) in the case of stock of any body incorporated within England and Wales, that body;

  (iv) in the case of stock of any body incorporated outside England and Wales or of any state or territory outside the United Kingdom, which is registered in a register kept in England and Wales, the keeper of that register;

  (v)   in the case of units of any unit trust in respect of which a register of the unit holders is kept in England and Wales, the keeper of that register; and

(e) if the interest charged is in funds in court, the Accountant General at the Court Funds Office.

4.89   The reason for service of the interim charging order on the judgment debtor, trustees (in the case of an interest under a trust), party who administers the register (in the case of stock) and Accountant General at the Courts Funds Office (in the case of funds in court) is self evident, since they are either a party with an interest in the asset or a party who is responsible for administering dealings in relation to the asset.

4.90   In addition, under CPR 75.3(2)(b) the court has power to direct service of the order on other creditors of the judgment debtor and the application notice (Form N379/N380) requires the applicant to state those other creditors of the judgment debtor of whom he is aware. The reason for this provision is that the court will not make a charging order where it is not equitable to do so and one of the factors which may be relevant in this regard is the solvency of the judgment debtor and the position of other creditors. This is discussed further in paras 4.153–4.166.

Land – service on spouses/co-owners

4.91 As the notes to the White Book observe,[1] no rule specifically requires service of the interim charging order on the judgment debtor's spouse where the property concerned is the matrimonial home and, while co-owners may often hold the legal estate jointly with the judgment debtor (and thus be trustees on whom service is required pursuant to CPR 73.5(1)(c)), this will not always be the case.[2] However, Form N379 requires[3] the judgment creditor to provide the names of other persons to be served with the interim charging order and the wording of the Form suggests that this includes any co-owners and persons with rights of occupation.[4] Therefore although the charging order ranks as a charge on the judgment debtor's beneficial interest in land rather than the land itself, best practice is also to serve the charging order on the judgment debtor's spouse in the case of the matrimonial home, and on any co-owners, tenants, licensees or on any other persons with a right of occupation to the property concerned.

[1]   Civil Procedure 2004, vol 1, para 73.0.5.
[2]   Where the spouse is also a creditor of the judgment debtor, or has a registered charge on the matrimonial home under Matrimonial Causes Act 1973, s 31, service on the spouse will be required in any event.
[3]   Judgment creditors are obliged to use Form N379 in relation to charging orders relating to land by virtue of CPR 73.3(4)(a) and PD 73.1(1.1).
[4]   Since in ticking the box 'No other person has an interest in the property' the judgment creditor is verifying that this includes co-owners, trustees and person with rights of occupation of the property.

Deadline for service

4.92 The documents[1] must be served not less than 21 days before the hearing for further consideration of the application.[2] In any event, the judgment creditor should proceed to serve the interim charging order as soon as possible in order to be protected in the event that the judgment debtor disposes of the property. In the case of land, the judgment creditor will have to take additional steps in order to be protected against third party purchasers of the judgment debtor's property.[3]

[1]   Namely the interim charging order, the application notice and any documents filed in support of the application (see para 4.88).
[2]   CPR 73.5(1).
[3]   See paras 4.100-4.132.

Certificate of service

4.93 CPR 6.3 makes provision for the court to serve the interim order but the judgment creditor may serve the order himself provided he notifies the court that he wishes to do so. The judgment creditor may wish to take advantage of this provision so that he can retain control over the time and method in which service is effected. Where he does so, he must either file a certificate of service at court at least two days before the hearing or produce a certificate of service at the hearing.[1]

[1]   CPR 73.5(2).

Effect of service of the interim charging order

4.94 The effect of service of the interim charging order will depend on the nature of the judgment debtor's property which is subject to the order.

Effect of interim order in relation to securities

4.95 Where a judgment debtor has been served with an interim charging order relating to his interest in securities, if that judgment debtor disposes of that interest the disposition shall not be valid as against the judgment creditor.[1] The importance of serving the interim charging order on the judgment debtor as soon as it has been obtained is therefore evident.

1 So long as the charging order remains in force: CPR 73.6(1)

4.96 Under CPR 73.5(1)(d), service of an interim charging order relating to an interest in securities must also be effected on the company or holder of the stock register. Once served with the order, that party must not permit any transfer of any of the securities or pay any dividend, interest or redemption payment relating to them unless the court gives permission.[1] Service of the order should therefore operate to prevent shares being registered in a third party's name.

1 CPR 73.6(2).

4.97 Further protection is given to the judgment creditor under CPR 73.6(3), which provides that if a company or keeper of a stock register who has been served with an interim charging order permits the securities charged to be transferred, he will be liable to pay the judgment creditor the value of the securities transferred or the amount of the dividend or interest payment made (unless such sum exceeds the judgment debt, in which case he will be liable for the amount necessary to satisfy the judgment debt in respect of which the charging order was made).[1]

1 If the company can show that the judgment debtor whose name appears on the stock register had no beneficial interest in the shares, it will not be liable for permitting the transfer of the shares: *Gill v The Continental Union Gas Co Ltd* (1871-72) LR 7 Exch 332, a case under JA 1838 but which contained like provisions to CPR 73.6(3).

4.98 Such protections may not be sufficient to ensure that assets are available to satisfy the judgment debt, however. Difficulties can be caused where the judgment debtor has disposed of the beneficial interest in his shares but this not has yet been reflected in the stock register. In *Hawks v McArthur*,[1] the court found that even though the judgment debtor and the transferees had transferred shares (for valuable consideration) in flagrant breach of the company's articles of association relating to share transfers, the transferees had equitable rights in the shares that preceded the equitable rights under the charging order (which had not been obtained until after the transfer). Accordingly, although the judgment debtor still held the legal title to the shares, a charging order could not be obtained.[2]

1 [1951] 1 All ER 22.
2 In such circumstances obtaining a freezing injunction earlier in the proceedings may assist in the preservation of assets.

Effect of interim order in relation to funds in court

4.99   If a judgment debtor disposes of his interest in funds in court that are subject to an interim charging order that has been served on him and on the Accountant General,[1] that disposition will not be valid as against the judgment creditor (so long as the charging order remains in force). However, note that there is no equivalent provision to CPR 73.6(3) imposing a liability on the Accountant General if funds which are subject to a charging order are improperly paid out of court.[2]

[1]   In accordance with CPR 73.5(1).
[2]   See further para 4.278 for a discussion of *Bath v Bath*, a case which considered whether the Court Funds Office should be liable in the event that funds are improperly paid out of court in breach of a stop order.

Effect of interim order in relation to land

4.100   As is the case with any unregistered charge over land, a sale to a bona fide purchaser without notice will defeat the charge. In order to be effective, the charging order must therefore be appropriately registered.

Registering a charging order over land

4.101   The means by which registration of a charging order over land is effected depends on both the nature of the judgment debtor's interest in the land that has been charged and whether the land is registered or unregistered. Registration should be effected as soon as the interim charging order has been obtained, rather than waiting for the final charging order, in order to prevent the charge being defeated by failure to register in the intervening period.

4.102   In practice, title to the vast majority of judgment debtors' property is registered. However, although all land in England and Wales is now subject to compulsory registration,[1] unregistered title is still occasionally encountered and will be for some time to come.

[1]   Since 1 December 1990 the whole of England and Wales has been subject to compulsory registration of title: Registration of Title Order 1989, SI 1989/1347. See the Land Registration Act 2002, s 4.

4.103   The mechanics for registration of a charging order over registered and unregistered land are governed by entirely different statutory regimes. In the case of registered land, this is governed by the Land Registration Act 2002 and in the case of unregistered land by the Land Charges Act 1972. The statutory regimes are mutually exclusive and charging orders affecting registered land cannot be protected under the Land Charges Act 1972.[1] The means by which a judgment creditor can determine whether land is owned by a judgment debtor and whether the title to the land is registered or unregistered are considered in Chapter 2.

[1]   LCA 1972, s 14 and Land Charges Rules 1974, r 13.

Registering a charging order over unregistered land

4.104 Assuming that an index map search reveals that the land is unregistered, COA 1979, s 3(2) provides that the Land Charges Act 1972 (LCA 1972) shall apply in relation to charging orders as they apply to other orders or writs for the purpose of enforcing judgments. The LCA 1972 requires the Chief Land Registrar to continue to maintain numerous registers noting interests that affect unregistered land. These registers include the register of pending actions and register of writs and orders affecting land,[1] which are considered in turn.

[1]   LCA 1972, s 1.

Register of pending actions

4.105 The register of pending actions allows the registration of 'any action or proceeding pending in court relating to land or any interest in or charge on land'.[1] This would include an application notice seeking a charging order. In most cases it will not be necessary to register the application notice itself because the interval between the issue of the application and the making of an interim charging order is normally very short.

[1]   LCA 1972, ss 5(1) and 17(1).

4.106 Where the judgment creditor has grounds to believe that the judgment debtor intends to deal with the land imminently, it may be appropriate to register the application (as distinct from the interim order) as a pending land action, although a related injunction should also be sought restraining the sale. However, bearing in mind the injunction will not confer any priority on the judgment creditor if the judgment debtor breaches the injunction, the application for the charging order should still be registered to secure the advantages of registration (see para 4.108). Where an application is made to register a pending action, it should be registered against the estate owner or other person whose estate or interest is intended to be affected[1] (see paras 4.114-4.116).

[1]   LCA 1972, s 5(4).

4.107 It is not possible to protect an application to obtain a charging order over a tenancy in common held in unregistered land as this falls outside the definition of land in LCA 1972 which excludes from its scope an 'undivided share in land' (see further paras 4.114-4.116).[1]

[1]   LCA 1972, s 17(1) and *Perry v Phoenix Assurance plc* [1988] 1 WLR 940. See further Megarry and Wade *The Law of Real Property* (6th edn, 2000), p 177.

Effect of registration as a pending action

4.108 Registration of the interim charging order as a pending action, where correctly registered, constitutes actual notice of the order.[1] However, where it is not registered it will only bind a purchaser with express notice of it.[2]

[1]   Law of Property Act 1925, s 198. See generally Megarry and Wade *The Law of Real Property* (6th edn, 2000), pp 185–186.
[2]   LCA 1972, s 5(7).

Practice and procedure for applying to register a pending action

4.109   The appropriate form to register an application for registration of a pending action is Form K3.[1] The fee is £1 per name.[2] The registration of a pending action ceases to have effect at the end of the period five years from the date on which it was made.[3] In the unlikely circumstances where protection is still required after this period, the registration can be renewed. Once this is done, the registration shall have effect for five years from the date of renewal.[4]

[1]   Land Charges Rules 1974 SI 1974/1286, r 5 and Sch 2. The form can be downloaded from the Land Registry website:www.landreg.gov.uk/publications/?pubtype=1. Instructions for completion of the form are provided with the form.
[2]   Land Charge Fees Rules 1990, SI 1990/327 Sch 1.
[3]   LCA 1972, s 8.
[4]   LCA 1972, s 8.

Register of writs and orders affecting land

4.110   Once an interim charging order has been made, it should be registered as a writ or order affecting land.[1] LCA 1972, s 6(1) provides that 'any writ or order affecting land issued or made by any court for the purpose of enforcing any judgment' may be registered in the register of writs and orders affecting land. This clearly includes either an interim or final charging order. In practice, the interim order should be registered to ensure that priority is not lost in between the time the interim charging order is made and the time the final charging order is made.

[1]   Otherwise the judgment creditor takes the risk of the registration of the application being vacated by the court. LCA 1972, s 5(10) and *Sowerby v Sowerby* (1982) 44 P & CR 192.

Sole owners

4.111   In some cases the property will belong solely to the judgment debtor, particularly where the judgment debtor is a corporate. Where this is the case, an interim charging order over unregistered land can properly be registered in the register of writs and orders affecting land.

Trusts of land

4.112   LCA 1972, s 6(1A) prohibits the registration of any writ or order affecting an *interest under* a trust of land[1] being registered as a writ or order affecting land.[2] In short, almost all charging orders imposed upon a beneficial interest under a trust relating to unregistered land are incapable of registration as a writ or order affecting land.[3] The reason for this is that a beneficial interest may be 'overreached' by a purchaser.[4]

[1]   The meaning of trust of land is considered in para 4.40.
[2]   In *Perry v Phoenix Assurance plc* [1988] 1 WLR 940, an undivided share in land (ie a tenancy in common) was held not to fall under the definition of land in LCA 1972. LCA 1972, s 6(1A) is much wider than just tenancies in common and covers almost all forms of co-ownership of

land. If the judgment creditor were to manage to register a charging order over tenancy in common this would not constitute actual notice of the charging order because it would have been registered contrary to LCA 1972 (Law of Property Act 1925, s 198(2)).

3   Neither can a Class C(iii) land charge (general equitable charge) be registered instead: Land Charges Act 1972, s 2(4) which excludes, among other things, any trust of land from the definition of a Class C(iii) land charge.

4   The process whereby a purchaser of a legal estate in land can take free of any beneficial interests in the land by paying the purchase monies to two or more trustees.

4.113 There are two possible ways for a judgment creditor in such a position to protect himself. First, where no sale of the property appears to be imminent, proceedings could be brought for an order for sale of the land pursuant to TLATA 1996, s 14. Those proceedings can then be registered as a pending land action under LCA 1972, s 5(1) (see paras 4.105–4.110). However, this should be done without delay because the judgment creditor has no protection before this is done. Secondly, and in the event that there appears to be a risk that the land might imminently be sold, a receiver could possibly be appointed over the judgment debtor's share of the land. However, given that it may not be possible to register the receiver's appointment as a pending land action, it is hard to see the advantages of this other than the fact it would act as an injunction restraining the judgment debtor from dealing with the land.

Registration against the name of the 'estate owner'

4.114 The entry is made against 'the name of the estate owner or other person whose land, if any, is affected by the order registered'.[1] Estate owner means 'the owner of the legal estate'.[2] In practice, the 'names should be that or those appearing on the [abstract of] title'[3] even if known by a different name or another name appears on his birth certificate.[4] This creates a difficulty for the judgment creditor who is unlikely to have access to the title deeds (unless the judgment arises out of a dispute concerning a transaction involving the judgment debtor's land). However, under the Pt 71 procedure, the judgment debtor could be ordered to produce the title deeds when he attends court to provide information about his means.[5] If any doubt remains, there is no reason why registration should not be made in more than one name.[6]

1   LCA 1972, s 6(2).
2   LCA 1972, s 17(1) and Law of Property Act 1925, s 205(1)(v).
3   *Oak Co-operative Building Society v Blackburn* [1968] Ch 730 at 742, CA (decided under the Land Charges Act 1925) and *Standard Property Investment plc v British Plastics Federation* (1987) 53 P & CR 25 at 32.
4   *Standard Property Investment plc v British Plastics Federation* (1987) 53 P & CR 25 at 35.
5   CPR 71.2(6)(b).
6   *Megarry's Manual of the Law of Property* (8th edn, 2002) p 102. Although in *Standard Property Investment plc v British Plastics Federation* (1987) 53 P & CR 25 at 30, Walton J suggested multiple registrations 'fills one with alarm' he stopped short of saying it could not be done.

4.115 An error in the name registered will be invalid against a purchaser who applies for an official search in the correct full names of the estate owner and receives a clear certificate of search.[1] However, an error in the name registered does not entirely invalidate the registration where the name given might fairly be described as a version of the proper names of an estate owner (such as Frank instead of Francis). Such a registration would be valid against someone who failed to make a search or who applied for an official search in the wrong name and received a clear certificate of search.[2] Registration will be wholly ineffective where it omits one of the names of the estate owner.[3]

[1] *Oak Co-operative Building Society v Blackburn* [1968] 1 Ch 730 at 743, CA (decided under the Land Charges Act 1925).
[2] *Oak Co-operative Building Society v Blackburn* [1968] 1 Ch 730 at 743, CA.
[3] *Diligent Finance Co Ltd v Alleyne* (1972) 23 P & CR 346 (omitted middle name).

4.116   The registration of a writ or order affecting land ceases to have effect at the end of the period five years from the date on which it was made.[1] If protection is still required after this period, the registration can be renewed and once this is done, the registration shall have effect for five years from the date of renewal.[2]

[1] LCA 1972, s 8.
[2] LCA 1972, s 8.

Effect of registration as a writ or order against land

4.117   Registration of the interim charging order as a writ or order against land, where correctly registered, constitutes actual notice of the order.[1] Where the charging order has not been registered it is void against a purchaser of the land even if the purchaser has actual notice of the charging order.[2]

[1] Law of Property Act 1925, s 198. See generally Megarry and Wade *The Law of Real Property* (6th edn, 2000) pp 185–186. As has been noted, if the judgment creditor were to manage to register a charging order over an interest under a trust of land this would not constitute actual notice of the charging order because it would have been registered contrary to LCA 1972.
[2] LCA 1972, s 6(4). Contrast pending actions which by virtue of LCA 1972, s 5(7) bind a purchaser with express notice even if not registered.

Practice and procedure for registering a writ or order

4.118   Where registration is required, the appropriate form for the registration of a writ or order is Land Registry Form K4.[1] The current fee for a registration or renewal of a registration is £1.[2] The register of land charges is a public register[3] and an official search of the register can be made using Land Registry Form K15.[4] The current fee for searches is £1 or £2 per name depending on how the search is carried out.[5]

[1] The form can be downloaded from the Land Registry website: www.landreg.gov.uk/publications/?pubtype=1. Instructions for completion of the form are provided with the form.
[2] Land Charges Fees Rules 1990, SI 1990/327, Sch 1.
[3] LCA 1972, s 9(1).
[4] Land Charges Rules 1974, r 3(2). The form can be downloaded from the Land Registry website: www.landreg.gov.uk/publications. Instructions for completion of the form are provided with the form.
[5] Land Charges Fees Rules 1990, SI 1990/327, Sch 1.

Cancellation of either a pending action or a writ or order affecting land

4.119 An application for cancellation of either a pending action or a writ or order affecting land is made using from K11.[1] This should be done where a final order is refused or the charging order is satisfied (either by sale or payment by the judgment debtor).

[1]   Land Charges Rules 1974, SI 1974/1286, r 10.

Registering a charging order over registered land

4.120 Protection of a charging order against registered land is relatively simple. Assuming that an index map search reveals that the land is registered, COA 1979, s 3(2) provides that the Land Registration Act 2002 (LRA 2002) shall apply in relation to charging orders as they apply to other orders or writs for the purpose of enforcing judgments.

4.121 Under LRA 2002 a charging order can be protected by either a notice or a restriction.[1] The Act imposes a duty to act reasonably when applying to register a notice or restriction and no application should be made without proper grounds. A failure to observe this duty may result in a claim for damages as the duty is owed 'to any person who suffers damage in consequence of its breach'.[2] This provision should present no difficulties for a judgment creditor who has applied for or obtained a charging order.

[1]   Under the Land Registration Act 1925, either a caution against dealings or notice would have been used: Land Registry Land Registration Act 2002 Fact Sheet 16.
[2]   LRA 2002, s 77.

Registration of the application or order?

4.122 The LRA 2002 provides that a pending land action[1] and a writ or order affecting land[2] can be protected by the entry of a notice.[3] The Land Registration Rules 2003 also provide that a pending land action[4] and a writ or order affecting land[5] can be protected by the entry of a restriction.[6] The practical significance of this is that both the application and the charging order can potentially be protected by either notice or restriction as appropriate.

[1]   Within the meaning of LCA 1972.
[2]   Of a type mentioned in LCA 1972, s 6(1)(a) (ie a writ or order issued by a court to enforce a judgment).
[3]   LRA 2002, ss 87(1)(a)-(b) and 32(1). See also LRA 2002, s 34(1) and Land Registration Rules 2003, r 172(1) and (3).
[4]   Within the meaning of LCA 1972.
[5]   Of a type mentioned in LCA 1972, s 6(1)(a) (ie a writ or order issued by a court to enforce a judgment).
[6]   LRA 2002, s 43(1)(c) and Land Registration Rules 2003, r 172(2)–(3).

Notices

4.123 Where the judgment debtor is the sole owner of the registered land, either the application notice or the interim charging order can be protected by the entry of a notice.[1] A notice is an entry in the register denoting a burden affecting the registered estate[2] and is registered against the registered estate affected by the interest.[3] Any notices will appear in the charges register of the registered title affected.[4] The fact that an interest is the subject of a notice does not necessarily mean that the interest is valid, but does mean that the priority of the interest, if valid, is protected.[5]

1   LRA 2002, ss 34(1) and 87(1).
2   LRA 2002, s 32(1).
3   LRA 2002, s 32(2).
4   Land Registration Rules 2003, r 84(1).
5   LRA 2002, s 32(1).

4.124   Notices can either be agreed or unilateral.[1] In the context of charging orders an agreed notice is available where the Land Registrar has been sent a certified or official copy of the interim charging order with the application.[2] Where, for whatever reason, a certified or official copy of the interim charging order cannot be provided (for example, because the judgment creditor has not yet received the sealed interim charging order from court), a unilateral notice can be registered instead because it does require proof of the interest to be provided to the Land Registrar at the time of registration.

1   LRA 2002, s 34(2). An agreed notice is something of a misnomer because it can be entered without the registered proprietor's consent where the Land Registrar is satisfied as to the validity of the applicant's claim: LRA 2002, s 34(3)(c).
2   See the Land Registration Rules 2003, r 81(1)(b) and the Land Registry Land Registration Act 2002 Fact Sheet 16 and Land Registry Practice Guide 19 (Dec 2004).

Agreed or unilateral notice?

4.125   A judgment creditor who can provide a certified or official copy of the sealed application notice or interim charging order is in principle free to apply for either an agreed notice or a unilateral notice.[1] The form of the notice makes no difference to priority. However, a unilateral notice must be notified to the registered proprietor by the Land Registrar[2] and the registered proprietor has an automatic right to apply for its cancellation.[3] Objections by the judgment debtor are often groundless but the Land Registrar is duty bound to consider them and will transfer them to the Adjudicator if the parties cannot agree.[4] By contrast, an application by the registered proprietor to cancel an agreed notice could only be made if the charging order has expired.[5] The inconvenience which may therefore be caused by an application for cancellation by the judgment debtor in the case of a unilateral notice should be weighed against the possibility that where the application to register is urgent (for example, the judgment creditor is aware of an impending dealing with the title), the Land Registry may refuse his application for an agreed notice (which would leave the priority of his interest unprotected until he could apply for a unilateral notice).[6] In these circumstances, the safer course is to apply for a unilateral notice in the first instance.

1   Land Registry Practice Guide 19 (Apr 2004): Notices, restrictions and the protection of third party interests in the register, pp 8–9.
2   LRA 2002, s 35(1).
3   LRA 2002, s 36(1) and Land Registration Rules 2003, r 86.
4   LRA 2002, s 73(7).
5   Land Registration Rules 2003, r 87.
6   Land Registry Practice Guide 19 (Dec 2004): Notices, restrictions and the protection of third party interests in the register.

4.126   The relevant form is Land Registry form AN1[1] for an agreed notice and form UN1[2] for a unilateral notice. The current application fee for either form of notice is £40.[3]

1   Land Registration Rules 2003, r 81(1)(a).
2   Land Registration Rules 2003, r 83. The form can be downloaded from the Land Registry website: www.landreg.gov.uk/publications. An annotated guide explaining how to complete both forms is available at www.landreg.gov.uk/assets/library/documents/formrx1_annotated.pdf.
3   Land Registration Fee Order 2004, SI 2004/595, Sch 3.

Cancellation of a notice

4.127   The beneficiary of a notice can apply for its removal using form UN2.[1] This should be done where a final order is refused or the charging order is satisfied (either by sale of payment by the judgment debtor).

1   LRA 2002, s 35(3) and Land Registration Rules 2003, r 85(1).

Beneficial interest in registered land held under a trust of land

4.128   Where an application notice is issued or an interim charging order is made over a beneficial interest in registered land held under a trust of land, the judgment creditor should apply for a restriction.[1] A restriction 'is an entry in the register regulating the circumstances in which a disposition of a registered estate or charge may be the subject of an entry in the register'.[2] Where a restriction is entered on the register, it confers no priority but no entry of the type prohibited by the restriction can be made otherwise than in accordance with the terms of the restriction.[3]

1   LRA 2002, s 43(1)(c) and Land Registration Rules 2003, r 172(2)–(3). Note also that LRA 2002, s 33(a)(i) provides that it is not possible to protect an interest under a trust of land by notice.
2   LRA 2002, s 40(1).
3   LRA 2002, s 41.

4.129   A charging order over a beneficial interest in registered land held under a trust of land may be registered as Form K[1] of the standard form of restrictions which appear as the Land Registration Rules 2003, Sch 4. It will be noted that the restriction only requires the judgment creditor to be given notice of any disposition and will not prohibit the disposition from being made.

1   Which provides that: 'No disposition of the [registered estate or registered charge dated [date]] is to be registered without a certificate signed by the applicant for registration or his conveyancer that written notice of the disposition was given to [name of person with the benefit of the charging order] at [address for service], being the person with the benefit of [an interim] [a final] charging order on the beneficial interest of (name of judgment debtor) made by the (name of court) on (date) (Court reference . . .).'

4.130   The relevant form for the registration of beneficial interest in registered land held under a trust of land is Land Registry Form RX1.[1] The current fee to apply to enter a restriction is £40.[2]

1   Land Registration Rules 2003, r 92(1). The form can be downloaded from the Land registry website: www.landreg.gov.uk/publications/?pubtype=1. An annotated guide explaining how to complete the form is available at www.landreg.gov.uk/assets/library/documents/formrx1_annotated.pdf.
2   Land Registration Fee Order 2004, SI 2004/595, Sch 3.

Cancellation of a restriction

4.131   The beneficiary of a restriction can apply for its removal using form RX3.[1] This should be done where a final order is refused or the charging order is satisfied (either by sale or payment by the judgment debtor).

1   Land Registration Rules 2003, r 97(1).

Outline applications to register a notice or restriction

4.132   Where an application to register an application notice or an interim charging order over registered land is urgent, a procedure known as an outline application can be made by oral application, telephone or electronic means to register a notice (agreed or unilateral) or a restriction.[1] The procedure is set out in the Land Registration Rules 2003, r 54. An outline application can only be made once the application notice has been issued or an interim charging order has been granted.[2] Essentially, an outline application allows an application for a notice or restriction to be registered immediately, usually by telephone, with the application papers that would normally be required when applying for a notice of restriction (see above) to follow. The appropriate application papers must be submitted by noon on the fourth business day following the day that the outline application was made. If the documents are not filed within that time, the application must be cancelled by the Land Registrar.[3] Every outline application is given an official reference number[4] which will need to be quoted when the application papers are filed.

1   Land Registry Practice Guide 12 (Jun 2004): Official searches and outline applications, pp 22–23.
2   Land Registration Rules 2003, r 54(2)(b).
3   Land Registration Rules 2003, r 54(6)-(8).
4   Land Registration Rules 2003, r 54(5).

Do charging orders also need to be registered at Companies House?

4.133   COA 1979, s 3(4) provides that a charge imposed by a charging order shall have the like effect as an equitable charge created by the debtor by writing under his hand. Where the judgment debtor is a company, the question therefore arises as to whether charging orders have to be registered with the registrar of companies pursuant to the Companies Act 1985, ss 395 and 396.[1]

1   Companies Act 1985, s 395(1) provides: 'Subject to the provisions of this Chapter, a charge created by a company registered in England and Wales and being a charge to which this section applies is, so far as any security on the company's property or undertaking is conferred by the charge, void against the liquidator or administrator and any creditor of the company, unless the prescribed particulars of the charge together with the instrument (if

any) by which the charge is created or evidenced, are delivered to or received by the registrar of companies for registration in the manner required by this Chapter within 21 days after the date of the charge's creation.' Section 396 sets out the charges to which s 395 applies.

4.134 This question was answered by the Court of Appeal in *Re Overseas Aviation Engineering (GB) Ltd,*[1] which held that charging orders did not have to be registered with the registrar of companies. Although *Re Overseas Aviation* was decided by reference to AJA 1956, s 35(3) and Companies Act 1948, s 95, the statutory forebears of COA 1979, s 3(2), (4) and the Companies Act 1985, ss 395–396 respectively, the language used in the former statutes has been substantially replicated and thus the case remains good law.

[1]   [1963] Ch 24.

4.135 Lord Denning gave four reasons as to why registration of charging orders over company property with the registrar of companies was not required:

(a) The language of AJA 1956, s 35(3) made clear that the only form of registration with which the judgment creditor has to comply was registration pursuant to the Land Charges Act 1925 (in the case of unregistered land) and the Land Registration Act 1925. Similarly, the language of COA 1979, s 3(2) refers only to registration under LCA 1972 and LRA 2002.
(b) The words 'the like effect' were ambiguous and are capable of meaning that the charging order is to have 'the like effect as a valid equitable charge'. They do not compel the judgment creditor to make any formal registration of the charge in order to give it validity, save for registration under the Land Charges and Land Registration Acts.
(c) Practical difficulties would arise since under the Companies Act 1948, s 98 the judgment debtor company would be under a duty to register the charging order within 21 days even though the interim charging order may have been obtained without notice. Similar difficulties would arise under Companies Act 1985, s 398.
(d) The legislature would not have intended to make such a change affecting companies and no other debtors except by an express change to the relevant companies legislation.

Objections to a final charging order

4.136 'Any person' who wishes to object to the court making a final charging order must file and serve on the applicant written evidence stating the grounds of his objections.[1] The category of persons who may object to a final charging order being made is not therefore simply confined to the judgment debtor and may include, for example, other creditors, persons with a beneficial interest in the property in the case of land, or conceivably even the issuer company in the case of a charging order made in relation to securities.

[1]   CPR 73.8(1).

4.137 The evidence opposing the final charging order must be filed and served at least seven days before the hearing.[1] A witness statement with, where relevant, supporting documents setting out the person's grounds for opposing the final charging order should be provided.[1]

1   CPR 73.8(1).

Burden of proof

4.138   The burden of proof is on the judgment debtor (or other person) to show why a final charging order should not be made.[1]

1   *Roberts Petroleum Ltd v Bernard Kenny Ltd (in liquidation)* [1982] 1 All ER 685. Similarly, in *Aero Properties v Citycrest Properties* [2003] All ER (D) 218 the court held that the burden of proving that an interim charging order should not be made final rested on the judgment debtor, although in that case it had not been discharged.

4.139   In *Nightingale Mayfair Ltd v Mehta*,[1] the court had to decide the preliminary issue of where the burden of proof lay once evidence had been filed to object to the making of a charging order absolute. The evidence in question sought to establish that the judgment debtor had no beneficial interest in the land concerned. In his judgment Blackburne J summed up the dicta in earlier authorities and held that it is for the judgment creditor initially to provide evidence that the interest to be charged is beneficially owned by the judgment debtor. At the interim charging order stage, the case for a charging order has been made out on the evidence before the court. It is then for the judgment debtor to adduce evidence as to why a final charging order should not be made. If he does so, the burden shifts back to the judgment creditor.[2] Blackburne J concluded the issue by summarising the position as follows:

> 'In short, as in litigation generally, the burden is "a swinging burden" ... This means no more and no less than that, as the evidence of varying weight develops before the court, the evidential burden of proof will remain with or shift to the person who will fail without further evidence. ... The initial burden is plainly on the judgment creditor. Thereafter the burden rests with whichever side will lose on the basis of the weight of the evidence then before the court.'

1   [1999] All ER (D) 1501.
2   While *Nightingale* concerned the provisions of RSC Ord 50, and in particular r 1(3) which provided that 'unless sufficient cause to the contrary be shown' the judgment debtor's interest should be charged (wording which is not replicated in Pt 73), there is no logical reason why the principles as to the burden of proof established in *Nightingale* should no longer apply.

4.140   In the case of land, the fact that the judgment debtor is the only registered proprietor is good prima facie evidence in favour of granting a charging order against him. Where the judgment debtor nonetheless seeks to defeat a charging order by claiming that he holds the property on trust for another and where the evidence is inconclusive, the court is likely to make a final charging order (and thus postpone the arguments as to whether there is in fact a trust to the hearing for the order for sale).[1] Alternatively, the court could direct a trial to determine the beneficial ownership of the property.[2]

1   *Barclays Bank v Forrester* [1987] CLY 2437.
2   See paras 4.144–4.147.

Hearing for further consideration of the application

4.141 At least 21 days after the interim charging order is made[1] there will be a hearing for further consideration of the judgment creditor's application for a charging order. The interim charging order is made without notice on the strength of the information contained in the judgment creditor's application notice. The purpose of the further consideration of the interim order is to enable the court to review the position inter partes.[2]

1 See para 4.92.
2 *Roberts v Kenny* [1983] 2 AC 192.

4.142 Part 73.8(2) provides:

'At the hearing the court may –
(a) make a final charging order confirming that the charge imposed by the interim charging order shall continue, with or without modification;
(b) discharge the interim charging order and dismiss the application;
(c) decide any issues in dispute between the parties, or between any of the parties and any other person who objects to the court making a final charging order; or
(d) direct a trial of any such issues, and if necessary give directions.

4.143 There are therefore a range of options open to the court at the hearing. The use of the word 'may' in CPR 73.8 shows that the court has a discretion to make the final charging order. This discretion is discussed at paras 4.148–4.193.

When will the court direct a trial of issues between the parties?

4.144 CPR 73.8(2)(c) makes it clear that the master[1] can decide any issues in dispute between the parties (or between any of the parties and any other person who objects to the court making a final charging order) at the hearing. The commentary in the White Book[2] observes that only exceptionally will it be necessary for the master to give directions and order a trial of any issue between the parties pursuant to CPR 73.8(2)(d).

1 Or district judge in the county court.
2 Civil Procedure 2004, vol 1, para 73.8.2.

4.145 The circumstances in which a trial of issues between the parties will be appropriate was considered by the Court of Appeal in *Rosseel NV v Oriental Commercial & Shipping Co (UK) Ltd* .[1] In that case there was a dispute as to whether the judgment debtor beneficially owned land against which a charging order had been made, or whether the land actually belonged to third parties. The court approved[2] a note to RSC Ord 50 (the procedural rule then applying to charging orders), which is repeated in Pt 73,[3] to the effect that if title to stock or shares which are subject to a charging order is disputed, an issue may be directed to be tried, and observed that the same principles should apply in relation to a dispute as to the beneficial ownership of land.[4] Parker LJ, who gave the lead judgment, concluded:

'Where there is a real dispute, it is, as it seems to me, necessary in order to do justice that an issue should be tried and the court can in the exercise of its power to regulate its own procedure direct such issue.'

1   (1991) Times, 11 October. The relevant issue on appeal was whether the judge had the power to direct trial of an issue under RSC Ord 50. The wording of CPR 73.8(2)(c) now makes clear that there is such a power but the principles discussed in the case are still relevant.

2   Parker LJ stated: 'The note is not based on any authority, but I would endorse it.'

3   Civil Procedure 2004, vol 1, para 73.8.3.

4   See eg *Nightingale Mayfair Ltd v Mehta and others*, discussed in para 4.139.

4.146   A mere assertion by the judgment debtor that a final charging order should not be made will not suffice.[1] Where there is serious doubt as to the judgment debtor's solvency, the court may make an order for an inquiry into this issue.[2]

1   *Newman v Rook* (1858) 4 CB 434, a case relating to garnishee orders, but similar principles should apply.

2   See *George Lee & Sons (Builders) Ltd v Olink* [1972] 1 All ER 359, a case relating to garnishee orders but similar principles should apply.

4.147   Where the court directs that there is an issue to be tried the practice is to adjourn the application to make the charging order absolute until after the decision on the issue.[1]

1   Civil Procedure 2004, vol 1, para 73.8.3 and *Rosseel NV v Oriental Commercial and Shipping (UK) Ltd* [1991] 2 Lloyd's Rep 625.

The court's discretion

4.148   As has been noted, the court has a discretion as to whether or not to make a charging order.[1] This discretion exists both when the court considers the application for an interim charging order and at the hearing for further consideration of the application, and there is no difference between the principles the court should apply in exercising that discretion at either stage.[2]

1   See para 4.20.

2   See para 4.83. Should the judgment creditor subsequently proceed to enforce the security by applying for an order for sale, the court has a further discretion as to whether to or not to make that order. See paras 4.215–4.217.

4.149   Under COA 1979, s 1(5) the court must take into account all the circumstances of the case in exercising its discretion to make a charging order, and in particular must consider any evidence before it as to the personal circumstances of the judgment debtor and whether any other creditor of the debtor would be likely to be unduly prejudiced by the making of a charging order. Each case is a matter for the individual judgment of the court in the circumstances of that particular case.[1]

1   *Roberts Petroleum Ltd v Bernard Kenny* [1983] 2 AC 192.

4.150   The leading case on the principles governing the court's discretion to make a charging order is the Court of Appeal decision in *Roberts Petroleum Ltd v Bernard Kenny Ltd (in liquidation)*[1] and the subsequent reversal of that decision in the House of Lords.[2] In giving the lead judgment in the Court of Appeal, Lord Brandon of

Oakbrook laid out the following principles as relevant to the court's exercise of its discretion under COA 1979:

'(1) The question whether a charging order nisi should be made absolute is one for the discretion of the court.

(2) The burden of showing cause why a charging order nisi should not be made absolute is on the judgment debtor.

(3) For the purpose of the exercise of the court's discretion there is, in general at any rate, no material difference between the making absolute of a charging order nisi on the one hand and a garnishee order nisi on the other.[3]

(4) In exercising its discretion the court has both the right and the duty to take into account all the circumstances of any particular case, whether such circumstances arose before or after the making of the order nisi.

(5) The court should so exercise its discretion as to do equity, so far as possible, to all the various parties involved, that is to say the judgment creditor, the judgment debtor, and all other unsecured creditors.'[4]

[1]   [1982] 1 All ER 685.
[2]   [1983] 2 AC 192.
[3]   Similar sentiments were expressed in the earlier Court of Appeal decision in *Rainbow v Moorgate Properties Ltd* [1975] 2 All ER 821 where Buckley LJ at 824 expressed the view: 'I for myself can see no difference between those considerations which are relevant to the question whether the discretion should or should not be exercised to make absolute a garnishee order and those considerations which are relevant to the question whether the court should or should not make absolute a charging order.'
[4]   [1982] 1 All ER 685 at 689.

4.151   The Court of Appeal's decision in *Roberts v Kenny* was subsequently reversed in the House of Lords but the principles set out above were not effected by that reversal and remain good law.[1]

[1]   Two further principles were set out by Lord Brandon of Oakbrook at 689 but the House of Lords subsequently overturned these: see the judgment of Lord Brightman, [1983] 2 AC 192 at 213. See para 4.162.

Developments following the interim charging order

4.152   It is clear that the court can take into account what has happened since the interim charging order in deciding whether to make the final charging order.[1]

[1]   *Roberts v Kenny* [1983] 2 AC 192. See also *Ropaigealach v Allied Irish Bank plc* [2001] EWCA Civ 1790 at [15] for a clear synopsis of the law on this point.

Undue prejudice to other creditors

4.153   The COA 1979 requires the court to take into account the likelihood that a charging order will cause undue prejudice to other creditors in considering whether to make the final charging order.[1] Because charging orders take effect as an equitable charge on the judgment debtor's property, a judgment creditor with the benefit of a charging order has an advantage over the unsecured creditors of the judgment debtor. The position of other judgment creditors will be particularly important when the judgment debtor is insolvent or facing the prospect of insolvency.

¹   COA 1979, s 1(5)(b).

4.154 In *Rainbow v Moorgate Properties Ltd*¹ the Court of Appeal had to consider how the court's discretion under AJA 1956, s 35² should be applied in an appeal against two charging orders absolute which had been made after the judgment debtor company had gone into creditors voluntary liquidation and subsequently petitioned for its own winding up.

¹   [1972] 2 All ER 821.
²   Although this case therefore predates COA 1979, it remains good law since the earlier statutory provisions were equivalent to those under COA 1979 for these purposes.

4.155 On the facts of that case, the Court of Appeal held that the judgment creditors' charging orders absolute could not stand. In considering the matter, Buckley LJ found that the considerations which are relevant to the exercise of the court's discretion to make a charging order absolute are the same as those which the court should apply in deciding whether to make a garnishee order absolute (now a final third party debt order), and cited his own judgment in the earlier Court of Appeal decision in *D. Wilson (Birmingham) Ltd v Metropolitan Property Developments Ltd*:¹

> 'The position is, I think, that a court in considering whether or not to exercise its discretion to make absolute a garnishee order in circumstances such as this must bear in mind, not only the position of the judgment creditor, the judgment debtor and the garnishee, but the position of the other creditors of the judgment debtor and must have regard to the fact that proceedings are on foot, and were on foot at the time the garnishee proceedings were launched for ensuring the distribution of the available assets of the judgment debtor company among the creditors pari passu.'²

¹   Bar Library Transcript No 383A of 1974.
²   [1975] 1 WLR 788 at 793.

4.156 On the facts in *Rainbow* the Court of Appeal found that, while the judgment creditors had not done anything wrong in seeking to obtain the charging orders absolute (not least since they had no knowledge of the judgment debtor's financial situation), the orders should be discharged. Buckley LJ stated:¹

> 'While I have much sympathy for the plaintiffs and quite understand that they are anxious that payment should be made, I think it is wrong, when the court is aware of the fact that the debtor is, or is likely to turn out to be, insolvent, that one creditor should be given an advantage over other creditors by an exercise of the discretion of the court under s 35 of the Administration of Justice Act 1956. … the court has to be satisfied that it is proper for the court, in the exercise of its discretion, to place [the judgment creditor's] at an advantage over other creditors. If there were no countervailing reasons the court would make charging orders in the present case but, in my judgment, there are countervailing reasons connected with the moratorium and the proposed scheme of arrangement which I have mentioned which in this case do make it improper to give the plaintiffs an advantage over other creditors.'

¹   [1972] 2 All ER 821 at 825.

Roberts v Kenny

4.157 The need to balance the conflicting interests of a judgment creditor seeking to exercise his right to enforce his judgment and the rights of all creditors in an insolvency to be treated equally were at the centre of the court's considerations in *Roberts v Kenny* in both the Court of Appeal and the House of Lords.

4.158 The Court of Appeal judgment in *Roberts v Kenny* described two further principles in addition to those set out in para 4.150, which related to the exercise of the court's discretion in the context of a judgment debtor's insolvency. These were overturned by the House of Lords on appeal. Before considering the reasons for that reversal, it is worth briefly summarising the facts in the case.

4.159 A judgment creditor of a company had obtained a charging order nisi over the land of the judgment debtor company. The judgment debtor company subsequently convened a meeting of its shareholders on short notice and resolved to put the company into voluntary liquidation. The question for the court was whether, in the circumstances, the court should exercise its discretion to make the charging order absolute. The High Court judge thought it should not and discharged the charging order but the Court of Appeal disagreed and reinstated the charging order.

4.160 In giving the lead judgment in the Court of Appeal, Lord Brandon of Oakbrook held that proof of the combination of circumstances that the judgment debtor is insolvent *and* that a scheme of arrangement has been set on foot by the main body of creditors and has a reasonable prospect of succeeding will generally justify the court in exercising its discretion by refusing to make the order absolute. However, in the absence of the combination of these circumstances, the court will generally be justified in exercising its discretion to make the order absolute. The judgment debtor appealed.

4.161 Lord Brightman, who gave the lead judgment in the House of Lords, noted that the Court of Appeal had correctly identified the conflict between two well-established principles of law that were central to the matters at issue in the case: first, a judgment creditor is in general entitled to enforce a money judgment which he has lawfully obtained against a judgment debtor by all or any of the means of enforcement prescribed by the relevant rules of court; secondly, when a judgment debtor (natural person or a corporate body) has become insolvent, all the unsecured creditors should be treated equally. Lord Brightman summarised both the question facing the court and his views on how it should be answered as follows:[1]

> 'The basic question which confronts the court when it is faced with an application by an execution creditor to convert an order nisi into an order absolute in a case such as the present is whether the asset in question should fall outside the statutory scheme which, by virtue of the liquidation is then in existence, or should be subject to that scheme. In the absence of persuasive authority to the contrary, and it will of course be necessary to consider the authorities, I would myself have thought that the court should exercise this discretion so that the asset falls within the statutory scheme. The purpose of the further consideration of the order nisi is to enable the court to review the position inter parties. At the date of the order nisi the court has made no irrevocable decision. If therefore

the statutory scheme for dealing with the assets of the company has been irrevocably imposed on the company by resolution or winding up order before the court has irrevocably determined to give the creditor the benefit of the charging order, I would have thought that the statutory scheme should prevail.'

¹   [1983] 2 AC 192 at 208.

4.162   Having reviewed the authorities¹ the House of Lords found that while each case was a matter for the individual judgment of the court in the circumstances of that particular case, the liquidation of a company is, without more, sufficient cause for the court to exercise its discretion not to make the final charging order. The liquidation brought into operation a statutory scheme for dealing with the assets of the company which in general should prevail. It was irrelevant whether the statutory scheme was achieved through the compulsory winding up of a company, or a resolution of a company in general meeting for voluntary winding up because in each case the statutory scheme should prevail. As Hale LJ put it in *Ropaigealach v Allied Irish Bank plc*:²

'Roberts Petroleum held, in effect, that one judgment creditor should not be able to steal a march on the other unsecured creditors by getting a speedy charging order nisi and thereby pre-empting the statutory insolvency scheme. That of course is all relevant to the matters in s 1(5)(b) of the 1979 Act.'³

¹   See para 4.163, n 1.
²   [2001] EWCA Civ 1790.
³   Or as Lord Brightman put it at 209 in *Roberts v Kenny*: 'I do not see why a creditor should gain an advantage merely because he has a revocable order for security at the time when the statutory scheme comes into existence.'

4.163   The same principles would apply if an individual is made bankrupt after the interim charging order is made but before the final charging order.¹

¹   By parity of reasoning and because the House of Lords in *Roberts v Kenny* expressly disapproved *Burston Finance Ltd (in liquidation) v Godfrey* [1976] 1 WLR 719, where the Court of Appeal found to the contrary. The House of Lords in *Robert v Kenny* also reviewed the decisions in *Hudson's Concrete Products Ltd v D B Evans (Bilston) Ltd* (1961) 105 S.J. 281, *D. Wilson (Birmingham) Ltd v Metropolitan Property Developments Ltd* [1975] 2 All ER 814 (where the judgment debtor's insolvency had intervened between the making of a garnishee order nisi and the hearing for further consideration, so that the court refused to make the garnishee order absolute) and *Rainbow v Moorgate Properties Ltd* [1975] 1 WLR 788 (where the court discharged a charging order because a judgment debtor had presented its own winding up petition prior to the charging order absolute being made), and criticised the interpretation that had been placed on these cases in *Burston* (which was to the effect that each contained significant circumstances in addition to the presentation of a winding up petition, notably the preparation of a scheme of arrangement or moratorium, from which it could be inferred that an understanding existed between creditors as to common forbearance from pressing ahead with individual remedies in the interests of all - 'a holding back of action for the common benefit').

4.164   Effectively, therefore, in circumstances where a judgment debtor is insolvent, a judgment creditor who is seeking a charging order must overcome a presumption that the statutory regime should prevail. However, each case will be a matter for the individual judgment of the court in the circumstances of that particular case. In *Re a*

Debtor (nos 31/32/33 of 1993), Calor Gas v Piercy[1] the court had to consider the position where a judgment creditor had obtained a charging order nisi after which proposals for individual voluntary arrangements had been made in relation to the judgment debtor's estate. Following presentation of the proposals, interim orders freezing the position of the debtor's estate were made in accordance with IA 1986, s 252 following normal practice.[2] The charging orders were then made absolute notwithstanding the fact that the interim orders were by then in place.

[1]   [1994] 2 BCLC 321.
[2]   IA 1986, s 252 provides: '(1) In the circumstances specified below, the court may, in the case
       of a debtor (being an individual) make an interim order under this section. (2) An interim
       order has effect that, during the period for which it is in force – (a) no bankruptcy petition
       relating to the debtor may be presented or proceeded with, and (b) no other proceedings, and
       no execution or other legal process, may be commenced or continued against the debtor or
       his property except with the leave of the court.'

4.165   The judge reviewed the House of Lords' decision in *Roberts v Kenny* and said:

> 'As I read *Roberts Petroleum Ltd v Bernard Kenny Ltd* [1983] 1 All ER 564, [1983] 2 AC 192 in considering whether an order should be made absolute after bankruptcy or liquidation almost as a course the order will be discharged. Yet where there is no supervening bankruptcy the court has a wider discretion than where there had already been a bankruptcy. Even in the latter case where there had already been a bankruptcy, the court is not deprived of all discretion in the matter and I take that from the passage of Lord Brightman's speech to which I referred (see [1983] 1 All ER 564 at 575, [1983] 2 AC 192 at 211).'

4.166   The judge then considered the circumstances in this case and, in particular, the personal circumstances of the debtor and whether any other creditor of the debtor would be likely to be unduly prejudiced. While he found that both factors pointed towards discharging the order, against those considerations there were special circumstances, which pointed in favour of upholding the master's decision to make the order absolute. These comprised the fact that the judgment creditor had been deprived of important statutory rights due to the manner in which the scheme had been implemented. These considerations, together with the delay and expense the judgment creditor had suffered as a consequence, tipped the balance in favour of upholding the charging order absolute.

4.167   Essentially the court will seek to ensure fairness among all creditors where insolvency has occurred or is in prospect and so will not allow an advantage to be conferred on one creditor by means of a charging order. Clearly, therefore, a judgment creditor must make careful enquiries to find out the financial state of the judgment debtor before seeking to obtain a charging order since otherwise he runs the risk of incurring costs in obtaining the charging order which may lead him to no advantage. The manner in which a judgment creditor can search for insolvency steps affecting a judgment debtor has been considered in Chapter 2

4.168   In some respects, this may seem to cause an element of unfairness to a creditor who has diligently obtained judgment and proceeded to take enforcement steps (incurring further costs in the process) only to have such diligence go unrewarded by the intervention of a statutory scheme on insolvency. Such grievances may seem particularly acute when the prospect of the judgment debtor's future insolvency were not apparent at the time the judgment and the interim charging order were obtained.

Personal circumstances of the judgment debtor

4.169   COA 1979 requires the court to take into account the personal circumstances of the judgment debtor in considering whether to make the charging order.[1] Financial hardship to the judgment debtor alone is unlikely to be sufficient for the court to exercise its discretion against making the charging order, since the starting point is that a judgment creditor is generally entitled to enforce a money judgment by any means of enforcement available.[2] However, where the charging order is being sought over a matrimonial or family home, the court will take into account not just the position of the judgment debtor but also the situation of the judgment debtor's family.[3] Difficulties therefore arise where the court is faced with competing claims over the family home made by a judgment debtor's spouse or former spouse and a judgment creditor.

1   COA 1979, s 1(5)(a).
2   *Roberts v Kenny* [1983] 1 All ER 564.
3   *Harman v Glencross* [1986] 1 All ER 545 at 561, per Fox LJ: 'It seems to me that 'the personal circumstances of the debtor' would include the fact that he is obliged to make provision for his wife and young children, that he has no property with which to do so apart from the equity of his share of the matrimonial home and that his former wife has no resources of her own of any consequence. But, if that is not so, those facts are included in the expression "all the circumstances of the case". So far as the wife is concerned, they are, I think, the most important factor.'

4.170   These competing claims were considered by the Court of Appeal in *First National Securities Ltd v Hegerty*.[1] In that case a matrimonial home was owned jointly by the judgment debtor and his wife. The judgment creditor obtained a charging order nisi on the husband's beneficial interest in the house. Shortly afterwards the wife commenced divorce proceedings and was joined as a party to the charging order proceedings. When the matter came before the master for further consideration of the charging order application, he refused to make the order absolute and discharged the order nisi. The judgment creditor appealed and Bingham J allowed the appeal and made the charging order absolute. He rejected an application on behalf of the wife that the matter should be transferred to the Family Division so that the wife's interest in the property could be determined under the Matrimonial Causes Act 1973, Pt II at the same time as the judgment creditor's claim for a charging order. The wife appealed.

1   [1985] QB 850.

4.171   The Court of Appeal found that there were not sufficient grounds for holding that Bingham J was so clearly wrong in exercising his discretion as he did that it should interfere with his decision and upheld the charging order absolute. In concurring with Bingham J's dismissal of the wife's submission that the charging order application should be transferred to the Family Division, Stephenson LJ held:

'I have, however, come to the conclusion (1) that the court should not use its powers under Part II of the Matrimonial Causes Act 1973 to override the claims of a creditor seeking security for a debt by a charging order; (2) that it should not discharge or vary a charging order so as to prefer a wife's claim to such a creditor's; (3) that it can, and often should postpone the enforcement of a charging order until the hearing of any application under s 30 of the Law of Property Act 1925, when the court can decide between the competing claims of wife and creditor.'

4.172 Accordingly, the court found that the subsequent application under Law of Property Act 1925 (LPA 1925), s 30 for an order for sale of the matrimonial home was the correct venue to consider the competing claims of the judgment creditor and the judgment debtor's spouse since the wife's possession of the house could not be disturbed until after that hearing. (LPA 1925, s 30 has now been replaced by TLATA 1996, s 14.)

4.173 By the time that the Court of Appeal came to give judgment in *Hegerty*, the first instance decision in *Harman v Glencross* had been given by Ewbank J.[1] The facts in *Harman* were that a husband and wife had purchased a house in their joint names but the marriage had broken down and the wife had petitioned for divorce. The wife commenced ancillary proceedings for a property adjustment order and other financial relief, served notice of severance of the joint tenancy, and subsequently obtained a decree nisi. Shortly afterwards, a creditor of the husband obtained judgment against him and then obtained a charging order absolute in respect of the husband's interest in the matrimonial home (in contrast to the situation in *Hegerty*, where the charging order nisi was obtained *before* the wife commenced divorce proceedings). However, the judgment creditor did not serve the application for the charging order on the wife or give her notice of it. When the wife discovered the existence of the charging order she applied under COA 1979, s 3(5) for it to be discharged, or in any event not enforced until the hearing of her application for ancillary relief. The charging order proceedings were then transferred to the Family Division to be heard by the same court hearing the wife's application for ancillary relief in her divorce proceedings.

[1]   [1984] 2 All ER 577.

4.174 The Family registrar ordered that the charging order was to be subject to any order made in the ancillary proceedings and further ordered, in the ancillary proceedings, that the husband's interest in the matrimonial home was to be transferred to the wife. The judgment creditor appealed against the variation of the charging order made by the Family registrar. The Court of Appeal therefore had to consider how the interests of the wife and children were to be balanced against the interests of the judgment creditor.[1]

[1]   The court also had to consider when, if at all, it was appropriate for the court to consider the wife's position when deciding whether to make a charging order in respect of a matrimonial home.

4.175 The Court of Appeal in *Harman*[1] first observed that the comments made by the Court of Appeal in *Hegerty* to the effect that the first instance decision of Ewbank J in Harman was wrong were obiter. This was because, first, *Hegerty* was not concerned with the exercise of the court's powers under the Matrimonial Causes Act 1973, and secondly, because the court in *Hegerty* had expressly disclaimed any intention to bind the Court of Appeal in *Harman*.

[1]   [1986] 1 All ER 545.

4.176   The Court then stated Lord Brandon's dictum in *Roberts v Kenny* that a judgment creditor is in general entitled to enforce a money judgment which he has lawfully obtained against a judgment debtor by all or any of the means of enforcement prescribed by the relevant rules of court, but noted that this proposition is qualified (for example, where the interests of other creditors must be taken into account). Having accepted that the court is properly concerned to protect the wife's right to occupy the matrimonial home, the Court went on to consider how that right should be protected. Balcombe LJ observed that the Court of Appeal in *Hegerty* had come to the view that the wife's right of occupation was adequately protected by LPA 1925, s 30 hearing, but observed that if the position is considered by the Family Division pursuant to her application for ancillary relief under the Matrimonial Causes Act 1973, there are a number of ways in which her right to occupy the matrimonial home can be protected. He observed that the position in *Harman* differed significantly from that in *Hegerty* in that divorce proceedings had been commenced before the charging order nisi was obtained, and concluded:[1]

> 'If a judgment creditor obtains his charging order nisi after the wife has filed her divorce petition (which will usually contain a prayer for ancillary relief), then unless the court which hears the application to make the charging order absolute is satisfied that the wife's rights will be adequately protected by the court's discretion under s 30 of the Law of Property Act 1925, bearing in mind the limitations of that section mentioned above, it seems to me that it will normally be appropriate to take the course taken in the present case, and to transfer the judgment creditor's application for a charging order to the Family Division so that it may be heard by the court hearing the wife's application for ancillary relief.'

[1]   [1986] 1 All ER 545 at 557–558.

4.177   Accordingly, there were no grounds for holding that the judge was wrong to exercise his discretion in the manner that he had and the court upheld the order making the charging order subject to the order made in the ancillary proceedings.

4.178   Balcombe LJ went on to set out[1] a number of general principles for how the courts should deal with the competing interests of a spouse and a judgment creditor in these circumstances:

(a)   Where a judgment creditor has obtained an interim charging order on the matrimonial home *before* the wife has started divorce proceedings, it is difficult to see why the court should refuse to make the final charging order, and the wife's right of occupation should be 'adequately protected' under LPA 1925, s 30.

(b)   Where the interim charging order has been made *after* the wife's petition, then on the application for a final charging order, unless it appears to the court that the circumstances are so clear that it is proper to make the order there and then, the usual practice should be to transfer the application to the Family Division so that it may he heard with the wife's application for ancillary relief to enable one court to be in a position to consider all the circumstances of the case. Of particular relevance in considering such transfer will be:

(i)   whether the value of the equity in the house is sufficient to enable the final charging order to be made and realised at once even though that may result in the wife and children being housed at a lower standard than they might reasonably have expected had only the husband's interests been taken into account against them. (For example, in *Llewellin v Llewellin*,[2] the court found that even if the charging order was made absolute and the charge was then realised by a sale of the house, the resultant proceeds of sale would clearly be sufficient to provide adequate alternative accommodation for the wife and children.)

   (ii) Failing that, the court should make only such order as may be necessary to protect the wife's right to occupy (with the children where appropriate) the matrimonial home. The normal course should then be to postpone the sale of the house for such period only as may be requisite to protect the right of occupation,[3] bearing in mind that the court is holding the balance, not between the wife and the husband, but between the wife and the judgment creditor.[4]

   (iii) Finally, the court should consider whether there is any point in denying the judgment creditor his charging order if the wife's rights of occupation could, in any event, be defeated by the judgment creditor making the husband bankrupt.[5]

(c) Once the final charging order has been made, it would normally require some special circumstance, (for example, as in *Harman*, where the wife had no notice of the charging order application) for the court to set the charging order aside under COA 1979, s 3(5).

[1]   [1986] 1 All ER 545 at 558–559.
[2]   [1985] CA Bound Transcript 640.
[3]   A form of '*Mesher*' order, from *Mesher v Mesher and Hall* [1980] 1 All ER 126.
[4]   Notably the judgment creditor in *Harman* was not prepared to accept a *Mesher* order.
[5]   The court found that this did not apply in *Harman* since the wife had given valuable consideration for the transfer of the property, but did not rule this out as a ground of objection if the facts had been different.

4.179 Fox LJ, who gave the second judgment in *Harman*, concurred with these principles but emphasised that the point of a transfer to the Family Division of an application for a charging order is simply to ensure that the court is fully apprised of all the circumstances of the case relating to the judgment debtor and his family – the application remained a charging order application and should not be treated as if it were the wife's application under the matrimonial jurisdiction.

4.180 A number of commentators have criticised the lack of coherence in these judgments.[1] A procedural decision as to which court should hear the application for a charging order may inevitably involve different factors being weighed in the balance. The cases show that under COA 1979, s 1(5) a wife's interests in the matrimonial home should be taken into account whenever the court is considering whether to make a charging order. Both *Hegerty* and *Harman* were decided before the Human Rights Act 1998 came into force. Human rights considerations may be a further factor in suggesting that where there is insufficient equity in a matrimonial home to enable the charging order to be enforced immediately while leaving sufficient funds to provide adequate protection for the wife's accommodation, the better approach is for the court to make the charging order subject to postponing the judgment creditor's right to enforce the charge for such period as is necessary to protect the spouse's and children's rights to occupy the matrimonial home.

[1]   See eg Warburton 'Victory for the sprinter' Conv 1986, July–August, 291–295.

4.181 This was the approach Waite J followed in *Austin-Fell v Austin-Fell*,[1] a case heard in the Family Division. In that case the court faced the familiar dilemma of striking a balance between the family security claimed by the wife and children in matrimonial proceedings and the commercial security claimed by a judgment creditor bank in charging order proceedings. In that case, the matrimonial home had been purchased in joint names but the husband's business subsequently got into serious financial difficulties and his bank obtained judgment against him. Later that year the husband and wife separated. The bank then obtained a charging order against the husband's share in the matrimonial home. The wife applied to discharge the charging order and also brought divorce proceedings. The registrar directed that the wife's application to discharge the charging order be heard at the same time as her application for financial relief in the divorce proceedings.

1   [1990] 2 All ER 455.

4.182 On the hearing of both applications the registrar, exercising the unfettered discretion conferred by both the Matrimonial Causes Act 1973, s 25(1) and COA 1979, s 1(5) to have regard to 'all the circumstances of the case', set aside the charging order and directed that the husband's half share of the matrimonial home be transferred to the wife. The registrar's decision was made on the ground that the wife's claim to the matrimonial home was overwhelming as against the husband and should prevail over a creditor's claim for security, and where it was not possible both to enforce the charging order and to provide adequate protection for the wife's accommodation, the charging order should be discharged to allow her to have the full equity in the property unencumbered by the charging order. The registrar also refused to allow the bank's security to be deferred so that the competing claims might be looked at again in a few years' time.

4.183 The bank appealed, contending that while it accepted the wife's need to house herself and her children, the bank's security ought not to be swept aside so completely. The bank therefore sought to preserve the charging order absolute it had obtained, but to delay its enforcement until the children reached maturity.[1] Waite J allowed the bank's appeal and granted a postponed enforcement order until the children reached maturity. The argument centred around what Balcombe LJ had meant in *Harman* by 'adequate protection' for the wife in considering whether to make a charging order. Waite J held that the interpretation the wife had sought to put on the guidelines laid down by the Court of Appeal in *Harman* were plainly perverse. He held:[2]

'When the judgments of the Court of Appeal in *Harman v Glencross* [1986] Fam. 81 are read as a whole in the context of the facts with which they were dealing, they plainly refute the idea that there can ever be automatic predominance for any claim: whether it be the wife's claim for permanent adequate protection of her right of accommodation or the creditor's claim for permanent protection of his debt. Every case depends, as Fox LJ said in *Harman v Glencross*, at p 104A, upon striking a fair balance between the normal expectations of the creditor and the hardship to the wife and children if a charging order is made. The use of the expression "hardship" in that formula necessarily implies that there will be instances in which the wife and/or children will be compelled, in the interests of justice to the judgment creditor, to accept a provision for their security of accommodation which falls below the level of adequacy.'

1   Ie a *Mesher* order, see para 4.178, n 3.
2   [1990] 2 All ER 455 at 460.

4.184 The right of occupation to be protected is not therefore permanent protection. As Balcombe LJ stated in *Harman*, where a judgment creditor seeks an alternative to immediate enforcement via a *Mesher* type postponed enforcement order, such an order ought not to be refused save in exceptional circumstances. Inevitably, such an order may involve hardship on both sides (for the wife, in having to pay off accumulated interest on the charge during the postponement period, and for the judgment creditor, in having to wait for its money). Nonetheless:[1]

'A postponed enforcement order nevertheless represents the fairest balance between the competing claims of wife and creditor, in the endeavour which the court has to make to give some effect to both, and that is the order which I propose to direct.'

1   [1990] 2 All ER 455 at 463.

Hardship to the judgment creditor

4.185 The *Harman* case made clear that the court will take into account evidence of hardship that will be suffered by the judgment creditor if a charging order which is not immediately enforceable is not granted.[1] In that case the judgment creditor had not submitted any evidence as to his means. Similarly, in *Austin-Fell* the judgment creditor bank's personal circumstances were not taken into account since the bank acknowledged that it had the protection of substantial resources on which loss of the security for the relatively small debt concerned would make little dent.[2] However, a judgment creditor who will suffer hardship if the charging order is not granted would be well-advised to submit evidence as to this hardship in the event that the application for a charging order is opposed or sought to be varied or discharged.

1   [1986] 1 All ER 545 at 553.
2   [1990] 2 All ER 455 at 462.

Judgment debt not immediately payable

4.186 As has been noted, the court has the power to make a charging order in respect of a judgment debt which is not yet immediately payable.[1] However, the question remains how the court should exercise its discretion in such circumstances. In *Robinson v Bailey*[2] the court had to consider whether a charging order should be available to secure an order for specific performance whereby the judgment debtor was ordered to pay £50 a year quarterly to the judgment creditor. The judgment creditor sought to obtain a charging order over the judgment debtor's local loan stock which was valued at over £3,000.[3]

1   COA 1979, s 1(1) and see para 4.31.
2   [1942] Ch 268.

3 In *Robinson*, a pre-COA 1979 case, the court, somewhat reluctantly, assumed it had jurisdiction to make a charging order notwithstanding that the judgment debt is not yet immediately payable on the basis of earlier case law. That the court now has such jurisdiction is clear from the wording of COA 1979, s 1(1).

4.187 Simonds J held that the court's jurisdiction must be exercised 'only with the greatest care' where a charging order is intended to secure future payments and the court must be guarded in exercising it.[1] On the facts in *Robinson*, Simonds J refused to grant the charging order, stating:

> 'I cannot conceive that it would be proper for the court, by reason of an apprehended future failure of the defendant to satisfy the terms of the judgment, to lock up so disproportionate an amount of his property to satisfy so small a debt.'

In his view, a charging order should not be used as a 'lever' to force a judgment debtor to comply with a future (and in that case contingent) obligation.

1 Simonds J also appears to have been influenced by the fact that the future payments were conditional on the continued life of the judgment creditor.

4.188 However, the fact that the value of the judgment debtor's asset is disproportionately greater than the amount of the judgment debt will not of itself be a bar to a charging order if, in all the circumstances of the case, the judge considers it is proper to make the order. In *Archer v Williams*[1] a 'penniless' defendant was ordered to pay £2,500 damages. A charging order was granted over a defendant's home in respect of that judgment debt, and although the value of the defendant's home is not revealed in the judgment, it is likely to have been considerably in excess of £2,500. Mr Justice Jackson expressly acknowledged the relative modesty of the sum of damages compared to the defendant's equity in her home, when making the charging order:

> 'It seems to me that, considering all the circumstances of the case, and considering the relatively modest sum involved in comparison with the equity in the defendant's house, the proper order is for this court to make a charging order against the defendant's house in the sum of £2,500. I make such an order, because I consider that that is the only proper exercise of this court's discretion. I do so without any enthusiasm in view of the defendant's circumstances.'

1 [2003] EWHC 1670.

Judgment debt payable by instalments

4.189 As has been noted, the High Court has the power to make a charging order in respect of a judgment debt which is payable by instalments.[1] Whether the court will exercise its discretion to do so will depend on the circumstances of the case. In *Mercantile Credit Co Ltd v Huxtable*[2] the Court of Appeal held that a court cannot be faulted for exercising its discretion in favour of not making a charging order against a debtor's property where it is clear that he properly complied with the terms of an order for the payment of a judgment debt by instalments.[3] The White Book[4] refers to *Mercantile Credit* and states:

'The fact, however, that a debtor is up to date in complying with an order by instalments is likely to be a relevant factor in the exercise of the court's discretion to make or refuse a charging order. (*Mercantile Credit Co Ltd v Ellis*).'[5]

1   COA 1979, s 1(1). See para 4.30.
2   (1987) Times, 1 April.
3   Obiter, the court held that although it had not been necessary to decide the point in that case, it would have found that there was no jurisdiction to make a charging order as long as the instalments were being regularly paid by the judgment debtor. However, it should be noted that *Mercantile Credit* concerned a decision of the county court, to which County Courts Act 1984, s 86 would apply.
4   Civil Procedure 2004, vol 1, para 73.4.4.
5   This note was approved by the Court of Appeal in *Ropaigealach v Allied Irish Bank plc* [2001] EWCA Civ 1790, which referred to the notes to RSC Ord 50 at 50.1.20, which were in the same terms.

4.190   The position may be different where the instalment order is made after the interim charging order has been obtained. In *Ropaigealach v Allied Irish Bank plc*[1] the judgment creditor obtained a charging order nisi which was made absolute three months later. However, in the meantime an order for payment of the judgment debt by instalments had been made. The judgment debtor appealed against the charging order absolute on the grounds that, in light of the instalment order, the effect of County Courts Act 1984, s 86(1) was that the court had no jurisdiction to make the order. The County Courts Act 1984, s 86(1) provides:

'Where the court has made an order for payment of any sum of money by instalments, execution on the order shall not be issued until after default in payment of some instalment according to the order.'

1   [2001] EWCA Civ 1790.

4.191   The Court of Appeal dismissed the judgment debtor's appeal. Hale LJ held:

'I therefore conclude, as a matter of statutory construction, that there is jurisdiction to make a charging order absolute if a charging order nisi has been obtained before the instalment order was made. It is also tolerably clear that there is nothing wrong, in principle, with a charging order and an instalment order coexisting.'

4.192   While the court should take into account what has happened since the interim charging order was made in deciding whether to make the final charging order, this would include both the fact that the instalment order had been made and that the fact that the judgment creditor had submitted that it would not seek to enforce the sale of the property while the instalments were being met. The court noted that an instalment order provides for the method of payment by a judgment debtor, whereas a charging order gives security for the eventual payment of that debt. Accordingly, there were many circumstances in which it would be entirely sensible and satisfactory from both parties' points of view for an instalment order and a charging order to co-exist, particularly where, as in the circumstances of *Ropaigealach*, under the terms of the instalment order the debt will not be payable for many years (if at all), so that there is all the more reason to secure its eventual payment via a charging order.

4.193   While it is therefore open to the judgment debtor at the hearing for further consideration of the application (or subsequently) to seek to persuade the court not to make (or to discharge) a final charging order on the basis that he will pay off the judgment debt by instalments, the dicta in *Ropaigealach* suggest that such arrangements should not preclude a charging order being made. A judgment creditor faced with such a proposal who nonetheless wishes to obtain the security of a charging order could provide an undertaking to the court not to enforce the security through applying for an order of sale while the judgment instalments are being met.[1]

1   This could be made a condition of the order: see COA 1979, s 3(1).

Final charging order

4.194   Form N87 contains the standard form final charging order. The order will state that the interim charging order shall continue (subject to any modifications made by the final charging order, which will be stated) and that the judgment debtor's interest in the asset described in the order stands charged with a payment of the sum now owing under the judgment debt, together with any interests and the costs of the application. The order also provides that those costs are to be added to the judgment debt.

4.195   CPR 73.8(3) provides that if the court makes a final charging order which charges securities (other than securities held in court), the order will include a stop notice unless the court otherwise orders. Form N87 contains the appropriate wording.

Effective date of the final charging order

4.196   If the court proceeds to make a final charging order, that order operates from the date the interim charging order was made. In *Haly v Barry*[1] a judgment creditor had obtained a charging order nisi upon shares belonging to the judgment debtor. However, before he had obtained the charging order absolute, a decree was made for the administration of the judgment debtor's estate. The plaintiff in the administration suit sought an injunction to prevent the judgment creditor taking further steps in the execution which was refused. One of the grounds on which the plaintiff appealed to the Court of Appeal was that the judgment debtor's property was not charged until the charging order absolute had been made.

1   (1867-68) LR 3 Ch App 452.

4.197   The Court of Appeal dismissed the appeal on a number of grounds (some of which are no longer good law[1]) but in particular rejected the plaintiff's argument that a charging order should be considered as two orders such that the charging order nisi 'goes for nothing' unless it is followed by the charging order absolute. Page Wood, LJ held:[2]

'It is obvious that throughout these sections one order only is spoken of, which is at first to be an order nisi, and is afterwards to be made absolute.'

And later continued:[3]

'The statute directs the Judge to make an order nisi. If sufficient cause is shewn against it, it falls, but if not, it remains in force, and in the meantime it is operative, taking the fund out of the control of the debtor, and the only question remaining is, whether any sufficient cause can be shewn against making it absolute.'

1   See further para 4.264.
2   (1867-68) LR 3 Ch App 452 at 456.
3   (1867-68) LR 3 Ch App 452 at 457.

4.198   While *Haly* concerned the provisions of the Common Law Procedure Act 1852 (the statutory regime then governing charging orders), the modern day provisions of COA 1979 similarly refer to the court making 'an' order.[1]

1   See COA 1979, s 1(1).

4.199   *Haly* was followed in *Brereton and Wife v Edwards*[1] but was heavily criticised in subsequent cases[2] in relation to its conclusions concerning the interaction between charging orders and the insolvency regime. However, *Haly* remains good law in so far as it lays down the principle that when a final charging order is made it is to be treated as an order which has been effective since the date of the interim charging order.[3]

1   (1888) LR 21 QBD 226.
2   See the Court of Appeal's decision in *Burston Finance Ltd (in liquidation) v Godfrey* [1976] 1 WLR 719, which was itself disapproved by the House of Lords in *Roberts Petroleum Ltd v Bernard Kenny Ltd (in liquidation)* [1983] 2 AC 192, but not on this point.
3   See the Court of Appeal's comments in *Ropaigealach v Allied Irish Bank plc* [2002] 03 EG 130, at para 11: 'A charging order absolute takes effect from the date of the charging order nisi: see *Haly v Barry* (1868) LR 3 Ch App 452, which is still good law on this point.'

Costs

4.200   CPR 45.6 provides that the fixed costs recoverable against the judgment debtor on the making of a final charging order under CPR 73.8.2(a) are £110 plus any reasonable disbursements in respect of search fees and the fee for registration of the order. These costs are also secured under the charging order.[1]

1   See para 4.29.

4.201   Where judgment debtor (or some other person) objects to the final charging order being made, the judgment creditor may have incurred further costs in relation to the issues between the parties (for example, as a consequence of having to prepare and file written evidence disputing the judgment debtor's case or in connection with the trial of an issue). In such circumstances the successful judgment creditor should seek an order at the hearing in relation to the recovery of those additional costs, which are outside the fixed costs regime.[1]

1   The general rule is that the court should make a summary assessment of the costs at the conclusion of a hearing lasting not more than one day unless there is good reason not to. Each party who intends to claim costs should prepare a written statement of costs which should follow as closely as possible Form N260. The statement must be signed by the party or his legal representative and must be filed at court with copies served on any party from whom recovery of costs is sought. Filing and service must be done as soon as possible and in any event at least 24 hours before the date fixed for the hearing. See further Pt 44.

Discharge or variation of the charging order

4.202   COA 1979, s 3(5)[1] provides:.

'The court by which a charging order was made may at any time, on the application of the debtor or of any person interested in any property to which the order relates, make an order discharging or varying the charging order.'[2]

[1]   Equivalent provisions exist in relation to charging orders made under the Council Tax (Administration and Enforcement) Regulations 1992, SI 1992/613, whereby a local authority may apply to the county court for a charging order over a dwelling in respect of which council tax arrears are outstanding in excess of £1,000.

[2]   Council Tax (Administration and Enforcement) Regulations 1992, reg 51(4) make equivalent provision in relation to charging orders made under those regulations.

4.203   The use of the word 'may' in COA 1979, s 3(5) clearly shows that the court has a discretion to discharge or vary a charging order.

Who can apply?

4.204   A person interested in the property to which the charging order relates will obviously include the judgment debtor, but will also include the judgment debtor's spouse, even where it is the husband's beneficial interest in the matrimonial home that has been charged and the charging order does not encroach upon the wife's beneficial interest.[1] A trustee in bankruptcy or liquidator would similarly appear to fall within the category of interested persons within COA 1979, s 3(5).[2]

[1]   *Harman v Glencross* [1986] 1 All ER 545.

[2]   However, note the comments of Williamson H, QC in *Banque Nationale de Paris plc v Montmand Ltd* (1999) Times, 7 September. See also the commentary on *Jelle* in para 4.205.

Subsequent insolvency of the judgment debtor

4.205   In *Jelle Zwemstra Ltd v Walton and Stuart*,[1] the court considered how the discretion to discharge a charging order should be exercised upon a judgment debtor's subsequent bankruptcy. In that case, a charging order absolute had been obtained against a judgment debtor's only asset, his home. Approximately ten months later the judgment debtor was declared bankrupt and his trustee in bankruptcy discovered that the judgment debtor had a large number of other creditors whose debts had accrued before the charging order had been made absolute but who were not apparent when the charging order was made. The trustee in bankruptcy applied to discharge the charging order on the grounds that it unfairly prejudiced the other creditors as it effectively took up all of the judgment debtor's recoverable assets.

[1]   [1997] CLY 3002.

4.206   The court held that it would not exercise its direction to discharge the charging order. The court accepted that it had the power to do so, noting that although IA 1986, s 346 allowed a judgment creditor to retain the benefit of a completed execution that was obtained prior to a bankruptcy, the court nevertheless has a discretion to discharge or vary a charging order at any time pursuant to COA, s 3(5). The court noted that there was no direct authority on how that discretion should be exercised,[1] and said that while regard must be had to the interests of all creditors, the grounds for setting aside a valid charging order absolute must be more compelling than those for setting aside a charging order nisi. An order discharging or varying a charging order should not be made unless the injustice caused to the other creditors in not discharging or varying the charging order substantially outweighed the injustice that would be caused to the judgment creditor if the charging order were set aside.

[1]   While observing that *Roberts v Kenny* provided guidance on how the discretion should be exercised
      when insolvency intervenes between the interim charging order and final charging order.

4.207   In the circumstances of *Jelle*, the court found that the charging order should not be set aside. In reaching this conclusion, the court considered the following factors to be relevant: the judgment creditor had pursued its debts through the courts while the other creditors had not done so; the charging order had been made nearly a year before the judgment debtor became bankrupt; and there was no evidence that the judgment creditor was trying to 'steal a march' on other creditors.

Procedure

4.208   CPR 73.9 sets out the procedure for making an application to set aside or discharge a charging order. The application should be made in accordance with Pt 23.

4.209   The application must be made to the court that made the charging order.[1] The court may direct that any interested person be joined as a party to such an application or that the application be served on any such person.[2]

[1]   CPR 73.9(1).
[2]   CPR 73.9(2).

4.210   Any order discharging or varying a charging order must be served on all persons on whom the charging order was required to be served.[1]

[1]   CPR 73.9(3).

4.211   Where a charging order has been protected by an entry registered under LCA 1972 or LRA 2002, an order discharging the charging order may direct that the entry be cancelled.[1] The party who applied for the discharge would be well advised to include such provision in the draft order.

[1]   COA 1979, s 3(6).

Appeal

4.212   As many of the cases cited in this chapter illustrate, a judgment debtor may also seek to appeal the making of a charging order. However, a higher court will be reluctant to interfere with the exercise of a lower court's discretion and the final order will not be set aside unless wrong in principle.[1]

[1]   *Wicks v Shanks* (1893) 67 LT 109. In *Harman v Glencross*, the Court of Appeal decided not
      to interfere with the lower court's exercise of its discretion even though Fox LJ (with whom
      Mustill LJ concurred) stated that he would have exercised it differently.

ORDER FOR SALE

4.213   Once the judgment creditor has obtained the charging order he will have security for the payment of his debt. However, this will not of itself result in the judgment creditor receiving funds in settlement of the judgment debt. Where the judgment creditor is not prepared to wait for the judgment debtor to sell the property, he will need to take further steps to enforce the charge and satisfy the judgment debt. Separate proceedings must be issued under CPR Pt 8 in order to do this.

Jurisdiction to make an order for sale

4.214   Where the judgment debtor is the sole owner of the charged property, the court's jurisdiction to grant an order for sale falls within the inherent equitable jurisdiction of the court by virtue of the fact the charging order takes effect as an equitable charge.[1] Where the judgment debtor co-owns the property with another person, the judgment creditor must make an application for an order for sale under TLATA 1996, s 14.[2] This provides:

'(1) Any person who is a trustee of land or has an interest in a property subject to a trust of land may make an application to the court for an order under this section.
(2) On an application for an order under this section the court may make any such order (a) relating to the exercise by the trustees of any of their functions (including an order relieving them of any obligation to obtain the consent of, or to consult, any person in connection with the exercise of any of their functions), or (b) declaring the nature or extent of a person's interest in property subject to the trust, as the court thinks fit.'

---

[1]   COA 1979, s 3(4) and *Tennant v Trenchard* (1868-9) LR 4 Ch App 537.
[2]   TLATA 1996, s 14 is not relevant where the property is solely owned by the judgment debtor: *Pickering v Wells* [2002] 2 FLR 798.

A further discretion

4.215   A judgment creditor with the benefit of a charging order is a person 'with an interest in a property subject to a trust of land' for the purposes of TLATA 1996, s 14 and therefore has standing to apply for an order for sale. This was decided by the case of *Midland Bank plc v Pike*,[1] where the court held that a judgment creditor with a charging order on the share of a co-owner in the proceeds of sale of land is a 'person interested' under LPA 1925, s 30.[2] LPA 1925, s 30 has now been replaced by TLATA 1996, s 14 but the position remains unaltered.[3]

---

[1]   [1988] 2 All ER 434.
[2]   LPA 1925, s 30 provided '(i) If the trustees for sale refuse to sell or to exercise any of the powers conferred by either of the last two sections, or any requisite consent cannot be obtained, any person interested may apply to the court for a vesting or other order for giving effect to the proposed transaction or for an order directing the trustees for sale to give effect thereto, and the court may make such order as it thinks fit.'
[3]   Since the statutes refer to '*any person interested*' and '*any person ... who has an interest*' respectively.

4.216 CPR 73.10(1) provides:

'Subject to the provisions of any enactment, the court may, upon a claim by a person who has obtained a charging order over an interest in property, order the sale of the property to enforce the charging order.'

The use of the word 'may' in the procedural rules, like the equitable jurisdiction and statutory provision founding the court's jurisdiction to make an order for sale, indicates that the court has a further and separate discretion as to whether or not to grant the order for sale.

4.217 An order for sale can be a draconian step in the case of land, particularly where the property in question is the judgment debtor's home. As will be seen from the discussion of the case law which follows, the court will consider all the circumstances of the case in deciding whether to exercise this discretion. Relevant factors are likely to be the judgment debtor's conduct, the prospects of the debt being paid without the sale, the size of the judgment debt, the value of the property, and, in the case of land, whether the property is the judgment debtor's home and whether there are any co-owners of the property.

Orders for sale under LPA 1925, s 30

4.218 While the principles governing the court's discretion to make an order for sale under LPA 1925, s 30 have now been supersedcd by TLATA 1994, s 14 regime, it is worth reviewing the case law relating to the former statutory provision to gain an understanding of the history and development of the court's jurisprudence in this area.

4.219 As has been noted, in *Harman v Glencross* the Court of Appeal held that a spouse's right of occupation should be adequately protected by LPA 1925, s 30. Under the old LPA 1925, s 30 regime, the general principle was that the judgment creditor's interests should prevail except where there were 'exceptional circumstances'. In *Re Citro (Domenico) (a bankrupt)*[1] the court had to consider the position between the interests of a trustee in bankruptcy and an innocent spouse. Nourse LJ held as follows:

'Where a spouse who has a beneficial interest in the matrimonial home has become bankrupt under debts which cannot be paid without the realisation of that interest, the voice of the creditors will usually prevail over the voice of the other spouse and a sale of the property ordered within a short period. The voice of the other spouse will only prevail in exceptional circumstances. No distinction is to be made between a case where the property is still being enjoyed as the matrimonial home and one where it is not. What then are exceptional circumstances? As the cases show, it is not uncommon for a wife with young children to be faced with eviction in circumstances where the realisation of her beneficial interest will produce enough to buy a comparable home in the same neighbourhood, or indeed elsewhere. And, if she has to move elsewhere, there may be problems over schooling and so forth. Such circumstances, while engendering a natural sympathy in all who hear of them, cannot be described as exceptional. They are the melancholy consequences of debt and improvidence with which every civilised society has been familiar.'

1   [1991] Ch 142 at 157.

4.220 A trustee in bankruptcy is, however, under a statutory duty to realise the assets of the bankrupt. There is no such duty upon a chargee under a charging order. However, in *Lloyds Bank plc v Byrne & Byrne,*[1] the court found that the same considerations as in *Re Citro* apply to the respective interests of chargees and innocent spouses. Parker LJ held:

'... I accept that the statutory duty of the trustee is a powerful factor to be borne in mind when considering the exercise of discretion, but I cannot accept that it justifies any change in approach. Moreover, the position of a chargee may well be more powerful. If the sale is postponed the chargee creditor will suffer a postponement of the full amount of what may be a very large and increasing debt, whereas on a bankruptcy each individual creditor may suffer very little... In my judgment, this is wholly a matter of discretion and there is no difference in principle between the case of a trustee in bankruptcy and that of a chargee.'

1   [1993] 1 FLR 369.

4.221 In *Barclays Bank plc v Hendricks*[1] the judgment debtor had separated from his wife and left the matrimonial home of which the wife was co-owner to move into another house owned by the wife alone. The judgment debtor owed various sums of money to the bank who obtained a charging order absolute against the husband's interest in the first house and sought an order pursuant to LPA 1925, s 30 for the sale of the house. An order was made for the property to be sold at a price not less than £200,000. The wife appealed from the order and asked the court to exercise its discretion to defer sale of the house until her children, who were then 10 and 13, had reached the age of 18 or finished full-time education. She contended that if she were forced to vacate her present home she would have to compel her husband to leave the second house to make way for her and that might bring their present amicable arrangements to an end so that he would cease to make the mortgage repayments on the first house. Moreover, the children did not wish to leave their current home which was nearer to their school and friends.

1   [1996] 1 FLR 258.

4.222 Laddie J reviewed the decisions in *Re Citro* and *Lloyds Bank v Byrne*. He first observed that since the judgment debtor husband had now left the matrimonial home, the only collateral purpose under the trust for sale arising under LPA 1925 on which the wife could rely no longer existed.[1] Accordingly, the wife had to be able to show exceptional circumstances if her wish to remain in the first house were to prevail over the interests of the judgment creditor. Laddie J concluded there were no such circumstances. The fact that the wife owned another house and moving her children there would not even involve them changing schools meant that she was in a comparatively favourable position. Further, the fact that the order for sale would only result in the judgment creditor recovering some 20% of its judgment debt did not mean the order for sale should not be granted.

¹ The court contrasted the position in *Abbey National v Moss* [1994] 1 FLR 307, where the collateral purpose under the LPA 1925 trust for sale was that one co-owner could remain in occupation until she died, such that no order for sale was granted on application by a judgment creditor of the other co-owner, who had obtained a charging order.

Moratorium before possession

4.223 Laddie J went on to observe that when a court makes an order for the sale of a property in such circumstances, it still has to decide precisely when the innocent spouse must leave the home, and that no guidance had been given in the High Court or the Court of Appeal as to the factors which should be taken into consideration in determining the length of the moratorium period. In his view:

'It seems to me that the period before the innocent spouse has to give up possession should be such as to allow sufficient time to facilitate the departure from the property without adding unnecessarily to the distress and dislocation which will, in any event, be suffered by the innocent spouse and the children. However, any such period should be as short as possible in the circumstances and any period more than a few weeks should be avoided if it is likely to cause significant hardship to the chargee.'

4.224 In this case, the date by which the wife was ordered to vacate the house was postponed in order to avoid the move taking place in the middle of the children's school terms. Similarly, in *Pickering v Wells*¹ the court ordered that an order for sale should be postponed for a period of three months to allow the judgment debtor sufficient time to carry out negotiations to obtain a mortgage to pay off the judgment debt. There is no reason why such a moratorium should not be equally applicable under TLATA 1996, s 14 regime.

¹ [2002] 2 FLR 798.

Orders for sale under TLATA 1996, s 14

4.225 As has been noted, trusts for sale and LPA 1925, s 30 have now been replaced by TLATA 1996. The relevant provisions of TLATA 1996, s 14 are set out at para 4.214. TLATA 1996, s 15 provides:

'15 Matters relevant in determining applications
(1) The matters to which the court is to have regard in determining an application for an order under section 14 include—
(a) the intentions of the person or persons (if any) who created the trust,
(b) the purposes for which the property subject to the trust is held,
(c) the welfare of any minor who occupies or might reasonably be expected to occupy any land subject to the trust as his home, and
(d) the interests of any secured creditor of any beneficiary.
...
(3) In the case of any other application, other than one relating to the exercise of the power mentioned in section 6(2), the matters to which the court is to have regard also include the circumstances and wishes of any beneficiaries of full

age and entitled to an interest in possession in property subject to the trust or (in case of dispute) of the majority (according to the value of their combined interests).'

4.226   TLATA 1996, s 15 has therefore introduced a change in the law in relation to the way in which the court will exercise its power to order a sale at the suit of a chargee of the interest of one of the beneficial owners of the property. It prescribes the matters which the court must take into account on an application for such an order for sale and states that the interests of a secured creditor (which includes a judgment creditor with a charging order over one co-owner's beneficial interest) are only one of the matters the court should consider in determining whether to make an order for sale. While even under LPA 1925, s 30 regime the court would consider the purpose for which the property subject to the trust was held in determining whether an order for sale should be made,[1] the court must also now take into account the welfare of minors in occupation of the land as their home as well as the intentions of those who created the trust.

[1]   See eg the judgment of Evans-Lombe J quoted in *Bankers Trust Co v Namdar* (unreported) 18 July 1995 and the judgment of Laddie J in *Barclays Bank plc v Hendricks* [1996] 1 FLR 258 at 263.

4.227   This change of position in the law was expressly acknowledged by Neuberger J in *Mortgage Corporation v Shaire*.[1] In that case a chargee of a husband's beneficial interest in the matrimonial home applied for an order for sale under TLATA 1996, s 14. The husband had since died and his wife, the co-owner, opposed the application on the grounds that since TLATA 1996, s 15 required the court to take into account factors other than just the interests of the chargee when making an order for sale, the chargee's desire for such an order should not necessarily prevail over her desire to remain in the home.

[1]   [2001] Ch 743.

4.228   Neuberger J enumerated no less than eight reasons why TLATA 1996 had introduced a change in the law. In summary, these were as follows:

(a)   Had there been no intention to change the law, it is hard to see why Parliament had set out in TLATA 1996, s 15(2), (3) the factors which have to be taken into account specifically, albeit not exclusively, when the court is asked to exercise its jurisdiction to order a sale.

(b)   Parliament could not have intended to confirm the law as laid down in *Lloyds Bank v Byrne* while specifying that the interest of a chargee is only one of four specified factors to be taken into account in TLATA 1996, s 15, not least since there is no suggestion that the interest of a chargee is to be given any more importance than the interests of the children residing in the house.[1]

(c)   There is nothing in the language of TLATA 1996 to suggest that in the absence of a strong reason to the contrary, the court should order sale in the case of a trust of land (in contrast to the name 'trust for sale' and the law as it developed under the LPA 1925 regime).

(d)   Parliament clearly considered that a different approach is appropriate in a case where one of the co-owners was bankrupt and a case where one of the co-owners had charged his interest,[2] in contrast to the former regime where the court found that it should adopt precisely the same approach in both cases (*Citro* and *Byrne*).

(e) The Court of Appeal had indicated that TLATA 1996 was intended to change the law.[3]

(f) There is support for this view in the leading textbooks.[4]

(g) The views expressed in the Law Commission report which gave rise to TLATA 1996 support this view.[5]

(h) Indications of judicial dissatisfaction with the state of the former law and suggestions that the balance should be tipped somewhat more in favour of families and against banks and other chargees.[6]

---

[1] See also the observations of Mr D Oliver QC (sitting as a judge in the High Court) in *Pickering v Wells* [2002] 2 FLR 798 regarding TLATA 1996, ss 14 and 15: 'Those statutory provisions were introduced in order to mitigate the perceived harshness of the common law rule that the interests of those who are entitled to seek an order for sale are prima facie paramount.'

[2] By comparison of TLATA 1996, s 15(2) and (3) with the Insolvency Act 1986, s 15(4) and the new s 335A.

[3] From the obiter sentence in the judgment of Peter Gibson LJ in *Banker's Trust Co v Namdar* [1997] CA Transcript No 349, whereby the judge concluded that the wife's appeal against an order for sale had to be refused in light of the reasoning in *Citro and Byrne*, but observed: 'It is unfortunate for Mrs Namdar, that the very recent Trusts of Land and Appointment of Trustees Act 1996 was not in force at the relevant time [ie at the time of the hearing at first instance]'. Neuberger J noted that this observation should be treated with caution.

[4] *Megarry and Wade* at para 9-064 and *Emmet on Title* (19th edn, January 1999 release) at para 22-035.

[5] Transfer of Land, Trusts of Land (Law Com No 181), 8 June 1989, in particular at paras 12.9 and 13.6 of the report and at note 143.

[6] Neuberger J observed that while Bingham LJ agreed with Nourse LJ in *Citro*, he expressed unhappiness with the result ([1991] Ch 142 at 161), and that Sir George Waller's dissatisfaction went so far as led him to dissent ([1991] Ch 142 at 161–163). The Court of Appeal in decision in *Abbey National plc v Moss* [1994] 2 FCR 587 also suggested a desire for a new approach.

4.229 Neuberger J concluded as follows:

'All these factors, to my mind, when taken together point very strongly to the conclusion that section 15 has changed the law. As a result of section 15, the court has greater flexibility than heretofore, as to how it exercises its jurisdiction on an application for an order for sale on facts such as those in *Re Citro* and *Lloyds Bank plc v Byrne & Byrne*. There are certain factors which must be taken into account (see s 15(1) and, subject to the next point, s 15(3)). There may be other factors in a particular case which the court can, indeed should, take into account. Once the relevant factors to be taken into account have been identified, it is a matter for the court as to what weight to give to each factor in a particular case.'

4.230 Having arrived at this conclusion, Neuberger J considered the question of the extent to which the old authorities remained good law in relation to how the court should exercise its discretion to make an order for sale. He observed:

'On the one hand, to throw over all the wealth of learning and thought given by so many eminent judges to the problem which is raised on an application for sale of a house where competing interests exist seems somewhat arrogant and possibly rash. On the other hand, where one has concluded that the law has changed in a significant respect so that the court's discretion is significantly less fettered than it was, there are obvious dangers in relying on authorities which proceeded on the basis that the court's discretion was more fettered than it now is. I think it would be wrong to throw over all the earlier cases without paying them any regard. However, they have to be treated with caution, in light of the change in the law, and in many cases they are unlikely to be of great, let alone decisive, assistance.'

After observing that the weight to be given to each of the factors the court had to take into account pursuant to TLATA 1996, s 15 was a matter for the court in each particular case, on the facts of *Mortgage Corporation*, Neuberger J declined to make an order until the parties had had an opportunity to consider the consequences of his conclusions on the law.

4.231 Each case will therefore be decided on its own particular facts and in appropriate circumstances banks or creditors will be able to obtain orders for sale over co-owned homes, particularly where there is evidence that the chargee is not being given proper recompense for being kept out of his money. In *Bank of Ireland Home Mortgages Ltd v Bell,*[1] a Court of Appeal case decided after *Mortgage Corporation*, the husband had left the property and the wife opposed the order for sale. At first instance the judge had refused an application for an order for sale made by a bank with the benefit of a mortgage over co-owned property. The bank appealed.

[1]   [2001] 2 FLR 809.

4.232 The Court of Appeal found that the judge at first instance had erred in the exercise of his discretion as to whether or not to make an order for sale and had both taken into account irrelevant considerations and not taken into account relevant considerations. In considering whether to make an order for sale of the property, the court first observed that the judge should consider the matters set out in TLATA 1996, s 15, which included the interests of a secured creditor, and the mortgagee bank was clearly entitled to protection in respect of its advances. The judge should also have given consideration to the fact that the debt was increasing daily, and that, as the wife's 10% beneficial interest in the property would be swallowed up on a sale, the bank would be entitled to all the proceeds of the sale. The judge had also erred in giving weight to irrelevant considerations, such as the intention that the property should be held on trust as a matrimonial home (since this intention had evaporated with the departure of the husband by the time that the bank had brought the possession proceedings) and the fact that there was a second chargee of the property. The fact that the couple's son resided in the property should only have been a very slight consideration given that he was almost 18 at the time of the trial. Whilst the wife's health was a relevant consideration, proper regard should have been given to a postponement of the sale of the property, rather than refusing to order the sale.

4.233 Peter Gibson LJ concluded:

'Prior to [TLATA 1996] the courts under s 30 of the Law of Property Act 1925 would order the sale of a matrimonial home at the request of the trustee in bankruptcy of a spouse or at the request of the creditor chargee of a spouse, considering that the creditors' interest should prevail over that of the other spouse and the spouse's family save in exceptional circumstances. The 1996 Act, by requiring the court to have regard to the particular matters specified in s 15, appears to me to have given scope for some change in the court's practice. Nevertheless, a powerful consideration is and ought to be whether the creditor is receiving proper recompense for being kept out of his money, repayment of which is overdue (see *The Mortgage Corp v Silkin and anor*; *The Mortgage Corp v Shaire and ors* [2000] 2 FCR 222, 80 P & CR 280). In the present case it is plain that by refusing sale the judge has condemned the bank to go on waiting for its money with no prospect of recovery from Mr and Mrs Bell and with the debt increasing all the time, that debt already exceeding what could be realised on a sale. That seems to me to be very unfair to the bank.'

4.234 Sir Christopher Staughton agreed with Peter Gibson LJ on this point. He said:

'Unless there is a sale in the foreseeable future, the bank will get no return for its money, and no repayment of principal, until such time as Mrs Bell wishes to leave the house or is compelled to do so. That would not be justice in this case. The bank is a beneficiary of the trust referred to in s 15 as much as Mrs Bell.'

4.235 TLATA 1996, ss 14 and 15 only apply where the property is co-owned. This protection will therefore be of no assistance to a judgment debtor who is the sole owner of the property. What protection is then open to a sole owner of property with children? Can he resist an application to enforce a charging order by arguing that his eviction and the eviction of his children from the family home would be a breach of their human rights?

Human rights issues

4.236 As has been noted in Chapter 1, the Human Rights Act 1998 (HRA 1998) incorporates into UK law the European Convention for the Protection of Human Rights and Fundamental Freedoms (ECHR). Under HRA 1998, s 6 it is unlawful for a court, as a public body, to act in a way that is incompatible with the ECHR rights and freedoms. The question therefore arises as to whether a judgment debtor can invoke human rights arguments to resist the enforcement of a charging order against his property.

4.237 It is important to recognise from the outset that powerful human rights arguments also operate in favour of the judgment creditor. Strasbourg jurisprudence has recognised the right of judgment creditors under the ECHR to have their judgment enforced as ancillary to the right to a fair trial that is guaranteed by ECHR, art 6.[1]

[1]   *Hornsby v Greece* (1997) 24 EHRR 250 (paras 40–41). See further Chapter 1.

4.238 Further, both of the rights that judgment debtors may seek to rely upon to resist enforcement being implemented over their property are qualified rights. Both art 8 (the right to respect for private and family life) and art 1 of Protocol 1 (the protection of property) are qualified in favour of the rights of others. Article 8(2) provides:

'There shall be no interference by a public authority with the exercise of this right except such as is in accordance with the law and is necessary in a democratic society in the interests of national security, public safety or the economic well-being of the country, for the prevention of disorder or crime, for the protection of health or morals, or for the protection of the rights and freedoms of others.'

4.239   Similarly, art 1 of Protocol 1 provides:

'Every natural or legal person is entitled to the peaceful enjoyment of his possessions. No one shall be deprived of his possessions except in the public interest and subject to the conditions provided for by law and by the general principles of international law.

The preceding provisions shall not, however, in any way impair the right of a State to enforce such laws as it deems necessary to control the use of property in accordance with the general interest or to secure the payment of taxes or other contributions or penalties.'

4.240   Clearly, the rights of judgment creditors to have their judgments enforced and the public interest in ensuring judgment creditors have this right fall within these qualifications.[1]

1   See also the European Commission decision in *K v Sweden* (Application No 13800/88).

4.241   As an initial point, it is worth considering at which stage in proceedings related to charging orders that a judgment debtor would be best advised to raise human rights arguments. Potentially, such arguments could be raised both at the hearing to decide whether to make a final charging order, or at the hearing for an order for sale.

4.242   In light of the European Court's decision *X v France*,[1] the better view is that such arguments should only be raised at the hearing for an order for sale, since it is only at that stage that there is a tangible interference with property. *X v France* concerned a complaint by an individual that the registration of a mortgage against him by tax authorities constituted a breach of art 1 of Protocol 1. The mortgage had been obtained to secure the payment of evaded taxes and fines that the individual might eventually be ordered to pay. The commission held that the mortgage was not a 'deprivation of his possessions' within the terms of art 1 of Protocol 1.[2] Since charging orders take effect as an equitable charge against the judgment debtor's beneficial interest,[3] the imposition of a charging order should not amount to a 'deprivation' of possessions under art 1 of Protocol 1.

1   (1982) 5 EHRR 298.
2   In addition, on the point of whether the mortgage constituted an interference with the individual's right to peaceful enjoyment of his possessions, the Commission held that given the purpose behind the mortgage, it was a measure authorised by the second paragraph of art 1 of Protocol 1. Since it was designed: 'to secure the payment of taxes or other contributions or penalties', such considerations would not apply in the case of a charging order obtained by a commercial judgment creditor.
3   COA 1979, s 3(4).

4.243   In any event, the court still has to consider the qualifications to both art 1 of Protocol 1 and art 8 in deciding whether enforcement of a charging order amounts to a breach of a judgment debtor's human rights. There is little case law on this question and much will depend on the facts of the case. An order for sale of vacant commercial property belonging to a corporate judgment debtor clearly has very different human rights implications to an order for sale of a house that serves as the family home of an individual judgment debtor.

4.244 Such arguments were raised in *Pickering v Wells*,[1] where the court had to consider one of the procedural requirements that existed prior to the introduction of Pt 73[2] relating to witness statements or affidavits in support of a claim for an order of sale of land subject to a charging order. The rules required that the witness statement or affidavit had to set out details of all persons in possession of the property and had to state whether a class F land charge, notice/caution under the Matrimonial Homes Act 1967 or a notice under the Matrimonial Homes Act 1983 had been registered and whether notice of the proceedings had been served on those in possession or those whose interests had been so registered.[3] The judgment debtor contended that these procedural requirements meant that the court was obliged to consider the welfare of her three children who lived in the property with her.

[1]   [2002] 2 FLR 798.
[2]   RSC Ord 88, r 5A(f).
[3]   Similar procedural requirements are now incorporated into the Practice Direction to Pt 73.

4.245 The court first observed that since the judgment debtor was the sole owner of the charged property, it was not obliged to take into account the interests of her children under TLATA 1996, ss 14 and 15. The purpose of the procedural requirements was to enable the court to take into account all the competing proprietary interests in the property. This did not extend to the welfare or needs of those in occupation. As regards possible human rights objections, this policy was:

> '. . . entirely consistent with the policy of the law that a creditor is entitled to be paid and to be paid in due time, and I do not believe that the introduction of Art 8 of the European Convention for the Protection of Human Rights and Fundamental Freedoms 1950 into English law through the Human Rights Act 1998 affects that position.
>
> Article 8 provides, first, that everyone has the right to respect for his private and family life, his home and his correspondence, and, secondly, that there should be no interference by a public authority with the exercise of this right, except such as is in accordance with the law and is necessary in a democratic society in the interests of national security, public safety or the economic well-being of the country, for the prevention of disorder or crime, for the protection of health or morals, or for the protection of the rights and freedoms of others.
>
> In my judgment, the interpretation that I have placed on Ord 88, r 5A, results in the enforcement of the charging order being in accordance with the law, and indeed being in accordance with the law for the protection of the right of Miss Wells to be paid the sum due to her.'

4.246 However, the court clearly left open further consideration of this issue by observing that the point was of sufficient importance to merit consideration by the Court of Appeal, although under the rules permission to appeal could not be granted in this case.

4.247   The approach the courts have taken in cases where a bankrupt has sought to oppose an order for sale of his property on the grounds of human rights issues may also provide some indication of how the courts are likely to deal with these arguments in the context of charging orders. In *Re Karia*[1] the defendant submitted that an order for sale would seriously interfere with his private and family life and in particular with his relationship with his daughter since he would no longer be able to provide access for her to stay at the flat. He also claimed that if the flat was sold, he would be rendered destitute and would lose his present employment, all of which would have a serious effect on his daughter's mental health and on their continuing relationship.

[1]   Unreported (2001) WL 1560733.

4.248   Lightman J held the claims as to the consequences of the sale had been exaggerated and that:

'those disadvantages to [the defendant] and to his daughter as a consequence of the sale in no way interfere with his human rights to respect to his private and family life. The jurisprudence of the European Court of Human Rights makes absolutely plain that there has to be a balancing exercise when there is some interference with the right to private and family life, between the entitlement of the individual to that right, and the interests, rights and freedoms of others. For this purpose the interests of creditors on a bankruptcy are factors which have to be counter-balanced against the interference with the individual's rights. The balancing exercise is essentially a matter for national legislation. The national legislation in this country in the form of section 335A of the Insolvency Act 1986 affects the balancing exercise. Under the English Insolvency Act, as I read it, the fact that there are these consequences of bankruptcy and of a sale in the bankruptcy do not constitute exceptional circumstances. They are, as the Registrar held, the melancholy consequences of a matrimonial separation, matrimonial strife and a bankruptcy. One cannot but have great sympathy for Mr Karia in wishing to maintain the existing status quo, with the benefits that flow from it in terms of his relationship with his daughter. But it seems to me clear that I must have regard and give effect to the provisions of the Insolvency Act. Those provisions make plain that in this predicament the interests of the creditors must come first. Those interests, and the interests of Mrs Karia, make plain that there must be a sale. I am more than comforted in reaching that conclusion by the fact that I do think that Mr Karia over-exaggerates the adverse consequences for him of such an order for sale. In my view, this case does not come within a mile of any unjustifiable interference with any of his or his daughter's human rights under the Article to which I have referred.'

4.249   While this judgment may therefore shed some light on the court's approach to human rights arguments in the context of enforcement of a charging order, the difference in approach that the courts should take as between trustees in bankruptcy and chargees has already been noted (see para 4.228). Under IA 1986, s 335A(3) the interests of the bankrupt's creditors should outweigh all other considerations unless the circumstances of the case are exceptional. As has been noted, there is no such provision in COA or in Pt 73, and there is nothing in TLATA 1996, s 15 to suggest that the interests of a chargee should be given any more importance than the interests of the children residing in the house.

4.250 The Effective Enforcement White Paper recommended that the availability of orders for sale following the imposition of a charging order be retained. It states:[1]

'We have concluded, in the light of all the evidence available to us, that the court has adequate discretion to refuse orders for sale if they would be unduly oppressive to a vulnerable debtor, and that orders for sale should be retained as part of the civil enforcement system.'

[1] At para 390.

4.251 The protection of vulnerable judgment debtors was a key focus for the civil justice review and it is notable that the White Paper concluded that 'existing judicial discretion is a sufficient safeguard for vulnerable judgment debtors'.[1] The White Paper reviews a 'package of safeguards'[2] which inform the judicial discretion to make an order for sale. The existence of such safeguards, together with judicial recognition of the judgment creditor's right to enforcement, may mean that a judgment debtor who seeks to oppose an order for sale on human rights grounds may face severe difficulties.

[1] At para 391.
[2] Including: (a) COA 1979, ss 1(5) and 3(1); (b) TLATA 1996, s 15; (c) *Mesher* type orders; (d) the decision in *Royal Bank of Scotland v Etridge* (No 2) [2002] 2 AC 773 (where it was held that a lender will not be able to enforce a charge over property where the consequence of non-compliance with the loan in respect of which the security was given was not explained to both chargees); (d) the decision in *Bank of Ireland Home Mortgages v Bell* [2001] 2 FLR 809; and (e) the requirement upon judgment creditors to name all known creditors, existing charge holders and beneficiaries when applying for an order for sale.

Procedure relating to an order for sale

4.252 CPR 73.10 sets out the procedure for enforcement of a charging order by sale. The judgment creditor must issue fresh proceedings under the Pt 8 procedure and further reference should be made to that Part.[1]

[1] CPR 73.10(3).

Which court?

4.253 A claim for an order for sale should be made in the court that made the charging order unless that court lacks jurisdiction to make an order for sale.[1] The County Courts Act 1984, s 23 sets out the equitable jurisdiction of the county court. Section 23(c) provides that a county court shall have all the jurisdiction of the High Court to hear and determine proceedings for enforcing any charge provided the amount owing in respect of the charge does not exceed the county court limit, which is £30,000.[2] Where a claim for an order for sale to enforce a charging order is being brought in the High Court, the proceedings should be started in Chancery Chambers in the Royal Courts of Justice or a Chancery District Registry.[3]

1   CPR 73.10(2).
2   At present, no order has been made under the relevant provisions of the County Court Act
    1984 setting the county court limit for these purposes. However, under the Interpretation
    Act 1978, s 17(2)(b) the County Courts Jurisdiction Order 1981, SI 1981/1123 applies and
    sets a limit of £30,000 in respect of a county court's equity jurisdiction.
3   73 PD, para 4.2. The Practice Direction lists the location of the various Chancery district registries.

Evidence in support of the claim

4.254   A copy of the charging order must be filed with the claim form.[1] The following
information must also be contained in the written evidence filed in support of the
claim[2] and the claimant must take all reasonable steps to obtain this information
before issuing the claim:[3]

(a)   identify the charging order and the property sought to be sold;
(b)   state the amount in respect of which the charge was imposed and the amount due
      at the date of issue of the claim;
(c)   verify, so far as known, the debtor's title to the property charged;
(d)   state, so far as the claimant is able to identify –
      (i)   the names and addresses of any other creditors who have a prior charge or
            other security over the property; and
      (ii) the amount owed to each such creditor; and
(e)   give an estimate of the price which would be obtained on sale of the property.
(f)   if the claim relates to land, give details of every person who to the best of the
      claimant's knowledge is in possession of the property; and
(g)   if the claim relates to residential property –
      (i)   state whether –
            (A)   a land charge of Class F; or
            (B)   a notice under s 31(10) of the Family Law Act 1996, or under any provision
                  of an Act which preceded that section,[4]
            has been registered; and
      (ii) if so, state –
            (A)   on whose behalf the land charge or notice has been registered; and
            (B)   that the claimant will serve notice of the claim on that person.

It may therefore be necessary for the judgment creditor to undertake Part 71
proceedings (Orders to obtain information from a judgment debtor – see Chapter 2)
before making the application.

1   CPR 73.10(4).
2   CPR 73.10(5) and PD 73, para 4.
3   PD 73, para 4.4.
4   The Family Law Act 1996, s 31(10) provides for the registration of matrimonial home rights.

Form of the order for sale

4.255   Sample forms of orders for sale are set out in the Appendix to the Practice
Direction for Pt 73. The two sample forms are an order for sale following a charging
order where the property is solely owned by the judgment debtor, and an order for
sale following a charging order where the property is owned by the judgment debtor

and another person. However, the sample orders are for guidance only and are not prescribed forms of order - they may be adapted or varied by the court to meet the requirements of individual cases.[1]

[1]   PD 73, para 4.5.

4.256   The order for sale will allow the judgment debtor one last chance to pay the judgment debt since it will provide that the part of the order providing for the sale will not take effect if the judgment debtor pays the amount secured by the charge together with the costs of the application for the order for sale and interest by a specified date. Failing that, the property will be sold for a sum not less than that specified in the order. The order will also set out a date by which possession of the property must be delivered to the judgment creditor.

Mechanics of sale

4.257   The order should also set out the mechanics whereby the judgment creditor can carry out the sale and transfer the legal title to a third party purchaser. In the sample forms in Appendix A to the Practice Direction to Pt 73, this is done by:

(a)   in the case of an order for sale following a charging order where the property is solely owned by the judgment debtor, creating and vesting in the judgment creditor a legal term in the property pursuant to LPA 1925, s 90;[1] and

(b)   in the case of an order for sale following a charging order where the property is owned by the judgment debtor and another person, appointing the judgment creditor (or his solicitor) to convey the property under the Trustee Act 1925, s 50.

[1]   The inclusion of such provision is vital since it enables the judgment creditor to convey the judgment debtor's legal estate. LPA 1925, s 90(1) (Realisation of equitable charges by the court) grants the court the power to create and vest in the judgment creditor a legal term of years to enable him to carry out a sale of the land once an order for sale has been made. The judgment creditor will then have power to sell the land by virtue of LPA 1925, s 101(1). The length of the term is usually 3,000 years in the case of freehold property. In the case of leasehold property it will depend on the length of the judgment debtor's leasehold interest.

Proceeds of sale

4.258   The order for sale should also provide how the proceeds of sale are to be applied by the judgment creditor:

(a)   where the property is solely owned by the judgment debtor, the judgment creditor should first pay off the costs and expenses of effecting the sale, then any prior charges, before retaining the amount due to him under the order for sale then paying the balance (if any) to the judgment debtor.

(b)   where the property is owned by the judgment debtor and another person, the judgment creditor should first pay off the costs and expenses of effecting the sale, then any prior charges, then divide the remaining proceeds between himself and the judgment debtor's co-owner in accordance with the beneficial entitlements, before retaining the amount due to him under the order for sale from the judgment debtor's share, then paying the balance (if any) to the judgment debtor.

Redemption of charge once an order for sale has been made

4.259   As has been noted in para 4.256, the order for sale will provide the judgment debtor with one last chance to pay off the judgment debt and redeem the charge. A judgment debtor may seek to retain possession of the property by paying the judgment debt when, for example, a judgment creditor has exchanged contracts for the sale of land to a purchaser but before the completion of that sale has taken place. However, the judgment debtor's right to redeem the charge will be barred once an unconditional contract for the sale of the charged property has been entered into (ie following exchange of contracts in the case of land).[1] It may still be advisable to ask the court to draw up the order for sale to state expressly that that once contracts have been exchanged, any purported redemption of the judgment debt by the judgment debtor will be of no effect.

[1]   *Property & Bloodstock Ltd v Everton* [1968] Ch 94.

Interaction with the insolvency regime

4.260   The effect a judgment debtor's insolvency (or prospective insolvency) will have on the exercise of the court's discretion to make a charging order has been considered at paras 4.148-4.169. The effect of a judgment debtor's supervening insolvency in an application to discharge a charging order is discussed at paras 4.205–4.207.

4.261   Chapter 1 considers generally the interaction between the enforcement and insolvency regimes relating to corporate and individual judgment debtors. This section considers the application of the rules set out in IA 1986, ss 183 and 346 relating to the 'completion' of charging orders for the purposes of bankruptcy and winding up.

4.262   As is explained further in Chapter 1, pursuant to IA 1986, ss 183 and 346, unless a judgment creditor has completed a process of execution against goods or land before the commencement of the winding up or bankruptcy of a judgment debtor, he will be deprived of the benefit of that execution as against a liquidator or trustee in bankruptcy. For these purposes an execution against goods or land is completed by the making of a charging order under COA 1979, s 1.[1]

[1]   IA 1986, ss 183(3)(a) and (c) and 346(5)(a) and (b).

4.263   What these sections leave unclear is whether an execution against land is 'completed' when an interim charging order is obtained, or whether it is not completed until the final charging order has been made. Since the court may not have had the opportunity to consider 'all the circumstances of the case' (as it is required to do under COA 1979, s 1(5)) until the hearing for further consideration of the application, the wording of COA 1979 would suggest that 'completed' for the purposes of IA 1986 should be read as a reference to the final charging order.

4.264   In *Roberts v Kenny* the House of Lords considered the question of when a charging order was completed for the purposes of the Companies Act 1948 (CA 1948), s 325, which was the statutory predecessor of IA 1986 and in similar terms. CA 1948, s 325 disentitled a creditor to retain the benefit of an execution unless he had completed the execution before the commencement of a winding up. CA 1948, s 325(2) deemed an execution against land to be completed by the appointment of a receiver. (As has been noted in the introduction to this chapter, the need to appoint a receiver once a charging order had been obtained was removed following the entering into force of COA 1979.) The judgment creditor sought to argue that the execution was deemed to be complete once it had obtained the charging order nisi and an order for the appointment of a receiver. Lord Brightman rejected that submission:[1]

'The argument is formidable but I do not think it is correct. When the section speaks of an execution against land being 'deemed to be completed ... by the appointment of a receiver' I think that it is looking at a final order of the court effecting such appointment, and not at an order which is made provisionally, ex parte, pending further consideration by the court when the application is heard inter partes. I would expect to find clear words if I am to construe 'completion,' even 'deemed completion,' as comprehending a mere interim appointment of a receiver which is made ex parte and is not a final appointment. "Completion" of execution infers an element of finality. In the case of execution against goods, there must be both seizure and sale. In the case of an attachment of a debt there must be receipt of the debt. A debt due to the judgment debtor would not be paid to the judgment creditor under a garnishee order which was merely nisi. The argument based on section 325 is at best an argument by analogy to what the position would be if the order were made absolute and the liquidator invoked this section. I think the argument founders because it is based on a misconstruction of the section.'

[1]   [1983] 2 AC 192 at 213.

4.265 This passage from *Roberts v Kenny* was cited in *Coutts and Co v Clarke*,[1] where the Court of Appeal considered when a charging order is complete for the purposes of IA 1986, ss 183 and 346. The court found that execution is complete for the purposes of IA 1986 when the final charging order has been obtained. Lord Justice Peter Gibson referred to the passage from Lord Brightman's judgment above and held:[2]

'To my mind those remarks and that reasoning plainly support the approach of the judge, and are quite inconsistent with the remarks to which I have referred in the *Haly* case, which must be treated as no longer of validity. The recognition by Lord Brightman that the order nisi created an immediate charge and converted the creditor into a secured creditor did not detract from the fact that the order was defeasible if sufficient cause were shown. The argument that the execution was complete on the making of the order nisi was specifically rejected. For similar reasons it seems to me clear that the execution was not complete by a mere order nisi rather than an order absolute. The specific references to a charging order in s 183 and s 346, and the completion of the execution, must in my judgment be construed now consistently with the reasoning in Roberts, and in the absence of an element of finality there is no completion of execution for the reasons which Lord Brightman gave.'

[1]   [2002] EWCA Civ 943.
[2]   At [39].

STOP ORDERS AND STOP NOTICES

4.266 COA 1979, s 5(2) provides:

'The power to make rules of court under section 1 of, and Schedule 1 to, the Civil Procedure Act 1997 shall include power by any such rules to make provision—
(a) for the High Court to make a stop order on the application of any person claiming to be entitled to an interest in prescribed securities; and
(b) for the service of a stop notice by any person claiming to be entitled to an interest in prescribed securities.'[1]

[1] COA 1979, s 5(2) was substituted by the Civil Procedure (Modification of Enactments) Order 2002, SI 2002/439, arts 2, 5(a) and came into force on 25 March 2002 (see SI 2002/439, art 1.)

4.267 Those rules of court are contained in sections II and III of Pt 73, which provide that the court may make a stop order or a stop notice (respectively) on the application of a person claiming to be entitled to an interest in prescribed securities. 'Prescribed securities' are defined in COA 1979, s 5(1) as 'securities (including funds in court) of a kind prescribed by rules of court made under this section'. In summary:

(a) A stop order may be obtained in relation to funds in court and securities. A stop order relating to securities has the effect of preventing dealings in securities and may also prohibit the payment of any dividend or interest relating to such securities. A stop order relating to funds in court will prohibit dealings with the funds or any income on them.
(b) A stop notice may only be obtained in relation to securities. It has the effect of preventing any dealings in the securities without first giving 14 days' notice to the person who obtained the order (usually the judgment creditor).

4.268 The purpose of a stop order is to afford the applicant an opportunity to take whatever further steps he considers appropriate to secure his claim to the relevant assets. Similarly, the requirement to provide notice to the party who obtained a stop notice before dealing in securities affords the applicant the opportunity to assert his claim to the securities. In many cases, the next step is likely to be an application for a charging order over the securities or funds in court. However, it may be that the judgment creditor is not yet in a position to apply for a charging order, perhaps because the sums due to him are not yet ascertained.[1] Stop orders and notices are not therefore means of enforcement but rather methods whereby the judgment creditor can take steps to preserve a judgment debtor's assets so that they are available for enforcement. (This and other means of preserving a judgment debtor's assets for enforcement purposes are discussed in Chapter 1.) However, as the relevant primary legislation and procedural rules are the same as in relation to charging orders, stop orders and stop notices are covered in outline in this chapter for convenience.

[1] See further paras 4.22–4.23.

Stop orders

4.269 A stop order is 'an order of the High Court not to take, in relation to funds in court or securities specified in the order, any of the steps listed in s 5(5) of the [COA 1979]'.[1] Those prohibited steps[2] are:

(a) the registration of any transfer of the securities;
(b) in the case of funds in court, the transfer, sale, delivery out, payment or other dealing with the funds, or of the income thereon;
(c) the making of any payment by way of dividend, interest or otherwise in respect of the securities; and
(d) in the case of a unit trust, any acquisition or dealing with the units by any person or body exercising functions under the trust.

[1]   CPR 73.11. See also COA 1979, s 5(1).
[2]   COA 1979, s 5(5)

Procedure for applying for a stop order

4.270 Part 73 prescribes two methods of obtaining a stop order. Where there are existing proceedings, the application should be made by application notice under Pt 23.[1] Where there are no existing proceedings in the High Court, the application for a stop order should be made by Pt 8 claim form.[2]

[1]   CPR 73.12(2)(a).
[2]   CPR 73.12(2)(b).

Funds held in court – procedure

4.271 Where an order has been made that funds should be paid into court, a stop order can be obtained.[1]

[1]   In *Shaw v Hudson* (1879) 48 LJ Ch 689 the court held that a stop order can even be obtained notwithstanding that the funds have not yet been paid into court. However, where there are no funds in court and there is no order for payment of funds into court, a stop order cannot be obtained: *Wellesley v Mornington* (1863) 11 WR 17.

4.272 A stop order relating to funds in court may be made on the application of any person:[1]

(a) who has a mortgage or charge on the interest of any person in the funds; or
(b) to whom that interest has been assigned; or
(c) who is a judgment creditor of the person entitled to that interest.

[1]   CPR 73.12(1)(a).

4.273 The applicant should produce to the court a certificate proving that the funds actually are held in court. A judgment creditor should also produce evidence of his title to the funds, which should usually appear from the proceedings in the cause.[1]

[1]   Civil Procedure 2004, vol 1, para 73.13.4.

Service of the application notice/Part 8 claim form

4.274   The application for a stop order relating to funds in court must be served on every person whose interest may be affected by the order applied for and the Accountant General at the Court Funds Office.[1] Thus, in addition to serving the Accountant General, the applicant should also serve the application notice on the judgment debtor, any mortgagee or chargee of the funds in court, an assignee of the interest in the funds and any other party with an interest in the funds in court. The certificate of funds issued by the Accountant General must state particulars of any charges or restraints on the fund of which the Accountant General is aware, which should assist the judgment creditor in ascertaining the relevant parties to be served.[2]

1   CPR 73.12(3). See also COA 1979, s 5(4).
2   Court Funds Rules 1987, r 63(1).

Service of the stop order

4.275   Anomalously, Pt 73 does not set out the parties on which the stop order (as opposed to the application notice or claim form) should be served.[1] However, it would seem that the stop order should be served on the same parties as prescribed in relation to the application notice.

1   As has been noted, COA 1979, s 5(4) states that the rules of court made by virtue of COA 1979, s 5(2) '*shall* prescribe the person or body on whom a copy of any stop order or a stop notice is to be served.' (Emphasis added)

Effect of a stop order relating to funds in court

4.276   The effect of a stop order over funds held in court is to prohibit the transfer, sale and delivery out, payment or other dealing with the funds (or any part of them) or any income on the funds.[1] However, the granting of a stop order by the court does not determine the rights of the parties competing for the funds in court, it merely maintains the status quo. (For this reason it is not necessary to state that a stop order is made 'without prejudice' *Lucas v Peacock*.[2])

1   CPR 73.13.
2   (1846) 9 Beav 177.

4.277   As regards the priority acquired by a stop order, the general rule is that the party with the earlier stop order has priority over a party with a later stop order (rather than the date or nature of any underlying charge).[1]

1   There is considerable case law on how to determine the priority acquired by a stop order and relevant citations are contained in Civil Procedure 2004, vol 1, para 73.13.8.

Funds improperly paid out of court

4.278   In *Bath v Bath*,[1] the court considered the question of whether a judgment creditor would have a claim against public funds in the event that funds in court which were subject to a stop order were paid out in disregard of a judgment creditor's rights. In that case, the judgment creditor with an interest in the funds failed to obtain a stop order and the court did not have to decide the question, thus the court's comments are strictly obiter. However, it is interesting to note that the court expressed the view that where a judgment creditor's rights under a stop order were disregarded due to administrative error amounting to negligence, there would be no such right of recourse. In the court's view, there would have to have been 'some act of misfeasance or carelessness attributable to the Paymaster-General himself' for a cause of action to lie.

1   *Bath v Bath* [1901] 1 Ch 460.

Securities – procedure

4.279   A stop order relating to securities (other than securities held in court) may be made on the application of any person claiming to be beneficially entitled to an interest in the securities.[1]

1   CPR 73.12(1)(b)

4.280   In order to ensure that the stop order drawn up by the court provides the best possible protection for the application, the application for a stop order over securities should clearly set out the securities to which it relates, and the name in which the securities stand. The application should also specify the steps to be prohibited in relation to the securities.[1] To obtain the best possible protection, the applicant for a stop order over securities should ask the court to prohibit the registration of any transfer of the securities and the making of any payment by way of dividend, interest or otherwise in respect of the securities. If the securities are units in a unit trust, the applicant should ask the court to prohibit any acquisition of, or other dealing with, units by any person or body exercising functions under the trust.

1   CPR 73.14 states that the court may prohibit all or any of the steps set out in that rule and it is advisable for the judgment creditor to set out clearly in the application the steps he seeks the court to prohibit.

Service of the application notice/Part 8 claim form

4.281   The application notice or Pt 8 claim form relating to a stop order relating to securities must be served on every person whose interest may be affected by the order applied for and in addition, the person specified in CPR 73.5(1)(d),[1] namely:

(a)   in the case of stock for which the Bank of England keeps the register, the Bank of England;

(b)   in the case of government stock to which (i) does not apply, the keeper of the register;

(c)   in the case of stock of any body incorporated within England and Wales, that body;

(d)   in the case of stock of any body incorporated outside England and Wales or of any state or territory outside the UK, which is registered in a register kept in England and Wales, the keeper of that register; and

(e)   in the case of units of any unit trust in respect of which a register of the unit holders is kept in England and Wales, the keeper of that register.

1   CPR 73.12(3). See also COA 1979, s 5(4).

Service of the stop order

4.282   The stop order shall specify the securities to which it relates, the name in which the securities stand, the steps which may not be taken, and whether the prohibition applies to the securities only or to the dividends or interest as well.

4.283   As has been noted, Pt 73 does not set out the parties on which the stop order (as opposed to the application notice or claim form) should be served, but it would seem that the stop order should be served on the same parties as prescribed in relation to the application notice. However, the process of transferring shares or paying a dividend may involve more parties than just the company in which the stock is held. For example, many companies delegate such functions to service providers who keep their registers (for example, Computershare) and the payment of interest on bonds often involves paying agents to pay the interest. In order to ensure the stop order is effective, the judgment creditor should serve the stop order on any person who is likely to play a part in any of the activities prohibited in the order, which may involve serving persons additional to those set out in CPR 73.5(1)(d). This requires forethought as to how the prohibited activity will be administered in practice.

Effect of a stop order relating to securities

4.284   A stop order relating to securities (other than securities held in court) may prohibit all or any of the following:

(a)   the registration of any transfer of the securities;
(b)   the making of any payment by way of dividend, interest or otherwise in respect of the securities; and
(c)   in the case of units of a unit trust, any acquisition of or other dealing with the units by any person or body exercising functions under the trust.

Variation or discharge of a stop order

4.285   The court has a discretion to discharge or vary a stop order on the application of 'any person' claiming to have a beneficial interest in the funds or securities to which a stop order relates.[1] Such applications are not therefore confined to the judgment creditor or judgment debtor, but could include, for example, the spouse of a judgment debtor. The application should be made in accordance with Pt 23. The application notice seeking the variation or discharge must be served on the person who obtained the stop order.[2]

[1]   CPR 73.15(1).
[2]   CPR 73.15(2).

Stop notices

4.286   A stop notice is 'a notice issued by the court which requires a person or body not to take, in relation to securities specified in the notice, any of the steps listed in s 5(5) of the [COA 1979], without first giving notice to the person who obtained the notice'.[1] A stop notice cannot be obtained in relation to funds or securities held in court[2] (however, a stop order can be obtained in relation to such securities).

[1] CPR 73.19. See also COA 1979, s 5(1).
[2] CPR 73.16(b).

4.287 The steps which are prohibited by a stop notice are set out in para 4.284. A stop notice may also (and will, unless the court considers otherwise) be included in a final charging order which relates to securities (other than securities held in court).[1]

[1] CPR 73.17 and CPR 73.8(3).

4.288 A stop notice is different in purpose and effect from a stop order in that it is essentially a temporary measure which has the effect of preventing any dealings in the securities without first giving 14 days' notice to the person who obtained the order. However, once such notice is given, the person on whom the stop notice is served must not, by reason of the notice alone, refuse to register a transfer of the stock after the 14-day notice period has expired.[1] The 14-day period therefore affords the judgment creditor the opportunity of securing his judgment by making an appropriate application to the court within that time-frame. The appropriate application is usually a charging order on the securities.

[1] CPR 73.18(2)(b). See further para 4.295.

Procedure

4.289 CPR 73.17(1) provides that 'The High Court may, on the request of any person claiming to be beneficially entitled to an interest in securities, issue a stop notice'. The application should therefore be made to the High Court. The use of the word 'may' in CPR 73.17(1) indicates that the court has a discretion as to whether to issue the stop notice. However, the application will be dealt with without a hearing and CPR 73.17(3) provides that if a court officer considers that the request for a stop notice complies with the requirements of CPR 73.17(2), he 'will' issue a stop notice.

4.290 An applicant makes the request for a stop notice on the basis of a claim to be 'beneficially entitled' to an interest in the securities.[1] The White Book[2] observes that 'there must therefore be some beneficial interest in the stock sought to be affected, comprised in some document or legal instrument in writing'. Written evidence will also need to be filed with the request for a stop notice substantiating the applicant's claim.

[1] CPR 73.17(1).
[2] Civil Procedure 2004, vol 1, para 73.17.1.

4.291 A request for a stop notice must be made by filing:[1]

(a) a draft stop notice; and
(b) written evidence which –
   (i) identifies the securities in question;
   (ii) describes the applicant's interest in the securities; and
   (iii) gives an address for service for the applicant.

[1] CPR 73.17(2).

4.292   A sample form of stop notice is annexed as Appendix B to the Practice Direction to Pt 73. The stop notice must be addressed to a particular person or body concerned. For the reasons set out in para 4.283, in order for the stop notice to achieve the desired effect, it may be necessary to request more than one stop notice to ensure that every party who may be involved in the activity of which the applicant seeks to have notice is served. Again, this will require forethought before making the application. The name and address of the person claiming to be beneficially entitled to an interest in the securities should then be inserted in the draft notice, followed by the securities concerned and the name(s) in which they stand.

Service of the stop notice

4.293   The applicant must serve copies of the stop notice and his written evidence on the person to whom the stop notice is addressed.[1] A stop notice takes effect when it is served.[2] It remains in force until it is withdrawn or discharged in accordance with CPR 73.20 or CPR 73.21[3] (see further paras 4.297–4.298).

1   CPR 73.17(4).
2   Ie when it is served in accordance with CPR 73.17(4), see CPR 73.18(1)(a).
3   CPR 73.18(b).

Effect of a stop notice

4.294   A stop notice requires its addressee to take notice that the applicant claims to be beneficially entitled to an interest in the specified securities and requires the addressee to refrain from registering a transfer of the securities or from paying any dividend or interest in respect of the securities (where applicable) without first giving 14 days' notice to the applicant.

4.295   As noted above, a stop notice does not therefore operate as an absolute prohibition on the addressee from taking those steps. Rather, while a stop notice is in force, the person on whom it is served must not register a transfer of the securities described in the notice or take any other step restrained by the notice without first giving 14 days' notice to the person who obtained the stop notice.[1] However, once he has given the required notice, the person on whom the stop notice has been served must not, by reason only of the notice, refuse to register a transfer or to take any other step, after the 14-day notice period has expired.[2] Accordingly, in the absence of any other restriction (resulting from steps taken by the applicant to protect its beneficial interest in the securities in question), the addressee should then register the transfer or take any other relevant steps.

1   CPR 73.18(2)(a). While the CPR contains no stipulation as to the form such notice should take, best practice may be to provide such notice in writing to the address given by the applicant on the stop notice.
2   CPR 73.18(2)(b).

Amendment to stop notice

4.296 If the applicant finds that he has incorrectly described the securities in a stop notice which has been obtained and served he may request an amended stop notice.[1] Such request should be made and the amended stop notice served in accordance with the procedure set out in CPR 73.17 (see para 4.293).[2] The amended stop notice takes effect when it is served on the addressee.[3] During the intervening period the securities in which the applicant had a beneficial interest may have been transferred, and so it is crucial that the original stop notice accurately specifies the securities in question, or that steps are taken to correct the error as soon as possible.

1   CPR 73.19(1).
2   CPR 73.19(1).
3   CPR 73.19(2).

Withdrawal of stop notice

4.297 An applicant who has obtained a stop notice may withdraw it by serving a request for its withdrawal on both the person or body on whom the stop notice was served and the court which issued the stop notice.[1] The request must be signed by the person who obtained the stop notice and his signature must be witnessed by a practising solicitor.[2] It is unlikely that a judgment creditor applicant would wish to withdraw a stop notice save in circumstances where the judgment debt has been satisfied through other means (for example, payment of the sums owed by the judgment debtor or recourse to other forms of enforcement).

1   CPR 73.20(1)
2   CPR 73.20(2)

Discharge or variation of stop notice

4.298 As with charging orders and stop orders, it is possible for a stop notice to be varied or discharged. The court has a discretion to make an order varying or discharging the stop notice on the application of any person claiming to be beneficially entitled to the securities to which a stop notice relates.[1] Such parties may include not just the judgment debtor but third parties claiming a beneficial interest in the securities.

1   CPR 73.21(1).

4.299 The application must be made to the court which issued the stop notice in question.[1] The application should be made in accordance with Pt 23. The application notice should be served on the person who obtained the stop notice.[2]

1   CPR 73.21(2).
2   CPR 73.21(3).

CHAPTER 5

Writs of fieri facias

INTRODUCTION

5.1 A writ of fieri facias[1] is a command to a High Court enforcement officer, formerly known as a sheriff, to seize and sell sufficient of a judgment debtor's goods to satisfy a money judgment and the costs of enforcement. It is more commonly known by its shortened name, the writ of fi fa.[2]

[1]   Fieri facias derives from the Latin 'quod fieri facias de bonis' meaning 'which you shall cause to be made of the goods'. The term is one of the few Latin terms to survive the introduction of the Civil Procedure Rules 1998.

[2]   Pronounced 'fy fay'.

5.2 Writs of fi fa are an ancient remedy. The statutory origins of this form of writ can be traced back as far as the Damages Execution Act 1285.[1] Blackstone, writing in the eighteenth century, described a writ of fi fa as follows:

> 'THE next species of execution is against the goods and chattels of the defendant; and is called a writ of fieri facias, from the words in it where the sheriff is commanded, quod fieri faciat de bonis,[2] that he cause to be made of the goods and chattels of the defendant the sum or debt recovered. This lies as well against privileged persons, peers, &c, as other common persons; and against executors or administrators with regard to the goods of the deceased. The sheriff may not break open any outer doors, to execute ... this ... writ: but must enter peaceably; and may then break open any inner door, belonging to the defendant, in order to take the goods. And he may sell the goods and chattels (even an estate for years, which is a chattel real) of the defendant, till he has raised enough to satisfy the judgment and costs: first paying the landlord of the premises, upon which the goods are found, the arrears of rent the due, not exceeding one year's rent in the whole. If part only of the debt be levied on a fieri facias, the plaintiff may have a capias ad satisfaciendum[3] for the residue.'[4]

[1]   The preamble to the Damages Execution Act 1285 suggests that the Act provided for a new method of enforcement which did not previously exist. It states: 'WHEREAS of late our Lord the King ... considering that divers of this Realm were disherited, by Reason that in many Cases, where Remedy should have been had, there was none provided by [the King] nor

his Predecessors.' The Act itself states: 'WHEN Debt is recovered or knowledged in the King's Court, or Damages awarded, it shall be from *henceforth* in the Election of him that sueth for such Debt or Damages, to have a Writ of Fieri facias unto the Sheriff for to levy the Debt of the Lands and Goods; (2) or that the Sheriff shall deliver to him all the Chattels of the Debtor (saving only his Oxen and Beasts of his Plough) and the one half of his Land, until the Debt be levied upon a reasonable Price or Extent. (3) And if he be put out of that Tenement, he shall recover by a Writ of Novel disseisin, and after by a Writ of Redisseisin, if need be.'

2 See para 5.1, n 1. This dates from a time when the writ directed to the sheriff was written in Latin.

3 *Capias ad satisfaciendum* was a writ issued after judgment to arrest and imprison a judgment debtor until the judgment creditor's claim was satisfied: *Blackstone's Commentaries on the Laws of England* (1765-1769), vol 3, pp 414-417. The right to imprisonment for non-payment of debts was largely abolished by the Debtors Act 1869: see Chapter 1.

4 *Blackstone's Commentaries on the Laws of England* (1765–1769), vol 3, p 417.

5.3 The modern form of writ of fi fa is clearly recognisable from Blackstone's description, as are the descriptions of the limitations on a sheriff's rights of entry.[1]

1 See paras 5.149–5.191. The priority of a landlord who has levied distress for rent over the writ of fi fa is also recognisable.

5.4 The threat of a writ of fi fa may in itself be enough in some cases to secure payment of a judgment debt. Writs of fi fa are, by their very nature, intrusive and public, involving attendance at a judgment debtor's home or business premises by an enforcement officer and seizure and sale of the judgment debtor's goods. These factors may underlie the enduring popularity of the writ of fi fa as a method of enforcement. Judicial statistics reveal that the writ of fi fa is by far the most commonly used method of enforcement in the Queen's Bench Division of the High Court (both in and outside London) accounting for over 97% of all enforcement proceedings between 1999 and 2003. During that period, the Queen's Bench Division issued an average of nearly 50,000 writs of fi fa per year.[1]

1 1999: 44,592 writs of fi fa issued (95% of all enforcement proceedings); 2000: 49,465 writs of fi fa issued (97% of all enforcement proceedings); 2001: 53,248 writs of fi fa issued (98% of all enforcement proceedings); 2002: 50,687 writs of fi fa issued (99% of all enforcement proceedings); 2003: 41,652 writs of fi fa issued (99% of all enforcement proceedings). Similarly, the warrant of execution is by far the most popular method of enforcement in the county court.

5.5 The antiquarian nature of this method of enforcement has attracted both judicial comment and calls for reform.[1] Such calls may finally be answered if the proposals put forward in the March 2003 'Effective Enforcement' White Paper[2] are adopted.[3] The White Paper proposed that the powers and duties of enforcement officers should be codified and the enforcement industry should be subject to far greater regulation. Some of these proposals were implemented by the Courts Act 2003 (CA 2003) and High Court Enforcement Officers Regulations 2004.[4] CA 2003 brought about the replacement of sheriffs by High Court enforcement officers, the abolition of the territorial limitations which applied to sheriffs, and drew together various provisions which had previously been scattered across a number of statutes into CA 2003, Sch 7. However, at present the change of name from sheriff to enforcement officer is largely cosmetic and an enforcement officer continues to retain all the duties, powers, rights, privileges and liabilities that a sheriff formerly had at common law.[5] At the time of writing, it is not known if or when the remainder of the White Paper's proposals will be implemented.[6]

[1]   See eg the judgment of Judge Roger Cooke at first instance in *McLeod v Butterwick* [1996] 1 WLR 995 at 997: 'I am bound to say that the issues disclosed on this motion are of some fascination, if only to an antiquarian. They reveal the law of execution, as it still is in England and Wales, as based, in many cases, upon very ancient authority. None the worse for that, but some of the principles that emerge and, indeed, the gaps which the law of execution reveals in modern conditions, lead one to hope that it is an area of the law that will sooner rather than later attract the attention of the Law Commission.'

[2]   Effective Enforcement: Improved methods of recovery for civil court debt and commercial rent and a single regulatory regime for warrant enforcement agents (March 2003) Cm 5774.

[3]   See further paras 5.334–5.339.

[4]   SI 2004/400, as amended by SI 2004/673.

[5]   CA 2003, Sch 7, para 4(2).

[6]   Wilson *'Who Shot the Sheriff'* LSG 2004, 101(16), 31 refers to an Enforcement Officer Bill proposed for some time in 2005.

5.6   In a move that perhaps foreshadows greater regulation, the National Standards for Enforcement Agents (the National Standards) were prepared by the Lord Chancellor's Department[1] in May 2002. The National Standards are aimed at all public and private enforcement agents, the enforcement agencies that employ them, and major creditors who use their services. The National Standards were designed 'to share, build on and improve existing good practice and thereby to raise the level of professionalism across the whole sector'. While they are not legally binding, they are used in this chapter as guidance for best practice.

[1]   Now the Department for Constitutional Affairs.

Outline of procedure

5.7   The procedural rules relating to writs of fi fa are found in the Rules of the Supreme Court 1965 (RSC) Ords 46 and 47.[1] The powers and duties of High Court enforcement officers generally continue to be governed by the common law.[2]

[1]   Preserved in the Civil Procedure Rules 1998, Sch 1.

[2]   See also CA 2003, s 99 and Sch 7, and the High Court Enforcement Officers Regulations 2004, SI 2004/400.

5.8   A further reason for the popularity of the writ of fi fa as a method of enforcement may be the relatively straightforward nature of the process. Once a judgment or order for the payment of a sum of money has been given by the court, a writ of fi fa may generally be issued without the permission of the court[1] and without prior notice to the judgment debtor. Issue of the writ is, in most cases, simply a matter of producing the correct documents to the court officer of the appropriate court and paying the fee for issue. The writ will command the enforcement officer to seize the judgment debtor's goods and raise from them the sums detailed in the writ in order to pay the judgment creditor.

[1]   See further paras 5.71-5.88.

5.9   Upon receipt of the writ, the enforcement officer will prepare a warrant, which is a summary of the command in the writ of fi fa for use by his agent. The warrant is sealed by the enforcement officer and bears his name and date of issue.[1] The enforcement officer's agent will subsequently attend the judgment debtor's premises to effect seizure of the judgment debtor's goods. Having seized the goods, the enforcement officer's agent will generally either remove the goods or, more commonly, enter into a walking possession agreement allowing the judgment debtor to retain possession of his goods.[2] If an arrangement cannot be reached for satisfaction of the judgment debt, the enforcement officer will then arrange for a sale of the goods to raise the sums detailed in the writ.

[1]   Keith, Podevin and Sandbrook *The Execution of Sheriffs' Warrants* (2nd edn, 1995) pp 14–15. The use of sheriff's warrants explains why many of the cases on writs of fi fa refer to a 'warrant' being produced by a sheriff's officer. Such warrants should not be confused with county court warrants of execution.

[2]   The concept of walking possession is considered at paras 5.216–5.235. Where a walking possession agreement cannot be agreed, a hybrid practice exists which is explained at paras 5.228–5.229.

Writs of execution

5.10   The writ of fi fa is just one of a number of so called 'writs of execution'. In addition, the Civil Procedure Rules 1998 (CPR) provide for writs of possession,[1] writs of delivery,[2] and any further writ in aid of other writs of execution.[3]

[1]   RSC Ord 45, r 3.
[2]   RSC Ord 45, r 4.
[3]   RSC Ord 46, r 1. CCR Ord 26 also provides for warrants of execution, delivery and possession.

5.11   As has been noted in Chapter 1, this book is concerned with the enforcement of high value, money judgments in the High Court. Writs of possession and delivery are concerned with the recovery of land and goods, respectively, and are considered in outline in Chapter 1.[1] Where a judgment creditor is entitled to enforce a judgment in respect of land or property through a writ of possession or writ of delivery, he may also issue a writ of fi fa to enforce payment of any costs or damages awarded under the judgment.[2] This chapter concerns the use of writs of fi fa in the enforcement of money judgments. A writ of fi fa is only available in the High Court, although a similar procedure known as a warrant of execution is available in the county court.[3]

[1]   As are writs of sequestration, which involve the seizure of a contemnor's assets.
[2]   RSC Ord 47, r 3(2).
[3]   See CCR Ord 26.

Distress for rent and arrest

5.12   Seizure of goods to satisfy a judgment debt is by no means a unique method of debt enforcement. Distress for rent is an ancient remedy allowing a landlord to seize and sell a tenant's goods to pay arrears of rent. There are many similarities between distress for rent and writs of fi fa, and many of the cases on distress for rent are equally applicable to writs of fi fa. (However, a note of caution should be sounded in this regard since distress for rent is a self-help remedy that does not require the court's permission, whereas writs of fi fa are a form of judicial writ. The courts often take a stricter view on rights of entry for distress than they do as regards an enforcement officer's rights of entry because the enforcement officer has the authority of the court to levy execution of the writ.) Following initial entry and seizure, the rights of an enforcement officer executing a writ of fi fa and a bailiff levying distress for rent are also very similar, although differences remain. Cases on arrest can also be instructive as to how writs of fi fa operate, particularly in relation to rights of entry.

Judgments where a writ of fi fa is not available

5.13   Where a judgment stipulates payment within a certain time or by a certain date, a writ of fi fa will not issue until that time has elapsed.[1] Where a judgment provides for quantified damages plus costs to be assessed, the creditor can issue a writ of fi fa to enforce payment of the damages (which are known) and provided he waits at least eight days following issue of that writ, may issue another writ of fi fa to enforce payment of the assessed costs.[2]

1   RSC Ord 46, r 6(4)(b) states that no writ of execution shall be sealed unless the court officer who seals it is satisfied that the period, if any, specified for payment of the judgment debt has expired.
2   RSC Ord 47, r 3(1).

GOODS CAPABLE OF SEIZURE

5.14   There are two central aspects to the process of seizure: what goods can be seized, and what amounts to seizure? The question of what can be seized is considered first. This will enable a judgment creditor to decide whether a writ of fi fa is a suitable enforcement method. The question of what, as a matter of law, amounts to seizure is considered at paras 5.192–5.199.

What goods can be seized?

5.15   At common law, a judgment debtor's goods and chattels could be taken in execution under a writ of fi fa only if they were capable of sale.[1] Statute now provides that *any* goods belonging to a judgment debtor can be seized unless they are *exempt goods*. CA 2003, s 99 and Sch 7, para 9 provide that an enforcement officer executing a writ of execution may seize:

'(a) any goods of the execution debtor that are not exempt goods; and
(b) any money, banknotes, bills of exchange, promissory notes, bonds, specialties or securities for money belonging to the execution debtor.'

The nature of 'exempt goods' is discussed in paras 5.26–5.41.

1   *Francis v Nash* (1815) Cas T H 53 (giving the example of 'deeds, writings etc'). Judgments Act 1838, s 12 extended the powers of seizure to 'Money or Bank Notes, (whether of the Governor and Company of the Bank of England, or of any other Bank or Bankers,) and any Cheques, Bills of Exchange, Promissory Notes, Bonds, Specialties, or other Securities for Money'.

5.16   CA 2003 does not define 'goods' for the purposes of that Act. However, the property which may be seized by a writ of fi fa is extremely wide and includes any form of personal property regardless of size.

Goods must belong to the judgment debtor

5.17 Only goods belonging to the judgment can be taken in execution.[1] Goods in the judgment debtor's premises which are subject to a hire purchase agreement cannot therefore be seized (see paras 5.43–5.44). Where a third party makes claim to goods that have been seized in execution by an enforcement officer, the matter can be resolved through interpleader proceedings (see paras 5.276–5.296).

[1]   CA 2003, s 99 and Sch 7. For the common law position see *Glasspoole v Young* (1829) 9 B & C 696 at 700, per Lord Tenterden CJ (decided under former legislation).

Seizure of money and other financial instruments

5.18 Money and other financial instruments are expressly stated to be capable of seizure in CA 2003, Sch 7, para 9(2)(b) . Under Judgments Act 1838, s 12[1] special rules apply to seizure of the judgment debtor's money, banknotes, bills of exchange, promissory notes, bonds, specialities or securities for money.

[1]   To which minor amendments were made by CA 2003 but which was largely unaltered.

Seizure of money

5.19 To be capable of seizure by writ of fi fa, the money or banknotes must be in the judgment debtor's possession[1] and not merely payable to him[2] or in the hands of a third party or trustee.[3] The appropriate method of enforcement in the case of a debt payable to a judgment debtor by a third party is a third party debt order (see Chapter 3). Where money or banknotes have been seized, the enforcement officer must pay that money, or sufficient of it to satisfy the judgment debt, to the judgment creditor.[4]

[1]   *Robinson v Peace* (1838) 7 Dowl 93 at 94.
[2]   *Brown v Perrott* (1841) 4 Beav 585.
[3]   *Robinson v Peace* (1838) 7 Dowl 93 at 94 (purchase moneys for sale of property paid to a third party to be held for the use of the judgment debtor) and *France v Campbell* (1841) 9 Dowl 914 (money deposited in court by the judgment debtor in one action cannot be paid to the execution creditor in another action).
[4]   Judgments Act 1838, s 12.

Seizure of bills of exchange, promissory notes, bonds, specialities or securities for money

5.20 If the seizure is related to bills of exchange,[1] promissory notes, bonds, specialities[2] or securities for money[3] (referred into in this section as financial instruments), the enforcement officer must hold the financial instruments as security for the judgment debt.[4] He has the power to sue in his own name for recovery of the sums payable or secured under the financial instruments when the time for payment arrives.[5] However, the enforcement officer is not obliged to sue under a financial instrument unless he is indemnified by the judgment creditor for the costs and expenses associated with prosecuting such a claim in the form of a bond with two sufficient sureties provided by the judgment creditor.[6] A payment by the person liable under the financial instrument to the enforcement officer is a good discharge of his liability under it. Any surplus after payment of the judgment creditor and payment of the execution officer's fees and expenses should be paid to the judgment debtor.[7]

1   A cheque is a bill of exchange. However, dealings in cheques are heavily restricted by the Cheques Act 1992 which inserted s 81A into the Bills of Exchange Act 1882 to make account payee cheques non-transferable and only valid between the parties.
2   A speciality is an obligation contracted by matter of record or instrument under seal.
3   A life assurance policy has been held not to be a security for money and therefore not capable of seizure under previous legislation: *Re Sargent's Trusts* (1879) 7 LR Ir 66.
4   Judgments Act 1838, s 12.
5   Judgments Act 1838, s 12.
6   Judgments Act 1838, s 12.
7   Judgments Act 1838, s 12.

5.21   The 2003 White Paper recommends that enforcement officers be trained in order to ensure that the proper value of financial instruments is recognised.[1]

1   See para 172.

Trust assets

5.22   Goods held on trust for the judgment debtor cannot generally be seized by an enforcement officer.[1] However, where the whole beneficial interest in the goods is vested in the judgment debtor a writ of fi fa can be used. As Bailhache J explained in *Stevens v Hince*:[2]

'The proposition that a judgment creditor could not under a [writ of] fi fa seize chattels in which the judgment debtor had only an equitable interest, though true as a general rule, did not apply... where the whole beneficial interest in the chattels was vested in the judgment debtors. In these circumstances, the judgment debtors were not entitled to rely on the existence of the trust in order to defeat the judgment creditor.'

1   *Caillaud v Estwick* (1794) 2 Anst 381.
2   [1914] WN 148.

Interests in land

5.23   Freehold land clearly falls outside the scope of the property described in CA 2003 that may be seized by an enforcement officer executing a writ of execution.[1] However, there is case law to the effect that a debtor's interest in a lease (ie as lessee or tenant) may be seized and sold under a writ of fi fa.[2] This is because historically a lease was classified as a form of personalty known as a chattel real.[3]

1   See paras 5.15–5.16.
2   See eg *Doe d Westmoreland and Perfect v Smith* (1827) 1 Man & Ry KB 137.
3   See further *Woodfall on Landlord and Tenant*, paras 16.178–16.183.

5.24   While it may be arguable as to whether the case law on this point remains good law, from a practical perspective the question arises as to how an enforcement officer would 'take possession' of a lease. Even where seizure of the demised premises can be effected, if the judgment debtor is not willing to vacate the premises, the practical likelihood of effecting a sale of the leasehold interest without vacant possession may be minimal. For these reasons, a charging order is the preferable method of enforcement against a judgment debtor's leasehold interest.[1]

[1] See further Chapter 4. By contrast where the judgment debtor's interest is that of landlord and gives him the right to a stream of rental income from a property, equitable execution (which is discussed in Chapter 6) may be a useful form of enforcement.

Fixtures

5.25 Certain sorts of property belonging to the judgment debtor may be fixtures, which will have lost their character as chattels and become part of the land. If so, they will not be capable of seizure under a writ of fi fa. What constitutes a fixture is a question of land law and is dealt with in detail in specialist works.[1] However, one of the main issues is likely to be the degree of physical attachment the property has to the land.[2]

[1] Megarry and Wade *The Law of Real Property* (6th edn, 2000) pp 928–938.
[2] See eg *Hulme v Brigham* [1943] 1 KB 152 where the court held that printing machines weighing from 9 to 12 tons, but which were secured by their own weight, were chattels rather than fixtures.

Exempt goods

5.26 Exempt goods are defined in CA 2003, Sch 7, para 9(3) as:

'(a) such tools, books, vehicles and other items of equipment as are necessary to the execution debtor for use personally by him in his employment, business or vocation;

(b) such clothing, bedding, furniture, household equipment and provisions as are necessary for satisfying the basic domestic needs of the execution debtor and his family.'

5.27 This provision replicates (save for one small change in terminology)[1] the Supreme Court Act 1981 (SCA 1981), s 138, which it replaces.[2] A similar provision applies in respect of a bankrupt under the Insolvency Act 1986.[3]

[1] The words 'that person' are replaced by 'execution debtor'.
[2] Repealed by CA 2003, Sch 8, para 264.
[3] Which exempts tools of the trade and household items from the definition of the 'bankrupt's estate' in terms almost identical to CA 2003, Sch 7, para 9(3).

Tools of the trade

5.28 It is clear from the wording of CA 2003, Sch 7, para 9(3) that a factual assessment of what is 'necessary' will have to be made on a case by case basis. The question of what tools and equipment were necessary to a judgment debtor for use by him personally in his business was considered by the Court of Appeal in *Toseland Building Supplies Ltd v Bishop t/a Bishop Groundworks*[1] construing the near identical provisions of SCA 1981, s 138. The question in that case was whether a JCB mechanical digger was exempt from seizure. The evidence adduced indicated that that the judgment debtor ran a groundwork business which typically involved digging trenches for the footings of buildings, or digging out and laying a driveway. The judgment debtor owned the JCB and it was used regularly. He claimed that it was essential for him to own a JCB digger because it enabled him to respond very quickly to enquiries that entailed using such a digger during the course of building work and his business would not, from a practical point of view, have been viable if he had to hire a vehicle. There was evidence that the judgment debtor personally used the digger but, importantly, there was also evidence that his employees did so.

1   Unreported, 28 October 1993, CA.

5.29 On the facts, the court held that the JCB digger was not 'for use personally by him in his employment, business or vocation'. As the judge put it at first instance:

'The idea behind the legislation in my view is and always has been to protect the tools of the trade of the individual worker. In this type of case, involving as it does a vehicle, I can well understand that if, for example, a motorcycle courier of the kind that one sees so frequently these days, who owns his own motorcycle and hires himself out to go and deliver documents in various places, then that motorcycle will be protected. So too would a van owned and driven solely by a person in which he drove about making deliveries in the course of his work as a delivery man.'

However, on the facts of *Toseland* the JCB was not exempt because it was also used by the judgment debtor's employees and was not therefore for use by the judgment debtor 'personally'.

5.30 The Court of Appeal agreed with the judge at first instance. The Court stressed that the statutory provision was clear and the court should not seek to define the words, which were plain and did not require further elaboration. Rather, the statutory wording should be interpreted in the light of the facts of the particular case. In line with these principles, a disc jockey has been held to be able to claim the tools of the trade exemption for the records, tapes and CDs he uses for his work.[1] However, where a judgment debtor owns equipment which is also used by his employees in the course of his business, the exemption is unlikely to apply for the reasons provided in *Toseland*.

1   *Brookes v Harris* [1995] 1 WLR 918 at 921.

Burden of demonstrating that goods are exempt

5.31 In considering whether a judgment debtor's property is exempt the Court of Appeal in *Toseland* also held that:[1]

'Prima facie all the judgment debtor's goods are liable to seizure under a writ of fieri facias. If a judgment debtor claims the benefit of a statutory exemption, the burden of showing that the exemption applies rests squarely on him.'

1   Unreported, 28 October 1993, CA. Followed in *Moffat v Lemkin (formerly High Sheriff of Greater London)* (unreported, 24 November 2003).

5.32   Such provision is logical because there is no way in which a sheriff could know what tools are necessary for use by the judgment debtor personally in his employment or business and no way in which he could know what tools are used by him personally.[1]

[1]   *Moffat v Lemkin (formerly High Sheriff of Greater London)* (unreported, 24 November 2003).

Household necessities

5.33   The exemption for household necessities provided in CA 2003, Sch 7, para 9(3)(b) is unlikely to be relevant in a commercial enforcement context because the judgment creditor will be seeking high value items in satisfaction of his judgment debt. However, the same principles of construction of the statutory provisions on a case-by-case basis as set in *Toseland* should apply.

Dealing with exempt property

5.34   There is no legal requirement for an enforcement officer to point out to the judgment debtor goods which are likely to be exempt from seizure. In *Moffat v Lemkin (formerly High Sheriff of Greater London)* the judge commented:[1]

> 'I do not accept that there is any such duty upon the Sheriff to [the judgment debtor] although I do accept that it would, certainly to a layman, be monstrous for a sheriff to sell goods which were likely tools of trade without any warning.'

[1]   *Moffat v Lemkin (formerly High Sheriff of Greater London)* (unreported, 24 November 2003).

5.35   The standard notice of seizure, which must be left with the judgment debtor by the enforcement officer (Form No 55 'Notice of Seizure'), draws attention to the statutory exemptions and sets them out on the reverse of the Form.[1] (The steps which should be taken by a judgment debtor who seeks to rely on the statutory 'exempt goods' provisions are discussed in paras 5.286-5.291.) The Effective Enforcement White Paper proposes that the enforcement agents will have 'a general responsibility to direct the debtor to tell him or her which goods are exempt', although whether this will go beyond the current directions contained in the Notice of Seizure is unclear.

[1]   See further paras 5.200–5.204.

5.36   The 2003 White Paper also suggests that a limit be set on the aggregate value of goods which are exempt from seizure because they fall within the tools of the trade exemption. In addition, it proposes that it should be acceptable for very expensive goods (including tools of the trade) to be taken and replaced with similar goods of a lesser value.[1] Whether these proposals are implemented remains to be seen.

[1]   See paras 168–171. This is already permitted in the case of bankruptcy: Insolvency Act 1986, s 308(1).

5.37   The National Standards impose other requirements on enforcement agents executing writs. These include not removing anything clearly identifiable as belonging to, or for the exclusive use of, a child, and enforcement officers taking reasonable steps to satisfy themselves that the value of the goods seized does not exceed the value of the debt and charges owed.

Specific exemptions

5.38   In addition to the tools of the trade and household necessities exemptions provided by CA 2003, there are a number of specific exemptions which apply in the case of particular types of property.

Bills of sale

5.39   A bill of sale is a document evidencing the sale (an 'absolute bill') or grant of security (a 'security bill') *by an individual* over certain sorts of chattel where the seller/chargor still retains possession of the chattel. Their purpose was to create a public register to show where chattels in the possession of one person and apparently owned by him had been sold to, or secured in favour of, another. Bills of sale must be registered and the statutory formalities contained in the Bills of Sales Acts 1878 and 1882 must be carefully followed or the bill may be void.

5.40   Provided the transferee has no notice of the unexecuted writ,[1] goods in which the property has been transferred by means of a bill of sale are protected from seizure because the transferee will constitute a good faith purchaser for value (see paras 5.133–5.139). In practice, bills of sale are rarely encountered because the stringent formalities surrounding their creation are so cumbersome. A judgment debtor who attempts to use a bill of sale as a means of evading execution against his goods is as likely to fall foul of the statutory formalities as to execute a bill of sale successfully.

[1]   *Gladstone v Padwick* (1871) LR 6 Exch 203 at 209.

5.41   Where a judgment debtor does assert that goods are exempt from seizure because they have been transferred pursuant to a bill of sale, it will be worth a judgment creditor checking that the formalities have been correctly followed and that the bill of sale has been duly registered since otherwise the bill may well be void. The register of bills of sale is a public register[1] and is kept at the Action Department Room in room E10 at the Royal Courts of Justice.[2] The register is arranged alphabetically by grantor[3] and can be inspected[4] to determine whether a bill of sale has been validly registered. The current search fee is £5 per name.[5]

[1]   Bills of Sale Act 1878, s 16.
[2]   Queen's Bench Guide, para 12.4.1.
[3]   Bills of Sale Act 1878, s 12.
[4]   RSC Ord 95, r 4.
[5]   Civil Proceedings Fees Order 2004, SI 2004/3121, Sch 1, para 9.2.

Crown

5.42   A writ of fi fa cannot be executed against the Crown to enforce payment of money or costs.[1] Instead, a separate procedure exists, which is set out in the Crown Proceedings Act 1947, s 25(1)–(3) (see paras 1.132–1.134).

[1]   Crown Proceedings Act 1947, s 25(4). See also RSC Ord 77, r 15(1).

Hire purchase, conditional sales and finance leasing of business equipment[1]

5.43 Many forms of business equipment are acquired by means of trade finance. Common financing techniques include hire purchase,[2] conditional sales[3] and finance leasing.[4] (Similarly, household goods can be purchased on hire purchase agreements, though this is less likely to be relevant in the context of commercial enforcement.) While the commercial and legal terms of hire purchase, conditional sales and finance leasing will differ, what they have in common is that title is either retained by the hirer or seller (or in the case of the finance lessor, title never leaves him) and the contract will typically provide that in the event of execution being levied the agreement will terminate and an immediate right to retake possession arises. Strictly, therefore, hire purchase and other like goods are not 'exempt' from seizure but rather are not available for execution because they do not belong to the judgment debtor (see para 5.17). In any event, it will be important to ascertain the ownership of the type of goods which are commonly subject to financing agreements before levying execution in order to avoid wasted costs of execution or potential liability to the true owner. The use of Pt 71 proceedings (Orders to obtain information about a judgment debtor's assets) may assist in this regard. Part 71 proceedings are described in Chapter 2 as are other means of ascertaining whether goods are subject to hire purchase.

[1]   See generally Goode *Commercial Law* (3rd edn, 2004) pp 700–737.
[2]   A hire purchase contract is an agreement to hire equipment under which the hirer agrees to pay the agreed instalments for the use of the equipment over an agreed term. It typically provides that at the end of the agreed term the hirer has the option, but not the obligation, to purchase the equipment. See Goode *Commercial Law* (3rd edn, 2004) pp 713–719.
[3]   A conditional sale agreement is an agreement for sale under which title is retained by the seller until payment has been made in full or other conditions prescribed in the agreement are met. It differs from hire purchase because the buyer is contractually committed to buy, whereas under a hire purchase agreement he has an option but not an obligation to purchase. See Goode *Commercial Law* (3rd edn, 2004) pp 709–713.
[4]   A finance lease is an agreement to hire equipment over a period usually equivalent to the estimated life of the equipment in return for 'rental' payments. At the end of the finance lease, the lessee will not be permitted to acquire the equipment otherwise it would convert the agreement to one of hire purchase. Instead, the lessor will sell the equipment (which will typically have a small residual value) and will pay or credit any amounts raised against a future transaction. See Goode *Commercial Law* (3rd edn, 2004) pp 721–737.

5.44 Where an enforcement officer seizes the goods and sells them *with notice* of the hirer's, lessor's or seller's interest, he will be liable to the hirer, lessor or seller, as the case may be.[1] The statutory protection afforded to an enforcement officer with no notice of the interest of a third party is considered at paras 5.264–5.271.

[1]   *Jelks v Hayward* [1905] 2 KB 460.

Landlords/distraint

5.45 Unpaid landlords may have rights over a tenant judgment debtor's chattels that are held on the leased property which take priority over a judgment creditor executing a writ of fi fa. Detailed analysis of a landlord's right to distress for rent is outside the scope of this book.[1] However, goods which have been seized in distress for rent cannot then be seized in execution of a writ of fi fa.[2] Conversely, goods that have been seized under a writ of fi fa cannot be taken in distress, as they are in the custody of the law.[3]

1   See further *Woodfall on Landlord and Tenant*, paras 9.712-9.187 and Keith, Podevin and Sandbrook *The Execution of Sheriffs' Warrants* (2nd edn, 1995), pp 149–156.
2   *Haythorne v Bush* (1834) 2 C&M 689 and *Reddell v Stowey* (1841) 2 Mood & R 358.
3   See eg *Re Mackenzie* [1899] 2 QB 566 at 573–574, CA.

5.46   Even if the landlord has not distrained, statute provides that a landlord may claim unpaid rent before goods may be removed in execution of a writ of fi fa. The Landlord and Tenant Act 1709, s 1 prohibits the removal of goods seized by an enforcement officer until the landlord's rent in arrears (not exceeding one year's rent) had been paid by the execution creditor.[1] The Act effectively impounds the goods for the landlord's benefit and they cannot be removed until he has been paid.[2] In the case of tenancies for less than a year, the Execution Act 1844, s 67 provides that four terms' arrears of rent (for example, four weeks' or four months') may be claimed by the landlord.

1   *Re Mackenzie* [1899] 2 QB 566 at 574, CA.
2   *Re Mackenzie* [1899] 2 QB 566 at 574, per Lord Lindley MR, CA.

5.47   However, a judgment creditor has no duty of inquiry to ascertain if rent is unpaid[1] and can levy execution against a tenant unless he is notified of a claim by the landlord for unpaid rent. Once an enforcement officer has notice of unpaid rent, the duties of the enforcement officer are as described by Lord Esher MR in *Thomas v Mirehouse*:[2]

'When notice has been given by the landlord to the sheriff that rent is due, it becomes the duty of the sheriff under the statute not to sell anything upon the demised premises till the rent has been paid. Even if there are goods upon the demised premises of a value many times exceeding the amount of rent due his duty is the same. He must refuse to sell the smallest part of the goods until the claim of the landlord is satisfied.'

1   *Re Mackenzie* [1899] 2 QB 566 at 574, CA.
2   *Thomas v Mirehouse* (1887) 19 QBD 563, CA.

5.48   In practice, the enforcement officer will send a notice to the judgment creditor advising that unpaid rent is due.[1] If the judgment creditor provides the sum due, the enforcement officer will pay the landlord and proceed with the execution. If the judgment creditor is not prepared to pay the unpaid rent then the enforcement officer will withdraw and cannot be called on to infringe the statute.[2] Whether the judgment creditor will be prepared to pay off the rent arrears will depend on the amount of the rent owed and the likely recovery from the judgment debtor's goods.

1   A useful specimen notice can be found in Keith, Podevin and Sandbrook *The Execution of Sheriffs' Warrants* (2nd edn, 1995) p 156.
2   *Thomas v Mirehouse* (1887) 19 QBD 563, CA.

5.49   Were an enforcement officer to breach his duty and sell without paying the unpaid rent, he would incur liability under statute to the landlord for wrongful removal.[1] The amount of the rent is prima facie the measure of the damages. However, it is open to the enforcement officer to show that the value of the goods removed was not sufficient to pay the rent in mitigation of damages, in which case the loss to the landlord by the removal of the goods, or their value to him at the time of the removal, becomes the measure of damages.[2]

1 *Re Mackenzie* [1899] 2 QB 566 at 574, CA.
2 *Thomas v Mirehouse* (1887) 19 QBD 563, CA.

5.50 However, assuming that there are sufficient goods to cover all amounts owed, the enforcement officer may add the amount of rent paid to the landlord to the amounts owed under the writ and seize and sell sufficient goods to cover the whole amount.[1]

1 *Re Mackenzie* [1899] 2 QB 566 at 575, CA.

5.51 It is also worth noting that the government has proposed the abolition of the priority accorded to landlords in respect of distress for rent in the Effective Enforcement White Paper.[1]

1 Effective Enforcement White Paper, para 205.

Partnerships

5.52 A writ of fi fa can only be executed against the assets of a partnership where judgment has been entered against the firm.[1] Partnership property cannot be seized to satisfy the debt of one partner.[2] Where there is a dispute as to whether assets are owned by the partnership or an individual partner, interpleader proceedings may be necessary[3] (see paras 5.276–5.296).

1 Partnership Act 1890, s 23(1) and *Peake v Carter* [1916] 1 KB 652 at 655.
2 Instead, a judgment creditor of a partner may obtain a charging order on that partner's interest in the partnership property (Partnership Act 1890, s 23(2)).
3 *Peake v Carter* [1916] 1 KB 652.

Railway rolling stock and plant

5.53 The Railway Companies Act 1867 exempts certain railway rolling stock and plant used by a railway company[1] from seizure under a writ of fi fa after a railway has been open to public traffic.[2] The exemption covers 'engines, tenders, carriages, trucks, machinery, tools, fittings, materials, and effects constituting the rolling stock and plant used or provided by a company for the purposes of the traffic on their railway, or of their stations or workshops.' The appropriate procedure for enforcement is to seek the appointment of a receiver or manager under the special mechanism provided by the statute.[3]

1 See definition in the Railway Companies Act 1867, s 3.
2 Railway Companies Act 1867, ss 4–5. The exemption is for any 'execution at law or in equity'.
3 Railway Companies Act 1867, s 4.

5.54 Key system assets[1] in the London Underground are also exempted by statute from seizure.[2]

1 Defined in the Greater London Authority Act 1999, s 213.
2 Greater London Authority Act 1999, s 216(4).

Goods amenable to seizure

5.55 As has been noted, any goods belonging to the judgment debtor can be seized in execution provided they are not 'exempt goods' or subject to any of the specific exemptions mentioned above. However, in the context of the enforcement of high value judgment debts, particular types of assets are worthy of further consideration.

Aircraft

5.56 Aircraft can be seized under a writ of fi fa. A copy of the warrant must be attached outside the plane and another in the cockpit. The exterior copy is to advise people entering the aircraft of the seizure and the interior copy to alert the pilot that it is subject to a seizure.[1]

1   Keith, Podevin and Sandbrook *The Execution of Sheriffs' Warrants* (2nd edn, 1995) p 39.

5.57 Seizure of an aircraft can be complicated, not least because different parts may have different ownership, some or all of which may be subject to finance leases, charges or mortgages. Accordingly, an enforcement officer should ensure that the aircraft does indeed belong to the judgment debtor before he takes action to seize it. The means of identifying aircraft owned by the judgment debtor is considered in Chapter 2. The identification of an enforcement officer with a proven track record of aircraft seizure is likely to be essential.

Farms

5.58 Executing a writ of fi fa over farm goods raises particular issues. Animals can be seized under a writ of fi fa. However, in a commercial enforcement scenario, execution is only likely to be worthwhile in the case of a large number of animals or animals of high value. The animals must also be properly looked after following seizure, which will add to the costs and complexities of enforcement, and the enforcement officer can charge the judgment creditor the full cost associated with caring for the animals.[1]

1   High Court Enforcement Officers Regulations 2004, SI 2004/400, Sch 3, para 5.

5.59 Growing crops can be seized under a writ of fi fa, but only if they were produced by human labour.[1] However, case law reveals some fairly arbitrary distinctions as to what constitutes 'human labour'. An enforcement officer would appear to be able to seize corn[2] or potatoes[3] but not trees[4] growing fruit[5] or grass[6] as these have been held not to be produced by human labour. However, once trees have been felled it seems they can be seized.[7]

1   *Evans v Roberts* (1826) 5 B&C 829.
2   *Evans v Roberts* (1826) 5 B&C 829 at 840.
3   *Evans v Roberts* (1826) 5 B&C 829 at 840.
4   *Rodwell v Phillips* (1842) 9 M&W 501 at 505.
5   *Rodwell v Phillips* (1842) 9 M&W 501 at 505.
6   *Evans v Roberts* (1826) 5 B&C 829 at 832.
7   *Rodwell v Phillips* (1842) 9 M&W 501 at 505.

5.60 Special rules apply where the judgment debtor is a tenant farmer and there exists a covenant or written agreement with the landlord not to remove various produce[1] from the land. A tenant farmer has a statutory duty to notify the enforcement officer of the agreement with the landlord and inform him of the name and address of the landlord.[2] Even if no notice is given, the enforcement officer has a duty to inquire whether such restrictions exist.[3] An enforcement officer with notice of such an agreement must not remove or sell the produce[4] without first notifying the landlord that he has taken possession of it.[5] The produce can, however, be sold where a buyer agrees to purchase on the terms of the original covenant or written agreement.[6]

1   Sale of Farming Stock Act 1816, s 1 provides that the following produce may not be removed: 'straw threshed or unthreshed, or any straw of crops growing, or any chaff, colder, or any turnips, or any manure, compost, ashes, or seaweed, in any case whatsoever; nor any hay, grass or grasses, whether natural or artificial, nor any tares or vetches, nor any roots or vegetables, being produce of such lands.'
2   Sale of Farming Stock Act 1816, s 2.
3   Sale of Farming Stock Act 1816, s 5.
4   Sale of Farming Stock Act 1816, s 1.
5   Sale of Farming Stock Act 1816, s 2.
6   Sale of Farming Stock Act 1816, s 3.

5.61 Under the Agricultural Credits Act 1928, a farmer may create an agricultural charge over farm stocks and assets. The County Court Rules 1981 (CCR) have a specific provision dealing with the procedure to be followed before levying a county court warrant of execution[1] against a farmer. CCR Ord 26, r 3 provides that:

'If after the issue of a warrant of execution the district judge for the district in which the warrant is to be executed has reason to believe that the debtor is a farmer, the execution creditor shall, if so required by the district judge, furnish him with an official certificate, dated not more than three days beforehand, of the result of a search at the Land Registry as to the existence of any charge registered against the debtor under the Agricultural Credits Act 1928.'

1   The county court equivalent of a writ of fi fa.

5.62 Neither the CPR nor the RSC contain an equivalent provision. However, an execution creditor takes subject to any charges on the property and so will take subject to an agricultural charge. For this reason, when executing a writ of fi fa against a farmer, a search should be made for charges registered under the Agricultural Credits Act 1928. All agricultural charges must be registered at HM Land Registry[1] within seven days, or they will be void against any person other than the farmer.[2] Registration constitutes actual notice of the charge to all persons.[3] The register is a public register[4] and a search can be obtained by completing HM Land Registry form AC6[5] and sending it to the Agricultural Credits Department at the address specified on the form.[6] The fee for the search is currently 50p.[7]

1   Agricultural Credits Act 1928, ss 9(1) and 9(2).
2   Agricultural Credits Act 1928, s 9(1).
3   Agricultural Credits Act 1928, s 9(8).
4   Agricultural Credits Act 1928, s 9(4).
5   Agricultural Credits Regulations 1928, SI 1928/667, reg 2.
6   The address for applications set out in the Agricultural Credits Regulations 1928, SI 1928/667, reg 5 is obsolete.
7   Agricultural Credits Fees Order 1985, SI 1985/372, reg 2.

Clergy

5.63   Where the judgment debtor is a member of the clergy and appears to have no goods against which a writ of fi fa can be executed, a writ of *fieri facias de bonis ecclesiasticis* can be delivered to the bishop of the judgment debtor's diocese for execution.[1] However, such procedure is unlikely to be relevant in the context of commercial enforcement and is outside the scope of this book.

1   RSC Ord 47, r 5.

Goods in bond

5.64   An enforcement officer can seize goods belonging to the judgment debtor wherever they are held in England and Wales. Goods of the judgment debtor held in warehouses owned by third parties are no exception.

5.65   However, practical difficulties may arise in the case of warehouse goods in that they may be subject to a conditional sale or retention of title agreements and may not therefore belong to the judgment debtor (see paras 5.43–5.44). Furthermore, if the warehouseman is owed any sums by the judgment debtor, he may have a lien over the goods which will allow him to retain possession until he is paid. Goods belonging to the judgment debtor which are subject to a lien by a third party are capable of seizure but will remain subject to the lien.[1] Practically, therefore, the enforcement officer will be unable to remove them for the purposes of sale as the prospects of achieving a sale may be low where the goods remain subject to the lien. (By contrast, where the judgment debtor has a lien over goods which are owned by a third party, neither the goods nor the lien are capable of seizure.)[2]

1   *Duncan v Garratt* (1824) 1 C & P 169; *Jacobs v Latour* (1828) 5 Bing 129 at 132; *Proctor v Nicholson* (1835) 7 C & P 67; and *The Ile de Ceylan* [1922] P 256 at 258.
2   *Legg v Evans* (1840) 6 M&W 36. The lien is a mere personal interest in the goods which cannot form the subject matter of a sale.

Motor vehicles

5.66   Motor vehicles of any type can be seized under a writ of fi fa (as can caravans).[1] The question of whether a judgment debtor could claim the vehicle is a tool of his trade is considered at paras 5.28-5.32. Before seizing a vehicle, an enforcement officer will check with DVLA to ascertain the identity of the registered keeper of the vehicle.[2] Although the registered keeper of a vehicle is not necessarily the owner, it is likely to give a good indication of ownership. In addition, vehicles are often subject to various forms of hire purchase agreement, and if so cannot be seized by writ of fi fa.[3] Appropriate inquiries should therefore be made in this regard.[4]

1   This is the case even if it is the judgment debtor's home: *Lloyds and Scottish Finance Ltd v Modern Cars and Caravans (Kingston) Ltd* [1996] 1 QB 764. For safety reasons a caravan should not be removed when occupied: *Cave v Capel* (1954) 1 QB 367. A judgment debtor may be able to argue that a caravan has become a fixture to land, in which case a writ of fi fa is not the appropriate means of levying execution.
2   It is intended that enforcement officers will shortly have direct access to the DVLA database in order to check the identity of the registered keeper of a vehicle.

3   See paras 5.43–5.44.
4   See further, para 2.66.

Machinery

5.67 Machinery in a factory, however large, can be seized provided it is a chattel and not a fixture (see para 5.25). If machinery is very large or heavy or both, a specialist enforcement officer with experience of valuing such assets and, if necessary, with the facilities to arrange removal and storage should be consulted. It may also be necessary to apply to consider an auction of the goods to take place on the judgment debtor's premises (see paras 5.253–5.255).

Ships

5.68 It is possible to proceed against a ship by way of fi fa[1] and an enforcement officer can seize a ship or a 'share' of a ship.[2] Where the debtor owns only some of the shares in a ship, the officer can still seize the ship as a whole and sell just that share.[3] Under certain circumstances the master and crew can claim a lien over the ship (commonly for unpaid wages). Some of these liens operate *in rem* and will take priority over a judgment debtor's claim to enforcement against a ship, even if already seized by an enforcement officer.[4]

1   *The James W Elwell* [1921] P 351; *The Joannis Vatis (No 2)* [1922] P 213; and *The Ile de Ceylan* [1922] P 256.
2   Merchant Shipping (Registration of Ships) Regulations 1993, SI 1993/3138, reg 2(5) provides that the property in a ship to be registered in the Register of British Ships shall be divided into 64 'shares'.
3   *The James W Elwell* [1921] P 351 at 368–369.
4   *The Ile de Ceylan* [1922] P 256 at 258, and contrast *The James W Elwell* [1921] P 351 at 369–370.

PROCEDURE FOR OBTAINING A WRIT OF FI FA

5.69 The procedural rules for obtaining a writ of fi fa have not yet been amended and are contained in RSC Ord 46 and RSC Ord 47.[1]

1   Preserved in CPR, Sch 1.

High Court jurisdiction

5.70 A writ of fi fa can only be issued in the High Court. As has been noted, a similar procedure known as a warrant of execution is available in the county court. A writ of fi fa can be obtained using a county court judgment but the judgment must first be transferred to the High Court (see Chapter 1).[1]

1   Transfer can also be arranged by sending the judgment to the Sheriffs Lodgment Centre, or other firms of enforcement officers who offer this service, who will arrange the transfer and the issue of a writ of fi fa for a small fee.

Where permission to issue is required

5.71   The general rule is that permission is not needed to issue any writ of execution. However, RSC Ord 46, r 2(1) sets out the circumstances in which a writ of execution may not issue without the permission of the court. These are:

(a)   where six years or more have elapsed since the date of the judgment or order;
(b)   where any change has taken place, whether by death or otherwise, in the parties entitled or liable to the execution under the judgment or order;
(c)   where the judgment or order is against the assets of the deceased person coming into the hands of his executors or administrators after the date of the judgment or order and it is sought to issue execution on such assets;
(d)   where under the judgment or order any person is entitled to a remedy subject to the fulfilment of any condition which it is alleged has been fulfilled; or
(e)   where any goods sought to be seized under a writ of execution were in the hands of a receiver appointed by the court or a sequestrator.

5.72   Most of the categories set out in RSC Ord 46, r 2(1) are relatively self-explanatory. The requirement for permission to issue a writ where a court appointed receiver or sequestrator hold goods is to avoid committing a contempt of court. The requirement for permission where six years or more have elapsed since the date of the judgment warrants further consideration, not least since the identification of assets of value can take years, particularly in a fraud case.

Permission to issue a writ of fi fa after six years

5.73   It should be noted at the outset that an application to issue execution more than six years following the date of judgment, or to extend the time for execution, has been held not to be time-barred by the Limitation Act 1980, s 24(1) (which prohibits the bringing of an action on a judgment after the expiration of six years).[1] The court has a discretion as to whether to grant permission to issue a writ of execution. RSC Ord 46, r 2(1) gives no guidance as to how this court's discretion to grant permission to issue a writ of fi fa where more than six years have elapsed since the date of judgment will be exercised. It is, however, clear that obtaining such permission is 'no mere formality'.[2]

[1]   *National Westminster Bank plc v Powney* [1991] Ch 339 at 357, CA; *Duer v Frazer* [2001] 1 WLR 919; and *Lowsley v Forbes* [1999] 1 AC 329 at 342, HL. This is because the Limitation Act 1980, s 24(1) is concerned with a fresh action on a judgment.
[2]   Civil Procedure 2004, vol 1, para 46.2.2.

5.74   In *National Westminster Bank v Powney*[1] the Court of Appeal held that delays in the administration of justice which were outside the control of the parties, such as a delay of two years and ten months which had been necessary to determine an application to set aside, would be proper grounds for the court to grant permission for a fresh writ to be issued outside the six-year period.[2] While each case will turn on its own facts, in *Duer v Frazer*[3] the court held that it:[4]

'would not, in general, extend time beyond the six years save where it is demonstrably just to do so. The burden of demonstrating this should, in my judgment, rest on the judgment creditor. Each case must turn on its own facts but, in the absence of very special circumstances such as were present in *National Westminster Bank plc v Powney* [1991] Ch 339, the court will have regard to such matters as the explanation given by the judgment creditor for not issuing execution during the initial six-year period, or for any delay thereafter in applying to extend that period, and any prejudice which the judgment debtor may have been subject to as a result of such delay including, in particular, any change of position by him as a result which has occurred. The longer the period that has been allowed to lapse since the judgment the more likely it is that the court will find prejudice to the judgment debtor.'

1   [1991] Ch 339 at 361-362, CA.
2   *National Westminster Bank Plc v Powney* [1991] Ch 339 at 361–362, CA. Although the case was concerned with a county court warrant of possession, the relevant county court rule under consideration by the Court of Appeal (CCR Ord 26, r 5(1)) contains an almost identical provision to RSC Ord 46, r 2(1).
3   [2001] 1 WLR 919, QBD.
4   *Duer v Frazer* [2001] 1 WLR 919 at 925.

5.75   The court in *Duer* also found no basis on which a judgment of a foreign court that has been registered in this country should be treated any differently to an English judgment in this regard.[1]

1   *Duer v Frazer* [2001] 1 WLR 919 at 925.

5.76   The Court of Appeal revisited the question of the exercise of this discretion in *Patel v Singh*.[1] In that case the judgment creditor had obtained judgment against the judgment debtor on 8 September 1992 and believed the defendant had subsequently moved to Germany and was working there. Six months after she became aware that the defendant was in England, on 1 May 2002, she applied to issue a writ of fi fa outside the six-year time limit. Peter Gibson LJ, giving the judgment of the Court of Appeal, refused permission:

'In my judgment, therefore, consistently with what this court said in *Powney*, the court must start from the position that the lapse of six years may, and will ordinarily, in itself justify refusing the judgment creditor permission to issue the writ of execution, unless the judgment creditor can justify the granting of permission by showing that the circumstances of his or her case takes it out of the ordinary. That may be done by showing the presence of something in relation to the judgment creditor's own position, or, as Sir Anthony Evans suggested in the course of the argument, in relation to the judgment debtor's position. Thus the judgment creditor might be able to point, for example, to the fact that for many years the judgment debtor was thought to have no money and so was not worth powder and shot but that, on the judgment creditor winning the lottery or having some other change of financial fortune, it has become worthwhile for the judgment creditor to seek to pursue the judgment debtor.'

The court also pointed out that in accordance with the CPR the exercise of its discretion should be informed by the overriding objective of enabling the court to deal with cases justly.

1   *Patel v Singh* [2002] EWCA Civ 1938.

5.77   The fact that the judgment debtor had moved to Germany and since returned was not seen by the Court as an adequate grounds for granting permission to issue:[1]

> 'I can understand that when she discovered Mr Singh had moved to Germany she regarded that as an obstacle to her proceeding on her writ of execution. The obvious thing for her to have done at that point would have been to go to an English solicitor to obtain help. The solicitor would perhaps have advised her to register her judgment in Germany as a signatory, like this country, to the Brussels Convention, and as to the steps that could be taken to discover Mr Singh's whereabouts in Germany. But, as Mr Crosfill frankly accepted, she appears to have done nothing at all once she discovered that Mr Singh was in Germany.'

[1]   [2002] EWCA Civ 1938 at [25].

5.78   The basic message is clear: a judgment should be enforced expeditiously and, if it is not, the judgment creditor will only have himself to blame if the court refuses him permission to issue a writ of fi fa after the initial six-year period. The Court of Appeal's judgment in *Patel* would suggest there is effectively a presumption against granting that permission and that, barring court delays, it will be for the judgment creditor to show why the presumption should be rebutted. However, where the judgment creditor can demonstrate that the reason why enforcement had not taken place is because it was thought that the judgment debtor had no assets but that his financial circumstances have since changed, permission is likely to be granted (provided that the reason assets had not been discovered earlier was not attributable to a lack of resolve by the judgment creditor to discover them). In any event, a judgment creditor who is approaching the sixth anniversary of the judgment and who wishes to preserve his full rights to enforcement might be better advised to bring a fresh action on the judgment within the six-year limitation period[1] to reset the time limit.[2]

[1]   Limitation Act 1980, s 24(1).
[2]   *Bank of Scotland v Bennett* [2004] All ER (D) 417 (Jul).

Where another enactment or rule requires permission

5.79   The specific situations where permission is required to issue a writ of fi fa set out in RSC Ord 46, r 2(1) are without prejudice to all other occasions where it has been enacted or rules that provide that a person is required to obtain the permission of the court for the issue of a writ of execution or otherwise to enforce a judgment or order.[1]

[1]   RSC Ord 46, r 2(2).

5.80   There are a number of enactments which require the permission of the court for execution to issue.[1] Many of these are unlikely to be relevant in a commercial enforcement scenario.[2] However, of particular importance are various provisions of the Insolvency Act 1986, which are considered in Chapter 1. Various rules concerning partnerships also require the court's permission before execution may issue.[3]

[1]   RSC Ord 46, r 2(2) makes specific reference to the Reserve and Auxiliary Forces (Protection of Civil Interests) Act 1951, s 2, which protects the interests of persons called up or volunteering for certain naval, military or air force service. However, this is unlikely to be relevant in a commercial enforcement context.

² Though less likely to be relevant in the context of commercial enforcement, it is worth noting that permission of the county court to bring enforcement proceedings is needed where the county court has made an attachment of earnings order to secure the payment of a judgment debt (Attachment of Earnings Act 1971, s 8(2)(b)).

³ See RSC Ord 81, rr 5(4)–(5) and 6.

Making the application for permission

5.81 An application for permission to issue a writ of execution may be made in accordance with CPR Pt 23.¹ However, the application need not be served on the judgment debtor unless the court directs otherwise.²

¹ RSC Ord 46, r 4(1).
² RSC Ord 46, r 4(1).

5.82 The application should be supported by a witness statement or affidavit¹ containing the following information:

(a) the judgment or order to which the application relates;²

(b) in the case of a money judgment, the amount originally due under the judgment or order and the amount due at the date of the application (ie any post-judgment interest should be calculated to the date the application is issued);³

(c) where the judgment or order is over six years old, the reasons for the delay in enforcing the judgment or order;⁴

(d) where there has been a change in parties entitled or liable to execution, a description and explanation of this change;⁵

(e) where the judgment or order is against the assets of a deceased person and have come into the hands of his executors or administrators after the date of the judgment or order, a statement that a demand to satisfy the judgment or order was made on the person liable to satisfy it and he refused or failed to do so;⁶

(f) where under the judgment or order the judgment creditor is entitled to a remedy subject to the fulfilment of any condition which is alleged has been fulfilled, a statement that a demand to satisfy the judgment or order was made on the person liable to satisfy it and he refused or failed to do so;⁷ and

(g) any other information which is necessary to satisfy the court that the applicant is entitled to proceed to execution on the judgment or order and that the person against whom it is sought to issue execution is liable to execution on it.⁸

¹ RSC Ord 46, r 4(2).
² RSC Ord 46, r 4(2)(a).
³ RSC Ord 46, r 4(2)(a).
⁴ RSC Ord 46, r 4(2)(b).
⁵ RSC Ord 46, r 4(2)(c).
⁶ RSC Ord 46, r 4(2)(d).
⁷ RSC Ord 46, r 4(2)(d).
⁸ RSC Ord 46, r 4(2)(e).

Fee for application for permission to issue

5.83 Where the application for permission to issue is made without notice the fee is £50.¹ Where the court directs that the application must be made on notice, the fee is £100.²

1   The Civil Proceedings Fees Order 2004, SI 2004/3121, Sch 1, para 2.7.
2   The Civil Proceedings Fees Order 2004, SI 2004/3121, Sch 1, para 2.6.

Discretion to grant permission

5.84   The court has a discretion to grant permission to issue a writ of execution where permission is required.[1] At the hearing, the court can grant or refuse permission or may order a trial of any issue or question which is necessary to determine the rights of the parties.[2] Thus, for example, where new evidence which has come to light as to a judgment debtor's means is disputed, the court may order a 'mini-trial' to determine this issue.

1   RSC Ord 46, r 4(3) provides that the court hearing such application '*may*' grant permission.
2   RSC Ord 46, r 4(3).

Costs of the application for permission to issue

5.85   The court may impose such terms as to the costs of the application for permission to issue as it thinks just.[1] A successful judgment creditor should therefore seek an order to recover the costs incurred in connection with the application for permission to issue, particularly where a trial to determine issues between the parties has been necessary.

1   RSC Ord 46, r 4(3).

Further application possible if permission refused

5.86   If an application for permission to issue a writ of execution is refused, a second application is still possible. However, any subsequent application should not be granted unless it is founded on material which was not before the court on the first application.[1]

1   *WT Lamb & Sons v Rider* [1948] 2 KB 331 at 334, CA, per Scott LJ.

Order for permission lasts one year

5.87   An order granting permission to issue a writ of execution is valid for one year.[1] Where the writ is not issued within one year after the date of the order granting such permission, the order shall cease to have effect.[2] However, the expiration of this order does not preclude the making of a fresh order granting permission for the issue of a writ of fi fa.[3]

1   RSC Ord 46, r 2(3).
2   RSC Ord 46, r 2(3).
3   RSC Ord 46, r 2(3).

Even where permission is granted, judgment interest limited to six years

5.88   Where execution of a judgment is permitted after the expiry of six years from the date of judgment, the recovery of interest on the judgment debt is limited to six years' interest.[1]

1   *Lowsley v Forbes* [1999] 1 AC 329, HL. See further paras 7.102–7.112.

APPLICATION FOR A WRIT OF FI FA

5.89 The issue of a writ of fi fa is an administrative process and does not involve a judicial decision.[1] Issue of the writ takes place on its being sealed by a court officer. The judgment creditor will need to file the following documents at court:

(a) a request for issue of the writ (known as a praecipe);[2]
(b) a draft writ of fi fa;
(c) the judgment or order on which the writ is to issue;[3] and
(d) where the writ may not issue without permission of the court, the order granting such permission.[4]

The requirements for the praecipe and draft writ of fi fa are considered below.

1 Unless permission to issue is required.
2 RSC Ord 46, r 6(2).
3 Or an office copy: RSC Ord 46, r 6(4)(a)(i).
4 Or evidence that order has been granted: RSC Ord 46, r 6(4)(a)(ii).

Judgments against a state

5.90 In addition, where judgment or failure to acknowledge service has been entered against a state,[1] a writ can only be sealed on evidence that the state has been served in accordance with CPR 40.10[2] and that the judgment has taken effect.[3]

1 See State Immunity Act 1978, s 14 for the definition of 'state'.
2 Which provides that where a claimant obtains default judgment on a claim against a state where the state failed to file an acknowledgment of service, the judgment does not take effect until two months after the state has been served with a copy of the judgment and evidence in support of the application to enter default judgment.
3 RSC Ord 46, r 6(4)(a)(iii).

Which court?

5.91 The documents listed in para 5.89 (and 5.90 where appropriate) should be filed in the 'appropriate office.' This is defined in RSC Ord 46, r 6 as one of the following:

(a) where the proceedings in which execution is to issue are in a District Registry, that Registry;
(b) where the proceedings are in the Principal Registry of the Family Division, that Registry;
(c) where the proceedings are Admiralty proceedings or commercial proceedings which are not in a District Registry, the Admiralty and Commercial Registry;
(d) where proceedings are in the Chancery Division, Chancery Chambers; and
(e) in any other case, the Central Office of the Supreme Court.

Accordingly, the appropriate office for Queen's Bench Division proceedings is the Central Office of the Supreme Court.

5.92 Both the High Court and county court have jurisdiction to order the seizure and sale of the judgment debtor's goods.[1] Where the judgment creditor seeks to enforce a county court judgment for £5,000 or more wholly or partly by execution against goods then the judgment must be enforced in the High Court.[2] The £5,000 upper limit is curious because ordinarily only claims with a financial value over £15,000 can be made in the High Court.[3]

1   CA 2003, Sch 7 and CCA 1984, s 85.
2   High Court and County Courts Jurisdiction Order 1991, SI 1991/724, art 8(1)(a). Unless the judgment was made in proceedings arising out of an agreement regulated by the Consumer Credit Act 1974, in which case they shall be enforced only in the county court: High Court and County Courts Jurisdiction Order 1991, SI 1991/724, art 8(1A).
3   High Court and County Courts Jurisdiction Order 1991, SI 1991/724, art 4A.

5.93   Where the judgment creditor seeks to enforce a county court judgment for less than £600 wholly or partly by execution against goods, it may only be enforced in the county court.[1] Where the judgment creditor seeks to enforce a county court judgment for amounts greater than £600 but less than £5,000 wholly or partly by execution against goods, it can be enforced in either the High Court or county court.[2]

1   High Court and County Courts Jurisdiction Order 1991, SI 1991/724, art 8(1)(b).
2   High Court and County Courts Jurisdiction Order 1991, SI 1991/724, art 8(1)(c).

5.94   The rules relating to transfer of proceedings between the High Court and the county court are dealt with in Chapter 1.

Praecipe

5.95   A praecipe[1] is a request for issue of a writ of execution containing particulars of the writ requested and must be filed with the court.[2] For a writ of fi fa the praecipe takes the form of PF 86.[3] The praecipe must be signed by or on behalf of the judgment creditor's solicitor or, if the judgment creditor is acting in person, by him.[4]

1   Defined in the *Oxford English Dictionary* (ed J A Simpson and E S C Weiner, 2nd edn, 1989) as: '[a] note containing particulars of a writ which must be filed with the officer of the Court from which the writ issues, by the party asking for the writ, or by his solicitor.'
2   RSC Ord 46, r 6(2).
3   This states: 'Seal a writ of fieri facias directed to the sheriff of (County) against the (party) (name and address) on a judgment [or order] dated (date) for the sum of £ debt and £ costs and interest. Endorsed to levy £ and interest at (insert rate) per annum from (date) and costs of execution.' The form has not yet been updated to refer to an enforcement officer and should be amended accordingly.
4   RSC Ord 46, r 6(3).

Judgments or orders expressed in foreign currency

5.96   Where the judgment or order is expressed in a foreign currency the praecipe and the draft writ of fi fa[1] will require amendment. The Queen's Bench Guide provides guidance as to how this should be done.[2] This derives from Practice Direction (Judgment: Foreign Currency)[3] and should also apply in the Chancery Division.

1   See para 5.106. This applies to English judgments expressed in a foreign currency. Note that where enforcement of a foreign registered judgment is sought, form PF 63 should be used.
2   Paragraph 11.2.4.
3   [1976] 1 WLR 83 at 85–86.

5.97 The praecipe should be endorsed with the following certificate:

'I/We certify that the rate current in London for the purchase of [state the unit of foreign currency in which the judgment is expressed] *at the close of business on* [state the nearest preceding date to the date of issue of the writ of fieri facias] was [state exchange rate] *to the £ sterling and at this rate the sum of* [state amount of the judgment debt in the foreign currency] *amounts to £* [state the sterling amount of the judgment debt].'

5.98 The rate to be used is not specified but the closing rates from the Financial Times and Reuters are commonly used in commercial cases.

Draft writ of fi fa

5.99 The draft writ of fi fa should be prepared using the most appropriate of the following Practice Forms:[1]

Form	Type of writ of fi fa
PF 53	Writ of fieri facias
PF 54	Writ of fieri facias on order for costs
PF 56	Writ of fieri facias after levy of part
PF 57	Writ of fieri facias against personal representatives
PF 58	Writ of fieri facias de bonis ecclesiasticis
PF 62	Writ of fieri facias to enforce Northern Irish or Scottish judgment
PF 63	Writ of fieri facias to enforce foreign registered judgment

---

1   RSC Ord 45, r 12.

5.100 Form PF 53 is most likely to be used in the context of commercial enforcement. Where judgment has been given but costs remain to be assessed, the judgment creditor may wish to levy for the judgment debt and issue a separate writ of fi fa for his costs once assessed. Where the judgment creditor simply wishes to recover quantified costs (for example, where costs have been awarded in relation to a non-money judgment), PF 54 should be used. If goods belonging to the judgment debtor have been seized in partial satisfaction of a judgment debt under an earlier writ of fi fa and a further writ is sought, PF 56 should be used. The date of the earlier writ and details of the enforcement officer to whom it was addressed should be provided on the form. Where a foreign judgment has been registered for enforcement in England and Wales, PF 63 requires that details of that judgment and the statute pursuant to which it was registered[1] be provided.

---

1   That is under the Administration of Justice Act 1920, the Foreign Judgments (Reciprocal Enforcement) Act 1933 or the Civil Jurisdiction and Judgments Act 1982. See further Chapter 1.

5.101   Very little of form PF 53 requires amendment. The title heading should be completed to match the title of the original action and where the judgment has been transferred to the High Court from the county court there is space to insert the date of the Certificate of transfer. A writ of fi fa is issued in the name of the monarch and contains an endorsement to this effect.[1] The Lord Chancellor acts as witness to the writ of fi fa. The full name of the current Lord High Chancellor should be inserted.[2]

[1]   Form PF 53 states: 'ELIZABETH THE SECOND, by the Grace of God, of the United Kingdom of Great Britain and Northern Ireland and of Our other realms and territories Queen, Head of the Commonwealth, Defender of the Faith.'
[2]   How long this provision will continue remains to be seen in light of the government's proposals to abolish the post of Lord Chancellor. Constitutional Reform: A Supreme Court for the United Kingdom (July 2003).

5.102   The writ should be addressed to an individual enforcement officer or the enforcement officers for a particular district of England and Wales. The choice of enforcement officer is considered further below in paras 5.112–5.118.

5.103   The schedule to the draft writ sets out the date and amount of the judgment debt together with any costs and interest less any amounts received by the judgment creditor. If the judgment has been transferred from the county court to the High Court, interest should be calculated at the county court rate from the date of the original county court judgment until the date of the certificate of transfer and the amount inserted at paragraph 5 of the schedule. Post-judgment interest should also be inserted in section A of the schedule (or post-certificate of transfer interest in the case of transferred county court judgments). In the High Court this is generally at 8% per annum pursuant to the Judgments Act 1838, s 17 and accrues from the date of the judgment on the amount of the sub-total. (Judgment interest is considered in detail in Chapter 7).

5.104   Any payments received by the judgment debtor before the issue of the writ should be entered in paragraph 6 of the schedule so that the amount to be levied is reduced accordingly. If this is not done, it could constitute excessive execution.[1] The CPR also requires that any amounts received after the issue of the writ should immediately be notified to the enforcement officer in writing.[2] As a precaution, the enforcement officer should also be notified by telephone to ensure that he does not levy excessive execution in the meantime.

[1]   See paras 5.206–5.210.
[2]   PD 70, para 7.2.

Address(es) for enforcement

5.105   The judgment creditor should set out in the draft writ the address or addresses which the enforcement officer should visit in order to levy execution. An enforcement officer named in a writ can seize the judgment debtor's goods wherever they are located in England and Wales and this includes at the premises of third parties. Completion of the draft writ is the opportunity for the judgment creditor to direct the enforcement officer to the location of the judgment debtor's assets. The judgment creditor should set out all known premises where goods of the judgment debtor can be found, if necessary supplemented by a covering letter giving further detail. If the writ of fi fa is endorsed with an inaccurate address for seizure of the judgment debtor's goods and the endorsement misleads the enforcement officer into seizing goods belonging to a third party, the judgment creditor will be personally liable for trespass for the wrongful seizure.[1] (However, if the endorsement is correct and the enforcement officer seizes goods which later turn out to belong to a third party, the judgment creditor will not be liable for the wrongful seizure and the enforcement officer alone will be liable for trespass.[2]) Care must therefore be taken in completing the endorsement and the judgment creditor should be certain that goods belonging to the judgment debtor are located at the addresses given. Such information could be obtained from the judgment debtor in Part 71 proceedings (see Chapter 2).

1   *Marris v Salberg* (1889) LR 22 QBD 614, CA (where the solicitor incorrectly stated on the writ of fi fa that the debtor resided at a certain address, which was in fact not his address but that of his father).
2   *Condy v Blaiberg* (1891) 7 TLR 424.

Judgments or orders expressed in a foreign currency

5.106 Where the judgment or order has been expressed in a foreign currency, the schedule to the writ of fi fa should also be amended to insert a new paragraph immediately following that stating the amount of the judgment or order in the foreign currency (ie immediately after paragraph 2 of the schedule in form PF 53) as follows:

'3. Amount of the sterling equivalent as appears from the certificate endorsed on the praecipe for issue of the writ £ [ ].'

5.107 There are special rules concerning judgment interest on judgments expressed in a foreign currency which are considered in Chapter 7.

Return

5.108 The writ also commands the enforcement officer to indorse the writ with a statement of the manner in which he has executed it immediately after execution and to send a copy of the statement to the judgment creditor. This is known as a 'return' and provides the judgment creditor with information as to the steps taken by the enforcement officer.

Fee for the issue of writ of fi fa

5.109 The court fee for issue of a writ of fi fa is £50.[1]

1   The Civil Proceedings Fees Order 2004, SI 2004/3121, Sch 1, para 6.1.

Issue of a writ of fi fa

5.110 The writ is issued when it is sealed by a court officer of the appropriate office.[1] The writ will not be sealed unless the documents listed in para 5.89 (and 5.90

where appropriate) have been produced to the court.[2] In addition, the court officer authorised to seal the writ must be satisfied that the period (if any) specified in the judgment for payment of the judgment debt has expired. Every writ of fi fa will bear the date of the day on which it was issued.[3] The court seal will indicate the date of issue.

[1] RSC Ord 46, r 6(1). See para 5.91.
[2] RSC Ord 46, r 6(4)(a).
[3] RSC Ord 47, r 6(5).

Fixed costs

5.111 Where the court grants a writ of fi fa, the judgment creditor will only be entitled to recover his fixed costs.[1] The amount of fixed costs allowed are any court fee[2] and a fixed sum in respect of the costs of execution of £51.75.[3] Where an application for permission to issue a writ of fi fa is required the costs of this application can also be claimed (see para 5.85).

[1] CPR 45.2(1)(c).
[2] RSC Ord 62, Appendix 3, Part III, para 2A.
[3] RSC Ord 62, Appendix 3, Part III, para 5.

DELIVERY TO AN ENFORCEMENT OFFICER

5.112 The judgment creditor should deliver the sealed writ to an enforcement officer for execution. CA 2003 divides up England and Wales into districts.[1] The districts correspond with the postal areas for England and Wales and are prescribed by statutory instrument.[2] A writ of execution issued from the High Court may be directed:[3]

'(a) if only one enforcement officer is assigned to the district in which the writ is to be executed, to that officer;

(b) if two or more enforcement officers are assigned to that district, to those officers collectively; or

(c) to a named enforcement officer who, whether or not assigned to that district, has undertaken to execute the writ.'

[1] CA 2003, Sch 7, para 1.
[2] High Court Enforcement Officers Regulations 2004, SI 2004/400, reg 3 and Sch 1. Previously, a sheriff was confined to his 'bailiwick' which referred to areas broadly correlating to pre-1974 county boundaries.
[3] CA 2003, Sch 7, para 3(1).

Abolition of bailiwicks

5.113 CA 2003 ended the regional monopoly formerly enjoyed by sheriffs since the effect of the above provisions is to grant a judgment creditor complete freedom to use any authorised enforcement officer, irrespective of the district to which he is assigned, provided the enforcement officer agrees to enforce the writ. It was formerly the case that a sheriff could only enforce writs of fi fa in his own county or 'bailiwick.' The change in the law was intended to widen the choice of enforcement officers available to judgment creditors and increase competition.[1] In the case of a judgment debtor with assets in more than one district, either an enforcement officer authorised in all those districts should be chosen or an individual enforcement officer who is willing to enforce in all the required districts.[2]

[1]   Effective Enforcement White Paper, March 2003, para 48.
[2]   Some enforcement officers are authorised in all districts and have a nationwide network of agents. A further consequence of the abolition of the bailiwick system is that an enforcement officer, unlike his predecessor the sheriff, has no duty to appoint a deputy resident in London.

Selecting an enforcement officer

5.114   The nature of commercial enforcement work means that seizure of large, delicate or highly valuable assets may be required. Some associations of enforcement officers, such as Sherforce, have nationwide coverage and a network of specialist contractors available who can remove and store large, delicate or highly valuable assets. There are, however, other service providers and the liberalisation of the territorial boundaries of enforcement officers may well see the emergence of a number of large commercial operations. Where the seizure is likely to be particularly specialist, the judgment creditor and his advisers should consider which enforcement officer is best resourced to meet the particular demands of the case. Directories containing details of all current enforcement officers, the districts to which they have been assigned and the addresses to which writs of execution should be sent are available for inspection at the Royal Courts of Justice, the district registries of the High Court, and county courts.[1] The list can also be downloaded from the Department for Constitutional Affairs' website.[2]

[1]   High Court Enforcement Officers Regulations 2004, SI 2004/400, reg 14.
[2]   www.dca.gov.uk/enforcement/enforcedir.pdf.

To allocate or not to allocate?

5.115   The judgment creditor can either direct the writ of fi fa to a particular enforcement officer or specify a district of England and Wales for allocation. Where the execution relates to specialist or high-value assets (such as paintings or a yacht), the judgment creditor will probably wish to choose an individual enforcement officer with appropriate expertise and resources in seizing and, where necessary, removing and storing such goods. However, where the work is more routine, he may be content for the writ simply to be allocated to an enforcement officer in the appropriate district of England and Wales.

Options where an individual enforcement officer is not chosen

5.116   Where an individual enforcement officer is not selected, there are two options for allocation.[1] For a small fee[2] the judgment creditor can send the original judgment[3] or even a completed writ of fi fa to the Sheriffs Lodgment Centre which will issue the writ and send it to an appropriate enforcement officer for execution. The Sheriffs Lodgment Centre will then send the writ to one of its own nationwide network of enforcement officers. The Sheriffs Lodgment Centre is a commercially run enterprise and gives the judgment creditor greater control over the process through services such as a secure online progress monitor known as 'Track-O-Meter' (which allows the progress of execution to be tracked, questions to be asked and further addresses for levy to be provided). Updates can also be obtained by telephone from the Sheriffs Lodgment Centre's call centre.

1   Note that form PF 53 states that where a judgment creditor simply directs the writ to the enforcement officers authorised for a particular district of England and Wales, the writ should be sent to the National Information Centre for allocation. The Sheriffs Lodgment Centre is an alternative to this.
2   Details of the fees are available on the Sheriffs Lodgment Centre website. See the Appendix to this chapter for contact details.
3   Or completed writ of fi fa where the judgment creditor wishes to carry out this step himself.

5.117   Alternatively, a judgment creditor may send the sealed writ to the state-run National Information Centre for Enforcement, which will automatically allocate it to an enforcement officer for the relevant district using the 'cab rank principle'. There is no fee charged by the National Information Centre for Enforcement.

5.118   Contact details for both the National Information Centre for Enforcement and the Sheriffs Lodgment Centre are set out in the Appendix to this chapter.

Authorisation of enforcement officers

5.119   The changes introduced by CA 2003 not only renamed sheriffs as enforcement officers but also changed the appointment arrangements which had been in place since the Sheriffs Act 1887. An enforcement officer must now be authorised to act as such by the Lord Chancellor or a person acting on his behalf.[1] Enforcement officers are often solicitors although this is not a legal requirement.[2]

1   CA 2003, Sch 7, para 2(1).
2   Keith, Podevin and Sandbrook *The Execution of Sheriffs' Warrants* (2nd edn, 1995) p 4. The enforcement officer will usually have a number of enforcement agents who physically execute writs on his behalf (see para 5.9).

5.120   Regulations now govern the conditions to be met by individuals seeking to be authorised as enforcement officers and the circumstances in which such authorisation can be terminated.[1] An enforcement officer must be an individual.[2] He must make a written application for authorisation to act as an enforcement officer, listing detailed information about himself and about his application (including his relevant experience, business plan, relevant insurance polices, membership of professional bodies and policies in relation to the selection and employment of staff). Certain matters will disqualify an individual from acting as an enforcement officer.[3]

1   High Court Enforcement Officers Regulations 2004, SI 2004/400.
2   CA 2003, Sch 7, para 2(1).
3   Namely: conviction for a serious criminal offence, unpaid fines, an unsatisfied court judgment, an undischarged bankruptcy, a recent disqualification from acting as a company director, or past or present involvement in any business relating to the purchase or sale of debts: High Court Enforcement Officers Regulations 2004, SI 2004/400, para 4.

5.121 Once an individual has been authorised to act as an enforcement officer he remains under a continuing duty to meet certain requirements, such as completing required training, holding relevant insurance policies, maintaining a separate bank account into which monies recovered are to be paid in and out, and producing annual audited accounts.[1] The authorisation to act as an enforcement officer may be terminated at any time by the Lord Chancellor.[2]

[1] High Court Enforcement Officers Regulations 2004, SI 2004/400, para 8.
[2] On the grounds set out in High Court Enforcement Officers Regulations 2004, SI 2004/400, para 12(2).

5.122 These appointment provisions could be the subject of yet further change if the proposals in the 2003 Effective Enforcement White Paper to set up a statutory body regulating the licensing and conduct of enforcement agents come into force.

VALIDITY AND RENEWAL OF WRIT

5.123 Once issued, a writ of fi fa is valid for 12 months from the date of issue.[1] Where it has not been completely executed by that time, the court may from time to time order that it be extended for a period of 12 months at any one time.[2] The court also has a discretion to extend a writ after it has expired.[3]

[1] RSC Ord 46, r 8(1).
[2] RSC Ord 46, r 8(2).
[3] RSC Ord 46, r 8(2).

5.124 The priority of a writ (see paras 5.306-5.312) that has been extended in this way is determined by reference to the date on which it was originally delivered to the enforcement officer.[1] The court will consider the effect on priority when deciding whether to allow an extension:[2]

'In such a situation a court dealing with an application for extension would no doubt consider whether it was just that a creditor who had allowed his writ to expire without application should be permitted to retain his priority, for it is necessary to remember that priorities are a matter of equity. That priority is not necessarily lost by a temporary invalidity of a writ is, however, clear.'

[1] RSC Ord 46, r 8(4).
[2] *Bankers Trust Co v Galadari* [1987] 1 QB 222 at 226-227.

5.125 Before an extended writ is executed, it must be re-sealed by the court office with the date of the order extending its validity. Alternatively, the judgment creditor must serve a sealed notice on the enforcement officer to whom the writ is directed to inform him that the extension order has been made.[1] If a sealed notice is used, Form No 71 should be used.[2]

[1] RSC Ord 46, r 8(3).
[2] RSC Ord 46, r 8(3).

Interpleader automatically extends a writ

5.126 Where an interpleader application is brought (see paras 5.276–5.296), the validity of the writ of fi fa will be automatically extended until 12 months from the conclusion of the interpleader application.[1]

1   RSC Ord 46, r 8(6).

EFFECT OF A WRIT OF FI FA

5.127 The effect of a writ of fi fa on the judgment debtor's goods is set out in CA 2003, Sch 7, para 8, which provides as follows:

'(1) Subject to sub-paragraph (2), the writ binds the property in the goods of the execution debtor from the time when the writ is received by the person who is under a duty to endorse it.

(2) The writ does not prejudice the title to any goods of the execution debtor acquired by a person in good faith and for valuable consideration.

(3) Sub-paragraph (2) does not apply if the person acquiring goods of the execution debtor had notice, at the time of the acquisition, that—

(a) the writ, or

(b) any other writ by virtue of which the goods of the execution debtor might be seized or attached, had been received by the person who was under a duty to endorse it but had not been executed.

(4) Sub-paragraph (2) does not apply if the person acquiring goods of the execution debtor had notice, at the time of the acquisition, that—

(a) an application for the issue of a warrant of execution against the goods of the execution debtor had been made to the district judge of a county court, and

(b) the warrant issued on the application—

(i) remained unexecuted in the hands of the district judge of the court from which it was issued, or

(ii) had been sent for execution to, and received by, the district judge of another county court and remained unexecuted in the hands of that district judge.

(5) In sub-paragraph (1) "property" means the general property in goods (and not merely a special property).

(6) For the purposes of sub-paragraph (2) a thing shall be treated as done in good faith if it is in fact done honestly (whether it is done negligently or not).

(7) Any reference in this paragraph to the goods of the execution debtor includes anything else of his that may lawfully be seized in execution.'

5.128 This provision has a long history. It originates from the Statute of Frauds 1677, s 16[1] as later modified by the Mercantile Law Amendment Act 1856 (which added the good faith purchaser defence).[2] These provisions were replaced by the Sale of Goods Act 1893, s 26[3] and then SCA 1981, s 138[4] which was itself replaced by CA 2003, Sch 7, para 8. The similarity in the wording of earlier versions of the statutory provision and the modern form means that cases interpreting the statutory predecessors of CA 2003, Sch 7, para 8 remain relevant.

¹ Which provided that: '[A] Writ of Fieri facias or other Writ of Execution shall *bind the Property of the Goods* against whom such Writ of Execution is sued forth, but from the Time that such Writ shall be delivered to the Sheriff, Under-Sheriff or Coroners, to be executed: And for the better Manifestation of the said Time, the Sheriff, Under-Sheriff and Coroners, their Deputies and Agents, shall upon the Receipt of any such Writ, (without Fee for doing the same) endorse upon the Back thereof the Day of the Month and Year whereon he or they receive the same.' (Emphasis added) Repealed by the Sale of Goods Act 1893, s 60 and Schedule.

² Which provided that: 'No Writ of Fieri facias or other Writ of Execution, and no Writ of Attachement against the Goods of a Debtor, shall prejudice the Title to such Goods acquired by any Person bonâ fide and for a valuable Consideration before the actual Seizure or Attachment thereof by virtue of such Writ; provided such person had not, at the Time when he acquired such Title, Notice that such Writ, or any other Writ by virtue of which the Goods of such Owner might be seized or attached, had been delivered to and remained unexecuted in the Hands of the Sheriff, Under Sheriff, or Coroner.' (Emphasis added)

³ Which provided that: 'A writ of fieri facias or other writ of execution against goods *shall bind the property in the goods* of the execution debtor as from the time when the writ is delivered to the sheriff to be executed; and, for the better manifestation of such time, it shall be the duty of the sheriff, without fee, upon the receipt of any such writ to endorse upon the back thereof the hour, day, month, and year when he received the same. Provided that no such writ shall prejudice the title to such goods acquired by any person in good faith and for valuable consideration, unless such person had at the time when he acquired his title notice that such writ or any other writ by virtue of which the goods of the execution debtor might be seized or attached had been delivered to and remained unexecuted in the hands of the sheriff.' (Emphasis added) In s 62(1) 'property' was defined as 'the general property in goods, and not merely a special property'. Repealed by SCA 1981, s 152 and Sch 7.

⁴ Repealed by CA 2003, s 109(1) and Sch 8, para 264. The wording is almost identical to that in CA 2003.

Writ 'binds the property in the goods of the execution debtor'

5.129   The fact that a writ of fi fa 'binds the property in the goods of the execution debtor' refers to the enforcement officer's legal right to seize sufficient of the judgment debtor's goods to satisfy the amount specified in the writ following his receipt of it.[1] Although the judgment debtor continues to own the goods until any sale by the enforcement officer[2] and can legally deal with the goods,[3] if the judgment debtor transfers his goods after receipt of the writ by an enforcement officer, the goods will be taken subject to the enforcement officer's continuing right to seize them.[4] The enforcement officer's right to seize will apply to any subsequent transferee other than a purchaser in good faith for value[5] (see further paras 5.133-5.139).

¹ *Lloyds and Scottish Finance Ltd v Modern Cars and Caravans (Kingston) Ltd* [1966] 1 QB 764 at 781, per Edmund Davies J (decided under the Sale of Goods Act 1893, s 26).

² *Payne v Drewe* (1804) 4 East 522 at 541; *Giles v Grover* (1832) 9 Bing 127 at 138-139, 141, 158-160, 176-177, 208, 263, 280 and 284; *Lucas v Nockells* (1833) 10 Bing 151 at 182; *Samuel v Duke* (1838) 3 M & W 623 at 628-629; *Woodland v Fuller* (1840) 11 AD & El 859 at 866-868; *Re Davies ex p Williams* (1872) 7 Ch App 314 at 317; *Lloyds and Scottish Finance Ltd v Modern Cars and Caravans (Kingston) Ltd* [1966] 1 QB 764 at 775-776 (all decided under previous legislation).

³ *Re Davies, ex p Williams* (1872) 7 Ch App 314 at 317.

⁴ *Payne v Drewe* (1804) 4 East 522 at 538-540; *Lucas v Nockells* (1833) 10 Bing 157 at 182; *Samuel v Duke* (1838) 3 M & W 623 at 628-629; *Woodland v Fuller* (1840) 11 AD & El 859 at 866-868; *McPherson v Temiskaming Lumber Company* [1913] AC 145 at 155-156, PC (construing the Ontario Execution Act which was similar to the Sale of Goods Act 1893, s 26 in force in England at the time); *Lloyds and Scottish Finance Ltd v Modern Cars and Caravans (Kingston) Ltd* [1966] 1 QB 764 at 780-781.

5   See eg *Payne v Drewe* (1804) 4 East 522 at 538 (construing the Statute of Frauds Act 1677,
     s 16); *Re Cooper* [1958] 1 Ch 922 at 928-929 (construing the Sale of Goods Act 1893, s 26)
     and *Lloyds and Scottish Finance Ltd v Modern Cars and Caravans (Kingston) Ltd* [1966]
     1 QB 764 at 780–781 (construing the Sale of Goods Act 1893, s 26).

5.130   The binding effect of the writ is expressed to extend to the 'goods of the
execution debtor'. The term 'goods' includes 'anything else of [the execution debtor]
that may lawfully be seized in execution'[1] and thus extends to 'money, banknotes,
bills of exchange, promissory notes, bonds, specialties or securities for money
belonging to the execution debtor', which are also liable to seizure by an enforcement
officer.[2]

1   CA 2003, Sch 7, para 8(7).
2   CA 2003, Sch 7, para 9(2). Under previous legislation the separate treatment of goods to
     money and other choses in action lead the court in *Johnson v Pickering* [1908] 1 KB 1, CA
     to hold that money was to be treated differently from goods and that the money was only
     actually bound upon seizure as opposed to the time of receipt by an enforcement officer.
     This is no longer the case.

'Received by the person who is under a duty to endorse it'

5.131   The writ will bind the property of the judgment debtor from the time it is
received by the person who is under a duty to endorse it, ie the enforcement officer.[1]
An enforcement officer is under a duty to endorse the writ as soon as possible after
receiving it.[2] Where the writ is directed to two or more enforcement officers (see para
5.112), the endorsement will be made by the individual who is responsible for allocating
its execution to one of those officers as soon as possible after receiving it.[3] A writ is
endorsed simply by writing the date and time that it was received on the back.[4] An
enforcement officer cannot charge for endorsing a writ.[5] The process of endorsement
is important not only for determining the time and date at which the writ binds the
goods of the judgment debtor but also in determining the priority of a number of writs
issued on the same day (see paras 5.306–5.312).

1   CA 2003, Sch 7, para 8(1).
2   CA 2003, Sch 7, para 7(1).
3   CA 2003, Sch 7, para 7(2).
4   CA 2003, Sch 7, para 7(4).
5   See CA 2003, Sch 7, para 7(5).

5.132   The receipt of the writ of fi fa by an enforcement officer is not an event of
which, in ordinary circumstances, the judgment debtor or indeed a third party is likely
to be aware.[1] For this reason, the enforcement officer will often send a notice to the
judgment debtor informing him of the writ shortly after receipt. This serves two
purposes. First, it informs the judgment debtor that the goods are bound by the writ
and, secondly, it is intended to spur the judgment debtor into paying the judgment
debt before the enforcement officer pays a visit. However, there is no legal obligation
on the enforcement officer to make this notification and if it suspected that the notice
will simply tip off the judgment debtor to conceal his goods or dispose of them, the
enforcement officer should be asked not to send the notice and to levy execution as
soon as possible.

1   *Gladstone v Padwick* (1871) LR 6 Exch 203 at 210.

Good faith purchasers

5.133 Clearly, some safeguards are required to protect purchasers who have acquired goods from a judgment debtor having no idea that a writ of fi fa has been issued against the judgment debtor and received by an enforcement officer. Thus where a party has in good faith and for valuable consideration purchased goods from a judgment debtor, his title to those goods will not be prejudiced by the existence of the writ unless he had notice at the time of the acquisition that a writ had been received by an enforcement officer and remained unexecuted.[1] For the purposes of this provision, 'in good faith' means honestly (whether or not done negligently).[2]

1   CA 2003, Sch 7, para 8(3), or alternatively, where he knew that there was an unexecuted county court warrant of execution against the judgment debtor's goods, CA 2003, Sch 7, para 8(4).
2   CA 2003, Sch 7, para 8(7).

5.134 However, the protection afforded to good faith purchasers is narrower than it first seems because it only applies where the writ 'has not been executed'. This is vividly illustrated by the facts of the leading modern case of *Lloyds and Scottish Finance Ltd v Modern Cars and Caravans (Kingston)* Ltd.[1] Although that case was decided applying the Sale of Goods Act 1893, s 26 the relevant provisions of that Act are not materially different to those contained in CA 2003, Sch 7, para 8.[2]

1   [1966] 1 QB 764.
2   See para 5.128, n 3.

5.135 In *Lloyds and Scottish Finance Ltd* the judgment debtor owned a caravan in which he lived with his family. A sheriff's officer attended the caravan to execute a writ of fi fa. The sheriff's officer was admitted to the caravan, read the warrant and explained the reason for his visit. The judgment debtor's wife claimed that she owned the caravan and its contents and signed a form of claim to that effect. Since it was inappropriate to remain in possession, the judgment debtor was asked to sign a walking possession agreement, which he refused to do. The judgment debtor and his wife were told not to move the caravan and were handed a card bearing the name of the sheriff's officer's employers on which the sheriff's officer wrote on the reverse the title of the action and with the words 'We hold a High Court Execution against you.' This was held to amount as a matter of law to seizure of the caravan.[1]

1   What amounts in law to seizure is considered further at paras 5.192–5.199.

5.136 The sheriff's officer returned a further six times to check the caravan was still there. On the seventh visit, two months after the first visit, he found the caravan had disappeared. In fact the judgment debtor had sold the caravan to the defendants, who were caravan dealers, the day before. Shortly afterwards the defendants sold the caravan to the plaintiffs, a hire-purchase company, who immediately let it out on hire-purchase. A few days before that sale, the defendants had learned from the sheriff's officers of the existence and delivery of the writ of fi fa against the judgment debtor. The sheriff's officers subsequently traced the whereabouts of the caravan, took possession from the lessee under the hire-purchase contract, and sold it paying the proceeds to the judgment creditors.

5.137 The plaintiffs sued the defendant for breach of warranty because they had stated in the contract of sale that their title to the caravan was unencumbered. On the facts of the case, the loss fell with the defendants because the plaintiffs succeeded in their claim for breach of warranty against them. However, as part of their defence, the defendants had contended that they had acquired good title free of the sheriff's right of seizure relying on the proviso in the Sale of Goods Act 1893, s 26 that a writ would not prejudice the title of a good faith purchaser for valuable consideration unless at the time of acquisition the purchaser had notice that such a writ *'had been delivered to and remained unexecuted in the hands of the sheriff'*. The essence of their contention was that because there had been no payment of the judgment debt by the judgment debtor or sale by the Sheriff consequent to the writ, the writ remained 'unexecuted'. Edmund Davies J rejected this contention:[1]

> 'I propose to deal with this submission briefly. The proviso must of necessity be limited in its operation to the ambit of the section which it qualifies. When, by the opening words of the section, it is provided that "A writ of fieri facias... shall bind 'the property in the goods of the execution debtor...," this simply means that on delivery of the writ the sheriff acquires a legal right to seize sufficient of the debtor's goods to satisfy the amount specified in the writ (Samuel v Duke). The proviso, accordingly, does no more than protect a purchaser of the goods against that right of seizure if the stated conditions are fulfilled. But it has no scope for operation where an actual seizure of the debtor's goods has already been effected; and where this has occurred, it is immaterial whether or not the purchaser from the debtor had notice of the seizure, or even of the writ. Furthermore, by its wording the proviso relates only to a writ "by virtue of which the goods of the execution debtor might be seized," and where such an essential step in execution as actual seizure has already been effected, it is, I hold, impossible to regard the writ as one which still "remained unexecuted in the hands of the sheriff."[2] In my judgment, accordingly, the defendants are not saved by the proviso.'

[1]   [1966] 1 QB 764 at 780–781.
[2]   CA 2003, Sch 7, para 8(3) now reads 'had been received by the person who was under a duty to endorse it but had not been executed'.

5.138   In summary, where an enforcement officer has received but not executed a writ of fi fa by seizure, a person who acquires those goods in good faith for valuable consideration and without notice of the writ will acquire good title. However, where the writ of fi fa has been executed by seizure, no person can purchase the goods without them being liable to further seizure by the enforcement officer.

5.139   The fact that 'execution' often involves little more than a visit from an enforcement officer and a notional seizure with the judgment debtor being left in possession of the goods creates difficulties for a purchaser of goods. If the judgment debtor does not tell the purchaser that execution has been levied by an enforcement officer, the purchaser has no way of knowing that execution has taken place. In such circumstances he may acquire the judgment debtor's goods entirely innocently and pay full price for them, only to find that the enforcement officer is able to seize them and sell them. The fact that the purchaser may have a claim for breach of express or implied warranty as to title[1] against the judgment debtor may provide little comfort faced with an impecunious judgment debtor. However, this position perhaps seems less harsh when it is remembered that the general rule at common law is *nemo dat quod non habet.* [2]

1 See the Sale of Goods Act 1979, s 12 (implied terms about title).
2 No one can give what he does not have.

The nature of the judgment creditor's interest after seizure

5.140 The nature of the judgment creditors' right or interest in the goods after seizure has taken place has been described in some cases as a form of security. Initially this was in the context of the Bankruptcy Act 1869 but has subsequently been interpreted as a more general principle:[1]

'It is very true that the property in goods seized under a fi. fa. remains in the execution debtor until sale: *Giles v Grover.*[2] But it is no less true that after seizure and before sale the execution creditor is as regards those goods in the position of a secured creditor: see *ex parte Williams*[3] and *Slater v Pinder.*[4] He had a legal right as against the execution debtor – ie owner of the goods – to have the goods sold and to be paid out of the proceeds of sale.'

1 *Re Clarke* [1898] 1 Ch 336 at 339, CA, per Lindley MR. See also *McPherson v Temiskaming Lumber Co Ltd* [1913] AC 145 at 155, PC and *The James W Elwell* [1921] P 351 at 369–370.
2 (1832) 9 Bing 128.
3 (1872) 7 Ch App 314. The court was construing the Bankruptcy Act 1869, s 12. Sir G Mellish LJ stated at 316–317: 'The effect of seizure, therefore, is, that upon seizure the sheriff ceases to have merely a right to seize, and acquires a qualified property in the goods like that of a factor who is under advances, and from whom the goods may be claimed back on payment of those advances. This qualified property differs from a mortgage, inasmuch as at law the mortgagee has an absolute title to the property, and the title of the debtor is only in equity; but in this case there is at law a qualified property with a power of sale. The Court of Exchequer held, in *Slates v. Pinder*, that when the goods have been seized by the sheriff, the creditor has a security upon them. Are we to hold that he has a security upon them before they are seized? ... A mere right to seize property cannot properly be called a security.'
4 (1871) LR 6 Exch 228. The court was construing the Bankruptcy Act 1869, s 12 and held that a 'creditor holding a security' included an execution creditor who has seized before an act of bankruptcy has been committed.

5.141 The exact nature of a judgment creditor's security interest in the goods once they have been seized is a matter of some debate[1] although in *Peck v Craighead* it was held to be a security right 'not unlike a lien'.[2] Whatever the proper legal characterisation, the interest allows an enforcement officer who has effected seizure to follow the seized goods into the hands of third parties who have purchased the goods after seizure, retake possession and sell those goods in order to pay the judgment creditor (though in certain circumstances these rights will be defeated by a judgment debtor's insolvency) (see paras 5.313–5.326).

1 See eg Walton 'Execution Creditors – (Almost) the Last Rights in Insolvency' (2003) 32 CLWR 179.
2 [1995] 1 BCLC 337 at 341, per M E Mann QC sitting as a deputy judge of the High Court.

Other exceptions to the binding nature of a writ of fi fa

5.142   The circumstances in which the judgment debtor's insolvency will defeat the binding effect of a writ of fi fa are considered in paras 5.313–5.326. In addition, Crown writs will take priority over the binding effect of a writ of fi fa issued by a subject.

Crown priority

5.143   The Crown can use any method of enforcement available to a subject.[1] Accordingly, the Crown may use any writ of execution, including a writ of fieri facias, to enforce a judgment debt.[2] Where it does so, the Crown writ will take priority over the writ of a subject unless the judgment debtor's goods have been seized and sold, in which case the subject may retain the proceeds.[3] It follows that goods that have been seized by an enforcement officer under a writ of fi fa but not yet sold are liable to be seized by the Crown at any time up to sale. If this happens, the enforcement officer must sell the judgment debtor's goods and satisfy any amounts owed to the Crown in priority to the judgment creditor executing the writ of fi fa.[4]

[1]   CPA 1947, s 26(1).
[2]   RSC Ord 46, r 1.
[3]   *R v Sloper* (1814) 6 Price 114 at 121 and *Giles v Grover* (1832) 9 Bing 128 at 154, per Alderton J, HL.
[4]   *Grove v Aldridge* (1832) 9 Bing 428 at 429.

Priority of Crown distraint for unpaid taxes

5.144   The priority of Crown writs is of limited practical importance because the Crown has available to it a large number of forms of statutory distraint which in practice provide the Crown with a far simpler and cheaper method of enforcement than bringing civil proceedings followed by enforcement. Unsurprisingly, most of these forms of statutory distraint relate to distraint for unpaid tax or fines.[1]

[1]   The most important forms for present purposes relate to income tax, capital gains tax, corporation tax, VAT and any Customs and Excise duty (other than vehicle excise duty). See respectively the Taxes Management Act 1970, s 61(1) and the Distress for Customs and Excise Duties and Other Indirect Taxes Regulations 1997, SI 1997/1431, reg 4(1).

5.145   As regards income tax, the Taxes Managements Act 1970, s 62 provides that the goods or chattels belonging to a debtor who owes moneys for unpaid PAYE, or deductions required to be made with respect to sub-contractors, are subject to restrictions before they can be removed or sold by an enforcement officer under a writ of fi fa. If a demand[1] for the tax has been made by a tax inspector, the judgment debtor's goods or chattels may not be removed or sold by the enforcement officer until the amounts due are paid to the tax collector. If such sums are not paid to the tax collector within ten days of the demand, the collector himself can seize and sell the chattels and goods of the debtor regardless of the prior seizure under the writ of fieri facias. There is no equivalent of provision in respect of other taxes.

[1]   The demand can be made for up to one year's unpaid taxes.

Abolition of Crown priority

5.146 The 2003 Effective Enforcement White Paper proposes that in the light of the Enterprise Act 2002 (in which Crown preference was abolished for the purposes of insolvency), the priority which Crown debts have with regard to writs of fi fa should also be removed.[1]

[1]   Paragraph 204.

STAGES OF EXECUTION OF A WRIT

5.147 It is convenient to break down the process of executing a writ into three stages:

(a) entry into the premises to effect seizure of the goods;
(b) seizure of goods; and
(c) securing or impounding the goods seized. [1]

[1]   This analysis was used in the context of distress for rent by Morritt LJ in *McLeod v Butterwick* [1998] 1 WLR 1603 at 1607. It is more conceptually helpful than the division suggested in *Martimore v Cragg* (1878) 3 CPD 216 at 219: (1) the delivery of the writ to the sheriff; (2) seizure; (3) the possible payment of money after seizure; (4) if no payment, sale.

5.148 In summary, entry is concerned with the rules governing an enforcement officer's right to go onto premises to take possession of the judgment debtor's goods. Seizure is concerned with the means by which an enforcement officer may obtain possession of the judgment debtor's goods. Securing and impounding is concerned with the enforcement officer's retention of possession of the judgment debtor's goods once seized. As will be seen, where a walking possession agreement is used, seizure and securing or impounding are for all practical purposes a single step.

ENTRY INTO PREMISES

5.149 An enforcement officer has all the duties, powers, rights, privileges and liabilities that a sheriff would have had at common law.[1] The common law rules concerning rights of entry therefore continue to apply to enforcement officers. Many of the cases relevant to an enforcement officer's rights of entry concern arrest or distress for rent. The court treats many of the principles arising from those cases as equally applicable to the execution of writs of fi fa by an enforcement officer.[2]

[1]   CA 2003, Sch 7, para 4(2).
[2]   See eg *Southam v Smout* [1964] 1 QB 308 where the Court of Appeal treated the rules on entering a third party's dwelling-house to execute a warrant of arrest as substantially the same as those applicable to a sheriff or bailiff levying execution or distress and *McLeod v Butterwick* [1998] 1 WLR 1603, CA where the Court of Appeal held that the common law rules on rights of re-entry for bailiffs levying distress for rent and those applicable to sheriff's officers executing a writ of fi fa were substantially the same.

5.150 At common law, an enforcement officer has the right to enter the judgment debtor's house and premises to levy execution.[1] He may also enter the premises of third parties where the judgment debtor's goods are being held for this purpose.[2] In other words, the enforcement officer is authorised to do things that would otherwise constitute a trespass in order to levy execution.[3] In many cases, gaining entry will be entirely straightforward because the judgment debtor will be at the premises and will admit the enforcement officer. However, the judgment debtor may not be at the premises when the enforcement officer attends. Alternatively, he may refuse to allow the enforcement officer entry.

1   *Semayne's Case* (1604) 5 Co Rep 91a, resolution 4; *Ratcliffe v Burton* (1802) 3 Bos & P 223 at 228; *Kerbey v Denby* (1836) 1 M & W 336.
2   *Semayne's Case* (1604) 5 Co Rep 91a, resolution 5.
3   *Long v Clarke* [1894] 1 QB 119, CA.

5.151   Although an enforcement officer can seize the judgment debtor's goods wherever he finds them, the goods will most commonly be at the judgment debtor's house or place of business. Given that a commercial enforcement case could either involve an individual or a corporate judgment debtor, it is necessary to consider the rules applicable to both.[1]

1   They also require that enforcement agents should always produce relevant identification on request, such as a badge or ID card, together with a written authorisation to act on behalf of the creditor.

The use of force to gain initial entry to the judgment debtor's house

5.152   Gaining initial access to a judgment debtor's home, particularly with the use of force, is one of the most glaring human rights issues raised by this method of enforcement. The human rights implications of forced entry to a person's home have always been recognised by the common law, which starts from the principle that every man's house is his castle.[1] This means that a judgment debtor has, subject to certain conditions, a privilege against an enforcement officer entering his house without his consent.

1   In *R (on the application of Bempoa) v London Borough of Southwark* [2002] EWHC 153 (Admin) at [11], a judicial review case considering the enforcement of a possession order in breach of an undertaking, Munby J equated the principle that every man's house is his castle with ECHR, art 8 and Protocol 1, art 1.

5.153   The leading case, and the starting point for considering an enforcement officer's rights of entry, is the 1604 decision in *Semayne's Case*.[1] *Semayne's Case* starts from the principle that every man's house is his castle:

'1.   The house of every one is his castle, and if thieves come to a man's house to rob or murder, and the owner or his servants kill any of the thieves in defence of himself and his house, it is no felony and he shall lose nothing ...
4.   Where the door is open the sheriff may enter, and do execution at the suit of a subject ... It is not lawful for the sheriff, on request made and denial, at the suit of a common person, to break the defendant's house, scil, to execute any process at the suit of a subject.
5.   The house of any one is only a privilege for himself, and does not extend to protect any person who flies to his house, or the goods of any other which are

brought there, to prevent a lawful execution and to escape the process of the law: in such cases after request and denial, the sheriff may break the house.

6.   If the sheriff might break open the door to execute civil process, yet it must be after request made …'

¹   (1604) 5 Co Rep 91a.

5.154   The 'house' referred to in *Semayne's Case* means 'dwelling-house'. It does not include other buildings such as barns or outhouses not connected with a dwelling-house, or those within the curtilage of the dwelling-house, which *may* be broken open in order to levy execution.¹ The judgment debtor's house refers to the place he normally resides and he need not necessarily own it.² However, it will not protect a judgment debtor who seeks to evade enforcement by transferring his goods to another's house: the 'privilege' that a judgment debtor enjoys to deny entry to his house for the purposes of the execution is strictly construed and will not be extended.³

¹   *Hodder v Williams* [1895] 2 QB 663 at 667, CA.
²   *Lee v Gansel* (1774) 1 Cowp 1 (an arrest case).
³   *Lee v Gansel* (1774) 1 Cowp 1 at 6, per Lord Mansfield CJ (an arrest case).

5.155   Accordingly, if an enforcement officer makes a request to be allowed to enter the judgment debtor's house and is refused, he must not use force to gain initial entry to a house.¹ In theory at least this would allow a determined judgment debtor to resist execution indefinitely. In practice, the enforcement officer will keep returning until the judgment debtor allows him in.

¹   *Semayne's Case* (1604) 5 Co Rep 91a, resolution 4; *Lee v Gansel* (1774) 1 Cowp 1 at 5–6 (an arrest case); *Aga Kurboolie Mahomed v R* (1843) 4 Moo PCC 239 at 246, PC; *Hodder v Williams* [1895] 2 QB 663 at 666, CA; *Southam v Smout* [1964] 1 QB 308 at 321, CA; and *McLeod v Butterwick* [1998] 1 WLR 1603 at 1617, CA.

5.156   The supposed reason for the privilege is that if 'the outer door of a man's house were broken open by process, it would leave the family within unprotected from thieves and robbers'.¹ The law considers it much better to wait for another opportunity to gain entry than 'do an act of violence, which may probably be attended with such dangerous consequences'.² In light of the modern practice of enforcement officers securing the premises with a new lock on leaving, the avoidance of violent confrontation is now the more convincing rationale.³

¹   *Hodder v Williams* [1895] 2 QB 663 at 666, CA. See also *Lee v Gansel* (1774) 1 Cowp 1 at 7 (an arrest case).
²   *Lee v Gansell* (1774) 1 Cowp 1 at 6, per Lord Mansfield CJ (an arrest case)
³   *McLeod v Butterwick* [1998] 1 WLR 1603 at 1615–1616, CA.

5.157   In order to gain access to the grounds of the judgment debtor's house, an enforcement officer may walk over the land to the front door.¹ He is also permitted to climb over a wall or fence provided he does not damage it.²

¹   *Long v Clarke* [1894] 1 QB 119 at 121, per Lord Esher MR, CA (a distress case).
²   *Long v Clarke* [1894] 1 QB 119 at 123–124, per Kay LJ, CA (a distress case).

5.158   Where the outer door of a house is open, the enforcement officer may pass through it to gain access.¹ Similarly, where the outer door is unlocked, the enforcement officer may enter provided no force is required.² However, the use of a locksmith to effect entry is unlawful,[3] as would be the use of a landlord's pass-key.[4] It is also unlawful for an enforcement officer who discovers a hole in a door or pane of glass to put his hand through the hole to open the door or window.[5] However, if there is a hole in the house itself, for example because there is building work going on, then the enforcement officer may use it to enter.[6]

1 *Semayne's Case* (1604) 5 Co Rep 91a, resolution 4; *Kerby v Denby* (1836) 1 M & W 336 (an arrest case); and *Southam v Smout* [1964] 1 QB 308 at 321, CA.
2 *Ryan v Shilcock* (1851) 7 Exch 72 (a distress case); *Nash v Lucas* (1867) LR 2 QB 590 at 594 (a distress for rent case); *Boyd v Profaze* (1867) 16 LT 431 at 432; and *Crabtree v Robinson* (1885) 15 QBD 312 at 314 (a distress for rent case).
3 *McLeod v Butterwick* [1998] 1 WLR 1603, CA.
4 *Welch v Kracovsky* (1919) 3 WWR 361 (British Columbia CA).
5 *Ryan v Shilcock* (1851) 7 Exch 72 at 76–77, per Pollock CB (a distress case).
6 *Long v Clarke* [1894] 1 QB 119 at 121, CA , per Lord Esher MR (a distress case). See also *Whalley v Willamson* (1836) 7 Car & P 294.

5.159 In *Southam v Smout* Lord Denning MR provided the following summary:[1]

'It seems to me that the law now is that where... a sheriff's officer enters by virtue of his warrant to effect civil process, he may not break the door, in the sense that he may not break it physically. If it is locked, bolted or barred, he must not open it: he is forbidden to do so. But if it is open and ajar, or if it is closed and can be opened by the peaceable means of lifting the latch or turning the knob or just by gently pushing, in those circumstances he can lawfully enter because there he is not breaking. The difference between the two cases is this, that in the case where a man locks, bolts or bars his door, he makes it clear that no one is to come in. Whereas if he leaves it open, or if he just shuts it and all that is needed is to turn the handle or lift the latch or give it a push, then he gives an implied invitation to all people who have lawful business to come in.'

Pearson LJ added that peaceable means would not include using a key where the door was locked if there was no authority from the householder to make use of the key.[2]

1 *Southam v Smout* [1964] 1 QB 308 at 322–323, CA.
2 *Southam v Smout* [1964] 1 QB 308 at 329, CA.

Gaining initial entry to a judgment debtor's house through a window

5.160 The Court of Appeal in *Southam* rationalised the various forms of peaceful entry on the basis of an implied licence granted by a householder to enter on lawful business. If this is the true rationale for what qualifies as peaceable entry, it casts doubt on the older authorities which sanction entering a judgment debtor's home through a window. It is clear that an enforcement officer must not break a window to gain access to a house.[1] Similarly, it is unlawful to gain entry through a closed window, even if it is unfastened, because the opening of the window is treated as forceful.[2] However, earlier authorities held that where a window is open or partly open, the enforcement officer may use it to gain access provided it does not require any further force to be used.[3] In one case, entry was held to be lawfully effected by entering a house a few doors off until they came upon the debtor's roof and effected entry by opening a skylight which was slightly open.[4]

1   *Lee v Gansel* (1774) 1 Cowp 1 at 5–6 (an arrest case) and *Boyd v Profaze* (1867) 16 LT 431 at 432.

2   *Nash v Lucas* (1867) LR 2 QB 590 at 594 (a distress for rent case). During argument Lush J pointed out that 'The ground of holding entry through a closed but unfastened door to be lawful, is, that access through the door is the usual mode of access, and that the licence from the occupier to any one to enter who has lawful business may therefore be implied from his leaving the door unfastened. Entry through a window is not the usual mode of entry, and therefore no such licence can be implied from the window being left unfastened.' See also *Hancock v Austin* (1863) 14 CBNS 634 and *Attack v Bramwell* (1863) 3 B&S 520 at 529 (a distress case where entry via a fastened window was found unlawful).

3   *Nixon v Freeman* (1860) 5 H&N 647 at 653, per Pollock CB; *Nash v Lucas* (1867) LR 2 QB 590 at 594 (a distress for rent case); *Boyd v Profaze* (1867) 16 LT 431 at 432; *American Concentrated Must Corpn v Hendry* (1893) 68 LT 742 at 743 (a distress for rent case); *Long v Clarke* [1894] 1 QB 119; and *Crabtree v Robinson* (1885) 15 QBD 312.

4   *Miller v Tebb* (1893) 9 TLR 515, CA (a distress case).

5.161   Pearson LJ in *Southam* considered that obtaining entry through 'ordinary means' would not include going through a window.[1] *Clerk and Lindsell on Torts* conclude from *Southam* that the authorities on entering through a window are no longer good law.[2] However, the point did not arise in *Southam* so Pearson LJ's comments are strictly obiter and, as the editors of *Clerk and Lindsell* recognise, the leading case on entry through a partially open window[3] was not cited to the court. Professor Beatson in his March 2000 review on bailiff's law[4] considered entering through windows still to be in accordance with the law,[5] although he went on to recommend in his June 2000 Report[6] that entry should only be allowed by normal means, which should not include through a window unless it is a French window.[7] The government has recommended legislation to the same effect.[8] In light of the potential human rights implications of entry through a window to gain access to a judgment debtor's home,[9] the case for putting the position on a firm statutory footing is a strong one.

1   *Southam v Smout* [1964] 1QB 308 at 329, CA.
2   (18th edn, 2000) p 871.
3   *Crabtree v Robinson* (1885) 15 QBD 312 (a distress for rent case).
4   Independent Review of Bailiff Law: A Consultation Paper (March 2000).
5   Independent Review of Bailiff Law: A Consultation Paper (March 2000) p 24.
6   Independent Review of Bailiff Law: Report (June 2000).
7   Beatson Independent Review of Bailiff Law: Report (June 2000) p 36.
8   Effective Enforcement: Improved methods of recovery for civil court debt and commercial rent and a single regulatory regime for warrant enforcement agents (March 2003) p 39.
9   See paras 5.327–5.333 for a discussion of human rights issues.

Use of force to gain initial entry to the judgment debtor's house where entry resisted

5.162   If the judgment debtor physically resists the enforcement officer's initial entry to his house, it is not lawful for the enforcement officer to effect entry using force, for example, by jamming his foot in the door and forcing it open[1] or using an object to jam the door.[2] This is because there is no real difference between a door which is momentarily opened but sought to be closed and can only be fully opened by violence, and a door which is shut and which can only be opened by violence.[3]

1   *Vaughan v McKenzie* [1969] 1 QB 557 at 562, DC.

2   *Boyd v Profaze* (1867) 16 LT 431 at 432 (use of a pair of shears).
3   *Vaughan v McKenzie* [1969] 1 QB 557 at 562, per Lord Parker CJ, DC.

Goods on the debtor's person

5.163   An enforcement officer cannot take 'wearing apparel on a man's person'.[1] In practice this is likely to mean that clothes and jewellery being worn by the judgment debtor on their person may not be seized. The principle may also extend to all goods 'in the actual use and possession' of the judgment debtor, such as a parcel or luggage.[2] In *Storey v Robinson*[3] it was held illegal to distrain a horse where the debtor was riding it. (By analogy, it would be unlawful to levy execution in respect of a vehicle in which the judgment debtor was sat.)

1   *Sunbolf v Alford* (1838) 3 M&W 248 at 254, per Parke B.
2   *Sunbolf v Alford* (1838) 3 M&W 248 at 252, per Lord Cabinger CB. The case concerns an
      innkeeper's lien and during the judgments the judges consider what can be seized under a writ
      of fi fa. These comments may therefore be restricted to innkeeper's liens.
3   (1795) 6 Term Rep 138 (a distress case).

Use of force to gain initial entry to commercial premises

5.164   Gaining entry to premises that are not dwelling-houses is much more straightforward. It is clear that the privilege against forcible entry only extends to a dwelling-house and does not cover a building which is not connected to the dwelling-house or outside its curtilage.[1] While it would therefore be unlawful to use force to enter a shed or garage of a house, forced entry to offices, warehouses, factories and workshops is permissible. Care should be exercised in respect of commercial premises near or in the grounds of a house because they may be defined as a dwelling-house for legal purposes rendering the use of forcible entry illegal. Examples would be businesses run from a building on the grounds of a house or shops which have living accommodation above them.[2]

1   *Hodder v Williams* [1895] 2 QB 663 at 667, CA. See also *Penton v Brown* (1664) 1 Keble
      699.
2   In the Canadian case *Hudson v Fletcher* (1909) 12 WLR 15 at 21 it was held to be unlawful
      entry where the sheriff's officer forced open one of the outer doors of a store which had an
      upstairs apartment occupied by the plaintiff. This decision was reached even though there
      was no access between the living quarters and store and the living quarters were reached by
      external stairs.

The use of force once inside the judgment debtor's premises

5.165   Once an enforcement officer has lawfully entered a judgment debtor's house, he may use force to open any inner doors.[1] Similarly, force may be used to open an inner window as it is treated as equivalent to an inner door.[2] The original policy reason for this rule is that that provided the outer door is not broken, breaking the inner doors of a house will not expose the inhabitants 'to insult and violence from without'.[3] In *Lee v Gansel*, an arrest case,[4] General Gansel was a lodger renting a number of rooms on two floors in a large house which opened onto a communal staircase. The owner also lived in the house and both men entered the property using a shared front door. General Gaskel complained that his arrest was illegal because the officers arresting him had entered peaceably through the front door but had forced entry to his bedroom which, like all the other rooms he rented, opened onto the communal staircase. The court found that his arrest was legal because the door to his bedroom was an inner door and the use of force to effect entry was legal since any other conclusion would have meant that General Gaskell had four outer doors.[5]

1   *Lee v Gansel* (1774) 1 Cowp 1 at 7.
2   *Lloyd v Sandilands* (1818) 8 Taunt 250.
3   *Lee v Gansel* (1774) 1 Cowp 1 at 7, per Lord Mansfield.
4   The case was cited in *Hodder v Williams* [1895] 2 QB 663 at 666 as applicable to writs of fi fa.
5   *Lee v Gansel* (1774) 1 Cowp 1 at 8–9, per Lord Mansfield (an arrest case). In the Canadian case of *Welch v Kracovsky* (1919) 3 WWR 361 the British Columbian Court of Appeal disapproved this aspect of the reasoning on the basis that many modern houses have numerous outer doors because they are often converted into apartments.

5.166   The court did, however, consider the difficulties associated with defining an inner door and suggested that 'if what was one house originally comes to be divided into separate tenements, and there is a distinct outer door to each, they will be separate houses.'[1] In other words, where a house has been converted into apartments and there is one outer door and also doors to gain access to individual apartments, the doors used to gain access to the individual apartments will count as outer doors and cannot be opened with force. The same would be true of purpose built apartments.[2]

1   *Lee v Gansel* (1774) 1 Cowp 1 at 8, per Lord Mansfield (an arrest case).
2   *Welch v Kracovsky* (1919) 3 WWR 361 (British Columbia CA).

5.167   Once entry has been effected, closets, cupboards and trunks can also be broken open by the enforcement officer while levying execution[1] as these are treated as equivalent to inner doors.[2] It seems that the enforcement officer need make no prior demand before using force.[3] However, while not a legal requirement, there is no reason why he should not do so if the judgment debtor is present and willing to open them.

1   *R v Bird* (1679) 2 Show KB 87 and *Hutchinson v Birch* (1812) 4 Taunt 620 at 625.
2   *Hutchinson v Birch* (1812) 4 Taunt 620 at 625, per Mansfield CJ.
3   In the arrest case of *Ratcliffe v Burton* (1802) 3 Bos & P 223, the court held that a prior demand was necessary before a sheriff who had gained peaceable entry through the front door forced the inner doors of the defendant's house in search of him when the sheriff was uncertain whether he was in the house. However, in *Hutchinson v Birch* (1812) 4 Taunt 620, the court held that this principle did not apply to sheriffs levying execution under a writ of fi fa. At 626 of that judgment Chambre J stated 'I do not see how execution could proceed, if the officer were to stop between the opening of every drawer and box, to make a fresh demand for the next to be unlocked.'

5.168   If a luckless enforcement officer becomes locked inside the judgment debtor's property and there is no-one to open the door to permit him to exit, he may use force to escape.[1] No prior demand is necessary on the grounds there is no-one on whom a demand could be made.[2] Similarly, he may rescue someone else who has become locked in.[3]

1   *Pugh v Griffith* (1838) 7 Ad & EL 827.
2   *Pugh v Griffith* (1838) 7 Ad & EL 827.
3   *White v Wiltshire* (1619) Cro Jac 555.

Entering third party premises

5.169   An enforcement officer has the right to enter the premises of third parties if goods belonging to the judgment debtor are held there.[1] However, caution should be exercised in this regard since if the judgment debtor's goods are not located there, the enforcement officer will be liable for trespass. In *Southam v Smout* Lord Denning MR explained the relevant legal principles:[2]

> '[the] law on this point seems to be now well settled that a sheriff's officer, when he goes into a stranger's house to execute process, enters at his peril, to this extent, that if the defendant's goods are actually there that he is to take … then he is justified by the event. But if the goods are not there … then he is guilty of a trespass. It seems illogical. It might be said that if he had reasonable cause to think the goods were there …, that should be sufficient justification. But not so, as I read the authorities. It would be putting far too much power into the hands of sheriff's officers or bailiffs if it was open to them to excuse an entry by saying they had reasonable grounds. They might go and invade a person's house too easily without justification. Therefore the law has made it plain, to discourage them from any unwarranted intrusion, that they are only justified if they are sure the person is there or the property is there. They are only justified if that in fact proves to be the case.'

---

[1]   *Biscop v White* (1600) Cro Eliz 759; *Semayne's Case* (1604) 5 Co Rep 91a, resolution 5; and *Cooke v Birt* (1814) 5 Taunt 765 at 771, per Dallas J.
[2]   *Southam v Smout* [1964] 1 QB 308 at 323, CA. See also *Morrish v Murrey* (1844) 13 M & W 52 (an arrest case).

5.170   What this case does not address is whether force may be used to enter a third party's premises. Both *Southam* and before it *Biscop v White*[1] establish that entry may be made peaceably at the risk of being a trespasser if the goods of the judgment debtor are not found. *Semayne's Case* states that where goods have been moved to the *house* of stranger to prevent lawful execution, the enforcement officer may effect entry by force although he must first make a demand to enter.[2] The correctness of this proposition is questioned by *Clerk and Lindsell*[3] relying on passages in the cases of *Cooke v Birt*[4] and *Morrish v Murrey*.[5] However, the passage relied on in *Cooke v Birt*,[6] while establishing that entry can be made to a third party's house through an open door, does not seem to be making any decision about whether force can be used. In any event, that case was not a case about entry of a third party's house so any comments are strictly obiter. Similarly, the passage referred to in *Morrish v Murrey*[7] would not appear to be on point because it relates to the breaking of inner doors. It therefore seems that after a demand and refusal, force can be used to break the outer door of a stranger's house where the judgment debtor's goods have been moved to the premises of the stranger to prevent lawful execution. Other commentators certainly proceed on this basis.[8] Again, in light of the potential human rights implications of such a course of action, legislative clarification would be welcome. The 2003 White Paper envisages that in the future prior judicial authority will always be required for forcible entry to third party premises.[9]

---

[1]   *Biscop v White* (1600) Cro Eliz 759.
[2]   *Semayne's Case* (1604) 5 Co Rep 91a, resolution 5. See para 5.153.

3   (18th edn, 2000), p 871.
4   (1814) 5 Taunt 765 at 770, per Gibbs CJ.
5   (1844) 13 M&W 52 at 56, per Pollock CB.
6   (1814) 5 Taunt 765 at 770, per Gibbs CJ and 771, per Dallas J.
7   (1844) 13 M&W 52 at 56, per Pollock CB.
8   Keith, Podevin and Sandbrook *The Execution of Sheriffs' Warrants* (2nd edn, 1995) p 27;
     Kruse *Distress & Execution: A Guide to Bailiff's Law and Practice* (1998) p 69; Kruse *The
     Law of Seizure of Goods: Debtors Rights and Remedies* (2000) p 98; vol 17(1) *Halsbury's
     Laws of England* (4th edn, 2002) p 74.
9   'Effective Enforcement' White Paper, para 167.

5.171   Having effected entry, an enforcement officer may break inner doors of a
third party's premises, although again he does so at his peril because suspicion that
the defendant's goods are there is not enough to justify his entry if in fact the goods
are not there.[1]

1   *Johnson v Leigh* (1815) 6 Taunt 246 (an arrest case).

5.172   It may also be worth noting that there is authority to the effect that the
house of the personal representatives of a deceased judgment debtor is not considered
that of a third party because this would be a natural place to find the deceased
judgment debtor's goods. Accordingly, an enforcement officer searching will not be
liable for trespass even if he finds no goods there.[1]

1   *Cooke v Birt* (1814) 5 Taunt 765 at 771, per Dallas J.

Re-entry

5.173   An enforcement officer has a right to re-enter the judgment debtor's premises
in order to remove goods for the purposes of sale.[1] The question of whether force
may be used to effect re-entry will depend on the circumstances.

1   *McLeod v Butterwick* [1998] 1 WLR 1603 at 1618, CA.

5.174   The leading modern authority on an enforcement officer's rights of re-entry
is the Court of Appeal decision in *McLeod v Butterwick*.[1] The case was a combined
appeal concerned with a bailiff's rights of re-entry to commercial premises on levying
distress for rent, and sheriffs' officers' rights of re-entry to a dwelling-house on
levying execution under a writ of fi fa. In both cases the initial entry had been made
peaceably. However, in both cases when the officers returned some time later to
remove the debtor's goods and found the debtor's premises locked, re-entry was
effected with the help of a locksmith and therefore by force. There was no issue in
either appeal of the debtor deliberately locking the premises to defeat execution
because, in each case, the debtors had no prior warning of the intended re-entry and
had simply locked their doors when they went out. The issue was whether it was
lawful to effect re-entry by force in each case.

1   [1998] 1 WLR 1603, CA.

5.175   Morritt LJ gave the judgment of the Court of Appeal. Having explained that
it was common ground in both appeals that the initial entry must be peaceful,[1] he first

considered the law on bailiffs' rights of re-entry when levying distress for rent and concluded that:[2]

> '... a bailiff is not entitled to re-enter by force except where, having gained entry peaceably, he was expelled by force or he has been deliberately excluded by the tenant. What amounts to deliberate exclusion must be recognised on a case by case basis. It will include cases where the tenant knowing of the intended visit deliberately locks the door and goes away or when invited to admit the bailiff refuses to do so. But, in my view, it does not include the case of a tenant who has no knowledge of an intended visit by the bailiff at any particular time and locks his premises in the ordinary way and goes about his business as normal.'

1   Since in the case of the writ of fi fa, the judgment debtor's premises were a dwelling house, and in the case of levying distress for rent there is no right to forcible entry (to domestic or commercial premises).
2   *McLeod v Butterwick* [1998] 1 WLR 1603 at 1616, CA.

5.176   Morritt LJ then surveyed the law on re-entry for enforcement officers and concluded:[1]

> 'The statutory power conferred by [SCA 1981, s 138][2] authorises the sheriff to seize goods. It contains no express power to make forcible entry and I see no grounds for implying one. Nor does the common law recognize such a power in the case of a dwelling house. Accordingly, in my view, and for substantially the same reasons a sheriff is entitled forcibly to re-enter a dwelling house in the same circumstances as a bailiff, disregarding the statutory restrictions I referred to earlier, but not otherwise. I should reiterate, in case it is not clear already, that this conclusion is confined to re-entry to a dwelling house. If and in so far as a sheriff may forcibly enter premises other than a dwelling house I see no reason why he may not re-enter such premises in a similar fashion.'

1   *McLeod v Butterwick* [1998] 1 WLR 1603 at 1619, CA.
2   Now replaced by CA 2003, Sch 7, para 8.

5.177   Accordingly, the use of force to gain re-entry to a dwelling house is unlawful unless the enforcement officer has been expelled by force or deliberately excluded by the judgment debtor. However, in the case of commercial premises, where an enforcement officer has gained initial entry (whether or not by force) he may use force to gain re-entry to remove the goods for the purposes of sale.

5.178   It is of note that in *McLeod* no 'walking possession' agreement had been entered into between the judgment debtor and the enforcement officer. The nature of walking possession agreements and their impact on rights of re-entry are considered in paras 5.216–5.235.

Is the seizure and sale invalidated by an unlawful entry?

5.179   Even if the original entry or re-entry was unlawful, the removal and sale of the goods is still lawful.[1] As Judge Roger Cooke put it at first instance in *McLeod v Butterwick*:[2]

'I really do not entertain any doubt. In a very old case in the 18th century called *Lee v. Gansel* (1774) 1 Cowp. 1 at 6 Lord Mansfield CJ held quite clearly, and following, indeed, earlier authority, "that breaking open the outer door was a trespass, but that taking away the goods was lawful." That short passage alone seems to me at least to settle the issue of whether the sheriff can sell the goods. To my mind, notwithstanding any defects that there might have been (and I will come, presently, to whether there were in the entry into the house), there can be no doubt that the seizure of the goods was effective and the goods may be sold.'

1   *Lee v Gansel* (1774) 1 Cowp 1 at 6 (an arrest case); *Percival v Stamp* (1853) 9 Exch 167; *Hooper v Lane* (1857) 6 HL Cas 443 at 550; and *McLeod v Butterwick* [1998] 1 WLR 1603 at 1628, CA.

2   [1996] 1 WLR 995 at 997-998; affirmed [1998] 1 WLR 1603 at 1628, per Morritt LJ: 'The statutory right to sell continues to subsist and I see no reason to inhibit its exercise.'

5.180   The Court of Appeal concurred on this point and dismissed the judgment debtor's application for an injunction to restrain the sheriff from selling the goods, notwithstanding the fact the court had found they had been seized unlawfully:[1]

'In these circumstances, I do not see how an injunction to restrain the sale of the goods so seized and now stored in a warehouse off Mrs McLeod's premises could be justified. Mrs McLeod has not paid the judgment debt and, apparently, has no intention of doing so. As pointed out in *Lee v Gansel*, 1 Corp. 1, though the re-entry may have been wrongful the removal of the goods was not. The statutory right to sell continues to subsist and I see no reason to inhibit its exercise.'

1   *McLeod v Butterwick* [1998] 1 WLR 1603 at 1628, ICA.

5.181   He went on to observe that the judgment debtor may have a right to damages in consequence of the unlawful entry. However, assuming the enforcement officer makes good any damage to the property in effecting forcible entry (for example, by using a locksmith to effect entry and replacing the locks with new locks on leaving the premises) it is unclear what loss a judgment debtor would sustain as a consequence of a lawful seizure of goods to make payment of the judgment debt. However, the court observed that a criminal sanction may also lie pursuant to the Criminal Damage Act 1971. The National Standards require that enforcement agents may only gain access to goods without the use of unlawful force and must not misrepresent their powers (which would include their powers of entry).

Practice of forced entry

5.182   In practice, an enforcement officer should use a locksmith to assist him in gaining forced entry to commercial premises. Afterwards, he will replace the locks and re-secure the premises. The enforcement officer will invariably seek the approval of the judgment creditor before effecting a forced entry and will seek the judgment creditor's agreement to pay for the costs of the locksmith to secure the premises on leaving and any other damage caused by the forced entry.[1] The judgment creditor (and his advisers) should ensure that the proposed entry is lawful before providing such sanction since otherwise they may end up as joint tortfeasors.

¹   *Working with the Sheriff: What you can expect the Sheriff to do for you; what you can do for help*: available from the Sheriffs Lodgment Centre, for which contact details are available in the Appendix.

Reform of the law of forcible entry [1]

5.183   It will be apparent from the discussion above that the rules concerning entry are antiquated and in need of some clarification and rationalisation. Some of the distinctions drawn between lawful and unlawful entry are somewhat slight.

¹   See also Beatson *Independent Review of Bailiff's Law: A Consulation Paper* (March 2000); Beatson *Independent Review of Bailiff's Law: Report* (June 2000); *Towards Effective Enforcement: A Single piece of bailiff law and regulatory structure for enforcement* (July 2001) and 2003 White Paper.

5.184   The Effective Enforcement White Paper proposes legislation to clarify the law in this area and sets out general procedures for entry. The Paper recognises that allowing an enforcement officer entry to a judgment debtor's premises is necessary to ensure that judgment debts are not rendered unenforceable and that continuous refusal by a judgment debtor to allow entry will mean that enforcement cannot take place. Normal entry will be by unlocked outer doors (including French windows but not through other windows), and includes normal access to the outer door, for example by way of the drive or garden. Forcible entry to commercial premises will remain permissible for enforcement officers and the Paper proposes that forcible entry to domestic premises should be permitted with prior judicial authority. In the case of third parties' premises, normal entry (ie by unlocked outer doors) will not require judicial permission but the enforcement officer should be certain that the goods are on the premises before attempting to enter. The Paper also proposes that judicial permission should be sought in all cases where forcible entry of third party premises is intended.[1]

¹   Effective Enforcement White Paper, paras 163–167.

Exempt premises

5.185   Certain premises are exempt from execution.

Diplomatic privilege

5.186   Execution may not be levied at diplomatic premises[1] or at the private residence of a diplomatic agent.[2]

¹   Diplomatic Privileges Act 1964, Sch 1, art 22. See further Chapter 1.
²   Diplomatic Privileges Act 1964, Sch 1, art 30. See further Chapter 1.

Royal and Crown privilege

5.187 Goods at royal residences are exempt from execution[1] as are goods at government premises. (Crown immunity is considered in Chapter 1).

[1]   *Winter v Miles* (1809) 10 East 578.

Police assistance

5.188 The police must assist an enforcement officer in the execution of a writ if requested to do so.[1] Such assistance may be advisable where forcible entry is intended or in other situations in which a breach of the peace is likely.

[1]   CA 2003, Sch 7, para 5.

Obstructing a High Court enforcement officer

5.189 A person who resists or intentionally obstructs an enforcement officer or his agent while executing a High Court writ is now guilty of an offence under the Criminal Law Act 1977, s 10.[1] As yet there have not been any cases on the ambit of this offence and there is no guidance provided as to what exactly 'resisting' or 'intentionally obstructing' entails – for example, it is unclear whether a judgment debtor intentionally refusing to allow an enforcement officer access to his home would constitute resisting or obstructing for the purposes of this offence.

[1]   As amended by CA 2003, Sch 8, para 189.

Right to remain on the judgment debtor's premises

5.190 The writ of fi fa gives the sheriff the right to remain on the judgment debtor's premises for a reasonable time in order to take possession of the goods but no longer.[1]

[1]   *Watson v Murray* [1955] 2 QB 1 at 17; *Ash v Dawnay* (1852) 8 Exch 237; and *Reed v Harrison* (1778) 2 Wm Bl 1218.

5.191 What constitutes a 'reasonable time' will depend on the nature of the goods seized and the method by which the enforcement officer takes possession – evidently it may take longer for an enforcement officer to remove goods from the judgment debtor's premises for storage than for the judgment debtor to sign a walking possession agreement.

SEIZURE

5.192 The nature of goods that can be seized by writ of fi fa has been considered at paras 5.15-5.68. This section considers what, as a matter of law, amounts to a valid seizure by an enforcement officer.

What amounts to seizure?

5.193   The question as to whether there has been effective seizure is one of fact[1] and will therefore depend on the circumstances of the case. Some act must be done to demonstrate that a seizure has been made.[2] However, it is clear that very simple acts are sufficient to effect a valid seizure.[3] It is not necessary for the officer to take the goods into his physical possession[4] or even have physical contact with the goods seized.[5] However, simply touching the goods intended to be seized without producing the writ or informing anyone of the seizure does not amount to a valid seizure.[6]

[1]   *Re Cooper* [1958] 1 Ch 922 at 928 and 930 and *Lloyds and Scottish Finance Ltd v Modern Cars and Caravans (Kingston) Ltd* [1966] 1 QB 764 at 776.
[2]   *Balls v Pink* (1845) 9 Jur 304 at 305.
[3]   *Re Cooper* [1958] 1 Ch 922 at 928.
[4]   *Re Cooper* [1958] 1 Ch 922 at 927. Clearly, if it were necessary then walking possession would be impossible.
[5]   *Gladstone v Padwick* (1871) 6 LR 203 at 212.
[6]   *Re Williams, ex p Jones* (1880) 42 LT 157.

5.194   In *Nash v Dickenson*[1] it was held not to amount to a valid seizure where a sheriff's officer merely went with a warrant to the defendant's premises and, without saying or doing anything more, produced the warrant and demanded the debt and costs together with poundage and expenses of levy. By contrast, in *Bissicks v The Bath Colliery Company Ltd*[2] it was held to be a valid seizure where a sheriff's officer went to the debtor's house, showed him the warrant and demanded payment, and told him that in default of payment a man must remain in possession and that further proceedings would be taken. Donaldson J sought to reconcile *Nash* and *Bissicks* in *Brintons Ltd v Wyre Forest District Council*,[3] a case that concerned distress for local rates. In that case the bailiff had entered the debtor's premises and stated nothing more than that he had come to levy distress for the rates and for costs. He did not state that he had seized any goods or take steps amounting to taking possession. Donaldson J reviewed the authorities and held as follows:[4]

> 'In relation to the execution of a warrant of fieri facias the dividing line between what is and what is not a seizure is shown by comparing *Nash v Dickenson* (1867) L.R. 2 C.P. 252 which seems to me to be indistinguishable from the present case and *Bissicks v Bath Colliery Co Ltd* (1877) 2 Ex.D. 459 and on appeal (1878) 3 Ex.D. 174 which is distinguishable because the sheriff's officer threatened to leave a man in possession of the goods and both parties treated the action of the sheriff's officer as having amounted to a seizure. The claim to poundage on this basis therefore fails.'

[1]   (1867) LR 2 CP 252.
[2]   (1877) 3 Ex D 174, CA.
[3]   [1997] 1 QB 178.
[4]   [1977] 1 QB 178 at 181.

5.195   The court in *Brintons* therefore concluded that something more than attending the judgment debtor's premises, producing the writ and demanding payment is necessary for seizure to be effected.

5.196 In *Re Cooper*[1] it was held that seizure had been effected by the sheriff's officer coming upon the judgment debtor's farm and indicating to an employee of the judgment debtor that he was levying an execution on two tractors and handing him two forms inviting the judgment debtor to enter into a walking possession agreement. Similarly, in *Lloyds and Scottish Finance Ltd v Modern Cars and Caravans (Kingston) Ltd*[2] it was held that seizure was validly effected when a Sheriff's officer demanded payment of the debt, told the debtor he had come to levy execution, proffered for signature a walking possession agreement and warned the judgment debtor not to move his property (a caravan). Edmund Davies J noted that whether seizure has taken place will be a question of fact in each particular case. However, he referred to certain guiding principles which had evolved over the years and which were summarised in *Halsbury's Laws of England*, from which he quoted in his judgment:[3]

> 'For an act of the sheriff or his bailiff to constitute a seizure of goods, it is not necessary that there should be any physical contact with the goods seized; nor does such contact necessarily amount to seizure. An entry upon the premises on which the goods are situate, together with an intimation of an intention to seize the goods, will amount to a valid seizure, even where the premises are extensive and the property seized widely scattered, but some act must be done sufficient to intimate to the judgment debtor or his servants that a seizure has been made, and it is not sufficient to enter upon the premises and demand the debt. Any act which, if not done with the authority of the court, would amount to a trespass to goods, will constitute a seizure of them when done under the writ.[4]
>
> In the light of the authorities cited in support of this passage, I hold that on April 14 there was a seizure by the sheriff's officer of the caravan and its contents as against the judgment debtor. He did not merely demand payment of the debt (as was done in *Nash v Dickinson*) but, having entered and told the debtor that he had come to levy execution and read out his warrant, he handed him the written intimation already referred to. Furthermore, he proffered for signature a "walking possession" agreement, and he warned Wood and his wife that the caravan must not be moved.'

1   [1958] 1 Ch 922 at 928.
2   [1966] 1 QB 764.
3   [1966] 1 QB 764 at 776-777.
4   *Halsbury's Laws of England* (3rd edn, 1956) vol 16, p 55.

5.197 The court in *Lloyds and Scottish Finance* rejected the proposition that the enforcement officer should have done more, such as asking the judgment debtor's family to leave the caravan and then locking it up or towing it away. Given that the judgment debtor had refused to sign the walking possession agreement and that his wife asserted ownership of the caravan, such a course of action would have been unrealistic and would have run a risk of involving the sheriff in liability to pay damages for wrongful execution, wrongful imprisonment and trespass against the person. Nor was it realistic for him to have remained in the caravan or to camp outside on the caravan site. Further, the fact that he had been refused consent to walking possession supported the view that he was levying execution.

The extent of the seizure

5.198   When seizure takes place it seizes all goods on the judgment debtor's premises.[1] It has been said that 'a sheriff's officer upon entering a house to execute a *fieri facias* ... seizes everything therein'.[2] However, such statements should be treated with caution since the writ only authorises the enforcement officer to seize goods belonging to the judgment debtor in order to raise the sums detailed in the writ. Seizing all the judgment debtor's goods may amount to 'excessive' execution (see paras 5.206–5.210).

1   However, see the further commentary at paras 5.206-5.210 as to excessive execution.
2   See also *Bissicks v The Bath Colliery Company Ltd* (1877) 3 Ex D 174 at 175, per Bramwell LJ.

5.199   The width of this principle that seizure potentially applies to all the goods on the judgment debtor's premises is illustrated by *Gladstone v Padwick*[1] where the judgment debtor was the Duke of Newcastle. The Duke's lands consisted of a mansion house and grounds. On the grounds of the mansion house was a farm which was a mile away from the house. The sheriff's officer attended the Duke's mansion house and informed those there that all goods on the estate were seized and a possession man was left in possession. The farm was not visited until the next day when a possession man[2] was left in place. A dispute arose as to whether goods on the farm had been validly assigned under a bill of sale which had been executed after the seizure at the mansion house. It was held that the seizure effected at the mansion house 'was effectual over the whole extent of the property.'[3] Martin B held that:[4]

> 'I am of opinion that, where property is all one holding, as it was here, if the sheriff goes and makes known at the mansion-house or dwelling-house of the occupier that he is come to seize, and does, so far as words and intention can go, seize all the goods on that holding, he has done enough ... Here it was all one holding; and when the sheriff, being present at the house with the writ of execution, says, "I seize everything on this holding," enough is done to constitute a seizure of the whole.'

1   (1871) 6 LR Exch 203 at 212, per Bramwell B.
2   Former practice entailed leaving a man on the judgment debtors' premises where seized goods were not removed pending sale.
3   (1871) 6 LR 203 at 210.
4   (1871) 6 LR 203 at 212, per Bramwell B.

Notice of seizure

5.200   When first executing a writ of fi fa, the enforcement officer must either deliver to the judgment debtor, or leave at each place where execution is levied, a notice informing the judgment debtor of the execution.[1] The notice to be used is form PF 55.

1   RSC Ord 45, r 2.

5.201   The notice informs the judgment debtor that a formal seizure of the goods at the address named in the notice has been made and the goods seized are now in the custody of the enforcement officer. It states that the goods must not be removed, sold or otherwise disposed of and that this will remain the position until the judgment debt has been paid in full.

5.202 The notice draws the judgment debtor's attention to 'exempt goods'[1] which are not subject to the seizure and sets out the statutory provision on the reverse of the notice.[2] The notice states that the judgment debtor must send full details in writing to the enforcement officer within five days (or such greater period as the court may on the judgment debtor's application allow) of any goods falling within the statutory exemption. It also provides that the enforcement officer should be informed of any goods seized which do not belong to the judgment debtor (as must the true owner) and any goods which are subject to a hire purchase agreement. Similarly, the judgment debtor is required to inform the enforcement officer if another bailiff seizes, levies or distrains the goods or if any insolvency application is made against him.

[1] See paras 5.26-5.37
[2] Form PF 55 refers to SCA 1981, s 138(3A) which should now be a reference to Court Act 2003, Sch 7, para 9(3). At the time of writing the form had yet to be updated.

5.203 The notice will enclose a standard form 'walking possession' agreement (see paras 5.216–5.235) and states that the judgment debtor should read and sign the agreement to acknowledge the seizure then return it to the enforcement officer. The notice warns the judgment debtor that failure to do so may result in the removal of the goods seized without further notice pending disposal by public auction.

5.204 The notice will set out the amount of judgment debt, the costs of execution, interest and fees and charges of the enforcement officer or alternatively will state that the judgment debtor should contact the enforcement officer to be told the sum due. The notice warns the judgment debtor that if payment is not made and the execution proceeds, the enforcement officer will attend and remove the goods seized for sale by public auction or as the court may direct. The notice will be signed and dated by the enforcement officer, who will also provide his contact address.

Inventories and receipts for goods seized and removed

5.205 Both the notice of seizure and the National Standards require that an enforcement officer produce an inventory of the goods seized and that it is left with the judgment debtor or at the judgment debtor's premises. This is also envisaged by the Effective Enforcement White Paper.

Trading concerns and 'excessive' execution

5.206 The writ of fi fa authorises the enforcement officer to seize 'any' goods of the judgment debtor[1] and to raise from those goods the sums set out in the Schedule to the writ. However, it may be the case that the value of the entirety of the goods on the judgment debtor's premises far exceeds the sums payable by the judgment debtor under the writ. If so, this will constitute excessive and therefore wrongful execution. In *Gawler v Chaplin*[2] the sheriff's officers seized goods belonging to the judgment debtor of greater value than was due under this writ knowing that these sums could be met with only partial seizure. Parke B held:[3]

> 'in the first instance, the duty of the sheriff is confined to seizing goods that would reasonably be sufficient, if sold, to pay the sum indorsed on the writ - that is, the debt, interest upon the debt, poundage and expenses; and if the sheriff seizes more, prima facie he is a wrongdoer.'

[1]   CA 2003, Sch 7, para 9(2)(a).
[2]   (1848) 2 Exch 503.
[3]   (1848) 2 Exch 503 at 507.

5.207   Where a writ of fi fa is executed in respect of commercial premises, such as a shop, the stock contained on the premises may well be far more extensive than necessary to satisfy the judgment debt in respect of which the writ was issued. Historically, one way in which enforcement officers have sought to address this is by taking possession of all the goods through a walking possession agreement but agreeing with the judgment debtor that he may continue to trade provided he pay to the sheriff the money taken from such trade less whatever was required for staff wages.

5.208   In *Re Dalton (a bankrupt)*[1] a sheriff's officer had obtained a signed walking possession agreement in respect of the entire stock of a grocer's shop and orally agreed that the judgment debtor could continue to trade but that he must not sell any of the goods in the store room in bulk and that if he sold any of them in the ordinary course of business he must replace them.[2]

[1]   [1963] 1 Ch 336, DC.
[2]   This is almost like an oral floating charge.

5.209   The Court of Appeal observed that while such practice appeared common, it should not be followed:[1]

> 'It appears from the evidence in the present case and from *Watson v Murray & Co. Ltd* that it is quite common in the case of executions at retail shops for execution to be levied on the entire stock, but with walking possession and permission to continue normal retail trading. Where this initially involves excessive and therefore wrongful and tortious execution, the practice, though perhaps convenient and not really damaging to the debtor, seems to us to be one which should not be followed. An appropriate amount of the stock should be seized. Permission to dip into the seized stock if required for normal trading would of course tend to reduce the value of the execution: but it should not in practice be difficult to put a limit on the value of the amount of such seized stock sold in any day or longer period and to arrange in the course of visits under the walking possession agreement either to receive the proceeds of sale or to replenish the stock by a further levy.'

[1]   [1963] 1 Ch 366 at 346.

5.210   If there is considered to be any benefit in allowing the judgment debtor to continue trading, care must be taken in this kind of arrangement otherwise the enforcement officer risks being deemed to have abandoned possession (see paras 5.239–5.241). The practical guidance arising from the Court of Appeal's judgment in *Re Dalton* seems to be as follows:

(a) if there are more goods than the writ requires, the enforcement officer when preparing his inventory should only identify sufficient goods to meet the full amount due under the writ of fi fa;

(b) the permission to sell the stock should not be for *all of the stock* noted in the inventory otherwise the enforcement officer will be deemed to have abandoned possession. Instead, a limit to the goods which may be sold in the course of normal trading should be agreed. Any agreement reached should be recorded in a letter which should be counter-signed by the judgment debtor. Alternatively it could be noted on the inventory that stock will change and a note of the agreement on use of stock should be made (again it is helpful for the judgment debtor to sign the inventory);

(c) the enforcement officer should return regularly to collect the proceeds of sale or to make further levies to make sure that any new stock is covered by the seizure. It may be sensible, if only for evidential reasons, for a new walking possession agreement to be signed on each visit and an updated inventory produced. At the very least the original inventory should be updated (and the judgment debtor should again sign); and

(d) if it becomes clear from a repeat visit by the enforcement officer that the judgment debtor is clearly not replenishing stock, then the enforcement officer should make a physical seizure and remove the stock to be sold.

Date and time of seizure

5.211 A writ of execution must not be executed on a Sunday, Good Friday or Christmas Day, unless the court orders otherwise.[1] In addition, the National Standards recommend that enforcement should not take place on Bank Holidays unless the court so orders and that ideally enforcement should be carried out between 6.00 am and 9.00 pm or at any time during trading hours. The National Standards also recommend that enforcement agents respect the religion and culture of others at all times. This means being aware of dates of religious festivals and considering whether enforcement on any day of religious or cultural observance or during any major religious or cultural festival is appropriate.[2]

[1]   RSC Ord 46, PD, para 1.1.
[2]   The 2003 White Paper notes at para 162 that '*it would be problematic to seek to identify all religious festivals and adherents to all religions*' and that further guidance is needed on religious and cultural sensibilities in a Code of Practice.

Return to a writ of execution

5.212 As noted at para 5.108, the writ requires the enforcement officer to make a return, which is a statement as to the manner in which the writ was executed that is indorsed on the writ and a copy sent to the judgment creditor. In practice, the more sophisticated enforcement officers allow enforcement to be tracked online or for updates to be obtained by telephone. If the enforcement officer fails to make the return, the judgment creditor can serve a notice on the officer requiring him to do so.[1] The enforcement officer must respond within the time stipulated in the notice. Where the enforcement officer fails to comply with such notice, the judgment creditor may apply to the court for an order requiring him to do so.[2]

1   RSC Ord 46, r 9.
2   RSC Ord 46, r 9(2).

SECURING OR IMPOUNDING GOODS SEIZED

5.213   After seizure of goods under a writ of fi fa, the enforcement officer has a duty to retain possession of the judgment debtor's goods pending sale.[1] Historically, an enforcement officer would have retained possession by either leaving a man guarding the goods on the premises (known as 'close possession') or physically removing them to be stored at the parish pound pending auction.

1   *Ackland v Paynter* (1820) 8 Price 95.

5.214   This practice was inconvenient and added to the costs of the enforcement process, while only nominal fees are recoverable for leaving a man in close possession.[1] As a result, close possession and removal of goods are now only rarely used and instead widespread use is made of 'walking possession' agreements under which the goods are left in the possession of the judgment debtor provided the judgment debtor agrees not to dispose of them. This practice grew up from distress for rent[2] but has since been adopted by enforcement officers levying execution.

1   See Distress for Rent Act 1737, s 10: 'And whereas great difficulties and inconveniences frequently arise to landlords and lessors and other persons taking distresses for rent, in removing the goods and chattels or stock distrained off the premises, in cases where by law they may not be impounded and secured thereupon, and also to the tenants themselves many times, by the damage unavoidably done to such goods and chattels or stock in the removal thereof: Be it enacted by the authority aforesaid, that... it shall and may be lawful to and for any person or persons lawfully taking any distress for any kind of rent, to impound or otherwise secure the distress so made, of what nature or kind soever it may be, in such place or on such part of the premises chargeable with the rent as shall be most fit and convenient for the impounding and securing such distress.' Various forms of statutory distress permit the use of walking possession agreements.
2   High Court Enforcement Officers Regulations, SI 2004/400, Sch 3, para 5 only allows £3 per person per day where a person is left in physical possession of goods seized.

5.215   Possession can therefore now be maintained by leaving a man on the judgment debtor's premises with the goods, under a walking possession agreement or by physical removal of the goods. In addition, where a judgment debtor refuses to sign a walking possession agreement and the goods are left in the judgment debtor's possession, the enforcement officer can also maintain possession by visiting periodically[1] to check the goods have not been moved in order to rebut any allegation of abandonment of possession (see paras 5.239-5.241).

1   See eg *National Commercial Bank of Scotland v Arcam Demolition and Construction Ltd* [1966] 2 QB 593.

Walking possession

5.216 Under 'walking possession' a judgment debtor signs a written agreement which provides that the goods are allowed to remain on the judgment debtor's property on the understanding that they have been seized and will not be removed except by the enforcement officer or with his permission. The agreement also grants the enforcement officer permission to re-enter the premises at any time to inspect the goods or remove them to allow sale. Where a walking possession agreement is used, this process collapses the historic distinction between seizure of the goods and securing and impounding them (in contrast to physical removal and impounding, where the distinction remains).

Standard form walking possession agreement

5.217 The High Court Enforcement Officers Regulations 2004 include a standard form walking possession agreement which an enforcement officer may use to take walking possession of the goods.[1] The operative parts of the agreement comprise a request from the judgment debtor to the enforcement officer not to leave a possession man on the judgment debtor's premises in close possession of the goods[2] seized under the writ of execution in consideration for which the judgment debtor undertakes, pending withdrawal or satisfaction of the writ:

(a) not to remove the goods or any part of them nor to permit their removal by any person not authorised by the enforcement officer;
(b) to inform any person who may visit the judgment debtor's premises for the purpose of levying any other execution or distress that the enforcement officer is already in possession of the judgment debtor's goods under the writ; and
(c) to notify the enforcement officer immediately of any such visit.

The agreement also authorises the enforcement officer or a person acting on his behalf, pending the withdrawal or satisfaction of the writ, to re-enter the judgment debtor's premises at any time for the purpose of inspecting the goods or completing the execution of the writ (see paras 5.230–5.234).

[1] SI 2004/400, Sch 4, reg 15.
[2] See para 5.213 for the meaning of this expression.

5.218 The High Court Enforcement Officers Regulations 2004 are silent as to the legal effect of a walking possession agreement, which continues to be governed by the common law. The 2003 White Paper proposes that the parties' obligations under a walking possession agreement should be made express in any enforcement legislation.[1]

[1] Effective Enforcement White Paper, paras 174–176.

5.219 The fee charged where an enforcement officer takes walking possession under a standard form walking possession agreement is £0.25 per day.[1]

[1] High Court Enforcement Officers Regulations 2004, SI 2004/400, Sch 3, para 5(2).

Legal effect of a walking possession agreement

5.220   As has been noted in para 5.196, in *Lloyds and Scottish Finance* the court held that a sheriff who had entered a judgment debtor's premises and requested that a judgment debtor sign a walking possession agreement had taken sufficient steps to amount to a valid seizure of the judgment debtor's goods, even where the judgment debtor refused to sign the agreement. In that case, because the judgment debtor would not sign the walking possession agreement, the sheriff had to visit periodically in order to remain in possession of the goods.[1] However, where a walking possession agreement has been signed there is no need for the enforcement officer to make periodic visits and he will not be taken to have abandoned possession given the existence of the agreement.[2]

1   In *McLeod v Butterwick* [1996] 1 WLR 995 at 999, at first instance, Judge Roger Coche called this arrangement '*walking possession*' even though there was no written agreement.
2   *National Commercial Bank of Scotland Ltd v Arcam Demolition and Construction Ltd* [1966] 2 QB 593. Although that case considered the earlier form of walking possession agreement set out in the Sheriffs' Fees (Amendment) Order 1956, SI 1956/502 (partly repealed) the comments apply equally to the current form since it is almost identical.

Who should sign the walking possession agreement?

5.221   In many cases the walking possession agreement will be signed by the judgment debtor and the standard form walking possession agreement indicates that it should be signed by the judgment debtor. However, this is not strictly necessary. The agreement need only be signed by a 'responsible person' in the premises. In *National Commercial Bank of Scotland v Arcam Demolition and Construction Ltd*[1] judgment had been obtained against a married man and a writ of fi fa issued against him. The sheriff's officer went to a house occupied by the husband and his wife and children and took possession of the contents of the house believing them to be the property of the husband. The sheriff's officer did not wish to remain in close possession and asked the husband to sign a walking possession agreement. The husband refused to do so on the basis that the goods had been sold to a third party some time before the judgment had been made against him. The sheriff's officer withdrew but over the next few weeks visited the house frequently and on one visit five and a half weeks later, when the husband was away, the sheriff's officer persuaded the wife to sign a walking agreement.

1   [1966] 2 QB 593.

5.222   Lord Denning MR held:

'But I do not think it necessary, in point of law, for the agreement to be made by the judgment debtor himself. It is sufficient if it is made by any responsible person in the house. Take the simple case where the only person in the house is a caretaker. It would suffice if the caretaker signed a form saying that he would not permit the goods to be removed and would inform the bailiff if anyone tried to remove them. It would not be necessary for the caretaker to have the authority of the judgment debtor. So here it was sufficient for the wife to agree that the goods would not be removed. She was a responsible person in the house. She could see to it that the goods were not removed: or, if anyone attempted to remove them, she could tell the bailiff. She did not need her husband's authority for the purpose. The agreement signed by her was good enough to give "walking possession," even though the judgment debtor did not authorise it, or even objected to it.'

Davies LJ and Russell LJ agreed.

5.223 The National Standards provide that an enforcement officer must withdraw from domestic premises if the only person present is, or appears to be, under the age of 18. However, they can ask when the debtor will be home, except where the only persons present at the domestic premises are children who appear to be under the age of 12, in which case they should withdraw without making any inquiries at all. In *Lumsden v Burnett*, a distress for rent case, the Court of Appeal held that a child of 13 was unable to sign a walking possession agreement on behalf of her father.[1] The Court of Appeal seemed to treat the question as one of agency, finding that the child had no express or implied authority to sign. Given that the age of capacity for the purposes of contract is generally 18[2] it is doubtful that a minor could enter into a walking possession agreement in any event.

[1]   [1898] 2 QB 177 at 181 and 185.
[2]   Family Law Reform Act 1969, s 1.

Can a walking possession agreement be agreed orally?

5.224 In *In Re Dalton*[1] the court found that the written walking possession agreement had been varied orally. While it may also be possible for a walking possession agreement be entered into orally, the risk of a finding that the agreement is invalid is that the enforcement officer has abandoned possession if he makes no further visits to the seized goods. Given the difficulties of proving that an oral agreement has been made, and the risks inherent in relying upon it, this is not advisable.

[1]   [1963] Ch 336.

Can a walking possession be posted in the judgment debtor's absence?

5.225 As has been noted, the notice of seizure (PF 55) encloses a standard form walking possession agreement. PF 55 must either be delivered to the judgment debtor or left at each place where execution is levied.[1]

[1]   RSC Ord 45, r 2.

5.226 In *Evans v Ribble Borough Council*,[1] a distress for unpaid community charges case, the court held that a walking possession agreement cannot be made effective by posting it in the judgment debtor's absence.[2] In that case the bailiff attended the debtor's home and discovered that she was not at home. He posted a number of papers through her door, including a walking possession agreement which the bailiff had signed. The court found that this was wholly ineffective as a method of securing and impounding the debtor's goods because a walking possession agreement is designed to ensure that possession of goods is maintained only once entry and seizure had been validly effected. As the bailiff had not entered the property and taken possession of the goods, the walking possession agreement by definition could not take effect.

1   [1992] 1 QB 757.

2   Although that case was concerned with distress for unpaid community charges, which is governed by special statutory rules, it is clear that the judge was prepared to assume that his decision was in principle equally applicable to *all* cases of distress: [1992] 1 QB 757 at 763.

5.227   While a writ of fi fa binds the goods at the time of delivery to the enforcement officer,[1] the binding only gives a *right of seizure*, it does not dispense with the need for the enforcement officer to effect seizure of the goods. Accordingly, the same principles should apply in the case of a writ of fi fa and posting a walking possession agreement in the judgment debtor's absence will not be effective.

1   See paras 5.127–5.146.

What if the judgment debtor refuses to agree to walking possession?

5.228   Where a debtor refuses to sign a walking possession agreement, the enforcement officer can retain possession of goods either by visiting the judgment debtor's premises periodically to check the goods have not been moved[1] or by physically removing them.

1   As in *Lloyds and Scottish Finance* [1966] 1 QB 764. Alternatively, a man can be left in close possession but in light of the minimal costs recoverable, this is unlikely to be an attractive option: see para 5.299.

5.229   Where the goods are left with the judgment debtor and periodic visits are made, the visits will only add to the ultimate costs of enforcement, which are recoverable from the judgment debtor. Such visits are also likely to be an unwelcome disturbance to a judgment debtor and these factors may be persuasive in encouraging the judgment debtor to sign the walking possession agreement.

Re-entry under walking possession agreement

5.230   The standard form walking possession agreement expressly authorises an enforcement officer, or a person acting on his behalf, to re-enter the judgment debtor's premises at any time and as often as the enforcement officer may consider necessary for the purpose of inspecting the goods or completing the execution of the writ. The standard form walking possession agreement for writs of fi fa is silent as to the use of force to effect re-entry. Historically, forms of walking possession agreement expressly authorised forceful re-entry[1] but when a standard form was introduced in 1953,[2] the reference to the use of force disappeared. The same is also true of walking possession agreements used by bailiffs for levying for distress for rent.

1   See eg the form of walking possession agreement set out in the judgment of Hillbery J in *Watson v Murray & Co* [1955] 2 QB 1 at 9, which stated, that: 'I hereby authorize and

empower you and your representative to re-enter my house and premises... and *if necessary to use force for that purpose.*' (Emphasis added.)

2   Sheriffs' Fees (Amendment) Order 1956, SI 1956/502, Sch 1.

5.231   In *McLeod v Butterwick,*[1] the combined appeal concerning the use of force to effect re-entry in the case of distress for rent and under writs of fi fa, a walking possession agreement had been entered into in the distress case but not in the case of the writ of fi fa. The distress for rent walking possession agreement provided simply that the bailiff 'may re-enter the premises at any time while the distraint is in force'.

1   [1998] 1 WLR 1603.

5.232   When the tenant was out, the bailiff had effected forcible re-entry relying on the wording 'may re-enter the premises at any time' in the walking possession agreement. The Court of Appeal was unequivocal in its rejection of the contention that this wording permitted forcible re-entry:

> 'The bailiff relies on the use of the unqualified words 'at any time.' He submits that they mean just that, so that the right is not dependent on the consent of the tenant or the presence of other circumstances sufficient to justify a forcible re-entry. I do not accept that submission. It cannot have been intended by the parties that the bailiff should be entitled, without notice, to break in at any time of day or night. If such a power were intended then it would require to be expressed in plain terms. That is certainly the case if the power were conferred by a statute: *Grove v Eastern Gas Board* [1952] 1 K.B. 77, 82. In my view, it would not be right to attribute an intention on the part of the tenant to confer such wide-ranging rights on the bailiff without clear expression. I do not think that the use of the words 'at any time' is sufficient, for they deal with time not method and must be read against the background of being a prescribed form which superseded the form previously in common use which expressly referred to the use of force'.[1]

1   [1998] 1 WLR 1603 at 1616.

5.233   Morritt LJ found that following initial entry and seizure the rights of a sheriff were very similar to those applicable to bailiffs.[1] However, it is unclear whether his findings on walking possession were strictly included, particularly since no walking possession agreement had been entered into in the writ of fi fa appeal. In any event, given that the modern wording for a writ of fi fa walking possession agreement is so similar to that before the court in *McLeod,*[1] it would be surprising if a different rule applied. The standard form of walking possession agreement used in the case of writs of fi fa would not therefore seem to confer rights on an enforcement officer to effect forcible re-entry.

1   [1998] 1 WLR 1603 at 1617.
2   It provides: 'to re-enter my premises at any time and as often as you may consider necessary.'

5.234   The distress for rent rules in force at the time in *McLeod* provided that the form of walking possession agreement might be 'used with such variations as circumstances may require'. The current distress for rent rules contain an identical provision.[1] Morritt LJ also observed obiter in *McLeod* that, subject to any question of duress, a tenant might lawfully agree that a bailiff might re-enter by force.[2] It would therefore seem that the *distress for rent* walking possession agreement *can* be amended to include a provision to allow forcible re-entry and this would be effective provided it is expressed in plain terms. By contrast, reg 15 of the High Court Enforcement Officers Regulations 2004[3] simply provides that: 'Schedule 4 to these Regulations sets out the form of an agreement under which an enforcement officer may take walking possession of goods.' This does not make it express whether the form of agreement may be varied and it is therefore uncertain whether an express provision for forcible re-entry in a walking possession agreement would be effective. If such a provision is included, it would need to be made in plain terms.

[1]   Distress for Rent Rules 1988, SI 1988/2050, r 2(2).
[2]   [1998] 1 WLR 1603 at 1613.
[3]   SI 2004/400.

Breach of the walking possession agreement

5.235   If the judgment debtor breaches the walking possession agreement and sells his goods, the enforcement officer will be able to follow the goods into the hands of subsequent transferees, even if they are good faith purchasers for value (see paras 5.133–5.141).

Physical removal and impounding

5.236   Where the judgment creditor believes that the judgment debtor may act in breach of a walking possession agreement by removal of the goods, serious consideration should be given to physical removal and storage of the goods by the enforcement officer pending sale. While the enforcement officer can retake the goods of which he is in possession under a walking possession agreement if they are moved or sold, he would first have to locate them, and this may not be possible, particularly where the goods have been removed from the jurisdiction. High value items which can easily be moved, such as jewellery, paintings and antiques, may be at particular risk. Where the goods have been sold, if the enforcement officer does locate them and retakes possession this may lead to litigation, however ill-conceived, over whether title has passed. The practical message is that prevention may be simpler than cure.

5.237   However, the costs that will be incurred through removal and storage of the goods should be considered carefully by the judgment creditor and his solicitor before such steps are taken because the enforcement officer is entitled to charge the sums actually paid in this regard.[1] While these sums are ordinarily deductible from the proceeds of sale of the judgment debtor's goods, the enforcement officer may sue the judgment creditor for his fees if he is unable to recover them from the judgment debtor (see para 5.304).

[1]   High Court Enforcement Officers Regulations 2004, SI 2004/400, Sch 3, para 5(3).

Receipts for goods seized and removed

5.238   The National Standards require that a receipt should be given for any goods actually removed (in addition to producing an inventory).

Abandonment

5.239   A judgment debtor may seek to resist enforcement of a writ of fi fa on the grounds that the enforcement officer has abandoned possession of the goods. If an enforcement officer abandons possession of the judgment debtor's goods once they have been seized, they will no longer be subject to the writ. The enforcement officer will potentially be liable to the judgment creditor for damages in these circumstances.[1]

1   *Ackland v Paynter* (1820) 8 Price 95 and *Blades v Arundale* (1813) 1 M & S 711.

5.240   The question of whether there has been abandonment is one of fact.[1] Evidence that the enforcement officer or his agent was absent from the judgment debtor's premises will be considered prima facie evidence of abandonment.[2] However, as has been noted, the enforcement officer will not be taken to have abandoned the goods where they remain on the judgment debtor's premises under a walking possession agreement (in which case no further visits need be made by the enforcement officer). Even where there is no walking possession agreement, there will be no abandonment provided the enforcement officer makes periodic visits to the judgment debtor's premises to rebut any suggestion of abandonment. In *Lloyds and Scottish Finance Ltd v Modern Cars and Caravans (Kingston) Ltd*,[3] seven visits in two months were held sufficient to rebut any suggestion of abandonment, although this will ultimately be a question of fact in each case.

1   *Bagshawes Ltd v Deacon* [1898] 2 QB 173.
2   *Ackland v Paynter* (1820) 8 Price 95.
3   [1966] 1 QB 746.

5.241   In *McLeod v Butterwick*[1] the judgment debtor contended that there had been an abandonment of possession by the sheriff's officer because no walking possession agreement had been signed and the enforcement officer did not visit the goods for eleven months because there were ongoing interpleader proceedings. The Court of Appeal rejected this contention:[2]

'If, over a long period, there is simply silence and inactivity by the sheriff I can easily see that there is abandonment of possession. But I find it very difficult to see in this case how there could be. There were long and continuing interpleader proceedings. I have only briefly summarised what happened, but there were numerous steps over months. Central to a sheriff's interpleader and, indeed, his bothering to start the proceeding at all, is the concept that he is seeking to establish possession, though over what he does not know; what he needs is the court's direction to tell him what he is entitled to retain. Indeed, the final order in the interpleader was that the sheriff would release his possession of certain items, which would scarcely be necessary if he had abandoned possession of them. I find in the context of those proceedings and the immediate activity by the sheriff following the determination by the deputy judge on 13 December, that it is very difficult to say that the sheriff abandoned possession of the goods.'

1   [1998] 1 WLR 1603, CA.
2   [1996] 1 WLR 995 at 999–1000; affirmed [1998] 1 WLR 1603 at 1628, CA.

Reform of securing and impounding

5.242   The Effective Enforcement White Paper proposes[1] simplifying the law on seizure and impounding in favour of what it terms 'taking legal control of goods'. Taking legal control of goods would include any of the following:

(a) by agreement (formerly walking possession);
(b) by securing goods on the premises (for example, locking them in a room or close possession); and
(c) by removal from the premises.

1   Para 175.

5.243   Provision of an inventory, which either lists every item seized or states that all goods on the premises have been seized, will also become mandatory.[1] At the time of writing there were not yet any proposals for implementation of these reforms.

1   Para 178.

PAYMENT BY THE JUDGMENT DEBTOR

5.244   It is open to the judgment debtor to make payment of the amount due under the writ at any time. The notice of seizure explains that the sums set out in the writ are due and that payment may be made to the enforcement officer by cash or bankers draft (or cheques provided the enforcement officer agrees), failing which the execution will proceed and the judgment debtor's goods will be sold.

5.245   As a matter of practice, where the judgment creditor consents, the enforcement officer may also agree to accept payment of the judgment debt by instalments. Whether this should be agreed will depend on the circumstances and what available assets the judgment debtor has to satisfy the writ. Where there are insufficient assets to cover the full amount, it may make sense to accept payments by instalments. Human rights arguments may also weigh in favour of this course (see paras 5.327–5.333).

Effect of payment by a judgment debtor

5.246   Once the judgment debtor has paid the judgment debt, his obligations under that judgment or order are extinguished.[1] A person who issues a writ of fi fa after payment[2] or after a valid tender[3] is liable for trespass. Similarly, a person issuing a writ of fi fa for a sum greater than the amount actually due at the time of issue would also be liable for trespass. Solicitors issuing writs on behalf of their client should be aware that this liability extends to them too. In *Clissold v Cratchley*[4] a solicitor and his client were found liable for trespass where the judgment debt had been paid in full at another of the solicitor's offices three hours before they issued a writ of fi fa in the High Court, even though neither of them knew of that payment. If neither the judgment creditor nor any person authorised by him to receive money in payment of the judgment debt is within the jurisdiction, a stay of execution will be granted on payment of the judgment debt into court.[5]

1   *Clissold v Cratchley* [1910] 2 KB 244, CA.
2   *Clissold v Cratchley* [1910] 2 KB 244, CA.
3   *Cubitt v Gamble* (1919) 35 TLR 233, KBD.
4   [1910] 2 KB 244.
5   *Re a Debtor* [1912] 1 KB 53 at 62, CA.

SALE

5.247 Following seizure the judgment debtor's goods must be sold unless the judgment debtor tenders payment to avoid the sale. The enforcement officer is not entitled to hand over the judgment debtor's goods to the judgment creditor[1] nor to keep them himself and pay off the judgment creditor.[2] The normal procedure for the sale of goods is by public auction although, with the permission of the court, goods can also be sold by private tender. Following sale, the sums specified in the writ should be paid over to the judgment creditor. However, this payment should only be made after a holding period of 14 days to comply with the provisions of the Insolvency Act 1986 (see paras 5.316–5.317 and 5.322–5.323).

1   *Thomson v Clerk* (1596) Cro Eliz 504.
2   *Waller v Weedale* (1604) Noy 107.

Second hand value

5.248 One practical point to bear in mind is that the second-hand value of most goods is usually only a small percentage of their original purchase price. The contents of the average family home may be unlikely to yield significant sums and there may be human rights objections where the sums raised by the sale of such items are wholly disproportionate to the judgment debt (see paras 5.327–5.333). This is reflected in the National Standards, which provide that enforcement agents should take all reasonable steps to satisfy themselves that the value of the goods impounded in satisfaction of the judgment is proportional to the value of the debt and charges owed. In a commercial enforcement scenario, the judgment creditor is likely to be looking to locate high value items that will yield significant sums when sold.

Sale by public auction

5.249 Sale of the judgment debtor's goods must be made by public auction unless the court orders otherwise.[1] It is a statutory requirement that a sale by public auction must be publicly advertised during the three days preceding the day of sale and on the day of sale itself.[2] (However, a sale made in breach of these requirements will not be invalidated until set aside by the court.[3])

1   CA 2003, Sch 7, para 10(2)(a).
2   CA 2003, Sch 7, para 10(2)(b). There is no requirement to defer sale for a period of at least five days following the date of seizure as is required under a county court warrant of execution in the case of a writ of fi fa.
3   *Crawshaw v Harrison* [1894] 1 QB 79.

Time for the auction to be held

5.250   The sale by auction must take place within a reasonable time after seizure. No precise time is specified in CA 2003. The Effective Enforcement White Paper proposes that no goods should be sold until the expiration of seven calendar days following the day when the enforcement agent took legal control of the goods. However, one week's delay has been held to be unreasonably long where a sheriff received notice of an act of bankruptcy by the judgment debtor and failed to make inquiries to verify the act of bankruptcy.[1] An enforcement officer cannot delay a sale even though he thinks it might be beneficial to do so. In *Re Sheriff of Essex, Terell v Fisher*,[2] it was held that delaying execution so as to enable the judgment debtor to continue his business (even though the sheriff believed that doing so would better enable the judgment debtor to raise the money to pay judgment debt) could not be justified. If the judgment creditor wishes to allow the judgment debtor to carry on business then a walking possession agreement could be used (see paras 5.216-5.235).

1   *Ayshford v Murray* (1870) 23 LT 470.
2   (1862) 10 WR 796.

5.251   Where the judgment creditor[1] (or the judgment debtor[2]) can show that he has suffered damage as a consequence of an unreasonable delay in the sale, the enforcement officer will be liable to him in damages. Thus where, for example, the goods seized are perishable or depreciate in value, the sale should take place without undue delay.

1   *Ayshford v Murray* (1870) 23 LT 470.
2   *Carlile v Parkins* (1822) 3 Stark 163.

Proper price to be obtained

5.252   The enforcement officer must put the seized goods up for sale for a reasonable price. He must not conduct the sale so as to prevent the goods fetching such a price as might otherwise be obtained nor will it be acceptable to sell them to the highest bidder if the price is very much below their value.[1] If an adequate price cannot be obtained, the sale should be adjourned.[2]

1   *Keightley v Birch* (1814) 3 Camp 521, where the court found that the sheriff should have waited for 'a venditioni exponas, the meaning of which is 'sell for the best price you can obtain'.
2   See *Edge v Kavanagh* (1888) 24 LRI (Ireland) where a sale was set aside on the grounds that the sheriff had not taken reasonable and proper care to advertise the sale and the farm was therefore sold at an undervalue (£5 rather than £600 valuation).

Holding auction on judgment debtor's premises

5.253 An enforcement agent cannot sell the goods on the judgment debtor's premises without the debtor's consent, except where a sale elsewhere is impossible. In *Watson v Murray*[1] the sheriff took possession of a judgment debtor's stock in her ladies and children's outfitters shop. In the run up to the auction, the sheriff's officers stuck posters on the windows advertising the auction, locked the judgment creditor from the premises where they had lotted goods for the auction, opened the premises to the public for viewing the items to be auctioned, and proceeded to start the auction in the shop (although it was stopped as the judgment debt was paid). The court found that the sheriff was liable for trespass in respect of these actions. The court held:[2]

> 'At common law the sheriff's duty is to remove the goods to some place where they can be safely kept until they are sold, but I cannot find any English authority which decides that he can, if he chooses, use the debtor's premises for the purpose of holding a sale there. It does not appear to me that in this case it is established that it was impossible to hold the sale anywhere else than on the plaintiff's premises. It was, no doubt, extremely difficult in the particular circumstances to arrange for it elsewhere, and no doubt the defendants decided that it was expedient to hold the sale at the plaintiff's shop; but the plaintiff objected and they knew that she objected. They must in those circumstances, it seems to me, show that they had a legal right to do what they did notwithstanding the plaintiff's objection.
>
> ...
>
> It may be that if the sheriff can show that it was not possible to sell the goods except on the debtor's premises, it would be lawful for him so to do. Part of his duty is to sell the goods so as to make of them sufficient to satisfy the debt which is the subject of the writ of fi fa. which he has to execute, and the law will not require of him that which is impossible. But the defendants in this case have not established that it was impossible to remove and sell the goods away from the plaintiff's premises. They have shown that by the concessions they had made to the plaintiff it had become extremely difficult for them so to do before an act of bankruptcy by the plaintiff was committed, but their evidence does not amount to more than this.'

[1]   [1955] 2 QB 1.
[2]   *Watson v Murray & Co* [1955] 2 QB 1 at 17-19.

5.254 However, while the sheriff was found liable for trespass, the court held it was difficult to say what damage the plaintiff suffered as a consequence. The court rejected the judgment creditor's contention that the posters were so injurious to her business that she was obliged finally to sell up and close down, observing that it was not possible to decide the extent to which this would inevitably have been caused by her grave financial difficulties. As a consequence only nominal damages were awarded.

5.255 It may be in the judgment debtor's interests to agree to a sale on the premises because this attracts significantly lower fees from the enforcement officer.[1] The Effective Enforcement White Paper proposes that the sale of the judgment debtor's goods may take place on the judgment debtor's commercial premises unless the debtor makes a written request that it takes place elsewhere, and may take place on domestic premises with the consent of the debtor.[2]

1   High Court Enforcement Officers Regulations 2004, SI 2004/400, Sch 3, para 6(1)(b).
2   Paragraph 185.

Proportionality

5.256   The Independent Review of Bailiff Law Report[1] recommended that 'where there are insufficient distrainable goods on the premises to cover the expenses and 10% of the debt, or £50, whichever is the lesser, the goods should not be sold.'[2] However, this recommendation was not accepted in the Effective Enforcement White Paper on the basis that the sale of an item at auction will always vary. Nevertheless, the White Paper recommended that enforcement officers consider the principle of proportionality when enforcing writs and do not seize goods when it is obvious that the sale of such goods will not meet the expenses of the officer and some of the debt.[3] A failure to do so may also be in breach of a judgment debtor's human rights (see paras 5.327–5.333).

1   Independent Review of Bailiff Law Report, June 2000.
2   2003 White Paper, para 187.
3   2003 White Paper, para 187.

Private sale

5.257   Sale other than by public auction requires the permission of the court.[1] The judgment creditor, judgment debtor or the enforcement officer are all entitled to apply to the court for a sale to take place other than by public auction.[2] The application must be made under CPR Pt 23 and the application notice must contain a short statement of the grounds for the application.[3] The enforcement officer may have experience of which goods are likely to reach higher prices under private contract than at public auction.

1   CA 2003, Sch 7, para 10(2)(a).
2   RSC Ord 47, r 6(1).
3   RSC Ord 47, r 6(2).

Notice of other execution creditors

5.258   Where an enforcement officer has notice of another execution or executions in respect of the judgment debtor's goods, the court will not consider an application for permission to sell privately until notice of that application has been given to the other execution creditor or creditors.[1] An execution creditor given notice in this way has a right to be heard on the application for a private sale.[2]

1   CA 2003, Sch 7, para 10(3).
2   CA 2003, Sch 7, para 10(4).

5.259   Where the applicant is the judgment debtor or judgment creditor, the enforcement officer must, if requested by the applicant, inform him whether he knows of any other writs of execution against the goods of the judgment debtor and provide a list of any such writs. This list should be produced by the applicant at the hearing.[1]

1   RSC Ord 47, r 6(3).

5.260   The application notice must be served on the judgment creditor, judgment debtor, enforcement officer and any other person who has issued a writ of execution in respect of the judgment debtor's goods at least four days before the hearing.[1] Any person on whom the application notice is served can attend and be heard at the hearing.[2]

1   RSC Ord 47, r 6(4).
2   RSC Ord 47, r 6(7).

Private sale made without leave of the court

5.261   In *Crawshaw v Harrison*[1] a sale of the judgment debtor's goods took place by private contract with the judgment debtor's consent but without the leave of the court. This was held valid against a subsequent execution creditor unless set aside by the court. In the words of Wright J:[2]

'The section [s 145 of the Bankruptcy Act 1883] does not say that … the sale shall be ipso facto void. The sale, it is true, is irregular, and might upon a proper application by any person who is injured by the irregularity be set aside, while it may be that such person would also have an action against the sheriff for his breach of duty. But no steps have been taken in the present case to set the sale aside. The goods, therefore, are not the goods of the debtor, and the plaintiff is not entitled to succeed.'

1   In *Crawshaw v Harrison* [1894] 1 QB 79 the court was considering the Bankruptcy Act 1883, s 145 (now repealed), which provided: 'Where the sheriff sells the goods of a debtor under an execution for a sum exceeding twenty pounds (including legal incidental expenses), the sale shall, unless the Court from which the process issued otherwise orders, be made by public auction, and not by bill of sale or private contract, and shall be publicly advertised by the sheriff on and during three days next preceding the day of sale'. This provision is substantially the same as the requirements of CA 2003, Sch 7, paras 10(1)-(2).
2   [1894] 1 QB 79 at 82.

Protection of enforcement officers and purchasers

5.262   CA 2003, Sch 7, para 11 provides a measure of statutory protection to an enforcement officer who sells goods found in the possession of the judgment debtor at the time of seizure and which are sold without any claims having been made to them. The protection is qualified rather than absolute. For reasons that will be explained, purchasers of such goods are granted absolute protection. Paragraph 11 states:

'(1) This paragraph applies if—
(a) a writ of execution has been issued from the High Court,
(b) goods in the possession of an execution debtor are seized by an enforcement officer or other person under a duty to execute the writ, and

(c) the goods are sold by that officer without any claims having been made to them.

(2) If this paragraph applies—

(a) the purchaser of the goods acquires a good title to them, and

(b) no person is entitled to recover against the officer or anyone acting under his authority—

(i) for any sale of the goods, or

(ii) for paying over the proceeds prior to the receipt of a claim to the goods, unless it is proved that the person from whom recovery is sought had notice, or might by making reasonable enquiry have ascertained, that the goods were not the property of the execution debtor.

(3) Nothing in this paragraph affects the right of a lawful claimant to any remedy to which he is entitled against any person other than the enforcement officer or other officer charged with the execution of the writ.

(4) "Lawful claimant" means a person who proves that at the time of sale he had a title to any goods seized and sold.

(5) This paragraph is subject to sections 183, 184 and 346 of the Insolvency Act 1986.'

History of the provision

5.263   In *Singh v Kenyan Insurance Ltd*[1] the Privy Council were asked to consider Kenyan legislation which derived from the Bankruptcy and Deeds of Arrangement Act 1913, s 15. The wording of the 1913 Act was the same in all material respects to the current wording contained in CA 2003, Sch 7, para 11 set out above. Lord Reid, giving the advice of the Privy Council, explained the history of the Bankruptcy and Deeds of Arrangement Act 1913, s 15 and the apparent mischief which it was passed to remedy:

'In construing section 45(3) it is proper to bear in mind the position before the passing of section 15 of the English Act of 1913, from which it is copied. A bailiff or other officer was only entitled to seize and sell goods which belonged to the execution-debtor, but it was often difficult for him to ascertain the ownership of goods in the possession of the debtor and he might without negligence sometimes seize and sell goods which did not in fact belong to the debtor. He gave no warranty of title of the goods which he sold. A purchaser could seldom know or ascertain to whom the goods belonged but he had to take the risk of the true owner appearing and recovering the goods from him while he could not recover the price which he had paid for them. This was made clear in *Crane & Sons v Ormerod*. And the liability of the bailiff or other officer when he made a mistake was made clear in *Jelks v Hayward*. Section 15 of the 1913 Act must have been enacted to deal with that position ...'

---

[1]   [1954] AC 287, PC.

Goods sold not the property of judgment debtor

5.264   As Lord Reid explained, as a practical matter an enforcement officer will often genuinely not know that goods found in the possession of a judgment debtor may belong to another. A purchaser at an auction is in no better position.

5.265   Two principal consequences follow from the modern statutory provisions where an enforcement officer sells goods found in a judgment debtor's possession in respect of which no claims are made by any other person. The first is that the purchaser acquires good title to the goods sold to him.[1] The second is that no claim can be made against the enforcement officer (or anyone acting under his authority) for any sale of the goods or for paying over the proceeds prior to the receipt of a claim to the goods unless it can be shown that the enforcement officer had notice or might reasonably have ascertained that the goods did not belong to the judgment debtor.[2]

[1]   CA 2003, Sch 7, para 11(2)(a).
[2]   CA 2003, Sch 7, para 11(2)(b).

5.266   The statutory protection afforded to purchasers under the provisions of CA 2003, Sch 7, para 11 and its forebears has come under attack on a number of occasions. In *Curtis v Maloney*[1] the plaintiff had left his boat with wainwrights who subsequently got into financial difficulties and had judgment entered against them. A sheriff executing a writ of fi fa seized the boat and sold it at public auction. The claimant sought to recover the boat from a purchaser who had bought it at the auction. The plaintiff contended that his right to recovery against the defendant (the purchaser) was preserved by the wording of Bankruptcy and Deeds of Arrangement Act 1913, s 15, which is in all material respect identical to the wording of CA 2003, Sch 7, para 11. In essence, the plaintiff contended that, notwithstanding the clear statutory provision that the purchaser acquired good title, his rights against the purchaser defendant were preserved because the wording in the statute[2] provided only for the extinguishing of his rights as the 'true owner' as against a sheriff.[3]

[1]   [1951] 1 KB 736.
[2]   Bankruptcy and Deeds of Arrangement Act 1913, s 15 provided: 'Where any goods in the possession of an execution debtor at the time of seizure by a sheriff, high bailiff, or other officer charged with the enforcement of a writ, warrant, or other process of execution, are sold by such sheriff, high bailiff, or other officer, without any claim having been made to the same, the purchaser of the goods so sold shall acquire a good title to the goods so sold, and no person shall be entitled to recover against the sheriff, high bailiff, or other officer, or anyone lawfully acting under the authority of either of them, except as provided by the Bankruptcy Acts 1883 and 1890, for any sale of such goods or for paying over the proceeds thereof, prior to the receipt of a claim to the said goods unless it is proved that the person from whom recovery is sought had notice, or might by making reasonable inquiry have ascertained that the goods were not the property of the execution debtor: Provided that nothing in this section contained shall affect the right of any claimant who may prove that at the time of sale he had a title to any goods so seized and sold to any remedy to which he may be entitled against any person other than such sheriff, high bailiff, or other officer as aforesaid.'
[3]   Ie the plaintiff relied on a construction of the then equivalent of CA 2003, Sch 7, para 11(3), namely 'nothing in this paragraph affects the right of [the true owner] to any remedy to which he is entitled against any person *other than the enforcement officer or other officer charged with the execution of the writ*'. (Emphasis added.)

5.267   The Court of Appeal unanimously rejected this interpretation of the statute. They concluded that the reference to a purchaser acquiring 'good title'[1] could only mean good title against the world, which included the original owner. The Court held that to read the terms of the statute otherwise would render the reference to 'good title' meaningless.

[1]   Now CA 2003, Sch 7, para (11)2(a).

5.268   The decision in *Curtis v Maloney* was approved by the Privy Council in *Singh v Kenyan Insurance Ltd.*[1] In *Singh*, the owner of a motor omnibus which had been seized and sold at auction in satisfaction of a third party's debt sought to recover it from the purchaser. In that case, the 'true owner' sought to attack the purchaser's title by reference to statutory provisions the equivalent of which are now contained in CA 2003, Sch 7, para 11(2).[2] The 'true owner' contended that the reference in the statute to 'unless it is proved that the person from whom recovery is sought ...' should be construed to mean that 'the purchaser of the goods acquires good title to them ... unless it is proved that the person from whom recovery is sought [ie the purchaser] had notice or might reasonably have ascertained that the goods did not belong to the judgment debtor.'

[1]   [1954] AC 287, PC.
[2]   *Singh* concerned the wording of Banking Ordinance 1930, s 45(3), which is in identical terms to the provisions of Bankruptcy and Deeds of Arrangement Act 1913, s 15, set out in para 5.266, n 2 above.

5.269   The Privy Council rejected this interpretation. They held that the words 'from whom recovery is sought' (now contained in CA 2003, Sch 7, para 11(2)) only referred to the enforcement officer and not to a purchaser. As Lord Reid explained:[1]

'Moreover, the realities of the situation make that construction probable: one would expect ... [an enforcement officer] to be required to make reasonable inquiry, but it is difficult to see what reasonable inquiry as to title could be expected of a person who intended to bid for goods at a sale by auction.'

[1]   [1954] AC 287 at 299, PC.

5.270   The Privy Council in *Singh* also rejected the interpretation of what is now the Courts Act 2003, Sch 7, para 11(3) that was contended for by the 'true owner' in *Curtis v Maloney* (see para 5.266 above) on the basis that it would nullify the enactment.

5.271   As Lord Reid recognised, this interpretation of what is now CA 2003, s 11 and Sch 7 means that even a purchaser who had notice of the original owner's title can take free of it:

'... their Lordships must therefore hold that the subsection gives a good title to purchasers whether or not they had notice of the true position. It was hardly disputed that "a good title" must mean a title good against the true owner. Their Lordships think it right to add that it is not impossible to find reasons which might have led the legislature to confer such an unusual right on purchasers. It may have been thought necessary to give every encouragement to bidders at such sales by auction. There would be very few cases where a bidder in fact had notice of the true position and the possibility of constructive notice may have been neglected. It may have been thought advantageous to assure all purchasers that they could buy without risk even if that meant that in some cases the true owner would be deprived of one of his remedies.' [1]

[1]   [1954] AC 287 at 299, PC.

Claim by true owner against judgment debtor

5.272   So far only claims by the true owner of the goods against the enforcement officer and purchaser have been considered. The true owner of the goods may also have claims against the judgment debtor (for allowing the goods to be sold) and the judgment creditor (for receiving the proceeds of sale). Indeed, in *Curtis v Mahoney*[1] Denning LJ held that what is now the Courts Act 2003, Sch 7, para 11(3):

'is to be explained by the anxiety of the draftsman not to deprive the original owner of his remedy against any wrongdoer who had converted the goods before the sale. If it were not for the proviso, the execution creditor might have argued that the original owner's claim for money had and received was not preserved.'

[1]   [1954] AC 287 at 299, PC.

5.273   The notice of seizure[1] puts the judgment debtor on notice that he should inform the enforcement officer if any of the goods seized belong to another. If he does not do so and the goods are subsequently sold pursuant to the writ, he may be liable to the true owner in conversion since in failing to inform the enforcement officer as to the goods' true ownership he will have dealt with them in a manner inconsistent with their true ownership. However, a right to damages for conversion against a judgment debtor who has just had his goods seized and sold under a writ of fi fa is unlikely to prove an attractive method of seeking to recover any loss.

[1]   [1951] 1 KB 736 at 745.

Claim by the true owner against the judgment creditor

5.274   What is likely to be of more value is a claim by the true owner against the judgment creditor in respect of the proceeds of sale for monies had and received. In *Jones v Woodhouse*[1] the plaintiff had let furniture under a hire purchase agreement to the tenant judgment debtor. The furniture belonging to the plaintiff was seized along with other goods belonging to the judgment debtor. All of the furniture and goods were sold at public auction and the proceeds of sale were paid to the defendant, who was the judgment creditor. Even though the plaintiff was informed of the seizure by the judgment debtor some days before the sale, and did nothing about it until after the furniture had been sold, the plaintiff succeeded in an action for money had and received against the defendant judgment creditor.[2] However, since only about half the proceeds of sale emanated from the plaintiff's furniture, the plaintiff's claim was limited to that amount.

[1]   [1923] 2 KB 117.
[2]   McCardie J at [1923] 2 KB 117 at 126 considered that the Bankruptcy and Deeds of Arrangement Act 1913, s 15 (a provision similar to that contained in CA 2003) only protected the sheriff and purchaser but not the judgment creditor.

Insolvency

5.275   The protections set out in CA 2003, Sch 7, para 11 are expressed to be subject to Insolvency Act 1986, ss 183, 184 and 346. These provisions are concerned with the circumstances in which execution is effective against a bankrupt and a company in liquidation and are considered at paras 5.313–5.326.

ADVERSE CLAIMS AND INTERPLEADER[1]

5.276   After an enforcement officer has seized the judgment debtor's goods, a third party may claim that the goods seized belong to them rather than the judgment debtor. Claims vary from those by a spouse or a member of the judgment debtor's family, to claims by a rival creditor of the judgment debtor that the goods seized are subject to a hire purchase agreement.

1   Interpleader is considered in detail in *Halsbury's Laws of England* (4th edn Reissue, 2001), vol 37, paras 1419–1459.

5.277   A procedure known as interpleader provides a mechanism to deal with these types of disputes. The procedural rules are set out in RSC Ord 17.[1] They provide both a mechanism for the resolution of disputes as to the ownership of goods which have been seized and a means whereby the enforcement officer can obtain a degree of protection from claims for taking possession of the goods.

1   Preserved in CPR, Sch 1.

5.278   RSC Ord 17, r 1(b) provides:

'Where – . . .
(b) claim is made to any money, goods or chattels taken or intended to be taken by a sheriff in execution under any process, or to the proceeds or value of any such goods or chattels, by a person other than the person against whom the process is issued [ie the judgment debtor],......... the sheriff [or individual authorised to act as an enforcement officer under CA 2003], may apply to the court for relief by way of interpleader.'

Receipt of an adverse claim by the enforcement officer

5.279   The interpleader rules actively encourage the parties to agree matters informally between themselves.

5.280   Any person making an adverse claim to any goods seized, or intended to be seized, by the enforcement officer, or to the proceeds of sale of such goods, must give notice to the enforcement officer of his claim. The notice given must include his address and confirm that it is his address for service.[1]

1   RSC Ord 17, r 2(1).

5.281   If an adverse claim is received, the enforcement officer must forthwith give notice to the judgment creditor of the claim.[1] The notice that should be used is PF 23.

1   RSC Ord 17, r 2(2).

5.282 The judgment creditor has seven days from the receipt of the notice[1] to inform the enforcement officer whether he disputes or admits the claim. The response should be made using PF 24.

1   RSC Ord 17, r 3(7).

5.283 If the judgment creditor admits the claim, he is only liable for the enforcement officer's fees and expenses incurred prior to receipt of that notice. Where the enforcement officer receives a notice that a claim is admitted, the enforcement officer will withdraw from possession of the goods and is entitled to apply for an order restraining any claim being made against him for having taking possession of the goods.[1]

1   RSC Ord 17, r 2(4).

5.284 If the judgment creditor disputes the claim or fails to respond with seven days, or the interpleader claimant refuses to withdraw his claim, then the enforcement officer may interplead.[1] An enforcement officer's interpleader application should be made by application notice under CPR Pt 23[2] and the wording from PF 26 QB should be included. PF 26 QB includes a notice that the person claiming the goods must within 14 days of service serve on the judgment creditor and the enforcement officer a witness statement or affidavit specifying the money, goods and/or chattels claimed and setting out the grounds upon which such claim is based.[3]

1   RSC Ord 17, r 2(3).
2   RSC Ord 17, r 3(1). Although Ord 17, r 3 is somewhat unclear as to whether a claim form or application notice should be used, the form prescribed under CPR 4(1) for sheriff's interpleader (PF26 QB) is for use with an application notice.
3   RSC Ord 17, r 3(6).

The practical perspective

5.285 Interpleader can be a costly form of satellite litigation. While it is important that the judgment creditor is prepared to dispute dubious claims and maintain a healthy cynicism with regards to unidentified parties claiming to own goods, the judgment creditor and his advisers should also take a realistic approach about which of those claims to admit. For example, there is little to be achieved by disputing a bank or financial institution's claim that goods are subject to hire purchase where evidence of the agreement has been provided.

Claims to exempt goods

5.286 Interpleader proceedings are not generally concerned with any adverse claims to goods made by the judgment debtor.[1] However, there is an exception where the judgment debtor claims that the goods are exempt from seizure on the grounds that they are tools of the trade or household necessities (see paras 5.26–5.37).[2]

1   RSC Ord 17, r 1(2).
2   RSC Ord 17, r 2A(1). The rule still refers to SCA 1981, s 138(3A) (repealed) which is now CA 2003, Sch 7, para 9(3).

5.287   If the judgment debtor claims that goods seized, or intended to be seized, by an enforcement officer are exempt from seizure he must give notice in writing to the enforcement officer. The notice must be given within five days of the seizure and should identify all those goods in respect of which he makes a claim for exemption and the grounds of such claim in respect of each item.[1] Where the tools of the trade exemption is relied on, the court will not just accept the judgment debtor's claim (even on affidavit) that a whole category of goods are exempt, he will be required to demonstrate that they are for use by him personally and necessary for his business.[2]

1   RSC Ord 17, r 2A(1).
2   *Moffat v Lemkin (formerly High Sheriff of Greater London)* (unreported), 24 November 2003.

5.288   Having received a notice that the judgment debtor claims goods are exempt from seizure, the enforcement officer will notify the judgment creditor and any person who has given notice that he makes a claim to the goods. The judgment creditor and any claimant must inform the enforcement officer in writing within seven days of receipt of the notice whether he admits or disputes the judgment debtor's claim that the goods are exempt from seizure.[1]

1   RSC Ord 17, r 2A(2).

5.289   If the claim to exemption is admitted, or the persons notified fail to respond, the enforcement officer will withdraw from possession of the goods.[1]

1   RSC Ord 17, r 2A(3).

5.290   Where any of the parties notifies the enforcement officer that the claim to exemption is disputed, the enforcement officer must forthwith apply to the court for directions. The application for directions should be made by application notice in accordance with CPR Pt 23.[1] As part of this application the enforcement officer may seek an order restraining any claim against him in respect of seizure of the goods.[2]

1   RSC Ord 17, r 2A(5).
2   RSC Ord 17, r 2A(6).

5.291   At the hearing of the application, the court may determine the judgment debtor's claim summarily or give such directions for the determination of any issue raised by the claim as may be just.[1] If the matter is sufficiently complex, a trial of the issue may be required.

1   RSC Ord 17, r 2A(5).

Powers of the court

5.292   The court has a number of powers to help it resolve interpleader applications. In practice, how the court will approach the matter will depend entirely on the nature of the claim. If the claim is clearly spurious the court is likely to deal with it summarily. However, where the claim involves significant factual inquiry, the court is likely to require disclosure and witness statements.

Summary disposal

5.293 Where the question at issue is a question of law and the facts are not in dispute, the court may at the request of the parties summarily determine any question.[1]

1   RSC Ord 17, r 5(2).

Barring orders

5.294 Where the person making the claim to the goods is served with an application and fails to attend the hearing, or does appear but fails or refuses to comply with an order made in the proceedings, the court can forever bar him and his successors in title from claiming the goods.[1] If there are several claimants to the goods, the barring order does not affect the rights of the claimants between themselves.[2]

1   RSC Ord 17, r 5(3).
2   RSC Ord 17, r 5(3).

Power to sell goods

5.295 Where an enforcement officer has taken possession of goods and a claim is made that the goods are held by way of security for a debt, the court has the power to order the sale of goods and direct how the proceeds should be dealt with.[1] This is particularly useful for any property seized which has a charge over it.

1   RSC Ord 17, r 6.

Disclosure, trials and costs

5.296 The court can order a trial of an interpleader issue.[1] In addition the court can make any orders it thinks just in connection with interpleader proceedings, including orders for disclosure and further information[2] and costs.[3] Where the interpleader claimant fails to attend the hearing, the court can direct that the costs of the judgment creditor and enforcement officer are assessed by a master or district judge.[4] A number of standard form orders exist in connection with interpleader claims which can be used as appropriate.[5]

1   RSC Ord 17, rr 5(1)(b) and 11.
2   RSC Ord 17, r 10. Note that requests for further information can also be made.
3   RSC Ord 17, r 8.
4   RSC Ord 17, r 8(2).
5   PF 28 QB, PF 29 QB, PF 30 QB, PF 31 QB, PF 32 QB and PF 34 QB.

ENFORCEMENT OFFICERS' FEES

5.297 An enforcement officer is a private sector agent who is remunerated by charging fees calculated by reference to the recovery made. This is seen by many as one reason[1] why an enforcement officer is far more effective than his public sector counterpart, the county court bailiff, who is paid a flat salary.

¹   Another is that the county court bailiff is move likely to be faced with people who lack the means to pay.

5.298   In executing the writ, the enforcement officer must seize sufficient goods to satisfy the amount of the judgment debt, any interest payable, and the enforcement officer's own fees and expenses. Form PF 53, which contains the standard form writ of fi fa, states that an enforcement officer should seize sufficient of the judgment debtor's goods to raise the balance owing on the judgment debt and its associated costs and interest 'together with fees and charges to which you are entitled'.

Scale of fees

5.299   The scale of fees payable to an enforcement officer for executing writs of fi fa is set out in reg 13 of and Sch 3 to the High Court Enforcement Officers Regulations 2004.¹ The fee is made up of several components, which are summarised in the table below:

Fee	Amount Chargeable
Executing the writ ('poundage')	Percentage of amount recovered: 5% on first £100; 2.5% on amounts over £100.
Travel	Mileage allowance for travel to and from place of execution.²
Flat fee for seizure	£2 for each building or place of seizure.
Daily possession fee	£3 per day for close possession. £0.25 per day where a walking possession agreement is entered.
Removal and storage of goods	Actual cost (including the upkeep of animals that have been seized).
Sale of goods by public auction	Percentage fee on amounts realised.³ (This is designed to cover the auctioneer's commission and expenses.)
Sale of goods by private contract	Percentage fee on amounts realised.⁴

¹   SI 2004/400.
²   Currently 29.2p per mile up to a maximum of £50.
³   The fee is 15% on the first £100 realised, 12.5% on the next £900 realised and 10% on amounts realised above £1,000. If the auction is held on the judgment debtor's premises the fee is 7.5% on the sums realised plus expenses actually and reasonably incurred. Where no sale takes place but preparatory work has been done, the fee is 10% of the value goods if removed to the auctioneer's premises. Where the goods have not been removed from the judgment debtor's premises, the fee is 5% of the value of the goods plus expenses actually and reasonably incurred.
⁴   The fee is 7.5% on the first £100 realised, 6.25% on the next £900 realised and 5% on amounts realised above £1,000. Where work has been done preparing for a sale by auction, an additional sum not exceeding 2.5% of the value of the goods plus expenses actually and reasonably incurred.

5.300   The part of the fee for executing the writ that is a percentage of the amount recovered was historically known as 'poundage'. The position at common law regarding when an enforcement officer is entitled to payment of his fee is not altered by virtue of having a scale of fees set out in regulations.[1]

> 1   *Montague v Davies, Benachi & Co* [1911] 2 KB 595. The court was construing an order prescribing fees to be charged by a sheriff which contained provisions similar to the High Court Enforcement Officers Regulations 2004, SI 2004/400, para 13 concerning fees on withdrawal of a writ.

5.301   While unlikely to be relevant in the context of commercial enforcement, where a judgment or order is for less than £600, and does not entitle the judgment creditor to costs against the judgment debtor,[1] the enforcement officer will not be entitled to levy his fees or expenses. [1]

> 1   RSC Ord 47, r 4.

Responsibility for the fees

5.302   Where the execution of a writ of fi fa is completed by sale, the enforcement officer's fees may be deducted from the proceeds of sale.[1] However, not all writs of fi fa proceed as far as sale. Where the writ is satisfied or its execution stopped, the enforcement officer's fees must be paid by:

'(a)   the person upon whose application the writ was issued (ie the judgment creditor); or

(b)   the person at whose insistence the execution is stopped.'[2]

> 1   High Court Enforcement Officers Regulations 2004, SI 2004/400, reg 13(2). The writ also commands the enforcement officer to seize the judgment debtor's goods and raise therefrom the fees to which he is entitled.
> 2   High Court Enforcement Officers Regulations 2004, SI 2004/400, reg 13(3).

5.303   The poundage fee for 'executing' a writ of fi fa is payable by virtue of the fact that the enforcement officer has seized the goods.[1] This could be a very significant amount on a large seizure. If a writ is withdrawn because the judgment debtor agrees to pay the judgment debt, the liability for any fees payable to the enforcement officer should also be expressly agreed as part of that settlement. The amounts should be agreed with the enforcement officer before settling a figure with the judgment debtor. If not, the judgment creditor is likely to be landed with a large bill from the enforcement officer which he will not be in funds from the judgment debtor to pay.

> 1   *Bissicks v Bath Colliery* (1877) 2 Ex D 459.

5.304   The National Standards require that creditors must not request the suspension of a warrant or make direct payment arrangements with debtors without appropriate notification and payment of fees due to the enforcement agent. Where the enforcement officer is unable to recover his fees from the judgment debtor, for example because sale of the judgment debtor's goods raises insufficient funds, he may seek to recover them from the judgment creditor.[1] It seems he may not look to the solicitors for payment of his fees unless there is a specific contract to this effect.[2]

> 1   *Smith v Broadbent & Co* [1892] 1 QB 551 at 554.
> 2   *Royle v Busby* (1880) LR 6 QBD 171, CA.

Reform of enforcement officer's fees

5.305   Enforcement officers' fees is one area that could change significantly if the Effective Enforcement White Paper proposals are enacted. The proposed reforms envisage a fee structure based on payment of an up-front fee by the judgment creditor (fixed or variable, depending on the enforcement process undertaken) which is recoverable from the judgment debtor where enforcement is successful. The White Paper acknowledges that:

> 'An up-front fee marks a significant shift away from the ethics and mechanics of the existing fee structure and will require attitudinal and practical changes to the way enforcement is approached ...'[1]

1   Effective Enforcement White Paper, para 236.

PRIORITY OF WRITS

5.306   It sometimes happens that two judgment creditors deliver writs of fi fa in respect of the same judgment debtor to an enforcement officer closely together or even on the same day. The priority of writs of fi fa is determined on the basis that the person whose writ is first delivered to the enforcement officer takes priority.[1] This should be simple to determine given that an enforcement officer is obliged to endorse a writ with the time and date of delivery as soon as possible after receiving it.[2] If several writs are handed to the enforcement officer at the same time (for example, by one solicitor acting for several judgment creditors) the enforcement officer must execute them simultaneously.[3]

1   *Smallcomb v Buckingham* (1697) 1 Salk 320; *Hutchinson v Johnston* (1787) 1 TR 729 at 731; *Hunt v Hooper* (1844) 12 M & W 664 at 671.
2   CA 2003, Sch 7, para 7.
3   *Ashworth v Earl of Uxbridge* (1842) 12 LJ QB 39.

5.307   Where a writ has been extended under RSC Ord 46, r 8 (see paras 5.123–5.124) its priority shall be determined by reference to the date on which it was originally delivered to the relevant enforcement officer.[1]

1   RSC Ord 46, r 8(4).

5.308   If an enforcement officer executes the writs in the wrong order, a good faith purchaser for valuable consideration without notice of the writ will take good title[1] and the money from the sale will pass to the judgment creditor whose writ was executed.[2] However, the wronged judgment creditor will have a separate cause of action against the enforcement officer.[3]

1   CA 2003, Sch 7, para 8(2). See paras 5.133–5.141.
2   *Smallcomb v Buckingham* (1697) 1 Salk 320. This point comes out more strongly in the alternative report of the case at 5 Mod 376.
3   *Smalcomb v Buckingham* (1697) 1 Salkfield 320 and *Hunt v Hooper* (1844) 12 M&W 664 at 671.

5.309   Where several writs are to be executed against the same judgment debtor, there is no need for an enforcement agent to make separate seizures. One seizure will be made for the benefit of all, in order of priority.[1]

1   *Jones v Atherton* (1816) 7 Taunt 56.

5.310 If the enforcement agent has been told to suspend execution, as was the case in *Hunt v Hooper*,[1] then the request to suspend will be treated as a withdrawal of the writ and that judgment creditor will lose priority if another writ is delivered before the first is reactivated.[2]

1   (1844) 12 M&W 664 at 673.
2   *Smallcomb v Buckingham* (1697) 1 Salk 320 (this point comes out more strongly in the alternative report of the case at 5 Mod 376); *Hunt v Hooper* (1844) 12 M & W 664 at 673; and *Bankers Trust Co v Galandari* [1987] QB 222 at 227–228 and 229.

5.311 However, what if the suspension is not the judgment creditor's fault? In *Bankers Trust Co v Galandari*,[1] a lower court set aside the judgment. The judgment creditor therefore instructed the sheriff, who had already taken walking possession of the defendant's goods, to suspend the execution.[2] The judgment was later restored but in the meantime another writ of fi fa had been delivered to the sheriff in relation to the judgment debtor's goods. The judgment creditor sought directions from the court as to which writ should take priority. The Court of Appeal held that the priority of the original writ should be restored. In the words of Lord Justice Parker:[3]

'Where, as here, temporary invalidity is in no way due to the fault or voluntary action or inaction of the creditor but to the erroneous decision of the court, I have no doubt that this court should, if it can, ensure that, when the matter is put right, the creditor should not lose the benefit of what he has done under what has been held to be, throughout, a valid judgment.'

1   [1987] QB 222, CA.
2   CPR 70.6 provides that where a judgment is set aside, any enforcement of the judgment shall cease to have effect unless the court orders otherwise.
3   [1987] QB 222 at 227. See also Kerr LJ at [1987] QB 222 at 229.

5.312 *Hunt v Hooper*[1] was distinguished by the Court on the basis that execution was suspended voluntarily at the request of the judgment creditor rather than involuntarily because of an error made by a lower court. The Court of Appeal went on to offer the following guidance:[2]

'… where the judgment pursuant to which a fieri facias has been issued is set aside, it is the duty of the creditor so to inform the sheriff; that once so informed the sheriff cannot proceed with the execution unless and until the judgment is restored and he has been notified of the fact and that, if in the interim period he has had any dealings with the goods or their proceeds which would have been wrongful as against the creditor had the judgment not been set aside, he is not to be liable to the creditor in respect of such dealings.

If a creditor whose judgment has been set aside gives notice to the sheriff that the order to set aside is under appeal and thereafter the sheriff receives for execution another writ in respect of the same goods, he should not, in my view, proceed beyond possession without applying to the court for directions and giving notice to both creditors of such application.'

1   (1844) 12 M&W 664 at 673.
2   [1987] QB 222 at 278.

INSOLVENCY

5.313   Chapter 1 considers generally the interaction between the enforcement and insolvency regimes relating to corporate and individual judgment debtors. This section considers the application of the rules set out in the Insolvency Act 1986 (IA 1986), ss 183 and 346 relating to the 'completion' of execution by writ of fi fa for the purposes of winding up and bankruptcy and considers a number of statutory duties imposed on enforcement officers under IA 1986. Although similar provisions apply in the case of both winding up and bankruptcy, the provisions are drafted differently and are therefore considered separately.

WINDING UP

5.314   Chapter 1 notes that where a judgment creditor has issued execution against the goods of a company, and the company is subsequently wound up, he is not entitled to retain the benefit[1] of the execution or attachment against the liquidator unless he has completed the execution before the commencement of the winding up.[2] Execution is completed under a writ of fi fa by seizure and sale of the goods.[3] These rules are further refined by a number of specific duties imposed on enforcement officers by IA 1986 with respect to monies received by them under an execution.

[1]   The meaning of 'retain the benefit of the execution' has been considered in Chapter 1.
[2]   Insolvency Act 1981, s 183(1). The meaning of 'commencement of winding' up has been considered in Chapter 1.
[3]   Insolvency Act 1981, s 183(3)(a).

Duties of an enforcement officer under IA 1986, s 184 before sale

5.315   IA 1986, s 184(1)–(2) provides that where a company's goods are taken in execution and, before their sale or the completion of the execution (by the receipt or recovery of the full amount of the levy), notice in writing[1] is served on the enforcement officer that:

(a)   a provisional liquidator has been appointed;
(b)   a winding up order has been made; or
(c)   a resolution for voluntary winding up has been passed;

the enforcement officer must, on being so required, deliver the goods and any money seized or received in part satisfaction of the execution to the liquidator. Where this happens, the enforcement officer's fees are a first charge on the goods or moneys handed over to the liquidator who has a power to sell them or sufficient part of them to satisfy the charge. The insolvency practitioner has a right to insist that the enforcement officer's bill of costs be subjected to detailed assessment.[2]

[1]   Insolvency Rules 1986, SI 1986/1925, r 12.19(1)(a). The notice must be delivered by hand or sent by recorded delivery to the enforcement officer charged with the execution.
[2]   Insolvency Rules 1986, r 7.36(1).

Duties of an enforcement officer under IA 1986, s 184 after sale or receipt of moneys

5.316 IA 1986, s 184(3)–(4) imposes a holding period in respect of any moneys received by an enforcement officer under a writ of fi fa. Where a company's goods are sold or money is paid in order to avoid sale under a writ of fi fa in respect of a judgment for more than £500, the enforcement officer must deduct the costs of the execution from the proceeds of sale, or the money paid, and retain the balance for 14 days. If within the 14-day period a notice in writing[1] is served on the enforcement officer of:

(a) a petition for the winding up of the company having been presented; or
(b) of a meeting having been called at which there is to be proposed a resolution for voluntary winding up;
(c) and an order is made or a resolution passed (as the case may be);

the enforcement officer must pay the balance to the liquidator, who is entitled to retain it as against the judgment creditor. The insolvency practitioner has a right to insist that the enforcement officer's bill of costs for the costs he has deducted be subjected to detailed assessment.[2]

[1] Insolvency Rules 1986, r 12.19(1)(b). The notice must be delivered by hand or sent by recorded delivery to the enforcement officer charged with the execution.
[2] Insolvency Rules 1986, r 7.36(1).

5.317 IA 1986, s 184(5) grants the court a discretion to set aside the rights conferred on the liquidator under IA 1986, s 184 in favour of the judgment creditor to such extent and subject to such terms as the court thinks fit. In practice, the court is likely to be extremely reluctant to interfere and will wish to ensure that creditors of the same class are treated pari passu.

Good faith purchaser

5.318 IA 1986, s 183(2)(b) protects persons who purchase goods of the company in good faith from an enforcement officer by providing that such persons acquire a good title to the goods against the liquidator 'in all cases'.

Other forms of insolvency

5.319 The effect of administration, company voluntary arrangements and administrative receivership are considered in Chapter 1.

BANKRUPTCY

5.320 Chapter 1 notes that where the creditor of any person who is adjudged bankrupt has, before the commencement of the bankruptcy, executed against the goods of that person, that creditor is not entitled to retain the benefit of the execution,[1] or any sums paid to avoid it, unless the execution was completed, or the sums were paid, before the commencement of the bankruptcy.[2] Execution is completed under a writ of fi fa by seizure and sale of the goods.[3] The sale referred to must be a sale under the writ of fi fa and not a sale ordered in respect of interpleader proceedings.[4] Again, these rules are further refined by a number of specific duties imposed on enforcement officers by IA 1986 with respect to monies received by them under execution.

[1]   The meaning of 'retain the benefit of the execution' has been considered in Chapter 1.
[2]   IA 1981, s 346(1). The meaning of 'commencement of the bankruptcy' has been considered in Chapter 1.
[3]   IA 1981, s 346(5)(a).
[4]   *Heathcote v Livesley* (1887) 19 QBD 285 at 287, per Wills J (construing the similarly worded Bankruptcy Act 1887, s 45).

Duties of an enforcement officer under IA 1986 before sale

5.321   IA 1986, s 346(2) provides that if a notice in writing[1] is given to the enforcement officer that the judgment debtor has been adjudged bankrupt before the completion of the execution of a writ of fi fa, the enforcement officer must, on request, deliver to the official receiver or trustee of the bankrupt's estate the goods and any money seized or recovered in part satisfaction of the execution. As with a winding up, the enforcement officer's costs of the execution are a first charge on the goods or money so delivered and the official receiver or trustee may sell the goods or a sufficient part of them for the purpose of satisfying the charge.

[1]   Insolvency Rules 1986, r 12.19(1)(c). The notice must be delivered by hand or sent by recorded delivery to the enforcement officer charged with the execution.

Duties of an enforcement officer under IA 1986 after sale

5.322   IA 1986, s 346(3) provides that where an individual's goods are sold, or money is paid in order to avoid sale, under a writ of fi fa in respect of a judgment for more than £1,000,[1] and:

(a)   before the end of the period of 14 days beginning with the day of the sale or payment the enforcement officer is given written notice[2] that a bankruptcy petition has been presented in relation to that person; and

(b)   a bankruptcy order is or has been made on that petition;

the balance of the proceeds of sale or money paid, after deducting the costs of execution, shall be comprised in the bankrupt's estate in priority to the claim of the judgment creditor.

[1]   This is the amount prescribed under IA 1986, s 346(3) by the Insolvency Proceedings (Monetary Limits) (Amendment) Order 2004, SI 2004/547.
[2]   Insolvency Rules 1986, r 12.19(1)(d). The notice must be delivered by hand or sent by recorded delivery to the enforcement officer charged with the execution.

5.323   This provision is complemented by IA 1986, s 346 which requires enforcement officers to retain any moneys for 14 days beginning with the day of the sale or payment or while there is a pending bankruptcy petition of which he has been given notice. If a bankruptcy order is made on the petition, the enforcement officer must pay the moneys he is holding over to the official receiver or the trustee in bankruptcy.

5.324 IA 1986, s 346(6) grants the court a discretion to set aside the rights conferred on the official receiver or trustee under IA 1986, s 346(1)–(3) in favour of the judgment creditor to such extent and subject to such terms as the court thinks fit. In practice, the court is likely to be extremely reluctant to interfere and will wish to ensure that creditors of the same class are treated pari passu.

Good faith purchaser

5.325 The rights conferred by IA 1986, s 346 do not confer any power in the trustee of a bankrupt's estate to claim goods from a person who has purchased any goods from an enforcement officer in good faith.[1]

[1]   IA 1986, s 346(7).

Other forms of insolvency

5.326 The effect of individual voluntary arrangements and county court administration orders are considered in Chapter 1.

HUMAN RIGHTS

5.327 With the entry into force of the Human Rights Act 1998[1] (HRA 1998) the operation of writs of fi fa (and other forms of execution) must be viewed in the light of the provisions of the European Convention for the Protection of Human Rights and Fundamental Freedoms (ECHR).

[1]   On 2 October 2000 (SI 2000/1851).

5.328 The implications of HRA 1998 for the operation of the law of distress for rent and county court warrants of execution would appear to be greater than is the case for High Court writs of fi fa, particularly in the case of distress, where the rules governing this procedure have been criticised as arbitrary, artificial and obscure.[1] However, entry into a person's premises, especially in the case of their home, and seizure of their goods is a particularly intrusive form of execution and has potential human rights implications under ECHR, art 8 (the right to respect for private and family life and the home) and art 1 of the First Protocol (the right to peaceful enjoyment of possessions). It is important to note, however, that both of these rights are qualified rights. Article 8 provides:

'(1) Everyone has the right to respect for his private and family life, his home and his correspondence.

(2) There shall be no interference by a public authority with the exercise of this right except such as is in accordance with the law and is necessary in a democratic society in the interests of national security, public safety or the economic well-

being of the country, for the prevention of disorder or crime, for the protection of health or morals, or for the protection of the rights and freedoms of others.'

1   Law Commission Report *Landlord & Tenant Distress for Rent* (Law Com No 194) February 1991. The law relating to distress for rent contains no provision for certain types of goods to be exempt from distraint and there is no requirement that the goods seized be proportionate to the debt owed. Such criticism suggests that the law on distress for rent may fail to meet ECHR requirements for lawfulness. In the case of county court warrants of execution human rights challenges may also arise as a consequence of County Courts Act 1984, s 123. This provides that every registrar shall be responsible for the acts and defaults of the bailiffs appointed to assist him. The European Court of Human Rights decision in *McGonnell v United Kingdom* [2000] ECHR 28488/95 arguably puts into question whether a district judge's dual jurisdiction as chief bailiff and adjudicator of disputes that might arise between the judgment debtor and the bailiff or judgment creditor is compatible with art 6 of the ECHR (the right to a fair trial before an independent tribunal). The 2003 White Paper proposes amendment to County Courts Act 1984, s 123 in recognition of this potential conflict (see para 34).

5.329   Similarly, art 1 of the First Protocol provides:

'Every natural or legal person is entitled to the peaceful enjoyment of his possessions. No one shall be deprived of his possessions except in the public interest and subject to the conditions provided for by law and by the general principles of international law.

The preceding provisions shall not, however, in any way impair the right of a State to enforce such laws as it deems necessary to control the use of property in accordance with the general interest or to secure the payment of taxes or other contributions or penalties.'

5.330   In addition, as discussed further in Chapter 1, powerful human rights arguments also operate in favour of the judgment creditor in the context of execution. Enforcement is integral to the judgment creditor's right to a fair trial under ECHR, art 6.[1] Accordingly, consideration of the judgment debtor's rights under ECHR, art 8(1) and art 1 of the First Protocol must be balanced against the rights of the judgment creditor.

1   *Hornsby v Greece* (1997) 24 EHRR 250.

5.331   Strasbourg jurisprudence would indicate that execution by writ of fi fa is not per se in breach of art 8 or art 1 of the First Protocol. In *K v Sweden*[1] an applicant filed a complaint with the European Commission relating to the circumstances in which an enforcement officer had seized her property in execution against unpaid taxes and civil debts owed by the applicant's former husband. The applicant complained that the enforcement officer had entered her house while she was in hospital, had not informed her in advance, had changed the door lock and had left some of her belongings in disarray in breach of ECHR, art 8.

1   Application 13800/88.

5.332   The Commission found that the matters complained of did constitute an interference with the applicant's right to respect for her private life and her home within the meaning of ECHR, art 8(1), but that the interference was justified under the terms of ECHR, art 8(2). The Commission observed that '*in accordance with the law*' referred not simply to the provision being incorporated into domestic law, but rather to it being compatible with the rule of law. Arbitrary interference with the rights safeguarded by art 8 would not be compatible with the rule of law but a law which confers discretion is not itself incompatible, provided the scope of the discretion and the manner of its exercise are sufficiently clear having regard to the legitimate aim of the measure. In this case, the Swedish enforcement legislation was sufficiently precise and the fact that the seizure was subject to review by the courts gave the applicant adequate protection against arbitrary interference. Further, the protection of creditor's rights was a legitimate aim under art 8(2) and the interference was proportionate to the legitimate aim pursued. The Decision stated:

> 'The Commission notes that the bailiff's duties by their very nature were bound to cause some difficulties for the applicant and it finds that the manner in which the execution was effected would in normal circumstances be considered to be harsh. However, having regard to the circumstances of the present case, in particular the special problems connected with the enforcement of the claims against the applicant's former husband, the Commission finds that the procedure followed was not only in conformity with Swedish law but could also reasonably be regarded as proportionate to the legitimate aim pursued.'

5.333 In the case of commercial premises, it is hard to see how ECHR, art 8 arguments could arise. While art 1 of the First Protocol may be relevant, in *Gasus Dosier-und Fördertechnik Gmbh v Netherlands*[1] the European Court of Human Rights found that the grant to tax authorities of a power to recover tax debts against goods owned by certain third parties was not per se incompatible with the requirements of art 1, though the requirements of proportionality must be observed. While that case concerned enforcement by tax authorities rather than private creditors, it too would suggest that the procedure for seizure and sale contemplated by a writ of fi fa is not in breach of art 1 of the First Protocol. However, the Commission's observations in *K v Sweden* as to the need for the law to be clear and precise may suggest that reform of the law on entry may be needed, particularly in the case of entry to a judgment debtor's house through a window, to ensure compatibility with the human rights regime.

[1] [1995] ECHR 15375/89.

REFORM

5.334 The Civil Enforcement Review which began in March 1998 incorporated a review of the effectiveness of country court warrants of execution and High Court writs of fi fa.[1]

[1] As part of that review, Professor Jack Beatson QC of Cambridge University also provided a report to the Lord Chancellor on bailiff law, the *Independent Review of Bailiff Law Report* (June 2000). The scope of the Enforcement Review was broadened in March 2001 to look at structures for and the regulation of all civil enforcement agents.

5.335 The Effective Enforcement White Paper states at the outset:[1]

> 'It remains the Government's position that it may always be necessary to permit taking legal control of goods and the sale of such goods as part of the

enforcement regime in England and Wales. However, these actions should be undertaken in a reformed and regulated system, where efforts are made to ensure it is not used indiscriminately; our proposals for licences, increased professionalism and changes to the fee structure are intended to assist here.'

1   Introduction to Effective Enforcement White Paper.

5.336 It is intended that a new concept of 'taking legal control of goods' should be enacted to govern the actions of enforcement agents generally under a unified piece of legislation governing both rent arrears and enforcement of judgment debts. The concept of taking legal control of goods will apply irrespective of the form of control used and is a recognition that the conceptual distinction between seizure and impounding has largely been rendered obsolete by the use of walking possession agreements.

5.337 The Enforcement Review Green Paper 'Towards Effective Enforcement' published in July 2001 set out the government's proposals for a new class of enforcement agents and the Effective Enforcement White Paper[1] set out the government's proposals to codify the powers and duties of enforcement officers and to subject the enforcement industry to far greater regulation. A number of these proposals were implemented with the enactment of CA 2003 and the High Court Enforcement Officers Regulations 2004. While the Sheriffs Act 1887 has not been repealed, sheriffs no longer have any duty to execute writs and High Court writs of execution are now directed to High Court enforcement officers.[2] However, the new provisions largely re-state the law relating to High Court writs of execution and the common law continues to govern the rights, powers and obligations of enforcement officers.[3]

1   Effective Enforcement White Paper.
2   CA 2003, s 99 and Sch 7.
3   CA 2003, Sch 7, para 4(2).

5.338 The remaining proposals for reform contained in the Effective Enforcement White Paper relating to writs of execution envisage primary legislation, to codify enforcement law through a single piece of legislation, to regulate enforcement officers through a statutory body and to introduce a new fee structure for enforcement officers aimed at both enhancing the effectiveness of execution and incorporating safeguards against malpractice. It is also intended that the terminology relating to execution should be modernised, in line with the changes that have been seen with the introduction of CPR Pts 70–71. Many of the White Paper's proposals have been noted where relevant earlier in this chapter and the key changes envisaged (such as ensuring proportionality between the size of the debt and the sums raised by sale of the goods seized, a requirement to allow the debtor an opportunity to take advice or pay the debt before the goods are sold and reform of the law on entry) would appear to be driven, at least in part, by human rights considerations. The National Standards on Enforcement Agents[1] seem to foreshadow many of the proposed reforms and its endorsement by a wide variety of participants in the civil enforcement arena may signify a move to adopt the requisite practices and standards in advance of legislative change.

1   Prepared by the Lord Chancellor's Department in May 2002.

5.339 While as yet there is no draft bill before Parliament to enact the White Paper's proposals, an Enforcement Officers Bill has been suggested for some time in 2005.[1] The spectre of legislative reform is also likely to explain why the procedural rules relating to writs of fi fa, unlike the other methods of High Court enforcement, have not yet been updated through secondary legislation[2] and for the present continue to be governed by the Rules of the Supreme Court 1965.[3]

[1] Wilson 'Who shot the Sheriff?' LSG 2004, 101(16), 31.
[2] The procedural rules relating to receivers, oral examinations, third party debt orders and charging orders were updated by the Civil Procedure (Amendment No 4) Rules 2001, SI 2001/2792 and Civil Procedure (Amendment) Rules 2002, SI 2002/2058, which introduced CPR Pts 69–73.
[3] RSC Ords 46 and 47.

APPENDIX

Writs of fieri facias

Sheriffs Lodgment Centre

Address:	Sheriffs Lodgment Centre
	20-21 Tooks Court
	London
	EC4A 1LB
Telephone:	020 7025 2555
Fax:	020 7025 2556
Email:	info@sheriffslodgmentcentre.net
Website:	www.sheriffslodgmentcentre.net

National Information Centre for Enforcement

Address:	National Information Centre for Enforcement
	Westwood Park
	London Road
	Little Horkesley
	Colchester
	Essex
	CO6 4BS
	DX 3654 Colchester

CHAPTER 6

Appointing a receiver by way of equitable execution

INTRODUCTION

6.1   The appointment of a receiver by way of equitable execution is a form of equitable relief originally devised by the old Courts of Chancery.[1] Equitable execution was granted to aid the judgment creditor in enforcing his judgment where the property sought to be used to satisfy the judgment debt could not be reached by normal legal methods of execution,[2] such as a writ of fieri facias[3] or the now abolished writ of elegit.[4] As such, it is an example of the equitable maxim 'equity will not suffer a wrong to be without a remedy'.[5]

[1]   One of the courts exercising equitable jurisdiction before the Supreme Court of Judicature Acts 1873 and 1875 merged the courts which administered common law and equity into a single Supreme Court all of whose judges had power to administer both law and equity.
[2]   Para 11.7.1 of the Queen's Bench Guide states that: 'Equitable execution is a process which enables a judgment creditor to obtain payment of the judgment debt where the interest of the judgment debtor in property cannot be reached by ordinary execution.'
[3]   See Chapter 5.
[4]   See para 6.68, n 1.
[5]   Snell's Equity (31st edn, 2005) p 95 and Meagher *Gummow & Lehane's Equity Doctrines & Remedies* (4th edn, 2003) p 86.

6.2   As a rule of thumb, equitable execution is only available where other methods of legal enforcement are not available. Perhaps the most striking instances of its application are the appointment of a receiver over future debts payable to a judgment debtor or to enforce contractual rights of indemnity which a judgment debtor is refusing to exercise. Neither of these choses in action can be reached through third party debt orders or other forms of enforcement.

6.3   The effect of the order appointing the receiver by way of equitable execution is akin to an injunction restraining the judgment debtor from receiving the receivership property. It also authorises the receiver to collect in the property subject to the order. Neither the receiver nor the judgment creditor appointing him obtains any proprietary interest in the receivership property nor does the appointment make the judgment creditor a secured creditor. The receivership order therefore confers no priority on insolvency.

6.4 The High Court's power to appoint a receiver by way of equitable execution derives from Supreme Court Act 1981 (SCA 1981), s 37, which provides:

'The High Court may by order (whether interlocutory or final) grant an injunction or appoint a receiver in all cases in which it appears to the court to be just and convenient to do so.'

6.5 The bulk of the substantive law relating to equitable execution is found in a large body of case law, much of which was decided towards the end of the nineteenth and start of the twentieth century. Kekewich J referring to his efforts to determine how to apply the legal principles pertaining to equitable execution to a case before him in 1907, lamented that:[1]

'After consulting many authorities and pondering over the matter, I have come to the conclusion that full treatment of this question would require something in the nature of a lecture or treatise, which it is better to avoid unless absolutely necessary. My observations, therefore, do not pretend to be exhaustive. The authorities bearing on the point cannot be said to be wholly satisfactory, and the law must be taken to be still in the making.'

[1] *Ideal Bedding Co Ltd v Holland* [1907] 2 Ch 157 at 168.

6.6 Although some relatively recent decisions at first instance and by the Court of Appeal have settled some of the more doubtful propositions to be found in the older cases, equitable execution has not come under the sort of detailed scrutiny their Lordships recently applied to garnishee orders (now third party debt orders),[1] and there is still some truth to Kekewich J's lament about the law relating to equitable execution being 'still in the making'.

[1] In *Société Eram Shipping Co Ltd v Compagnie Internationale de Navigation* [2004] AC 260, HL and *Kuwait Oil Tanker Co SAK v Qabazard* [2003] UKHL 31, HL.

6.7 The procedural rules relating to the appointment of a receiver by way of equitable execution have recently been updated. They are now set out in the Civil Procedure Rules 1998 (CPR), Pt 69 and the accompanying Practice Direction, which both came into force on 2 December 2002.[1] The new procedural regime repealed and replaced the Rules of the Supreme Court 1968 (RSC) Ord 30 (Receivers) and RSC Ord 51 (Receivers: Equitable execution).[2]

[1] Civil Procedure (Amendment Rules) 2002, SI 2002/2058, r 26 and Sch 7.
[2] Civil Procedure (Amendment Rules) 2002, SI 2002/2058, r 36 and Sch 10.

Equitable execution distinguished from other receiverships

6.8 A receiver can be appointed in a variety of circumstances under English law and the appointment of a receiver by way of equitable execution is one type of receivership. However, equitable execution is *not* an insolvency process and equitable receivership should not be confused with receivers appointed under the insolvency legislation or by a creditor under a charge. Similarly, equitable receivership should not be confused with an interim receiver appointed to preserve assets (who performs a similar function to a freezing injunction except that the receiver physically collects assets to preserve them for any subsequent enforcement steps).[1] Equitable execution is about the appointment of a receiver to aid the *enforcement* of a judgment debt.

[1]   See generally *Commercial Litigation: Pre-Emptive Remedies*, paras A2-349–A2-369.

THE NATURE OF A RECEIVER

6.9   The classic judicial exposition on the nature of a receivership generally was given by Sir George Jessell MR in *Re Manchester and Milford Railway Co, ex p Cambrian Railway Co*:[1]

> 'A "receiver" is a term which was well known in the Court of Chancery, as meaning a person who receives rents or other income paying ascertained outgoings, but who does not, if I may say so, manage the property in the sense of buying or selling or anything of that kind. We were most familiar with the distinction in the case of a partnership. If a receiver was appointed of partnership assets, the trade stopped immediately. He collected all the debts, sold the stock-in-trade and other assets, and then under the order of the Court the debts of the concern were liquidated and the balance divided. If it was desired to continue the trade at all, it was necessary to appoint a manager, or a receiver and manager as it was generally called. He could buy and sell and carry on the trade. The same distinction was well known also in the working of mines. If a receiver only was appointed, the working of the mine was stopped, but if it was desired to continue the working of the mine, a receiver and manager was necessary. So that there was a well-known distinction between the two. The receiver merely took the income, and paid necessary outgoings, and the manager carried on the trade or business in the way I have mentioned.'

[1]   (1880) 14 Ch D 645 at 653, CA.

6.10   In short, a receiver is appointed merely to collect assets and to pay those outgoings strictly necessary for their upkeep. The issue of whether a receiver by way of equitable execution has a power of sale is considered in para 6.16. By contrast, a manager is appointed where it is desired that the business should continue operating. In spite of the distinction between a receiver and a manager, the two are often conflated. In particular, SCA 1981, s 37 refers only to a 'receiver', whereas Pt 69 states that references in its provisions to a 'receiver' include a manager.[1]

[1]   CPR 69.1(2).

Is a manager by way of equitable execution possible?

6.11   There is no direct authority on the question of whether a judgment creditor applying for equitable execution could ask the court to appoint the receiver as manager of the judgment debtor's business or contracts to allow the profits to be collected in to satisfy the judgment debt. The fact that a receiver can be appointed manager for one species of receiver does not necessarily mean that the same applies to all receivers, particularly in the case of a receiver appointed by way of equitable execution, which is in many ways a very different creature to other forms of receivership.

6.12   In *Edwards v Picard*,[1] a case concerning a judgment creditor's attempts to appoint a receiver over a patent that was not being exploited, Buckley LJ suggested obiter that a manager could *not* be appointed by way of equitable execution.[2]

1   [1909] 2 KB 908.
2   [1909] 2 KB 908 at 910–911.

6.13   However, in *SACI v Novokuznetsk Aluminium*,[1] one of the grounds on which the judgment debtors opposed the judgment creditor's application for the appointment of a receiver by way of equitable execution to receive payments owed to them under a supply contract was that this would effectively mean that the receiver was there to manage the supply contract for the benefit of the judgment creditors. Colman J found nothing in this point.[2]   He held:[3]

> 'I see no reason why this limited function [that is, the appointment of a receiver for the purpose of ascertaining what deliveries were to be made under the supply contract, what payments became due and collecting those payments] would involve the receiver in acting as manager of the supply contract or would impose on him a duty to enforce it.'

1   [1998] QB 406.
2   [1998] QB 406 at 421.
3   [1998] QB 406 at 411.

6.14   However, he continued that even if, as the judgment debtors contended, the appointment of a receiver would bring the judgment debtor's business to a standstill:[1]

> 'Impact on the judgment debtor's business is not a consideration material to the availability of legal process of execution and there is no reason in principle why it should be introduced as material to the availability of equitable execution.'

In any event, as a practical matter, the fact that the distinction between mere receipt and management may sometimes be blurred should not necessarily preclude the appointment of a receiver by way of equitable execution.

1   [1998] QB 406 at 421.

The nature of a receiver by way of equitable execution

6.15   Clear judicial statements as to the nature of equitable execution are thin on the ground. Sir George Jessell MR gave the following description in *Salt v Cooper*:[1]

> 'equitable execution … [is] a mere mode of doing that which the plaintiff asks the Court in every action to do, namely, to realize the debtor's property so as to produce the sum demanded.'

1   (1880) 16 Ch D 554 at 552.

6.16   A receiver appointed by way of equitable execution has no power to sell the judgment debtor's personalty[1] or to obtain a charge over it with a view to obtaining an order for sale.[2] The effect of an order appointing a receiver by way of equitable execution is considered in paras 6.102–6.117.

¹   *De Peyrecave v Nicholson* (1894) 71 LT 255; *Flegg v Prentis* [1892] 2 Ch 428 at 431 and *Ideal Bedding Co Ltd v Holland* [1907] 2 Ch 157 at 169.

²   *Ideal Bedding Co Ltd v Holland* [1907] 2 Ch 157 at 169. However, it should be noted that in the case of land, the court has in the past appointed a receiver by way of equitable execution to bring a claim in the name of a judgment debtor who is refusing to sell his interest in the land in order to force him to do so. See para 6.69.

Is equitable execution a form of execution at all?

6.17   Execution is a legal process by which the judgment creditor brings proceedings for his sole benefit to satisfy his judgment in whole or in part.¹ Equitable execution is technically a form of *equitable relief* to allow recovery of a judgment debt rather than a form of execution.² As Cotton LJ explained in *Re Shephard*:³

'Confusion of ideas has arisen from the use of the term 'equitable execution.' The expression tends to error. It has often been used by judges, and occurs in some orders, as a short expression indicating that the person who obtains the order gets the same benefit as he would have got from legal execution. But what he gets by the appointment of a receiver is not execution, but equitable relief, which is granted on the ground that there is no remedy by execution at law; it is a taking out of the way a hindrance which prevents execution at common law. ... The obtaining a receivership order is not taking out execution, it is obtaining equitable relief by a subsequent order, which must be made against someone against whom the Court has jurisdiction to make an order.'

¹   See eg *Re a Company (No 0022 of 1915)* [1915] 1 Ch 520 at 525.

²   *Re Shephard* (1889) 43 Ch D 131 at 137–138; *Levasseur v Mason & Barry* [1891] 2 QB 73 at 77, per Lord Coleridge and 79, per Lord Esher MR; *Re Potts* [1893] 1 QB 648 at 661; *Ideal Bedding Ltd v Holland* [1907] 2 Ch 157 at 169; *Morgan v Hart* [1914] 2 KB 183 at 187-188; *Bourne v Colodense* [1985] ICR 291 at 302.

³   (1889) 43 Ch D 131 at 135–136.

6.18   A reference to 'execution' in a statute¹ or document² may be construed to include equitable execution depending on the context. Therefore outside the context of insolvency (see paras 6.153-6.156), this may be a distinction without a difference.

¹   Eg in *Re a Judgment Debtor No 2176 of 1938* [1939] 1 Ch 601 at 604 a statutory reference to 'execution' was held to include equitable execution.

²   Eg in *Blackman v Fysh* [1892] 3 Ch 209, CA a clause in a will which referred to 'taken in execution by any process of law' was held to include equitable execution.

6.19   It follows from the fact that equitable execution is an equitable remedy that it is discretionary in nature.¹ However, this does not mean that the court's discretion is arbitrary. As Davey LJ put it in *Harris v Beauchamp Brothers*:²

'We should be sorry to limit by construction the beneficial jurisdiction of the Court to grant an injunction or make an order for a receiver where it is "just or convenient" to do so; but we conceive those well-known words do not confer an arbitrary or unregulated discretion on the Court, and do not authorize the Court to invent new modes of enforcing judgments in substitution for the ordinary modes.'

¹   *Bourne v Colodense* [1985] ICR 291 at 302.

²   *Harris v Beauchamp Brothers* [1894] 1 QB 801 at 809.

THE DEVELOPMENT OF THE MODERN JURISDICTION

6.20 Before the overhaul of the court system brought about by the Supreme Court of Judicature Act 1873 and the Supreme Court of Judicature Act 1875 (the Judicature Acts) the appointment of a receiver was a jurisdiction only exercisable by the Courts of Equity.[1] Common law courts had no jurisdiction to appoint receivers and relied upon methods of legal execution such as garnishment (now the third party debt order procedure), the writ of fieri facias and the now abolished writ of elegit.[2]

[1] *Snell's Equity* (31st edn, 2005) p 427. The Court of Chancery procedure prior to the Judicature Acts is explained by Sir George Jessell MR in *Anglo-Italian Bank v Davies* (1878) 9 Ch D 275 at 283: 'by issuing a writ of elegit, and, without obtaining a return, to file a bill in equity alleging that the Plaintiff had issued his writ of elegit, and that owing to legal impediments it could not be enforced at law, and asking for payment of the judgment debt by means of receiver. According to the practice the application for the receiver was made by interlocutory application before the hearing, and in a proper case it was granted.'

[2] See para 6.68, n 1.

6.21 The Judicature Acts brought about a significant rationalisation of the court system following which all divisions of the High Court were empowered to appoint a receiver by way of equitable execution.[1] Supreme Court of Judicature Act 1873, s 25 made the following provision for the granting of injunctions and the appointment of a receiver:

'A mandamus or an injunction may be granted or a receiver appointed by an interlocutory Order of the Court in all cases in which it shall appear to the Court to be just or convenient that such Order should be made; and any such Order may be made either unconditionally or upon such terms and conditions as the Court shall think just.'

[1] *Harris v Beauchamp Brothers* [1894] 1 QB 801 at 808.

6.22 This provision has been re-enacted in amended form over the years[1] and is now to be found in SCA 1981, s 37, which is in substantially the same terms (see para 6.4).

[1] Supreme Court of Judicature (Consolidation) Act 1925, s 45 repealed Supreme Court of Judicature Act 1873, s 25 and replaced it with: 'The High Court may grant a mandamus or an injunction *or appoint a receiver* by an interlocutory order in *all cases in which it appears to the court to be just or convenient so to do*. Any such order may be made either unconditionally or on such terms and conditions as the court thinks just.' (Emphasis added). This provision was repealed and re-enacted as SCA 1981, s 37.

6.23 In spite of some earlier dicta to the contrary,[1] the Supreme Court of Judicature Act 1873, s 25 was restrictively interpreted in a series of decisions of the Court of Appeal, which held that the court would not appoint a receiver where the old Court of Chancery would not have appointed a receiver prior to the Supreme Court of Judicature Act 1873.[2] In particular, where *legal* execution would not have been available because the judgment debtor's property was not amenable to such process, the Court of Chancery could not have granted equitable relief and so it seemed the post-Judicature Acts court could not do so.

[1] In *Anglo-Italian Bank v Davies* (1878) 9 Ch D 275 at 286 where Sir George Jessell MR stated that: 'I think that the Act of 1873, sect. 25, sub-sect. 8, has enlarged very much the powers which Courts of Equity formerly possessed of granting injunctions or receivers.' See also

Cotton LJ in the same case at 293, where he states: '[u]nder [s 25(8)] ... the Court may and does grant receivers when it never could have done so before.'

2   *Holmes v Millage* [1893] 1 QB 551 at 557-558, CA; *Harris v Beauchamp Brothers* [1894] 1 QB 801 at 810, CA; *Edwards & Co v Picard* [1909] 2 KB 903 at 905, CA; *Morgan v Hart* [1914] 2 KB 183 at 186 and 191, CA.

6.24   The Court of Appeal decision in *Parker v Camden London Borough Council*[1] questioned the correctness of the principle that the post-Judicature Acts courts were bound by the practices of the Court of Chancery prior to the Judicature Acts. Sir John Donaldson MR held[2] that:[3]

'[Counsel for the defendants] retorted by referring to *Harris v Beauchamp Brothers* [1894] 1 Q.B. 801 and submitting that it was only permissible to appoint a receiver in circumstances in which the Court of Chancery would have done so prior to 1873. For my part I do not accept that the pre-Judicature Act practices of the Court of Chancery or any other court still rule us from their graves'.

1   [1986] Ch 162.
2   [1986] Ch 162 at 172–173.
3   [1986] Ch 162 at 176 Browne-Wilkinson LJ concurred stating that the jurisdiction to appoint a receiver and manager under SCA 1981, s 37(1) was 'unlimited'.

6.25   However, *Parker* is not determinative of the issue because, as Sir John Donaldson MR made clear, that case was not concerned with a receiver by way of equitable execution but rather the court's power to appoint a receiver to enforce a landlord's breach of covenant.[1]

1   [1986] Ch 162 at 176. It also appears that only *Harris v Beauchamp* [1894] 1 QB 801 was cited to the court and not other relevant authorities.

6.26   In *Maclaine Watson v International Tin Council*,[1] the court had to consider whether it had jurisdiction to appoint a receiver by way of equitable execution over possible indemnity claims by the ITC against its members. Such claims could not be reached by any other form of enforcement available to the judgment creditor[2]. However, although he had earlier observed that the statutory provisions of SCA 1981, s 37 did not confer on the court power to appoint a receiver by way of equitable execution in a case where prior to the Judicature Acts no court could have granted such relief,[3] Millett J went on to conclude that there was 'no technical objection' to the appointment of a receiver by way of equitable execution in respect of the ITC's indemnity claims (although in the circumstances the order was not made because the judgment creditors had failed to show an arguable case for the claims).[4]

1   [1988] 1 Ch 1. Millett J's judgment was expressly approved by the Court of Appeal.
2   A claim to be indemnified by a third party is not amenable to garnishee proceedings (now the third party debt order procedure).
3   [1988] 1 Ch 1 at 17.
4   [1998] 1 Ch 1 at 21.

6.27   The issue of whether the court's power to appoint a receiver by way of equitable execution was confined to the practice of the Court of Chancery prior to the Judicature Acts arose directly in *Soinco S.A.C.I. v Novokuznetsk*.[1] In that case the judgment creditor sought the appointment of a receiver by way of equitable execution over payments that were due or that may in future have become due under a supply contract. One of the grounds on which the judgment debtors sought to oppose the application was that the pre-Judicature Acts courts could not have made such an appointment. Colman J, having extensively reviewed the authorities, held that he had jurisdiction to appoint a receiver by way of equitable execution and that it was just and convenient that he should do so. There were strong matters of principle in favour of this conclusion, since to conclude otherwise:[2]

> '... would involve treating the rules of the Court of Chancery before the Judicature Acts as carved in stone and as expressing immutable principles incapable of development beyond 1873 unless changed by Parliament. This must be wrong in principle. English law has traditionally developed by means of identifying broad but established juridical principles which have been extended incrementally to new factual situations when the interests of justice required such extension. The development of the law relating to Mareva injunctions[3] amply demonstrates that this developing process applies to equitable remedies as to any other.'

[1]   [1998] QB 406.
[2]   [1998] QB 406 at 420.
[3]   Now a freezing injunction.

6.28   Given that Colman J arguably departed from a number of earlier decisions of the Court of Appeal, it is possible the Court of Appeal could reach a different conclusion. However, this seems unlikely and the court's jurisdiction to appoint a receiver by way of equitable execution should not therefore be confined to the constraints laid down by the Court of Chancery prior to the Judicature Acts.

THE MODERN JURISDICTION TO APPOINT A RECEIVER BY WAY OF EQUITABLE EXECUTION

6.29   The modern requirements for the appointment of a receiver by way of equitable execution can be summarised as follows:

(a) there must be some difficulty, arising from the nature of the property, which precludes the use of legal methods of execution such as writs of fieri facias, third party debt orders and charging orders but which can be overcome by the appointment of a receiver; *or*

(b) there must be some 'special circumstances' justifying appointment such as to render it practically very difficult, if not impossible, for the judgment creditor to obtain the fruits of his judgment in the absence of equitable execution; and

(c) although the property to be the subject of the receivership may be either legal or equitable in nature, it must be capable of assignment and not otherwise inalienable; and

(d) the costs of the receivership must be proportionate to the likely recovery; and

(e) the court will not appoint a receiver where it is satisfied that such appointment would be fruitless because there is nothing for the receiver to collect in.

6.30   Each of these requirements is considered in more detail below. (a) and (b) should be treated as alternatives. (a) is concerned with the impossibility of enforcement at law. (b) is concerned with situations where, although the asset may as a matter of law be subject to other forms of enforcement, this would be very difficult, if not impossible, in practice.

(a) Difficulty arising from the nature of the property which precludes the use of legal methods of execution but which can be overcome by the appointment of a receiver

6.31 The requirement for 'some ... difficulty, arising from the nature of the property, which precludes execution at law but which can be overcome by the appointment of a receiver',[1] has been variously described in the cases as 'some legal difficulty in the way of enforcing the usual legal remedy'[2] or a 'hindrance which prevents execution at ... law'.[3] In essence, what this requirement means is that the property cannot be obtained using the ordinary legal methods of execution, such as a writ of fieri facias, third party debt order or a charging order. As Lord Esher MR once put it:[4]

'Is it just or convenient that such an order should be made, when there is available a clear and usual mode of realizing the judgment [at law] by a writ of fi. fa? I think that, where there is no impediment shewn in the particular case to the realization of the judgment by the ordinary mode of execution at law, it is not shewn to be just or convenient to appoint a receiver and to substitute for the ordinary known practice of execution by fi. fa. another practice, viz., the appointment of a receiver, which to be effectual must be followed by a further order for sale of the goods.'

1   *Maclaine Watson v ITC* [1988] 1 Ch 1 at 17 and see also *Morgan v Hart* [1914] 2 KB 183 at 188.
2   *Manchester and Liverpool District Banking Co v Parkinson* (1888) 22 QBD 173 at 177 and in similar terms in *Holmes v Millage* [1893] 1 QB 551 at 555 and *Re Watkins* (1879) 8 Ch D 252 at 257–258.
3   *Re Shephard* (1889) 43 Ch D 131 at 135-136 and *Edwards v Co v Picard* [1909] 2 KB 903 at 910.
4   *Manchester and Liverpool District Banking Co v Parkinson* (1888) 22 QBD 173 at 175.

6.32 Thus, in *Soinco S.A.C.I. v Novokuznetsk*[1] a receiver by way of equitable execution was appointed in respect of present and *future payments* due under a supply contract because it was not possible to garnish the future payments[2]. In *Bourne v Colodense Ltd*,[3] the Court of Appeal appointed a receiver to bring a claim to enforce an indemnity against legal costs which judgment debtor was refusing to enforce to meet a costs order made in favour of the judgment creditor on the basis that an indemnity, like a future debt, was not the sort of property amenable to garnishment at law. Such limitations in legal methods of enforcement give rise to the equity entitling the court to appoint a receiver by way of equitable execution to overcome the difficulty.

1   [1998] QB 406.
2   In that case the court was also influenced by the conduct of the judgment debtors and the company with whom they had contracted under the supply contract, which appeared to be endeavouring to 'smother' its indebtedness to the judgment debtors and otherwise behave in such a way as to shield the judgment debtor's assets from enforcement in England.
3   [1985] ICR 291.

6.33 The requirement for a difficulty precluding other methods of enforcement is recognised by the CPR, which require that the evidence in support of an application to appoint a receiver by way of equitable execution must give details of why the judgment cannot be enforced by any other method.[1]

1   PD 69, para 4.1(3)(d).

(b) 'Special circumstances' justifying appointment

6.34 Equitable execution will not be allowed by the court *simply* because it would be a more convenient method of satisfying the judgment debt than the usual methods of legal execution.[1] 'Special circumstances' must exist such as to render it practically very difficult, if not impossible, for the judgment creditor to obtain the fruits of his judgment in the absence of equitable execution. As Davey LJ put it in *Harris v Beauchamp Brothers*:[2]

> 'The learned counsel for the plaintiff boldly argued, that, if you have got a subject-matter which might be made available for the satisfaction of the judgment debt, you may have a receiver, if it is a better mode of getting it in than the usual mode. In our opinion, this is wrong.
>
>   Various modes are provided by common law and statute for enabling a judgment creditor to obtain payment of his debt, and the Rules of Court contain elaborate provisions for giving effect to such modes of enforcing a judgment. … [I]n our opinion, if any more convenient process is to be established, it ought to be by the Legislature and not by the Court.'

1   *Harris v Beauchamp Brothers* [1894] 1 QB 801 at 807.
2   [1894] 1 QB 801 at 807.

6.35 The requirement for something more than simple convenience to justify equitable execution was met in the Court of Appeal decision in *Goldschmidt v Oberrheinsche Metallwerke*.[1] In that case the judgment debtor was a German manufacturing company with no assets in England other than unknown amounts owed by its English customers. The judgment creditor had no means of ascertaining the particulars of any such debts and therefore could not provide an affidavit in support of an application to garnish the debts. It was not possible to conduct an oral examination of the judgment debtor to ascertain this information as it was not within the jurisdiction. In addition, there was evidence that the judgment debtor was endeavouring to collect in the amounts owed by the judgment debtor company's English customers to avoid their being available for execution in England. Vaughan Williams LJ, who gave the judgment of the Court, found that there were special circumstances entitling the judgment creditor to equitable execution since without the appointment, it would have been 'practically very difficult, if not impossible, to obtain any fruit of his judgment'.[2]

1   [1906] 1 KB 373, CA.
2   [1906] 1 KB 373 at 375.

6.36 However, in the absence of special circumstances, the court will not appoint a receiver. In *Morgan v Hart*[1] the judgment debtor had no property available for execution except furniture and effects from his home, which he had removed and stored in a large furniture repository. The judgment creditor's solicitor interviewed the owner of the repository who admitted the judgment debtor's furniture and effects were stored in the repository but stated that the sheriff would be unable to seize them under a writ of fieri facias because they could not be distinguished from other people's furniture and he would not give any assistance in this regard. The Court of Appeal refused to appoint a receiver because the purpose of the order was not execution but to keep the property where it was until the judgment creditor could obtain disclosure as to which of the furniture and effects belonged to the judgment debtor. The court observed that judgment creditor would have been better advised to seek an order for such disclosure.[2]

1   [1914] 2 KB 183, CA.
2   [1914] 2 KB 183 at 190–191.

6.37   In the Canadian case of *Manning Wanless Building Supplies Ltd v Puskas and Flemke*[1] the court held that the fact that the collection of monthly rents owed to the judgment debtor would require a series of garnishee applications qualified as 'special circumstances'. Similarly, in *Soinco S.A.C.I. v Novokuznetsk*[2] a receiver was appointed over future payments under a supply contract. The judgment debtors had sought to argue that one reason an order for the appointment of a receiver by way of equitable execution should not be granted was that there was nothing to stop the plaintiffs applying for a series of garnishee orders as and when the debts became due.[3] The court rejected the judgment debtors' arguments and made the order.[4]

1   (1962) 39 WWR 672 (Can).
2   [1998] QB 406.
3   [1998] QB 406 at 411.
4   [1998] QB 406 at 423. The fact that information as to the operation of the supply contract and what payments were due or would become due in future would be unobtainable without an order for the appointment of a receiver by way of equitable execution was one of a number of factors that influenced the court.

(c) Property must be capable of assignment and not otherwise inalienable

6.38   This requirement is considered in relation to the types of assets that can be subject to equitable execution at paras 6.46–6.47.

(d) The costs of the receivership must be proportionate to the likely recovery

6.39   At common law, it is well established that equitable execution should only be granted '*in cases where the amount of the judgment debt warrants the expense*'.[1] This is now a procedural requirement for equitable execution. The Practice Direction to Pt 69 states:[2]

'Where a judgment creditor applies for the appointment of a receiver as a method of enforcing a judgment, in considering whether to make the appointment the court will have regard to –

(1) the amount claimed by the judgment creditor;
(2) the amount likely to be obtained by the receiver; and
(3) the probable costs of his appointment.'

1   *I v K* [1884] WN 63.
2   PD 69, para 5.

6.40   The Practice Direction also requires that the written evidence in support of an application for the appointment of a receiver must give details of the value and likely income of the property it is intended the receiver should get in. These provisions are considered further in the context of the evidence required in support of the application at paras 6.83-6.90.

(e) The court will not appoint a receiver where the court is satisfied that it would be fruitless because there is nothing for the receiver to collect in

6.41   Equity does not act in vain. Therefore where it cannot be shown that the appointment of a receiver by way of equitable execution will be an effectual and useful method of enforcing the judgment debt, it will not be made.

6.42   In *Edwards & Co v Picard*[1] a majority of the Court of Appeal held that a receiver should not be appointed where the judgment creditor sought an order for the appointment of a receiver of all rents, profits and moneys receivable in respect of the judgment debtor's interest in three English patents in or towards satisfaction of the judgment debts. The judgment debtor had no other property in the jurisdiction. However, there was no evidence before the court that any licences had been granted in respect of which royalties were receivable or that any business was being carried on by the use of the patents. Vaughan Williams LJ held that the patent merely conferred a right to exclude others from manufacturing in a particular way and using a particular invention. He concluded that there was no property of the patentee judgment debtor for the receiver to receive and that the order should not therefore be made.[2] Similarly, Buckley LJ concurred that no order should be made because there was nothing receivable.[3] Fletcher Moulton LJ, dissenting, thought that the court did have jurisdiction to make the order and, while acknowledging that 'it is true in general that it would not appoint a receiver without a probability that the appointment would be effectual and useful',[4] thought that justice in that case was so strongly on the side of the judgment creditor that the appointment should be made 'as soon as possible in order that nothing may escape' the receiver.[5] While Fletcher Moulton LJ may have been seeking to push the principle too far, where a patentee has a right to claim damages for patent infringement or a right to fees under the terms of a licence that has been granted, there would appear to be property amenable to equitable execution.[6]

It seems that the principle that the appointment should not be fruitless is not offended where the property will or may be received in the future, such as where the judgment debtor has a reversionary interest under a will (see para 6.59).

1   *Edwards v Co v Picard* [1909] 2 KB 903. See also *I v K* [1884] WN 63 where Field J held that a receiver should only be granted where 'there is something for the receiver to receive'

and *Bourne v Colodense* [1985] ICR 291 at 302, per Dillon LJ: 'it is plain that the court would not appoint a receiver if the court were satisfied that the appointment would be fruitless because there was nothing for the receiver to get in'.

2   [1909] 2 KB 903 at 906.

3   [1909] 2 KB 903 at 910. However, Buckley LJ's obiter comments at 910 that a receiver could not sue for infringement of a patent or non-payment of licence fees seem in contradiction to that court's later decision that a receiver could be appointed to enforce an indemnity claim under an insurance contract.

4   [1909] 2 KB 903 at 908.

5   [1909] 2 KB 903 at 909.

6   However, see the comments of Buckley LJ: [1909] 2 KB 903 at 909–910.

ASSETS AMENABLE TO EQUITABLE EXECUTION

6.43   Because of the nature of equitable execution and the fact that there must be some legal or practical difficulty which precludes legal methods of execution, the circumstances in which equitable execution will be available are more easily defined negatively rather than positively. The starting point is that if the property can be reached by writ of fieri facias, third party debt order or charging order, then this method of enforcement should generally be used in preference to equitable execution.

Interest can be legal or equitable in nature

6.44   A number of the older authorities state[1] or appear to state[2] that the court only has jurisdiction to appoint a receiver by way of equitable execution where the judgment debtor holds only an equitable interest in the asset which, if it had been a legal interest, could have been reached by execution at law. This view was firmly rejected by Millett J in *Maclaine Watson v International Tin Council*[3] whose judgment was expressly approved by the Court of Appeal.[4] The test was simply 'that there should be no way of getting at the fund except by the appointment of a receiver'.[5]

1   *Anglo-Italian Bank v Davies* (1878) 9 Ch D 275 at 285, per Sir George Jessell MR and 289, per Brett LJ; *Salt v Cooper* (1880) 16 Ch D 544 at 552, per Jessell MR; *Holmes v Millage* [1893] 1 QB 551 at 555, per Lindley LJ; *Cadogan v Lyric Theatre Ltd* [1894] 3 Ch 338 at 341, per Lord Herschell LC; *Edwards v Co v Picard* [1909] 2 KB 903 at 910, per Buckley LJ.

2   See Millett J's critical analysis of a number of earlier authorities in *Maclaine Watson v International Tin Council* [1988] 1 Ch 1 at 19-21.

3   [1988] 1 Ch 1 at 20–21.

4   [1989] 1 Ch 253 at 270, per Ralph Gibson LJ, 284, per Nourse LJ and 284, per Kerr LJ.

5   [1986] 1 Ch 1 at 20, approving the judgment of Chitty J in *Westhead v Riley* (1883) 25 Ch D 413.

6.45   In the case of land, it is specifically provided by statute that both legal and equitable interests can be the subject of equitable execution.[1]

1   See paras 6.67–6.69.

Interest must be capable of assignment

6.46   The property in respect of which an order for equitable execution is sought must be capable of assignment and not otherwise inalienable. This is because a 'party who gets equitable execution gets nothing more than his judgment debtor can give him'.[1] In practical terms, the judgment creditor should enquire whether the property has any statutory, common law or contractual restrictions on assignment which make the property inalienable. If there are such restrictions, it will not be possible for the court to appoint a receiver by way of equitable execution.

[1] *Ridout v Fowler* [1904] 1 Ch 658 at 661, per Farwell J.

6.47 An exhaustive list of the types of property which are *not* capable of assignment is outside the scope of this book. The following types of property have been found not to be capable of assignment and therefore not amenable to the appointment of a receiver by way of equitable execution:

(a) Pensions: orders for equitable execution in respect of army pensions[1] and maintenance payments have been refused on the grounds of non-assignability.[2] Many forms of pensions are rendered unassignable by statute.[3]

(b) Salaries: salaries of public officers are unassignable on public policy grounds at common law[4] and there are statutory restrictions on the assignment of army, navy or air force pay[5] as well as the wages of seamen.[6] Although not explicitly on the basis of lack of assignability, it has been held that a receiver cannot be appointed over future salary.[7] The proper mechanism for attaching a judgment debtor's salary or pension is an attachment of earnings order, which is considered in Chapter 1 (General rules on enforcement of judgments).

(c) Contractual restrictions: contractual restrictions on assignability which are binding upon the judgment debtor will also be fatal to equitable execution. This is illustrated by *Field v Field*,[8] where an attempt to appoint a receiver to make an election on behalf of the judgment debtor to receive a lump sum under a pension scheme was refused because the judgment debtor's interest in the fund contained a prohibition on assignment.[9]

[1] *Lucas v Harris* (1886) 18 QBD 127 where an attempt was made to appoint a receiver to collect an army pension which by virtue of the now repealed Army Act 1881, s 141 was unassignable. The equivalent modern statutory provisions are Army Act 1955, s 203(1), Air Force Act 1955, s 203(1) and Naval Discipline Act 1957, s 128G(1) which respectively render void, inter alia, any purported assignment of an army, air force or navy pension. The statutory provisions cover not just pensions but, inter alia, any pay, grant or allowances payable to any person in respect of his or any other person's service in Her Majesty's military, air forces or navy. See also *Crowe v Price* (1889) 22 QBD 429, where the Court of Appeal refused to allow equitable execution where a trustee in bankruptcy had collected pension payments and paid them into court but where the bankruptcy order was later set aside. The court held that the payments were still pension payments until received by the pensioner and reduced into possession and therefore still unassignable. The position is different once the pension payments have been received by the pensioner and paid into the pensioner's bank account. In these circumstances the amounts in the pensioner's bank account have been reduced into possession and lost their character as pension and become part of the pensioner's ordinary money. Accordingly, the pension payments in the bank account can be garnished in the usual manner: *Jones & Co v Coventry* [1909] 2 KB 1029, DC.

[2] *Watkins v Watkins* [1896] P 222, CA; *Paquine v Snary* [1909] 1 KB 688, CA; *J Wallis Ltd v Legge* [1923] 2 KB 240, CA. See generally *Halsbury's Laws of England* (4th edn, 2003 reissue), vol 6, para 87.

[3] These include pensions of public officers. The more obviously relevant examples include: military pensions (see n 1 above); police pensions (Police Pensions Act 1976, s 9); parliamentary pensions (Parliamentary Pensions (Consolidation and Amendment) Regulations

1993, SI 1993/3253, reg R1(1)); civil service superannuation schemes (Superannuation Act 1972, s 5(1)); NHS pensions (National Health Service Pension Scheme Regulations 1995, SI 1995/300, reg T3(1)); judicial pensions (Judicial Pensions (Preservation of Benefits) Order 1995, SI 1995/634, art 7) and clergy pensions (Church of England Pensions Regulations 1988, SI 1988/2256, reg 29(2)). Guaranteed Minimum Pensions under an occupational pension scheme are unassignable by virtue of Pension Schemes Act 1993, s 159. Occupational pension schemes themselves are also unassignable under Pensions Act 1995, s 91.

4   See *Halsbury's Laws of England* (4th edn, 2003 reissue) vol 6, para 85.
5   See 6.47, n 3.
6   Merchant Shipping Act 1995, s 34.
7   *Holmes v Millage* [1893] 1 QB 551. The Court of Appeal decided the case on the basis that future salary could not be reached at law or in equity.
8   [2003] 1 FLR 376.
9   [2003] 1 FLR 376 at 382. The case was decided on the basis of lack of assignability and the question of whether a receiver could make elections on the judgment debtor's behalf was left open. For a critique of the decision, see Gee *Commercial Injunctions* (5th edn, 2004), pp 468–471.

Residual category

6.48   Assuming therefore that:

(a) no method of legal execution (that is, no writ of fieri facias, third party debt order or charging order) is available in respect of the property; and

(b) the judgment debtor's property is capable of assignment,

there is no closed list of assets which potentially can be subject to equitable execution. However, the property must be specifically identified, it is not permissible to ask for a receiver to be appointed over *all* the judgment debtor's assets.[1]

This section focuses on those instances of equitable execution that have come before the courts that are likely to be relevant to a commercial enforcement scenario. Receivers appointed over personalty are dealt with first, followed by a discussion of receivers appointed over land, which are governed by special statutory provisions.

1   PD 69, para 4.1(2).

Receivers over personalty

Future payments

6.49   As has been noted, in *Soinco S.A.C.I. v Novokuznetsk*[1] it was held that future payments to a judgment debtor under a supply contract could be subject to equitable execution. Colman J explained that:[2]

'[t]he function of such a receiver would be to require the [payor under the supply contract[3]] to pay over to him all sums that become due for payment to [the judgment debtor] under the supply contract as and when they fall due. The receiver would then accumulate the payments up to the amount of the judgment debt and interest and then pay over that amount to the [judgment creditors] in discharge of the judgment debt.'

¹ [1998] QB 406. Noted (1997) 10(7) Insol Int 53.
² [1998] QB 406 at 410.
³ A company that there was evidence to show was controlled by the same individuals as the judgment debtor: see [1998] QB 406 at 423.

6.50   The judgment creditors' application for equitable execution was based on the impediments in their ability to satisfy the debt by the use of garnishee proceedings (now third party debt orders). In particular:

(a) the judgment creditors had no information as to *what* sums were or would become due or accruing due under the supply contract or *when* they would become due or accruing due;

(b) garnishee proceedings would only attach debts due or accruing due at the time of the garnishee order nisi (now an interim third party debt order). The judgment creditors' inability to ascertain when amounts fell due or accruing due precluded them from using garnishee proceedings: if the application was paid too soon, they may get nothing; too late, and the judgment debtors may have paid the sums away;

(c) there was evidence that the payor and the judgment debtors were seeking to 'smother' the payments due under the supply contract by making advance prepayments which could be set off against the sums payable under the supply contract so as to make the payments owed to the judgment debtor 'garnishee proof'.

6.51   Colman J had considerable sympathy with the judgment creditors' submission, that in light of these circumstances, it would be both just and convenient to appoint a receiver for the purpose of ascertaining what payments were due under the supply contract, and he dismissed the judgment debtor's objection that such appointment would involve the receiver in acting as manager of the supply contract (see paras 6.13–6.14). The bulk of his judgment was devoted to a review of earlier authorities in light of the judgment debtor's other key objection, namely that the court had no jurisdiction to appoint a receiver by way of equitable execution over future debts because it was bound by the position prior to the Supreme Court of Judicature Act 1873 when the Court of Chancery had no such jurisdiction. As discussed at para 6.27, Colman J eventually rejected this submission and found that there *was* jurisdiction to appoint a receiver by way of equitable execution to receive future debts as well as debts accruing due at the date of the order. Having concluded thus, he continued:¹

'… the question that has to be answered is whether future debts have intrinsic characteristics which would justify excluding them from this remedy. In approaching this question it is necessary to keep in mind that the purpose of such a remedy would be to supplement legal process of execution by garnishee proceedings. Since that process does not apply to future debts and since it cannot be commenced in anticipation of debts becoming accruing due at a later stage, there is much to be said for the availability of a remedy which would enable the judgment creditor to acquire information as to future debts to enable him to effect collection from third parties as and when they fell due.'

¹ [1988] QB 406 at 421.

6.52   As has been noted, Colman J made short shrift of the judgment debtor's argument that such appointment would bring the judgment debtor's business to a standstill.[1] Similarly, he found little merit in the judgment debtor's argument that questions of double jeopardy may arise with the payor under the supply contract having to pay the debts twice over, since the receiver's powers to apply to the court for directions would safeguard the paying party's position.[2] He also felt there were independent positive justifications for making the order sought connected to the development of the Mareva or freezing injunction jurisdiction.[3]

[1]   See para 6.14.
[2]   [1998] QB 406 at 421–422.
[3]   [1998] QB 406 at 422.

Future trust payments to a beneficiary

6.53   It was suggested in *Webb v Stenton*[1] that where the judgment debtor was a beneficiary under a trust and was entitled to future income payable half-yearly from trustees, the income could be collected by the appointment of a receiver by way of equitable execution.[2] However, *Webb v Stenton* concerned an application for a garnishee order[3] and thus the court's comments are strictly obiter. Further, doubt as to the validity of these remarks were expressed by Colman J in *Soinco S.A.C.I. v Novokuznetsk*:[4]

'On the face of it, these remarks in favour of the appointment of a receiver appear to be directly inconsistent with many subsequent Court of Appeal decisions. It may be that they can be explained on the basis that the property in that case consisted of future payments (not yet to be made) by trustees to a beneficiary with a life interest under a will and was therefore of an equitable nature which attracted the equitable remedy in question. Having regard to the fact that in the present case there is no question of the property being of an equitable nature, I do not consider that these remarks have any relevance, if indeed they were correct.'

[1]   (1883) 11 QBD 518.
[2]   (1883) 11 QBD 518 at 519, per Cave J at first instance, 530-531, per Fry LJ and 531, per Lindley LJ (concurring).
[3]   Which was refused on the basis that there was no debt owing or accruing by the trustees when the debt was applied for.
[4]   [1998] QB 406 at 417.

6.54   However, given the court's conclusion in *Soinco* that payments that became due as a consequence of future payments made under a supply contract should be amenable to equitable execution, it is difficult to see why a right to future income under a non-discretionary trust should not also be so amenable. Different considerations may arise where the trust is discretionary, and it should also be borne in mind that the terms of the trust may have provisions forfeiting a beneficiary's interest in the event that equitable execution is sought in respect of his interest.

Refusal to exercise a contractual right

6.55   A receiver by way of equitable execution can be appointed to enforce a contractual right that the judgment debtor is refusing to exercise.[1] This most commonly arises where the judgment debtor has a right under a contract of indemnity and is refusing to exercise this right.

¹ *Bourne v Colodense* [1985] ICR 291, CA; *Maclaine Watson & Co v ITC* [1988] 1 Ch 1; *Allied Irish Bank v Ashford Hotels Ltd* [1997] 3 All ER 309, CA.

6.56 In *Bourne v Colodense*¹ the judgment debtor was a trade union member and had, as he was entitled to do under the trade union rules, applied for financial support by the union to bring a claim against his employer. The trade union agreed to give financial support in the litigation and instructed a solicitor to act on his behalf. The claim failed and costs were awarded against the judgment debtor personally but on the understanding that he would be put in funds to pay the costs order by the trade union. The judgment debtor himself had no assets to satisfy the judgment debt and flatly refused to seek reimbursement from the trade union to pay the costs order.

¹ [1985] ICR 291.

6.57 The employer judgment creditor applied to appoint a receiver by way of equitable execution to bring proceedings in the name of the judgment debtor to enforce the indemnity for costs or the contractual right which they contended the union had given the judgment debtor. The Court of Appeal held that the judgment debtor had an arguable indemnity or contractual right from his trade union in respect of the costs order made against him and was therefore prepared to uphold the order appointing the receiver, since if the indemnity or contractual right could be established, this would satisfy the judgment creditor's costs order.¹

¹ In *Soinco S.A.C.I. v Novokuznetsk* [1998] QB 406 at 419–420 Colman J pointed out that a number of key authorities did not appear to have been cited to the Court in *Bourne*. However, he declined an invitation from counsel to ignore the case on the basis it was decided per incuriam and in any event referred to the later decision in *Maclaine Watson*, which gave full consideration to the authorities.

6.58 By statute¹ the court has power to make a costs order directly against non-parties to the proceedings, such as the trade union in *Bourne*, thereby removing the need for recourse to equitable execution in such circumstances. However, *Bourne* is authority for the wider principle that equitable execution can be used to bring proceedings in the judgment debtor's name to enforce contractual rights of indemnity in respect of the judgment debtor's liabilities. This was illustrated in *Maclaine Watson & Co v International Tin Council*.² In that case the judgment creditors had obtained a judgment debt of some £6m against the International Tin Council (the ITC). The ITC was a treaty organisation whose members consisted of various states including the UK government. The judgment creditors were seeking to appoint a receiver by way of equitable execution to bring proceedings in the name of the ITC to attempt to enforce an indemnity said to arise from its member states in respect of the judgment debt. A receiver was ultimately refused because any indemnity claim by the ITC was not justiciable before the English courts. However, Millett J, after a full consideration of the authorities, was prepared to treat *Bourne* as authority for the appointment of a receiver by way of equitable execution to enforce a claim to an indemnity.³ Although the issue did not arise before the subsequent appeal to the Court of Appeal, all members of the Court of Appeal expressly approved the reasoning of Millett J.⁴ It should also be noted that any claim that the appointment of a receiver by way of equitable execution to enforce the judgment debtor's claim would be contrary to the rules on maintenance and champerty would be likely to fail since the judgment creditor clearly has a genuine commercial interest in the enforcement of the indemnity.[5]

1   SCA 1981, s 51 and CPR 48.2(1)(a). In *Hamilton v Al Fayed (No 2)* [2003] 3 QB 1175, at 1203–1204 Hale LJ suggested *obiter* that a third party costs order is not usually made against a trade union because the expectation is that the trade union will pay voluntarily. Presumably where it does not, as in *Bourne v Colodense*, the court has a discretion to make a direct costs order against the trade union rather than use the more circuitous route of appointing a receiver by way of equitable execution. In *Murphy v Young & Co* [1997] 1 WLR 1591 at 1601 Phillips LJ issued guidance on making a costs order under SCA 1981, s 51 against, inter alia, a trade union. On the power to award costs against non-parties generally see *Cook on Costs* 2005.

2   *Maclaine Watson & Co v International Tin Council* [1988] 1 Ch 1.

3   *Maclaine Watson & Co v International Tin Council* [1988] 1 Ch 1 at 21.

4   *Maclaine Watson & Co v International Tin Council* [1989] 1 Ch 253.

5   *Bourne v Colodense* [1985] ICR 291 at 301–302, per Lawton LJ and 303, per Dillon LJ.

Reversionary interest under a will

6.59   Equitable execution is possible in respect of any capital or income which the judgment debtor may become entitled to in future under a reversionary interest under a will.[1]

1   *Macnicoll v Parnell* (1887) 35 WR 773, DC; *Fuggle v Bland* (1883) 11 QBD 711; *Flegg v Prentis* [1892] 2 Ch 428; *Tyrrell v Painton* [1895] 1 QB 202, CA; *Ideal Bedding Co Ltd v Holland* [1907] 2 Ch 157.

Funds held in court

6.60   In *Westhead v Riley*,[1] Chitty J appointed a receiver by way of equitable execution over taxed costs which were due to be paid to the judgment debtor from a fund held at court. Such appointment would no longer be necessary as funds standing to the benefit of a judgment debtor in court can now be made available to a judgment creditor using the procedure set out in CPR 72.10.[2] Alternatively, a charging order could be sought.[3]

1   (1881) 25 Ch D 413.

2   See further Chapter 3 (Third party debt orders). While a third party debt order cannot be obtained in respect of such sums, CPR 72.10 provides an alternative method whereby such funds can be paid in satisfaction of a judgment debt.

3   See Chapter 4 (Charging orders).

Foreign assets

6.61   There are no cases where a receiver by way of equitable execution has been appointed over foreign assets. However, receivers appointed under debentures have been appointed over foreign assets. In *Re Maudslay, Sons & Field*[1] the claimant debenture holders appointed a receiver over the company's assets which included a debt due to the company by a French firm. When another creditor brought proceedings in France to attach the debt due to the company by the French firm, the debenture holders applied to restrain the French proceedings on the basis that they interfered with the receiver's possession. Cozens-Hardy J held that there was no contempt:[2]

'So long as the property is within the territorial jurisdiction of the Court, there is no difficulty, at least in theory, in putting the receiver in actual possession. And when the receiver is in possession, the Court does not allow his possession to be interfered with without leave. For example, no judgment creditor of the company would be allowed to levy execution upon the property of the company in England now in the possession of the receivers. It is well settled that the Court can appoint receivers over property out of the jurisdiction. This power, I apprehend, is based upon the doctrine that the Court acts in personam. The Court does not, and cannot attempt by its order to put its own officer in possession of foreign property, but it treats as guilty of contempt any party to the action in which the order is made who prevents the necessary steps being taken to enable its officer to take possession according to the laws of the foreign country. See *Keys v Keys*, where special directions were given to a receiver as to the best mode of getting in an Indian debt; and *Smith v Smith*, where it was pointed out that a receiver of property in Jersey and in France would have to recover possession according to the laws of those countries; and in *Houlditch v Marquis of Donegal* the House of Lords held that the Court of Chancery in Ireland ought to appoint a receiver in a suit instituted to carry into effect a decree of the Court of Chancery in England by which a receiver had been appointed over estates in Ireland. In other words, the receiver is not put in possession of foreign property by the mere order of the Court. Something else has to be done, and until that has been done in accordance with the foreign law, any person, not a party to the suit, who takes proceedings in the foreign country is not guilty of a contempt either on the ground of interfering with the receiver's possession or otherwise.'

1   [1990] 1 Ch 602.
2   [1990] 1 Ch 602 at 611–612.

6.62   Although the case is authority for the proposition that receivers appointed under a debenture can be appointed over foreign assets, it illustrates the practical difficulties inherent in so doing. The receiver was effectively powerless when proceedings were brought in France over the assets which were theoretically within the scope of his appointment. One possible solution is for the court to direct the judgment debtor to take steps to facilitate the receiver to take possession of the asset in accordance with the foreign law.[1] However, faced with a recalcitrant judgment debtor who has already ignored one court order by not satisfying the judgment debt, such directions may prove of limited utility.

1   [1910] WN 218.

6.63   In *Soinco S.A.C.I. v Novokuznetsk*[1] one of the numerous grounds on which the judgment debtors objected to the appointment of a receiver by way of equitable execution over payments due or to become due under a supply contract was that the payor company was a Guernsey company and a receiver could not collect in assets outside the jurisdiction.[2] Colman J found that the judgment creditor's application was made on the basis that the situs of all the debts was England, since that was where the Guernsey company carried on business, so there was no reason why the receiver should be concerned with amounts payable abroad.[3] However, at a later passage in the judgment he considered a further argument from the judgment debtors that the order should not be made where there was serious risk of the third party payor facing double jeopardy by being sued for the debt in the foreign jurisdiction where the debt was still payable despite having already paid the receiver.[4] Colman J found:[5]

> 'This argument is, in my judgment, quite unconvincing. Half the attraction of the remedy of the appointment of a receiver is that it is inherently capable of great flexibility. In particular, if any question of double jeopardy arose in respect of any particular debt when it fell due for payment, that matter could be referred to the court for further consideration, a fortiori where, as in this case, the third party debtor, the Guernsey company, is already a party to the action. The court could then satisfy itself as to how real the danger of double jeopardy was and, if necessary, vary the receiver's mandate. I would only add that in the present case there is, at least at present, no real evidence of risk of double jeopardy.'

1   [1998] QB 406.
2   [1998] QB 406.
3   [1998] QB 406 at 412.
4   The judgment debtors contrasted the position under equitable execution with that which applied in relation to garnishee proceedings whereby the courts had a discretion as to whether to garnish a foreign debt. However, this is no longer the law following the House of Lords' decision in *Société Eram Shipping Co Ltd v Compagnie Internationale de Navigation* [2004] 1 AC 260, which effectively held there is no jurisdiction to garnish a foreign debt. See further Chapter 3 (Third party debt orders).
5   [1998] QB 406 at 422.

6.64   However, where a real risk of double jeopardy could be demonstrated to the court, it seems unlikely that the court would be prepared to appoint a receiver by way of equitable execution over a foreign debt. It is a fundamental principle of both English law and private international law that the laws of the country in which a debt arises may discharge a debt and that such discharge will be an effectual answer to the claim not only in that country but in every other country. Further, the discharge of a debt or liability by the law of a country other than that in which the debt arises does not relieve the debtor in any other country.[1] The problem of effective discharge will therefore invariably arise in all equitable execution cases which seek to collect foreign payments.

1   *Ellis v M'Henry* (1871) LR 6 CP 228 at 234. The relevant passage of the judgment was approved by the House of Lords in *Société Eram Shipping Co Ltd v Cie Internationale de Navigation* [2004] 1 AC 260.

Interest in partnership property

6.65   Where a judgment has been obtained against a partner, it is possible for the judgment creditor to appoint a receiver of that partner's interest in the partnership property and profits. The Partnership Act 1890 (PA 1890), s 23(2) provides that:

> 'The High Court, or a judge thereof, … may, on the application by summons of any judgment creditor of a partner, make an order charging that partner's interest

in the partnership property and profits with payment of the amount of the judgment debt and interest thereon, and may by the same or a subsequent order appoint a receiver of that partner's share of profits (whether already declared or accruing), and of any other money which may be coming to him in respect of the partnership, and direct all accounts and inquiries, and give all other orders and directions which might have been directed or given if the charge had been made in favour of the judgment creditor by the partner, or which the circumstances of the case may require.'

6.66 The procedure for obtaining a charging order under PA 1890, s 23(2) is set out in RSC Ord 81, r 10.[1] The application must be made in accordance with Pt 23[2] and every application notice issued and order made on such application must be served on the judgment debtor and on such of his partners as are within the jurisdiction.[3] In practice, the application may be for both a charging order to charge the partner's share of the partnership property and to appoint a receiver to receive the partnership income.

1   As preserved in CPR, Sch 1.
2   RSC Ord 81, r 10(1).
3   RSC Ord 81, r 10(3). This provision affords the other partners the opportunity to exercise their statutory right to redeem the interest charged or purchase the partnership interest in the event of a sale.

Receivers over land

6.67 Unless land belonging to the judgment debtor has some income stream associated with it, a charging order will normally be the appropriate method of enforcing a judgment against land. Appointing a receiver by way of equitable execution over land is regulated by special statutory rules.

6.68 Historically, receivers could only be appointed over *equitable* interests in land because legal interests in land could be taken at law by the writ of elegit.[1] The Administration of Justice Act 1956 abolished the writ of elegit[2] and extended the jurisdiction to appoint a receiver by way of equitable execution in respect of all legal estates and interest in land.[3] This is still the position today whereby the provisions in the Administration of Justice Act 1956 concerning receivers were repealed and re-enacted by SCA 1981.[4] SCA 1981, s 37(4) provides that:

'The power of the High Court to appoint a receiver by way of equitable execution shall operate in relation to all legal estates and interests in land; and that power—
(a) may be exercised in relation to an estate or interest in land whether or not a charge has been imposed on that land under section 1 of the Charging Orders Act 1979 for the purpose of enforcing the judgment, order or award in question; and
(b) shall be in addition to, and not in derogation of, any power of any court to appoint a receiver in proceedings for enforcing such a charge.'

1   A writ of elegit was a form of execution created by the Damages Execution Act 1285 which allowed the sheriff to take 'all the Chattels of the [judgment] Debtor (saving only his Oxen and Beasts of his Plough) and the one half of his Land'. The writ of elegit was extended to

cover all the judgments debtor's land by the Judgments Act 1838, s 11. Bankruptcy Act 1883, s 146 removed the sheriff's right to take the goods of the judgment debtor and restricted the writ of elegit to land only. For a historical perspective, see *Blackstone's Commentaries on the laws of England* (1765–1769) vol 3, pp 419–420.

2   Administration of Justice 1956, s 34(1). Section 34(2) also repealed the Law of Property Act 1925, s 195(1)–(3) and (5) which provided that judgments entered up in SCA 1981 operate as equitable charges on all the land of the judgment debtor. Section 195(3) provided that the judgment creditor had to wait a year from the entering up of judgment before being entitled to enforce the statutory charge and if the judgment debtor became bankrupt before the year was up, the judgment creditor had no priority. A similar regime had also existed under the Judgments Act 1838, ss 11 and 19.

3   Administration of Justice 1956, s 36(1).

4   SCA 1981, s 152(4) and Sch 7.

6.69   In other words, equitable execution can be granted without the need to apply for a charging order and, even where a charging order has been made, the court may also appoint a receiver by way of equitable execution. In practice, the appointment of a receiver probably has no advantage over a charging order unless there is some periodic income stream or profits associated with the property for the receiver to collect.[1] While a receiver by way of equitable execution could be appointed to make an application *in the judgment debtor's name*[2] under Trusts of Land and Appointment of Trustees Act 1996, s 14[3] for the sale of the property, this could also be achieved by obtaining an order for sale under a final charging order. In practice, it is likely that where a judgment debtor owns land with an associated income stream the judgment debtor should apply for both a charging order (to charge the judgment debtor's interest in the land) and an order for appointment of a receiver by way of equitable execution (to obtain the income from the land).

1   In contrast to a charging order, the appointment of a receiver will not impose a charge on the property and place the judgment creditor in the position of a secured creditor. See paras 6.153–6.156.

2   If the action is brought in the name of the receiver rather than the judgment debtor he will not have sufficient interest under the Trusts of Land and Appointment of Trustees Act 1996, s 14: *Stevens v Hutchinson* [1953] Ch 299 at 305 where the court was considering the Law of Property Act 1925, s 30 (the predecessor of the Trusts of Land and Appointment of Trustees Act 1996, s 14).

3   *Levermore v Levermore* [1979] 1 WLR 1277 at 1281–1282 where the court was considering Law of Property Act 1925, s 30 (the predecessor of Trusts of Land and Appointment of Trustees Act 1996, s 14).

Rents

6.70   Where the judgment debtor owns a property in which there are tenants in possession paying rent, a receiver by way of equitable execution would serve a useful purpose by being able to collect the rents which could not otherwise easily be reached. A charging order does not extend to cover income from the land and the third party debt order procedure would require a proliferation of orders after each instalment of rent because it requires a 'debt due or accruing due to the judgment debtor' before an order can be made.[1] Following the Canadian case of *Manning Wanless Building Supplies Ltd v Puskas and Flemke*,[2] the need for a proliferation of third party debt orders is likely to be grounds for an order for the appointment of a receiver by way of equitable execution.

1　See further Chapters 3 and 4.
2　(1962) 39 WWR 672 (Can).

Registering the appointment of a receiver over land

6.71　In order to be effective,[1] the order appointing a receiver by way of equitable execution over land should be registered. The land registration system is considered in detail at paras 4.101–4.132 and this section simply deals with the mechanics of registration. The method of protecting an order appointing a receiver over land depends on whether the land is registered or not.

1　Since otherwise a bona fide purchaser without notice could take free of the order.

Unregistered land

6.72　In the case of unregistered land, an application should be made to have the order appointing the receiver registered in the register of writs and order affecting land.[1] Registration of the order constitutes actual notice of the order irrespective of whether a potential purchaser actually inspects the register.[2] Where a charging order has already been obtained and registered under Land Charges Act 1972, s 6, it is not necessary to register an order appointing a receiver by way of equitable execution.[3] Where registration is required, the appropriate form for the registration of a writ or order is Land Registry Form K4[4] and the fee is £1.[5]

1　Land Charges Act 1972, s 6(1)(b). The entry is made against the name of the estate owner or other person whose land is affected by the order: Land Charges Act 1972, s 6(2). The meaning of 'estate owner' is considered at paras 4.114–4.115.
2　Law of Property Act 1925, s 198.
3　SCA 1981, s 37(5). This section disapplies Land Charges Act 1972, s 6(4) which would otherwise render the receivership order void as against a purchaser for failure to register the order.
4　The form can be downloaded from the Land Registry website: www.landreg.gov.uk/publications/?pubtype=1. Instructions for completion of the form are provided with the form.
5　Land Charges Fees Rules 1990, Sch 1.

Registered land

6.73　An application to protect an order appointing a receiver should be made to enter a restriction which 'is an entry in the register regulating the circumstances in which a registered estate or charge may be the subject of an entry in the register'.[1] A court appointed receiver is entitled to apply for a restriction to be registered[2] in Form L[3] or N[4] of the standard form of restrictions which appear in the Land Registration Rules 2003, Sch 4. Where a restriction is entered on the register, no entry of the type prohibited by the restriction can be made otherwise than in accordance with the terms of the restriction.[5] The relevant form for the registration of a receiver is Land Registry Form RX1[6] and the fee is £40.[7]

1　Land Registration Act 2002, s 40(1).
2　Land Registration Act 2002, s 43(1)(c) and Land Registration Rules 2003, r 93(s).

3   The substance of which provides: 'No disposition [or specify details] of the registered estate [(other than a charge)] by the proprietor of the registered estate [, or by the proprietor of any registered charge,] is to be registered without a certificate.'

4   The substance of which provides: 'No disposition [or specify details] of the registered estate [(other than a charge)] by the proprietor of the registered estate [or by the proprietor of any registered charge] is to be registered without a written consent.'

5   Land Registration Act 2002, s 41. The form can be downloaded from the Land Registry website: www.landreg.gov.uk/publications/?pubtype=1. An annotated guide explaining how to complete the form is available at http://www.landreg.gov.uk/assets/library/documents/formrx1_annotated.pdf.

6   Land Registration Rules 2003, r 92(1).

7   Land Registration Fee Order 2004, SI 2004/595, Sch 3, Part 1.

LIMITATIONS OF EQUITABLE EXECUTION

6.74   It has been noted at the outset that equitable execution generally will not be available when some other method of enforcement can be used against the judgment debtor's assets. It also is not possible for equitable execution to be obtained against the Crown.[1] Crown Privilege and other general limitations on enforcement are considered in Chapter 1.

1   Crown Proceedings Act 1947, s 25(4) and RSC Ord 77, r 16(1)(c).

PRACTICE AND PROCEDURE

6.75   The procedural rules relating to the appointment of a receiver by way of equitable execution are set out in CPR Pt 69 and the accompanying Practice Direction. (The provisions of Pt 69 apply to most forms of court-appointed receiver, not simply receivers by way of equitable execution.[1]) The application for appointment of a receiver by way of equitable execution should also be made in accordance with the provisions of CPR Pt 23.

1   See further *Kerr and Hunter on Receivers and Administrators* (18th edn, 2005) pp 119–120.

When can the court appoint a receiver?

6.76   The court may appoint a receiver before proceedings have started, in existing proceedings, or on or after judgment.[1] This chapter is concerned with the appointment of a receiver by way of equitable execution once judgment has been obtained. It follows from the use of the words '*on* or after judgment' that the judgment creditor may apply for judgment as soon as judgment is given, assuming he is in a position to do so.

1   CPR 69.2(1)(a)–(c).

Which court?

6.77   A receiver can be appointed by way of equitable execution in any division of the High Court.[1] Part 69 contains no provision as to the court in which the application should be made. However, in line with the general rules on applications, the application should be made to the court where the claim was started[2] unless the claim has since been transferred, in which case it should be made to the court to which the claim was transferred.[3] If an application for an order for appointment of a receiver is made after proceedings to enforce the judgment have begun, it must be made to the court that is dealing with those enforcement proceedings.[4]

1   Note that in the Family Division, the RSC continues to apply in respect of application to appoint a receiver.
2   CPR 23.2(1).
3   CPR 23.2(2).
4   CPR 23.2(5).

With or without notice?

6.78   An application to appoint a receiver may be made without notice.[1] Generally, the application will be made on notice and the judgment creditor will serve a copy of the application notice and evidence in support on the judgment debtor. However, where the judgment creditor also seeks a related in injunction because, for example, he fears dissipation of the judgment debtor's assets, the application should be made without notice (see paras 6.93–6.94).

1   CPR 69.3.

Application notice

6.79   An application to appoint a receiver by way of equitable execution should be made by application notice in accordance with Pt 23.[1] Part A of the application notice should use wording based on that set out in Form No 82,[2] which provides that the application is:

'... for an order that [a receiver be appointed] [(name and address) be appointed receiver][3] in this claim to receive the rents, profits and moneys receivable in respect of the interest of the (party) in the following property, namely (describe the property) in or towards satisfaction of the moneys and interest due to the (party) under the judgment [or order] in this claim dated (date) and for an order that the costs of this application be paid by the (party) to the (party).'

1   CPR 23.3(1).
2   CPR 4(1).
3   In most applications for a receiver by way of equitable execution, a named individual should be given. An exception might be where there is evidence of dissipation and a related injunction is sought at the same time making the identification of a named receiver impractical.

6.80   Where a related injunction is sought[1] the same application notice must be used for both the application for the receivership order and the injunction.[2]

1   See paras 6.91–6.95.
2   PD 69, para 3.1.

Draft order

6.81   A draft order should be included with the application notice.[1] Form No 84 is a standard form order[2] and seems to be largely based on cases of considerable antiquity.[3] In preparing the draft order the judgment creditor should bear in mind that a receiver appointed by way of equitable execution is very much a creature of the court's order. It is vital that thought is given at an early stage as to what steps the receiver is likely to need to take to secure and collect the judgment debtor's property and that appropriate provisions are sought in the order. While not every situation can be foreseen in advance, and directions can be sought by the receiver from time to time if needed,[4] it will save time and legal costs if the order making the appointment also gives the receiver sensible powers framed with the receivership property in mind.

[1]   This is required where possible in the Queen's Bench Division or Chancery Division and mandatory in the Commercial Court. See the notes to N244 (standard application notice), N244(CC) (Commercial Court application notice) and CPR 23.7(3)(b).

[2]   CPR 4(1).

[3]   Similar to the orders reported in *Wells v Kilpin* (1874) LR 18 Eq 298; *Salt v Cooper* (1880) 16 Ch D 544 at 545; *Levasseur v Mason & Barry* [1891] 2 QB 73 at 74; *Re Potts* [1893] 1 QB 648 at 649; *Cadogan v Lyric Theatre* [1894] 3 Ch 338 at 344; *Holmes v Millage* [1893] 1 QB 551 at 551 and *Croshaw v Lyndhurst* [1897] 2 Ch 154 at 154; *Re Marquis of Anglesey* [1903] 2 Ch 727 at 728; *Re Parbola* [1909] 2 Ch 437 at 438; *Lord Ashburton v Nocton* [1914] 2 Ch 211 at 212.

[4]   See para 6.143.

6.82   Annex 3 of Appendix 4A of the Chancery Guide 2002 sets out the powers and duties of a receiver generally and these may form a useful starting point for a judgment creditor who is considering amendment of the standard form order to ensure that a receiver by way of equitable execution will have adequate powers to satisfy the judgment debt. By way of example, where a receiver is appointed to enforce an indemnity, the following factors should be given consideration:

(a) the receiver will need permission to bring proceedings to enforce the indemnity;

(b) he will also need permission to bring such proceedings in the name of the judgment debtor;

(c) where necessary, he will also need permission to instruct counsel and/or solicitors in connection with the claim.

What evidence is required in support?

6.83   Paragraphs 4 and 5 of the Practice Direction to Pt 69 provide guidance on the evidence required by the court in support of an application to appoint a receiver. It should be borne in mind that much of the evidence required is focused on demonstrating that enforcement will not only be effective but cost effective. The application must demonstrate to the court that the enforcement will realise sufficient assets to justify the costs associated with appointing a receiver.

General requirements as to evidence in support of an application for a receiver

6.84 The evidence in support of the application must be in writing.[1] It must explain the reasons why the appointment is required and give details of the property over which it is proposed the receiver will get in.[2] When identifying the property, the evidence should estimate the value of the property and the amount of income it is likely to produce.[3] In a commercial enforcement scenario, the amounts at stake are likely to justify the expense of the appointment of a professional valuer (or accountant) depending on the type of receivership property. The court will also require evidence of the identity of the individual being proposed to act as receiver and demonstrating his suitability[4] (see paras 6.138–6.141). Finally, if the court is being asked to appoint a receiver without the receiver being required to provide security, certain further evidence is required as to why it is necessary for the court to allow the receiver to act without giving security (see para 6.125).

1   CPR 69.3(b) and PD 69, para 4.1.
2   CPR PD 69, para 4.1(2).
3   CPR PD 69, para 4.1(2)(a)–(b).
4   CPR PD 69, paras 4.2–4.4.

Evidence specific to equitable execution

6.85 In addition to the general evidence required in support of an application for a receiver, there are some specific requirements where the application is to appoint a receiver by way of equitable execution. Para 4.1(3) of the Practice Direction to Pt 69 provides that details must also be given of:

(a)   the judgment which the applicant is seeking to enforce;
(b)   the extent to which the debtor has failed to comply with the judgment;
(c)   the result of any steps already taken to enforce the judgment; and
(d)   why the judgment cannot be enforced by any other method.

6.86 As regards (a) the judgment should be summarised in the supporting witness statement. The requirement for (b) is directed at determining whether the judgment debtor has taken any steps to satisfy the judgment and, if he has, what those steps are. In most cases this requirement will be satisfied by a statement in the supporting witness statement that the judgment debtor has not paid the judgment debt and that it remains unpaid. Where the judgment debtor has made some payment towards satisfaction of the judgment debt, this should be explained to the court.

6.87 (c) and (d) are directed at demonstrating to the court that enforcement is either *practically* impossible by normal methods of legal execution or that they would be *legally* impossible. Where other methods of enforcement have been attempted but have failed, or where enforcement in any other way is legally or practically impossible, this will be relevant to the exercise of the court's discretion and should be fully explained to the court.

6.88 Paragraph 5 of the Practice Direction to Pt 69 goes on to explain that the court will have regard to the amount claimed by the judgment creditor, the amount likely to be obtained by the receiver, and the probable costs of his appointment in considering whether to make the appointment. There is a clear onus on the judgment creditor to demonstrate to the court that the receivership will not only be effective but that it will justify the cost of appointing a receiver.[1] If there is a dispute about any of these matters, the court could order an inquiry before making the appointment.[2]

[1]   In this respect, the Practice Direction echoes both the overriding objective (CPR 1.1(2)(b), CPR 1.1(c)(i), and the common law (see para 6.39, n 1).
[2]   Chapman and Counsell *Chancery Practice and Procedure* (2001) pp 106 and 336.

6.89   As regards the receiver's likely costs, a quotation should be sought from the proposed receiver. Alternatively, the court should be provided with evidence of the proposed receiver's hourly rates together with an estimate of the projected time commitments of the receivership.

6.90   It is likely much of the judgment creditor's evidence will be directed at demonstrating the likely recovery that the judgment creditor expects to be made by the appointment of a receiver. This is where effective use of the methods of obtaining information as to the judgment debtor's assets discussed in Chapter 2 may be a vital precursor to any application for the appointment of a receiver by way of equitable execution.

Related injunctions and orders

6.91   The court has power to grant a related injunction when it appoints a receiver by way of equitable execution. Where an injunction is sought, the written evidence in support of the application must explain why an injunction is needed. To ensure that committal proceedings are possible if the injunction is breached, a penal notice should be endorsed on the order[1] and the order should also be served personally.[2]

[1]   RSC Ord 45, r 7 and PD 40B, para 9.1. The form of the penal notice is set out in PD 40B, para 9.1.
[2]   RSC Ord 45, r 7. Form PF 141 (witness statement of personal service) should be used for this purpose.

6.92   Alternatively, an ancillary order requiring the judgment debtor to disclose documents relating to the receivership property could be made, as was ordered by the court in *Soinco*. Where such an order is sought, the reasons why this is necessary should be explained. For example, in *Soinco*[1] a recent history of unexplained payments to the judgment debtor, evidence that the judgment debtor was seeking to 'smother' the future debts, evidence that the judgment debtor and the payor were controlled by the same family, and the fact that information as to the payments that would become due under the supply contract was otherwise unobtainable, were all factors to which the court had regard in making the disclosure order.

[1]   [1998] QB 406 at 423.

Injunction pending the hearing of the application

6.93   A special procedure exists where the judgment creditor fears that the judgment debtor may dispose of the property *before* the receivership application can be heard.

In these circumstances the court may grant an injunction restraining the judgment debtor from assigning, charging or otherwise dealing with the property until after the hearing of the receivership application.[1]

1   Queen's Bench Guide, paras 11.7.3–11.7.5.

6.94   The Queen's Bench Guide contemplates that such an injunction is likely to be sought where the judgment debtor is in financial difficulties and may dissipate his assets.[1] Where an injunction to prevent dissipation of assets is sought, evidence of dissipation should be provided.[2] The judgment creditor need not give notice of this application, which will normally be dealt with without a hearing. If the master is satisfied with the evidence he will make an order based on Form No 83 granting an injunction until a hearing can take place in respect of the application for the appointment of a receiver.[3]

1   Queen's Bench Guide, para 11.7.3(6).
2   Queen's Bench Guide, para 11.7.3(6) and *Lloyd's Bank Ltd v Medway Upper Navigation Co* [1905] 2 KB 359, CA.
3   Queen's Bench Guide, para 11.7.4.

6.95   Again, to ensure that committal proceedings are possible if the injunction is breached, a penal notice should be endorsed on the order[1] and the order should also be served personally.[2]

1   RSC Ord 45, r 7 and PD 40B, para 9.1. The form of the penal notice is set out in PD 40B, para 9.1.
2   RSC Ord 45, r 7. Form PF 141 (witness statement of personal service) should be used for this purpose.

Fees

6.96   The fee for issuing an application to appoint a receiver by way of equitable execution is currently £100 for each party against whom the order is sought.[1] From 1 April 2005, all cheques should be made payable to 'HMCS' or 'Her Majesty's Courts Service' instead of 'Her Majesty's Paymaster General' or 'HMPG' as was previously the case.

1   The Civil Proceedings Fees Order 2004, SI 2004/3121, Sch 1, para 6.3(a).

Hearing of the application

6.97   Following service on the judgment debtor of the application notice or, in cases where a related injunction has not been sought, Form No 83 (which sets a hearing date and grants an injunction in the meantime), a hearing for consideration of the application will take place.

6.98   At the hearing of the application to appoint the receiver the master will, if he thinks fit, make an order based on Form No 84.[1]

1   Queen's Bench Guide, para 11.7.6.

Who must be served with the order?

6.99   CPR 69.4 explains who the judgment creditor must serve with the order, namely:

(a)   the person appointed as receiver;

(b)   unless the court orders otherwise, every other party to the proceedings; and

(c)   such other persons as the court may direct.

Cross-undertaking in damages

6.100   One matter which may arise at the hearing is whether the judgment creditor should be required to give a cross-undertaking in damages.[1] Where a related injunction is sought, a cross-undertaking will be required unless the court orders otherwise.[2] However, even where a related injunction is not sought, a cross-undertaking may be sought against the judgment creditor at the hearing of the application to appoint a receiver.

1   A cross-undertaking in damages is an undertaking given by an applicant to pay any damages which the respondent(s) (or any third party served with or notified by the order) may later be found by the court to have suffered.

2   See PD 25, para 5.1(1) which, by virtue of CPR 25.2(b), would include interim remedies granted after judgment. Form No 83, which sets a hearing date to consider appointing a receiver and grants an injunction in the meantime, contains cross-undertaking wording.

6.101   It is clear from the Court of Appeal decision in *Allied Irish Bank v Ashford Hotels Ltd*[1] that the court has jurisdiction, in appropriate circumstances, to require the judgment creditor to give a cross-undertaking in damages for the benefit of third parties as a condition of appointing a receiver by way of equitable execution. However, it is hard to draw any firm conclusions from this case other than the fact that the court has such jurisdiction. The only general guidance as to the exercise of discretion given by the Court of Appeal was whether it is 'just to make the order sought', although it should be noted that even counsel for the parties seeking the cross-undertaking stopped short of contending that a cross-undertaking would be required in *every* case where a receiver by way of equitable execution is sought. Presumably, in the absence of direct authority the court would be guided by the principles developed in relation to freezing injunctions. The standard form order appointing a receiver by way of equitable execution[2] does not contain any sort of cross-undertaking and so would require amendment where such an undertaking is sought.

1   [1997] 3 All ER 309, CA.

2   Form No 84.

EFFECT OF APPOINTMENT OF A RECEIVER BY WAY OF EQUITABLE EXECUTION

6.102   An order for equitable execution empowers the receiver to collect the property specified in the order.[1]

1   *Re Dickinson* (1888) 22 QBD 187 at 192.

No proprietary effect

6.103   An order appointing a receiver by way of equitable execution operates 'in personam' not 'in rem'.[1] That is, it confers upon the judgment creditor purely personal rights against the judgment debtor.[2]

1   *Giles v Kruyer* [1921] 3 KB 23 at 25; *Re Whiteheart* (1971) 116 Sol Jo 75.
2   *Stevens v Hutchinson* [1953] 1 Ch 299 at 305.

6.104   The order does not have any proprietary effect and does not give the judgment creditor any rights over the judgment debtor's property.[1] In particular, it does not make the judgment creditor a secured creditor by creating any mortgage, charge[2] or lien[3] over the judgment debtor's property. It 'is simply an uncompleted process to obtain payment of money'.[4] The judgment creditor only receives an interest in the judgment debtor's property when the receiver finally pays the money to the judgment creditor in satisfaction of the judgment debt.[5]

1   *Re Potts* [1893] 1 QB 648 at 652.
2   *Re Potts* [1893] 1 QB 648 at 661 and 662; *Tyrrell v Painton* [1895] 1 QB 202 at 206; *Re Marquis of Anglesey* [1903] 2 Ch 727 at 730; *Ridout v Fowler* [1904] 1 Ch 658 at 662; affd CA [1904] 2 Ch 93; *Re a Debtor* [1909] 1 KB 430 at 434; *Re Whiteheart* (1971) 116 Sol Jo 75; *Allied Irish Bank v Ashford Hotels Ltd* [1997] 3 All ER 309 at 313. In *Re Whiteheart* (1971) 116 Sol Jo 75 it was held *obiter* that it was arguable that where the order appointing the receiver stated the receiver should receive the moneys 'in or towards satisfaction' of the judgment debt that this might create a charge in favour of the judgment creditor once the moneys had been received by the receiver. However, any such charge could not affect the moneys where they are still held by a third party which was the situation that the court was being asked to consider.
3   *Re Dickinson* (1888) 22 QBD 187 at 190, per Lord Esher MR: 'How can the possession of a receiver establish a lien in favour of the creditor at whose instance he was appointed? Does the receiver hold the goods so as to give the creditor possession of them? He holds the goods as agent for the Court, not for the creditor. There cannot, therefore, be a possessory lien of the creditor. Is there any other lien? In my opinion the receiver appointed under such an order does not hold the goods for the creditor at all; he holds them for the court in order that it may decide the right to them.' In the same case at 192 Fry LJ explained that '... the order creates no lien on the debtor's property in favour of the receiver, and it certainly creates none in favour of the judgment creditors, who have no possession of the property.'
4   *Re Potts* [1893] 1 QB 648 at 661.
5   *Re Potts* [1893] 1 QB 648 at 653 and *Re Whiteheart* (1971) 116 Sol Jo 75.

Receiver takes subject to prior incumbrancers

6.105   The receiver will take possession of the judgment debtor's property subject to any prior incumbrances.[1] The meaning of incumbrance in this context was considered by Romer J in *Jones v Barnett*,[2] where it was held to be a claim, lien or liability attached to the property. This would include prior charges or mortgages over the property.

1   *Wells v Kilpin* (1874) LR Eq 298 at 300; *Salt v Cooper* (1880) 16 Ch D 544 at 554 (trustee in bankruptcy appointed moments before a receiver by way of equitable execution containing the usual prior incumbrancers wording); *Searle v Choat* (1884) 25 Ch D 723 at 726; *Cadogan v Lyric Theatre* [1894] 3 Ch 338 at 343, per Lord Herschell LC, 343, per Lindley LJ and 344.
2   [1899] 1 Ch 611 at 620. See further *Stroud's Judicial Dictionary of Words and Phrases* (6th edn, 2000) vol 2, 1263-1265.

6.106   The standard order appointing a receiver, Form No 84, which has been granted since at least the 1870s,[1] expressly preserves the rights of prior incumbrancers.[2]

1   See para 6.81, n 3.

2   Form No. 84 states that:
     '(2) this appointment shall be without prejudice to the rights of any prior incumbrancers
     upon the said property who may think proper to take possession of or receive the same by
     virtue of their respective securities or, if any prior incumbrancer is in possession, then
     without prejudice to such possession.'

6.107   An example of prior incumbrances taking priority is provided by *Searle v Choat*.[1] In that case the judgment creditor obtained an order that the receiver should be appointed to receive the rents and profits of certain leasehold houses. The judgment debtor's interest in the leases took the form of the equity of redemption in the leases, which had been mortgaged to the plaintiff. The order mirrored the standard form. The plaintiff had previously taken possession in his capacity as mortgagee and instructed the tenants to pay over their rent to him. Subsequently, the receiver served a notice on the tenants requiring the tenants to pay the rents to him. The Court of Appeal held that the receiver should not have acted as he did:[2]

> '...I am of opinion that what was done by the receiver was wrong. He was appointed without prejudice to the rights of prior incumbrancers, and he ought not to have taken possession as against [the plaintiff]. His first notice recites correctly the order appointing him receiver, and he knew that the Plaintiff was a prior incumbrancer, and yet he gives notice to the tenants to pay their rents to him. This notice would entirely prevent any reasonable tenant from paying his rent to [the plaintiff], who as mortgagee in possession, was entitled to receive it. That being so, I think the proceedings of the receiver were wrong and were in violation of his duty and of the rights of the present Plaintiff.'

1   (1884) 25 Ch D 723.
2   (1884) 25 Ch D 723 at 726.

6.108   Similarly, *Re Parbola*[1] a mortgagee had obtained a foreclosure order nisi prior to the judgment creditor obtaining an order for a receiver which was, in accordance with the standard form, subject to the rights of prior incumbrancers. The court held that the receiver:[2]

> 'being pro tanto an assignee of the equity of redemption; ... must be content to take his interest in the equity of redemption in the state in which he finds it, namely, as bound by the [foreclosure order nisi], and he must redeem on [the redemption date].'

1   [1909] 2 Ch 437.
2   [1909] 2 Ch 437 at 439.

6.109   In *Levasseur v Mason & Barry*[1] the court considered the question of priority in respect of liens. Some copper belonging to a French company was in the possession of an English company who had a lien upon it. A receiver was appointed over the copper and shortly afterwards the French company became insolvent and liquidators were appointed. The copper was sold, the lien paid, and the balance of the moneys were paid into court. The issue before the court was who was entitled to the remainder of the proceeds of sale. Because the copper had been sold and the lien paid, the question of who had priority as between the receiver and the holder of the lien was not a live issue but the Court of Appeal unanimously accepted that the receiver could only have taken the goods once the lien had been satisfied.[2]

¹   [1891] 2 QB 73.
²   [1891] 2 QB 73 at 77–78, per Lord Colderidge CJ, 78, per Lord Esher MR and 82, per Fry LJ.

Order operates as an injunction against the judgment debtor

6.110   The order appointing a receiver by way of equitable execution operates as an injunction against the judgment debtor from receiving the property over which the receiver is appointed¹ and prevents the judgment debtor from dealing with property to the prejudice of the judgment creditor.² However, the order appointing a receiver by way of equitable execution is not in fact an injunction,³ it simply has the *effect* of an injunction.

¹   *Re Sartoris's Estate* [1892] 1 Ch 11 at 22; *Tyrrell v Painton* [1895] 1 QB 202 at 206; *Re Marquis of Anglesey* [1903] 2 Ch 727 at 731; *Ridout v Fowler* [1904] 1 Ch 658 at 663–664; affd [1904] 2 Ch 93, CA; *Ideal Bedding Ltd v Holland* [1907] 2 Ch 157 at 169–170; *Re a Debtor* [1909] 1 KB 430 at 434; *Stevens v Hutchinson* [1953] 1 Ch 299 at 305; *Allied Irish Bank v Ashford Hotels Ltd* [1997] 3 All ER 309 at 313.
²   *Re Marquis of Anglesey* [1903] 2 Ch 727 at 731. In *Ideal Bedding Ltd v Holland* [1907] 2 Ch 157 at 170 Kekewich J declined counsel's invitation to reject Swiften Eady J's comments on this point and 'venture[d] to think this statement of the law will eventually prove sound'. In *Morgan v Hart* [1914] 2 KB 183 at 186 Buckley LJ stated that 'The order [appointing the receiver] has no effect except that which is equivalent to an injunction restraining the debtor from dealing with the [property subject to the order]'. In *Soinco S.A.C.I. v Novokuznetsk* [1998] 1 QB 406 at 412 Colman J, while forming no concluded view on the matter, stated: 'I do not exclude the possibility that injunctive relief ... might be devised which would have the effect of curbing what is in substance if not in form an arrangement for the disposal by [the judgment debtor] of assets which would otherwise be available for execution.'
³   As is evident from the standard form of order (form No 84).

Discharge and set-off

6.111   Since the order appointing a receiver has the effect of an injunction restraining the judgment debtor from receiving the property and from dealing with property to the prejudice of the judgment creditor, the judgment debtor would be breaching the order if he were to continue to accept payments from his debtor or purport to give good discharge.¹ The judgment debtor is also prohibited from setting off any debt owed to him by a third party against a debt that he owed to that third party in lieu of taking payment.²

¹   *Re a Debtor, ex p the Peak Hill Goldfield Ltd* [1909] 1 KB 430 at 436; *Giles v Kruyer* [1921] 3 KB 23 at 26-27.
²   *Re a Debtor, ex p the Peak Hill Goldfield Ltd* [1909] 1 KB 430 at 437. See also *Soinco S.A.C.I. v Novokuznetsk* [1997] QB 406 at 412.

Effect on third parties with notice of the order

6.112   An order appointing a receiver by way of equitable execution only acts as an injunction against the *judgment debtor* from receiving the property over which the receiver is appointed. In *Giles v Kruyer*¹ the court held that the order does not act as an injunction against *third parties,* even where the third parties are subsequently notified of the order.[2]

¹   [1921] 3 KB 23.
²   Unless this is specifically provided for.

6.113   *Giles v Kruyer* followed an earlier decision by the Court of Appeal on similar facts.[1] The judgment creditor had recovered judgment against the judgment debtor, but as his costs remained unsatisfied he obtained an order for the appointment of a receiver by way of equitable execution in March 1919. The order for the appointment of a receiver by way of equitable execution was made in the absence of the bank where the judgment debtor held an account. In April that year a copy of the order was served on the bank where the judgment debtor had, at the date of service, a sum on deposit. The bank then heard nothing further of the matter and in December 1919 paid to the judgment debtor the amount standing to her credit. The judgment creditor sought an order that the bank should pay to the receiver the amount standing to the judgment debtor's credit in March 1919 with interest. Greer J refused to make the order:[2]

'I am bound, moreover, not merely by the decision in *In re Potts*, but by the ratio decidendi of the Court in giving judgment, and I think that decision shows that the order appointing the receivers, made in the absence of the bank, in no way affects the rights or duties of the bank, and that the bank being, if I may so describe it, untouched by the order are entitled, after it is made, to do anything they could have done before it was made, unless indeed steps were taken to make the order binding upon them. The order appointing the receivers is an order inter partes, it is in no sense an order creating rights or duties in rem, and consequently the person in possession of the fund or the debt, as the case may be, is in nowise limited as regards his rights or duties in reference to the debt by the appointment of the receivers. It is quite true, as was pointed out by Mr Bennett on behalf of the plaintiff, that the order operates as an injunction to restrain the defendant from receiving the money, but that is not decisive, because, as is pointed out in *In re Potts*, the bank are not restrained from paying the money to the defendant; there is no obligation imposed upon them at all; the position is one in which equitable execution has started, but has not gone far enough to affect the rights or duties of the bank. As pointed out by Lord Esher in that case the persons in possession of the fund, over which a receiver had been appointed in their absence, were under no obligation not to pay the fund to the person originally entitled.'

¹   *Re Potts* [1893] 1 QB 648.
²   [1921] 3 KB 23 at 25.

6.114   The court further held that refusing the order for the bank to pay over the sum again to the judgment creditor was in accordance with justice since the order for appointment of a receiver by way of equitable execution had been in place for eight months and, rather than having taken any steps to make the order binding on the bank, the judgment creditor had allowed the bank to forget all about it.[1]

¹   [1921] 3 KB 23 at 25.

6.115   The correctness of this decision has been questioned by distinguished commentators.[1] In the more recent case of *Allied Irish Bank v Ashford Hotels Ltd*[2] the

Court of Appeal held that the effect of an order for appointment of a receiver by way of equitable execution on third parties who had notice of it *was* to prevent them discharging any liability that they had to the judgment debtor by payment to the judgment debtor rather than the receiver.[3] However, *Giles v Kruyer* does not appear to have been cited to the Court of Appeal in that case.

¹   *Kerr and Hunter on Receivers and Administrators* (18th edn, 2005) p 142 where it is suggested that the case can only be supported on the footing that the debt should have been garnished and that the judgment creditor had no equity of which to complain but conceding that this ground is not mentioned in the case.
²   [1997] 3 All ER 309, CA.
³   [1997] 3 All ER 309 at 313–314, CA.

6.116   The court in *Giles v Kruyer* placed great store on the fact that the third party bank had not been present at the application for the order for appointment of a receiver by way of equitable execution as the basis for holding that the order should in no way affect the bank's rights and obligations. While it may seem clear that, absent clear wording, the order should not operate as an injunction so as to place third parties who make payments which are not in accordance with the terms of the order in contempt of court, it seems less clear that the mere fact that a third party was not before the court when an order was made should be a sound basis for holding that that order cannot in any way affect the rights of a party who has notice of it. As has been noted, the standard form of order for appointment of a receiver by way of equitable execution has remained unchanged for well over a hundred years. Amendment to the wording of the standard order to make clear provision for its effect on third parties, as is now the case with the wording of standard form freezing injunctions, would be helpful.

6.117   For the present, the court has power to grant whatever injunction is necessary to prevent third parties receiving property subject to an order for appointment of a receiver by way of equitable execution.[1] If there are concerns that a third party may deal with property in such a way as to defeat the order, a related injunction should be sought.

¹   *Ideal Bedding Ltd v Holland* [1907] 2 Ch 157 at 170; *Stevens v Hutchinson* [1953] 1 Ch 299 at 305; *Soinco S.A.C.I. v Novokuznetsk* [1998] 1 QB 406 at 412.

Interference with a receiver¹

6.118   A receiver appointed by way of equitable execution is an officer of the court rather than an agent of the judgment creditor.[2] Interference with a receiver in possession of the receivership property is therefore a contempt of court if done without the permission of the court,[3] since interference with the court's officer is treated as an interference with the court itself.[4] The interference can be by a party to the proceedings or by a third party.[5]

¹   See generally *Arlidge, Eady & Smith on Contempt* (2nd edn, 1999) pp 716 and 718–720 and Miller *Contempt of Court* (3rd edn, 2000) pp 601–604.
²   *Re Dickinson* (1888) 22 QBD 187 at 190.
³   See *Arlidge, Eady & Smith on Contempt* (2nd edn, 1999) pp 718–720.
⁴   *Defries v Creed* (1865) 34 LJ Ch 607 at 608.

⁵   *Dixon v Dixon* [1904] 1 Ch 161 at 163.

6.119   It is well established that interference with a receiver in possession without the court's prior permission can constitute a contempt of court[1] even if the interfering party claims better title than the judgment creditor.[2]   In *Ames v The Trustees of the Birkenhead Docks*, interference was stated to include intercepting and preventing payments that the receiver had been appointed to receive:[3]

> 'There is no question but that this Court will not permit a receiver, appointed by its authority, and who is therefore its officer, to be interfered with or dispossessed of the property he is directed to receive, by anyone, although the order appointing him may be perfectly erroneous; this Court requires and insists that application should be made to the Court, for permission to take possession of any property of distinction (which could not be maintained if it were attempted, which it is not by counsel at the Bar although suggested by the affidavits), that this rule only applies to property actually in the hands of the receiver. If a receiver be appointed to receive debts, rents, or tolls, the rule applies equally to all these cases, and no person will be permitted, without the sanction or authority of the Court, to intercept or prevent payment to the receiver of the debts, rents, or the tolls, which he has not actually received but which he has been appointed to receive.'

¹   *Angel v Smith* (1804) 9 Ves Jun 336 at 338; *Evelyn v Lewis* (1844) 3 Hare 472 at 474; *Tink v Rundle* (1847) 10 Beav 318; *Ward v Smith* (1848) 6 Hare 309; *Hawkins v Gathercole* (1852) 1 Drewry 12 at 17; *Defries v Creed* (1865) 34 LJ Ch 607 at 608.
²   *Evelyn v Lewis* (1844) 3 Hare 472 at 474; *Hawkins v Gathercole* (1852) 1 Drewry 12 at 17; *Ranfield v Ranfield* (1860) 1 Dr & AM 310 at 314;
³   (1855) 20 Beav 332 at 353. See also *Parker v Pocock* (1874) 30 LT 458.

6.120   An interference with a receiver can take many forms including: bringing proceedings against the receiver,[1] asserting a superior right to the property,[2] a sheriff seizing goods under a writ of fieri facias,[3] another judgment creditor applying to appoint a sequestrator,[4] and removing property from the land.[5]

¹   *Angel v Smith* (1804) 9 Ves Jun 336 at 338 (a claim for ejectment).
²   *Johnes v Claughton* (1822) Jac 572.
³   *Russell v East Anglican Railway Co* (1850) 3 Mac & G 104; *Lane v Stern* (1862) 3 Giff 629. This is reflected in RSC Ord 46, r 2(1)(e) which provides that a writ of execution may not issue without the permission of the court where any goods sought to be seized are in the hands of a receiver appointed by the court or a sequestrator.
⁴   *Hawkins v Gathercole* (1852) 1 Drewry 12 (the modern equivalent would probably be the appointment of a second receiver by way of equitable execution).
⁵   *Fripp v Bridgewater and Taunton Canal Co* (1845) 3 WR 356.

6.121   An action will not constitute interference where the right in question was exercised *prior* to the appointment of the receiver[1] or where the right was being asserted at the time of the appointment[2] because the appointment will not affect that right.[3] Neither will it constitute a contempt to interfere with property over which a receiver has been appointed where the order makes the appointment conditional on the provision of security and the security has not yet been provided. This is because the receiver cannot be said to have taken possession before giving security.[4]

¹   *Defries v Creed* (1865) 34 LJ Ch 607 at 608.

2   *Johnes v Claughton* (1822) Jac 572 (rights of common asserted after the appointment).
3   *Evelyn v Lewis* (1844) 3 Hare 472 at 474.
4   *Edwards v Edwards* (1876) 2 Ch D 291 at 296.

6.122   Once a receiver has been appointed, the permission of the court must first be obtained before a right to receivership property is asserted, even if the right is asserted by bringing a claim or making an application to assert the right.[1] Where the court has not granted prior permission for the claim to be made, it may grant an injunction to restrain proceedings taken without permission.[2] This is the case even where the claimant was unaware of the appointment or where the claimant's right is clear.[3] Accordingly, the appropriate way for a party who considers the order appointing the receiver to have been wrongly obtained to proceed is to apply to set aside the order appointing the receiver, since any other step may constitute interference.[4]

1   *Evelyn v Lewis* (1844) 3 Hare 472 at 474; *Hawkins v Gathercole* (1852) 1 Drewry 12 at 17-19; *Re Maidstone Palace of Varieties* [1908] 2 Ch 283 at 286.
2   *Evelyn v Lewis* (1844) 3 Hare 472 at 474; *Tink v Rundle* (1847) 10 Beav 318.
3   *Evelyn v Lewis* (1844) 3 Hare 472 at 474.
4   *Russell v East Anglican Railway Co* (1850) 3 Mac & G 104 at 117–118; *Ames v The Trustees of the Birkenhead Docks* (1855) 20 Beav 332 at 353.

6.123   The sanction for interference as constituting contempt is a fine, imprisonment or sequestration. However, in practice the court does not usually make an order for a committal but orders the interfering party to pay the costs and expenses caused by the improper conduct.[1] In addition the court will usually also grant an injunction ordering that the property is returned to the receiver and restraining the party from interfering further[2] (or accept an undertaking in lieu).[3]

1   *Russell v East Anglican Railway Co* (1850) 3 Mac & G 104 at 120-121; *Lane v Stern* (1862) 3 Giff 629 at 632; *Perkes v Landon* (1988) 15 NSWLR 408 at 412–415 (NSW Sup Ct).
2   *Russell v East Anglican Railway Co* (1850) 3 Mac & G 104 at 120-121; *Ames v The Trustees of the Birkenhead Docks* 20 Beav 332 at 354.
3   *Hawkins v Gathercole* (1855) 1 Drewry 12 at 20.

GENERAL ISSUES RELATING TO RECEIVERSHIP

6.124   The remainder of this chapter considers general issues that apply to any form of receiver, namely: the provision of security, remuneration, who can be appointed receiver, a receiver's powers and duties, a receiver's rights to seek directions, and discharge. Such topics are the subject of specialist works and the following sections are intended as an overview.

Provision of security

6.125   Under CPR 69.5 the court has a discretion as to whether or not to require the receiver to provide security. Where the judgment creditor is asking the court to allow the receiver to act without security, the evidence in support of the application must explain why.[1] No guidance is given on the exercise of this discretion.

1   PD 69, para 4.1(4).

6.126   The provision of security is a potential expense of equitable execution. CPR 69.5(1) provides:

'The court may direct that before a receiver begins to act or within a specified time he must either –
(a)   give such security as the court may determine; or
(b)   file and serve on all parties to the proceedings evidence that he already has in force sufficient security,
to cover his liability for his acts and omissions as a receiver.'

6.127   The order appointing a receiver will normally give directions regarding security[1] and specify the date by which the receiver must give security or file and serve evidence to satisfy the court that he already has security in force.[2]

1   PD 69, para 6.2.
2   PD 69, para 7.1.

6.128   The form of the security is different depending on whether the receiver is a licensed insolvency practitioner or not.

Licensed insolvency practitioner

6.129   If the receiver is a licensed insolvency practitioner, unless the court directs otherwise, security will be in the form of the bond provided by him under the Insolvency Practitioner Regulations 1990[1] and extended to cover his appointment as a court appointed receiver.[2]   The bond must be in the form prescribed by Sch 2 to the Regulations.   Written evidence of the bond, the sufficiency of the bond's cover and the fact that the bond covers the appointment of the receiver as a court appointed receiver must be filed at court.[3]

1   SI 1990/439, Pt III and Sch 2.   The regulations relate to the compulsory security requirements applying to licensed insolvency practitioners before they are qualified to act as set out in IA 1986, s 390(3)(a)–(b).
2   CPR 69 PD, para 7.2(1).
3   CPR 69 PD, para 7.3(1).   Appendix 4A of the Chancery Guide 2002 states that '[w]here security is given by bond, written evidence of the extended bond and the sufficiency of its cover must be filed in Room 7.09 in accordance with the requirements of Pt 69 PD 7.3(1)'.

Not a licensed insolvency practitioner

6.130   Where the judgment creditor seeks to appoint someone other than a licensed insolvency practitioner as receiver, security will be required in the form of a guarantee[1] entered into with a bank or insurance company[2] in a form approved by the court.[3]   The Chancery Division has a declared practice on guarantees.[4]

1   CPR 69 PD, para 7.2(2).
2   In the Chancery Division, Appendix 4A of the Chancery Guide 2002 states that this will be one of the four main clearing banks or Zurich GSG Ltd.
3   CPR 69 PD, para 7.3(2).   Model forms of guarantee are referred to in the Queen's Bench Guide and Chancery Guide 2002.
4   Appendix 4A of the Chancery Guide 2002 states that: '[t]he guarantee must then be engrossed and executed, ie signed by the receiver and signed and sealed by the bank or insurance

company. It should then be lodged in Chancery Chambers, Room TM 7.09, Royal Courts of Justice, Strand London WC2A 2LL. It will then be signed by the Master and endorsed with a certificate of completion of security and placed on the court file.'

Date by which security must be provided

6.131 The order appointing a receiver should specify the date by which the receiver must give security or file and serve evidence to satisfy the court that he already has security in force.[1] The judgment creditor should ensure that this date is a workable one and gives sufficient time for either the evidence of the bond or for the executed guarantee to be filed.

[1]   CPR 69 PD, para 7.1.

Amount of the security

6.132 The CPR do not give any guidance on the amount of security that will be required by the court where security is required. CPR 69.5 simply refers to 'such security as the court may determine ... to cover his acts and omissions as a receiver', thereby providing the court with a wide discretion to fix the amount of security.

Failure to provide security

6.133 A failure by the receiver to give the security determined, or to provide proof that sufficient security is in place, is grounds for the removal of the receiver.[1] The rules do not specify what effect the failure to provide security has on the effectiveness of the receivership. However, at common law, where there has been a failure to provide security, the appointment of a receiver is 'not effectual till the security is given. It is a conditional appointment, and the giving of security is a condition precedent'.[2] Until security is given '... the title of the receiver was not complete, and he could not give a receipt or obtain the money'.[3] However, once the failure to provide security has been corrected by the provision of security, the order relates back to the date on which it was originally made.[4]

[1]   CPR 69.5(2).
[2]   *Ridout v Fowler* [1904] 1 Ch 658 at 662.
[3]   *Ridout v Fowler* [1904] 1 Ch 658 at 662.
[4]   *Re Watkins* (1879) 13 Ch D 252 at 260 CA and *Ridout v Fowler* [1904] 1 Ch 658 at 661.

Remuneration of the receiver

6.134 A receiver may only charge for his services if the court so directs and specifies the basis on which he is remunerated. The court has a discretion to specify who is responsible for paying the receiver and the fund or property from which the receiver is to be remunerated.[1]

[1]   CPR 69.7(2).

6.135   It has already been noted that the evidence in support of the application requires that the probable costs of the receiver's appointment be covered. The standard form order suggests that the receiver be limited to a fixed percentage of the judgment amount or amounts collected by the receiver (whichever is less).[1] The method of remuneration is something that should be addressed at the application to appoint a receiver and spelt out in the order.

1   See Form No 84, para 6.

6.136   Where the court directs that the amount of the receiver's remuneration is to be determined by the court, the receiver will only able to recover his remuneration after such determination.[1] The receiver, or any other party, can apply at any time for such a determination to take place.[2] CPR 69.7(4) sets out the factors that the court will normally use to determine a receiver's remuneration.[3] The Practice Direction to Pt 69 specifies the procedure for determining the receiver's remuneration. The court has power to refer the determination of the receiver's remuneration to a costs judge.[4]

1   CPR 69.7(3)(a) and PD 69, para 9.3.
2   CPR 69.7(3)(b).
3   Para 9.2 PD 69.
4   CPR 69.7(5).

Receivership expenses

6.137   Expenses incurred by the receiver are distinct from his remuneration. Accordingly, they should be accounted for as part of his account for the assets he has recovered (see para 6.144).[1]

1   PD 69, para 9.6.

Who can be appointed a receiver?

6.138   A receiver must be an individual.[1] Accordingly, although a receiver may be a partner or employee of a firm, or a director or employee of a company, the order must appoint a named individual rather than appointing the firm or company itself. The court will require certain particulars of the proposed receiver as part of the evidence required in support of the application. Para 4.2 of the Practice Direction to Pt 69 provides:

'In addition, the written evidence should normally identify an individual whom the court is to be asked to appoint as receiver ('the nominee'), and should –
(1)   state the name, address and position of the nominee;
(2)   include written evidence by a person who knows the nominee, stating that he believes the nominee is a suitable person to be appointed as receiver, and the basis of that belief; and
(3)   be accompanied by written consent, signed by the nominee, to act as receiver if appointed.'

1   CPR 69.2.

Discretion concerning the nominee

6.139 The court has a discretion as to the identity of the individual proposed to act as receiver.[1] If the applicant does not nominate a person to be appointed as receiver, or if the court decides not to appoint the nominee, the court may order that a suitable person be appointed as receiver. Alternatively, the court may direct any party to nominate a suitable individual to be appointed.

[1] See PD 69, para 4.3.

Qualifications and disqualifications from acting as receiver

6.140 There are a number of cases concerning receivers which qualify the court's power to appoint certain individuals as receivers.[1] Although in practice qualified insolvency practitioners are often appointed as receivers, there is nothing to preclude the claimant himself being appointed as a receiver, as the standard form of order, Form No 84, illustrates. However, the Court of Appeal has described it as 'a settled rule that one of the parties to the cause shall not be appointed receiver without the consent of the other party unless a very special case is made'.[2] In practice, it is unlikely that the judgment debtor would consent to the judgment creditor being appointed receiver unless he could be persuaded that it would save costs. Given the potential liabilities that could be incurred by a receiver for his acts and omissions, a judgment creditor in a commercial enforcement situation would be well-advised to appoint a professional such as a licensed insolvency practitioner. The appointment of the judgment creditor as receiver would presumably only be appropriate where there are no complex legal steps required before he could collect in the property over which he was being appointed receiver.[3] In any event, if the judgment creditor were appointed as receiver, he would not be entitled to remuneration.[4]

[1] See further Picarda *The Law Relating to Receivers, Managers and Administrators* (3rd edn, 2000) ch 22.
[2] *Re Lloyd* (1879) 12 Ch D 447 at 451, CA, per Sir George Jessell MR.
[3] In *Allied Irish Bank v Ashford Hotels Ltd* [1997] 3 All ER 309, CA, a partner from a city law firm was appointed to act as receiver to enforce an indemnity.
[4] *Cummins v Perkins* [1899] 1 Ch 16 at 18, per Kekewich J. The Court of Appeal upheld Kekewich J's order but without considering this point.

6.141 Further, the court will not appoint as a receiver an individual who would have a conflict of interest in so acting. An important practical example of this principle is that the claimant's solicitor may not act as the receiver. The reason behind this was explained by Sir George Jessell MR in *Re Lloyd*:[1]

'It is improper for this simple reason: The duty of the solicitors of the Plaintiff is to check the receiver's accounts. It is so much their duty that as a general rule no one else does so. The solicitor of the Plaintiff attends on the taking of the receiver's account. Now, how is it possible that the firm can properly discharge that duty when one of the firm is himself the receiver? It is obviously a case where his interest will conflict with his duty, and that consideration alone, in my opinion, makes the appointment improper ...'

[1] *Re Lloyd* (1879) 12 Ch D 447 at 451 and also 453–454, per Cotton LJ, CA.

Receiver's powers and duties

6.142   As has been noted, a receiver is a creature of the court order appointing him. The receiver's powers and duties are largely defined by the terms of the order appointing him.[1] The essential point is that a receiver must have the court's permission to take almost any step or incur any costs. This reinforces the importance of ensuring that the order appointing the receiver, and any subsequent directions, are adequate for the steps likely to be taken by the receiver.

1   When a receiver is appointed in the Chancery Division the receiver should be provided with a copy of Appendix 3 to Appendix 4A of the Chancery Guide 2002 (powers and duties of receivers).

The receiver's right to seek directions

6.143   If the receiver is in any doubt as to what his powers and duties are, he should seek directions from the court. A receiver may apply to the court at any time for directions to assist him in carrying out his functions as a receiver.[1] The application should be made by application notice in accordance with CPR Pt 23[2] unless non-contentious, in which case the application can be made by letter (and the court may reply by letter).[3] Where directions are given, the court may also direct the receiver to serve the directions and application for directions on any person.[4] The receiver is invariably given permission to apply for this purpose.[5]

1   CPR 69.6(1).
2   PD 69, para 8.1.
3   PD 69, paras 8.2–8.3. The receiver need not serve the letter and reply on the parties unless directed to do so. The court can also direct that a receiver who applies by letter for directions should file and serve an application notice.
4   CPR 69.6(2).
5   See Form No 84, para 9.

Receiver's accounts

6.144   The court may order a receiver to prepare accounts either by a specified date or at specified intervals.[1] Form No 84 provides that:

'(5) the receiver shall on (date - 3 months after the date of order), and at such other times as may be ordered by the Master/District Judge pass his accounts, and shall on (date - 4 months after the date of order), and at such further and other times as may be ordered by the Master/District Judge pay the balance or balances appearing due on the accounts, or such part as shall be certified as proper to be paid, such sums to be paid in or towards satisfaction of what shall for the time being be due in respect of the judgment signed (date) for the sum of £ debt and £ costs, totalling £.'

1   CPR 69.8(1) and PD 69, para 10.1.

Inspection of documents relevant to preparation of accounts

6.145   A party served with the accounts may apply for an order permitting him to see any document in the possession of the receiver relevant to the accounts, although he should not do so without first asking for the document to be provided voluntarily.[1] If an order for inspection is made, the usual time limit for compliance will be to allow inspection within seven days of being served with the order and for copies to be provided within seven days of receipt of a request (provided the party has undertaken to pay the reasonable cost of making and providing the copy).[2]

[1]   PD 69, para 10.2.
[2]   PD 69, para 10.3.

Challenging the accounts

6.146   If the accounts are disputed there is a mechanism for objecting provided for by the rules.[1] If necessary an inquiry can be held to resolve disputes about the receiver's accounts.[2]

[1]   CPR 69.8(3)–(6).
[2]   CPR 69.8 (final unnumbered para) and CPR PD 40.

Non-compliance by the receiver

6.147   If the receiver does not comply with any rule, practice direction or direction of the court, the court can order him to attend a hearing to explain his failure to comply.[1] At the hearing, the court may make any order it considers to be appropriate in the circumstances, including: termination of the receiver's appointment, reducing or entirely disallowing the receiver's remuneration and ordering the receiver to pay any party's costs.[2] If the receiver's default is failure to comply with an order to pay a sum of money into court, the court can order interest at any rate it considers appropriate for the time he is in default.[3]

[1]   CPR 69.9(1).
[2]   CPR 69.9(2).
[3]   CPR 69.9(3).

Termination of the receiver's appointment

6.148   A receiver can be removed by the court and replaced by another receiver at any time.[1] A failure to provide security or satisfy the court that he has such security in place within the time specified by the court is grounds for termination.[2] An order terminating the appointment of a receiver may:
   (a)   require him to pay into court any money held by him; or
   (b)   specify the person to whom he must pay any money or transfer any assets still in his possession; and
   (c)   make provision for the discharge or cancellation of any guarantee given by the receiver as security.[3]

[1]   CPR 69.2(3).
[2]   CPR 69.5(2).
[3]   CPR 69.11(1).

6.149   Any order terminating the appointment of a receiver must also be served on all parties originally served with the order appointing the receiver.[1]

¹   CPR 69.11(2).

Application for discharge

6.150   A receiver or any party may apply for the receiver to be discharged on completion of his duties.[1] In the case of equitable execution, this will be when all available property has been collected in or the judgment entirely satisfied. The application seeking discharge should be served on all parties originally served with the order appointing the receiver.[2] An order discharging the appointment of a receiver may:

(a)   require him to pay into court any money held by him; or

(b)   specify the person to whom he must pay any money or transfer any assets still in his possession; and

(c)   make provision for the discharge or cancellation of any guarantee given by the receiver as security.[3]

¹   CPR 69.10(2).
²   CPR 69.10(2).
³   CPR 69.11(1).

6.151   Any order discharging the receiver must also be served on all parties originally served with the order appointing the receiver.[1]

¹   CPR 69.11(2).

Costs

6.152   Equitable execution is outside the fixed costs regime under CPR Part 45.[1] Instead, provided the application to appoint a receiver lasts less than a day, the court should be invited to make a summary assessment of the costs at the conclusion of a hearing, which the court is supposed to do unless there is good reason not to.[2] Each party who intends to claim costs should prepare a written statement of costs which should follow as closely as possible Form N260. The statement must be signed by the party or his legal representative and must be filed at court with copies served on any party from whom recovery of costs is sought. Filing and service must be done as soon as possible and in any event at least 24 hours before the date fixed for the hearing.[3]

¹   CPR 45.1(2)(c) states that CPR, Pt 45 (fixed costs) applies where a judgment creditor has taken steps under Pts 70-73 to enforce a judgment or order. CPR 70.2 provides that the relevant practice direction sets out methods of enforcing judgments or orders for the payment of money. One of the methods set out in PD 70, para 1.1(5), is the appointment of a receiver under Pt 69. However, there is no amount of fixed costs provided for equitable execution in the table to CPR 45.6 (fixed enforcement costs).
²   See CPR Pt 44.
³   General rules about costs are set out in Pt 44 and the accompanying Practice Direction, which should be referred to for the specific provisions.

INTERPLAY WITH THE INSOLVENCY REGIME

6.153 There is no modern authority on the effect of insolvency on a receiver by way of equitable execution. Although IA 1986, ss 183 and 346 both refer to the fact that priority on insolvency in respect of land is achieved by the appointment of a receiver, this would seem to be a hangover from when priority on insolvency in respect of a charging order could only be obtained on the appointment of a receiver.[1]

> 1   *Re Overseas Aviation Engineering (GB) Ltd* [1963] Ch 24, CA. As IA 1986, ss 346(5)(b) and 183(3)(c) recognise, the making of a charging order is now effective to confer priority on insolvency and the appointment of a receiver is no longer necessary.

6.154 The real issue is whether the appointment of a receiver by way of equitable execution falls within IA 1986, ss 183 and s 346 at all. As has already been noted in Chapter 1, IA 1986, ss 183 and 346 have a long history and derive from similar provisions in the various Bankruptcy and Companies Acts. The application of the Bankruptcy Act 1883, s 45 to equitable execution, which is one of the historical antecedents of IA 1986, s 346, was considered in *Re Potts*.[1] In that case, the judgment creditor sought and obtained a receiver by way of equitable execution in respect of Potts' share of the residuary estate under his mother's will. Two months later Potts was declared bankrupt on his own petition. The judgment creditor sought a declaration that it was a secured creditor of Potts by virtue of the order for the appointment of a receiver by way of equitable execution and that it had therefore obtained priority over his general creditors on insolvency. At first instance Vaughan Williams J also considered an argument that equitable execution was a form of execution and that it had been completed for the purposes of the Bankruptcy Act 1883, s 45, which provided that:

> '(1) Where a creditor has issued execution against the goods or lands of a debtor, or has attached any debt due to him, he shall not be entitled to retain the benefit of the execution or attachment against the trustee in bankruptcy of the debtor, unless he has completed the execution or attachment before the date of the receiving order, and before notice of the presentation of any bankruptcy petition by or against the debtor, or of the commission of any available act of bankruptcy by the debtor.
> (2) For the purposes of this Act, an execution against goods is completed by seizure and sale; an attachment of a debt is completed by receipt of the debt; and an execution against land is completed by seizure, or, in the case of an equitable interest, by the appointment of a receiver.'

> 1   [1893] 1 QB 648.

6.155 Vaughan Williams J was clearly unimpressed by the judgment creditor's argument:[1]

> 'I am of opinion that the applicants are not entitled to the order for which they ask. The case was argued principally with reference [Bankruptcy Act 1883, s 45], and it was contended that equitable execution of the character in this case is execution within the meaning of s 45, and that the execution had been completed, and that under those circumstances the applicants were by the very terms of the section entitled to the benefit of the execution. In my judgment the position of the applicants is not that of creditors who have issued execution

within the meaning of the section. I think the section only applies to the cases which are specified in it, and that this is not one of those cases.'

¹   [1893] 1 QB 648 at 650.

6.156   In other words equitable execution fell entirely outside the Bankruptcy Act 1883, s 45. The Court of Appeal upheld the first instance decision and unanimously concurred that a receiver by way of equitable execution did *not* make the judgment creditor a secured creditor since the order did not amount to a 'mortgage, charge or lien on the property of the debtor'.¹ Given the similarity of the wording of the Bankruptcy Act 1883, s 45 to its modern counterpart, IA 1986, s 346, it seems that bankruptcy will defeat a receiver appointed by way of equitable execution. Since IA 1986, s 183 is in similar terms to IA 1986, s 346, the same should also follow in the case of the winding up of a company.

¹   Although the Court of Appeal affirmed the judgment of Vaughan Williams J, it disposed of the case on the basis that a receiver by way of equitable execution did not make the judgment creditor a secured creditor.

CHAPTER 7

Interest on judgments

INTRODUCTION

7.1   Once judgment has been obtained, it may be some time before the judgment debtor makes payment and, where the judgment debtor fails to pay, enforcement proceedings may take months or even years to reach fruition. In order to compensate the judgment creditor for the time during which he has been deprived of the sums owed to him, statute provides that interest will accrue on a judgment once it has been given.

7.2   Where the judgment is of high value, the amount of interest which could potentially accrue will be significant. Judgment for these purposes includes costs orders, ie awards made in relation to the costs of the litigation itself and also on the costs associated with enforcing the judgment debt. Provided the judgment debtor has sufficient assets to meet both the judgment debt and interest, the latter can therefore provide a valuable source of compensation.

7.3   The interest with which this chapter is concerned is interest that is awarded on High Court judgments. This chapter does not cover interest that can be claimed prior to the commencement of proceedings or arising during the course of proceedings but before judgment is given.[1] Neither does this chapter cover interest on judgments in the county court, to which separate rules apply.[2] However, it is worth noting that with certain exceptions, county court judgments over £5,000 carry interest at the same rate as High Court judgments.[3]

---

[1]   A claimant will usually seek to claim interest pursuant to Supreme Court Act 1981, s 35A, which gives the court a discretion to award interest. A party will only be entitled to interest if this is specifically pleaded and the basis for the plea for interest (ie contract, statute or other basis) is set out in the statement of case. Details of the rate of interest claimed, the time period, the total interest to the date of calculation and the daily rate thereafter should be included.

[2]   Judgment interest on county court judgments is provided for by County Courts Act 1984, s 74 and the County Courts (Interest on Judgment Debts) Order 1991, SI 1991/1184.

[3]   See the County Courts (Interest on Judgment Debts) Order 1991, SI 1991/1184, paras 2 and 5, which provides that county court judgments over £5,000 carry interest at the same rate as specified in Judgments Act 1838, s 17. Prior to this, county court judgments did not carry interest.

Application to the Crown

7.4 Pursuant to the Crown Proceedings Act 1947 (CPA 1947), s 24(1), judgment debts due from or to the Crown carry interest in the same way as any other judgments.[1]

[1] CPA 1947, s 24(1) provides: 'section 17 of the Judgments Act 1838 (which provides that a judgment debt shall carry interest) and section 44A of the Administration of Justice Act 1970 (which enables the court to order an appropriate rate for a judgment debt expressed in a currency other than sterling) shall apply to judgment debts due from or to the Crown.'

PERIOD OF INTEREST

7.5 The general rule in respect of interest on High Court judgments is set out in the Judgments Act 1838 (JA 1838), s 17. This section has been amended over time, most recently as part of the Woolf reforms by the Civil Procedure (Modification of Enactments) Order 1998.[1] Broadly, the section now provides that all High Court judgments shall carry interest unless the court otherwise disallows it.

[1] SI 1998/2940.

7.6 JA 1838, s 17 (as amended) reads:

'(1) Every judgment debt shall carry interest at the rate of 8% per annum from such time as shall be prescribed by rules of court until the same shall be satisfied, and such interest may be levied under a writ of execution on such judgment.
(2) Rules of court may provide for the court to disallow all or part of any interest otherwise payable under subsection (1).'

As is explained further in paras 7.62-7.65, the current interest rate on sterling judgment debts (known as the 'judgment rate') is 8% per annum.

7.7 The reference in JA 1838, s 17(1) to 'such time as shall be prescribed by rules of court' means that this provision must now be read in conjunction with the Civil Procedure Rules 1998 (CPR),[1] r 40.8, which provides:

'(1) Where interest is payable on a judgment pursuant to section 17 of the Judgments Act 1838 ..., the interest shall begin to run from the date that judgment is given unless –
(a) a rule in another Part or a practice direction makes different provision; or
(b) the court orders otherwise.
(2) The court may order that interest shall begin to run from a date before the date that judgment is given.'

[1] SI 1998/3132.

7.8 The effect of the amendments to JA 1838, s 17, read with the provisions of CPR 40.8, is to grant the court considerable discretion in the *period* for which it awards interest and a flexibility that it previously did not have when making awards of interest.[1]

[1] See *O'Connor v Amos Bridgman Abattoirs Ltd* (1990) Times, 13 April, a decision prior to these modifications, where it was held that it would be helpful if the court had some discretion under JA 1838, s 17 as to whether to award interest on damages and costs but that it lacked such a discretion.

7.9 Although CPR 40.8(2) only makes reference to the discretion of the court to order that interest shall run from before judgment, JA 1838, s 17(2) and CPR 40.8(1)(b) appear to grant the court a discretion to order that interest on a judgment shall run from whatever date the court sees fit, whether before or after judgment, and including a discretion to order that interest is not payable at all.

7.10 The court's discretion under JA 1838, s 17 and CPR 40.8 is a new one and, at the time of writing, no cases have considered the provisions of CPR 40.8. It therefore remains to be seen how the court's power to award interest from a time other than when judgment is given will be used in practice.

When is a judgment 'given' for the purposes of CPR 40.8?

7.11 CPR 40.7 provides that 'a judgment or order takes effect from the day when it is given or made, or such later date as the court may specify'. It therefore seems that, unless the court orders otherwise, a judgment is 'given' for the purposes of CPR 40.8(1) when it is pronounced in court, and not on the date when the judgment or order is drawn up and sealed, which may be a number of days or even weeks later. Where the court reserves judgment and an advance copy is sent to the parties judgment will be given on the date that the judgment is actually handed down, and not the date the parties were sent the draft judgment.[1]

[1]   *Prudential Assurance Co Ltd v McBains Cooper (a firm)* [2000] 1 WLR 2000 at 2008, per Brooke LJ, CA.

7.12 CPR 40.2(2)(a) provides that every judgment must 'bear the date on which it is made'. However, as will be seen in paras 7.15 to 7.22, certain types of judgment and orders have historically created particular problems in determining when interest begins to accrue under JA 1838, s 17.

Meaning of 'judgment debt' under JA 1838, s 17

7.13 In order for interest to accrue under the provisions of the JA 1838, the judgment must therefore fall within the meaning of 'judgment debt'.[1] The following judgments and orders have all been held to be judgment debts:

(a)   orders for damages (once assessed);[2]
(b)   consent orders (except Tomlin orders);[3]
(c)   orders to make payments by instalments;[4]
(d)   judgments first made on appeal;[5] and
(e)   costs orders.[6]

[1]   Administration of Justice Act 1970, s 44A, which is considered at paras 7.66–7.68, also requires that a non-sterling judgment must be a 'judgment debt' within the meaning of JA 1838, s 17 and so the comments in this section apply equally to that section.
[2]   See paras 7.15–7.17.
[3]   See paras 7.18–7.21.
[4]   See para 7.22.
[5]   See paras 7.25–7.32.
[6]   See paras 7.33–7.57.

7.14 The type of judgment or order may therefore impact upon the judgment interest which is awarded. In addition, various enactments provide that orders and awards made under them should carry interest at the same rate as under JA 1838, s 17.[1] However, these are outside the scope of this book, which is concerned with the enforcement of high value High Court judgments. By way of exception, paras 7.95-7.98 below deal briefly with the interest payable on arbitration awards in light of the prevalence of arbitration as a method of commercial dispute resolution.

[1]   Examples include Proceeds of Crime Act 2002, s 12 (confiscation orders), Electricity Act 1989, s 27A (penalties imposed on licence holders), and National Lottery Act 1998, s 2(13) (penalties imposed on licence holders).

Orders for damages and judgments determining liability only

7.15 As has been noted, orders for damages once assessed will fall within the meaning of 'judgment debt' for the purposes of JA 1838, s 17. Where a claimant succeeds on the issue of liability but the court leaves damages to be assessed, the issue arises of how interest is to be determined. When does interest cease to run under Supreme Court Act 1981, s 35A(1)(b) (which applies until 'the date of judgment') and begin to run under JA 1838, s 17 (which applies once 'judgment is given')?

7.16 In *Thomas v Bunn*,[2] the House of Lords held that interest under JA 1838, s 17 begins to run from the date of the final judgment assessing damages and not from the earlier date of judgment determining liability.[3] Lord Ackner explained the court's interpretation of the statute as follows:[4]

> 'the judgment referred to in section 17 of the Judgments Act 1838 does not relate to an interlocutory or interim order or judgment establishing only the defendant's liability. The judgment contemplated by that section is the judgment which quantifies the defendant's liability.'

[1]   [1991] 1 AC 362, HL, in which the House of Lords overruled *Borthwick v Elderslie Steamship Co Ltd (No 2)* [1905] 2 KB 516, CA, and disapproved the dictum of Eve J in *Ashover Fluor Spar Mines Ltd v Jackson* [1911] 2 Ch 355 and dicta in *Hunt v R M Douglas (Roofing) Ltd* [1990] 1 AC 398, HL. It should, however, be noted that this case was decided on the pre-1998 wording of JA 1838, s 17, which provided that judgment debts would carry interest 'from the time of entering up judgment', rather than the current provisions, which provide for interest on judgment debts 'from such time as shall be prescribed by rules of court'.

[2]   The position is made express in the county court by the County Courts (Interest on Judgment Debts) Order 1991, para 2(2), SI 1991/1814, which provides that '[i]n the case of a judgment or order for the payment of a judgment debt, ... the amount of which has to be determined at a later date, the judgment debt shall carry interest from that later date.'

[3]   [1991] 1 AC 362 at 381, per Lord Ackner, HL.

7.17 The logic behind this approach – the so called 'allocatur rule' – is that the assessed damages take account of inflation between the judgment on liability and the judgment assessing damages. It would therefore be unfair to award interest during that period.[1] While there have been no cases on this, following the reasoning in *Thomas v Bunn*, judgment interest on an inquiry for an account of profits will presumably only run from the date the account of profits is quantified, rather than the date liability was established and the inquiry ordered.

1   See the judgment of Turner J in *Lindop v Goodwin Steel Castings Ltd* (1990) Times, 19 June for an explanation of the reasoning behind the application of the allocatur rule.

Consent orders

7.18   With the exception of Tomlin orders, which are discussed next, orders for the payment of money given by consent will accrue interest in the same way as a contested judgment or order for the payment of money.

Tomlin orders

7.19   Tomlin orders stay proceedings on the terms of settlement that have been agreed between the parties. They are expressly recognised by CPR 40.6(3)(b)(ii).[1] A Tomlin order simply provides that:[2]

'And the parties having agreed to the terms set out in the attached schedule

IT IS BY CONSENT ORDERED

That all further proceedings in this claim be stayed except for the purpose of carrying such terms into effect

AND for that purpose the parties have permission to apply.'

As the order itself states, the detailed terms of settlement are set out (or referred to) in a schedule to the order.

1   Which refers to 'an order for the stay of proceedings on agreed terms, disposing of the proceedings, whether those terms are recorded in a schedule to the order or elsewhere'.   The predecessor to this rule, RSC Ord 42, r 5A(2)(b)(iii), provided: 'the stay of proceedings upon terms which are scheduled to the order but which are not otherwise part of it (a "Tomlin order")'.
2   Chancery Guide 2002, para 9.16.

7.20   The effect of a Tomlin order is to stay the proceedings, which are only kept on foot for the limited purpose of allowing a party to enforce the terms of the schedule of the order under the permission to apply provision. One of the terms agreed in the schedule will usually provide for the payment of a sum of money by one party to the other. However, the schedule to the Tomlin order is simply a record of the contractual terms agreed by the parties and those terms do not themselves form part of the order of the court. Accordingly, they are not enforceable as a judgment debt under JA 1838, s 17.[1]

1   In *Horizon Technologies International Ltd v Lucky Wealth Consultants Ltd* [1992] 1 WLR 24 at 29, PC, Sir Maurice Casey described a Tomlin order in the following terms: 'It is, of course, a feature of [Tomlin orders] that the schedule forming the basis of the stay of proceedings is not part of the order: it is simply a record of the compromise reached between the parties.'

7.21   If one party is not observing the terms agreed between them, the other will need to make an application under the permission to apply provision to give effect to the order.[1] If the relevant term is for a party to pay a sum of money to the other, an application must be made for an order for payment of that sum so that judgment can be entered. Once such judgment is obtained, the question arises as to whether interest under JA 1838, s 17 is available for the period between the Tomlin order being made and the subsequent judgment enforcing the Tomlin order. It follows from the nature of a Tomlin order that judgment interest will only be available from the date the judgment ordering payment of the sums agreed in the schedule to the Tomlin order is obtained. However, in an appropriate case, the court would have a discretion under CPR 40.8 to vary the period of interest including 'to run from a date before the date [that] judgment is given'.[2] It remains to be seen whether breach of a Tomlin order would be an appropriate basis for the court to exercise this discretion.[3]

1   *Dashwood v Dashwood* [1927] WN 276.
2   CPR 40.8(2). See paras 7.5–7.10.
3   If the obligation to pay a sum of money is contained in the order itself, this should be enforceable as a judgment debt and interest will begin to run in the normal way. It is common to include any costs which require assessment in the body of the order rather than the schedule because the provision for costs would otherwise be unenforceable. Para 9.16 of the Chancery Guide 2002 refers to the order being drawn up 'with any appropriate provision in respect of costs'.

Payments by instalments

7.22   Where an order is made for payment of a judgment debt by instalments, interest is not payable on any of the instalments until they fall due. In *Caudery v Finnerty*[1] it was held that interest under JA 1838 did not accrue on a judgment debt that was ordered by consent to be paid in instalments. However, interest would accrue on outstanding instalments if the instalments were not paid when due.[2]

1   (1892) 61 LJQB 496, DC.
2   The position is made express in the county court by the County Courts (Interest on Judgment Debts) Order 1991, SI 1991/1184, para 3, which provides that interest on payments by instalments will not accrue on the amount of any instalment until it falls due.

Specific rules applying to particular forms of judgment

DEFAULT JUDGMENTS AGAINST STATES

7.23   Under CPR 40.10 a default judgment does not take effect against a state until two months after service on the state of the judgment. Interest under JA 1838, s 17 does not, therefore, begin to run until the judgment has taken effect.

COUNTY COURT JUDGMENT TRANSFERRED TO HIGH COURT

7.24   As has been noted in Chapter 1, if a judgment in the county court has been transferred to the High Court for the purposes of enforcement, the judgment will be treated as a judgment or order of the High Court *'for all purposes'* under the County Courts Act 1984, s 42(5)(b). It therefore follows that, following transfer, interest will accrue on the same basis as if the judgment were a High Court judgment (ie under JA 1838, s 17). However, the question arises as to whether judgment interest accrues at the county court rate up until the date of transfer and at the High Court rate thereafter. At present, this question would appear to be largely academic in the case of sterling money judgments over £5,000 since the rates of interest are identical[1] even if they are awarded on different statutory bases.[2] In the case of non-sterling money judgments over £5,000, the court's discretion to award interest at a different rate to that provided for in JA 1838, s 17 is substantially the same in both the county court and High Court, even though the court's discretion again derives from different statutory bases.[3]

1   They both carry interest at the rate provided for in JA 1838, s 17.
2   See para 7.3, n 2 and n 3.
3   See para 7.67, n 2.

Judgments made on appeal

7.25   Another important question is the effect on judgment interest of judgment being awarded for the first time on appeal, either in the Court of Appeal or House of Lords.

Court of Appeal

7.26   The cases considered in paras 7.26–7.28 were all decided before the introduction of the CPR. It should therefore be borne in mind that the court now has a much broader discretion on judgment interest than it had previously.[1]

1   See paras 7.5–7.10.

7.27   As a general rule, where the claimant fails at trial, but obtains judgment for damages on appeal to the Court of Appeal, judgment interest runs from the date of the Court of Appeal decision. In *Borthwick v Elderslie Steamship Co Ltd (No 2)*,[1] Romer LJ held that:[2]

'The judgment in favour of the plaintiff must be treated as of the date on which it was given in the Court of Appeal, subject to the right of that Court to antedate its judgment.'

1   [1905] 2 KB 516, CA.
2   [1905] 2 KB 516 at 521, CA.

7.28   Although the Court recognised it had a right to antedate its judgment, it decided that the right was only to be exercised sparingly.[1] Similarly, in *Belgian Grain and Produce Co Ltd v Cox & Co (France) Ltd*,[2] Bankes LJ held:[3]

'If we were to accede to this request, there are very few cases in which we should not be asked to do the same thing. While we have jurisdiction to make the order [that interest runs from a date prior to the judgment of the Court of Appeal], there must be something exceptional to justify it.'

1   [1905] 2 KB 516 at 521, CA.
2   (1919) 1 Ll L Rep 256, CA.
3   (1919) 1 Ll L Rep 256 at 258, CA.

House of Lords

7.29   The provisions of the CPR do not apply to appeals heard by the House of Lords[1] and so there is no reason to suppose that pre-1999 cases are diminished in terms of authority.

> 1   CPR 2.1 provides that the CPR apply to all proceedings in: (a) the county courts, (b) the High Court and (c) the Civil Division of the Court of Appeal. The Practice Directions for Civil Appeals to the House of Lords do not deal with awards of interest.

7.30   In the House of Lords, the crucial factor as to the date from which judgment interest should run is whether or not the ultimately successful party won at first instance. In *Nitrate Producers Steamship Co v Short Bros,*[1] the plaintiffs lost at first instance and in the Court of Appeal but succeeded in the House of Lords. On a subsequent application, the plaintiffs obtained an order from the judge at first instance that interest should run from the date of the first instance decision. The House of Lords held that this approach was wrong. Lord Buckmaster, giving the leading judgment, said:[2]

> 'Where judgment is for the first time directed to be entered in favour of any litigant party in this House, the date which that judgment will bear must be the date when the order is made. It is, of course, a totally different proposition where the effect of the order here is to restore a judgment of the Court of first instance which has been reversed by the Court of Appeal. In that case the judgment of the Court of first instance is expressly restored and remains standing as from the date when it was pronounced.'

> 1   (1922) 12 Ll L Rep 1, HL.
> 2   (1922) 12 Ll L Rep 1 at 2, HL.

7.31   In summary, the current position from the claimant's perspective is that judgment interest will run from the decision that was first successful. The position is summarised in the following table:[1]

Court of first instance	Court of Appeal	House of Lords	When interest runs from
Win	Win	Win	First instance
Lose	Win	Win	Court of Appeal
Lose	Lose	Win	House of Lords
Win	Lose	Win	First instance

> 1   Different rules apply to costs, which are considered in paras 7.52–7.57.

7.32   As has been noted, however, the CPR introduced a discretion for the High Court and the Court of Appeal to order that interest should run on a judgment from a date other than that on which the party is first successful.[1]

> 1   CPR 40.8(1)(b) and (2). See paras 7.5–7.10.

INTEREST ON COSTS

7.33 Prior to the CPR, the general rule was that interest on costs orders under JA 1838, s 17 began to run from the date when the costs in question were originally ordered, even though the costs had not been taxed. This contrasted with the rules regarding interest following judgments on liability only (see paras 7.15–7.17 above), which require damages to be assessed before interest begins to run.[1]

---

1   It is worth noting that in relation to the county court, the County Courts (Interest on Judgment Debts) Order 1991, SI 1991/1184, para 2(2) provides that: '[i]n the case of a judgment or order for the payment of a judgment debt, other than costs, the amount of which has to be determined at a later date, the judgment debt shall carry interest from that later date.' This rule also applied in the case of interim judgments under which one party is ordered to pay costs. See *Taylor v Roe* [1894] 1 Ch 413.

7.34 The rule was established following the decision of the House of Lords in *Hunt v RM Douglas (Roofing) Ltd.*[1] In *Hunt*, the House of Lords considered a long line of authority stretching back 150 years to the case of *Fisher v Dudding*.[2] Their Lordships overruled earlier decisions which had favoured the allocatur rule (namely that interest on costs should only run from the date on which they were quantified, ie the date of the taxing master's or costs officer's certificate).[3] The House of Lords instead concluded that the incipitur rule (namely that interest should run from the date of the costs order) was the more appropriate method of achieving a just outcome. The incipitur rule found favour primarily because it is the unsuccessful party to the litigation who has caused the costs to be incurred and so the incipitur rule should provide a desirable stimulus for cases to be dealt with efficiently.[4]

---

1   [1990] 1 AC 398, HL.
2   (1841) 9 Dowl 872.
3   Specifically, *Hunt* overruled the Court of Appeal decisions in *K v K* [1977] Fam 39, CA and in *Erven Warnink BV v J Townend & Sons (Hull) Ltd (No 2)* [1982] 3 All ER 312, CA.
4   [1990] 1 AC 398 at 415–416, HL.

7.35 The courts have acknowledged that neither the allocatur or the incipitur rule dealt with the issue of interest on costs satisfactorily. The inconsistency between the rule which applied to interest on costs and the rule which applied to interest on orders for damages following interlocutory judgments was acknowledged by Lord Ackner in his subsequent judgment in *Thomas v Bunn*[1] where he stated:[2]

'I accept that it is an anomaly that an order for payment of costs to be taxed[3] is construed for the purpose of section 17 [JA 1838] as a judgment debt, even though, before taxation has been completed, there is no sum for which execution can be levied. However, the courts have accepted since its enactment that section 17 does apply to such an order and, for the reasons set out in my speech in Hunt's case, the balance of justice favours continuing so to treat such an order.'

---

1   [1991] 1 AC 362, HL.
2   [1991] 1 AC 362 at 380, HL.
3   Now detailed assessment: see CPR 44.7.

A new discretion – CPR 44.3(6)(g)

7.36   The CPR introduced a new discretion in relation to interest on costs under Pt 44. CPR 44.3 provides that the court has a discretion as to the costs it awards and CPR 44.3(6)(g) makes the following provisions as to interest:

'The orders which the court may make under this rule include an order that a party must pay – ...

(g)   interest on costs from or until a certain date, including a date before judgment.'

7.37   Accordingly, the courts have a wide discretion to make orders for interest on costs from or until specified dates, including from a date before judgment. Paragraph 11.2(5) of the Chancery Guide 2002 makes express reference to the court's power to award interest from a date before the date of the order: 'so compensating the receiving party for the delay between incurring the costs and receiving a payment in respect of them.'[1]

1   Substantially the same wording is found at para 2.5.10 of the Queen's Bench Guide.

7.38   There have been a number of cases considering this rule since the introduction of the CPR, although it seems likely that further refinement will follow.

7.39   The court considered whether to apply CPR 44.3(6)(g) in *Amoco (UK) Exploration Co v British American Offshore Ltd (No 2)*.[1] In that case, Langley J stated obiter:[2]

'[I]t may well be appropriate, at least in substantial proceedings involving commercial interests of significant importance ... that the court should award interest on costs under [CPR 44.3(6)(g)] where substantial sums have inevitably been expended perhaps a year or more before an award of costs is made and interest begins to run on it under the general rule. ... I have no difficulty in accepting that costs of such an order [£16m] have had to be financed and paid over a substantial period of time.... I would consider it appropriate in principle to award interest upon such costs from payment to judgment.'

1   [2001] All ER (D) 327 (Nov).   Considered in *Rambus Inc v Hynix Semiconductor UK Ltd* [2004] All ER (D) 587 (Jul).
2   [2001] All ER (D) 327 (Nov) at [10].

7.40   However, the facts of the case were such that the court did not have to reach a final decision on how the rule would be applied.[1]

1   The parties were also in litigation on related issues in the courts of Texas and the judge considered that, by making an award under the rule, there was a risk of double recovery.

7.41   In *Amec Process and Energy Ltd v Stork Engineers & Contractors BV (No 3)*,[1] Thornton J considered Langley J's words on the application of CPR 44.3(6)(g) and stated:

'I agree with these sentiments and that they are directly applicable to this case since the costs, although not in the Amoco scale, are still huge in size and much of those costs were incurred many years ago.'

1   [2002] All ER (D) 48 (Apr).

7.42 The court went on to 'adopt a broad brush' approach and awarded interest on the whole of the costs but only for half of the period of the litigation at a rate of 6%, and judgment rate interest on costs from the date of judgment.

7.43 In *Powell v Herefordshire Health Authority*[1] the defendant health authority admitted negligence in April 1994 and judgment was entered by consent. Quantum was not resolved until June 2001, over seven years later. Costs were awarded to the claimant on the standard basis and the costs judge concluded that interest on costs should run from April 1994 in accordance with JA 1838, s 17. The defendant appealed.

[1]   [2003] 3 All ER 253, CA.

7.44 The Court of Appeal considered whether interest on costs should run from the April 1994 judgment, the June 2001 damages assessment, or whether CPR 44.3(6)(g) allowed the costs judge to award interest from some other date (the latter being a point which neither party had raised). The Court of Appeal held that CPR 44.3(6)(g) gave the costs judge a discretion to look at the dates when the costs had been incurred and to come to a conclusion which 'fitted the justice of the circumstances of the case'.[1] However, no definitive guidance was provided by the Court as the parties came to an agreement on costs.

[1]   [2003] 3 All ER 253 at 254.

7.45 In *Seashore Marine SA v Phoenix Assurance plc, The Vergina (No 3)*[1], Aikens J considered both the court's new discretion under the CPR to vary the date from which interest under the JA 1838 is to run and the apparent inconsistency of logic applied by the House of Lords in the decisions of *Thomas v Bunn* and *Hunt v RM Douglas (Roofing) Ltd*.[2] The claimant in that case was seeking enhanced interest and indemnity costs, having beaten its Pt 36 offer, and the case contains a detailed analysis of both costs and interest. On the facts of the case, counsel agreed that the court could make an order using its discretion under the CPR, the net effect of which was that statutory interest under JA 1838 ran on both the principal amount and costs from the date of the judgment on liability. Aikens J stated:[3]

> 'The effect of the two [House of Lords'] decisions on this case, therefore, would be that the rates of interest awarded under Rule 36.21(2) and (3) would run until the date of this judgment (i.e. July 31, 2001), rather than the one dealing with liability, which I handed down on May 16, 2001. That would make some difference in the interest recoverable by the claimant. However, counsel also pointed out that the Court has power to set a date from which interest on a judgment will run under s. 17 of the Judgments Acts that is *before* the date of the judgment: see CPR Part 40.8(1)(b) and (2). Furthermore, under CPR 44.3(6)(g), the Court has power to award interest on costs from a date *before* judgment. It was therefore agreed by Counsel on July 31, 2001 that I could make an order that Judgment Act interest would run from May 16, 2001 on: (i) the principal sum awarded plus interest, including the enhanced CPR Part 36.21(2) interest; and (ii) costs, including the pre-judgment interest on costs awarded under CPR Part 36.21(3). After some discussion it was agreed that I should order that, for the purposes of the accrual of interest under s. 17 of the Judgments Act, the date of this judgment would be deemed to be May 16, 2001. So the order drawn

has provided that Judgment Act interest on the sums identified above will run as from May 16, 2001.'

1   [2003] 3 All ER 253.
2   [2002] 1 Lloyd's Rep 238.
3   [2002] 1 Lloyd's Rep 238 at 248.

7.46   The court has been asked to consider the application of CPR 44.6(3)(g) in several cases in which the successful party has claimed interest on costs for a period prior to judgment. In *Somatra Ltd v Sinclair Roche & Temperley*,[1] Morison J could see no reason why he should not exercise his discretion under CPR 44.3(6)(g) to award the successful claimant interest on its costs 'to reflect the commercial reality that [the claimants] have lost the use of the money which they otherwise would have been able to spend in earning yet more money'. The judge further ordered that interest should run at the commercial rate of 1% over base rate on the claimant's costs.[2]

1   [2002] All ER (D) 231 (Oct).
2   The court's discretion to vary the rate of interest on a judgment debt is discussed at paras 7.69–7.71.

7.47   Morison J's judgment in *Somatra* does not deal with the interest *period* since it does not specify from or until when that interest should have run but it is presumed that Morison J intended interest to run for the period from the date on which the costs had been incurred (costs had been billed and paid on a monthly basis) until the date of judgment. This was substantially the approach taken by the Court of Appeal in exercising its powers under CPR 44.3(6)(g) in *Bim Kemi AB v Blackburn Chemicals Ltd (costs)*,[1] where the successful party was awarded interest on its costs at a rate of 1% over base rate from the date of each costs invoice to the date of the trial judgment, with interest to accrue at the judgment rate thereafter.

1   [2003] EWCA Civ 889.

7.48   In *Douglas v Hello! Ltd (No 7)*,[1] Lindsay J considered *Bim* and gave further guidance on the period during which interest on costs should be ordered under CPR 44.3(6)(g):

'the more appropriate dates, when one is seeking to measure the extent to which a party has been out of pocket, would be the dates on which the invoices were actually paid. As to when such interest should stop, it seems to me that the appropriate time would be when interest on costs is replaced by judgment interest.'

1   [2004] EWHC 63 (Ch).

7.49   In both *Somatra* and *Bim Kemi*, the court ordered a different rate of interest on costs paid before the date of the costs order. Arguably, the scope of the discretion given to the court by CPR 44.3(6)(g), when read in conjunction with JA 1838, s 17, is only to vary the *period* of the interest not the *rate* of interest on a judgment debt. It remains to be seen whether this apparent tension will be resolved through case law.

7.50   In conclusion, although the incipitur rule that costs should run from the date of the costs order (rather than the date on which costs are assessed) probably remains the starting assumption when assessing interest on costs orders, the courts are increasingly willing to make alternative orders where the costs and time periods involved are sufficiently large and a party has been out of pocket for a significant period of time.

Delay in applying for detailed assessment

7.51 It should also be noted that a party who delays unnecessarily in bringing detailed assessment proceedings under Pt 74 may have any interest that he would otherwise be entitled to under JA 1838, s 17 disallowed in whole or in part.[1]

1   CPR 47.8(3) and 47.14(5)(b).

Costs – reversals in the Court of Appeal and the House of Lords

7.52 The general principles regarding interest on a judgment debt following reversal on appeal are summarised in the table in para 7.31. The question of when interest is to run on costs orders where a decision has been reversed by either the Court of Appeal or the House of Lords has been considered in a number of pre-CPR cases. At least prior to the CPR, the general rule was that if a decision was reversed in the Court of Appeal, the successful party was entitled to interest on his costs from the date of the Court of Appeal's decision. Likewise, if a decision was reversed in the House of Lords, the successful party was only entitled to his costs from the date of the House of Lords' decision. This has led to some injustice and there are a number of cases in which the courts have tried to circumvent the general rule.

7.53 In *Kuwait Airways Corpn v Iraqi Airways Co (No 2)*,[1] the Court of Appeal reversed a decision that had been made in the plaintiff's favour at first instance. The plaintiffs were ordered to pay the costs of proceedings before both courts. The defendants, relying on the discretion the court had under RSC Ord 42, r 3(2) to vary the date from which the date a judgment or order takes effect, sought to obtain interest on those costs from the date of the first instance decision, rather than the date of the Court of Appeal judgment.

1   [1994] 1 WLR 985, CA.

7.54 The Court of Appeal held that it did have a discretion to backdate its costs order to the date of the judgment at first instance so that interest could be claimed from the date of the judgment at first instance and went on to find that it would ordinarily be just to backdate the part of the order that relates to costs at first instance to the date of the first instance judgment. In this case, however, the court only partially backdated the order for costs at first instance, having taken into consideration the unusually high interest rates at the time of the first instance decision.

7.55 However, the House of Lords disagreed when their Lordships considered the question of backdating interest on costs in the 1997 case of *Nykredit Mortgage Bank plc v Edward Erdman Group Ltd (No 2)*.[1] The plaintiff lenders had been awarded damages at first instance for loss caused by the defendant's negligent valuation. The Court of Appeal dismissed the defendants' appeal but the House of Lords allowed it and ordered, among other things, that the plaintiff pay the defendant's costs in the Court of Appeal on the issue of quantum.

1   [1997] 1 WLR 1627, HL.

7.56 The House of Lords then considered from when interest should run on the defendant's costs in the Court of Appeal. The House of Lords rejected the defendant's claim that interest on these costs should run from the date of the Court of Appeal decision and, in doing so, overruled the Court of Appeal's decision in *Kuwait Airways Corpn v Iraqi Airways Co (No 2)*. The House of Lords concluded that there was no discretion to backdate interest on costs by backdating the date of the order, '*however desirable it might be for the court to have* [such a] *power*'.[1]

1   [1997] 1 WLR 1627 at 1636, per Lord Nicholls.

7.57 However, as has been noted, these cases were all decided before the introduction of the CPR. CPR 44.3(6)(g)[1] now appears to give the High Court and the Court of Appeal precisely the discretion that the House of Lords had decided was not available in 1997.

1   See paras 7.36 and 7.37.

Orders for costs of detailed assessment

7.58 Where detailed assessment proceedings are required, costs can be ordered in respect of those proceedings.[1] The question arises as to when interest begins to run on the costs of these proceedings. The Practice Direction to Pts 43–48 provides that interest on the costs of detailed assessment proceedings shall begin to run from the date of the default, interim or final costs certificate, as the case may be.[2]

1   CPR 47.18. The Practice Direction to Pts 43–48, para 45.1 states: '[a]s a general rule the court will assess the receiving party's costs of the detailed assessment proceedings and add them to the bill of costs.'
2   Practice Direction to Pts 43–48, para 45.5(1).

Costs following specific procedures[1]

7.59 In certain circumstances, costs orders are deemed to have been made by the court. These circumstances are set out in CPR 44.12, which provides that a costs order will be deemed to have been made:

'(1) Where a right to costs arises under –
(a) rule 3.7 (defendant's right to costs where claim struck out for non-payment of fees);
(b) rule 36.13(1) (claimant's right to costs where he accepts defendant's Part 36 offer or Part 36 payment);
(c) rule 36.14 (claimant's right to costs where defendant accepts the claimant's Part 36 offer); or
(d) rule 38.6 (defendant's right to costs where claimant discontinues).'

1   See further paras 7.72–7.75 on Pt 36 offers.

7.60 CPR 44.12(2), which is self-explanatory, provides:

'(2) Interest payable pursuant to section 17 of the Judgments Act 1838 … on the costs deemed to have been ordered under paragraph (1) shall begin to run from the date on which the event which gave rise to the entitlement to costs occurred.'

Costs awarded against the Crown

7.61 As noted in Chapter 1, the Crown has certain immunities from enforcement steps being taken against it by virtue of CPA 1947. However, the CPA 1947, s 24(2) provides that:

'Where any costs are awarded to or against the Crown in the High Court, interest shall be payable upon those costs unless the court otherwise orders, and any interest so payable shall be at the same rate as that at which interest is payable upon judgment debts due from or to the Crown.'

RATE OF INTEREST

7.62 The courts' power to alter the *period* for which interest is payable has been noted at paras 7.5-7.10. This section considers the *rate* of interest that applies to the judgment.

Rate of interest – sterling judgments

7.63 Where the judgment is a sterling judgment, the *rate* of interest will depend on whether there is a contractual agreement between the parties on the rate of interest which is to run after judgment. In the absence of contractual variation, the statutory rate will apply.

7.64 The interest rate applicable under JA 1838, s 17 now derives from statutory instruments made under the Administration of Justice Act 1940 (AJA 1970), s 44, which provides:

'The Lord Chancellor may by order made with the concurrence of the Treasury direct that section 17 of the Judgments Act 1838 (as that enactment has effect for the time being whether by virtue of this subsection or otherwise) shall be amended so as to substitute for the rate specified in that section as the rate at which judgment debts shall carry interest such rate as may be specified in the order.'

7.65 The judgment rate has been amended from time to time by various orders issued under AJA 1970, s 44. The current rate is fixed at 8% per annum by virtue of the Judgment Debts (Rate of Interest) Order 1993.[1] The following table sets out the historic rates of interest which have applied under JA 1838, s 17:

Judgment date	Rate of interest per annum	Authority
before 20 April 1971	4%	Judgments Act 1838, s 17
post 20 April 1971	7.5%	Judgment Debts (Rate of Interest) Order 1971, SI 1971/491[2]
post 1 March 1977	10%	Judgment Debts (Rate of Interest) Order 1977, SI 1977/141
post 3 December 1979	12.5%	Judgment Debts (Rate of Interest) Order 1979, SI 1979/1382
post 9 June 1980	15%	Judgment Debts (Rate of Interest) Order 1980, SI 1980/672
post 8 June 1982	14%	Judgment Debts (Rate of Interest) Order 1982, SI 1982/696
post 10 November 1982	12%	Judgment Debts (Rate of Interest) (No 2) Order 1982, SI 1982/1427
post 16 April 1985	15%	Judgment Debts (Rate of Interest) Order 1985, SI 1985/437
post 1 April 1993	8%	Judgment Debts (Rate of Interest) Order 1993, SI 1993/564

---

[1]   SI 1993/564.
[2]   This increase was made under AJA, s 44, which implemented the recommendations of the Report of the Committee on the Enforcement of Judgment Debts (Payne Committee Report) (1969) Cmnd 3909.

Rate of interest – judgments expressed in a foreign currency

7.66   Judgments awarded by the English courts can be expressed in a foreign currency.[1] Where this is the case, the court has a discretion to alter the rate of judgment interest. The rules are set out in AJA 1970, s 44A,[2] which provides as follows:

'(1) Where a judgment is given for a sum expressed in a currency other than sterling and the judgment debt is one to which section 17 of the Judgments Act 1838 applies, the court may order that the interest rate applicable to the debt shall be such rate as the court thinks fit.
(2) Where the court makes such an order, section 17 of the Judgments Act 1838 shall have effect in relation to the judgment debt as if the rate specified in the order were substituted for the rate specified in that section.'

[1]   See further Chapter 1.
[2]   Inserted by Private International Law (Miscellaneous Provisions) Act 1995, s 1.

7.67   Therefore provided the judgment is for a 'judgment debt' to which JA 1838, s 17 applies,[1] the court may vary the rate of interest which would otherwise normally be awarded under JA 1838, s 17 if the judgment were a judgment expressed in sterling. A party who believes that a different rate should apply in the case of a non-sterling judgment should therefore apply to the court under AJA 1970, s 44A to vary the rate otherwise applicable under JA 1838, s 17.[2]

[1]   See paras 7.13–7.24.

2   Similar rules apply to county court judgments, although the jurisdiction arises under different legislation. Interest on non-sterling county court judgments is provided for by County Courts Act 1984, s 74(5A) and the county courts (Interest on Judgment Debts) Order 1991, SI 1991/1184. With certain exceptions, the County Courts (Interest on Judgment Debts) Order 1991, para 5(2) provides that, in the case of non-sterling county court judgments over £5,000, the 'County Court may order that the rate of interest shall be such rate as the court thinks fit … and, where the court makes such an order, section 17 of the Judgments Act 1838 shall have effect in relation to the judgment debt as if the rate specified in the order were substituted for the rate specified in that section'.

7.68   At the time of writing, no cases have yet been decided under AJA 1970, s 44A. However, where judgment is given in a foreign currency, the court may well be prepared to consider the rate of interest at which that currency could be borrowed by the successful party in the country in which the debt should have been paid. The court's willingness to award judgments in currencies other than sterling and the increasing prevalence of transactions where payment is required in Euros may well lead to an increase in the recourse to the provisions of AJA 1970, s 44A by judgment creditors.

Can the court vary the rate of interest under JA 1838, s 17?

7.69   Other than in the case of non-sterling judgments (as discussed above), the court does *not* have a discretion to alter the judgment rate. This could be particularly significant if the statutory rate of interest has increased since the judgment creditor was awarded judgment and the judgment debtor has yet to satisfy some or all of his judgment debt. At the time of writing, the judgment rate had remained unchanged at 8% per annum since 1 April 1993, so, at present, the issue may be largely academic. However, it may become relevant if the statutory rate changes in future.

7.70   The question of whether the court had a discretion to alter the judgment rate arose in *Rocco Giuseppe & Figli v Tradax Export SA*.[1] Although the court was considering two arbitration awards in that case, under the provisions of the Arbitration Act in force at the time, the awards carried interest at the same rate as a judgment debt.[2] At the time the awards were made the judgment rate was 10%. However, the award was not paid until nearly four years later, during which time the judgment rate had subsequently increased to 12.5% and then 15% by two successive orders made under AJA 1970, s 44. The judgment creditor contended for a construction of the applicable legislation that allowed him to claim the increases in the rates of interest that had occurred in the period between the awards being made and their subsequent payment.

1   [1984] 1 WLR 742.
2   Arbitration Act 1950, s 20. In *Rocco Giuseppe & Figli v Tradax Export SA* [1984] 1 WLR 742 at 747, Parker J expressly found that the fact he was considering an arbitration award rather than a judgment was irrelevant as the award was to be 'treated exactly like a judgment'.

7.71   Parker J held that the applicable judgment rate is the rate specified in the order made under AJA 1970, s 44 in force at the date judgment is given. The court has no power to vary the judgment rate in force at the date judgment is given even if a new order altering the judgment rate is made after judgment has been given. This approach was apparently affirmed by the Court of Appeal in *McPhilemy v Times Newspapers*

Ltd[1] which is discussed in para 7.74. However, as has been noted at para 7.49, the court seems implicitly to have taken a different approach in both the *Somatra* case and *Bim Kemi* case, where the court ordered a different rate of interest to the judgment rate on costs paid before the date of the costs order. It remains to be seen how this is developed in the case law.

1   [2002] 1 WLR 934 at 945, per Chadwick LJ, CA.

Can the court vary the judgment rate if a claimant beats a Pt 36 offer?

7.72   Part 36 contains a number of rules about the costs and interest consequences of offers to settle made in the course of litigation. In particular, CPR 36.21(2) provides that:

'The court may order interest on the whole or part of any sum of money (excluding interest) awarded to the claimant at a rate not exceeding 10% above base rate for some or all of the period starting with the latest date on which the defendant could have accepted the offer without needing the permission of the court.'

7.73   CPR 36.21 applies where a defendant is held liable for more, or the judgment in favour of a claimant is more advantageous to the claimant, than the proposals contained in the claimant's Part 36 offer. The question arises as to whether CPR 36.21 grants the court a power to vary the rate at which interest is to be awarded in respect of any period *after* judgment.

7.74   In *McPhilemy v Times Newspapers Ltd (No 2)*,[1] the Court of Appeal held that the statutory rate of interest on judgments cannot be altered by the court even when a claimant does better than he proposed in his Pt 36 offer. The Court of Appeal held that the court has no power under CPR 36.21(2) to make such an order in relation to the payment of interest after judgment, and that interest on damages and costs thereafter was payable at the judgment rate. Chadwick LJ held:[2]

'The power to fix the rate at which interest is payable on judgment debts has been conferred on the Lord Chancellor by section 44 of the Administration of Justice Act 1970 and is exercisable by him with the concurrence of the Treasury. I can see no reason why Parliament should have intended to confer on the courts, indirectly through rules made by the Civil Procedure Rule Committee under section 1(1) of the Civil Procedure Act 1997, power to vary in individual cases a rate fixed under the 1970 Act; nor any reason why a power to fix the rate at which interest is payable on judgment debts could be required for the purpose of "securing that the civil justice system is accessible, fair and efficient": see section 1(3) of the 1997 Act. Nor can I see why a party who fails to pay a judgment debt, which (ex hypothesi) the court has ordered that he should pay, should pay more, or less, interest on that debt because, in the litigation which has led to that order, the other party has, or has not, made an offer to which rule 36.21 applies. The point was not addressed at any length in the argument on the cross-appeal, but, for my part, I am not persuaded that the court has power to make an order under paragraph (2) of rule 36.21 for the payment of interest on the amount of the jury's award in respect of any period after judgment, or to make an order under paragraph (3)(b) for the payment of interest on costs in respect of any period after judgment.

Interest thereafter, on damages and costs, will be payable at the judgment rate, under section 17 of the 1838 Act [JA 1838], in the ordinary course.'

1   [2002] 1 WLR 934, CA.
2   [2002] 1 WLR 934 at 945, CA.

7.75 The court does, however, have a discretion to vary the period for which interest is awarded under CPR 36.21(2). The court may award interest under CPR 36.21(2) from the latest date on which the defendant could have accepted the Pt 36 offer without needing the permission of the court, until the date on which judgment is given.

Variation by contract?

7.76 Many commercial agreements, and in particular loan agreements and security documents, provide that interest shall be paid at a contractually agreed rate both before and after any judgment.[1] The contract may provide for interest to be payable at the same rate post-judgment as applied pre-judgment, or may provide for a higher rate of interest to become payable post-judgment.[2] In these circumstances, the question that arises is whether post-judgment interest will run at the contractually agreed rate or at the statutory rate. Whether the contractual rate of interest is awarded or not will depend on the proper construction of the contract.

1   See further Fuller *Corporate Borrowing Law and Practice* (2nd edn, 1999) paras 5.2.2(a) and 5.2.3. Lord Millett observed in *Director General of Fair Trading v First National Bank plc* [2002] 1 AC 481 at 505-506, HL: '[such a] term is not only a standard term in non-negotiable loans to consumers, but in commercial loans freely negotiated between parties on equal terms and acting with professional advice. I venture to think that no lawyer advising a commercial borrower would dream of objecting to the inclusion of such a term, which merely reinforces and carries into effect what the parties themselves would regard as the essence of the transaction.' This case is considered in paras 7.89–7.92.
2   Note that where the contract provides for a higher rate of interest than the judgment rate to be payable post-judgment, there is a risk that courts could construe the interest provision as a penalty clause. See *Lordsvale Finance plc v Bank of Zambia* [1996] QB 752.

7.77 In *Re European Central Railway Company, ex p Oriental Financial Corpn*[1] the statutory rate was held to prevail over the contractual rate. In that case the defendant issued debentures carrying interest at 6%. The claimant, a debenture holder, brought an action for recovery of the debt and interest and subsequently sought to enforce the judgment obtained. The Court of Appeal held that, following judgment, the original debt had become merged in the judgment, meaning that it no longer existed independently but had become fused with the judgment itself. As a result, the claimant was only entitled to interest at the statutory rate, which at the time was 4%. Bramwell J explained the court's analysis as follows:[2]

'[By virtue of the judgment] a fresh debt is created with different consequences. The judgment is now the charge.'

1   (1876) 4 Ch D 33, CA.
2   (1876) 4 Ch D 33 at 38, CA.

7.78 He explained the apparent injustice as follows:[1]

'It is said that it is a hardship upon the Appellants, because they are worse off by reason of their diligence in bringing the action. But they were not compelled to bring the action; they brought it in order to obtain the advantage of an execution.'

1   (1876) 4 Ch D 33 at 38, CA.

7.79 In *Re Sneyd, ex p Fewings*[1] the Court of Appeal reached similar conclusions to the Court in *Re European*. In *Re Sneyd* a mortgage deed contained a covenant by the mortgagor to pay interest at 5% if the principal sum remained unpaid after the date on which the mortgage was due to be redeemed. The court had held that, as from the date of the judgment, the mortgagee was only entitled to interest at the statutory rate of 4%. The often-quoted dicta of Fry LJ explains the court's reasoning:[2]

'When there is a covenant for the payment of a principal sum, and a judgment has been obtained upon the covenant for that sum, it is plain that the covenant is merged in the judgment, and, if there is a covenant to pay interest which is merely incidental to the covenant to pay the principal debt, that covenant also is merged in a judgment on the covenant to pay the principal debt. Of course a covenant to pay interest may be so expressed as not to merge in a judgment for the principal; for instance, if it was a covenant to pay interest so long as any part of the principal should remain due either on the covenant or on a judgment. … [I]n *Popple v Sylvester* there was an independent covenant for the payment of interest, and I held, as a matter of construction, that that covenant remained in force so long as any principal money could be recovered by the mortgagee in an action for the foreclosure or the redemption of the mortgage. On the other hand, there are cases which shew that, if there is no distinct covenant of that kind to pay interest, the subsidiary covenant for payment of interest falls with the covenant for payment of the principal. That is well illustrated by In re European Central Railway Company.'

1   (1883) 25 Ch D 338, CA.
2   (1883) 25 Ch D 338 at 355–356, CA.

7.80 It is therefore clear that it is possible by express wording to ensure that the interest covenant survives any judgment by agreeing that interest should be paid, as Fry LJ put it, 'so long as any part of the principal should remain due either on the covenant or on a judgment'. The wording frequently included in covenants to pay interest in loan agreements is '*as* well after as before any judgment'[1] or its more modern variant 'after as well as before any judgment'. This wording is a clear example of a so-called 'independent covenant', and will not become merged in a judgment.

1   This was the wording used in the Land Registration Act 1925, s 28(1)(b) (Implied covenants in charges). This section was repealed by the Land Registration Act 2002.

Non-express wording

7.81 In the absence of express wording, the question of whether the interest covenant merges in a judgment is more complex. It will be a question of fact in each case and the issue turns on the distinction to be drawn between, on the one hand, a covenant to pay interest that is '*merely incidental*' to the covenant to pay the principal debt and, on the other, an '*independent covenant*' to pay interest. The House of Lords decision in *Economic Life Assurance Society v Usborne*[1] sheds light on this distinction.

1   [1902] AC 147, HL. The dicta of Fry LJ in *Ex p Fewings* were approved at 149–150, per the Earl of Halsbury LC.

7.82   Their Lordships emphasised in *Usborne* that the question is purely one of the construction of the relevant documents in each case.[1] The facts of *Usborne* were that the parties had entered into a mortgage containing a covenant to repay the principal on a set date with interest of 5%. If the principal was not repaid on that date, the mortgagors covenanted to pay interest at a rate of 5% for so long as the principal remained unpaid. The House of Lords held that, on a true construction of the mortgage deed in question, the plaintiff was entitled to retain its security until it had been repaid both the capital and interest at the contractually agreed rate.[2] As will be seen, the reference to the retention of security is crucial to the analysis.

1   [1902] AC 147 at 150–151, per the Earl of Halsbury LC and 154–155, per Lord Davey who described the issue of construction as '*the only question in the case*'.
2   This reversed the decision of the Master of the Rolls and the Court of Appeal in Ireland on this point in *Usborne v Limerick Market Trustees* [1900] 1 IR 85.

7.83   Lord Davey drew a distinction between a personal remedy, which is extinguished or merged on judgment,[1] and an action on a security. Lord Davey approved the reasoning[2] of the judgment of Fry LJ in *Popple v Sylvester*[3] (another case in which the courts considered a covenant to pay interest under a mortgage following a judgment) as follows:[4]

'[In *Popple*] the question had to be considered whether the covenant for the payment of the interest was an independent covenant or a covenant which was merely ancillary to the payment of the principal money, and the learned judge ... came to the conclusion that it was an independent covenant which was not merged in or extinguished by the judgment obtained upon the principal covenant. But why did he come to that conclusion? Because the form of the covenant was to pay interest as long as anything was due upon the security. ... He said, because something was due upon the security, ergo, that was an independent subsisting covenant. My Lords, that appears to me to put the law upon a very sound and right footing.'

1   [1902] AC 147 at 152, HL.
2   [1902] AC 147 at 152. It seems that Lord Davey may have entertained some doubts as to whether Fry LJ correctly applied the law to the facts in *Popple*.
3   (1882) 22 Ch D 98, CA.
4   [1902] AC 147 at 152–153, HL.

7.84   The covenant in *Usborne* was held to be an independent covenant because, as Lord Davey explained:[1]

'according to the true construction ... it is not security to secure the performance of the covenant, but it entitles the mortgagees to sit upon their deeds, as we used to say, or to hold their security until they have been paid every penny of the … [judgment debt], together with interest measured by what is expressed in the covenant.'

¹   [1902] AC 147 at 155, HL.

7.85 Following *Usborne,* if, on its proper construction, the covenant to pay interest requires the judgment debtor to pay interest for so long as *sums remain due for repayment of the principal,* only the statutory rate of interest will be recoverable by the judgment creditor after judgment has been given. This is because the covenant to repay the principal will cease to exist when it becomes merged in the judgment and so no interest will continue to be payable under the interest covenant.

7.86 By contrast, if, on its proper construction, the covenant to pay interest requires the judgment debtor to pay interest for so long as *any sums remain due on the security for repayment of the principal,* the contractually agreed rate of interest will be recoverable by the judgment creditor after judgment has been given. This is because the covenant to secure the repayment of the principal will survive judgment and so interest will continue to be payable under the interest covenant.

7.87 The matter was further considered by the Court of Appeal in *Ealing London Borough v El Isaac.*¹ Templeman LJ considered the judgment of Lord Davey in *Usborne* and stated:²

'It appears, therefore, that merger has a very restricted operation. It does not, as appears from the *Usborne* case which I have just cited, apply to security. It does not apply to what is said to be an independent covenant and in most mortgages and deeds of borrowing these days care is taken to make the covenant an independent covenant.'

¹   [1980] 2 All ER 548, CA.
²   [1980] 2 All ER 548 at 551, CA.

7.88 Templeman LJ's statement that merger 'does not apply to security' can be seen as a highly distilled summary of the principle that merger will not apply to an interest covenant that is expressed to remain in force for as long as principal sums remain due on the security held.

7.89 The issue of a contractually agreed rate of interest was most recently considered by the House of Lords in *Director General of Fair Trading v First National Bank plc.*¹ The bank had a standard term in its consumer loan agreements providing for interest to run at the contractual rate: 'until payment after as well as before any judgment (such obligation to be independent of and not to merge with any judgment).'

¹   [2002] 1 AC 481, HL.

7.90 An agreement was reached between the bank and the judgment debtors to pay the debt by instalments. Interest had not been included in the instalments. The bank did, however, include in its loan agreement a term stipulating that should the borrower default on his repayments, interest would continue to be payable at the contractual rate until any judgment obtained by the bank was discharged. Where the court extended time for repayment of a loan, the borrower therefore remained liable for the interest which had accrued during that extended period after all the instalments due under the judgment had been paid. The Director General of Fair Trading argued that the term imposing the interest was unfair under the Unfair Terms in Consumer Contracts Regulations 1994.[1]

[1]   SI 1994/3159.

7.91   The House of Lords agreed that a situation where a debtor could pay all the instalments ordered by the court and still face a claim for interest accruing during the payment of those instalments was unacceptable. It was not, however, 'unfair' within the meaning of Unfair Terms in Consumer Contracts Regulations 1994 and judgment was given in favour of the bank. Lord Bingham of Cornhill considered the question of the effect of the bank's wording concerning interest accruing after judgment, and it is worth setting out the relevant passage from the judgment at length: [1]

> 'The bank's stipulation that interest shall be charged until payment after as well as before any judgment, such obligation to be independent of and not to merge with the judgment, is readily explicable. At any rate since *In re Sneyd; Ex p Fewings* (1883) 25 Ch D 338, not challenged but accepted without demur by the House of Lords in *Economic Life Assurance Society v Usborne* [1902] AC 147, the understanding of lawyers in England has been as accurately summarised by the Court of Appeal in the judgment under appeal [2000] QB 672, 682:
>
>> "It is trite law in England that once a judgment is obtained under a loan agreement for a principal sum and judgment is entered, the contract merges in the judgment and the principal becomes owed under the judgment and not under the contract. If under the contract interest on any principal sum is due, absent special provisions the contract is considered ancillary to the covenant to pay the principal, with the result that if judgment is obtained for the principal, the covenant to pay interest merges in the judgment. Parties to a contract may agree that a covenant to pay interest will not merge in any judgment for the principal sum due, and in that event interest may be charged under the contract on the principal sum due even after judgment for that sum."
>
> To ensure that they were able to recover not only the full sum of principal outstanding but also any interest accruing on that sum after judgment as well as before, it became the practice for lenders to include in their credit agreements a term to the effect of the term here in issue. If such a provision had not been included, a lender seeking to enforce a loan agreement against a borrower in the High Court would suffer prejudice only to the extent that the statutory rate of interest on judgment debts at the material time is lower than the contractual interest rate, because the High Court has, since 1838, had power to award statutory interest on a judgment debt until payment.'

[1]   [2002] 1 AC 481 at 487–488, HL.

7.92   Lord Millett observed that the clause was only necessary because of the 'artificial' reading of the covenant to pay interest that the Court of Appeal had reached in *Re Sneyd*:'[1]

> 'The substance of the transaction in the present case is self-evident. It is a loan repayable by instalments with interest on the balance from time to time outstanding

until the whole of the principal is repaid. The borrower would have no difficulty in understanding this. Nor would he think it unfair. If his attention were drawn to the impugned term, ie that interest should continue to be paid on the outstanding balance after as well as before judgment, he might well be surprised at the need to spell this out, but he would surely not be at all surprised by the fact. It is what he would expect. The term does not affect the substance of the transaction, which is that the borrower should continue to pay interest on the principal from time to time outstanding, nor does it impose any further or unexpected liability upon him not inherent in the basic transaction. It is included only to protect the lender from the (to modern eyes artificial) meaning placed on a covenant to pay interest by the Court of Appeal in *In re Sneyd; Ex p Fewings* (1883) 25 Ch D 338, where a covenant to pay interest on the balance of the principal sum from time to time remaining unpaid was construed as meaning remaining due under the covenant, so that it fell when the covenant was subsumed in the judgment.'

1   [2002] 1 AC 481 at 505, HL.

7.93 In summary, it is clear that it is possible for contracting parties to agree that a different rate of interest from the statutory rate will apply after judgment. However, the contractually agreed rate of interest will continue to be payable following a judgment where the contract contains a so-called 'independent covenant' expressly stating that the contractually agreed rate will prevail after judgment. Where the contract contains no such covenant, the courts will construe the contract to determine whether the contractual rate will continue to be payable after a judgment. Where the parties have agreed that interest will be payable at a contractual rate for as long as sums remain due on the security for the debt, the courts have held that the contractually agreed rate continues to be payable after any judgment.

Contractually agreed rate lower than the statutory rate

7.94 There is as yet no case law addressing the question of whether a judgment creditor can enforce at the statutory rate where the parties have contractually agreed that a lower rate than the statutory rate will apply after judgment. However, in the absence of other considerations, there seems to be no reason why the parties would not be held to be bound by their original bargain under the principles explained above.

Interest rate on arbitration awards

7.95 Arbitration is an important method of commercial dispute resolution and is widely employed as an alternative to court proceedings in the commercial sphere. Under English arbitration law, the basic rule regarding the award of interest is party autonomy: the parties are free contractually to agree on the powers of the tribunal as regards the award of interest.[1] This could be provided for in the arbitration agreement itself or under the rules of the arbitration[2] incorporated by reference into the arbitration agreement.

1   Arbitration Act 1996, s 49(1).
2   See, by way of example, the LCIA rules, art 26.6.

7.96 Unless otherwise agreed by the parties to the arbitration agreement, the default position is that a tribunal is granted a statutory discretion to award interest on any award or costs under Arbitration Act 1996, s 49(4), which states:

'The tribunal may award simple or compound interest from the date of the award (or any later date) until payment, at such rates and with such rests as it considers meets the justice of the case, on the outstanding amount of any award (including … any award as to costs).'

7.97 This provision is much broader than was previously the case[1] and it is clear that it grants the tribunal an extremely broad discretion to award simple or compound interest[2] on any arbitral award or costs and at such rates as it considers meet 'the justice of the case'. Unlike a civil court awarding interest on a judgment debt,[3] s 49(4) does not permit a tribunal to award interest on the arbitral award for a period beginning *before* the date of the award. However, the tribunal has broad powers under the Arbitration Act 1996, s 49(3) to award interest up to the date of the award, mirroring those of the civil courts to award interest prior to judgment.[4] In practice, it seems that arbitral awards and costs tend to include interest at the judgment rate.[5]

[1] Previously, the Arbitration Act 1950, s 20 provided that: 'A sum directed to be paid by an award shall, unless the award otherwise directs, carry interest as from the date of the award and at the same rate as a judgment debt.' In *Timber Shipping Co SA v London & Overseas Freighters Ltd* [1972] AC 1, the House of Lords held that an arbitrator is permitted only to decide whether or not an award should carry interest at the rate applicable to a judgment debt and not to determine the rate at which such interest should be carried. The wording of the Arbitration Act 1996, s 49(4) clearly operates to make this distinction redundant.

[2] Interest is compounded by adding all interest due at that date to the capital sum on which interest is being paid when carrying out the interest calculation.

[3] Compare the position under CPR 40.8(2) discussed in para 7.7–7.10.

[4] See para 7.1, n 1.

[5] *Russell on Arbitration* (22nd edn, 2003) para 6–146.

7.98 Under the Arbitration Act 1996, s 66 an arbitral award may, by leave of the court, be enforced as if it were a judgment or order of the court.[1] Where leave is given, judgment may be entered in terms of the award.[2] The award is enforced by a summary procedure set out in CPR Pt 62. In order to enforce any interest for a period after the date of the award, CPR 62.19 requires the applicant to file a statement giving the following particulars:

'Where an applicant seeks to enforce an award of interest the whole or any part of which relates to a period after the date of the award, he must file a statement giving the following particulars:
(a) whether simple or compound interest was awarded;
(b) the date from which interest was awarded;
(c) where rests were provided for, specifying them;
(d) the rate of interest awarded; and
(e) a calculation showing –
   (i) the total amount claimed up to the date of the statement; and
   (ii) any sum which will become due on a daily basis.'

[1] See Chapter 1.

[2] Arbitration Act 1996, s 66(2).

WHEN DOES INTEREST STOP RUNNING?

7.99   It is clear that interest will stop accruing when the judgment debt is paid in full. This is made clear by JA 1838, s 17(1) which states that '[e]very judgment debt shall carry interest at the rate of 8 per cent per annum ... until the same shall be satisfied'.[1] When only part of the judgment debt is satisfied by taking enforcement steps, it follows that interest will continue to accrue on the unpaid balance until that too is satisfied.[2]

[1]   A similar provision applies in the county court under the County Courts (Interest on Judgment Debts) Order 1991, SI 1991/1184, para 2(1), which provides that 'a judgment shall, to the extent it remains unsatisfied, carry interest ... from the date on which the relevant judgment was given'.

[2]   The position is made express in the county court under the County Courts (Interest on Judgment Debts) Order 1991, SI 1991/1184, para 4, which provides that '[w]here a judgment creditor takes proceedings in a county court to enforce payment under a relevant judgment, the judgment debt shall cease to carry interest thereafter, except where those proceedings fail to produce any payment from the debtor in which case interest shall accrue as if those proceedings had never been taken'.

7.100   Money paid into court and which is ordered to be used in partial satisfaction of a judgment debt will not be considered paid to the judgment creditor until it is received by the judgment creditor from the court. In *Parsons v Mather and Platt Ltd*,[1] the plaintiff obtained judgment and damages of £400,000 on 21 May 1975. The defendants had already paid £300,000 into court the previous year and the court ordered that this sum be paid out in partial satisfaction of the judgment debt. The defendants paid the remaining £100,000 on 11 June 1975. The £300,000 that had been paid into court was not released to the plaintiff until 10 July 1975.

[1]   [1977] 1 WLR 855.

7.101   The plaintiff then claimed interest. Much of the argument concentrated on when judgment had been 'entered up' but the court also held that the money paid into court, and directed to be paid in partial satisfaction of a judgment debt, was not considered paid until it was released to the judgment creditor. Accordingly, the defendants were held liable to pay interest on the sum of £300,000 under JA 1838, s 17 from the date of judgment to the date on which the monies were released to the plaintiff by the court. (Interest also ran, of course, on the sum of £100,000 from 21 May to 11 June.) The court held that it would also have been unjust to deny the plaintiff interest when he had not actually received payment. Furthermore, the judge noted that the interest that had accrued on the £300,000 held in court had been paid out to the defendants and that 'the probabilities are ... that the interest earned [on the monies held in court] will be greater than the statutory interest due'.

Limitation Act 1980, s 24

7.102   Limitation Act 1980 (LA 1980), s 24 provides:

'(1) An action shall not be brought upon any judgment after the expiration of six years from the date on which the judgment became enforceable.

(2) No arrears of interest in respect of any judgment debt shall be recovered after the expiration of six years from the date on which the interest became due.'

Lowsley v Forbes

7.103 LA 1980, s 24 was considered by the House of Lords in *Lowsley v Forbes*.[1] In that case, the plaintiff had obtained judgment for £70,000 on 2 February 1981. For reasons not relevant to the decision, the defendant then left the country. At the time, the applicable rate of interest for judgment debts was 15%. By 9 July 1992, the judgment debt had grown to £184,199 if it were correct to allow 11½ years' interest at the rate of 15% on the judgment debt. However, if only six years' interest could be claimed, the judgment debt would have been £133,000.

[1]   [1999] 1 AC 329, HL.

7.104 Lord Lloyd of Beswick, with whom all their Lordships agreed, defined the questions for their Lordships as follows:

'The first question is whether section 24(1) bars execution of a judgment after six years, or whether it only bars the bringing of a fresh action on the judgment. If the answer is, as the plaintiffs contend, that it only bars a fresh action, the second question is whether, when a judgment is executed after six years, interest on the judgment is limited under section 24(2) to a period of six years before the date of execution.'[1]

[1]   [1999] 1 AC 329 at 334, HL.

7.105 The answer to the first question as to the meaning of LA 1980, s 24(1) has already been considered in Chapter 1: their Lordships held that the word 'action' referred to the bringing of a fresh action on the judgment but did not refer to execution steps. Accordingly, it is possible to enforce a judgment even if it is more than six years old.

7.106 As to the second question (namely whether interest on a judgment is limited under LA 1980, s 24(2) to a period of six years before the date of execution when the judgment is executed *after* six years), Lord Lloyd of Beswick held:[1]

'With regret, however, I cannot agree with the Court of Appeal on the second question. There would seem to be no reason why the relevant words in section 24(2) "no arrears of interest ... shall be recovered" should not be given their ordinary meaning, so as to bar execution after six years in respect of all judgments. It is what the words say. "Recovered" has a broad meaning. It is not confined to recovery by fresh action . . .
So as to the second question I prefer the decision of Tuckey J, who held that section 24(2) limits recovery [of interest] by way of execution on all judgments to a period of six years, including the judgment in this case.'

[1]   [1999] 1 AC 329 at 342, HL.

7.107 Accordingly, the effect of LA 1980, s 24(2) is to allow only six years' worth of interest on a judgment to be recovered by way of execution. On the facts of *Lowsley*, the statutory limitation of the plaintiff's ability to recover interest on the judgment to only six years reduced the amounts that could be recovered from £184,199 to £133,000.

Action on a judgment to reset limitation period

7.108   Where the period of six years following a judgment is approaching expiry, the claimant[1] should consider what action it can take to protect its position. The claimant has two options: to enforce the judgment, or to bring a fresh action on the judgment. Whereas the right to enforce can in theory be exercised at any time, albeit with only six years of interest available, the right to bring a fresh action on a judgment expires after six years under LA 1980, s 24(2). The fresh action will be for the original debt plus all interest due on the debt up to that time. If the further judgment is given, the interest due between the date of the original judgment and the new judgment will be incorporated into the new judgment, and interest will run on this combined sum as from the date of the second judgment.[2]

1   Or defendant where judgment is given on a counterclaim.
2   See *ED & F Man (Sugar) Ltd v Haryanto (No 3)* (1996) Times, 9 August, CA, in which Leggat LJ rejected the arguments that allowing an action on a judgment was defeating the intention of LA 1980 and that the practice had become obsolete due to the available procedures for execution of a judgment. For a recent example, see *Bank of Scotland v Bennett* [2004] EWCA Civ 988, CA.

An exception to the normal limitation rule – charging orders

7.109   It should be noted that an entirely different principle applies where a judgment creditor who has obtained a charging order seeks to recover more than six years' interest out of the proceeds of enforcing his security. In *Ezekiel v Orakpo,*[1] the plaintiff had obtained a charging order on the defendant's property having previously obtained judgment for the sum of £20,733.27. After an 'unexplained lapse' of 11 years (and nearly 14 years since the judgment itself), the plaintiff sought to enforce the charging order, by which time the interest alone amounted to a sum of over £40,000. The defendant sought to argue that the effect of LA 1980, s 24(2) was to limit the plaintiff to six years' interest prior to the application to enforce the charge.[2]

1   [1997] 1 WLR 340, CA.
2   The defendant also sought to argue that the plaintiff was limited to six years' interest prior to the application to enforce the charge by virtue of LA 1980, s 20(5), which states: 'No action to recover arrears of interest payable in respect of any sum of money secured by a mortgage or other charge shall be brought after the expiration of six years from the date on which the interest became due.' The court rejected this argument on the basis that this section was directed at forbidding a mortgagee to recover by action a sum of interest after more than six years – it did not preclude him from relying on his security in order to recover it.

7.110   As is described further in Chapter 4 (Charging orders), a charging order takes effect as an equitable charge over the judgment debtor's property and renders the judgment creditor in the position of a secured creditor. Millett LJ, who gave the lead judgment of the Court of Appeal in *Ezekiel v Orakpo,* noted:[1]

'It is important to recognise at the outset what was the true nature of the plaintiff's application in 1993. He was not bringing an action upon the judgment debt which he had obtained in 1979. He was not even seeking to enforce execution of that judgment. He did that when he applied for and obtained the Charging Order in 1982. In 1993 he was a secured creditor with the statutory equivalent of an equitable charge. He was taking action to recover what was due to him, not as a judgment creditor, but as a secured creditor.'

1   [1997] 1 WLR 340 at 346–347, CA.

7.111   The Court held that a judgment creditor who is seeking to enforce his rights as a secured creditor under a charging order is not seeking to enforce a judgment (that process had come to an end when he obtained the charging order). Millett, LJ held:[1]

'In my judgment neither s 24(2) nor that case[2] is relevant to the question which we have to decide, which is whether a secured creditor who holds a charging order can recover more than six years' interest out of the proceeds of enforcing his security. By doing so, he is not bringing an action on the judgment; nor, is he seeking to enforce the judgment whether by a process of execution or otherwise. He is enforcing his rights as a secured creditor under the equitable charge which was created by the charging order.'

1   [1997] 1 WLR 340 at 350, CA.
2   This was a reference to *Lowsley v Forbes* [1999] 1 AC 329, HL, in which the judgment debtor also sought to rely to preclude the judgment creditor from recovering more than six years' interest. Millett LJ rejected this argument on the grounds that *Lowsley* concerned a different application to that under consideration in *Ezekiel*, namely an application to bring enforcement proceedings (rather than a judgment creditor taking steps to enforce his rights as a secured creditor).

7.112   Accordingly, a judgment creditor who has obtained a charging order can recover more than six years' interest out of the proceeds of enforcing his security.[1]

1   The County Courts (Interest on Judgment Debts) Order 1991, SI 1991/1184, para 4(2), carves out charging orders from the more general rule in para 4(1) that judgment interest ceases once successful enforcement steps are taken.

Insolvency of judgment debtor

7.113   If the judgment debtor becomes insolvent after judgment has been given but prior to the judgment being satisfied, the general rule is that judgment interest will cease to run from the commencement date of the formal insolvency proceedings.[1]

1   Insolvency Rules 1986, r 4.93(1) (winding up), r 2.88(1) (administration) and r 6.113(1) (bankruptcy).

7.114   In the (unlikely) event that there is a surplus of assets remaining after payment in full of the debts proved in the relevant insolvency proceedings, post-insolvency interest will be payable on the judgment debt at the rate specified in JA 1838, s 17 unless there is contractual agreement to pay a higher rate (in which case the contractual rate will apply).[1]

1   Insolvency Act 1986, s 189(2) (winding up), Insolvency Rules 1986, SI 1986/1925, r 2.88(7) (administration) and Insolvency Act 1986, s 328(4) (bankruptcy).

PRACTICE AND PROCEDURE

7.115   If a judgment creditor wishes to claim statutory interest on a judgment debt, he must include a claim for interest, detailing the amount claimed, the period of interest, and the relevant rate of interest, in his application or request to issue enforcement proceedings.[1]

1   PD 70, para 6.

REFORM

7.116   The Law Commission reported on pre-judgment interest in February 2004.[1] The report considered whether Parliament should legislate to facilitate the award of compound interest by the courts, as opposed to the simple interest awards usually made under the present law, and does not concern itself with post-judgment interest, nor is there any indication that the Law Commission plans to address this issue in the future. The argument in favour of compound interest (that it is fairer, particularly where the rate applied is high or where interest is awarded over a lengthy period) would also apply to interest awarded after judgment and it may be that this is an issue that is addressed by the courts and parliament in the future.

1   Pre-Judgment Interest on Debts and Damages, Law Com No 287, 23 February 2004.

7.117   The application of a fixed statutory rate of interest in force at the time of judgment as the basis for awarding judgment is a relatively blunt instrument. By contrast, the recent approach of the courts to pre-judgment awards of interest is to apply a rate which broadly represents the commercial rate. One of the disadvantages of having a fixed rate of interest on judgment debts is that, where this rate is lower than the commercial rate prevailing at any point in time, judgment debtors are in a position where they would be better delaying payment and waiting to see if enforcement steps are taken than taking steps to pay the judgment. There would appear to be no inherent reason why the flexible approach towards pre-judgment awards could not be applied to calculations of interest post-judgment, possibly by calculating the rate by reference to the Bank of England base rate, with a premium added to encourage prompt compliance with judgments. However, there are no current proposals to implement such a reform.

7.118   By contrast, the courts' discretionary powers regarding the period for which interest is awarded on both costs and damages awards create flexibility and it will be interesting to see how the courts continue to develop and apply this discretion in future. At present, its exercise seems to be confined to cases involving considerable costs or lengthy time periods and may therefore be relevant in commercial enforcement scenarios. This is perhaps because the use of these discretionary powers in cases involving smaller sums or shorter time periods may result in overly complex interest calculations and an inefficient use of the courts' resources.

Index